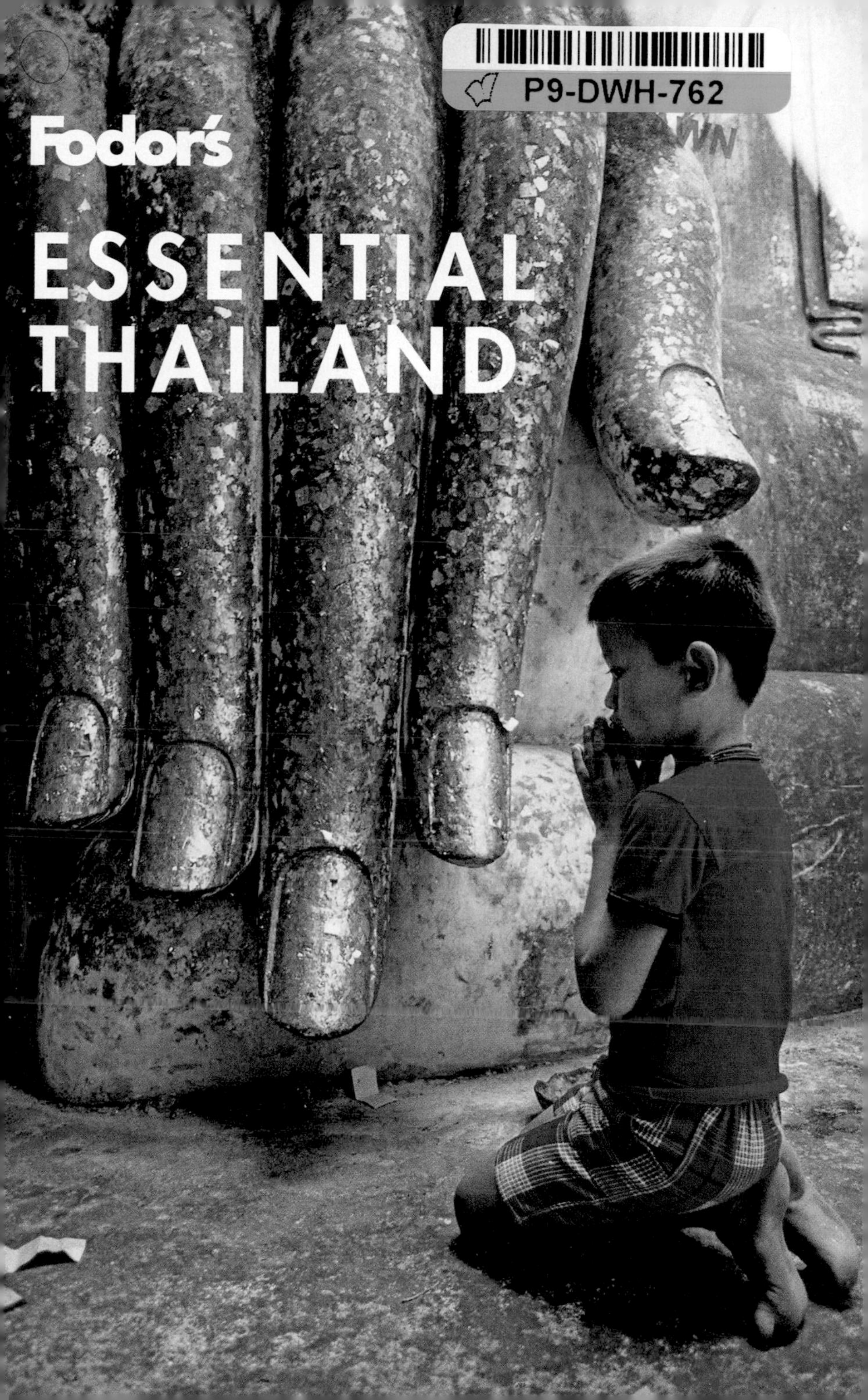
Fodor's
ESSENTIAL
THAILAND

Welcome to Thailand

Thailand conjures images of white-sand beaches and cerulean waters, peaceful temples, and lush mountain jungles. In Bangkok, a 21st-century playground, the scent of spicy street food fills the air, and the Grand Palace recalls the country's traditions. Outside the capital, the wonders of the countryside enchant, whether you are trekking to remote villages in the northern hills, exploring Ayutthaya's splendid ruins, or diving in the waters of the idyllic southern coast. The unique spirit of the Thai people—this is the "land of smiles," after all—adds warmth to any visit.

TOP REASONS TO GO

★ **Beaches:** Pristine strands and hidden coves bring vacation daydreams alive.

★ **Food:** Rich curries, sour-spicy tom yum soup, and tasty pad thai are worth savoring.

★ **Architecture:** Resplendent stupas and pagodas evoke the glory of ancient kingdoms.

★ **Spas:** Luxurious retreats offer indulgences such as world-renowned Thai massage.

★ **Trekking:** A trek to a remote mountain village to visit hill tribes is a memorable experience.

★ **Shopping:** Iconic night markets sell everything from hand-carved crafts to handbags.

Contents

Fodor's Features

MAPS

South East Asia
INDIA
CHINA
MYANMAR
LAOS
VIETNAM
THAILAND
Silchar
Imphal
Chindwin
Baoshan
Kunming
Xingyi
Yuxi
Hong (Red)
Gejiu
Nanning
Mekong
Simao
Ha Giang
Lao Chi
Pingxiang
Jinghong
Da (Black)
Thai Nguyen
Viet Tri
Bac Giang
Cam Pha
HANOI
Hong Gai
Haiphong
Ayeyawady
Salween
Shwebo
Monywa
Mandalay
Myingyan
Bagan
Chauk
Taunggyi
Yaynangyoung
Meuang Xai
Sittwe
20° N
Magway
Gulf of Tonkin
Kyaukphyu
NAY PYI DAW
Luang Prabang
Chiang Rai
Allanmyo
Phayao
Taungoo
Sayabouly
Chiang Mai
Nan
Pyay
Pyu
Paksan
Lampang
Ping
Phrae
VIENTIANE
Letpadan
Nong Khai
Hinthada
Uttaradit
Loei
Udon Thani
Thakhek
Bago
Yandoon
Sukhothai
Sakhon Nakhon
Pathein
Tak
Phitsanulok
Yangon
Thongwa
Wakema
Mae Sot
Savannakhet
Hue
Labutta
Mawlamyine
Mudon
Khon Kaen
Phyarpon
Da Nang
Kyaik ka me
Gulf of Martaban
Chaiyaphum
Nakhon Sawan
Bua Yai
Bay of Bengal

15° N
10° N
95° E
100° E
105° E
INDIA
Port Blair
CAMBODIA
THAILAND
Ye
Uthai Thani
Nakhon Ratchasima
Sisaket
Pakse
Loc Buri
Surin
Ayutthaya
Saraburi
Dawei
Kanchanaburi
Prachin Buri
Play Ku
BANGKOK
Aranyaprathet
Sisophon
Siem Reap
Ratchaburi
Phetchaburi
Tonle Sap
Pattaya
Battambang
Cha Am
Mergui
Hua Hin
Chanthaburi
Pursat
Kompong Chhnang
Kampong Cham
Koh Chang
Hon Quan
PHNOM PENH
Krong Koh Kong
Gulf of Thailand
Takeo
Phan Thiet
Kampot
Kaoh Rung
Chau Doc
Ho Chi Minh City
Chumphon
Long Xuyen
My Tho
Vung Tau
Koh Tao
Rach Gia
Can Tho
Koh Phangan
Koh Samui
Soc Trang
Surat Thani
Bac Lieu
Ca Mau
ANDAMAN SEA
SOUTH CHINA SEA
Nakhon Si Thammarat
Koh Phuket
Phuket
Thung Song
Kon Phi Phi
Trang
Koh Lanta Ya
Songkhla
Hat Yai
Yala
Narathiwat
Kota Bharu
Myanmar
Laos
Thailand
Cambodia
0
100 mi
0
100 km

Chapter 1

EXPERIENCE THAILAND

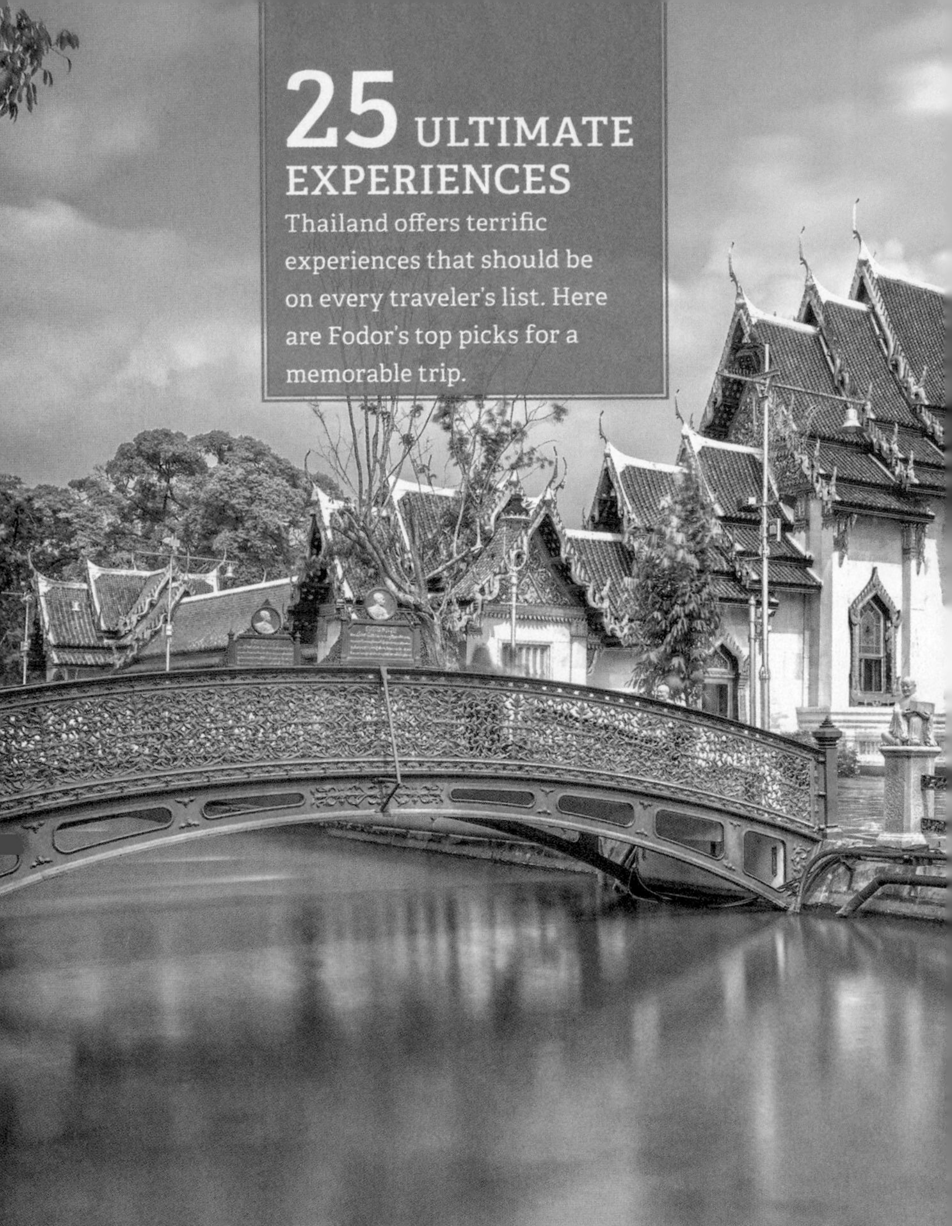

1 Bangkok's Famous Temples

There are over 400 temples in Bangkok so start with the famous ones: Wat Phra Kaew or the Temple of the Emerald Buddha, within the Grand Palace; Wat Pho or Temple of the Reclining Buddha, with its 141-ft-long gold-leaf Buddha; and Wat Benjamabophit, covered in Italian marble and featured on the 5 baht coin. *(Ch. 3)*

2 Kanchanaburi

Just a couple of hours by train from Bangkok, Kanchanaburi is famous for its seven-tiered waterfall within Erawan National Park. Swim, hike, and visit caves here and then visit the nearby Bridge on the River Kwai. *(Ch. 4)*

3 The Hill Tribes

Thailand's hill tribes make their homes in the mountainous regions of the north. Avoid the tourist traps and book a guide to take you to more remote villages to see tribes living as they have for centuries. *(Ch. 8)*

4 Festivals

Experience Thailand's rich traditions and rituals through a festival like Yi Peng, when thousands of candlelit paper lanterns are released into the sky and river along with all of the previous year's ills and misfortunes. *(Ch. 7)*

5 Ayutthaya

Destroyed in the late 1700s, the Thai- and Khmer-style ruins of Thailand's second capital now form Ayutthaya Historical Park and evoke the city's lost grandeur. *(Ch. 4)*

6 Island Hopping Around Krabi

Hire a longtail boat to explore breathtaking scenery, white sandy beaches, turquoise waters, limestone cliffs, and incredible coral reefs. *(Ch. 6)*

7 Doi Inthanon

Thailand's highest peak rises majestically over a national park of staggering beauty, popular with birders, nature lovers, and hikers, day-tripping from Chiang Mai. *(Ch. 7)*

8 Snorkel and Dive

Thailand's Andaman Coast offers some of the best snorkeling and dive sites in the world with crystal clear waters, abundant marine life, and spectacular underwater scenery. *(Ch. 6)*

9 Mae Hong Son Loop

Thailand's famous trail runs from Chaing Mai to Mae Hong Son via Pai and winds through spectacular mountain scenery along the way. *(Ch. 8)*

10 Thai Massage

Widely available in temples, markets, jungle hideaways, and luxury resorts, Thai massage treatments can be rigorous, even painful but pleasant.

11 Floating Markets

Vendors in straw hats peddle everything from caramelized crickets and samurai swords to herbal potions and silk at floating markets like Damnoen Saduak. *(Ch. 4)*

12 Pai

A popular stop along the Mae Hong Son Loop, this peaceful town ensconced in nature has a WWII Memorial Bridge, caves, a canyon, and a hippy scene. *(Ch. 8)*

13 Khao Sok National Park

One of the most spectacular landscapes in Thailand, remote Khao Sok offers lush greenery with rare flora and fauna and towering mountain ranges. *(Ch. 5)*

14 Khao San Road

Touristy and crowded with overpriced souvenirs, Bangkok's most famous shopping thoroughfare is still a must with its hustle and bustle, lively bars, and street food. *(Ch. 3)*

15 Sky Bar

Bangkok is famous for its rooftop bars, especially Sky Bar, with its breathtaking views of the Chaophraya River and a cocktail named for the *Hangover* movie filmed here. *(Ch. 3)*

16 Silk

Chiang Mai and silk are synonymous and at several workrooms along San Kamphaeng Road, you can learn how silk is made and buy quality silk clothing and home decor items. *(Ch. 7)*

17 Similan and Surin Islands

Unspoiled beaches and crystal-blue waters with a diversity of marine life, these remote island paradises are popular for diving, fishing, and hiking. *(Ch. 6)*

18 Cooking Class

Learn a few fundamentals and the history of Thai cuisine while you master an authentic green curry, a hot-and-spicy soup, or pad thai. *(Ch. 3)*

19 Sukhothai

This ancient city's impressive 13th-century ruins with Khmer- and Hindu-influenced scripture and architecture are relatively unspoiled by the ages. *(Ch. 8)*

20 Lopburi Monkeys

Lopburi has an unusually large monkey population and they like to gather around monuments like Phra Prang Sam Yot. They also like to steal your food or shoes! *(Ch. 4)*

21 Chiang Mai

Northern Thailand's largest city offers significant temples, trekking trails that lead to the Hill Tribes, and bustling night markets that are a riot of sounds and smells. *(Ch. 7)*

22 Koh Chang

Mountainous Koh Chang, or Elephant Island, is part of a national park and many of its beaches and villages are only accessible by boat, making them unspoiled paradises. *(Ch. 5)*

23 Phetchaburi

Khao Long Cave overflows with Buddhas, including a 32-ft reclining Buddha, and is best visited in the morning when the sun reflects off of the brass icons. *(Ch. 4)*

24 Chiang Rai

This city is a must for its access to the Golden Triangle and the surrounding hill tribes, as well as its glistening and spectacular White Temple, Wat Rong Khun. *(Ch. 8)*

25 Street Food

Join locals gathered around street stalls slurping noodles, devouring curries, sticky rice, and spicy som tam, and snacking on panfried insects. *(Ch. 3)*

WHAT'S WHERE

1 Bangkok. In this boomtown of contrasts where old-world charm meets futuristic luxury, you can dine at street stalls or ritzy restaurants, visit the jaw-dropping Grand Palace, and shop at Chatuchak Weekend Market or Pathumwan's designer malls. At night there are hip mega-clubs and Patpong's famous red lights, as well as quieter romantic restaurants and wine bars.

2 Around Bangkok. Petchaburi has ancient temples and a royal retreat, while Thailand's oldest city, Nakhon Pathom, is home to Phra Pathom Chedi, the world's tallest Buddhist stupa.

3 The Gulf Coast Beaches. Thailand's two shores have alternating monsoon seasons, so there's great beach weather *somewhere* year-round. The Gulf has Pattaya's nightlife and the island trio of Koh Samui (good sailing), Koh Pha Ngan (full-moon revelry), and Koh Tao (diving). The coastal drive to Trat is a pleasant, winding trip through the countryside. And south to Pattani, adventurers will find infrequently visited regions off the primary tourist circuit.

4 Phuket and the Andaman Coast. Highlights of this spectacular coastal region include Phuket, Phang Nga Bay (with James Bond Island), and Krabi, which is a paradise for divers, rock climbers, and foodies.

5 Chiang Mai. This moat-encircled city is riddled with temples and markets, and deserves a lingering stop in any tour of the north. Wander the narrow alleys and brick roads of the old city, then dine in the university area alive with hip young crowds.

6 Northern Thailand. Chiang Rai is a chilled-out regional center and the gateway to the Golden Triangle, where Laos, Myanmar (Burma), and Thailand meet. Thailand's first capital, Sukhothai, has carefully restored ruins.

7 Cambodia. No Southeast Asia trip is complete without a visit to the temple ruins of Angkor. The capital, Phnom Penh, is a vibrant city with a thriving food scene. Cross the Tonle Sap (the great lake) to communities living in floating houses, or laze on Cambodia's spectacular coastline. There is also plenty to interest hikers, birders, and wildlife buffs.

8 Laos. Photogenic rivers, mountainous countryside, and the dreamy feeling of going back in time are major reasons to make the trip across the border. World Heritage sites Luang Prabang and Champasak both have beautiful temples and the Plain of Jars will wow any archaeology enthusiast.

CHINA
Hong (Red)
Mekong
Salween
Shwebo
Mandalay
Jinghong
Ha Giang
Pingxiang
VIETNAM
Da (Black)
Myingyan
Bagan
MYANMAR
Bac Giang
HANOI
Haiphong
Sittwe
Ayeyawady
Meuang Xai
Luang Prabang
Plain of Jars
NAY PYI DAW
Chiang Rai
LAOS
Gulf of Tonkin
Allanmyo
Chiang Mai
Phayao
Sayabouly
Pyay
Pyu
Paksan
Bengal
Lampang
VIENTIANE
Phrae
Letpadan
Mekong
Loei
Thakhek
Sukhothai
Udon Thani
Yangon
Bago
Phitsanulok
Khon Kaen
Savannakhet
Labutta
Mudon
Mae Sot
THAILAND
Hue
Kyaik ka me
Chaiyaphum
Bua Yai
Ye
Uthai Thani
Pakse
Nakhon Ratchasima
Lop Buri
Champasak
Ayutthaya
Saraburi
Dawei
Kanchanaburi
Prachin Buri
Angkor Wat
Nakhon Pathom
BANGKOK
Siem Reap
Sisophon
Petchaburi
Tonle Sap
CAMBODIA
Pattaya
Mergui
Chanthaburi
Pursat
Kampong Cham
Trat
Koh Chang
Kompong Chhnang
PHNOM PENH
Krong Koh Kong
ANDAMAN SEA
Takeo
Chumphon
Kampot
Ho Chi Minh City
Koh Tao
Gulf of Thailand
Koh Phangan
Koh Samui
Bac Lieu
THAILAND
Surat Thani
Krabi
Nakhon Si Thammarat
Koh Phuket
Thung Song
Phuket
Trang
Songkhla
Hat Yai
Pattani
Narathiwat
0
100 mi
0
100 km
MALAYSIA
1
2
3
4
5
6
7
8

10 Things to Eat and Drink in Thailand

PANANG (PEANUT) CURRY
Panang curry uses fragrant red curry as a base and adds ground peanuts for creaminess and depth. A topping of basil and strips of fragrant Makrut lime leaf contrast the peanutty stick-to-your-ribs aspect of this dish. Thick, sweet, tasty, and commonly paired with chicken.

PANDAN CAKE
The comfort and familiarity of sponge cake with the distinctly Southeast Asian addition of the juice of the beloved pandan plant, which is extracted by squeezing or pulverizing the long, narrow leaves. Added to pound cake it provides a shock of green color and a very pleasant aroma.

FRESH POMEGRANATE JUICE
Juice stands abound in the street markets of Thailand and no juice is quite as easy to spot as that of the pomegranate. Squeezed fresh, it's tart, blood red, and quenching. Some stands may sell pre-squeezed juice or may add in other flavors or juices. If you want to make sure you get the real stuff find a stand that makes the juice right in front of you using fresh fruit.

THAI ICED COFFEE
Black-as-midnight Thai coffee is poured over ice and mixed with thick, sweet condensed milk to make a drink that's impossible not to fall in love with. It's fantastically delicious and exceptionally easy to find, which is great because between the caffeine, the sugar, and the sheer tastiness of it, it's easy to become addicted.

BASIL CHICKEN WITH FRIED EGG

Tossed in a smoking wok with chicken and chilies, basil holds both its texture and flavor to produce a fragrant, herbal stir fry that knocks the socks off of any sad carryout you've had in the past. Park yourself on a stool built for a toddler and always get the fried egg.

KHAO PHAT

Thai fried rice takes on many forms depending on available ingredients and personal preference. What is consistent is that it's made with jasmine rice and maintains a decidedly Thai flavor palate, meaning you'll find fish sauce, eggs, garlic, onions, and sometimes a smattering of chopped herbs.

ROLLED ICE CREAM

This Instagram-friendly dessert was born on the streets of Thailand. Soft, near-liquid ice cream is spread on a chilled metal surface and scraped into tightly coiled rolls of deliciousness. Yes, it is super touristy, but it's also the perfect way to cool down on a sultry Thai night.

Khao phat

LARB

At its core larb is a simple dish made from finely chopped or ground meat (such as chicken) tossed with chopped mint and cilantro, onion, and chilies, and spritzed with lime juice. Eaten with rice or scooped up with lettuce, it's a wonderful meal and is something you'll seek again and again.

THAI BEER

Singha or Chang are great examples of the kind of beer found all across Asia—light, golden, and easily quaffable and the perfect match for hot and humid weather and flavorful, spicy food.

MANGO STICKY RICE

That most ubiquitous of Thai desserts, Mango Sticky Rice is a sticky pile of sweet and starchy short-grain rice which is topped by stunningly fresh mango, drizzled with sweetened coconut milk, and often studded with puffed rice. Don't be surprised if the mango is wildly better than anything you've had in the past—India and Southeast Asia produce some of the best mangoes in the world, including varieties that are too fragile to ship to other places. Eat it while you can, it's not going to be this good back home.

10 Things to Buy in Thailand

PARASOLS

Save for a few months in northern Thailand, it's always hot and the sun is *strong*. In addition to sunscreen, make like the Thais and use a parasol to protect yourself. You can find them at markets in Bangkok and Phuket and Bo Sang, just outside Chiang Mai's city center, is umbrella central.

COTTON TEXTILES

Thai silk gets most of the attention but skilled artisans in Thailand also produce beautiful cotton textiles. It has a few advantages over silk: it's less costly, it's heartier, and it's more versatile. The patterns vary; you'll find slim stripes, batik, and *mudmee* (Thai ikat).

LOCAL ALCOHOL

Among the country's many craft beers are Full Moon and its popular Chalawan Pale Ale, Taopiphop and its saison, and Dirty Forty's light-bodied pilsner, all stocked in convenience stores. For local rum, look for Chalong Bay and Magic Alambicrum brands. For gin, Bangkok-brewed Iron Balls gin.

COCONUT EVERYTHING

Straw-ready fresh coconuts are on the menu at most Thai restaurants, particularly on the islands where they're also sold on the beach and on the street. The country's production of coconuts—more than 750,000 tons annually—means grocery store shelves heave with ultra-fresh coconut water, shredded coconut, chips, milk, moisturizer, candy, baked goods, ice cream, and coconut oil.

HILL TRIBE HANDICRAFTS

Hill tribe handicrafts abound in Chiang Mai and these purses, clothing, home goods, and silver jewelry make great gifts. For bolts of hill tribe fabric, trim, embroidery, and beads, go to Chiang Mai's fabric district and look for stalls run by hill tribe women. Or hire a guide and drive out to hill tribe villages deep in the countryside to buy textiles directly from them.

SPICES

All grocery stores sell a good selection of spices and Bangkok's Little India, Pahurat, has various spice shops. Look for curry paste, Kaffir leaves, and galangal for curries, lemongrass for soups and curries, pandan leaves for desserts, and bird's eye chili and crushed chili for everything.

WOOD FURNITURE AND ACCESSORIES

Carved wood sculptures and pretty baskets made of water hyacinth are widely available but for wooden furniture and accessories, head to Chiang Mai. Drive out to Baan Tawai Village in Han Dong where vendors sell custom teak and mango furniture and can arrange shipping.

SILK

You can buy pretty scarves at markets like Chatuchak in Bangkok or Chiang Mai's night markets, but don't pay for authentic silk when you're likely getting polyester. In Bangkok, the Museum of Textiles and Jim Thompson House are reputable places to buy silk as is Lamphun outside Chiang Mai.

BEAUTY PRODUCTS

Thai beauty products may not get as much attention as Korean or French, but beauty lovers should still plan a haul. Look for Sunsilk hair masks, Water Angel masks, Smooth E cleansers, Lansing eye creams and serums, and Srichand Powder. Read packaging carefully as some products have whitening cream in them. Shop chain pharmacies, Siam Center mall, Beauty Buffet, and Oriental Princess.

COFFEE

Thailand grows Arabica beans in the north and Robusta in the south, with Arabica being the most popular. Go to Chiang Mai or Chiang Rai and arrange a coffee tour where you can buy beans directly from farmers and sip their brews on the spot. If you just want to sip one good cup after another and bring home a few bags of excellent beans, hit up specialty coffee shops in Chiang Mai and Bangkok.

10 Best Festivals in Thailand

YI PENG, NOVEMBER
This Chiang Mai festival of lanterns features the release of thousands of candlelit lanterns into the night sky in a magical scene that will take your breath—and the previous year's bad luck and misfortunes—away. Highlights include candlelit streets and Buddhist purification ceremonies.

UBON RATCHATHANI CANDLE FESTIVAL, JULY
Held at Thung Si Muang, this candle-carving festival marks the beginning of Buddhist Lent. Historically, monks carved ornate designs into donated candles. Today, there are competitions, festivities, and a procession that includes giant candles and the Royal Candle.

LOY KRATONG, NOVEMBER
This festival of lights falls on the full moon, and marks the end of the rainy season. Participants release lotus-shaped lanterns onto rivers to signify a release of past negative thoughts. The best places to witness this sacred ritual are Bangkok, Chiang Mai, and Old Sukhothai.

SONGKRAN, APRIL
Thailand's biggest and wettest festival marks the beginning of the Thai New Year on the Buddhist calendar. During this time locals and visitors throw buckets of water on each other, spray passersby with water pistols, and catapult water balloons. Although less fun, it's also customary to spend time with your elders.

FULL MOON PARTY, MONTHLY
This is one of Thailand's most notorious festivals held on the island of Koh Phangan next to Koh Samui. This rowdy all-night dance party starts at sunset on Haad Rin Beach and continues until dawn with a variety of music, dancers, and fire performers.

WONDERFRUIT MUSIC AND ARTS FESTIVAL, DECEMBER
Music lovers and free spirits flock to The Fields at Siam Country Club in the seaside city of Pattaya for Thailand's high-concept, eco-friendly Burning Man. Events include musical performances from a mix of international and local acts, interactive art installations, banquets by award-winning chefs, workshops on everything from wellness to sustainable architecture, and more. The four-day, carefully curated festival of experiences is 24 hours a day, cashless, and plastic-free.

A parade float in Chiang Mai's Flower Festival.

VEGETARIAN FESTIVAL, OCTOBER
This nine-day holiday from meat and other indulgences is an act of purification in the Chinese community and taken to extremes in Phuket, where acts like walking barefoot on hot coals, putting swords through cheeks, and other acts of self-mutilation represent carrying the sins of the community. Rituals are accompanied by fireworks, drums, processions, and delicious vegetarian cuisine. Not for the weak of heart or stomach.

CHIANG MAI FLOWER FESTIVAL, FEBRUARY
A three-day floral extravaganza to mark the end of the cold season, this colorful celebration held in Chiang Mai features the local Damask rose and extravagant displays of white and yellow chrysanthemums. The not-to-miss activity is the Saturday morning parade with blooming floats and dancers.

CHINESE NEW YEAR, JANUARY OR FEBRUARY
Yaowaraj, Bangkok's Chinatown, is the place to be for the giant annual party in the street to kick off Chinese New Year. Ornate dragon dancers, firecrackers, and elaborate, delicious Chinese banquets are everywhere, and people are dressed in red to ward off Nien, a mythical beast.

BIG MOUNTAIN MUSIC FESTIVAL, DECEMBER
Thailand's largest and most popular music festival brings over 70,000 people to The Ocean Khao Yai in Phetchaburi Province. Over the course of two days, there are over 200 performers on nine stages, including musicians and acts from around the world. Thai bands and artists prevail at BNFF, including Luk-Thung country music, Moh-Lam folk songs, and also modern genres.

10 Best Temples and Ruins in Thailand

WAT BENJAMABOPHIT
Built in 1899 and designed by the half-brother of then-king Chulalongkorn, this active temple with resident monks is one of Thailand's most dazzling temples with its glorious Italian Carrara marble courtyard, pillars, and its stepped-out roof and ornate finials.

LOPBURI
The ancient city of Lopburi, now inhabited by a lively population of monkeys features important ruins from the 12th century onward, when Lopburi (then Lavo) became part of the Khmer empire. Of special note are Wat Phra Sri Rattana Mahathat (12C), Prang Sam Yot (early 13C), and Bahn Vichien (17C).

WAT LAN KUAD
Of the 40,000 temples in Thailand, Wat Lan Kuad, literally "Temple of a Million Bottles," is surely the most unique. Monks painstakingly recycled more than 1.5 million beer bottles—mostly Heineken (green) and Chang (brown) and their caps into 20 buildings.

DOI SUTHEP
Legend has it that this gilded temple inside Chiang Mai's Doi Suthep National Park was built here in the late 14th century because an elephant carrying religious relics from Chiang Mai climbed up to the 3,542-foot summit and decided to stay. To get here, climb 304 steps, the staircase flanked by 16th-century balustrades in the shape of nagas (mythical snakes), or hop on the funicular.

AYUTTHAYA
Ayutthaya was the capital of Thailand (then Siam) for more than 400 years, until succeeded by Bangkok in the late 18th century. Despite its destruction by the Burmese in 1767, many of the stupas, temples, and carvings that fill the Historic City of Ayutthaya, a UNESCO World Heritage Site, are remarkably well preserved. Like Angkor Wat, the Historic City of Ayutthaya is quite spread out.

WAT KU TAO

This rarely visited temple was built in 1613 to inter the remains of Tharawadi Min, son of King Bayinnaung, who ruled the then-Lanna kingdom from 1578 to 1607. The temple incorporates Burmese design elements and a distinctive chedi (stupa) made up of five stone spheres, rising largest to smallest.

WAT RONG KHUN

Chiang Rai's striking white Marble Temple is a symbol of modern Thailand: a glittering contemporary art installation by artist Chaloemchai Kositpipat, built in the late 1990s to look like a Buddhist temple. The temple's intricately carved exterior is white to symbolize Buddha's purity.

WAT PHO

Just off the Chao Phraya River and right next to the Grand Palace, this temple is home to a 150-foot gold reclining Buddha with 10-foot feet covered with 108 auspicious signs of Buddha inlaid in mother-of-pearl. The complex also holds Bangkok's oldest university, with a monk-run Thai massage school.

PHANOM RUNG

This uncrowded Hindu Khmer temple complex built between the 10th and 13th centuries, sits on the rim of an extinct volcano. Admire the pretty lotus leaf-filled ponds and the carvings of Hindu gods Vishnu and Shiva, who are carved on the pediments and lintels of the entrance gates. Phanom Rung is part of a larger UNESCO site that includes the nearby 11th-century temple Prasat Muang Tam.

SUKHOTHAI HISTORICAL PARK

A massive late 20th century restoration project created the impressive Sukhothai Historical Park, a UNESCO World Heritage Site, which comprises the partially restored ruins of historical sites across five zones. The most important central zone was the royal part of the city and contains 21 temples interspersed among lotus-covered pools, canals, trees, and other greenery.

10 Best Temples and Ruins in Cambodia and Laos

WAT OUNALOM, CAMBODIA
This 15th-century temple is admired for its beauty and respected as the center for Cambodian Buddhism. The highlight here is a Chetdai dating to Angkorian times and said to contain hair from one of the Buddha's eyebrows. Join the resident monks in daily guided meditation sessions.

PLAIN OF JARS, LAOS
Little is known of the people who carved the hundreds, possibly thousands, of huge sandstone containers strewn across fields around the town of Phonsavan. These giant ancient vessels are swathed in mystery and surrounded by countryside that is scarred by the "Secret War."

PHA THAT LUANG, LAOS
This 147-foot-high, gilded stupa is the nation's most important cultural symbol, representing the unity of the Lao people. Built in 1566 by King Setthathirat to guard a relic of the Buddha's hair, the complex includes two brilliantly decorated temple halls and a long reclining Buddha.

PAK OU CAVES, LAOS
Set in limestone cliffs above where the rivers Mekong and Nam Ou meet, these two caves are filled with thousands of 16th-century Buddha statues. Both caves are reached by staircases, so the climb isn't difficult; your entrance fee includes a guide and flashlight, which you'll need for the dark upper cave. It's best to arrive via a tranquil boat ride along the Mekong.

WAT PHU, LAOS
Wat Phu translates to Mountain Temple, and it's built on three levels, with 11th to 13th century ruins on the lower and middle. This was originally a Hindu temple, later converted to Buddhism, so you'll see carvings on the lintels of deities Vishnu and Shiva. While level two has most of the impressive ruins, it's up top that you'll find the sanctuary, impressive stone carvings of an elephant and a crocodile, and views to the Mekong.

ANGKOR WAT, CAMBODIA
Arguably the most famous temple in Cambodia, if not all of Asia, Angkor Wat is one of approximately 50 temples within the Angkor Archeological Park, a UNESCO World Heritage Site—but it's by far the most well-known. Its breathtaking presence has impressed visitors for nearly 1,000 years, with a construction dating from sometime between B.C. 1113 and 1150. Originally a Hindu temple dedicated to Vishnu, Angkor Wat was converted to a Buddhist

The Banyon temple in Angkor, Cambodia.

temple in the 14th century and later served as the capital of the Khmer empire.

TA PROHM, CAMBODIA

This expansive Buddhist temple was first built around the mid-12th century and while it is maintained like all Angkor temples, the undisturbed roots of large banyan, fig, and kapok trees appear to grasp it mightily. Wooden walkways have been installed around the jungle's attempts to reclaim the temple.

BAYON, CAMBODIA

It's ok to feel uneasy at Bayon—with over 200 smiling stone faces staring at you, this Buddhist shrine is unlike anywhere else. Scholars believe the faces are all representations of Jayavarman VII, a powerful Khmer king of the late 12th century, and perhaps are a testament to the power of ego. Many well-preserved mythological scenes are still visible in the temple's bas-reliefs.

BUDDHA PARK, LAOS

Created by a shaman-artist in the 1950s, this delightfully trippy park features some 200 Buddhist and Hindu sculptures in all sizes and poses. Enter the mouth of a demon head and climb its three floors—representing hell, heaven, and Earth—for great views of the bizarre but attractive park.

PHNOM BANAN, CAMBODIA

Despite years of neglect and pillaging, this Angkor-era mountaintop temple is still worth a visit for its stunning views and intricate carvings. From the top of the temple, gaze out over lush rice fields, traditional villages, and dramatic mountains. Notable architectural features include carved lintels above doorways, and the five distinctive, intact towers of the temple, a key architectural element of Khmer temple design.

10 Best Snorkeling and Diving Sites in Thailand

KOH LIPE

Get your PADI certificate on Thailand's most southern island and explore its warm, uncrowded, aquamarine waters and more than 20 dive sites, including "Sting Ray City," "Stonehenge," 'Yong Hua Shipwreck," and "8 Mile Rock." Snorkelers will find beautiful marine life just offshore.

KOH TAO

A ferry ride from Koh Samui, Koh Tao Sail Rock is known as one of the best dive sites in all of Thailand for its "secret pinnacle." Aow Leuk offers prime snorkeling on the less-populated southern part of the island. Enter near the rocks on the right side for the best coral reef access.

KOH ROK ISLANDS

These two small, unspoiled islands, an hour from Koh Lanta, are part of Mu Loh Lanta Marine National Park and offer an abundance and diversity of marine life (with great turtle-spotting), some of the most pristine coral reefs in Thailand, and pretty beaches. Good for all levels.

HIN DAENG AND HIN MUANG

On the outer fringes of Mu Koh Lanta Marine Park and a three-hour trip from Koh Ngai, these famed diving sites are musts for experienced divers. Hin Daeng, known as Red Rock, and Hin Muang, known as Purple Rock, feature amazing color in the coral and anemones, steep walls, huge shoals of fish, whale and nurse sharks, tuna, barracuda, and more. Nearby Koh Ha (between Hin Daeng and Phi Phi) offers stunning caverns with stalactites and is a great spot for a night dive.

KOH PHI PHI

Snorkeling or diving around Koh Phi Phi's limestone cliffs is bucket-list stuff while in Thailand. Dive with leopard sharks at Shark Point, considered the best dive site at Koh Phi Phi, while Lana Bay and the Mosquito and Bamboo Islands offer rich and shallow coral reefs for snorkelers.

KOH CHANG

A haven for divers and those looking to get their PADI certification, Koh Chang is home to one of Thailand's largest shipwrecks, the HTMS *Chang*, making for an unforgettable diving experience. There are several rock pinnacles like Hin Luk Bat and Hin Rap where you can see the world's biggest fish, the whale shark. If you're looking to snorkel, make your way to Pearl Beach. Nearby islands like Koh Wai offer relatively

The HTMS *Chang* shipwreck

undisturbed islands and uncrowded dive sites with shallow, hard coral reef populated with stingrays, leopard sharks, and colorful reef fish.

KOH LARN

Aptly named Coral Island for its plentiful coral reefs, you'll find beautiful beaches and harmless tawny nurse sharks and blue spotted stingrays swimming just offshore. Head to Nual "Monkey" Beach for some more secluded snorkeling or any beach on the western part of the island for soft and hard corals.

KOH TALU

One of Thailand's few privately owned islands, snorkelers and divers off the pristine beaches at Koh Talu can see broad swaths of colorful fish thanks to the island's resident fish conservationist. Diving trips to nearby islands can also be arranged. The island's one resort has beachside bungalows, private beaches, snorkeling and diving opportunities, and guests can seed new coral in the reefs and contribute to sea turtle preservation efforts.

KOH SIMILAN

This group of nine islands with crystal-clear waters and a sea turtle sanctuary are protected national parks and only reachable by boat from November to April. Book a day tour or stay overnight at Pakarang Beach to snorkel islands four to nine from February on to see manta rays and whale sharks.

KOH KRADEN

This quiet island is off-the-beaten tourist track and known for its off-the-beach snorkeling. Enter the water in front of Ao Niang Resort and swim to a significant drop-off (that runs from the southern cape to the National Park headquarters) to find colorful corals and massive schools of fish.

10 Best Natural Wonders in Cambodia and Laos

TONLE SAP LAKE, CAMBODIA
One of Southeast Asia's biggest lakes, the Tonle Sap swells and shrinks seasonally based on fluctuations in the Mekong's water levels. Once a year, the lake's tributary experiences a reversal of flow that Cambodians celebrate with an exciting festival, Bon Om Touk, in November.

KOH RONG, CAMBODIA
One of the biggest islands off the southwest Cambodian coast still resists major development, and boasts 23 soft sand beaches where the bungalows and small resorts prefer to remain low key. Find dense jungle with great trekking and over 15 dive sites and stretches of reef offshore.

THE MEKONG RIVER, LAOS
The Mekong River has been Laos' lifeline for centuries and the stretch from Huay Xai to Luang Prabang remains the most popular way to experience the slow lifestyle of local river communities. The two-day trip stops in the village of Pak Beng before docking at Luang Prabang.

PHONGSALY, LAOS
This remote, less trafficked extreme northern corner of an already quiet country has some of Laos' most spectacular mountains, as well as dense forests containing an abundance of animal, bird, insect, and plant life. Trekking to the remote villages through these forest-covered roads and past rushing rivers is as close to the thrill of exploring virgin territory as it comes.

THAM KHONG LOR CAVE, LAOS
Over 200 miles south of Vientiane, the bustling Mekong River port of Tha Khek is known for its access to stunning surrounding countryside and access to natural attractions in Phu Hin Bun National Park, including the Blue Lagoon and the phenomenal Thanm Khong Lor cave. Riding a narrow boat through the dark, impressively long cave for up to an hour and then emerging to a wide green river, framed by lush green vegetation and limestone cliffs—and maybe buffalo cooling in the water—is an otherworldly experience.

KUANG SI FALLS, LAOS
An hour tuk-tuk ride from Luang Prabang, these stunning tiered falls offer cascades of milky-blue waters tumbling from lush jungle into perfectly formed pools where visitors can take a refreshing dip. Hike to the top where you will find quieter pools, incredible views of Lao countryside, and beautiful forest.

Kuang Si Falls, Laos

YEAK LAOM LAKE, CAMBODIA
This mystical lake, sacred to the Khmer Loeu hill tribes, occupies a volcanic crater and is bordered by lush jungle and beautiful wildlife. The emerald-hued lake is almost perfectly round, and at 154 meters deep, it's also extremely clear and clean. There are hammocks in huts lining its shore and wooden jetties from which to launch yourself into the cool waters.

Nature trails wind along the lakeside. A walk around the perimeter takes about forty minutes. Midway along the track, at the western end of the lake, there is a small visitor center where you can find local handicrafts; proceeds go directly to the local communities.

PHNOM KULEN NATIONAL PARK, CAMBODIA
This most sacred mountain in Cambodia, north of Angkor Wat, is a rewarding spot for a day hike with gorgeous waterfalls, archaeological sites such as the River of a Thousand Lingas which is strewn with phallic carvings, and the giant reclining Buddha in Preah Ang Thom.

KAMPI, CAMBODIA
The stretch of the Mekong running from Kampi, just north of Kratie, all the way to Laos is populated with the endangered freshwater Irrawaddy dolphins. Catching a glimpse of these rare creatures.

VIRACHEY NATIONAL PARK, CAMBODIA
A lush scenic jungle, best experienced on a tour so that you can spot rare wildlife, this park is home to an impressive two-tier waterfall, Bu Sra waterfall, a pristine and popular bathing and picnic spot. In Bang Lung, book at least a three-day trek led by English-speaking rangers for an authentic jungle experience.

Introduction to Thai Architecture

Though real architecture buffs are few and far between, you'd be hard-pressed to find a visitor to Thailand who doesn't spend at least a little time staring in slack-jawed amazement at the country's glittering wats and ornate palaces—and the elegant sculptures of the mythical beasts that protect them. As befits this spiritual nation, most of the fanfare is saved for religious structures, but you can find plenty to admire in the much simpler lines of the traditional houses of the Central Plains and northern Thailand. Look for small structures known as Spirit Houses which can be found on the grounds of many Thai homes. These miniature houses (often exact replicas of the houses to which they belong) are usually elevated on a pole like a birdhouse and festooned with flowers and incense to placate the spirits of the land.

WATS

Wat is the Thai name for what can range from a simple ordination hall for monks and nuns to a huge sprawling complex comprising libraries, bell towers, and meditation rooms. Usually the focal point for a community, it's not unusual for a wat to also be the grounds for village fêtes and festivals. Although most wats you come across symbolize some aspect of Thai-style Theravada Buddhism, examples of other architectural styles are relatively easy to find: Khmer ruins dot the Isan countryside to the east, while northern Thailand showcases many Burmese-style temples.

Wats are erected as acts of merit—allowing the donor to improve his karma and perhaps be reborn as a higher being—or in memory of great events. You can tell much about a wat's origin by its name. A wat *luang* (royal wat), for example, was constructed or restored by royals and may have the words *rat*, *raja*, or *racha* in its name (e.g., Ratburana or Rajapradit). The word *phra* may indicate that a wat contains an image of the Buddha. Wats that contain an important relic of the Buddha have the words *maha* (great) and *that* (relic) in their names. Thailand's nine major wat mahathats are in Chiang Rai, Chai Nat, Sukhothai, Phisanulk, Ayutthaya, Bangkok, Yasothon, Phetchaburi, and Nakhon Si Thammarat.

Thai wats, especially in the later periods, were seldom planned as entire units, so they often appear disjointed and crowded. To appreciate a wat's beauty you often have to look at its individual buildings.

Perhaps the most recognizable feature of a wat, and certainly a useful landmark when hunting them down, is the towering conelike *chedi*. Originally used to hold relics of the Buddha (hair, bones, or even nails), chedis can now be built by anyone with enough cash to house their ashes. At the base of the chedi you can find three platforms representing hell, Earth, and heaven, while the 33 Buddhist heavens are symbolized at the top of the tallest spire by a number of rings.

The main buildings of a wat are the *bot*, which contains a Buddha image and functions as congregation and ordination hall for the monks, and the *viharn*, which serves a similar function, but will hold the most important Buddha image. Standard bot and viharn roofs will feature three steeply curved levels featuring red, gold, and green tiles; the outer walls range from highly decorated to simply whitewashed.

Other noticeable features include the *mondop*, *prang*, and *ho trai*. Usually square with a pyramid-shape roof, the mondop is reminiscent of Indian temple architecture and serves as a kind of storeroom for holy artifacts, books, and ceremonial objects. The prang is a tall tower similar to the chedi, which came to Thailand by way of the Khmer empire and is used to store images of the Buddha. Easily identifiable by its stilts or raised platform, the ho trai is a library for holy scriptures.

Roofs, which are covered in glazed clay tiles or wooden shakes, generally consist of three overlapping sections, with the lower roof set at gentle slopes, increasing to a topmost roof with a pitch of 60 degrees. Eave brackets in the form of a *naga* (snakes believed to control the irrigation waters of rice fields) with its head at the bottom often support the lower edges of the roofs. Along the eaves of many roofs are a row of small brass bells with clappers attached to thin brass pieces shaped like Bodhi tree leaves.

During the early Ayutthaya period (1350–1767), wat interiors were illuminated by the light passing through vertical slits in the walls (wider, more elaborate windows would have compromised the strength of the walls and, thus, the integrity of the structure). In the Bangkok period (1767–1932), the slits were replaced by proper windows set below wide lintels that supported the upper portions of the brick walls. There are usually five, seven, or nine windows on a side in accordance with the Thai preference for odd numbers. The entrance doors are in the end wall facing the Buddha image; narrower doors may flank the entrance door.

PALACES

The Grand Palace has been the official residence of the Kings of Siam (and later Thailand) since 1782. Shots of the palace with its gleaming spires flood-lighted up at night fill every postcard stand, and it's arguably Bangkok's single most important tourist attraction.

Built in 1782 when King Rama I chose Bangkok as Siam's new capital, the Grand Palace is the only remaining example of early Ratanakosin architecture—Rama II and III chose not to initiate any large-scale construction projects in the face of economic hardship. A primarily functional collection of buildings, the compound contains the Royal Thai Decorations and Coin Pavilion, the Museum of Fine Art, and the Weapons Museum.

Also worth checking out while in the capital is what is believed to be the world's largest golden teak-wood building. The three-story Vimanmek Palace was moved from Chonburi in the east to Bangkok's Dusit Palace, and contains jewelry and gifts given as presents from around the world.

Rama IV led the revival of palace construction in the second half of the 19th century, overseeing the building of several royal getaways. Perhaps the most impressive of these is Phra Nakhon Khiri in the southern town of Phetchaburi. Known locally as Khao Wang, the palace sits atop a mountain with wonderful panoramic views. Sharing its mountain home are various wat, halls, and thousands of macaque monkeys. Klai Kangwon in nearby Hua Hin is still used as a seaside getaway for the royal family and as a base when they visit southern provinces. Built in 1926 by Rama VI, the two-story concrete palace's name translates as Far From Worries and was built in the style of European châteaux.

HOUSES

Traditional Thai houses are usually very simple and essentially boil down to three basic components: stilts, a deck, and a sloping roof. Heavy, annual monsoon rains all over the country necessitate that living quarters be raised on stilts to escape flooding; in the dry season the space under the house is typically used as storage for farming equipment or other machinery. The deck of the house is essentially the living room—it's where you can find families eating, cooking, and just plain relaxing.

As with wats, it's often the roofs of houses that are the most interesting. Lanna-style (northern Thailand) roofs, usually thatched or tiled, are thought to have evolved from the Thai people's roots in southern China, where steeply pitched roofs would have been needed to combat heavy snows. Although there's no real chance of a snowball fight in Thailand, the gradient and overhang allows for quick runoff of the rains and welcome shade from the sun.

These basics are fairly uniform throughout the country, with a few small adjustments to accommodate different climates. For example, roofs are steepest in areas with more intense weather patterns, like the Central Plains, and northern Thai houses have smaller windows to conserve heat better.

Thailand Today

ROYALTY AND THE GOVERNMENT

Thailand is a constitutional monarchy, in which the prime minister is head of government and the king head of state; in practice, the country is at present ruled by the government. Beloved King Bhumibol Adulyadej (King Rama IX), the world's longest-reigning head of state, died in October 2016. The country was in mourning for a year. He was succeeded by his only son, Prince Vajiralongkorn who is three times divorced, made his late poodle Foo Foo an air chief marshal, and was once described by his mother as "a bit of a Don Juan." Politically, Thailand is a country divided. Populist Thaksin Shinawatra, prime minister of Thailand from 2001 to 2006, inspired political rifts among Thais. In 2006 Thaksin was overthrown in a bloodless military coup and went into exile. A general election in 2007 brought in the pro-Thaksin People's Power Party. Many considered it to be a puppet for Thaksin. Political riots escalated in 2008, at times halting government operations and even temporarily shutting down the international airport. The worst broke out in April and May 2010, when the anti-government Red Shirts staged protests across Bangkok. For weeks business and politics remained at a standstill until the military crushed the protests. Nothing was resolved. Protesters went home but vowed to continue their fight against the government. In July 2011 Yingluck Shinawatra, the younger sister of Thaksin, became prime minister. She oversaw a contentious political period through May 7, 2014, when she was removed from office. After yet more protests, on May 20, 2014, the military implemented martial law, repealed the constitution, ousted several former cabinet members, and put a tight rein on the country with General Prayuth Chan-ocha at the helm. On April 2, 2015, the government lifted martial law and replaced it with a controversial security order that gives the military junta widespread powers. And the political drama marches on. Prayuth Chan-ocha remains prime minister of Thailand. Elections were meant to be held in November 2018, then February 2019, and are now scheduled for May 2019. The liberal Future Forward party, led by auto parts scion Thanathorn Juangroongruangkit and law lecturer Piyabutr Saengkanokkul, hopes to capture the youth vote. As of this writing, because parties other than the junta are not allowed to campaign, it remains to be seen whether the election will be fair or a farce. Note that Thailand's politics barely impact tourism, save for protests in Bangkok leading to traffic jams.

ETHNIC DIVERSITY

Throughout its history, Thailand has absorbed countless cultural influences, and is home to groups with Chinese, Tibetan, Lao, Khmer, Malaysian, Burmese, and other origins. Migrating tribes from modern-day China, Cambodia, Myanmar, and the Malay Peninsula were the region's earliest inhabitants. Ancient trade routes meant constant contact with merchants traveling from India, China, and other parts of Southeast Asia. Conflicts and treaties, continue to alter the country's borders and ethnicity. Contemporary Thailand's cultural richness comes from its ethnic diversity. Though Buddhism is the predominant religion, Hindu and animist influences abound, and there's a significant Muslim population in the south. Malay is spoken in the southern provinces, Lao and Khmer dialects of Thai are spoken in the northeast, and the hill tribes have their own dialects as well.

MYSTICISM

Many Thais believe in astrology and supernatural energy. The animist element of Thai spirituality dictates that everything, from buildings to trees, has a spirit. With so many spirits and forces out there, it's no surprise that appeasing them is a daily consideration. Thais often wear amulets blessed by monks to ward off evil, and they believe that tattoos, often of real or mythical animals, bring strength and protect the wearer. Newspapers solemnly report that politicians have consulted their favorite astrologers before making critical policy decisions. Businesses erect shrines to powerful deities outside their premises, sometimes positioned to repel the power of their rivals' shrines.

THE IMPORTANCE OF SANUK

That's the word for Thai fun. Thais believe that every activity should be fun—work, play, even funerals. Of course, this isn't always practical, but it's a worthy aim. Thais enjoy being together in large parties, making lots of noise, and—as sanuk nearly always involves food—eating. They are also guided by a number of other behavior principles. Many, such as jai yen (cool heart) and mai pen rai (never mind), are rooted in the Buddhist philosophies of detachment, and result in a noncon frontational demeanor and an easygoing attitude. Giving and sharing are important, since being generous is an act of merit making, a way of storing up points for protection in this life and in future lives.

WHAT'S HOT IN THAILAND NOW

Thailand has always had a flair for art, creativity, and fun. You'll find that today in everything from fashion to interior design to the clever ads blaring across BTS stations as you wait for your train. Sophisticated Thai architects and designers create some of the world's most inviting spaces, using a mix of traditional materials (teak, silk, stone, clay) with modern elements and elegant styling. Visit a chic spa for a perfect example of this. This is a country oriented toward youth, and young Thais are as hip and connected as ever, wearing the trendiest clothes and obsessing with the latest digital devices (and if any of your Apple accoutrements break during your visit, you'll quickly find all necessary replacements). There's a rapidly growing contemporary art scene scattered across Bangkok (check out the Museum of Contemporary Art and the Bangkok Art and Culture Centre near the National Stadium BTS) and in the university area of Chiang Mai. Food in Thailand is always trendy, and city chefs are adept at mixing Thai flavors with other cuisines, though that hasn't displaced the myriad street stalls slinging delicious, inexpensive Thai comfort fare; street eats never go out of style, with several stalls attracting international awards and attention. Bangkok's drinking scene has evolved in recent years, too, to include an influx of wine bars and craft beer venues that cater to locals and foreigners alike. And perhaps no other metropolis on Earth has quite the collection of rooftop sky bars as Bangkok—don't miss a cocktail on an open-air patio 30 floors or more above the cacophony below. If alcohol isn't your thing, Thailand is awash with slick third-wave coffee shops catering to java connoisseurs. These days you'll never have to go without that work-of art cappuccino in a Thai city. But some things never change. Bangkok is—and likely always will be—a city to experience on the street. There's no better way to get a feel for Bangkok than to spend the day jostling with crowds on the sidewalks, grazing from one food stall to the next, people-watching all the way. Too hot? Tired feet? There's always an ice-cold shopping mall around the next corner. Step inside and catch an ear-splittingly loud blockbuster movie before heading back into the chaos. Another thing never seems to change in Thailand: despite the country's repeated, ongoing political troubles, tourism and development seem never to stop. Thailand is consistently a favorite pick among foreign visitors, year after year.

THAILAND BEST BETS

Fodor's writers and editors have chosen our favorites to help you plan. Search individual chapters for more recommendations.

RESTAURANTS

BANGKOK

Appia, *$$$, Ch. 3*

Bo.Ian, *$$$$, Ch. 3*

Breeze, *$$$$, Ch. 3*

Gaggan, *$$$$, Ch. 3*

Isao, *$$$, Ch. 3*

Le Normandie, *$$$$, Ch. 3*

Lek Seafood, *$$, Ch. 3*

Mezzaluna, *$$$$, Ch. 3*

Paste Restaurant, *$$$$, Ch. 3*

Pen, *$$$$, Ch. 3*

Peppina, *$$$, Ch. 3*

Raan Jay Fai, *$$$, Ch. 3*

Soul Food Mahanakorn, *$$, Ch. 3*

Sra Bua by Kin Kin, *$$$$, Ch. 3*

Supanniga Eating Room, *$$, Ch. 3*

Suhring The Local, *$$$$, Ch. 3*

The Local, *$$$, Ch. 3*

T&K Seafood, *$$, Ch.2*

Zanotti, *$$$, Ch. 3*

THE GULF COAST BEACHES

Koti, *$$, Ch. 5*

PHUKET AND THE ANDAMAN COAST

Breeze at Cape Yamu, *$$$$, Ch. 6*

Kopitiam by Wilai, *$, Ch. 6*

Marina Villa, *$$, Ch. 6*

On the Rock, *$$$, Ch. 6*

Otto Bar & Grill, *$, Ch. 6*

Raya Restaurant, *$, Ch. 6*

Suay, *$$, Ch. 6*

Time for Lime, *$$, Ch. 6*

CHIANG MAI

Dash Teak House, *$$, Ch. 7*

David's Kitchen, *$$$$, Ch. 7*

Overstand, *$, Ch. 7*

Rachamankha, *$$$$, Ch. 7*

Temple House Lamphun, *$$, Ch. 7*

NORTHERN THAILAND

Coriander in Redwood, *$$, Ch. 8*

Sihouette, *$$, Ch. 8*

CAMBODIA

Cuisine Wat Damnak, *$$$$, Ch. 9*

Devantas Restaurant, *$, Ch. 9*

Divino, *$, Ch. 9*

Epic Arts Café, *$, Ch. 9*

Friends the Restaurant, *$, Ch. 9*

Mahob, *$$, Ch. 9*

Mie Café, *$$, Ch. 9*

Sandan, *$, Ch. 9*

ST 63 Bassac, *$, Ch. 9*

Tepui, *$$$$, Ch. 9*

The Sugar Palm, *$$, Ch. 9*

LAOS

Acqua, *$$, Ch. 10*

Apsara Restaurant, *$$, Ch. 10*

Carpe Diem, *$$, Ch. 10*

The Bamboo Lounge, *$, Ch. 10*

Kitchen by the Mekong, *$, Ch. 10*

La Signature, *$$$, Ch. 10*

L'Elephant Restaurant Francais, *$$$, Ch. 10*

Manda de Laos, *$$, Ch. 10*

Souphailan's Restaurant, *$, Ch. 10*

Tamarind Restaurant and Cooking School, *$, Ch. 10*

Tamnak Lao, *$, Ch. 10*

The River Resort Restaurant, *$, Ch. 10*

Villa Opera, *$$$, Ch. 10*

HOTELS

BANGKOK

The Okura Prestige, *$$$$, Ch. 3*

Chakrabongse Villas, *$$$$, Ch. 3*

COMO Metropolitan Bangkok, *$$$$, Ch. 3*

The Cabochon Hotel, *$$$$, Ch. 3*

Mandarin Oriental Bangkok, *$$$$, Ch. 3*

Marriott Hotel Sukhumvit, *$$$, Ch. 3*

Millenium Hilton Bangkok, *$$$$, Ch. 3*

Shangri-La Hotel Bangkok, *$$$$, Ch. 3*

Sofitel So Bangkok, *$$$$, Ch. 3*

The Siam Hotel, *$$$$, Ch. 3*

The St. Regis Bangkok, *$$$$, Ch. 3*

Tower Club at Lebua, *$$$$, Ch. 3*

AROUND BANGKOK

Classic Kameo Hotel, *$$, Ch. 4*

House of Passion, *$$, Ch. 4*

THE GULF COAST BEACHES

Emerald Cove Koh Chang, *$$$, Ch. 5*

Amari Ocean Pattaya, *$$$, Ch. 5*

Centara Grand Beach Resort and Villas, *$$$, Ch. 5*

Charm Churee Villa, *$$, Ch. 5*

Chiva-Som, *$$$$, Ch. 5*

Dusit Thani Hua Hin Hotel, *$$$, Ch. 5*

Four Seasons Koh Samui, *$$$$, Ch. 5*

InterContinental Pattaya Resort, *$$$, Ch. 5*

Poppies, *$$$$, Ch. 5*

Santiburi Resort and Spa, *$$$$, Ch. 5*

Six Senses Samui, *$$$$, Ch. 5*

The Place Luxury Boutique Villas, *$$$$, Ch. 5*

PHUKET AND THE ANDAMAN COAST

Aleenta Phuket Resort & Spa, *$$$$, Ch. 6*

Amanpuri Resort, *$$$$, Ch. 6*

Banyan Tree Phuket, *$$$$, Ch. 6*

COMO Point Yamu, *$$$$, Ch. 6*

Holiday Inn Resort, *$$, Ch. 6*

J.W. Marriott Resort & Spa, *$$$, Ch. 6*

Keemala, *$$$$, Ch. 6*

Koyao Island Resort, *$$$$, Ch. 6*

La Flora Resort & Spa, *$$$, Ch. 6*

Layana Resort & Spa, *$$$$, Ch. 6*

Pimalai Resort and Spa, *$$$$, Ch. 6*

Railei Beach Club, *$$, Ch. 6*

Rosewood Phuket, *$$$$, Ch. 6*

Sri Panwa, *$$$$, Ch. 6*

Thanyapura Health & Sports Resort, *$$, Ch. 6*

The Slate, *$$$, Ch. 6*

Zeavola, *$$$$, Ch. 6*

CHIANG MAI

Anantara Chiang Mai Resort, *$$$$, Ch. 7*

Banjai Garden, *$, Ch. 7*

Dhara Dhevi Chiang Mai, *$$$$, Ch. 7*

Muang Gudi Lodge, *$$, Ch. 7*

Rachamankha, *$$$$, Ch. 7*

Riverside Guest House, *$, Ch. 7*

NORTHERN THAILAND

Anantara Golden Triangle Elephant Camp & Resort, *$$$$, Ch. 8*

Chiang Dao Nest, *$, Ch. 8*

Four Seasons Tented Camp Golden Triangle, *$$$$, Ch. 8*

Legendha, *$$, Ch. 8*

Maekok River Village Resort, *$$, Ch. 8*

Reverie Siam Resort, *$$$, Ch. 8*

Sukhothai Heritage Resort, *$$, Ch. 8*

The Legend, *$$$, Ch. 8*

CAMBODIA

Amansara, *$$$$, Ch. 9*

Battambang Resort, *$$, Ch. 9*

Bric-a-brac, *$$, Ch. 9*

Heritage Suites Hotel, *$$$$, Ch. 9*

Knai Bang Chatt, *$$$$, Ch. 9*

Lazy Beach, *Koh Rong Samloen, $$, Ch. 9*

Rajabori Villas Resort, *$$, Ch. 9*

Rambutan Resort Phnom Penh, *$, Ch. 9*

Rambutan Resort Siem Reap, *$$, Ch. 9*

Samanea Beach Resort, *$$$, Ch. 9*

Shinta Mani Angkor, *$$$$, Ch. 9*

Sojourn Boutique Villas, *$$$$, Ch. 9*

Song Saa Private Island, *$$$$, Ch. 9*

The Pavilion, *$$, Ch. 9*

The Plantation, *$$, Ch. 9*

LAOS

Hotel 3 Nagas, *$$, Ch. 10*

Angsana Maison Souvannaphoum, *$$, Ch. 10*

Ansara Hotel, *$$$, Ch. 10*

La Folie Lodge, *$$$$, Ch. 10*

Residence Sisouk, *$$, Ch. 10*

Riverside Boutique Resort, *$$$, Ch. 10*

Satri House, *$$$$, Ch. 10*

Settha Palace, *$$$$, Ch. 10*

The River Resort, *$$$, Ch. 10*

Victoria Xiengthong Palace, *$$$, Ch. 10*

NIGHTLIFE

BANGKOK

Beam, *Ch. 3*

Havana Social, *Ch. 3*

Sky Bar, *Ch. 3*

Moon Bar, *Ch. 3*

Octave, *Ch. 3*

CHIANG MAI

North Gate Jazz Co-Op, *Ch. 7*

SHOPPING

BANGKOK

Chatuchak Weekend Market, *Ch. 3*

Jim Thompson Thai Silk Company, *Ch. 3*

Phahurat Market, *Ch. 3*

CHIANG MAI

Kad Kong Ta Market, *Ch. 7*

Night Bazaar, *Ch. 7*

Studio Naenna, *Ch. 7*

Wattana Art Gallery, *Ch. 7*

COOKING CLASSES

BANGKOK

Blue Elephant Cooking School, *Ch. 3*

Oriental Cooking School, *Ch. 3*

CHIANG MAI

Baan Thai Cookery School, *Ch. 7*

Chiang Mai Thai Cookery School, *Ch. 7*

Thai Farm Cooking School, *Ch. 7*

What to Read and Watch Before Your Trip

PREMIKA
This gloriously absurd Thai horror-comedy romp by Thai director Siwakorn Jarupongpa boldly asks the question: What if being bad at karaoke had consequences? *Deadly* consequences.

TROPICAL MALADY
This Cannes Jury Prize winner by one of Thailand's leading experimental filmmakers, Apichatpong Weerasethakul, is a blissfully unconventional work and a beguiling meditation on love and the animal nature of mankind.

THE OVERTURE
Based on the life of legendary court musician and master of the ranad-ek (Thai xylophone) Luang Pradit Pairo, this 2004 period drama takes place in the golden age of Thai classical music, the late 19th-century through the 1930s, when the playing of such music was banned by the government.

SHUTTER
After fleeing from the scene of a hit-and-run, a Bangkok photographer, Tun, and his frightened wife, Jane, are haunted by a ghostly figure that appears in the background of his pictures. Unrelenting dread permeates every frame of this 2004 horror movie from Thai filmmakers Banjong Pisanthanakun and Parkpoom Wongpoom.

ONG BAK: MUAY THAI WARRIOR
No CGI. No wires. Just inventive stunts and world-class fight choreography. The plot follows Ting (Tony Jaa) as he leaves his rural home for the big city of Bangkok in order to retrieve the stolen head of a sacred Buddha statue. Jaa's martial arts skills here drew comparisons to Bruce Lee and Jackie Chan.

THE LIONESS IN BLOOM: MODERN THAI FICTION ABOUT WOMEN
The short stories and excerpted novels in this collection explore topics as diverse as their Thai authors. Some are humorous and witty, some are bleak and heartbreaking. But they all provide a well-rounded look at what womanhood means to the women of Thailand.

FOUR REIGNS BY KUKRIT PRAMOJ
The story of this historical novel follows the life of Phloi, a woman who arrives at the royal palace as a young girl and minor courtier, and follows her as she experiences the reigns of four Chakri Kings. As Phloi observes the massive upheaval that culminated in the 1932 coup that forced the dissolution of the monarchy, she must decide how she, too, must adapt for a new, shifting age.

HUSH! A THAI LULLABY BY MINFONG HO
In this atmospheric Caldecott Honor-winning children's book, written in verse and charmingly illustrated, a mother entreats the animals that surround her home to be quiet and still as her baby sleeps. By book's end the mother and all the animals are sleeping but Baby, of course, is wide-awake.

JASMINE NIGHTS BY S. P. SOMTOW
This semi-autobiographical novel, set in the early 1960s, follows a young boy named Justin (but nicknamed Little Frog by his family) as he navigates between two lives. One is on his family's estate where he lives in the care of his eccentric aunts. The other takes him into a ruined house where he makes a game weaving science fiction, Homer, and spirits out of Thai mythology.

SIGHTSEEING BY RATTAWUT LAPCHAROENSAP
This collection of short stories marks the debut of Rattawut Lapcharoensap, a Thai-American writer who was only 26 at the time of its publication. Set in contemporary Thailand, Lapcharoensap's characters are sharply drawn and his stories illuminate the beauty in even the bleakest of places.

COUPS & THE KING

THAILAND'S TURBULENT HISTORY

by Karen Coates

Thais share a reverence for their king, Bhumibol Adulyadej, who has been the nation's moral leader and a unifying figure since 1946. Thais are also united by a deep pride in their country, a constitutional monarchy and the only Southeast Asian nation never colonized by Europeans. But this hasn't stopped political turmoil from roiling beneath the surface and erupting.

Though northeastern Thailand has been inhabited for about 2,500 years, it wasn't until 1238 that Thai princes drove the Cambodian Khmers out of central Thailand and established Sukhothai, the first centralized Thai state. There was conflict again in the late 14th century, when the rival state of Ayutthaya conquered Sukhothai. After over 400 years of power, Ayutthaya in turn was defeated by the Burmese in the late 18th century, and the Thais established a new capital in Bangkok.

As European influence in Southeast Asia grew, Thailand alternated between periods of isolation and openness to foreign trade and ideas. Western-style democracy was one idea that took hold in the early 20th century. But since then a pattern has emerged in Thai politics: a prime minister is elected, allegations of corruption surface, the public protests, and the leader is ousted.

King Rama V (1853–1910) and family

4,000–2,000 BC Rice first cultivated in Thailand

1238 Sukhothai kingdom founded

1350 Ayutthaya kingdom founded

4000 BC 1200 1300 1400

(top) Pottery found at Ban Chiang; (left) stone face at Bayon in Angkor Thom, Cambodia; (bottom) Khmer elephant-shaped box.

4000–2000 BC Bronze & Rice

Scientists think that northeastern Thailand was a hotbed for agricultural innovation. In fact, the Mon people from modern-day Myanmar who settled in Ban Chiang may have been Asia's first farmers. Archaeologists have found ancient pottery, bronze rings, spearheads, bracelets, and axes.

500–1400 Great Migrations

Historians believe the Thais' ancestors were the ethnic Tai people of southern China. The Tai migrated south into modern-day Thailand in waves, but the biggest southern push came after the Mongols invaded their kingdom in the 13th century. The fleeing Tai settled in the Mekong River Valley, inventing elaborate agricultural systems to farm rice. Around this time, the Khmers of what is today called Cambodia were extending the Angkor empire west into Thailand.

1238–1438 Sukhothai & the Golden Age

In 1238 chieftains established the first Thai kingdom at Sukhothai in central Thailand, kicking out the Khmer overlords. The Sukhothai kingdom united many Thai settlements and marked the beginning of a prosperous era when, legend has it, the rivers were full of fish, and the paddies were lush with rice. In the late 13th century, King Ramkhamhaeng created a writing system that is the basis of the modern Thai alphabet.

1511
Portuguese
arrive

1782
Capital moves to Bangkok

1767
Ayutthaya falls to Burmese invaders

1500 1600 1700

(left) Interior of Wat Po, Bangkok; (top) Royal jewelry from Ayutthaya; (bottom) Buddha statue from Ayutthaya.

1350–1767 Ayutthaya Kingdom

King Ramathibodi founded the kingdom of Ayutthaya, 45 miles up the Chao Phraya River from Bangkok, in 1350 and took over Sukhothai 25 years later. The king made Theravada Buddhism the kingdom's official religion and established the Dharmashastra, a legal code with roots in Hindu Indian texts. Ayutthaya, a city of canals and golden temples, became wealthy and prominent.

1511–1800S European Influence

The Portuguese were the first Europeans to arrive in Thailand, establishing an embassy in Ayutthaya in 1511. But they brought more than ambassadors: The Portuguese also brought the first chilies to the country, making a huge contribution to Thai cuisine.

Over the following centuries of European trade and relations, Thailand's kings charted a sometimes tenuous course of autonomy as their neighbors were colonized by the Portuguese, Dutch, English, and French.

1767–1809 Burmese Invasion & New Beginnings

In 1767 the Burmese sacked Ayutthaya, destroying palaces, temples, artwork, and written records. But within two years, General Phraya Taksin ran out the Burmese and established a new capital at Thonburi, which is today a part of Bangkok. Taksin became king but was forced from power and executed in 1782. After this coup, Buddha Yodfa Chulaloke the Great (known as Rama I) took control. He moved the capital across the river, where he built the Grand Palace in the image of past Thai kingdoms.

1893–1907
Territory ceded to French

1850 1875 1900

(left) King Mongkut with queen;
(top) *The King and I*;
(bottom) 19th-century tin coin.

1851–1931 *The King and I* & Beyond

In 1862, Anna Leonowens, an English schoolteacher, traveled to Bangkok with her son to serve as royal governess to King Mongkut's wives and children. Leonowens's memoirs inspired Margaret Landon's controversial novel Anna and the King of Siam, which in turn was the basis for the well-known Broadway musical The King and I and the subsequent film.

Thais were deeply offended by the film, which portrays the king as foolish and barbaric; The King and I was consequently banned in Thailand. A 1999 remake, Anna and the King, followed Leonowens's version of the story more closely, but Thais, who are extremely devoted to their royal family, still found this version culturally insensitive.

Mongkut (or Rama IV) earned the nickname "Father of Science and Technology" for his efforts to modernize the country. He signed a trade treaty with Great Britain, warding off other colonial powers while opening Thailand to foreign innovation.

After Rama IV's death in 1868, his son Chulalongkorn became king. Also called "Rama the Great," Chulalongkorn is credited with preserving Thailand's independence and abolishing slavery.

1932–41 Constitutional Era

Thailand moved toward Western-style democracy when young intellectuals staged a bloodless coup against King Prajadhipok (Rama VII) in 1931. Thailand's first constitution was signed that year and parliamentary elections were held the next. In the new system—a constitutional monarchy similar to England's—the king is still head of state, but he doesn't have much legal power.

In 1939 the government changed the country's name from Siam to Thailand. The new name refers to the Tai people; Tai also means "free" in Thai.

1939 Siam renamed Thailand | 1942 Alliance formed with Japan | 1944 Phibun ousted | 1932 First elections held | 1946 Rama IX crowned | 1959–75 Vietnam War

1925 — 1950 — 1975

(left) Bridge over the River Kwai; (top) U.S. pilot in Vietnam; (bottom) Postage stamp c. 1950 featuring king Bhumibol Adulyadej.

World War II

1941–46

In 1941, Japan helped Thailand win a territorial conflict with France over parts of French Indochina (modern-day Cambodia, Laos, and Vietnam.) Later that year, the Japanese demanded free passage through Thailand so that they could attack Malaya and Burma. In 1942, under the leadership of Phibun, a military general elected prime minister in 1938, Thailand formed an alliance with Japan.

The Japanese conquered Burma and began to construct the Thailand–Burma "Death Railway," so named because over 100,000 Asian forced-laborers and Allied POWs died while working on it. Meanwhile, an underground resistance called Seri Thai gathered strength as Thais turned against the Phibun regime and the Japanese occupation. Phibun was ousted in 1944 and replaced by a government friendly to the Allies.

In 1946 King Rama VIII was murdered. He was succeeded by his brother, the beloved Bhumibol Adulyadej (Rama IX) who was the world's longest serving head of state until his death in late 2016.

The Vietnam War

1961–75

While publicly staying neutral, the Thai government let the U.S. Air Force use bases throughout Thailand to bomb Laos and Cambodia between 1961 and 1975. Meanwhile, Bangkok and Thailand's beaches became playgrounds to thousands of soldiers on leave. The Westernization of Thai popular culture has roots in the Vietnam era, when restaurants and bars catered to beer- and Coke-drinking Americans.

(left) Protesters occupying the Government House garden. Bangkok, September 3rd 2008; (top) Banner demanding that ousted P.M. Thaksin Shinawatra and his wife return to Thailand to stand trial; (bottom) Samak Sundaravej.

1973–PRESENT

Unrest

A new democracy movement gained force in 1973, when protesters charged the streets of Bangkok after students were arrested on antigovernment charges. On October 14, protests erupted into bloody street battles, killing dozens. More violent outbreaks occurred on October 6th, 1976, and again in "Black May" of 1992, when a military crackdown resulted in more than 50 deaths.

In 2001, billionaire Thaksin Shinawatra was elected prime minister on a platform of economic growth and rural development. The year after he was elected, he dissolved the liaison between the Muslim southern provinces and the largely Buddhist administration in Bangkok, rekindling bloody unrest after years of quiet. The situation escalated until insurgents attacked a Thai army arsenal in early 2004; thousands have been killed in frequent outbursts of violence in southern Thailand.

In September 2006, Thaksin was ousted by a junta, which controlled the country until voters approved a new constitution and elected Samak Sundaravej prime minister. He was forced to resign months later and was quickly replaced by Somchai Wongsawat, Thaksin's brother-in-law.

The protests did not end there. In late 2008 Somchai was forced to step down, and Parliament voted in Abhisit Vejjajiva, leader of the opposition party. Since 2011, anti-government protests have increased, and 2014 saw a coup d'etat and the establishment of a military junta. Thailand's long voyage toward democracy is ongoing.

In 2016, King Bhumibol Adulyadej (Rama IX), the world's longest reigning monarch, died at age 88 after a long illness. The King was immensely popular and commanded great love and respect during his reign. He was seen as a leader who skillfully charted a course that put the monarchy at the center of Thai society, even as the country lurched between political crises and military coups. After a year of mourning, Bhumibol's son and successor, King Rama X or King Maha Vajiralongkorn Bodindradebayavarangkun ascended the throne.

Chapter 2

TRAVEL SMART THAILAND

Updated by
Barbara Woolsey

★ CAPITAL
Bangkok

POPULATION
69,199,763

LANGUAGE
Thai

€ CURRENCY
Thai Baht

COUNTRY CODE
66

⚠ EMERGENCIES
191 Police,
1155 Tourist Police,
1669 Ambulance

DRIVING
On the left

ELECTRICITY
220v/50 cycles; electrical plugs have two flat prongs (the same as in the U.S.)

TIME
11 hours ahead of New York during daylight savings time; 12 hours ahead in the winter

WEB RESOURCES
www.tourismthailand.org, www.bangkokpost.com

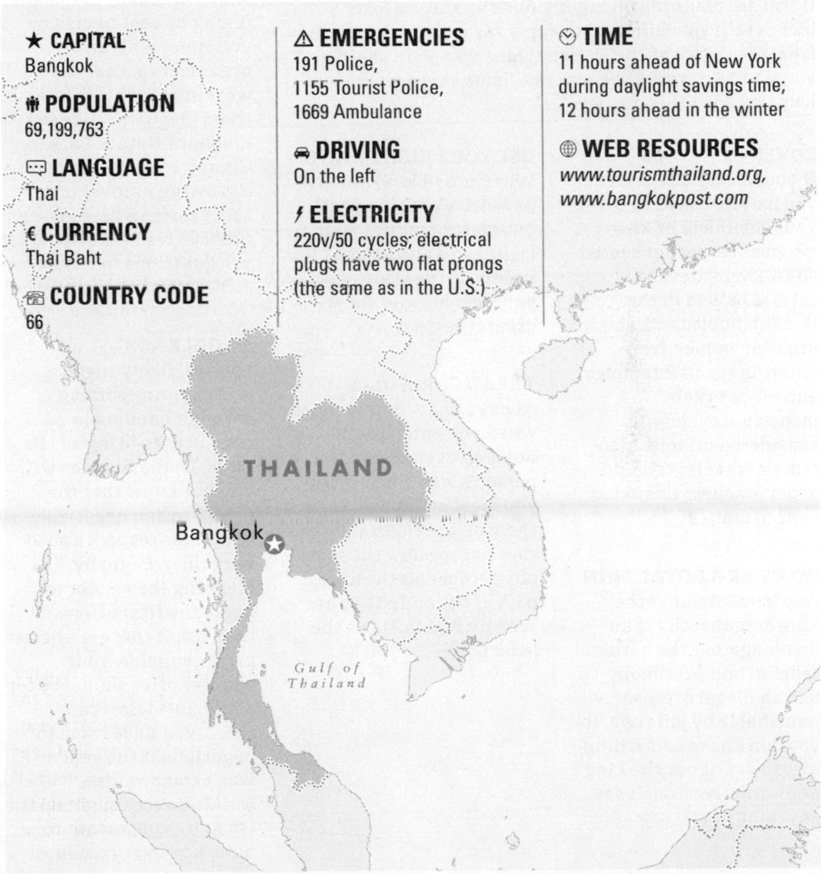

THAILAND
Bangkok
Gulf of Thailand

What You Need to Know Before You Visit Thailand

DON'T BUY ANYTHING WITH BUDDHA ON IT
While it isn't likely that you'll be arrested for buying a keychain featuring the image of the Buddha, you will notice signs throughout various cities that warn against disrespecting this Thai leader. Merchants who print his image on anything—from t-shirts to handbags and magnets—must source these goods from other countries, since Thailand bans the practice. If you want to be mindful of the rules of the region, it is recommended to avoid funding this form of sales. Also, don't get a tattoo of the Buddha; it is considered sacrilegious.

If you are planning on buying Buddha statues (over 5 inches tall) you will need to apply for an export permit from the Office of the National Museum. Plan ahead and allow 4 to 5 days for the process. Some shop owners will help you with this process.

COVER UP LADIES
If you're a female traveler, you may be asked to cover your shoulders or knees as a sign of respect at sacred sites. There are also certain beliefs in the Buddhist culture that prohibit women from entering specific temples entirely, as their menstrual cycles are considered unholy. Also, female travelers should avoid touching or sitting next to monks.

DON'T BE A ROYAL PAIN
Any insult against the king or monarchy is an insult against the national religion and patrimony and an illegal offense punishable by jail time. If you don't have something nice to say about the king or his relatives, don't say anything at all.

USE YOUR RIGHT HAND
When possible do not give or receive anything with your left hand; use your right hand and support it lightly at the elbow with your left hand to show greater respect.

TREAD CAREFULLY
Always remove your shoes when you enter a home. Do not step over a seated person's legs. Don't point your feet at anyone; keep them on the floor, and take care not to show the soles of your feet (as the lowest part of the body, they are seen by Buddhists as the least holy).

ELEPHANT ENCOUNTERS ARE A NO-NO
You may have visions of riding an elephant through the jungle but a debate is raging in Thailand, and internationally, as to the ethics of such animal interactions so you may want to reconsider that selfie. Tourism perpetuates the captivity of elephants but it also helps fund their care so you see the dilemma. Check your conscience and consider the welfare of these gentle giants before signing up for any kind of animal interaction. If you want to see an elephant in real life, it may be best to visit or volunteer with an organization that is working to rehabilitate these elephants, like the Elephant Nature Park in Chiang Mai. There are also a growing number of sanctuaries where you can observe rescued elephants; ask questions to ensure an ethical experience.

HAGGLE
You will likely spend a pretty penny sorting through handmade treasures to bring a little bit of Thailand home with you but know that the price is often negotiable and Thais respect a good bargainer. Begin by allowing the vendor to make the first offer, and then ask if there is a better price available. Your counter offer should be for about 30% less. From there, you have room to negotiate. If the vendor won't compromise, walking away might do the trick. It is important to note, however, that most

vendors make their income from selling these products, so while you shouldn't be short-changed yourself, you also don't want to insult them with a ridiculously low wager. Also, please don't bargain unless you plan to buy.

DON'T DRINK FROM THE TAP
Though you might watch a local sip, your digestive system likely isn't adjusted to the enzymes present in Thai aqua. Drink only bottled water, and use bottled or boiled water to brush your teeth.

TAKE THREE
Thais don't like anything done in twos, a number associated with death. Hence, you should buy three mangoes, not two, and stairways have odd numbers of stairs.

SLOW DOWN
Thais aim to live with a "cool heart" or jai yen—free from emotional extremes. Since being in a hurry shows an obvious lack of calm, they don't rush and aren't always punctual. Try to leave space in your itinerary for this relaxed attitude, since something will invariably happen to slow your progress.

PARK YOURSELF HERE
Thailand has 127 land and marine national parks with many rare species of flora and fauna. The National Park Wildlife and Plant Conservation Department *www.dnp.go.th/index_eng.asp* has some useful information on facilities, animal-spotting opportunities, notable features like waterfalls, and available cabin rentals or camping areas (you can book accommodation online), plus weather news and updates on which areas are closed. The more easily navigable site, *www.thainationalparks.com*, has even more info.

KID FRIENDLY
Thais dote on kids, so chances are you'll get extra help and attention when traveling with them, and the experience should be relatively problem-free. Powdered, canned, and pasteurized milk are readily available. Stomach bugs and infections thrive in the tropical climate. Basic cleanliness—washing hands frequently and making sure any cuts are treated with antibacterial ointment and covered—is the best protection against bacteria. Be careful while walking along sidewalks, where open manhole covers and people riding motorbikes can be hazardous.

THAI MASSAGE
Thai massage is an extremely rigorous, sometimes painful experience, and people with back, neck, or joint problems should not undergo it without seeking medical advice first. But it can also increase flexibility and provide relief to aches and pains. It's okay to ask if you want softer pressure (bow bow, kup/ka). Massages are booked by the hour, and aficionados say two hours is best to get the full benefit. In most shophouse parlors the masseuse will first bathe your feet and then give you a pair of pajamas to wear. You can remove your underwear or not—whatever makes you comfortable.

BATHHOUSE "MASSAGE"
Often classically ornate with names like Poseidon, barnlike bathhouses and saunas are fronts for prostitution. They offer the euphemistic "massage" for which Thailand has had a reputation since the Vietnam War. Luckily, they're fairly easy to avoid—masseuses are usually on display behind a glass partition, and the treatment menu will include options like "soapy massage."

PAUSE FOR THE ANTHEM
The national anthem is played twice a day, at 8am and 6pm. Every TV and radio station plays it, and it will be played over government building speaker systems, at the sky train and underground in Bangkok, bus stations, in parks, and in most other public places. Stop what you are doing and stand in silence. It takes less than a minute and is a small way to show respect to the Thai people and to the country you are visiting.

Getting Here and Around

Thailand is a long country, stretching some 1,100 miles north to south. Bangkok is a major Asian travel hub, so you'll likely begin your trip by flying into the capital. Relatively affordable flights are available from Bangkok to every major city in the country, and if you're strapped for time, flying is convenient and generally inexpensive. But train travel, where available, can be an enjoyable sightseeing experience if you're not in a rush, and Thailand also has a comprehensive bus system.

Air Travel

Bangkok is 17 hours from San Francisco, 18 hours from Seattle and Vancouver, 20 hours from Chicago, 22 hours from New York, and 10 hours from Sydney. Be sure to check your itinerary carefully if you are flying out of Bangkok—most low-cost carriers and domestic flights operate out of Don Mueang Airport, while Suvarnabhumi Airport remains the international hub. On popular tourist routes during peak holiday times, domestic flights in Thailand are often fully booked. Make sure you reserve well in advance of your travel date.

AIRPORTS

Thailand's gateway to the world, Bangkok, has two airports: Suvarnabhumi (pronounced soo-wanna-poom) International Airport (BKK), 30 km (18 miles) southeast of town, and Don Mueang International Airport (DMK), 25 km (15 miles) north of central Bangkok. Don Mueang is Bangkok's secondary international airport, handling both domestic and international flights and mostly low-cost carriers. Neither airport is close to the city, but both offer shuttle links and/or bus and taxi service throughout Bangkok. The smoothest ride to Suvarnabhumi is the Airport Rail Link, connecting the airport to the Skytrain and key areas of the city.

Chiang Mai International Airport, which lies on the edge of that city, has a large new terminal to handle the recent sharp increases in national and regional air traffic. Phuket Airport is Thailand's third-busiest airport (especially in summer) and is a major link to the southern beaches region, particularly the islands of the Andaman Coast.

Bangkok Airways owns and runs airports in Sukhothai, Trat, and Koh Samui. They have the only flights to these destinations, which can be expensive in high season.

AIRPORT TRANSFER

Shuttle service is available between Suvarnabhumi and Don Mueang airports. Bus service starts at 5 am and ends at midnight. Be warned that the transfer could take between 50 minutes to two hours depending on traffic. Other transportation options between the two airports include Uber and taxi. A taxi fare will run about B350 on the meter.

Bus Travel

Thai buses are cheap and faster than trains, and reach every corner of the country. There are usually two to three buses a day on most routes and several daily (or even hourly) buses on popular routes between major towns. Most buses leave in the morning, with a few other runs spaced out in the afternoon and evening. Buses leave in the evening for long overnight trips. Overnight buses are very popular with Thais, and they're a more efficient use of time, but they do crash with disturbing regularity, and many expats avoid them.

Avoid taking private bus company trips from the Khao San Road area. The buses are not as comfortable as public buses, they take longer, and they usually try to trap you at an affiliated hotel once you reach your destination. This is particularly the case for cross-border travel into Cambodia. There have also been many reports of rip-offs, scams, and luggage thefts on these buses over the years.

There are, generally speaking, three classes of bus service: cheap, no-frills locals on short routes that stop at every road crossing and for anyone who waves them down; second- and first-class buses on specific routes that have air-conditioning, toilets (sometimes), and loud chop-socky movies (too often); and VIP buses that provide nonstop service between major bus stations and have comfortable seats, drinks, snacks, air-conditioning, and movies. If you're setting out on a long bus journey, it's worth inquiring about the onboard entertainment—14 hours on a bus with continuous Thai pop karaoke VCDs can be torturous. Air-conditioned buses are usually so cold that you'll want an extra sweater. On local buses, space at the back fills up fast with all kinds of oversize luggage, so it's best to sit toward the middle or the front.

Bangkok has three main bus stations, serving routes to the north (Mo Chit), south (Southern Terminal), and east (Ekamai). Chiang Mai has one major terminal. All have telephone information lines, but the operators rarely speak English. It's best to buy tickets at the bus station, where the bigger bus companies have ticket windows. Thais usually just head to the station an hour before they'd like to leave; you may want to go a day early to be sure you get a ticket if your plans aren't flexible—especially if you hope to get VIP tickets. Travel agents can sometimes get tickets for you, but often the fee is more than half the cost of the ticket. All fares are paid in cash.

Car Travel

Car travel in Thailand has its ups and downs. Major thoroughfares tend to be congested, but the limited number of roads and the straightforward layout of cities combine to make navigation relatively easy. The exception, of course, is Bangkok. Avoid negotiating that tangled mass of traffic-clogged streets by hiring a driver.

Cars are available for rent in Bangkok and major tourist destinations. Nevertheless, even outside Bangkok hiring a driver is a small price to pay for peace of mind. If a foreigner is involved in an automobile accident, he or she—not the Thai—is likely to be judged at fault, no matter who hit whom.

If you do decide to rent a car, know that traffic laws are routinely disregarded. Bigger vehicles have the unspoken right-of-way, motorcyclists seem to think they are invincible, and bicyclists often don't look around them.

Rental-company rates in Thailand begin at about $40 a day for a jeep or $50 for an economy car with unlimited mileage. It's better to make your car-rental reservations when you arrive in Thailand, as you can usually secure a discount.

You must have an International Driving Permit (IDP) to drive or rent a car in Thailand. IDP's are not difficult to obtain, and having one in your wallet may save you from unwanted headaches dealing with local authorities. Check the AAA website for more info as well as for IDPs ($20) themselves.

Taxi Travel

Most Thai taxis now have meters installed, and these are the ones tourists should take. (Nevertheless, the drivers of Chiang Mai's small fleet of "meter" taxis often demand flat fees instead. Bargain.) Taxis waiting at attractions are more likely to demand a high flat fare than those flagged down on the street. Never enter any taxi until the price has been established or the driver agrees to use the meter. Whenever possible, ask at your hotel front desk what the approximate fare should be.

If you flag down a meter taxi and the driver refuses to use the meter, you can try to negotiate a better fare or simply get out. If you negotiate too much, he will simply take you on a long route to jack the meter price up. On the Grab app, you can also book taxis and private drivers for reasonable fixed prices.

Note: Guesthouses offer commission for customers brought in by drivers, so be wary of anyone telling you that the place where you booked a room is suddenly full. Smile and be courteous, but be firm about where you want to go. If the driver doesn't immediately take you where you want to go, get another taxi.

Train Travel

Though they're a bit slower and generally more expensive than buses, trains are comfortable and safe. They go to (or close to) most major tourist destinations, and many go through areas where major roads don't. The State Railway of Thailand has four lines, all of which terminate in Bangkok. Hua Lamphong is Bangkok's main terminal; you can book tickets for any route in the country there. (Chiang Mai's station is another major hub, where you can also buy tickets for any route.)

TRAIN ROUTES

The Northern Line connects Bangkok with Chiang Mai, passing through Ayutthaya, Phitsanulok, and Sukhothai. The Northeastern Line travels up to Nong Khai, on the Laotian border (across from Vientiane), and has a branch that goes east to Ubon Ratchathani. The Southern Line goes all the way south through Surat Thani (get off here for Koh Samui) to the Malaysian border and on to Kuala Lumpur and Singapore, a journey that takes 37 hours. The Eastern Line splits and goes to both Pattaya and Aranyaprathet on the Cambodian border. A short line also connects Bangkok with Nam Tok to the west, passing through Kanchanaburi and the bridge over the River Kwai along the way. (There's no train to Phuket; you have to go to the Phun Phin station, about 14 km [9 miles] from Surat Thani and change to a bus.)

TICKETS AND RAIL PASSES

The State Railway of Thailand offers two types of rail passes. Both are valid for 20 days of unlimited travel on all trains in either second or third class. The cheaper of the two does not include supplementary charges such as air-conditioning and berths. Ask at Bangkok's Hualamphong Station for up-to-date prices and purchasing; if the train is your primary mode of transportation, it may be worth it.

Even if you purchase a rail pass, you're not guaranteed seats on any particular train; you'll need to book these ahead of time through a travel agent or by visiting the advance booking office of the nearest train station. Seat reservations are required on some trains and are strongly advised on long-distance routes, especially if you want a sleeper on the Bangkok to Chiang Mai trip. Bangkok to Chiang Mai and other popular routes need to be booked several days in advance, especially during the popular tourist season between November and January, as well as during the Thai New Year in April. Tickets for shorter, less frequented routes can be bought a day in advance or, sometimes, right at the station before departure. Most travel agencies have information on train schedules, and many will book seats for you for a small fee, saving you a trip to the station.

The State Railway of Thailand's rather basic website has timetables, routes, available seats, and a booking system that doesn't always work. The British-based website Seat 61 (🌐 *www.seat61.com*) also has lots of helpful information about train travel in Thailand.

Other Travel

TUK-TUK TRAVEL

So-called because of their flatulent sound, these three-wheel cabs can be a more rapid form of travel through congested traffic. All tuk-tuk operators drive as if chased by hellhounds. Tuk-tuks are not very comfortable, require hard bargaining skills, are noisy, are very polluting, and subject you to the polluted air they create—so they're best used for short journeys, if at all.

If a tuk-tuk driver rolls up and offers to drive you to the other side of Bangkok for B20, think twice before accepting, because you will definitely be getting more than you bargained for. By dragging you along to his friend's gem store, tailor's shop, or handicraft showroom, he'll usually get a petrol voucher as commission. He'll tell you that all you need to do to help him put rice on his family's table is take a five-minute look around. Sometimes that's accurate, but sometimes you'll find it difficult to leave without buying something.

MOTORCYCLE TRAVEL

Many people rent small motorcycles to get around the countryside or the islands. A Thai city is not the place to learn how to drive a motorcycle. Phuket in particular is unforgiving to novices—don't think of driving one around there unless you are experienced. Motorcycles skid easily on wet or gravel roads. On Koh Samui a sign posts the year's count of foreigners who never made it home from their vacations because of such accidents. When driving a motorbike, make sure your vehicle has a rectangular sticker showing up-to-date insurance and registration. The sticker should be pasted somewhere toward the front of the bike, with the Buddhist year in big, bold numbers. You can rent smaller 100cc to 125cc motorcycles for only a few dollars a day. Dirt bikes and bigger road bikes, 250cc and above, start at about $25 per day.

SONGTHAEW TRAVEL

Songthaews are converted pickup trucks with two benches in the back and a metal roof. Thais ride songthaews both within a town and between towns. They aren't cheaper than local buses, but they are more frequent, will sometimes drive slightly out of their way to drop you nearer your destination, and are open air. Just stick out your hand as one passes, negotiate a price, and climb in back. Songthaews are often packed, and if all the seats are taken, Thais will just climb on the back and hang onto the railings. It's a bumpy ride on rural roads; for longer trips, you'll be more comfortable on the bus.

Before You Go

Passport

U.S. citizens arriving by air need only a valid passport, not a prearranged visa, to visit Thailand for less than 30 days. Technically, travelers need an outgoing ticket and "adequate finances" for the duration of their Thailand stay to receive a 30-day stamp upon entry, though authorities in Bangkok rarely check your finances. They do occasionally ask to see an outbound ticket. Tourists who arrive in Thailand by land from a neighboring country are now only eligible for a 30-day visa on arrival twice per year.

Visa

If you want to stay longer than one month, you can apply for a 60-day tourist visa through a Royal Thai embassy. The embassy in Washington, D.C., charges about $40 for this visa, and you'll need to show them a round-trip ticket and a current bank statement to prove you can afford the trip. Be sure to apply for the correct number of entries; for example, if you're going to Laos for a few days in the middle of your stay, you'll need to apply for two Thailand entries.

Immunizations

No vaccinations are required to enter Thailand, but we strongly recommend the hepatitis A vaccination as well as typhoid; and you should make sure your tetanus and polio vaccinations are up-to-date, as well as measles, mumps, and rubella.

Though many Western doctors recommend that you take antimalarials, many health-care workers in Thailand believe they can do more harm than good: they can have side effects and they are not 100% effective. Consult your physician for advice.

When to Go

HIGH SEASON $$$$

Thailand's high season runs from late November to February and is perfect for everything: the beaches in the south, trekking in the north, or exploring Bangkok. The northern nights are chilly in winter, generally in the 50s, but as low as freezing.

LOW SEASON $

Thailand is at its hottest from March to May. Pollution in the north can reach dangerous levels toward the end of the dry season in March and April. By April you can find good hotel deals, if you can stand the heat, though some hotels in less touristy areas shut down for the hot season.

VALUE SEASON $$

Thailand's rainy season starts in June and continues through the first half of November. City sightseeing is okay during these months but flooding can make rural areas inaccessible, and it's not a reliable time to plan a trek.

Safety

Thailand is generally a safe country, and millions of foreigners visit each year without incident. Avoid travel in the four southern provinces closest to the Malaysian border where Martial law is in effect.

Most Thai hardware stores sell a metal doorknob cup which is a handy security gadget that covers your doorknob and locks it in place with a padlock, keeping anyone from using a spare key or even twisting the knob to get into your room. A B300 investment, it's usable anywhere on your travels.

What to Pack for Thailand

BREATHABLE CLOTHING
The climate is hot and humid so you will want to pack clothes made of breathable fabrics like light cotton or linen. Drip-dry clothing is an especially good idea, because the tropical sun and high humidity encourage frequent changes of clothing. Lightweight but long-sleeve shirts and long pants will come in handy for visiting temples and also provide protection against insect bites.

WATERPROOF GEAR
If traveling in the rainy season a lightweight rain jacket or waterproof poncho is essential. If you plan to partake of water activites or just to spend a lot of time on the beach, bring a waterproof bag to keep your camera, phone, and wallet dry; it will also come in handy during the rainy season. A waterproof phone case is a good idea, too, if you plan to use your phone's camera when you travel.

LAYERS
A fleece sweater is welcome on cool evenings or in notoriously over-air-conditioned restaurants, cafes, buses, and trains.

PRACTICAL SHOES
The paths leading to temples can be rough, so bring sturdy walking shoes. Slip-ons are preferable to lace-up shoes, as they must be removed before you enter shrines and temples.

SUNSCREEN AND HAT
The tropical sun is powerful, and its effects long-lasting (and painful) so bring a hat and UV-protection sunglasses and sunscreen. Don't let a rainy season forecast fool you; you will still need to be protected from the sun.

A SARONG
Out of respect for the Buddhist culture, women are expected to cover up in temples. Pack a sarong to tie over shorts in such situations. It will also come in handy on the beach and as a head cover during tropical heat.

INSECT REPELLENT
As with most hot and humid countries, you will find a lot of mosquitos in Thailand. DEET-based insect repellent is preferable to avoid being bitten.

ANTI-DIARRHEAL PILLS
To be safe, pack "Bangkok Belly" busters such as Imodium (known generically as Loperamide) and soothers such as Pepto Bismol, as well as rehydration salts or solution such as Gastrolyte. Activated charcoal can also be helpful.

TRAVEL ADAPTER
Thai power outlets most commonly feature two-prong round or flat sockets; pack a universal travel power adapter to avoid complications.

LUGGAGE LOCK
If you plan to travel throughout Thailand, particularly if you plan to travel by bus, pack luggage locks to prevent tampering with your luggage.

VPN
If you're planning to work or stay connected while you travel, a portable VPN will ensure you won't get blocked from accessing certain sites. It also protects your passwords, credit cards, and identity while you travel.

Essentials

In smaller towns hotels may be fairly simple, but they will usually be clean and inexpensive. In major cities or resort areas there are hotels to fit all price categories. The least-expensive places may have a fan rather than air-conditioning. Breakfast is sometimes included in the room rate at hotels and guesthouses.

During the peak tourist season, hotels are often fully booked and rates are at their highest. During holidays, such as between December 30 and January 2, Chinese New Year (in January or February, depending on the year), and Songkran (the Thai New Year in April), rates climb even higher, and reservations are difficult on short notice.

Don't be reticent about asking for a special rate when booking. Though it may feel awkward to haggle, this practice is perfectly normal in Thailand. Often it will get you nothing, but occasionally it can save you up to 50% if you catch a manager in the right mood with a bunch of empty rooms.

APARTMENT AND HOUSE RENTALS

It is possible to rent apartments or houses for longer stays in most places in Thailand. Bangkok, Chiang Mai, Phuket, and Pattaya in particular have large expat and long-term tourist communities. Also, many hotels and guesthouses are willing to offer greatly reduced rates for long-term guests. Agents are available in all big cities and are used to helping foreigners.

GUESTHOUSES

Though the "guesthouse" label is tacked onto accommodations of all sizes and prices, guesthouses are generally smaller, cheaper, and more casual than hotels. They are often family-run, with small restaurants. The least-expensive rooms often have shared baths, and linens may not be included. At the other end of the spectrum, $35 will get you a room with all the amenities—air-conditioning, cable TV, en suite bathrooms, even Internet access—just about everywhere. Even if you're traveling on a strict budget, make sure your room has window screens or a mosquito net.

HOTELS

Thai luxury hotels are among the best in the world. At the other end of the scale, budget lodgings are simple and basic—a room with little more than a bed. Expect any room costing more than the equivalent of $35 a night to come with hot water, air-conditioning, and a TV. Southeast Asian hotels traditionally have two twin beds.

Dining

Thai food is eaten with a fork and spoon; the fork is used like a plow to push food into the spoon. Chopsticks are used only for Chinese food and noodle dishes. After you have finished eating, place utensils on the plate at the 5:25 position to show you are finished.

If you want to catch a waiter's attention, use the all-purpose polite word, *krup* if you are a man and *ka* if you are a woman. Beckoning with a hand and fingers pointed upward is considered rude; point your fingers downward instead.

Restaurant hours vary, but Thais eat at all times of day, and in cities you will find eateries open through the night. In Thailand breakfast outside the hotel often means noodle soup or congee. Street vendors also sell coffee, although die-hard caffeine addicts may not get enough of a fix; Thai coffee isn't simply coffee, but a combination of ground beans with nuts and spices.

The lunch hour is long—roughly 11:30 to 2—in smaller towns and rural areas, a holdover from when Thailand was primarily a country of rice farmers and everyone napped during the hottest hours of the day.

Tipping

Tipping is not a local custom, but it is expected of foreigners, especially at larger hotels and restaurants and for taxi rides. If you feel the service has been less than stellar, you are under no obligation to leave a tip.

In Thailand tips are generally given for good service, except when a price has been negotiated in advance. With metered taxis in Bangkok, however, the custom is to round the fare up to the nearest B5. Hotel porters expect at least a B20 tip, and hotel staff who have given good service are usually tipped. A 10% tip is appreciated at a restaurant when no service charge has been added to the bill.

Health

The most common vacation sickness in Thailand is traveler's diarrhea. It generally comes from eating contaminated food, be it fruit, veggies, or badly prepared or stored foods—really anything. Avoid ice unless you know it comes from clean water, uncooked or undercooked foods (particularly seafood, sometimes served raw in salads), and unpasteurized dairy products. Drink only bottled water or water that has been boiled for at least 20 minutes, even when brushing your teeth. The best way to treat "Bangkok Belly" is to wait for it to pass. Take Pepto-Bismol to help ease your discomfort, and if you must travel, take Imodium (known generically as Loperamide), which will immobilize your lower gut and everything in it. It doesn't cure the problem, but postpones it until a more convenient time. If "Bangkok Belly" symptoms include a high fever with stomach sickness, find a doctor.

Malaria and dengue fever are fairly rare in well-traveled areas. Malarial mosquitoes generally fly from dusk to dawn, while dengue carriers do the opposite; both are most numerous during the rainy season, as they breed in stagnant water. The best policy is to avoid being bitten. To that end, wear light-colored clothing and some form of insect repellent (preferably containing DEET). The ubiquitous bottles of menthol-scented Siang Pure Oil both ward off mosquitoes and stop the incessant itching of bites.

Dengue fever tends to appear with a sudden high fever, sweating, headache, joint and muscle pain (where it got the name "breakbone fever"), and nausea. A rash of red spots on the chest or legs is a telltale sign. Malaria symptoms include fever, chills, headache, sweating, diarrhea, and abdominal pain. A key sign is the recurrent nature of the symptoms, coming in waves every day or two.

Find a doctor immediately if you think you may have either disease. In Thailand the test for both is quick and accurate, and the doctors are accustomed to treating these diseases.

Great Itineraries

Highlights of Thailand: Bangkok, Beaches, and the North, 10 days

Almost every trip to Thailand begins in Bangkok, which is a good place to linger for a day or two, because some of the country's most astounding sights can be found in and around the Old City. After relaxing for a few days, you'll be ready for more adventures, so head to Thailand's second city, Chiang Mai. The surrounding countryside is beautiful, and even a short stay will give you a chance to visit centuries-old architecture and get lost among the lush forests of Doi Inthanon National Park.

DAYS 1 AND 2: BANGKOK

Experience the Old Thailand hiding within this modern megalopolis by beginning your first day with a tour of Bangkok's Old City, with visits to the stunning Grand Palace and Wat Po's Reclining Buddha. Later in the day, hire a longtail boat and spend a couple of hours exploring the canals. On the river you'll catch a glimpse of how countless city people lived until just a few decades ago, in wooden stilt houses along the water's edge. For a casual evening, head to the backpacker hangout of Khao San Road for a cheap dinner, fun shopping, and bar-hopping. For something fancy, take a ferry to the Mandarin Oriental Hotel for riverside cocktails and dinner at Le Normandie.

Start Day 2 with the sights and smells of Chinatown, sampling some of the delicious food along the way. Then head north to Jim Thompson's House, the silk mogul's former home and a fine example of a traditional teak abode, with antiques displayed inside. If you're up for more shopping, the malls near Siam Square are great browsing territory for local and international fashion, jewelry, and accessories. The malls also have a couple of movie theaters and a bowling alley—Siam Paragon even has an aquarium with sharks. CentralWorld, touted as "the largest lifestyle shopping destination," includes some 500 shops, 50 restaurants, 21 movie theaters, an office tower, hotel and more. Later grab a meal at Ban Khun Mae—tasty if a bit touristy—or local family favorite Inter Restaurant. Then if you've any energy left, head over to Lumphini Stadium for a Thai boxing match.

DAYS 3 TO 5: THE BEACHES

Most island destinations are within a few hours flying time from Bangkok. It's roughly an hour to Samui or Trat (jumping-off point for Koh Chang); an hour 20 minutes to Phuket and Krabi. Hua Hin is roughly a 3½-hour drive, a 3½ to 4½-hour railway journey, or a 4½-hour bus ride from Bangkok.

Get an early start and head down to the beach regions. Your choices are too numerous to list here, but Koh Samui, Phuket, and Krabi are all good bets if time is short because of the direct daily flights that connect them with Bangkok. Peaceful Khao Lak is only a two-hour drive from the bustle of Phuket, and Koh Chang is just a couple of hours by ferry from Trat Airport. Closer to Bangkok are Koh Samet (reached by 4 to 4½-hour drive and 30-minute ferry and Hua Hin reachable by car. But if you have at least three days to spare, you can go almost anywhere that piques your interest—just make sure the time spent traveling doesn't overshadow the time spent relaxing.

Samui, Phuket, and Krabi are also good choices because of the variety of activities each offers. Though Samui has traditionally been backpacker terrain, there are now a number of spa retreats on the island. You can also hike to a waterfall, careen

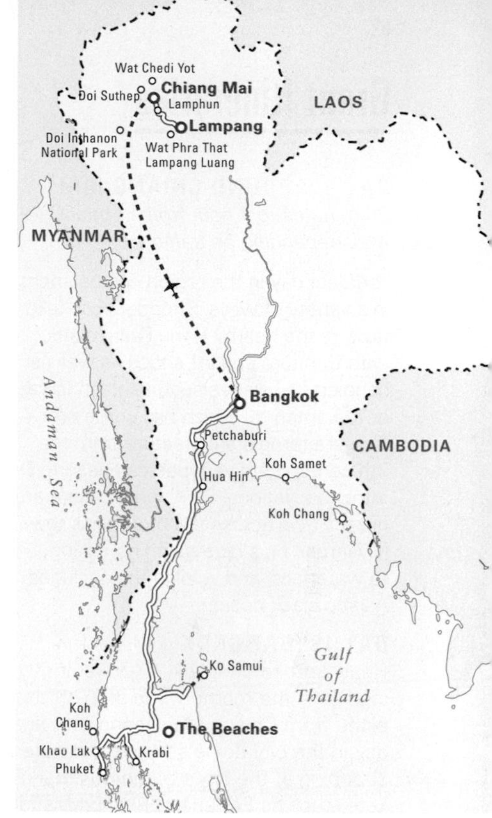

down a treetop zip line, or take a side trip to Ang Thong National Marine Park. There are dive shops on all the islands, with a number on Phuket. These offer diving and sometimes snorkeling trips to nearby reefs. There's great sailing around Phuket, too. On Krabi you can enjoy a relaxing afternoon and cheap beachside massage at gorgeous Phra Nang Beach; go rock climbing on limestone cliffs; kayak from bay to bay; and watch the glorious sunset from nearby Railay Beach.

DAY 6: CHIANG MAI

Chiang Mai is 1 hour by air, about 10 hours by bus or 12 to15 hours by train from Bangkok.

Though it shouldn't be a terribly taxing day, getting to Chiang Mai requires some travel time, so you should get an early start. Wherever you are, you'll most likely have to make a connecting flight in Bangkok; if you're pinching pennies, this actually works in your favor, because it's cheaper to book two separate flights on a low-cost airline than to book one ticket from a more expensive airline "directly" from one of the beach airports to Chiang Mai—you'll have to stop in Bangkok anyway. If you play your cards right, you should be in Chiang Mai in time to check into your hotel and grab a late lunch. Afterward stroll around the Old City, and in the evening go shopping at the night market or for a drink in trendy Nimmanhaemin Road, the university area.

DAY 7: CHIANG MAI

If traveling by songthaew, allow one hour from downtown Chiang Mai to Doi Suthep; if traveling by motorcycle or private car, allow ½ hour each way.

Spend the day exploring the city and visiting the dazzling hilltop wat of Doi Suthep. Ring the dozens of bells surrounding the main building for good luck. On the way back to Chiang Mai, drop in at the seven-spired temple called Wat Chedi Yot. Chiang Mai is famous for its massage and cooking schools, so if you're interested in trying a class in either— or just getting a massage—this is the place to do it.

DAY 8: LAMPANG

Lampang is 60 miles outside Chiang Mai, and the elephant center is midway between. Allow a full day.

An easy side trip from Chiang Mai, Lampang has some beautiful wooden-house architecture and a sedate way of getting around, in pony-drawn carriages.

A short ride out of town is one of northern Thailand's most revered temples, Wat Phra That Lampang Luang, which contains the country's oldest wooden building. It's an excellent example of classic Lanna architecture. Stroll through Kad Kong Ta market, eyeing pretty teak houses and munching on street fare.

Great Itineraries

DAY 9: AROUND CHIANG MAI

30 minutes to 1 hour from central Chiang Mai, depending on traffic.

Your last day in the region can be spent in a variety of ways. Shoppers can take taxis to the nearby Hang Dong district with furniture and art shops as well as handicrafts villages such as Baan Tawai; or to Lamphun, which has some pre-Thai-era temple architecture from the 7th century. Active types can head to Doi Inthanon National Park, where there are great views across the mountains toward Myanmar, plus bird-watching, hiking to waterfalls, and wildlife that includes Asiatic black bears.

DAY 10: BANGKOK

Head back to Bangkok. If you're not flying home the moment you step off the plane from Chiang Mai, spend your final day in the city doing some last-minute shopping at the city's numerous markets, such as Pratunam, Phahurat, and the weekend-only Chatuchak. Or just relax in Lumphini Park.

Three-Country Tour, 14 Days

It's possible to see three countries in two weeks, if you concentrate on a few highlights and are prepared to fly all over. Do you want to focus on cultural sites and cities? Do you need a few relaxing days at the beach? Determine your priorities first, then set your itinerary. Here is one possible route that will hit a bit of everything—Bangkok buzz, ancient temples, quiet beaches, and more.

DAY 1: BANGKOK

Follow Days 1 or 2 of the Essential Thailand itinerary.

DAYS 2–4 CHIANG MAI

1 hour 15 minutes from Bangkok. There are 45-plus direct flights daily.

Take an early evening flight from Bangkok and head to dinner and drinks on the ever-popular Nimmanhaemin Road, where Chiang Mai's students and trendy types hang out. The next day, tour the city's famous ancient temples including Wat Phra Singh, breaking for a tasty street-side lunch of khao soi (egg noodle curry) at Khao Soi Khun Yai. If you've got energy this afternoon, hire a car or catch a sangthaew up to Doi Suthep, the mountain temple overlooking the city. On the way stop at Studio Naenna to snap up beautiful textiles. If the weather is clear, it's a great spot to experience sunset. Eat dinner at one of the restaurants along the base of the mountain, or head back into the Old City. Overnight at Bussaba Bed and Breakfast Lodge for good value and local flavor.

The next day, hire a car for the two-hour drive to Doi Inthanon National Park. It can be a good 10-degrees cooler up here, where hiking trails, waterfalls and viewpoints beckon. Lunch at one of the local joints on the road leading up to the park.

DAYS 5–7: CHIANG MAI–LUANG PRABANG

1 hour 10 minutes. Book early on the one direct flight (Sun., Mon., Wed., Fri.).

Stop by Overstand Coffee for an Aussie brunch before your afternoon flight to Luang Prabang. You'll be there in time for a sunset drink on the Mekong. The entire UNESCO World Heritage city is accessible by foot, so wear sturdy shoes and plan full days of walking. Rise early on Day 7 (just before sunrise) to catch the parade of Buddhist monks out for their morning alms. Afterward you'll find enough temples, shops, and restaurants to keep you busy in the historical district. Spend a day taking in the views from Phu Si Hill, getting a massage at one of the town's many spas and perhaps trying your hand at a Lao cooking class. You can take a ferryboat across the Mekong and explore some of the old temple ruins directly across from the Luang Prabang Peninsula. Another option is to hire a boat upriver to the Pak Ou Caves, filled with Buddha statues. Plan on a full afternoon. After a riverside dinner, wander through the handicrafts market that sets up along Sisavangvong Road. Stay in the 3 Nagas Boutique hotel, in a UNESCO Heritage–protected mansion, or splash out on the Amantaka resort for your final night.

DAYS 8–10: LUANG PRABANG–SIEM REAP

1 hour 25 minutes. Book early on the one direct flight flight (Mon., Wed.-Sat.).

You'll want to arrange a tour of the Angkor Archaeological Park as soon as you arrive. (Any hotel can help you, or book direct with any tuk-tuk driver you see; one of the best ways to see the temples is to hire a tuk-tuk, so you can experience the scenes in open-air style.) Many visitors choose to spend at least one sunrise at Angkor Wat and one sunset on the hilltop Phnom Bakheng. The temple complex is vast, so talk to your guide, pick up one of the many freely available printed temple pamphlets, and design the itinerary that best suits your interests. If you have time after the second day at Angkor Wat, wander the old city and shop at the Psa Chas market. On your last night in Siem Reap, savor a modern Cambodian meal at Cuisine Wat Damnak.

DAYS 11–13: SIEM REAP–PHUKET

1 hour 30 minutes. Book early on the one direct flight (Sun., Mon., Wed., Fri.).

After multiple days pounding the grounds of temples, it's time for sand, sun (and shade!). Swim in crystal clear waters and laze under palm trees, fresh coconut in hand. The snorkeling and diving around Phuket are excellent, and any dive shop in town can arrange an excursion. You can also snorkel off Kata and Kata Noi beaches, but watch the current.

DAY 14: PHUKET—BANGKOK

1 hour 25 minutes. There are 40-plus direct flights daily.

Catch a flight to Bangkok, and connect to your flight home or spend another night shopping-eating-sightseeing in Thailand's scintillating capital city.

TIPS

- Temples and royal buildings, such as Bangkok's Grand Palace, require modest dress (no shorts or tank tops).
- Take a taxi to the Grand Palace or an express boat to nearby Tha Chang Pier. Wat Po is a 10-minute walk south. Hire a longtail boat to get to the canals and back at Tha Chang Pier. Khao San Road is a short taxi ride from the pier.
- Bangkok Airways owns the airport at Koh Samui, and flights there are relatively expensive due to taxes. Bangkok Airways runs most of the many daily flights, and these are slightly lower in price than Thai Airways. Nok Air, AirAsia, and Thai Lion also offer cheap flights to nearby Surat Thani or Nakhon Si Thammarat, from which you can take a ferry to the island.
- Late November through April is the best time to explore the Andaman Coast. For the Gulf Coast there's good weather from late November until August.
- Hotels in the south are frequently packed during high season and Thai holidays, so book in advance.

Contacts

VISITOR INFORMATION
Tourism Authority of Thailand. *www.tourismthailand.org.* **Discovery Thailand.** *www.discoverythailand.com.* **Tourism Cambodia.** *www.tourismcambodia.com.* **National Tourism Authority of the Lao People's Democratic Republic.** *www.tourismlaos.org.*

Embassy

Bangkok: U.S. Embassy. *02/205-4000* *th.usembassy.gov.* **Chiang Mai: U.S. Consulate.** *053/107-700* *th.usembassy.gov/embassy-consulate/chiang-mai.* **Cambodia: U.S. Embassy.** *kh.embassy.gov.* **Laos: U.S. Embassy.** *la.usembassy.gov.*

Visa

Ministry of Foreign Affairs. *www.mfa.go.th/main/en/home.* **Bangkok Immigration Office.** *http://bangkok.immigration.go.th/intro1.html.* **Chiang Mai Immigration Office.** *www.chiangmaiimm.com/en.*

Lodging

APARTMENT RENTALS
Airbnb. *www.airbnb.com.* **9apartment.** *www.en.9apartment.com.* **ThaiApartment.** *www.thaiapartment.com.*

Air Travel

AIRPORTS
Don Mueang Airport. *www.donmueangairport.com.* **Suvarnabhumi Airport.** *www.bangkokairportonline.com.* **Chiang Mai International Airport.** *www.chiangmaiairportonline.com.* **Phuket International Airport.** *www.phuketairportonline.com.* **Chiang Rai International Airport.** *www.chiangraiairportonline.com.*

CAMBODIA
Siem Reap International Airport. *rep.cambodia-airports.aero.* **Phnom Penh.** *pnh.cambodia-airports.aero.*

LAOS
Vientiane International Airport. *www.vientianeairport.com.*

REGIONAL CARRIERS
AirAsia. *www.airasia.com.* **Bangkok Airways.** *www.bangkokair.com.* **Cambodia Angkor Air.** *www.cambodiaangkorair.com.*

Taxi Travel

Grab Taxi. *www.grab.com/th*

Train Travel

BANGKOK
Airport Rail Link. *www.bangkokairporttrain.com.* **BTS Skytrain.** *www.bangkok.com/bts.* **MRT.** *www.bemplc.co.th.*

RAIL
Chiang Mai Railway Station. *www.thairailways.com/train-station.chiangmai.html.* **Hua Lamphong Railway Station.** *www.thairailways.com/train-station.bangkok.html.* **State Railway of Thailand.** *www.railway.co.th.*

National Parks

The National Park Wildlife and Plant Conservation Department. *www.dnp.go.th/index_eng.asp.* **Thai National Parks.** *www.thainationalparks.com.*

Health

HOSPITALS
Bangkok General Hospital, Bangkok. *662/310-3000* *www.bangkokhospital.com.* **Bumrungrad Hospital, Bangkok.** *662/066-8888* *www.bumrungrad.com.* **McCormick Hospital, Chiang Mai.** *053/921-777* *www.mccormick.in.th.* **Phuket International Hospital, Phuket.** *076/210-935* *www.phuketinternationalhospital.com.*

Chapter 3

BANGKOK

Updated by
Barbara Woolsey

Sights ★★★★★ | Restaurants ★★★★★ | Hotels ★★★★☆ | Shopping ★★★★☆ | Nightlife ★★★★☆

WELCOME TO BANGKOK

TOP REASONS TO GO

★ **The Canals:** They don't call it "Venice of the East" for nothing. Sure, boat tours are touristy, but the sights, from Khmer wats to bizarre riverside dwellings, are rare and wonderful.

★ **Street Food:** Bangkok may have the best street food in the world. Don't be afraid to sample the more exotic offerings. They're often fresher and better than the food you'd get at a hotel restaurant.

★ **Amazing Shopping:** Some of Asia's most high-tech malls sell high-end designer goods in amazing settings.

★ **Sky-High Sipping:** "Bar with a view" is taken to the extreme when you sip martinis in open-air spaces atop lofty towers.

★ **Temple-Gazing:** From the venerable Wat Po to the little wats that don't make it into guidebooks, Bangkok's collection of temples is hard to top.

Bangkok's endless maze of streets is part of its fascination and its complexity—getting around a labyrinth is never easy. Although the S-curve of the Chao Phraya River can throw you off base, it's actually a good landmark. Most of the popular sights are close to the river, and you can use it to get swiftly from one place to another. Also look at the Skytrain and subway to help you navigate and get around quickly.

1 The Old City. The Old City is the historic heart of Bangkok and home to opulent temples like Wat Po.

2 Banglamphu. North of the Old City, Banglamphu is mostly residential; it's known for pleasant strolls, diverse restaurants and vendors, and its famous backpacker hub—Khao San Road—which becomes a frenetic market by night and a huge water fight during Thai New Year.

3 Dusit. North of Banglamphu is this royal district, where elegant buildings line wide avenues. Dusit Park is one of the city's most appealing green spaces.

4 Thonburi. Across the river from the Old City is

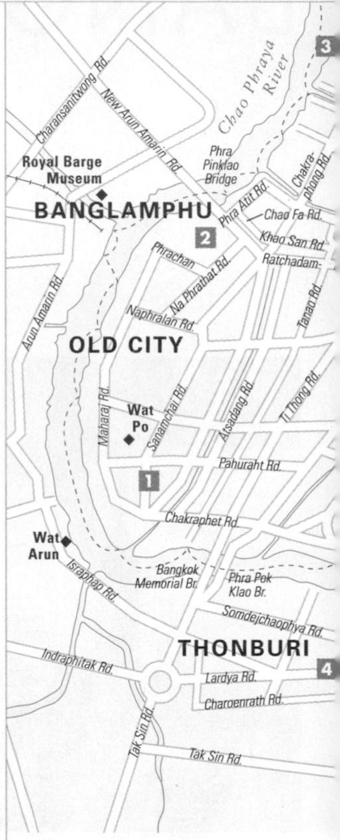

Thonburi, a mostly residential neighborhood, whose most notable attractions are the Royal Barge Museum and the spectacular Wat Arun.

5 Chinatown. East of the Old City in labyrinthine Chinatown are shops selling Buddhas and spices; the open-air fruit and vegetable markets here are among Bangkok's most vibrant.

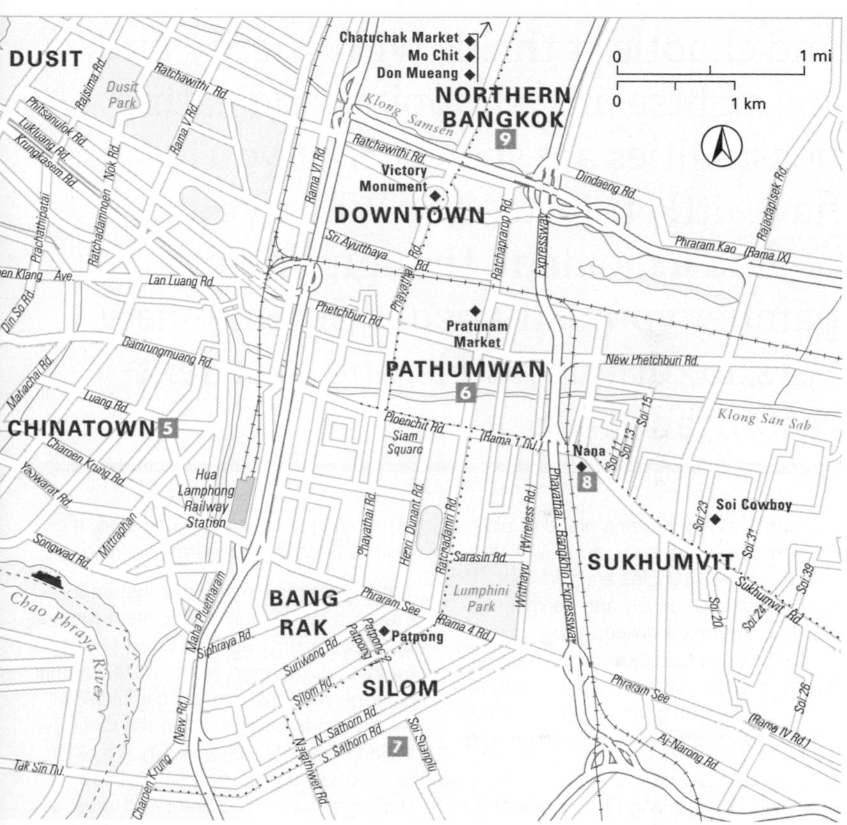

6 Pathumwan. This area, which can be considered Bangkok's downtown, is home to the city's greatest collection of shopping malls as well as the popular Pratunam clothing market.

7 Silom and Bang Rak. In this busy area you'll find Lumphini Park, Bangkok's largest park and a pleasantly green space to escape from the harried pace of the city. With many bars and restaurants, the Silom area also includes the infamous red-light district of Patpong. At the east end of Bang Rak lies the Chao Phraya River and many opulent hotels.

8 Sukhumvit. Sukhumvit Road is a bustling district filled with high-end restaurants, hotels, and shops, as well as the red-light areas of Nana and Soi Cowboy.

9 Northern Bangkok. This area includes the Victory Monument and all points north, such as the famous Chatuchak Weekend Market, the northern bus station of Mo Chit, and the budget air terminal at Don Mueang.

Bangkok, also known as the City of Angels and Venice of the East, will hit you like a ton of bricks. Hot, polluted, and chaotic, it thrills with energy, and the sightseeing, shopping, and eating possibilities are so vast that you'll have little time to rest. When you do find a moment, though, you can pamper yourself at spas, skyline-view bars, luxurious hotels, and excellent restaurants.

The city is a mesmerizing blend of old and new, East and West, and dizzying contradictions. Temples and red-light districts, languid canals and permanent gridlock, street-side vendors and chic upscale eateries, all exist side by side. Bangkok rarely fails to make an impression, and yes, you might need to spend a few days on the beach to recover from it all.

The Grand Palace, Wat Phra Kaew, and the Emerald Buddha are tops on most visitors' itineraries, and lesser-known temples, such as Wat Benjamabophit, the golden stupa of Wat Sakhet, and Wat Suthat all merit a look. Besides temples, there are plenty of niche touring possibilities. Take in a venom-extraction and python-feeding show at the snake farm at the Queen Saovabha Memorial Institute, or go to the nearby Jim Thompson House to learn all about the famed Thai silk industry. If architecture appeals to you, there is the Suan Pakkard Palace with its antique-teak-house collection. Even more astounding is Vimanmek Mansion, the world's largest golden-teak building.

The Old City is a major destination for travelers, as it's home to opulent temples like Wat Po and Wat Phra Kaew. Across the river is Thonburi, a mostly residential neighborhood, where you can find Wat Arun. At the northern tip of the Old City is Banglamphu, one of Bangkok's older residential neighborhoods. It's best known now for Khao San Road, a backpacker hangout, though the neighborhood has much more to offer, especially when it comes to street food. North of Banglamphu is Dusit, the royal district since the days of Rama V.

East of the Old City is Chinatown, a labyrinth of streets with restaurants, shops, and warehouses. Chinatown deserves at least a day on every travel itinerary—be sure to check out the sprawling Flower Market, hipster bars on Soi Nana, and the seafood restaurants on Yaowarat Road. Farther down the Chao Phraya River is bustling Silom Road, a major commercial district. Patpong, the most famous of several red-light districts, is also here. Bang Rak is home to some of the city's leading hotels: the Mandarin Oriental, the Peninsula, the Royal Orchid Sheraton, and the Shangri-La. To the north of Rama IV Road is Bangkok's largest green area, Lumphini Park.

Continue north and you reach Sukhumvit Road, Bangkok's downtown main vein. Thong Lor, farther east along Sukhumvit, is an "in" neighborhood for restaurants and nightlife. The Nana and Asok areas of Sukhumvit are now home to even busier red-light entertainment districts (Nana and Soi Cowboy) than Patpong. Farther south is the Sathorn district, where a smattering of trendy bars and eateries have also opened in recent years.

In all these neighborhoods you will find cuisine unrivaled for spice, taste, and variation. From multicourse meals to small bites from street vendors, the one constant here is food that's fresh and delicious at every level. You can lunch on superlative roast duck or wonton noodles on a street corner, and dine that evening on the sophisticated creations of world-class chefs. Your choices are by no means limited to spicy Thai either. There are excellent French, Italian, and other restaurants, and in 2017 Bangkok was bestowed Michelin stars for the very first time—you'd need a few months to survey all the options available.

Planning

WHEN TO GO

From late October to late February, when Bangkok is at its coolest (85°F) and driest, is the best time to visit. By April the humidity and heat create a sticky stew that lasts until the rains begin in late June.

PLANNING YOUR TIME

Bangkok's sights are very spread out and the heat, traffic, and chaos can be overwhelming. No wonder, then, that many visitors to Thailand quickly repair south to the islands. That said, two full days are the minimum for getting a quick fix of the country's dynamic capital, and three would be better. You just need to pace yourself. The Skytrain, subway, and river ferries will help you dodge some of the traffic, but the heat and urban sprawl can exhaust you. Don't try to pack too much into one day and you'll have more fun. Plan on half a day to take in the Grand Palace and Wat Po and another half to visit one or two other nearby sights. Later enjoy a meal along the riverside and have a drink at a skyscraper's rooftop bar. Another day could be well spent exploring Chinatown in the morning and the Jim Thompson House or Queen Saovabha Memorial Institute in the afternoon, followed by a dinner cruise on the river. Food lovers can take an extra day to explore the markets and hole-in-wall restaurants. If in town on the weekend, be sure to visit Chatuchak Market.

GETTING HERE AND AROUND

Bangkok has two main airports, multiple bus terminals, and a centrally located main railway station. Planes, buses, and trains connect Bangkok to all of Thailand's major cities and towns. Bangkok is large, so once here remember to pace yourself and take a break to escape the midday heat. The traffic is unbearable, so do yourself a favor and skip driving in the city.

AIR TRAVEL

Bangkok's Suvarnabhumi International Airport (pronounced "Su-wan-na-poom") is about 30 km (18 miles) southeast of the city. About 25 km (16 miles) north of the city is the former international airport, Don Mueang, which now receives many domestic flights and has become the terminal for budget airlines. A free shuttle service connects the two airports.

AIRPORTS Don Mueang International Airport ✉ *222 Vipavadee Rangsit Rd.* ☎ *02/535–1111* 🌐 *www.donmueangairport.com* Ⓜ *Subway: Chatuchak Park; Skytrain: Mo Chit, then taxi.* **Suvarnabhumi International Airport** ✉ *999 Bang Na-Trat Rd., Bang Phlii, Samut Prakan* ☎ *02/132–1888* 🌐 *www.bangkokairportonline.com* Ⓜ *Airport Link: Suvarnabhumi.*

AIRPORT TRANSFERS

Inexpensive and available around the clock, taxis are the most convenient way to get between downtown and the airport. **■TIP→ Make sure to have some baht on hand to pay for your taxi.** Get a taxi by heading to one of the taxi counters on Level 1, near Entrances 3, 4, 7, and 8. Take a number and state your destination to the dispatcher, who will lead you to your taxi. Allow 30 to 90 minutes to get downtown, depending on traffic and if your driver takes the expressway (you may want to request this to shorten the journey). A trip downtown will cost between B250 and B400, plus a B50 airport surcharge and any expressway tolls. **■TIP→ Avoid drivers who insist on a fixed price or refuse to turn on their meters.**

The Airport Rail Link system is your best option during rush hour. The express train (B150) takes 15 minutes to reach Makkasan Terminal, next to the Phetchaburi MRT subway stop. The regular commuter train (B45) takes about 26 minutes to the Phaya Thai BTS Station, convenient for those staying on the Skytrain line. The entrance to the system is on the airport's lower level.

Buses and minivans headed for Bangkok depart from the Airport Bus Station, which is reached in 10 minutes via a free shuttle bus you can catch at the front of the airport.

CONTACTS Airport Rail Link ✉ *Makkasan Station, New Petchaburi Rd.* ☎ *02/308–5600* 🌐 *www.srtet.co.th* Ⓜ *Subway: Petchaburi; Skytrain: Phaya Thai.* **Suvarnabhumi Airport Bus Station** ✉ *999, Moo 1, Suvarnabhumi Airport, Nang Prue, Samut Prakan* ☎ *02/134–4099* 🌐 *www.bangkokairportonline.com/node/56.*

BOAT TRAVEL

The Chao Phraya River is a great way to bypass the traffic that clogs most of the city. The vessels of Chao Phraya Express Boat (fares from B10 to B32, depending on distance) can get crowded, especially at peak times, but they're still far more pleasant than sitting in a taxi as it navigates bumper-to-bumper traffic. The company also operates a tourist boat that serves eight piers near sightseeing attractions. A one-day pass (B180) for this boat can also be used to board express boats.

CONTACTS Chao Phraya Express Boat ✉ *Saphan Taksin Pier, Bang Rak* ☎ *02/449–3000, 02/445–8888 hotline* 🌐 *www.chaophrayaexpressboat.com* Ⓜ *Skytrain: Saphan Taksin.*

BUS TRAVEL

Getting Here: Bangkok has three major terminals for buses headed from other parts of the country. Buses to and from Hua Hin, Koh Samui, Phuket, and points south and west arrive at the Southern Bus Terminal, in Thonburi. The Eastern Bus Terminal, called Ekkamai, is for buses headed to and from Pattaya, Rayong, and Trat provinces. Buses to and from Chiang Mai and points north arrive at the Northern Bus Terminal. Minivans to nearby destinations like Hua Hin, Cha-am, Pattaya, Kanchanaburi, and elsewhere depart from Victory Monument.

Bus companies generally sell tickets on a first-come, first-served basis. This is seldom a problem because service is frequent. The most comfortable buses are those of Nakhon Chai Air, which has its own terminal near Mo Chit. Nakhon Chai connects Bangkok with many destinations within Thailand.

Getting Around: Bangkok Mass Transit Authority provides bus service in the city. For a fare of B8 on non-air-conditioned

Tuk-Tuks

Though colorful three-wheeled tuk-tuks are somewhat of a symbol of Bangkok, they're really only a good option when traffic is light—otherwise you can end up sitting in gridlock, sweating, and sucking in car fumes. They're also unmetered, their drivers prone to overcharging; unless you are good at bargaining, you may well end up paying more for a tuk-tuk than for a metered taxi. Some tuk-tuk drivers drive like madmen, and an accident in a tuk-tuk can be scary. Expats are loath to enter a tuk-tuk, but for many tourists, a trip to Bangkok isn't complete without a ride.

■ TIP→ Watch out for unscrupulous tuk-tuk drivers who offer cut-rate tours, then take you directly to jewelry and clothing shops that pay them a commission. If a trip to Bangkok does not seem complete without a tuk-tuk adventure, pay half of what the driver suggests, insist on being taken to your destination, and hold on for dear life.

buses and B12 to B25 on air-conditioned ones, you can travel virtually anywhere in Bangkok. Air-conditioned microbuses charge B25. Most buses operate from 5 am to around 11 pm, but a few routes operate around the clock. You can pick up a route map at most bookstalls for B35, or just ask locals which bus is headed to your destination.

CONTACTS Bangkok Mass Transit Authority ✉ *131 Thiemruam-mitre Rd., Huay Khwang, Huai Khwang* ☎ *1348 hotline* 🌐 *www.bmta.co.th.* **Bangkok Southern Bus Station (Sai Tai Mai)** ✉ *Borommaratchachonnani Rd., Bangkok Noi* ☎ *02/894–6122* 🌐 *www.transitbangkok.com.* **Mo Chit Northern Bus Station** ✉ *Kamphaeng Phet 2 Rd., Chatuchak* ☎ *02/936–2852, 02/936–2842* 🌐 *www.transitbangkok.com.* **Nakhon Chai Air Bus Station** ✉ *333 Chatuchak Rd., Chatuchak, Chatuchak* ☎ *1624 booking number, 02/939–4999* 🌐 *www.nca.co.th* Ⓜ *Subway: Chatuchak Park; Skytrain: Mo Chit.*

SKYTRAIN AND SUBWAY TRAVEL

Although the BTS Skytrain covers just a fraction of the capital (it bypasses the Old City and Dusit, for example), it is surprisingly convenient for visitors, with routes above Sukhumvit, Silom, and Phaholyothin roads. **■ TIP→ If you are traveling between two points along the route, the Skytrain is by far the best way to go.** Rates run between B15 and B40. Like the Skytrain, the MRT subway covers only a small section of the city, but it's a great way to get from the city center out to the train stations. The subway runs daily from 6 am until midnight. Fares are from B16 to B44. Although the Skytrain and subway are separate entities and use different fare and ticketing systems, the two connect at three points: Sala Daeng Station and Silom Station, Asok Station and Sukhumvit Station, and Mo Chit Station and Chatuchak Station. **■ TIP→ During rush hour, long lines are common at ticket machines, especially at busier stations. Buying reloadable cards for the Skytrain and Metro for deposits of B100 each can save you time waiting. Cards can be returned at ticket offices for a refund.**

CONTACTS BTS Skytrain ✉ *1000 Phahonyothin Rd., Chatuchak* ☎ *02/617–7300, 02/617–7341 tourist information* 🌐 *www.bts.co.th.* **MRT Bangkok Metro** ✉ *189 Rama IX Rd., Huay Khwang* ☎ *02/354–2000, 02/6245200 information center* 🌐 *www.bangkokmetro.co.th.*

TAXI TRAVEL

Taxis can be an economical way to get around, provided you don't hit gridlock. Most taxis have meters, so avoid drivers whose cabs lack one or who claim that it is broken. The rate for the first 1 km (½ mile) is B35, with an additional baht for every 55 yards after that; a 5-km (3-mile) journey costs about B60. ■ **TIP→ Ask your concierge to write the name of your destination and its cross streets in Thai.**

Grab Taxi, a ride hailing app which acquired Uber in Southeast Asia, is also an easy option for getting around. Enter your location, your destination, and choose your preference of a motorbike, taxi, or private driver. A driver will be confirmed and should arrive in a matter of minutes. Fares are calculated according to distance and you can also choose to pay by cash or credit card. Rides don't cost much more than metered taxis and you won't need to worry about giving directions.

TRAIN TRAVEL

The central train station in Bangkok is Hua Lamphong, located near Chinatown and accessible by subway. Trains here connect Bangkok and many destinations within Thailand.

CONTACTS Hua Lamphong Station ✉ *Phra Ram IV Rd., Pom Prap Sattru Phai* ☎ *02/222–0175, 02/224–7788* 🌐 *www.railway.co.th* Ⓜ *Subway: Hua Lamphong.*

HEALTH AND SAFETY

For a city of its size, Bangkok is relatively safe; however, you still need to practice common sense. Don't accept food or drinks from strangers, as there have been reports of people being drugged and robbed. If you plan to enjoy a massage in your hotel room, put your valuables in the safe. Bangkok is no more dangerous for women than any other major city, but it's still best to avoid walking alone at night (take a taxi if you're out late).

■ **TIP→ Beware of hustlers who claim that your hotel is overbooked.** They'll try to convince you to switch to one that pays them a commission. Also avoid anyone trying to sell you on an overpriced taxi or limo. Proceed to the taxi stand; these taxis will use a meter.

Contact the Tourist Police first in an emergency. For medical attention, Bumrungrad Hospital and Bangkok Nursing Hospital are considered the best.

EMERGENCY SERVICES Ambulance ☎ *1669.* **Fire** ☎ *199.* **Police** ☎ *191.* **Tourist Police** ☎ *1155.*

HOSPITALS Bangkok Nursing Home Hospital ✉ *9/1 Convent Rd., Bang Rak* ☎ *02/022–0700* 🌐 *www.bnhhospital.com* Ⓜ *Subway: Silom; Skytrain: Sala Daeng.* **Bumrungrad Hospital** ✉ *33 Sukhumvit, Soi 3, Sukhumvit* ☎ *02/066–8888* 🌐 *www.bumrungrad.com* Ⓜ *Skytrain: Ploenchit.*

MONEY MATTERS

Major banks all exchange foreign currency, and most have easily accessible ATMs that accept foreign bank cards. Currency-exchange offices are common, but don't wait until the last minute. It's distressing to try to find one when you're out of baht.

RESTAURANTS

Thais are passionate about food, and love discovering out-of-the-way shops that prepare unexpectedly tasty dishes. Nowhere is this truer—or more feasible—than in Bangkok. The city's residents always seem to be eating, so the tastes and smells of Thailand's cuisine surround you day and night. That said, Bangkok's restaurant scene is also a minefield, largely because the relationship between price and quality at times seems almost inverse. For every hole-in-the-wall gem serving the best sticky rice, *larb* (meat salad), and *som tam* (the hot-and-sour green-papaya salad that is the ultimate Thai staple) you've ever had, there's an overpriced hotel restaurant serving touristy, toned-down fare. In general the best Thai food is found at the most bare-bones, even run-down restaurants, although there are famous, upscale places providing experimental twists.

If you want a break from Thai food, many other world cuisines are represented. Best among them is Chinese, although there's decent Japanese and Korean food as well. The city's ubiquitous noodle shops have their roots in China, as do roast-meat purveyors, whose historical inspiration was Cantonese. Western fare tends to suffer from the distance, although in the past few years some excellent trendy Western eateries have opened.

As with anything in Bangkok, travel time is a major consideration when choosing a restaurant. If you're short on time or patience, choose a place that's an easy walk from a Skytrain or subway station. **■ TIP→ The easiest way to reach a riverside eatery is often on a Chao Phraya River express boat.**

What It Costs In Baht

$	$$	$$$	$$$$
AT DINNER			
under B200	B200–B300	B301–B400	over B400

HOTELS

Bangkok offers a staggering range of lodging choices, and even some of the best rooms are affordable to travelers on a budget. The city has nearly 500 hotels and guesthouses, and the number is growing. In fact, competition has brought the prices down at many hotels; unfortunately, the service has suffered at some as a result of cutting corners to lower prices. Still, you'll feel more pampered here than in many other cities.

For first-class lodging, few cities in the world rival Bangkok. In recent years the Mandarin Oriental, The Peninsula, Shangri-La, and a handful of others have been repeatedly rated among the best in the world, with newer players like the Sofitel So and St. Regis receiving major accolades. If there were a similar comparison of the world's boutique hotels, Bangkok's would be near the top, too. These high-end hotels are surprisingly affordable, with rates comparable to standard hotels in New York or London. Business hotels also have fine service, excellent restaurants, and amenities like health clubs and spas.

Wherever you stay, remember that prices fluctuate enormously, and that huge discounts are the order of the day. Internet discounts are widely available, and booking online can often save you up to several thousand baht. **■ TIP→ Always ask for a better price, even when you are checking in.** Deals may be more difficult to come by during the high season from November through February, but during low season they're plentiful.

What It Costs In Baht

$	$$	$$$	$$$$
FOR TWO PEOPLE			
under B2,000	B2,000–B4,000	B4,001–B6,000	over B6,000

Hotels are concentrated in four areas: in Silom and Bang Rak (home to many riverfront hotels); around Siam Square and along Phetchaburi Road in Pathumwan; along Sukhumvit Road, which has the greatest number of hotels and an abundance of restaurants and nightlife; and in the Chinatown and the Old City neighborhoods, which have a smaller number of properties, most of which are affordable. Backpackers often head to Khao San Road, also home to some newer, more upmarket guesthouses.

NIGHTLIFE

The city that was once notorious for its raunchy sex trade is now entertaining a burgeoning class of professionals hungry for thumping discos, trendy cocktail

Where Should I Stay?

	NEIGHBORHOOD VIBE	PROS	CONS
North Bangkok	This relatively quiet business and residential neighborhood has plenty of local culture but few tourist attractions.	This is the closest neighborhood to Don Mueang, the domestic and low-budget carrier airport—helpful if you have an early flight.	It's a ways from downtown, which means you'll spend a lot on taxis getting to the city center. Public transportation options are limited.
The Old City, Banglamphu, and Dusit	These central neighborhoods are the historic heart of the city. Today they're full of places to stay in all price ranges.	Tons of dining and lodging options here to match any budget; you'll be near many major attractions, like the Grand Palace and Wat Benjamabophit.	May feel chaotic to some, too touristy to others. Not easily accessible by subway or Skytrain. Not the cheapest part of town.
Chinatown	The utter chaos of Chinatown is not for everybody. You'll be inundated by the sights and sounds—expect a lot of neon.	There are some good hotel deals here, the neighborhood is one of a kind, the food scene is great, and the street markets are fascinating.	Hectic and not the most tourist-friendly part of town. Limited hotel selection, terrible traffic, and public transportation options are not convenient.
Thonburi	You'll rub elbows with the locals in this mostly residential neighborhood across the river from the Old City.	Tucked away in peaceful seclusion from the noise and chaos of Bangkok; stellar river views.	Everything else is on the other side of the Chao Phraya, so expect to take the ferry a lot and spend more on taxis.
Pathumwan	The neighborhood that makes up Bangkok's "downtown," this sprawling area is full of markets and mega-malls and has several tourist attractions.	A shopper's paradise, and relatively convenient to subway and Skytrain. Many superposh hotels; this is the place to stay if you're traveling in style.	Horrible traffic—you'll run up a taxi tab sitting in gridlock. Most options are pricey and may be noisy, because there's lots of nightlife nearby.
Silom and Bang Rak	Another part of the central area, this neighborhood is the city's biggest business hub and also has the greatest concentration of restaurants. Nightlife is fun.	Popular area with travelers, so lots of comfortable restaurants and bars. Convenient subway–Skytrain connection here.	Can be clogged with traffic. Not the most authentic Thai experience, and because it's partially a business district, there's a lot of less-than-charming concrete.
Sukhumvit	This central tourist- and expat-heavy neighborhood is the nightlife area in Bangkok, and you'll find everything from Irish pubs to hostess bars. There's also a good restaurant scene here.	If you want to party, this is the place to be. A wide range of hotels here, from dirt cheap to über-ritzy, and public transit is convenient.	Fast-paced; some areas are noisy well into the night, and you may run into some shady dealings, though there are plenty of classier establishments here as well.

lounges, and swanky rooftop bars. There are also stricter rules that limit the sale of alcohol (11 am–2, 5–midnight from stores). Most bars and clubs close around 2 am, though nighthawks can probably find a place or two open until 5 or 6 am.

There are a few notable nightlife sections: the area off Sukhumvit Soi 55 (also called Soi Thonglor) is full of bars and nightclubs, and trendy and happening new places are springing up around Sathorn Road and the adjoining Suan Phlu.

If you want to take a walk on the wild side, Bangkok still has three thriving red-light districts: Patpong, Nana Plaza, and Soi Cowboy. Patpong, the largest and most touristy, includes three streets that run between Surawong and Silom roads. Nana Plaza, at Sukhumvit Soi 4, is packed with three floors of hostess bars, go-go clubs, and "ladyboy" clubs. Soi Cowboy, off Sukhumvit Road at Soi 21 (the Asok intersection), is where many expats go, finding it slightly more relaxed and less of a tourist trap than Patpong or Nana.

Even though it may not seem like it, live sex shows are officially banned and prostitution is illegal. The government doesn't always turn a blind eye, so exercise caution and common sense.

PERFORMING ARTS

A contemporary arts scene is relatively new to Thailand, but the last decade has seen great changes in the fine arts: artists are branching out into all kinds of media, and modern sculpture and artworks can be found in office buildings, parks, and public spaces. Music options range from piano concertos and symphonies to rock concerts and blues-and-jazz festivals.

Bangkok offers a variety of theater and dance performances, among them traditional puppet shows and masked dance dramas known as khon. For Thais classical dance is more than graceful movements. The dances depict tales from the religious epic *Ramakien*. Performances are accompanied by a woodwind called the piphat, which sounds like an oboe, as well as a range of percussion instruments. In addition to conventional theaters, many restaurants present classical dance.

ACTIVITIES

Thailand has an abundance of outdoor activities, but it's often difficult to find any within Bangkok. Due to elevated temperatures, Bangkok residents generally head to the malls on weekends to cool off. Soccer is immensely popular, and the Thai Premier League has matches at several stadiums around town during the season. Bangkok offers visitors one of the most intense spectator sports in the world, *muay Thai* (Thai kickboxing). This is the national sport. Seeing a match is a quintessential Bangkok experience.

SHOPPING

Many tourists are drawn to Bangkok for its relatively cheap silk, gems, and tailor-made clothes. But there are many other goods worth seeking out: quality silverware, fine porcelain, and handmade leather goods—all at prices well below those in Western shops. The already reduced prices can often be haggled down even further—haggling is mainly reserved for markets, but shopkeepers will let you know if they're willing to discount, especially if you start walking away.

Don't be fooled by a tuk-tuk driver offering to take you to a shop. Shop owners pay drivers a commission to lure in unsuspecting tourists. **■ TIP→ Patronizing reputable dealers will help you avoid getting scammed on big-ticket items like jewelry.**

Thai antiques and old images of the Buddha require a special export license; check out the Thai Board of Investment's website at 🌐 *www.boi.go.th/english* for

Two Days in Bangkok

Start your first day with the most famous of all Bangkok sights, the Grand Palace. In the same complex is the gorgeously ornate Wat Phra Kaew. Not far south of the Grand Palace is Bangkok's oldest and largest temple, Wat Po, famous for its enormous Reclining Buddha and for being a great place for a traditional Thai massage. Later take the ferry up to Banglamphu (get off at the Phra Athit pier), where you can enjoy a river walk at Santichaiprakarn Park and the Phra Sumen Fort before checking out the hip restaurants and bars that front Phra Athit Road, which parallels the river. From here lively Khao San Road and all of its shopping are just a short stroll away.

The next day start out in Chinatown, where you can spend hours browsing the food and spice markets, peeking into temples and shops, and just absorbing the atmosphere. Next work your way to the Chao Phraya River, ferry down to the Saphan Taksin Pier, and take a *klong* (canal) tour, which will give you a glimpse of the fascinating canal life in Bangkok. If it's a weekend, head to Kukrit Pramoj Heritage House; if it's a weekday, visit the Jim Thompson House. Take the Skytrain in the evening either to Silom or Sukhumvit Road, where great restaurants and bars await.

rules on exporting and applications to do so.

The city's most popular shopping areas are along **Silom Road and Surawong Road,** where you can find quality silk; **Sukhumvit Road,** which is rich in leather goods; **Yaowarat Road in Chinatown,** where gold trinkets abound; and along **Oriental Lane and Charoen Krung (New Road),** where there are many antiques shops. The shops around **Siam Square** and at the **World Trade Center** attract both Thais and foreigners. If you're knowledgeable about fabric, you can find bargains at the textile merchants who compete along Pahuraht Road in Chinatown and **Pratunam Road off Phetchaburi Road.** You can even take the raw material to a tailor and have something made.

VISITOR INFORMATION

Tourist Authority of Thailand

The Tourist Authority of Thailand, open daily from 8:30 to 4:30, is sometimes heavier on colorful brochures than hard information, but it can supply materials about national parks and out-of-the-way destinations. A 24-hour hotline provides information about attractions, festivals, and the arts. You can use the hotline to register complaints or request assistance from the Tourist Police. ✉ *1600 New Phetchaburi Rd., Ratchathewi* ☎ *02/250–5500, 1672 tourist hotline* 🌐 *www.tourismthailand.org* Ⓜ *Subway: Phetchaburi.*

The Old City

Sights

City Pillar Shrine

RELIGIOUS SITE | Somewhat in the shadow of grander nearby attractions like the Grand Palace and the Temple of the Emerald Buddha, this shrine is one of the most historically and culturally significant sites in the city. Just east of the Grand Palace compound, the City Pillar Shrine contains the foundation stone (Lak Muang) from which all distances in Thailand are measured. The stone is believed to be inhabited by a spirit that guards the well-being of Bangkok. The shrine is free to enter and frequented by locals who come here to pray, so behave and dress respectfully (knees and shoulders should be covered). ✉ *2 Lak Muang Rd., Phra Nakhon* ✣ *East of the Grand Palace compound.*

Democracy Monument

MEMORIAL | One of Bangkok's biggest and best-known landmarks, the monument anchors a large traffic circle three blocks from the eastern end of Khao San Road. Not frequented much by tourists, it commemorates the establishment of a constitutional monarchy in Thailand in 1932. ✉ *Ratchadamnoen Rd., at Dinso Rd., Old City* 🎫 *Free.*

Giant Swing

MEMORIAL | Originally built by King Rama I in 1784, this towering 27-meter (88-foot) wood structure has a great backstory but today it is just a random photo op. If you find yourself posing in front of it, or just walking by, know that it was once used in Hindu ceremonies where teams of men would launch themselves into the air and catch gold coins with their teeth; slingshotting them to good fortunes on heaven and Earth. The competitions were banned in 1935 after several fell to untimely deaths. ✉ *Bamrung Muang Rd., Phra Nakhon.*

★ Grand Palace

CASTLE/PALACE | This is Thailand's most revered spot and one of its most visited. King Rama I built this walled city in 1782, when he moved the capital across the river from Thonburi. The palace and adjoining structures only got more opulent as subsequent monarchs added their own touches. The grounds are open to visitors, but the buildings are not. They're used only for state occasions and royal ceremonies. On rare occasions, rooms in the Chakri Maha Prasat Palace—considered the official residence of the king, even though he does not live here—are sometimes open to visitors. Admission for the complex includes entrance to Dusit Palace Park. Note, proper attire (no flip-flops, shorts, or bare shoulders or midriffs) is required, if you forget, you will be loaned unflattering but more demure shirts and shoes at the entrance (deposit required). ✉ *Sanam Chai and Na Phra Lan Rd., Old City* ✣ *A few hundred meters east of Tha Chang ferry pier* ☎ *02/623–5500* 🌐 *www.palaces.thai.net* 🎫 *B500, includes admission to Wat Phra Kaew.*

National Gallery

MUSEUM | Although it doesn't get nearly as much attention as the National Museum, the gallery has a permanent collection of modern and traditional Thai art that is worth seeking out. There are also frequent temporary shows from around the country and abroad. To get to the gallery, walk down Na Phra That Road, past the National Theater and toward the river. Go under the bridge, then turn right and walk about 200 meters (650 feet); the gallery is on your left. The building used to house the royal mint. ✉ *4 Chao Fa Rd., Phra Nakhon* ☎ *02/281–2224* 🎫 *B200* ⏲ *Closed Mon. and Tues.*

National Museum

MUSEUM | There's no better place to acquaint yourself with Thai history than the National Museum, which also holds one of the world's best collections of Southeast Asian art. The exhibitions of Thai artworks and artifacts begin with the ceramic utensils and bronze ware of the Ban Chiang people (4000–3000 BC). Most of the masterpieces from the northern provinces are displayed here, not in museums there. ■ **TIP→ Free guided tours in English take place on Wednesday and Thursday, usually at 9:30 am.** ✉ *4 Na Phra That Rd., Phra Nakhon* ☎ *02/224–1333* 🌐 *www.mynmv.com/national-museum-bangkok* 🎫 *B200* ⏲ *Closed Mon. and Tues.* Ⓜ *Skytrain: Hua Lamphong.*

October 14 Memorial

MEMORIAL | The memorial honors Thais killed during a student-led uprising against military rule. That revolt began on October 14, 1973, and tributes to people killed in October 1976 and May 1992 in similar protests have also been incorporated. Although most of the inscriptions are written in Thai, the memorial is a sobering sight, especially being so close to the Democracy Monument, which acknowledges the establishment of the constitutional monarchy. Traffic is always whizzing about, the gate is often closed, and there seem to be no regular hours, though there are painting exhibitions at times. ✉ *Ratchadamnoen and Tanao Rds., Banglamphu* ✣ *2½ blocks west of Democracy Monument* 🎫 *Free.*

Queen Sirikit Museum of Textiles
MUSEUM | Within the Grand Palace complex, in the old Ministry of Finance building, this interesting little museum tells the story of Thai silk through a lovely display of the current queen's most celebrated outfits. There are daily silk-making demonstrations, and a particularly good gift shop. ✉ *Ratsadakorn-bhibhathana building, Old City* ✣ *Just inside main visitors' gate, Grand Palace* ☎ *02/225–9420, 02/225–9430* 🌐 *www.qsmtthailand.org* 🎫 *Included in Grand Palace ticket, or B150 for museum alone.*

★ **Wat Phra Kaew** (*Temple of the Emerald Buddha*)
RELIGIOUS SITE | No single structure within the Grand Palace elicits such awe as this, the most sacred temple in the kingdom. No other wat in Thailand is so ornate or so embellished with glittering gold. As you enter the compound, take note of the 20-foot-tall statues of fearsome creatures in traditional battle attire standing guard. Turn right as you enter the compound, where the inner walls are lively murals depicting Thailand's national epic the *Ramakien*. Several *aponsis* (half-woman, half-lion creatures) stand guard outside the main chapel, which has a gilded three-tier roof. Inside sits the Emerald Buddha. This most venerated image of Lord Buddha is carved from one piece of jade 31 inches high. ✉ *Sana Chai and Na Phra Lan Rds., Old City* ✣ *Near Tha Chang ferry pier* ☎ *02/224–3290* 🌐 *www.palaces.thai.net* 🎫 *B500, includes admission to Grand Palace and Vimanmek Mansion.*

Phony Guides

Be wary of phony tour guides who approach tourists offering tips about undiscovered or off-the-beaten-path places. Some will even inform you that the place you want to see is closed, suggesting that you should join them for a tour instead. Often these "tours"—offered at too-good-to-be-true prices—include a visit to a gem shop for more than a little arm-twisting. The majority of the fraudsters are to be found around the Grand Palace, Wat Po, and Khao San Road.

★ **Wat Po** (*Temple of the Reclining Buddha*)
RELIGIOUS SITE | The city's largest wat has what is perhaps the most unusual representation of the Buddha in Bangkok. The 150-foot sculpture, covered with gold, is so large it fills an entire viharn. Especially noteworthy are the mammoth statue's 10-foot feet, with the 108 auspicious signs of the Buddha inlaid in mother-of-pearl. Many people ring the bells surrounding the image for good luck. Behind the viharn holding the Reclining Buddha is Bangkok's oldest open university. A century before Bangkok was established as the capital, a monastery was founded here to teach traditional medicine. Around the walls are marble plaques inscribed with formulas for herbal cures, and stone sculptures squat in various postures demonstrating techniques for relieving pain. The monks still practice ancient cures, and the **massage school** is now famous. Thai massages (which can actually be painful, though therapeutic) cost B420 for one

hour. Appointments aren't necessary—you usually won't have to wait long if you just show up. Massage courses of up to 10 days are also available. ✉ *Chetuphon Rd., Old City* ☎ *02/225–9595* 🌐 *www.watpho.com* *B100.*

Wat Saket

RELIGIOUS SITE | A well-known landmark, the towering gold chedi of Wat Saket, also known as the Golden Mount, was once the highest point in the city. King Rama III began construction of this temple, but it wasn't completed until the reign of Rama V. On a clear day the view from the top is magnificent. Every November, at the time of the Loi Krathong festival, the temple hosts a popular fair with food stalls and performances. **■ TIP→ To reach the gilded chedi you must ascend an exhausting 318 steps, so don't attempt the climb on a hot afternoon.** ✉ *Chakkaphatdi Phong Rd., Old City* ☎ *02/621–2280* *B20.*

Restaurants

The Old City has every type of restaurant, including many holes-in-the-wall serving excellent food.

★ Raan Jay Fai

$$$ | **THAI** | To enjoy chef Jay Fai's award-winning dishes at her small open-air eatery, be prepared for upwards of a three-hour wait. Although the restaurant opens at 2:30, hopeful diners can put their names on a waiting list from 12:30, and although reservations via email or phone are possible, they're highly unlikely due to demand. **Known for:** pad khee mao (drunken noodles); lump crabmeat with curry; cult following. *$ Average main: B400* ✉ *327 Mahachai Rd., Phra Nakhon* ☎ *09/2724–9633* *jayfaibangkok@gmail.com* *No credit cards* *Closed Sun.*

Hotels

★ Chakrabongse Villas

$$$$ | **B&B/INN** | On the riverbank in an old part of the city, these traditional Thai houses were originally built up-country and then transported to the grounds of the Chakrabongse House, which was built in 1908. **Pros:** unique hotel experience; beautiful surroundings; large discounts during low season. **Cons:** fills up quickly; feels isolated; extremely expensive. *$ Rooms from: B6,700* ✉ *396 Maharaj Rd., Tatien* ☎ *02/222–1290, 02/622–1900* 🌐 *www.thaivillas.com* *4 rooms, 3 bed-and-breakfast rooms* *Free breakfast* *M Skytrain: Saphan Taksin, then river ferry.*

Phranakorn-Nornlen Hotel

$$ | **HOTEL** | Ideal for travelers seeking an artsy, off-the-beaten-track experience, this cute boutique guesthouse is in the old Phra Nakhon district. **Pros:** artsy setting; friendly and helpful staff; in a real Bangkok neighborhood well off the tourist track. **Cons:** far from Skytrain and subway; difficult to find; lacks pool, gym, and other hotel amenities. *$ Rooms from: B2,600* ✉ *46 Thewet, Soi 1, Phranakorn, Bangkhunprom, Krungkasem, Phra Nakhon* ☎ *02/628–8188* 🌐 *www.phranakorn-nornlen.com* *30 rooms* *Free breakfast.*

Riva Arun Bangkok

$$$ | **HOTEL** | This luxurious boutique hotel overlooking the Chao Phraya River favors elegant modern furnishings, perfect for couples seeking a romantic escape. **Pros:** near to Grand Palace and other attractions; rooftop restaurant; quiet and tucked down an alley. **Cons:** far from city center; expensive; very limited occupancy. *$ Rooms from: B5,200* ✉ *392/25-28 Maharaj Rd., Phra Nakhon* ☎ *02/221–1188* 🌐 *www.rivaarunbangkok.com* *28 rooms* *No meals.*

Royal Princess Larn Luang

$$ | **HOTEL** | This hotel with four restaurants of its own is situated for exploring

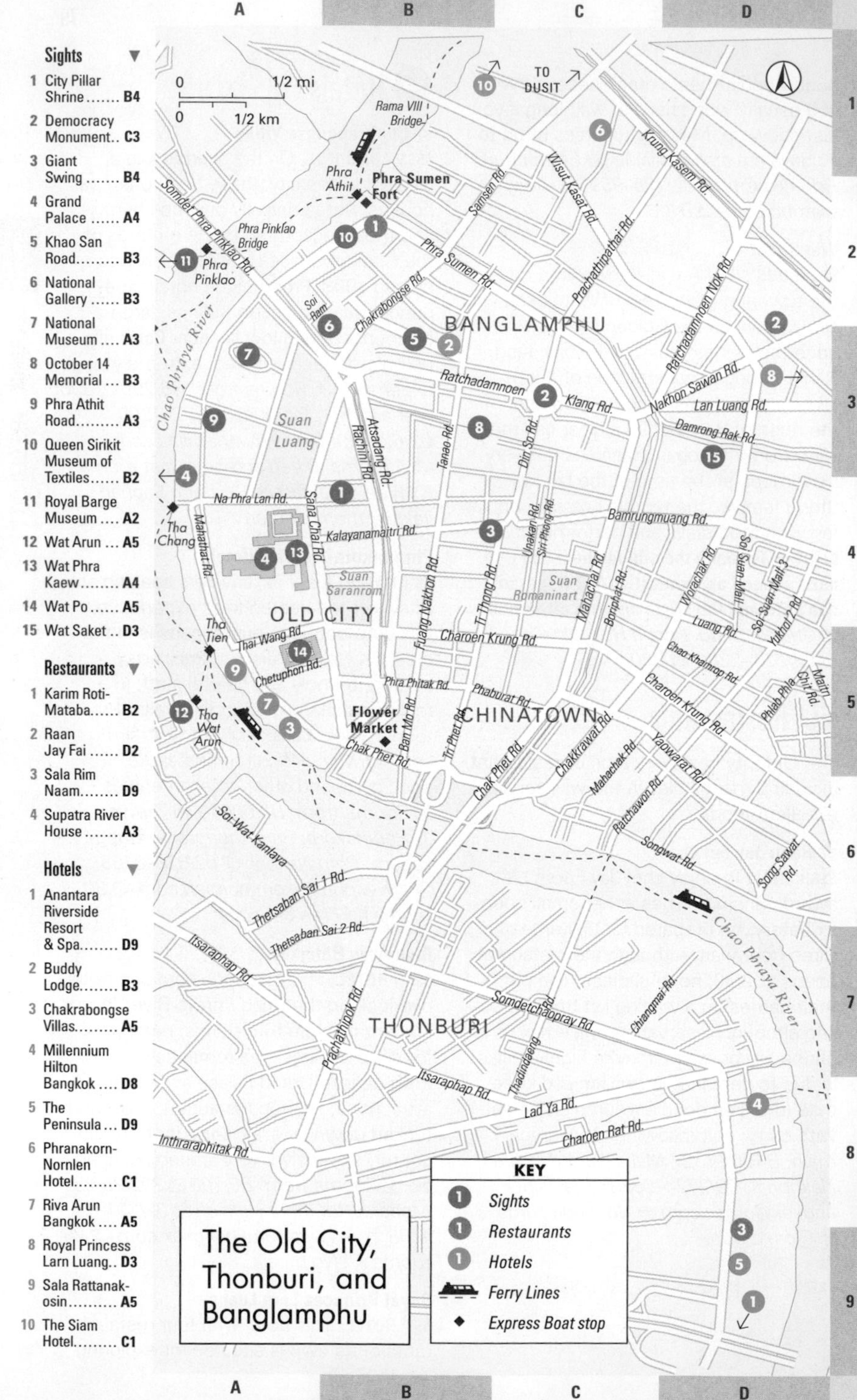

The Old City, Thonburi, and Banglamphu
A
B
C
D
1
2
3
4
5
6
7
8
9
Sights
1 City Pillar Shrine....... B4
2 Democracy Monument.. C3
3 Giant Swing B4
4 Grand Palace A4
5 Khao San Road......... B3
6 National Gallery B3
7 National Museum A3
8 October 14 Memorial ... B3
9 Phra Athit Road......... A3
10 Queen Sirikit Museum of Textiles...... B2
11 Royal Barge Museum A2
12 Wat Arun ... A5
13 Wat Phra Kaew........ A4
14 Wat Po A5
15 Wat Saket .. D3
Restaurants
1 Karim Roti-Mataba...... B2
2 Raan Jay Fai D2
3 Sala Rim Naam........ D9
4 Supatra River House A3
Hotels
1 Anantara Riverside Resort & Spa........ D9
2 Buddy Lodge........ B3
3 Chakrabongse Villas......... A5
4 Millennium Hilton Bangkok D8
5 The Peninsula ... D9
6 Phranakorn-Nornlen Hotel......... C1
7 Riva Arun Bangkok A5
8 Royal Princess Larn Luang.. D3
9 Sala Rattanakosin.......... A5
10 The Siam Hotel......... C1
0
1/2 mi
0
1/2 km
TO DUSIT
Rama VIII Bridge
Phra Athit
Phra Sumen Fort
Phra Pinklao Bridge
Phra Pinklao
Somdet Phra Pinklao Rd.
Samsen Rd.
Wisut Kasat Rd.
Krung Kasem Rd.
Prachathipathai Rd.
Phra Sumen Rd.
Chakrabongse Rd.
Soi Ram
BANGLAMPHU
Ratchadamnoen Nok Rd.
Nakhon Sawan Rd.
Lan Luang Rd.
Damrong Rak Rd.
Ratchadamnoen
Klang Rd.
Chao Phraya River
Suan Luang
Rachini Rd.
Atsadang Rd.
Tanao Rd.
Din So Rd.
Na Phra Lan Rd.
Tha Chang
Maharat Rd.
Sana Chai Rd.
Kalayanamaitri Rd.
Bamrungmuang Rd.
Unakan Rd.
Siri Phong Rd.
Suan Saranrom
Fuang Nakhon Rd.
Ti Thong Rd.
Suan Romaninart
Mahachai Rd.
Boriphat Rd.
Worachak Rd.
Soi Suan Mali 1
Soi Suan Mali 3
Yukhol 2 Rd.
OLD CITY
Tha Tien
Thai Wang Rd.
Chetuphon Rd.
Charoen Krung Rd.
Luang Rd.
Chao Khamrop Rd.
Maitri Chit Rd.
Phlab Phla
Phra Phitak Rd.
Phaburat Rd.
Tha Wat Arun
Flower Market
Ban Mo Rd.
Tri Phet Rd.
CHINATOWN
Chakkrawat Rd.
Charoen Krung Rd.
Chak Phet Rd.
Mahachak Rd.
Yaowarat Rd.
Ratchawong Rd.
Soi Wat Kanlaya
Songwat Rd.
Song Sawat Rd.
Thetsaban Sai 1 Rd.
Thetsaban Sai 2 Rd.
Itsaraphap Rd.
Prachathipok Rd.
Somdetchaopray Rd.
Chiengmai Rd.
THONBURI
Thadindaeng
Itsaraphap Rd.
Lad Ya Rd.
Charoen Rat Rd.
Inthraraphitak Rd.
KEY
Sights
Restaurants
Hotels
Ferry Lines
Express Boat stop

Dusit, the Old City, and Chinatown, and it's a short taxi ride from riverside eateries. **Pros:** beautiful pool area; fair number of creature comforts; quiet neighborhood. **Cons:** restaurants not outstanding; isolated location; smallish bathrooms. *Rooms from: B3,600* *269 Larn Luang Rd., Old City* *02/281–3088* *www.royalprincesslarnluang.com* *167 rooms* *Free breakfast.*

Sala Rattanakosin

$$ | **HOTEL** | Hidden down an alley filled with shophouses, this upcycled space features prestigious rooms with views of Wat Po and Wat Arun twinkling against the river. **Pros:** near Grand Palace and other attractions; excellent views; among newer accommodations in the area. **Cons:** far from city center; on the expensive side; rooms book up fast. *Rooms from: B3,600* *39 Maha Rat Rd., Phra Nakhon* *02/231–2589* *www.salarattanakosin.com* *16 rooms* *Free breakfast.*

★ The Siam Hotel

$$$$ | **RESORT** | Old Hollywood meets art deco at this family-owned property on the Chao Phraya, where ultraluxurious design pays homage to the postcolonial, early-1900s era of King Rama V, with black-and-white striped chairs and a library lined with limited-edition tomes. **Pros:** minutes from Grand Palace via private riverboat; exclusive, serene, and private; whimsical design. **Cons:** very pricey; a long way from public transportation; far from nightlife. *Rooms from: B17,070* *3/2 Thanon Khao, Vachirapayaabal, Dusit* *02/206–6999* *www.thesiamhotel.com* *28 rooms, 10 villas, 1 cottage* *Free breakfast* *Skytrain: Saphan Taksin, then hotel's private boat.*

Performing Arts

THEATER AND DANCE

National Theatre

DANCE | Classical dance and drama can usually be seen at the theater on the first Saturday and Sunday and the last Friday of every month at 1:30 and 5 pm. *Na Phra That Rd., Old City* *02/221–0171.*

Sala Chalerm Krung Royal Theatre

DANCE | **FAMILY** | A former student at the École des Beaux-Arts in Paris designed this theater in a style that might best be described as Thai deco. The venue hosts traditional khon, a masked dance-drama based on tales from the *Ramakien.* *66 Charoen Krung (New Rd.), Old City* *02/258–7578, 02/6238–1489* *www.salachalermkrung.com* *Skytrain: Saphan Taksin.*

Shopping

JEWELRY

Thailand is known for its sparkling gems, so it's no surprise that the country exports more colored stones than anywhere in the world. You'll find things you wouldn't find at home, and prices are far lower than in the United States. There are countless jewelry stores on Silom and Surawong roads. Scams are common, so it's best to stick with established businesses. **■ TIP→ Deals that seem too good to be true probably are.**

Johny's Gems

JEWELRY/ACCESSORIES | If you call first, this long-established firm will send a car—a common practice of the city's better stores—to take you to the shop near Wat Phra Kaew. The selection is massive, and you can order custom-designed pieces. *199 Fuengnakorn Rd., Phra Nakhon* *02/224–4065* *www.johnysgems.com* *Closed Sun.*

Lin Jewelers

JEWELRY/ACCESSORIES | The jewelry sold at this highly respected shop is more expensive than average, but so is the quality. *9 Charoen Krung (New Rd.), Soi 38, Bang Rak* *02/234–2819* *www.linjewelers.com* *Skytrain: Saphan Taksin.*

Cooking Classes

A Thai cooking class can be a great way to spend a half day—or longer. You won't become an expert, but you can learn a few fundamentals and some of the history of Thai cuisine. You can also find specialty classes that focus on things like fruit carving (where the first lesson learned is that it's more difficult than it looks) or hot-and-spicy soups. All cooking schools concentrate on practical dishes that students will be able to make at home, usually with spices that are internationally available, and all revolve around the fun of eating something you cooked (at least partly) yourself. ■ **TIP→ Book cooking classes ahead of time, as they fill up fast.** Most classes are small enough to allow individual attention and time for questions. Prices vary from B2,000 to more than B10,000.

Blue Elephant Cooking School. Long a favorite, and connected with the same-named restaurant, this school has a very friendly staff. The Thai dishes taught here are heavily Westernized. ✉ *233 S. Sathorn Rd., Sathorn* ☎ *02/673–9353* 🌐 *www.blueelephant.com* 🎫 *From B2,800 per half day* Ⓜ *Skytrain: Surasak.*

Oriental Cooking School. The cooking school at the Mandarin Oriental hotel is Bangkok's most established and expensive one, but the classes are fun and informative, and the dishes tend to be more interesting and authentic than those at other schools. Classes are taught in a beautiful century-old house across the river from the hotel. ✉ *Mandarin Oriental, 48 Oriental Ave., Bang Rak* ☎ *02/659–9000* 🌐 *www.mandarinoriental.com/bangkok* 🎫 *From B4,000 per half day* Ⓜ *Skytrain: Saphan Taksin then hotel boat.*

Banglamphu

In the northern part of the Old City, Banglamphu offers pleasant strolls, interesting markets, and Khao San Road, one of the world's best-known backpacker hubs. Visitors from dozens of countries populate the scene year-round, served by an equally diverse selection of restaurants and street vendors. During high season upwards of 10,000 people a day call the area home.

Sights

Khao San Road

NEIGHBORHOOD | This thoroughfare, whose name means "Shining Rice," has been the heart of the international backpacking scene for decades. In the past few years, stabs at trendiness have been made, with new outdoor bars, a glut of negligible Western restaurants, and some reasonably nice hotels sharing the space with the ubiquitous low-budget guesthouses, some of which aren't actually budget anymore. The road has become popular as well with Thais, who frequent the bars and watch the farang.

Sunset marks the start of a busy street market. Khao San is closed to traffic at night, making early evening the best time to stroll or sit back and people-watch. The frenetic activity can, depending on your perspective, be infectious or overwhelming. During Songkran, the Thai New Year, in mid-April, Khao San turns into one huge wet-and-wild water fight. Join in the fun only if you don't mind being soaked to the bone. ✉ *Khao San Rd.,*

Banglamphu ⊕ Between Chakrapong and Tanao Rds.; head southeast from Phra Athit ferry pier.

Phra Athit Road

NEIGHBORHOOD | Chao Phraya breezes cool the short path that leads from the Phra Athit ferry pier to Santichaiprakarn Park, a tree-lined spot at the northern end of Phra Athit Road. The park, a delightful place to sit and watch the river, contains **Phra Sumen Fort,** one of the two remaining forts of the original 14 built under King Rama I. Some of the buildings along Phra Athit Road itself date back more than 100 years. At night the street, a favorite of university students, comes alive with little bars and restaurants hosting live music. ✉ *Phra Athit Rd., Banglamphu ⊕ Take taxi, or Chao Phraya ferry to Phra Athit pier.*

Restaurants

Touristy Khao San Road is north of the Old City, though the tame Thai food available in this backpacker mecca is nothing to go out of your way for. Don't be afraid to sample the street food in the alleyways away from Khao San Road—it often makes for a memorable meal.

Karim Roti-Mataba

$ | **INDIAN** | In a century-old building across from Santichaiprakarn Park on the Chao Phraya, this little restaurant serves Indian and Thai-Muslim cuisine. The specialty, as the name suggests, is sizzling roti—unleavened, whole wheat flatbread—filled with your choice of vegetables, chicken, beef, fish, or seafood, or just sweetened with thick condensed milk. **Known for:** Thai-Muslim dishes like Massaman curry; air-conditioned seating; popular with tourists. *$ Average main: B60 ✉ 136 Phra Athit Rd., Banglamphu ☎ 02/282–2119 ⊕ www.roti-mataba.net ▭ No credit cards ⊙ Closed Mon.*

Hotels

Buddy Lodge

$$ | **HOTEL** | This colonial-style boutique hotel has contributed greatly to the trendiness of Khao San Road. **Pros:** happening location; comfortable rooms; cool clientele. **Cons:** nothing fancy; no subway or Skytrain access; exorbitant price for Khao San Road. *$ Rooms from: B2,000 ✉ 265 Khao San Rd., Banglamphu ☎ 02/629–4477 ⊕ www.buddylodge.com ⇨ 76 rooms ¦◎¦ No meals.*

Nightlife

Brown Sugar, one of Bangkok's longest-running jazz haunts, tops the list of bars in Banglamphu.

JAZZ BARS

Brown Sugar

MUSIC CLUBS | A good place to carouse over live jazz and occasionally blues, smoky Brown Sugar has been in business for over three decades. ✉ *469 Wanchat Junction, Phrasumen Rd., Banglamphu ☎ 02/282–0396, 089/499–1378 ⊕ www.brownsugarbangkok.com ⊙ Closed Mon.*

Shopping

FOOD

Nittaya Thai Curry Shop

FOOD/CANDY | To bring home a taste of Thailand, Nittaya Thai Curry Shop has premade, easy-to-prepare Thai curries and desserts that are packed in durable pouches. ✉ *136-40 Chakrabongse Rd., Banglamphu* Ⓜ *Subway: Hua Lamphong.*

MARKETS

Khao San Road

OUTDOOR/FLEA/GREEN MARKETS | Backpacker central in Banglamphu, this street has some of Bangkok's most enjoyable street shopping. If the plastic buckets of booze, harem pants, and cheesy souvenirs for sale, and all the cheap pad Thai don't make the trip here worth it, the

A B C D

Sights

1 Chitlada Palace....... D3

2 Wat Benjamabophit C4

Restaurants

1 Aw Taw Kaw Market...... D1

2 Dynasty..... D1

3 Kaloang Home Kitchen...... A2

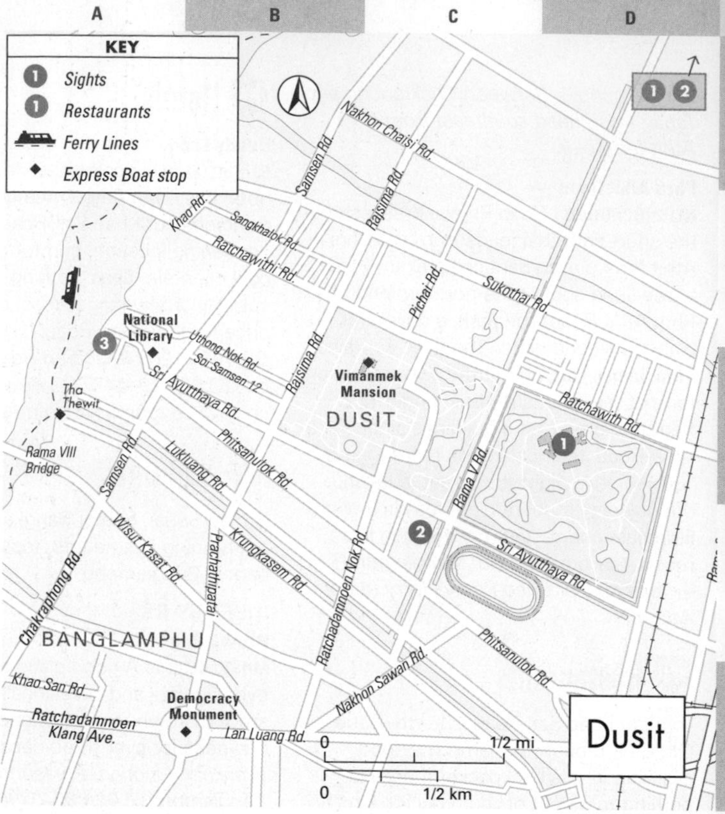

KEY

Sights

Restaurants

Ferry Lines

Express Boat stop

Nakhon Chaisi Rd.
Samsen Rd.
Rajsima Rd.
Khao Rd.
Sangkhalok Rd.
Ratchawithi Rd.
Pichai Rd.
Sukothai Rd.
National Library
Uthong Nok Rd.
Soi Samsen 12
Sri Ayutthaya Rd.
Rajsima Rd.
Vimanmek Mansion
DUSIT
Ratchawith Rd.
Tha Thewit
Phitsanulok Rd.
Rama VIII Bridge
Samsen Rd.
Lukluang Rd.
Rama V Rd.
Wisut Kasat Rd.
Krungkasem Rd.
Prachathipatai
Ratchadamnoen Nok Rd.
Sri Ayutthaya Rd.
Chakraphong Rd.
BANGLAMPHU
Phitsanulok Rd.
Khao San Rd.
Nakhon Sawan Rd.
Democracy Monument
Ratchadamnoen Klang Ave.
Lan Luang Rd.
0 1/2 mi
0 1/2 km

Dusit

people-watching will. ✉ *Khao San Rd., Banglamphu* ✣ *Between Chakrapong and Tanao Rds.; head southeast from Phra Athit ferry pier.*

Dusit and Northern Bangkok

More than any other neighborhood in the city, this area north of Banglamphu seems calm and orderly. Its tree-shaded boulevards and elegant buildings befit the district that holds Chitlada Palace, the official residence of the late king. The neighborhood's layout was the work of King Rama V, the first of the country's monarchs to visit Europe. He returned with a grand plan to remake his capital after the great cities he had visited. Dusit is a sprawling area, but luckily the major attractions are fairly close together.

Sights

Chitlada Palace

CASTLE/PALACE | The late King Bhumibol used to reside at this palace across from Dusit Park. Although it's closed to the public, the outside walls are a lovely sight, especially when lighted to celebrate his birthday, December 5, a national holiday. The extensive grounds shelter a herd of royal white elephants, though it's difficult to see them. ✉ *Ratchawithi Rd. and Rama V Rd., Dusit* Ⓜ *Skytrain: Victory Monument (take a taxi from the station).*

Wat Benjamabophit (*Marble Temple*)

RELIGIOUS SITE | Built in 1899, this wat is a favorite with photographers because of its open spaces and bright, shining marble. Statues of the Buddha line the courtyard, the magnificent interior has crossbeams of lacquer and gold, and an exquisite bronze seated Buddha is the focal point of the ordination hall's main altar. But Wat Benjamabophit is more than a glorious structure. The monastery here is a seat of learning that appeals to Buddhist monks with intellectual yearnings. ✉ *Nakhon Pathom Rd., Dusit* ☎ *02/282–9686* 🎫 *B20* Ⓜ *Skytrain: Victory Monument (take a taxi from station).*

Restaurants

Northern Bangkok is worth dining in only if you happen to be in the neighborhood for sightseeing, or if you really want to get to a part of the river that's off the beaten track.

★ Aw Taw Kaw Market
$ | THAI | FAMILY | Bangkok's best food bargains are found at this legendary spot in the Chatuchak market, where you are certain to be inundated with sights, sounds, and smells. Items are dished out in plastic bags so finding seats and utensils can be challenging—the trick is to buy something small at one of the few café-like establishments that have seats, plates, and cutlery, and then feast. **Known for:** traditional Thai-market atmosphere; fresh tropical fruits and vegetables; raw and cooked seafood. $ *Average main: B100* ✉ *Phaholyothin Rd., Chatuchak* 💳 *No credit cards* Ⓜ *Subway: Chatuchak Park; Skytrain: Mo Chit.*

Dynasty
$$$$ | CHINESE | This restaurant has long been a favorite among government ministers and corporate executives, both for its outstanding Cantonese cuisine and its private areas, perfect for business lunches or romantic dinners. The main dining room is elegant, with crimson carpeting, carved screens, lacquer furniture, and porcelain objets d'art. **Known for:** fantastic Peking duck; seasonal specialties like Taiwanese eels; dim sum. $ *Average main: B750* ✉ *Centara Grand at Central Plaza Lad Phrao, 1695 Phaholyothin Rd., Chatuchak* ☎ *02/541–1234* 🌐 *www.centarahotelsresorts.com/centaragrand/cglb/restaurant/dynasty-chinese-restaurant* Ⓜ *Subway: Phahon Yothin.*

Kaloang Home Kitchen
$$ | THAI | An alley near the National Library leads to this off-the-beaten-track restaurant on a ramshackle pier overlooking the Chao Phraya River. Kaloang Home Kitchen might not look like much with its plastic seats and simple tables, but it's a local favorite for waterfront breezes that keeping things comfortably cool, as well as generous grilled seafood platters and giant river prawns. **Known for:** no-frills dining; riverside location; well-priced seafood. $ *Average main: B200* ✉ *2 Sri Ayutthaya Rd., Dusit* ☎ *02/281–9228, 02/282–7581* 🌐 *www.kaloanghome.com.*

Nightlife

There aren't too many pubs frequented by foreigners around here, but the area around Victory Monument does have the long-running Saxophone, along with an excellent smattering of bars and pubs along the nearby Soi Rangnam.

BARS AND PUBS

Saxophone
BARS/PUBS | Popular with locals and expats, Saxophone hosts rhythm and blues, jazz, blues, rock, reggae, and sometimes ska bands. ✉ *3/8 Phayathai Rd., Victory Monument* ☎ *02/246–5472* 🌐 *www.saxophonepub.com* Ⓜ *Skytrain: Victory Monument.*

Performing Arts

THEATER AND DANCE

Siam Niramit
DANCE | This 2,000-seat theater presents *Journey to the Enchanted Kingdom of Siam,* a history of Thailand told in words and music. The 80-minute performance begins at 8 pm nightly. ✉ *19 Tiamruammit*

Continued on page 94

the Grand Palace

Thais regard their royal family with great respect, so it's no surprise that they hold the Grand Palace in high esteem. But the main attraction here is not a royal residence—it's Wat Phra Kaew (Temple of the Emerald Buddha), the home King Rama I built for the country's most revered idol. The temple is a reminder that in a country where everyone bows to the king, even the king bows to the Buddha.

---

by Lee Middleton

When Rama I was crowned in 1782, he wanted to celebrate the kingdom's renewed power. He moved the capital to Bangkok and set out to exceed the grandeur of Ayutthaya, once one of Asia's finest cities. The result was the dazzling Grand Palace compound, protected by a high white wall over a mile long. Rama I both ruled from and lived in the palace. Indeed, the royal family resided here until 1946, and each king who came to power added to the compound, leaving a mark of his rule and the era. Today, the Grand Palace compound's official use is for state occasions and ceremonies like coronations. The current monarch, King Bhumibol (Rama IX), lives in Chitralada Palace which is closed to the public and is in Bangkok's Dusit District, northeast of the palace.

GRAND PALACE COMPOUND

Mural at the Grand Palace.

The palace grounds and Wat Phra Kaew are open to visitors, but many of the buildings in the complex are not. If you arrive by boat, you will land at Chiang Pier (tha Chang). Make your way to the main entrance on Na Phra Lan Road. **Wat Phra Kaew** is the best place to begin your tour. Other highlights are **Phra Thinang Amarin Winichai Mahaisun** (Amarinda Winichai Throne Hall), **Chakri Maha Prasat** (Grand Palace Hall), **Dusit Maha Prasat** (Audience Hall), **Phra Thinang Borom Phiman** (Borom Phiman Mansion), and the **Wat Phra Kaew Museum**.

Phra Thinang Borom Phiman
5
1
Wat Phra Kaew
PRASAT PHRA DHEPBIDORN
HOR PHRA MONTHIAN DHARMA
PHRA MONDOP
PHRA WIHARN YOD
PHRA SIRATANA CHEDI
HOR PHRA NAGA
Shop
SALA SAHADAYA

1 Wat Phra Kaew. King Rama I built Wat Phra Kaew—now regarded as Thailand's most sacred temple—in 1785. The main building, called ubosoth, houses the Emerald Buddha. The ubosoth has three doors; only the king and queen are allowed to enter through the central door.

Wat Phra Kaew.

2 Phra Thinang Amarin Winichai Mahaisun. The only part of Rama I's original residence that's open to visitors is used today for royal events such as the king's birthday celebration. Inside this audience hall are an antique boat-shaped throne from Rama I's reign that's now used to hold Buddha images during ceremonies, and a second throne with a nine-tiered white canopy where the king sits. At the entrance, you'll see gold-topped red poles once used by royal guests to tether their elephants.

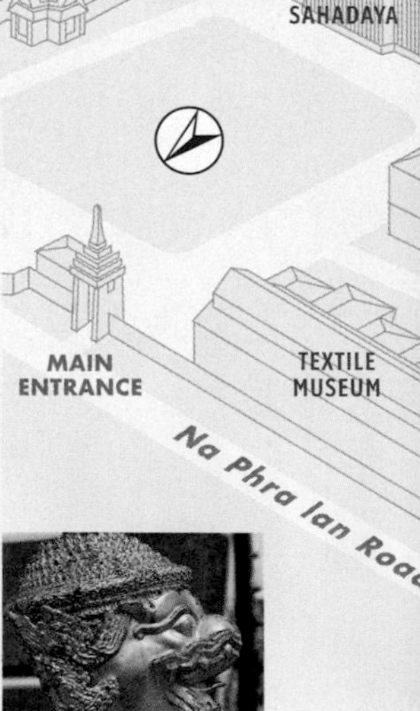

Golden statue.

3 Chakri Maha Prasat. Rama V's residence, built in 1882, is the largest of the palace buildings. The hybrid Thai–European style was a compromise between Rama V, who wanted a neoclassical palace with a domed roof, and his advisors, who thought such a blatantly European design was inappropriate. Rama V agreed to a Thai-style roof; Thais nicknamed the building farang sai chada or "the westerner wearing a Thai hat.

4 Dusit Maha Prasat. Built in 1784, the Audience Hall contains Rama I's original teak and mother-of-pearl throne. Today the hall is where Thais view royal remains, which are placed here temporarily in a golden urn.

5 Phra Thinang Borom Phiman. King Rama V built this French-style palace for his son (the future Rama VI) in 1903. Though later kings did not use the palace much, today visiting dignitaries stay here.

6 Wat Phra Kaew Museum. Stop by after touring the compound to learn about the restoration of the palace and to see the seasonal robes of the Emerald Buddha. Labels are in Thai, but free English tours occur regularly.

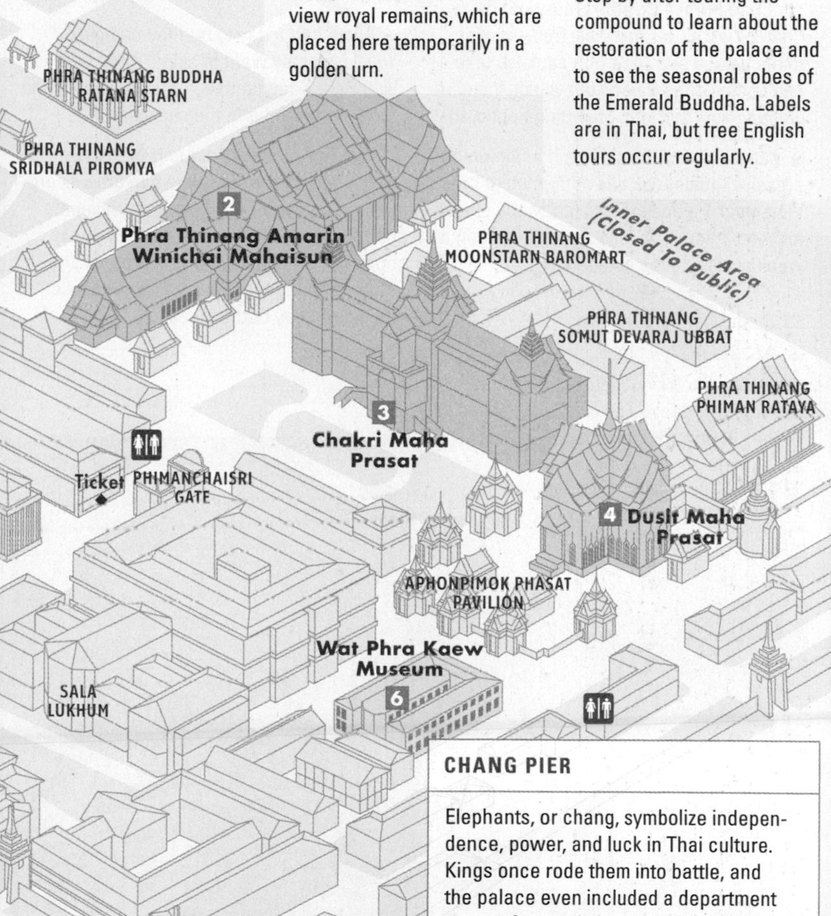

CHANG PIER

Elephants, or chang, symbolize independence, power, and luck in Thai culture. Kings once rode them into battle, and the palace even included a department to care for royal elephants. This pier is named for the kings' beasts, which were bathed here. Many elephant statues also grace the complex grounds. Notice how smooth the tops of their heads are—Thais rub the heads of elephants for luck.

TOURING TIPS

- Free guided tours of the compound are available in English at 10:00, 10:30, 1:30, and 2:00 daily; personal audio guides are available for B100 plus a passport or credit card as a deposit.

- The best way to get here is to take the Skytrain to Taksin Station and then board the Chao Phraya River Express boat to Chang Pier. It's a short walk from the pier to the palace entrance. You can also take a taxi to the Grand Palace but you may end up wasting time in traffic or getting ripped off.

- Admission includes a free (though unimpressive) guidebook and admission to the Vimanmek Palace in Dusit (currently closed for renovations), as long as you go within a week of visiting the compound.

- Don't listen to men loitering outside the grounds who claim that the compound is closed for a Buddhist holiday or for cleaning, or who offer to show you the "Lucky Buddha" or take you on a special tour. These phony guides will ultimately lead you to a gift shop where they receive a commission.

- Allow half a day to tour the complex. You'll probably want to spend three hours in Wat Phra Kaew and the other buildings, and another half-hour in the museums.

- Wat Phra Kaew is actually worth two visits: one on a weekday (when crowds are thinner and you can explore at a leisurely pace) and another on a Sunday or public holiday, when the smell of flowers and incense and the murmur of prayer evoke the spirituality of the place.

✉ Sana Chai Rd., Old City
☎ 02/224–1833
🎫 B500, admission includes entrance to Wat Phra Kaew, The Royal Thai Decorations & Coins Pavilion, and Museum of Textiles.
⏲ Daily 8:30–3:30.

The Grand Palace.

WAT PHRA KAEW

As you enter the temple compound, you'll see 20-foot-tall statues of fearsome creatures in battle attire. These are *yakshas*—guardians who protect the Emerald Buddha from evil spirits. Turn right to see the murals depicting the *Ramakien* epic. Inside the main chapel, which is quiet and heavy with the scent of incense, you'll find the Emerald Buddha.

Yaksha.

THE RAMAKIEN

The *Ramakien* is the 2,000-year-old Thai adaptation of the famous Indian epic the *Ramayana*, which dates from around 400 BC. Beginning at the temple's north gate (across from Phra Wihan Yot [the Spired Hall]) and continuing clockwise around the cloister, 178 mural panels illustrate the story, which, like most epics, is about the struggle between good and evil. It begins with the founding of Ayutthaya (City of the Gods) and Lanka (City of the Demons) and focuses on the trials and tribulations of Ayutthaya's Prince Rama: his expulsion from his own kingdom; the abduction of his wife, Sita; and his eventual triumph over the demon Tosakan.

Section of *Ramakien*.

Sita's Abduction

Rama's wife Sita is abducted by the evil demon king, Tosakan, ruler of Lanka. Disguising himself as a deer, Tosakan lures Sita to his palace. A battle ensues, forming a large part of the long and detailed epic, which concludes when Rama rescues Sita.

THE APSONSI

The beautiful gilded figures on the upper terraces of Wat Phra Kaew are *apsonsi*—mythical half-angel, half-lion creatures who guard the temple. According to Thai mythology, apsonsi inhabit the Himavant Forest, which is the realm between earth and the heavens.

Ramakien battle scene.

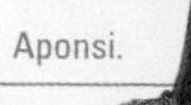

Aponsi.

THE EMERALD BUDDHA

Thailand's most sacred Buddha image is made of a single piece of jade and is only 31 inches tall. The statue, which historians believe was sculpted in Thailand in the 14th or 15th century, was at one point covered in plaster; in 1434 it was discovered in Chiang Rai as the plaster began to flake.

When the king of nearby Chiang Mai heard about the jade Buddha, he demanded it be brought to him. According to legend, the statue was sent to the king three times, but each time the elephant transporting it veered off to Lampang, 60 miles southeast of Chiang Mai. Finally the king came to the Buddha, building a temple at that spot.

The Buddha was kept at various temples in northern Thailand until Laotian invaders stole it in 1552. It stayed in Laos until the 18th century, when King Rama I captured Vientiane, the capital, reclaimed the statue, and brought it to Bangkok.

Perched in a gilded box high above the altar, the diminutive statue is difficult to see. This doesn't deter Thai Buddhists, who believe that praying before the Emerald Buddha will earn them spiritual merit, helping to ensure a better rebirth in the next life.

The king is the only person allowed to touch the Emerald Buddha. Three times a year, he changes the Buddha's robes in a ceremony to bring good fortune for the coming season. The Buddha's hot season attire includes a gold crown and jewels; in the rainy season, it wears a headdress of gold, enamel, and sapphires; and, in the cool season, it's adorned in a mesh robe of gold beads.

Emerald Buddha in hot season outfit.

Most Thais make an offering to the Buddha when they visit the temple. Inexpensive offerings, for sale outside the temple, generally include three joss sticks, a candle, and a thin piece of gold leaf stuck on a sheet of paper. At some wats, Thais stick gold leaves on the Buddha, but since that's not possible here, keep it as a souvenir or attach it to another sacred image (some elephant statues have gold leaves on their heads.) Light the candle from others that are already burning on the front alter, then light the incense with your candle.

WHAT'S A WAT?

A wat is a Buddhist temple or monastery, typically made up of a collection of shrines and structures in an enclosed courtyard, rather than a single building. Traditionally, monks reside in wats, but Wat Phra Kaew is a ceremonial temple, not a place of Buddhist study, so monks don't live here.

HONORING THE EMERALD BUDDHA

Thais usually follow an offering with three prostrations, or bows, to the Buddha. To prostrate, sit facing the Buddha with your legs folded or your feet tucked under you—then follow the sequence below. After prostrating you can sit in front of the Buddha in prayer or meditation for as long as you like.

1) Hold your hands together in a *wai* (palms together, fingers pointing up) at your heart.

2) Bring the *wai* up to touch your forehead,

3) Place your palms on the ground and bow your forehead until it's touching the ground between them.

4) Sit up, bring your hands back into a *wai* in front of your heart, and repeat.

TEMPLE ETIQUETTE

Even if you don't want to make an offering, pray, or prostrate, it's OK to linger in the temple or sit down. Here are a few other things to keep in mind:

- Appropriate dress—long-sleeved shirts and long pants or skirts—is required. Open-toed shoes must be "closed" by wearing socks. If you've come scantily clad, you can rent a sarong at the palace.
- Never point—with your hands or your feet—at the Emerald Buddha, other sacred objects, or even another person. If you sit down in the temple, make sure not to accidentally point your feet in the Buddha's direction.
- When walking around religious monuments, try to move in a clockwise direction. Thais believe that the right side of the body is superior to the left, so it's more respectful to keep your right side closer to sacred objects.
- Keep your head below the Buddha and anything else sacred. Thais will often bend their knees and lower their heads when walking past a group of older people or monks; it's a gesture of respect even if their heads aren't technically below the monks'.

Offerings.

Bargaining in Bangkok

Even if you've honed your bargaining skills in other countries, you might still come up empty-handed in Thailand. The aggressive techniques that work well in say, Delhi, won't get you very far in Bangkok. One of the highest compliments you can pay for any activity in the Land of Smiles is calling it *sanuk* (fun), and haggling is no exception. Thais love to joke and tease, so approach each bargaining situation playfully. Nevertheless, be aware that Thais are also sensitive to "losing face," so make sure you remain pleasant and respectful throughout the transaction.

As you enter a market stall, smile and acknowledge the proprietor. When something catches your eye, inquire politely about the price, but don't immediately counter. Keep your voice low—you're more likely to get a deal if it's not announced to the whole shop—then ask for a price just slightly below what you want. Don't get too cavalier with your counteroffer—Thai sellers generally price their wares in a range they view as fair, so asking to cut the initial price in half will most likely be seen as an insult and might end the discussion abruptly. In most cases the best you can hope for is 20% to 30% discount.

If the price the shopkeeper offers in return is still high, turn your smile up another watt and say something like, "Can you discount more?" If the answer is no, your last recourse is to say thank you and walk away. If you are called back, the price is still negotiable; if you aren't, maybe the last price quoted wasn't such a bad one after all.

—Molly Petersen

Rd., Huai Khwang ☎ *02/649–9222* 🌐 *www.siamniramit.com* 🎫 *B1,500; with dinner B1,850* Ⓜ *Subway: Thailand Cultural Center.*

Thailand Cultural Center

DANCE | The center hosts local and international groups, including opera companies, symphony orchestras, and modern dance and ballet troupes. ✉ *Ratchadaphisek Rd., Huai Khwang* ☎ *02/247–0028* Ⓜ *Subway: Thai Cultural Center.*

Shopping

DUTY-FREE SHOPPING

King Power International Group

DUTY-FREE | If you want the convenience of duty-free shopping, try King Power. You choose and pay for the items at the shop or online, then pick them up at Suvarnabhumi Airport when you depart Thailand (or simply take them with you). You need your passport and an airline ticket, and you need to make your purchase at least eight hours before leaving the country. The airport branch is open 24 hours. ✉ *King Power Complex, 8/2 Rangnam Rd., Phayathai, Ratchathewi* ☎ *1631 contact center, 02/205–8888* 🌐 *www.kingpower.com* Ⓜ *Skytrain: Victory Monument.*

MARKETS

★ Chatuchak Weekend Market

OUTDOOR/FLEA/GREEN MARKETS | You can purchase virtually anything at the city's largest market, including silk items in a mudmee (tie-dyed before weaving) design that would sell for five times the price in the United States. Despite its name the market is open from Wednesday through Sunday, though only the plant section is open on Wednesday and Thursday. It's best to come on Friday or the weekend—in the morning before the place gets too crowded and hot. An afternoon at JJ, as it is known by locals ("ch" is pronounced "jha" in Thai, so phonetically Chatuchak is Jatujak), is not for the faint of heart: up to 200,000 people visit each day, and there are more than 15,000 vendors. Keep your bearings by remembering that the outer ring has mainly new clothing and shoes, with some plants, garden supplies, and home decor. The next ring is primarily used (and some new) clothing and shoes plus accessories like jewelry, belts, and bags. Farther in are pottery, antiques, furniture, dried goods, and live animals. Be prepared with bottles of water, comfortable shoes, and make sure to print out a copy of the map of the market from the website. Strategically placed food vendors mean you don't have to stop shopping to grab a bite. ✉ *Phaholyothin Rd., Chatuchak* 🌐 *www.chatuchak.org* Ⓜ *Subway: Chatuchak Park; Skytrain: Mo Chit.*

Thonburi

Largely residential, Thonburi is where travelers go to take a ride along the city's ancient waterways. The riverbank area is currently undergoing major development with a landmark retail and residential development. Most of Thonburi beyond the riverbank is of little interest to visitors. Many locals claim it retains more "Thai-ness" than the rest of Bangkok, but you'd have to live here, or visit for a long time, to appreciate that.

Sights

Royal Barge Museum
MUSEUM | Splendid ceremonial barges are berthed on the Thonburi side of the Chao Phraya River. The boats, carved in the early part of the 19th century, take the form of mythical creatures in the *Ramakien*. The most impressive is the red-and-gold royal vessel called *Suphannahongse* (Golden Swan), used by the king on special occasions. Carved from a single piece of teak, it measures about 150 feet and weighs more than 15 tons. Fifty oarsmen propel it along the river, accompanied by flag wavers, two coxswains, and a rhythm-keeper. The museum is extremely difficult to find, so you may want to join a tour or take a taxi whose driver knows the area. **■TIP→ Steer clear of scam artists offering tours or claiming that the museum is closed.** ✉ *Khlong Bangkok Noi, 80/1 Th Arun Amarin, Thonburi* ☎ *02/424–0004* 🌐 *www.finearts.go.th/museumroyalbarges* 🎟 *B100.*

★ **Wat Arun** (*Temple of Dawn*)
RELIGIOUS SITE | If this riverside spot is inspiring at sunrise, it's even more marvelous toward dusk, when the setting sun throws amber tones over the entire area. The temple's design is symmetrical, with a square courtyard containing five Khmer-style prangs. All five prangs are covered in mosaics made from broken Chinese porcelain pieces. Energetic visitors can climb the steep steps to the top of the lower level overlooking the Chao Phraya; the less ambitious can linger in the small riverside park. ✉ *Arun Amarin Rd., Thonburi* ☎ *02/466–3167* 🎟 *B50* Ⓜ *Subway: Hualamphong (then river ferry).*

Restaurants

Thonburi has restaurants boasting unparalleled river views, along with dinner cruises.

Sala Rim Naam
$$$$ | **THAI** | Come to Sala Rim Naam to soak up the atmosphere, which includes a classical Thai dancing show nightly at 7:45 pm in an indoor pavilion, or the romantic mood of alfresco tables overlooking the river. The renditions of Thai food are rather Westernized, but the set dinners, buffet lunches, and à la carte

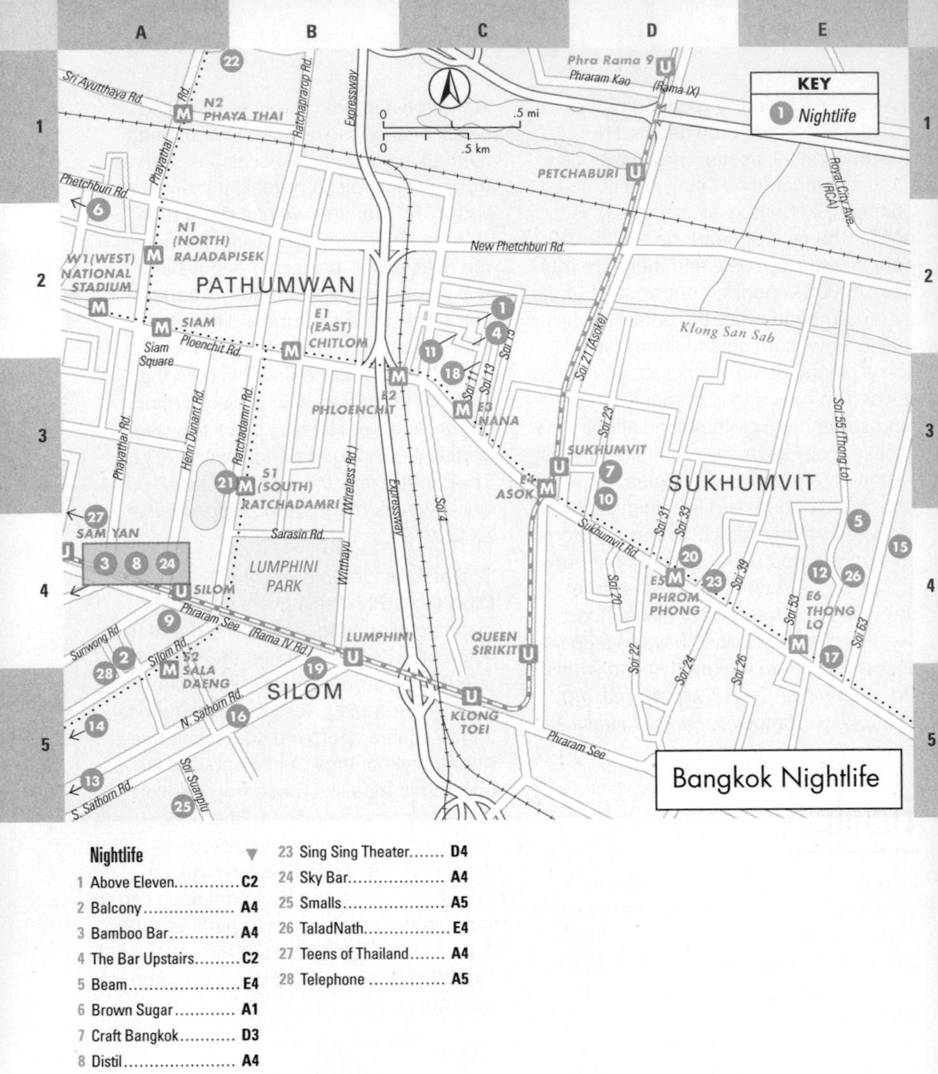

Nightlife

1	Above Eleven	C2
2	Balcony	A4
3	Bamboo Bar	A4
4	The Bar Upstairs	C2
5	Beam	E4
6	Brown Sugar	A1
7	Craft Bangkok	D3
8	Distil	A4
9	DJ Station	A4
10	Glow	D3
11	Havana Social	C2
12	J. Boroski	E4
13	Longtail Bar	A5
14	Maggie Choo's	A5
15	Mikkeller Bangkok	E4
16	Moon Bar	B5
17	Octave	E4
18	Oskar Bistro	C3
19	Park Society	B5
20	Royal Oak Pub	D4
21	St. Regis Bar	A3
22	Saxophone	B1
23	Sing Sing Theater	D4
24	Sky Bar	A4
25	Smalls	A5
26	TaladNath	E4
27	Teens of Thailand	A4
28	Telephone	A5

menus offer plenty of choices. **Known for:** riverside terrace; Thai dancing shows; extensive menu. *Average main: B500 ✉ Mandarin Oriental, 48 Oriental Ave., Bang Rak ☎ 02/659–9000 🌐 www.mandarinoriental.com/bangkok Ⓜ Skytrain: Saphan Taksin, then hotel boat.*

Supatra River House

$$$ | **THAI** | Located on the Chao Phraya River across from the Grand Palace, this charming restaurant is housed in the former home of Khunying Supatra, founder of Bangkok's express boat business. A free ferry from Maharaj Pier shuttles diners back and forth to enjoy impressive views and Thai cuisine, with multicourse prixe-fixe meals and à la carte options. **Known for:** riverside terrace; great for sunsets; steamed sea bass in soy or spicy lemon. *Average main: B330 ✉ 266 Soi Wat Rakhang, Arunamarin Rd., Siriraj ☎ 02/411–0305, 02/411–0874 🌐 www.bangkokriver.com/place/supatra-river-house/ Ⓜ Skytrain: Saphan Taksin, then river ferry.*

Hotels

Anantara Bangkok Riverside Resort & Spa

$$$$ | **RESORT** | Getting to the Anantara is a pleasant adventure in itself—free boats shuttle guests across the Chao Phraya from the Taksin Bridge. **Pros:** resort feel; lots of activities; great service. **Cons:** a hassle to get into the city; may feel too secluded; not all rooms have views. *Rooms from: B6,500 ✉ 257/1–3 Charoennakorn Rd., Thonburi ☎ 02/476–0022 🌐 www.bangkok-riverside.anantara.com 376 rooms Free breakfast Ⓜ Skytrain: Saphan Taksin, then hotel boat.*

★ Millenium Hilton Bangkok

$$$$ | **HOTEL** | Lording over the Chao Phraya, this flagship Hilton designed with cutting-edge flair competes successfully with Bangkok's other hotel giants but has far lower rates. **Pros:** snazzy amenities; cool pool area; all rooms have city and river views. **Cons:** rooms somewhat small; across the river from downtown pursuits; ferry service takes time. *Rooms from: B6,500 ✉ 123 Charoennakorn Rd., Klong San ☎ 02/442–2000 🌐 http://www3.hilton.com/en/hotels/thailand/millennium-hilton-bangkok-BKKHITW/index.html 543 rooms No meals Ⓜ Skytrain: Saphan Taksin.*

The Peninsula

$$$$ | **HOTEL** | The rooms at the Peninsula have plenty of high-tech gadgets, among them bathrooms with hands-free phones and mist-free TV screens, and bedside controls that dim the lights and close the curtains. **Pros:** beautiful pool; exceptional service; awesome views. **Cons:** most attractions are across the river; on-site dining not very good; outrageously expensive for Bangkok. *Rooms from: B17,000 ✉ 333 Charoen Krung (New Rd.), Klong San ☎ 02/020–2888 🌐 bangkok.peninsula.com 367 rooms, 65 suites No meals Ⓜ Skytrain: Saphan Taksin.*

Nightlife

The best reason to visit Thonburi is to take in the river views at some of the fancier hotel bars.

BARS AND PUBS

Longtail Bar

BARS/PUBS | This bar distinguishes itself with a tropical feel that is elusive in Bangkok—it will make you crave a mai tai by the river, either in a traditional sala or on outdoor sofas. You'll have to sail about 30 minutes downriver from the Saphan Taksin Skytrain stop on one of the Anantara resort's dedicated boats, which can be pleasant on a nice night. *✉ Anantara Bangkok Riverside, 257 Charoennakorn Rd., Samrae Thonburi, Thonburi ☎ 02/476–0022 🌐 www.anantara.com/en/riverside-bangkok/restaurants/longtail-bar.*

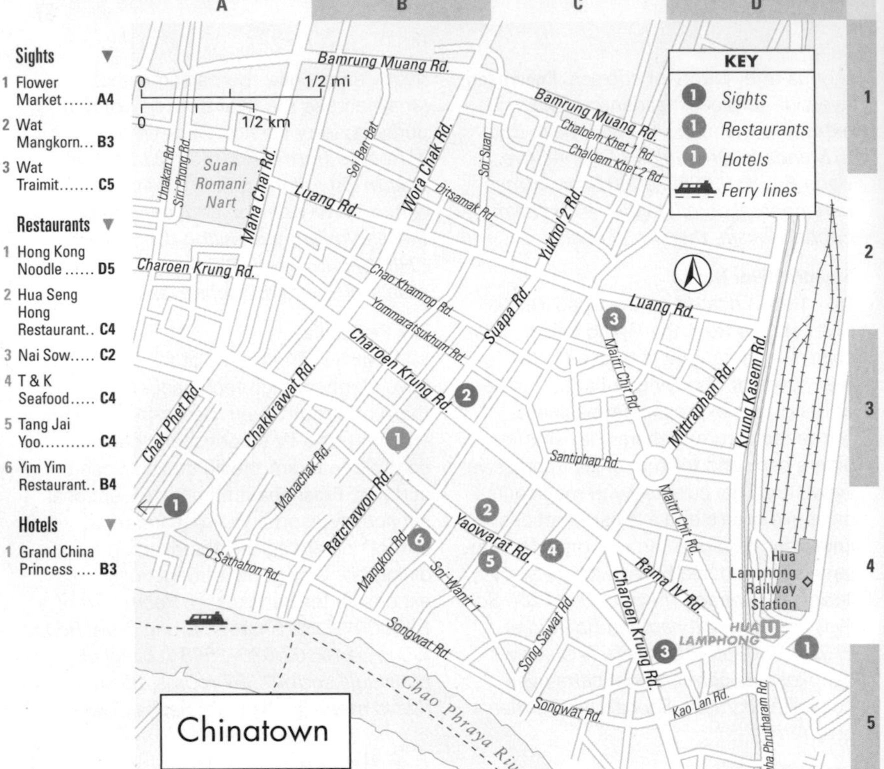

Chinatown

Almost as soon as Bangkok was founded, Chinatown started to form; it's the city's oldest residential neighborhood. Today it's an integral part of the city, bustling with little markets (and a few big ones), teahouses, restaurants, and recently, art galleries. Like much of the Old City, Chinatown is a great place to explore on foot. Meandering through the maze of alleys, ducking into herb shops and temples along the way, can be a great way to pass an afternoon, though the constant crowd, especially on hot days, does wear on some people.

Yaowarat Road, crowded with gold shops and excellent restaurants, is the main thoroughfare. Pahurat Road, Bangkok's "Little India," is full of textile shops, some quite literally underground. Many of the Indian merchant families on this street have been here for generations.

■ **TIP→ Getting to Chinatown is easiest by boat, but you can also start at the Hua Lamphong subway station and head west to the river.** The amount of traffic in this area cannot be overemphasized: avoid taking a taxi into the neighborhood if you can help it.

Sights

★ **Flower Market** (*Pak Khlong Talat*)
MARKET | This street lined with flower shops is busy around the clock, but it's most interesting at night when more deliveries are heading in and out. This is where individuals and buyers for restaurants, hotels, and other businesses purchase their flowers. Just stroll into the warehouse areas and watch the

action. Many vendors only sell flowers in bulk, but others sell small bundles or even individual flowers. As everywhere else where Thais do business, there are plenty of street stalls selling food. This very photogenic area that sees few tourists is well worth a visit. ✉ *Chakraphet Rd., between Pripatt and Yod Fa Rds., Pom Prap Sattru Phai* Ⓜ *Subway: Hua Lamphong.*

Wat Mangkorn (*Neng Noi Yee*)
RELIGIOUS SITE | Unlike most Bangkok temples, this one has a glazed ceramic roof topped with fearsome dragons. Neng Noi Yee is a Buddhist shrine, but its statues and paintings also incorporate Confucian and Taoist elements. The wat is especially appealing during Chinese New Year, when thousands of Thais visit the temple to burn incense and make merit. ✉ *Pom Prap Sattru Phai, Pom Prap Sattru Phai* ☎ *02/222–3975* Ⓜ *Subway: Hua Lamphong.*

★ **Wat Traimit** (*Temple of the Golden Buddha*)
RELIGIOUS SITE | The temple has little architectural merit, but off to its side is a small chapel containing the world's largest solid-gold Buddha, cast about nine centuries ago in the Sukhothai style. Weighing 5½ tons and standing 10 feet high, the statue is considered a symbol of strength and power. It's believed that the statue was brought first to Ayutthaya. When the Burmese were about to sack the city, it was covered in plaster. Two centuries later, still in plaster, it was thought to be worth very little; when it was being moved to a new Bangkok temple in the 1950s, it slipped from a crane and was left in the mud by the workmen. In the morning a temple monk, who had dreamed that the statue was divinely inspired, went to see it. Through a crack in the plaster, he saw a glint of yellow. In addition to the Buddha, Wat Traimit's museum devoted to Tha Chinese history is worth checking out. ✉ *Tri Mit Rd., Pom Prap Sattru Phai* ☎ *089/002–2700* 🌐 *www.wattraimitr-withayaram.com* 🎫 *B40 for statue, B100 for museum* Ⓜ *Subway: Hua Lamphong.*

Restaurants

Chinatown is impressive in large part for its food. The neighborhood draws huge crowds of Thais who spend big bucks on specialties like shark's fin and bird's nest, which you'll see advertised on nearly every restaurant's storefront. Most of the food is Cantonese; many of these restaurants are indistinguishable from what you'd find in Hong Kong. In the middle of Chinatown, just off Yaowarat, there's a massive Indian cloth market known as Phahurat, and many Indian restaurants do business nearby. Don't overlook Chinatown's street food, the noodle and dumpling shops, and the fruit and spice markets.

Hong Kong Noodle
$ | **CHINESE** | This famous noodle shop outside the Hua Lamphong subway station is perfectly placed for fueling up when you first get into Chinatown or on the way out. Thanks to an air-conditioned second floor, it's a little comfier than your average noodle stand, but still quite cheap, and the window offers great people-watching on the street below. **Known for:** convenient location; noodles and dim sum; cheap and satisfying dishes. Ⓢ *Average main: B99* ✉ *513–514 Rong Muang Rd., at Rama IV, Pom Prap Sattru Phai* ☎ *02/613–8977* 💳 *No credit cards* Ⓜ *Subway: Hua Lamphong.*

Hua Seng Hong Restaurant
$$$ | **CHINESE** | This expensive but worthwhile Chinatown classic takes you straight to Hong Kong with its excellent Cantonese roast meats, dim sum, and service that is authentically brusque. Hua Seng Hong has other locations across Bangkok, including at CentralWorld mall in the city center, but this is the original and most beloved for its bustling atmosphere—from inside to outside

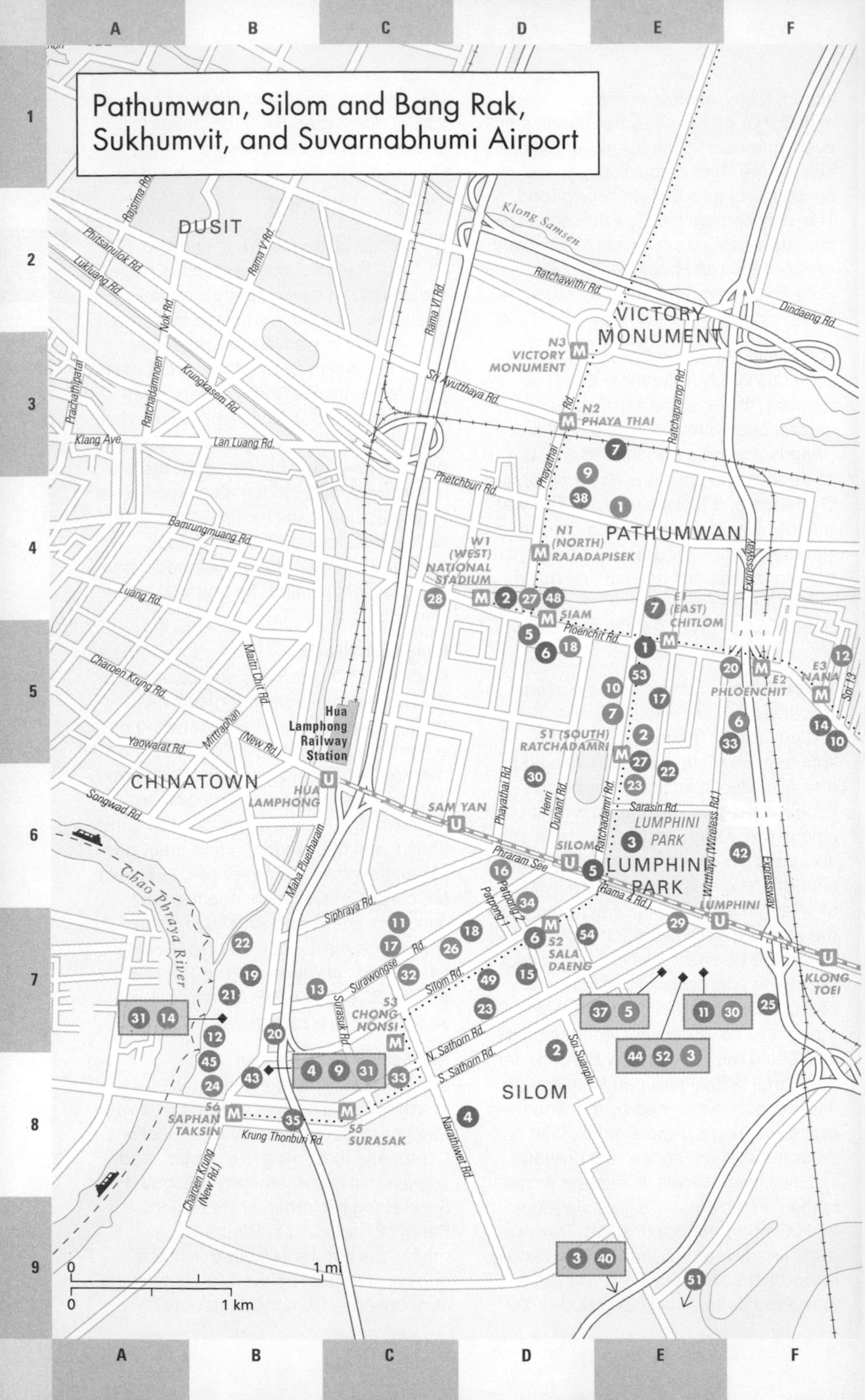
Pathumwan, Silom and Bang Rak, Sukhumvit, and Suvarnabhumi Airport
DUSIT
VICTORY MONUMENT
PATHUMWAN
CHINATOWN
LUMPHINI PARK
SILOM
Hua Lamphong Railway Station
Chao Phraya River
Klong Samsen
Ratchawithi Rd.
Dindaeng Rd.
Sri Ayutthaya Rd.
Phetchburi Rd.
Ploenchit Rd.
Rama VI Rd.
Rama V Rd.
Rajsima Rd.
Phitsanulok Rd.
Lukluang Rd.
Nok Rd.
Krungkasem Rd.
Ratchadamnoen
Prachathipatai
Klang Ave.
Lan Luang Rd.
Bamrungmuang Rd.
Luang Rd.
Charoen Krung Rd.
Yaowarat Rd.
Mittraphan
(New Rd.)
Maitri Chit Rd.
Songwad Rd.
Maha Pluetharam
Siphraya Rd.
Surawongse Rd.
Surasak Rd.
Silom Rd.
N. Sathorn Rd.
S. Sathorn Rd.
Narathiwat Rd.
Krung Thonburi Rd.
Charoen Krung (New Rd.)
Phayathai Rd.
Henri Dunant Rd.
Ratchadamri Rd.
Ratchaprarop Rd.
Sarasin Rd.
Witthayu (Wireless Rd.)
Phraram See (Rama 4 Rd.)
Patpong 1
Patpong 2
Soi Suanplu
Expressway
Soi 13
N3 VICTORY MONUMENT
N2 PHAYA THAI
N1 (NORTH) RAJADAPISEK
W1 (WEST) NATIONAL STADIUM
SIAM
E1 (EAST) CHITLOM
E2 PHLOENCHIT
E3 NANA
S1 (SOUTH) RATCHADAMRI
S2 SALA DAENG
S3 CHONG NONSI
S5 SURASAK
S6 SAPHAN TAKSIN
HUA LAMPHONG
SAM YAN
SILOM
LUMPHINI
KLONG TOEI
0 1 mi
0 1 km

KEY

- Sights
- Restaurants
- Hotels
- Rail lines
- MRTA (subway)
- BTS Sky Train
- River Bus

Sights

1 Erawan Shrine E5
2 Jim Thompson House .. D4
3 Lumphini Park............ E6
4 M.R. Kukrit's House..... D8
5 Queen Saovabha Memorial Institute D6
6 Siam Square............. D5
7 Suan Pakkard Palace ... E3

Restaurants

1 Appia.................... H6
2 Baan Khanitha & Gallery................ D7
3 Baan Klang Nam 2....... E9
4 Ban Chiang B8
5 Ban Khun Mae.......... D5
6 Banana Leaf............. D7
7 Big C...................... E4
8 Bo.lan H6
9 Breeze B8
10 Cabbages & Condoms................ F5
11 Celadon.................. E7
12 Ciao...................... B7
13 The Commons............ I5
14 Doo Rae.................. F5
15 Eat Me D7
16 55 Pochana.............. I7
17 Gaggan................... E5
18 Hai Som Tam Convent.. D7
19 Harmonique B7
20 Himali Cha Cha......... B7
21 Home Cuisine Islamic Restaurant.............. B7
22 Homo Kitchen E6
23 The House on Sathorn D7
24 Isao....................... G6
25 Issaya Siamese Club F7
26 Je Ngor's Kitchen....... G6
27 Jojo........................ E5
28 Kuppa G6
29 Le Dalat.................. G5
30 Le Du..................... D6
31 Le Normandie........... B7
32 Lek Seafood............ G9
33 Liu E5
34 The Local G5
35 Mezzaluna............... B8
36 My Choice I8
37 Nahm..................... E7
38 Once Upon a Time D4
39 Paste Restaurant H6
40 Pen E9
41 Peppina H6
42 Polo Fried Chicken....... F6
43 Prachak................. B8
44 Saffron E7
45 Salathip B8
46 Seafood Market......... H6
47 Soul Food Mahanakorn I6
48 Sra Bua by Kiin Kiin..... D4
49 Sühring.................. D7
50 Supanniga Eating Room . I6
51 Tawandang German Bakery E9
52 Vertigo E7
53 You & Mee................ E5
54 Zanotti................... D7

Hotels

1 Amari Watergate E4
2 Anantara Siam Bangkok E5
3 Banyan Tree Bangkok... E7
4 The Cabochon Hotel.... H6
5 COMO Metropolitan Bangkok E7
6 Conrad Bangkok F5
7 Courtyard by Marriott Bangkok E5
8 The Davis Bangkok..... G6
9 First House D3
10 Grand Hyatt Erawan..... E5
11 La Residence............ C7
12 The Landmark Bangkok F5
13 Ma Hotel................. B7
14 Mandarin Oriental Bangkok B7
15 Marriott Hotel Sukhumvit I7
16 Montien.................. D6
17 Narai Hotel C7
18 Novotel Bangkok on Siam Square......... D5
19 Novotel Suvarnabhumi Airport.................... I4
20 The Okura Prestige Bangkok E5
21 Pullman Bangkok Grande Sukhumvit...... G5
22 Royal Orchid Sheraton Hotel & Towers B7
23 The St. Regis Bangkok E6
24 Shangri-La Hotel Bangkok B8
25 Sheraton Grande Sukhumvit G6
26 Siam Heritage........... C7
27 Siam Kempinski......... D4
28 Siam@Siam C4
29 Sofitel So Bangkok E7
30 The Sukhothai Bangkok E7
31 Tower Club at Lebua.... B8
32 Triple Two Silom C7
33 W Bangkok............... C8
34 Wall Street Inn.......... D7
35 The Westin Grande Sukhumvit G5

Bangkok's Skyways

The Skytrain transformed the city when it opened on the late King Bhumibol's birthday in 1999. It now has more than 30 stations on two lines that intersect at Siam Square. Although the Skytrain bypasses many parts of the city, it is the speediest way to travel when its route coincides with yours. The fare is B15 to B52, depending on how far you plan to travel, and trains run from 5 am to midnight. Trains are still impressively clean and efficient, although they can get tremendously crowded at rush hour.

The sights in downtown Bangkok are spread out, but most are near Skytrain stations. Stations are generally about three minutes apart, so a trip from Chong Nonsi to National Stadium, which is four stations away, will take less than 12 minutes. At three stations—Chatuchak Park, Sukhumvit, and Saladaeng—the Skytrain intersects with the subway, which is convenient for some intercity travel.

on Chinatown's main vein, Yaowarat Road. **Known for:** delicious fatty duck; goose foot–and–abalone stew; combo specials and à la carte. *$ Average main: B350 ✉ 371–373 Yaowarat Rd., Samphanthawong ☎ 02/222–7053 🌐 www.huasenghong.co.th.*

Nai Sow

$ | **ASIAN** | This unassuming restaurant next to Wat Plaplachai has a steady clientele thanks to fast service and consistently excellent Chinese-Thai dishes prepared according to the owner's secret family recipes. The lighting and decor are lacking, but that can be forgiven when you taste the traditional tom yum goong or spicy shrimp soup, which some diehards deem to be the city's best. **Known for:** family business; very busy with no reservations accepted; specialties such as tom yum goong and the deep-fried taro dessert. *$ Average main: B150 ✉ 3/1 Maitrichit Rd., Pom Prap Sattru Phai ☎ 02/222–1539 Ⓜ Subway: Hua Lamphong.*

★ T & K Seafood

$$ | **THAI** | Proudly displaying the freshest catches on ice out front, this enormous and popular seafood restaurant with outdoor tables outside its bustling corner location opens daily at 4 pm and serves until as late as 1:30 am. Make your way through the evening crowds and take a number to secure your table—either against the sidewalk or inside. **Known for:** fresh shellfish like mussels and razor clams; classic Thai dishes like yellow curry crab; seating right on Yaowarat Road. *$ Average main: B300 ✉ 49–51 Phadungdao Rd., Samphanthawong ☎ 09/0658–6868 ⏲ No lunch Ⓜ Subway: Hua Lamphong.*

Tang Jai Yoo

$$ | **CHINESE** | This open-air ground-floor seafood restaurant is full of festive round tables and tanks containing live whole crabs, lobsters, and sea leech ready to be cooked in traditional Thai-Chinese style. There are lots of à la carte options from land and sea, but ordering off one of the many set menus is the best way to sample a variety of dishes. **Known for:** stewed turtle soup; whole roasted suckling pig; traditional Thai-Chinese. *$ Average main: B300 ✉ 85–89 Yaowapanit Rd., Samphanthawong ☎ 02/224–2167 Ⓜ Subway: Hua Lamphong.*

Yim Yim Restaurant

$$ | **CHINESE** | This second-floor restaurant has been serving Chinese cuisine for more than 70 years. Though it lacks the elegance of the hotel restaurants in the area—the dining room is simple and you have to walk through the dish-washing room to reach the bathroom—it's a solid option in the heart of Chinatown. **Known for:** simple decor; authentic Chinese; relaxed atmosphere. *$ Average main: ✉ 89 Passai Rd., off Yaowarat Rd. near intersection with Ratchawong Rd., Samphanthawong ☎ 02/224–2203, 02/224–2205 M Subway: Hua Lamphong.*

Hotels

Grand China Princess

$$$ | **HOTEL** | One good reason for staying in Chinatown is the chance to experience the sights and sounds of the city's oldest neighborhood. **Pros:** great city and river views; much Chinese food nearby. **Cons:** popular with big groups; neighborhood not overly tourist-friendly. *$ Rooms from: B4,400 ✉ 215 Yaowarat Rd., Bangkok ☎ 02/224–9977 ⊕ www.grandchina.com ⇆ 155 rooms, 22 suites 🍴 Free breakfast M Subway: Hua Lamphong.*

Shopping

MARKETS

Asiatique The Riverfront

SHOPPING CENTERS/MALLS | In a prime spot along the Chao Phraya River, this complex of eateries, bars, and shops occupies 10 old warehouses with retro and industrial themes. You can get here via a free shuttle boat from the Saphan Taksin Pier next to the Skytrain station of the same name. *✉ 2194 Charoenkrung Rd., Bangkor Laem ☎ 02/108–4488, 09/246–0812 ⊕ www.asiatiquethailand.com M Skytrain: Saphan Taksin, then free shuttle boat from nearby pier.*

Phahurat Market

OUTDOOR/FLEA/GREEN MARKETS | The Little India market near Chinatown is known for its bargain textiles. A man with a microphone announces when items at a particular stall will be sold at half price, and shoppers surge over to bid. It's best to come in the evening, when it's cooler and many street vendors sell snacks. *✉ Phahurat Rd., Phra Nakhon ✣ Near intersection of Chakraphet Rd., after Yaowarat M Subway: Hua Lamphong.*

Sampeng Lane Market

OUTDOOR/FLEA/GREEN MARKETS | Bangkok's best-known and oldest textile center—lots of fabrics here—is located in the heart of Chinatown. *✉ Soi Sampeng (Soi Wanit 1), Samphanthawong ✣ Off Yaowarat Rd. M Subway: Hua Lamphong.*

Pathumwan

Bangkok has many downtowns that blend into each other, but Pathumwan, which encompasses two major shopping areas, Siam Square and the Rajaprasong Junction, along with important attractions such as Erawan Shrine and the intriguing Jim Thompson House, is the closest thing to a "downtown" in Central Bangkok. Gaysorn Shopping Centre (for luxury goods) and the gigantic Central World mall are at Rajaprasong Junction, the intersection of Ratchadamri and Ploenchit roads. Among the numerous markets bearing Pathumwan addresses are the ones in Pantip Plaza—Thailand's biggest computer center and, with five floors of computer stores, an overwhelming shopping experience—and the Pratunam Market garment district. *See Shopping, below, for more about these malls and markets.*

Sights

Erawan Shrine (*San Phra Phrom*)

RELIGIOUS SITE | Completed in 1956, this is not a particularly old shrine by Bangkok standards, but it's one of the more active ones, with many people stopping by on their way home to pray to Brahma. Thai dancers in traditional dress and a small orchestra perform for a fee to increase the likelihood that your wish will be granted. Even with a traffic jam right outside the gates, though, the mix of burning incense, dancers, and worshippers is an intoxicating sight. Entry is free, but many leave a small donation. A crazed man smashed the main statue in early 2006 and then was beaten to death by people outside the shrine. More recently, the shrine was the scene of a bomb attack in mid-2015, in which 20 people, including tourists, were killed, and dozens injured. After both incidences, the shrine has been repaired and is as popular as ever. There are also fantastic views of the shrine from the Rajaprasong Skywalk up above, from where many visitors take pictures. ✉ *Ratchadamri and Ploenchit Rds., Pathumwan* 🎫 *Free (small donation customary)* Ⓜ *Skytrain: Chitlom.*

★ Jim Thompson House

HOUSE | Formerly an architect in New York City, Jim Thompson ended up in Thailand at the end of World War II after a stint at the Office of Strategic Services, the predecessor to the CIA. He eventually moved into silk and is credited with revitalizing Thailand's silk industry. This alone would have made him a legend, but his former home is also a national treasure. Thompson imported parts of several up-country buildings, some over a century old, to construct his compound. Three of six are still exactly the same as their originals, including details of the interior layout. With true appreciation and a connoisseur's eye, Thompson furnished the homes with what are now priceless pieces of Southeast Asian art. Adding to Thompson's notoriety is his disappearance: in 1967 he went to the Malaysian Cameron Highlands for a quiet holiday and was never heard from again.

The entrance to the house is easy to miss—it's at the end of an unprepossessing lane, leading north off Rama I Road, west of Phayathai Road (the house is on your left). A good landmark is the National Stadium Skytrain station—the house is north of the station, just down the street from it. An informative 30-minute guided tour starts every 15 minutes and is included in the admission fee. **■ TIP→ The grounds also include a silk and souvenir shop and a restaurant that's great for a coffee or cold-drink break.** ✉ *Soi Kasemsong 2, Rama I Rd., Pathumwan* ☎ *02/216–7368* 🌐 *www.jimthompsonhouse.com* 🎫 *B200* Ⓜ *Skytrain: National Stadium.*

Siam Square

STORE/MALL | Fashion, education, and diverse shopping converge in glitzy Siam Square in the heart of downtown. Thailand's most prestigious college, Chulalongkorn University, is here, along with neon-splashed malls, designer boutiques and trendy restaurants. At night along the sidewalk, a bohemian and latest-fashions outdoor market scene unfolds. ✉ *Thanon Rama I, Pathumwan* 🌐 *www.siamsquare.com* Ⓜ *Skytrain: Siam.*

Suan Pakkard Palace

CASTLE/PALACE | Eight antique teak houses built high on columns sit amid the undulating lawns and shimmering lotus pools of this engaging complex. The houses, which exhibit porcelain, stone heads, traditional paintings, and Buddha statues, were dismantled at their original sites and reassembled here. At the back of the garden is the serene Lacquer Pavilion, worth a look for its gold-covered paneling with scenes from the life of the Buddha. Academics and historians debate how old the murals are—whether they're from the reign of King Narai (1656–88) or from the first reign of the current Chakri Dynasty, founded by King Rama I (1782–1809). ✉ *352–354 Sri Ayutthaya Rd., Phaya Thai* ☎ *02/245–4934* 🌐 *www.suanpakkad.com* 🎫 *B100* Ⓜ *Skytrain: Phaya Thai (10-min walk east of station).*

Roaming the Waterways

Bangkok used to be known as the "Venice of the East," but many of the *klongs* (canals) that once distinguished this area have been paved over. Traveling along the few remaining waterways, however, is one of the city's delights. You'll see houses on stilts, women washing clothes, and kids going for a swim. Traditional wooden canal boats are a fun way to get around town.

Klong Saen Saeb, just north of Petchaburi Road, is the main boat route. The fare ranges from B10 to B20, depending on the distance, and during rush hour boats pull up to piers at one-minute intervals. Klong boats provide easy access to the Jim Thompson House and are a handy alternative way to get to Khao San Road during rush hour. The last stop is Pan Pha, which is about a 15-minute walk from the eastern end of Khao San Road.

Ferries (sometimes called river buses) ply the Chao Phraya River. The fare for these express boats is based on how far you travel; the price ranges from B10 to B32. The river can be an efficient way to get around as well as a sightseeing opportunity. Under the Saphan Taksin Skytrain stop, there is a ferry pier where passengers can cross the river to Thonburi for B3. Many hotels run their own boats from the pier at Saphan Taksin. From here you can get to the Grand Palace in about 10 minutes and the other side of Krungthon Bridge in about 15 minutes. Local line boats travel specific routes from about 6 am to 7 pm.

These boats stop at every pier and will take you all the way to Nonthaburi, where you'll find quaint, car-free Koh Kret. A pleasant afternoon trip when the city gets too hot, the island has a Mon community and specializes in pottery.

A Chao Phraya Tourist Boat day pass provides a fun introduction to the river, and at B180 for the day it's a bargain. One advantage of the tourist boat is that while traveling from place to place there's a running commentary in English about the historic sights along the river. The tourist boat starts at the pier under the Saphan Taksin Skytrain station, but you can pick it up at any of the piers where it stops, and you can get on and off as often as you like.

Longtail boats, so called for the extra-long propeller shaft that extends behind the stern, operate like taxis. Boatmen will take you anywhere you want to go for B300 to B500 per hour. The best place to hire these boats is at the Central Pier at Sathorn Bridge. A private trip up the old klongs to the Royal Barge Museum and the Khoo Wiang Floating Market starts at the Chang Pier near the Grand Palace. Longtails often quit running at 6 pm.

Restaurants

Unimaginably busy Pathumwan, which includes Siam Square, has a little bit of everything, from humble lunch stops to power-dining extravaganzas.

Ban Khun Mae

$ | **THAI** | **FAMILY** | Casually upmarket and aimed at tourists, this decades-old restaurant in Siam Square serves authentic Thai cuisine in an atmosphere a few notches above that of the simple family restaurants. What's best about Ban Khun Mae is a large dining area filled with big round tables, warm wood, and a few antique decorations, offering a comfortable and airy feel perfect for post-shopping relaxation. **Known for:** decor resembling a traditional Thai home; specialties like marinated chicken in pandan leaves; good wine list. *Average main: B150 458/6–9 Siam Sq., Soi 8, Rama I Rd., Pratunam 02/250–1952, 02/658–4112 up to 13 www.bankhunmae.com Skytrain: Siam.*

Big C

$ | **THAI** | The food court on the fifth floor of the Big C shopping mall offers a staggering selection of authentic Thai (and a few Chinese and Korean) dishes at rock-bottom prices, with virtually nothing exceeding B80. **Known for:** cafeteria-style service; Thai street food like spicy soups, and rice and noodle dishes; cheap yet satisfying eats. *Average main: B60 Big C Supercenter, 97/11 Ratchadamri Rd., Pratunam Opposite Central World Plaza 02/250–4888 www.bigc.co.th No credit cards Skytrain: Chitlom.*

★ **Gaggan**

$$$$ | **INDIAN** | Named Asia's best restaurant from 2015 to 2018, the headquarters of Chef Gaggan Anand serves progressive Indian cuisine with molecular gastronomy touches. The tasting menu, which ranges around 25 courses, is expensive by Bangkok standards but is worth it, especially considering rumors that Gaggan will close the restaurant in 2020 and start a new endeavor in Japan. **Known for:** tasting menus inspired by emojis; recommended booking at least three to five months in advance; cult following. *Average main: B6,500 68/1 Soi Langsuan, Pathumwan Near Ploenchit Rd. 02/652–1700 www.eatatgaggan.com No lunch Skytrain: Ploenchit.*

Home Kitchen (*Khrua Nai Baan*)

$ | **THAI** | **FAMILY** | A true hole-in-the-wall where friends gather to celebrate the simple act of enjoying meals together, this restaurant turns out excellent Thai-Chinese cuisine in the cozy setup of a former home. All the classics everyone should try at least once on a Bangkok trip are served here at reasonable prices, making it a favorite among Thais and expats alike living and working on the laid-back Lang Suan Road. **Known for:** traditional Thai dishes like tom yum goong and oyster omelet; balcony seating; close to Lumpini Park. *Average main: B150 94 Langsuan Rd., Soi 7, Pathumwan Just north of Lumphini Park 02/253–1888 www.khruanaibaan.com Subway: Lumphini.*

Jojo

$$$$ | **ITALIAN** | A romantic, candlelit outdoor patio and a sleekly contemporary indoor dining space set a stylish tone that's echoed in the equally refined Italian cuisine served at Jojo. Traditional antipasto, pastas, and so on are gussied up with modern flourishes and high-quality products imported from Europe and beyond, perfectly befitting the luxe surroundings of the prestigious St. Regis hotel where the restaurant is located. **Known for:** linguine with Canadian lobster; peerless wine list; tiramisu in a melting chocolate sphere. *Average main: B900 The St. Regis Bangkok, 159 Ratchadamri Rd., Pathumwan 02/207–7815 www.stregis.com/bangkok No credit cards Skytrain: Ratchadamri.*

Liu

$$$$ | **CHINESE** | **FAMILY** | You'll want to be spotted at this "neoclassic Chinese" restaurant whose contemporary-focused concept and design come from the creator of the equally snazzy Green T. House in Beijing. **Known for:** Chinese cuisine fusing different regional styles; dishes with fried frogs' legs; good for large groups. *Average main: B450 Conrad Bangkok, 87 Wittayu (Wireless Rd.), Pathumwan 02/690–9250, 02/690–9255 www.conradhotels.com/bangkok Skytrain: Ploenchit.*

Once Upon a Time

$$ | **THAI** | Period photos of the royal family, movie stars, and beauty queens cover the pink walls of this traditional Thai restaurant occupying two old teak houses down Soi 17 a ways. Antiques fill the dining rooms, and clothed tables are set up in the garden between the houses, creating the ideal laid-back setup for escaping Bangkok chaos while still being downtown. **Known for:** regional dishes like mieng kan (dried shrimp and various ingredients rolled in leaf); close to Pantip Plaza; away from traffic noise. *Average main: B250 ✉ 32 Phetchaburi, Soi 17, Ratchathewi ☎ 02/252–8629, 02/252–8629 Skytrain: Ratchathewi.*

★ Paste Restaurant

$$$$ | **THAI** | An upscale, intimate eatery run by experienced Australian-Thai husband-and-wife team, Bee Satongun and Jason Bailey, the award-winning Paste elevates traditional Thai food and flavors to a whole new level with fresh produce and technical flair. Located on the top floor of the high-end Gaysorn Village shopping mall, the restaurant is open for lunch and dinner, with à la carte and multiple tasting menus available. **Known for:** extensive wine list; plentiful vegetarian options; historical and royal inspirations. *Average main: B800 ✉ Gaysorn Village, 999 Ploenchit Rd. at Ratchadamri Rd., 3rd fl., Pathumwan ☎ 02/656–1003 ⊕ pastebangkok.com ⊗ No lunch Tues.–Sat. Skytrain: Chitlom.*

Polo Fried Chicken

$ | **THAI** | This legendary restaurant has been delighting diners with its chicken flavored with black pepper and plenty of golden-brown garlic for over 50 years. The restaurant is a bit hard to find—as you enter Soi Polo (Soi Sanam Khli), it's about 50 yards in on your left, but if you're reasonably close to Lumphini Park, Polo will deliver to your hotel for B30. **Known for:** frequented by Thais and foreigners alike; delicious sides like sticky rice and papaya salad; busy with workers at lunch. *Average main: B150 ✉ 137/1–2 Soi Polo (Soi Sanam Khli), Pathumwan ⊕ Off Wittayu (Wireless Rd.) ☎ 02/2655–8489 No credit cards Skytrain: Ploenchit.*

★ Sra Bua by Kiin Kiin

$$$$ | **THAI** | Luxurious and utterly unique, this restaurant based on Copenhagen's highly praised Kiin Kiin restaurant upends conventional wisdom about Thai cuisine and technique. Chef Henrik Yde-Andersen's tasting menus, priced at B1,850 for lunch and B3,200 for dinner, represent a veritable catalog of Thai flavors and dishes, though you may not recognize many of them through foams, emulsions, powders, and plenty of smoky liquid nitrogen. **Known for:** molecular gastronomy; winner of many fine-dining awards; experimental Thai cuisine. *Average main: B900 ✉ Siam Kempinski, 991/9 Rama I Rd., Pathumwan ☎ 02/162–9000 ⊕ www.kempinski.com/en/bangkok.*

You & Mee

$$ | **THAI** | Hotel restaurants in Bangkok often disappoint, but this casual street kitchen–inspired spot at the Grand Hyatt Erawan surprises with high-quality Thai food, and particularly northern Thai dishes, at reasonable prices. Come for the good range of noodles, curries, *khao tom* (rice soup) and congee, served à la carte or as buffet options, with premium add-ons such as lobster, crab, and braised beef available. **Known for:** northern dishes like khao soi (curry soup); fast service; central location. *Average main: B230 ✉ Grand Hyatt Erawan, 494 Ratchadamri Rd., Pathumwan ☎ 02/254–1234 ⊕ bangkok.grand.hyatt.com Skytrain: Chitlom.*

Amari Watergate

$$$ | **HOTEL** | The spacious and comfortable rooms at the Amari chain's Bangkok flagship are swathed in silks and other rich fabrics. **Pros:** many amenities; executive floor; massive pool. **Cons:** huge; impersonal feel; busy front desk.

$ *Rooms from: B4,700 ✉ 847 Phetchburi Rd., Pathumwan ☎ 02/653–9000 🌐 www.amari.com 569 rooms, 26 suites 🍴 No meals Ⓜ Skytrain: Chitlom.*

Anantara Siam Bangkok

$$$$ | **HOTEL** | One of Bangkok's more elegant hotels, the Anantara Siam still attracts local society for morning coffee and afternoon tea in the formal lobby, where a string quartet often plays. **Pros:** accessible location; great pool; magnificent tearoom. **Cons:** decor verges on stuffy; not all rooms have nice views; extremely pricey in season. $ *Rooms from: B13,550 ✉ 155 Ratchadamri Rd., Pathumwan ☎ 02/126–8866 🌐 siam-bangkok.anantara.com 354 rooms, 19 suites 🍴 Free breakfast Ⓜ Skytrain: Ratchadamri.*

Conrad Bangkok

$$$$ | **HOTEL** | Though this hotel is one of the largest in Bangkok, the service doesn't suffer—the staff is attentive, and the beautifully designed rooms are perfect down to the smallest detail. **Pros:** fun nightlife; sprawling pool area; attentive staff. **Cons:** huge; not on the river; 700 meters from Skytrain station. $ *Rooms from: B6,400 ✉ 87 Wittayu (Wireless Rd.), Pathumwan ☎ 02/690–9999 🌐 www.conradhotels.com/bangkok 391 rooms, 20 suites 🍴 No meals Ⓜ Skytrain: Ploenchit.*

Courtyard by Marriott Bangkok

$$ | **HOTEL** | Although it lacks the luxury of Bangkok's high-end lodgings, this reasonably priced Marriott property has a young, hip vibe. **Pros:** good value; family-friendly; convenient location. **Cons:** unremarkable room decor; not as luxurious as other Marriotts; just the standard amenities. $ *Rooms from: B4,000 ✉ 155/1 Soi Mahadlekluang 1, Ratchadamri Rd., Pathumwan ☎ 02/690–1888 🌐 www.marriott.com/hotels/travel/bkkcy-courtyard-bangkok 316 rooms 🍴 No meals Ⓜ Skytrain: Ratchadamri.*

First House

$ | **HOTEL** | Tucked behind the Pratunam Market, this lodging in the bustling garment district is an excellent value. **Pros:** reasonably priced; attractive rooms; close to Airport Rail Link station Ratchaprarop. **Cons:** not much natural light in rooms; neighborhood on the noisy side; no Skytrain or metro station nearby. $ *Rooms from: B1,900 ✉ 14/20–29 Phetchburi Rd., Soi 19, Ratchathewi ☎ 02/254–0300 🌐 www.firsthousebkk.com 100 rooms 🍴 Free breakfast Ⓜ Airport Link: Ratchaprarop.*

Grand Hyatt Erawan

$$$ | **HOTEL** | This stylish hotel hovers over the auspicious Erawan Shrine. **Pros:** easy access to many points in the city; world-class spa; nine restaurants. **Cons:** not on the river; often high occupancy; very busy lobby. $ *Rooms from: B5,900 ✉ 494 Ratchadamri Rd., Pathumwan ☎ 02/254–1234 🌐 www.bangkok.grand.hyatt.com 380 rooms, 44 suites 🍴 No meals Ⓜ Skytrain: Chitlom.*

Novotel Bangkok on Siam Square

$$ | **HOTEL** | Convenient to shopping, dining, and entertainment, this sprawling hotel is a short walk from the Skytrain central station, which puts much of the city within reach. **Pros:** good service; convenient location; cozy rooms. **Cons:** not many in-room amenities; busy front desk; large lobby with music stage and lots of action. $ *Rooms from: B3,500 ✉ 392/44 Siam Sq., Soi 6, Pathumwan ☎ 02/209–8888 🌐 www.novotelbkk.com 426 rooms 🍴 No meals Ⓜ Skytrain: Siam.*

★ The Okura Prestige Bangkok

$$$$ | **HOTEL** | Refreshingly different from Bangkok's other five-star hotels, the Okura Prestige boasts sleek minimalistic design, distinctly Japanese touches like comfy cotton yukata robes in every room, high-tech amenities, impressive downtown views, and a gorgeous 25th-floor infinity pool. **Pros:** chic Japanese design; direct link to Skytrain; excellent

Soi Boys

At many *sois* (side streets) you will find clusters of motorcycle taxis. Their drivers, called "soi boys," will take you anywhere in Bangkok, although they are best for short trips within a neighborhood. Many soi boys know their way around the city better than taxi drivers. Fares are not negotiable—the drivers have set rates to nearby points, usually a bit less than a taxi. Motorcycles can be dangerous; helmets, when available, are often nothing more than a thin piece of plastic without a chinstrap. The risks and discomforts limit their desirability, but motorcycles can be the best way to get around Bangkok if you're in a hurry and if the traffic is bad. Motorcycle taxis can also be hailed on the Grab app for cheaper than at stands, but often drivers don't speak much English, making pickups difficult if for some reason you can't find each other.

restaurants. **Cons:** pricey rooms; lobby not located on ground floor; not suitable for families. *Rooms from: B6,800* *57 Wittayu (Wireless Rd.), Pathumwan* *02/687–9000* *www.okurabangkok.com* *240 rooms* *Free breakfast* *Skytrain: Ploen Chit.*

★ The St. Regis Bangkok

$$$$ | HOTEL | The first hotel in Thailand to offer guests around-the-clock personal butler service, The St. Regis has always been all about pampering. **Pros:** centrally located; elegant rooms; personal butler service. **Cons:** expensive rates; can be a bit stuffy; lobby not on ground floor. *Rooms from: B9,000* *159 Ratchadamri, Pathumwan* *02/207–7777* *www.stregis.com/bangkok* *229 rooms* *No meals* *Skytrain: Ratchadamri.*

Siam Kempinski

$$$$ | HOTEL | The palatial Siam Kempinski combines sheer elegance with the feel of an escapist resort in the middle of the city. **Pros:** central location; some rooms have direct pool access; notable restaurants. **Cons:** pricey; no direct mall access from lobby; standard room rate doesn't include breakfast. *Rooms from: B15,500* *991/9 Rama I Rd., Pathumwan* *02/162–9000* *www.kempinski.com/bangkok* *303 rooms* *No meals* *Skytrain: Siam.*

Siam@Siam

$$$ | HOTEL | This boutique design hotel is definitely where the cool kids stay, but even those traveling with actual kids will feel welcome. **Pros:** great location; superhip crowd; creative rooms. **Cons:** can be noisy; some rooms have little natural light; decor might not be to everyone's taste. *Rooms from: B5,500* *865 Rama I Rd., Wang Mai, Pathumwan* *02/217–3000* *www.siamatsiam.com* *203 rooms* *Free breakfast* *Skytrain: Siam.*

Nightlife

The heart of Bangkok has fewer pubs than you'd imagine, but places like The St. Regis have great views, and Siam Square is home to dance spots like Concept CM2.

BARS AND PUBS

★ St. Regis Bar

BARS/PUBS | From this 12th-floor bar that overlooks the Royal Bangkok Sports Club, you can watch the horse races while sipping a Siam Mary, the Bangkok version of the Bloody Mary. The bar continues the age-old St. Regis tradition of Champagne sabering (opening a bottle using a saber), displayed nightly at 6. The afternoon tea here, with tiers of colorful treats, is also impeccable. ✉ *The St. Regis Bangkok, 159 Ratchadamri Rd., Pathumwan* ☎ *02/207–7777* 🌐 *www.stregis.com/bangkok* Ⓜ *Skytrain: Ratchadamri.*

JAZZ BARS

Maggie Choo's

MUSIC CLUBS | Hidden behind a basement noodle shop, Maggie Choo's is a Bangkok institution for its nightly live performances of jazz and other smooth tunes. The surreal feeling of being transported back to 1930s Shanghai, with heavy vault doors and ladies in embroidered cheongsams dangling on swings, is only amplified by the stiff cocktails. ✉ *Novotel Bangkok Fenix Silom, 320 Silom Rd., Bang Rak* ☎ *09/1772–2144* 🌐 *www.maggiechoos.com.*

Shopping

CLOTHING AND FABRICS

Thai silk gained its reputation only after World War II, when technical innovations made it less expensive. Two fabrics are worth seeking out: mudmee silk, produced in the northeastern part of the country, and Thai cotton, which is soft, durable, and easier on the wallet than silk. People who visit Bangkok might brag about a custom-made suit that was completed in just a day or two, but the finished product often looks like the rush job that it was. If you want an excellent cut, give the tailor the time he needs, which could be up to a week at a reputable place.

Greyhound

CLOTHING | This shop, part of a Thai fashion line, sells casual yet chic street wear. ✉ *Siam Paragon, 991/1 Rama 1 Rd., 1st fl., Pathumwan* ☎ *02/129–4358* 🌐 *www.greyhound.co.th* Ⓜ *Skytrain: Siam.*

Issue

CLOTHING | This hip local designer is inspired by the cultural influences of Thailand, from Buddhism to ancient royalty, within its threads. ✉ *226/10 Siam Sq., Soi 3, Pathumwan* ☎ *02/658–4416* Ⓜ *Skytrain: Siam.*

Marco Tailor

CLOTHING | One of the best custom-tailor shops in Bangkok, Marco Tailor sews a suit equal to those on London's Savile Row. It's not cheap, but it's cheaper than what you'd pay in London. ✉ *430/33 Siam Sq., Soi 7, Pathumwan* ☎ *02/252–0689* Ⓜ *Skytrain: Siam.*

Platinum Fashion Mall

CLOTHING | Fashionistas will fall in love with this mall packed with endless rows of tiny shops selling clothing, shoes, and accessories at wholesale prices. If you buy more things at one shop, you'll likely get a discount—especially for the same model in different colors. The only downside is you probably won't be allowed to try anything on. ✉ *222 Phetchburi Rd., Pathumwan* ✥ *Across from Pratunam Market* ☎ *02/121–8000* 🌐 *www.platinumfashionmall.com* Ⓜ *Skytrain: Siam.*

Prayer Textile Gallery

CLOTHING | Napajaree Suanduenchai studied fashion design in Germany, and more than two decades ago opened this business in her mother's former dress shop. She makes stunning items in naturally dyed silks and cottons and in antique fabrics from the farthest reaches of Thailand, Laos, and Cambodia. ✉ *197 Phayathai Rd., near Siam Sq., Pathumwan* ☎ *02/251–7549* 🌐 *www.prayertextilegallery.com* Ⓜ *Skytrain: National Stadium.*

Sretsis

CLOTHING | Three Thai sisters, darlings of the local design scene, created Sretsis, a feminine design label that has fashionistas around the world raving. ✉ *Central Embassy, 1031 Ploenchit Rd., 2nd fl., Pathumwan* ☎ *02/160–5874* 🌐 *www.sretsis.com* Ⓜ *Skytrain: Chitlom.*

MARKETS

Pratunam Market

OUTDOOR/FLEA/GREEN MARKETS | Hundreds of vendors selling inexpensive clothing jam the sidewalk each day here. The market is a popular destination for Indians, who drop by in the evening to sample the dozens of surrounding Indian, Nepali, and Pakistani restaurants. ✉ *Phetchaburi and Ratchaprarop Rds., Pathumwan* Ⓜ *Skytrain: Chitlom, Klong: Pratunam.*

SHOPPING CENTERS

Central Chitlom

CLOTHING | The flagship location of Thailand's largest department store chain has a good selection of jewelry, clothing, and fabrics, including a Jim Thompson silk shop. ✉ *1027 Ploenchit Rd., Pathumwan* ☎ *02/793–7777* 🌐 *www.central.co.th* Ⓜ *Skytrain: Chitlom.*

Central Embassy

CLOTHING | Fashionistas will find much to explore at one of Bangkok's newer shopping malls; from high-end international brands to Thai designers like Boyy and Disaya. The Eathai section offers street food nibbles and cooking ware displays, as well as the Thai cooking classes at Issaya Cooking Studio. ✉ *1031 Phloen Chit Rd., Pathumwan* ☎ *02/1605–9912* 🌐 *www.centralembassy.com* Ⓜ *Skytrain: Chitlom.*

Central World

SHOPPING CENTERS/MALLS | At more than 1 million square meters (nearly 11 million square feet), this monster claims to be Southeast Asia's biggest mall. It's packed with local and international retailers, as well as a multiplex cinema, a hotel, and many dining options. ✉ *999/9 Rama I Rd., Pathumwan* ☎ *02/021–9999* 🌐 *www.centralworld.co.th* Ⓜ *Skytrain: Chitlom.*

Gaysorn Village

CLOTHING | This upscale shopping center may outshine all the others with its white marble and chrome fixtures. You'll find European and local labels and lauded restaurants such as Paste and Riedel Wine Bar & Cellar. ✉ *999 Ploenchit Rd., Pathumwan* ✣ *At Ratchadamri Rd.* ☎ *02/656–1149* 🌐 *www.gaysornvillage.com* Ⓜ *Skytrain: Chitlom.*

MBK Center

SHOPPING CENTERS/MALLS | An impressive seven stories high, this is one of the busiest malls in the city. It's not as stylish as Siam Center—the main attractions are stores selling cheap clothes and electronics—but there are many other shops, as well as a movie theater, two food courts, and a bowling alley. ✉ *444 Phayathai Rd., Pathumwan* ✣ *At Rama I Rd.* ☎ *02/620–9000 call center* 🌐 *www.mbk-center.co.th* Ⓜ *Skytrain: Siam, Ratchathewi.*

Pantip Plaza

SHOPPING CENTERS/MALLS | This mall exists for the computer nerd in everyone. It houses an enormous number of shops selling computer hardware and software (some legal, most not). Shopping here can be overwhelming, but if you know what you're looking for, the bargains are worth it. **■ TIP→ Not all electronics will be compatible with what you have back home, so do your research.** ✉ *604/3 Phetchaburi Rd., Pathumwan* ☎ *02/256–0355* 🌐 *www.pantipplaza.com* Ⓜ *Subway: Phetchaburi; Skytrain: Chitlom.*

Siam Center

SHOPPING CENTERS/MALLS | Bangkok's young hipsters come here for the latest fashions. With one-of-a-kind handmade clothing, shoes, and accessories, this place oozes style, but be forewarned that the clothes are all made to Thai proportions, so they often run small. ✉ *Siam Tower, Rama I and Phayathai Rds., Pathumwan* ☎ *02/658–1000* 🌐 *www.siamcenter.co.th* Ⓜ *Skytrain: Siam.*

Siam Discovery

SHOPPING CENTERS/MALLS | After a slick renovation in 2016, this lifestyle mall reopened to much fanfare. It's full of shops selling funky international brands, with a heavy focus on fashion but also home ware and hobby items. ✉ *989 Rama I*

Rd., Pathumwan ⊕ At Phayathai Rd. ☎ 02/658–1000 🌐 www.siamdiscovery.co.th Ⓜ Skytrain: Siam.

Siam Paragon

SHOPPING CENTERS/MALLS | With 250 stores, including all the big international brands from Porsche to Chanel, this mall also has a multiplex cinema and tons of restaurants. Oh yes, and an underwater marine park where you can swim with sharks. ✉ *991/1 Rama 1 Rd., Pathumwan ☎ 02/610–8000 🌐 www.siamparagon.co.th Ⓜ Skytrain: Siam.*

SPAS

Anantara Spa

SPA/BEAUTY | A relaxing massage with warm oils is among the many treatments available at the Anantara Siam Bangkok. You can even arrange for a poolside massage. ✉ *Anantara Siam Bangkok, 155 Ratchadamri Rd., Pathumwan ☎ 02/126–8866 🌐 www.anantara.com/en/siam-bangkok/spa Ⓜ Skytrain: Ratchadamri.*

COMO Shambhala Urban Escape

SPA/BEAUTY | There's a wide range of treatments at this ultimate urban escape, but it's particularly known for its detox programs. The COMO Shambhala Bath treatment starts with an invigorating salt scrub, followed by a luxurious soak, a relaxing massage, and a glass of fresh juice to finish. ✉ *Metropolitan Hotel, 27 S. Sathorn Rd., Sathorn ☎ 02/625–3355 🌐 www.comohotels.com/en/metropolitanbangkok/wellness Ⓜ Subway: Lumphini; Skytrain: Sala Daeng.*

i.sawan Residential Spa and Club

SPA/BEAUTY | This spa's facilities are among the city's most cutting-edge, relaxing, and beautiful. The "residential spa cottages," luxurious suites clustered around a courtyard adjacent to the spa, have their own treatment spaces and seem worlds away from downtown Bangkok. Reasonably priced spa packages are available. ✉ *Grand Hyatt Erawan, 494 Ratchadamri Rd., Pathumwan ☎ 02/254–1234 🌐 www.hyatt.com/corporate/spas/I-Sawan-Residential-Spa-and-Club/en/home.html Ⓜ Skytrain: Ratchadamri.*

Silom and Bang Rak

The Silom area, with a mix of tall buildings, residential streets, and entertainment areas, is Bangkok's busiest business district. Some of the city's finest hotels and restaurants are in this neighborhood, which retains some charm despite being so developed and layered in concrete. Although the entire neighborhood across the Chao Phraya River falls under the postal code name and number of Bang Rak, locals are more likely to term places that are on Silom Road as Silom, on Sathorn Road as Sathorn, and call the area around the riverside Bang Rak.

Sights

Carpediem Galleries

MUSEUM | A vivacious, charismatic Singaporean woman owns this gallery that often exhibits oversize artworks. Though based in Sukhumvit, her gallery displays works south of Silom in Vino di Zanotti, a wine restaurant. ✉ *399 Nanglinchee Soi 9, Bangkok ☎ 089/115–4014, 08/1618–2890, 08/9115–4014 🌐 www.carpediemgalleries.com ⏲ By appointment only Ⓜ Skytrain: Chong Nonsi, then taxi.*

Lumphini Park

CITY PARK | Two lakes enhance this popular park, one of the biggest in the center of the city. You can watch children feed bread to the turtles, aerobics and tai chi classes, or teenagers rowing a boat to more secluded shores. During the dry season (from December to February), keep an eye and an ear out for Bangkok Symphony Orchestra's free "Concert in the Park" series, which starts at 5:30 pm each Sunday. There are many embassies in the immediate vicinity. The

Thai Massage

Traditional massage combines acupressure, reflexology, yoga, and meditation. Practitioners believe that 10 energy lines, called *sip sen*, link the body's meridian points. Blocked lines may lead to physical or spiritual ailments. Massage is thought to unblock the energy lines, clearing toxins and restoring balance to the body.

Where to Get a Massage

Outdoors: At markets, on beaches, and at temple fairs, masseurs and masseuses set up shop alongside street vendors. On the beach you'll lie on a mat; at the market you'll probably be seated in a street-side plastic or lounge chair set up for foot massage. Prices vary—a one-hour foot massage might cost as little as B100 at a temple fair or B250 on a popular beach.

Resort and Hotel Spas: For five-star pampering, head to upscale hotels and resorts, whose luxurious, tranquil spas offer an extensive array of massages, including Swedish massage, plus other treatments like tai chi and new-age therapies. Expect to pay at least B2,500 or more for an hour-long massage at a top Bangkok hotel—a lot by Thai standards, but still less than what you'd pay back home.

Shophouses: These ubiquitous massage parlors offer no-frills service. Expect to share a room with other patrons (curtains separate the cots); if you're getting a foot massage, you may be seated in the shop window. A two-hour massage costs at least B400. Though many shophouses are legitimate businesses, some offer "extra" sexual services; steer clear of treatments with suggestive names, like "special" or "full body" massage. You can also ask the concierge at your hotel to recommend a reputable place.

Temples: Some temples still have massage facilities, and massages are often provided to the elderly at no charge. At Wat Po in Bangkok you can receive a massage in an open-air pavilion for B420 an hour.

Urban Spas: A growing phenomenon, urban spas are more upscale than shophouse parlors. They're often located in old Thai houses, with contemporary Asian-style private treatment rooms. You'll have more options here: simple Thai massage is still on the menu (for B1,000 and up per hour), along with body scrubs, facials, and various other treatments.

Learn the Art of Massage

Bangkok's Wat Po is an acknowledged instruction center with an almost 200-year pedigree. A five-day, 30-hour course costs B9,500. You can get more information at 🌐 *www.watpomassage.com*.

—Sophie Friedman

Royal Bangkok Sports Club is just west of the park. ✉ *Rama IV Rd., Pathumwan* Ⓜ *Subway: Silom and Lumphini stations; Skytrain: Sala Daeng.*

M.R. Kukrit's House

HOUSE | Former Prime Minister Kukrit Pramoj's house reflects his long, influential life. After Thailand became a constitutional monarchy in 1932, he formed the country's first political party and was prime minister in1975 and 1976. (Perhaps he practiced for that role 12 years earlier, when he appeared with Marlon Brando as a Southeast Asian prime minister in *The Ugly American*.)

He died in 1995, and much of his living quarters—five interconnected teak houses—has been preserved. Throughout his life, Kukrit was dedicated to preserving Thai culture, and his house and grounds are monuments to a bygone era; the place is full of Thai and Khmer art and period furniture. The landscaped garden with its Khmer stonework is also a highlight. It took Pramoj 30 years to build the house, so it's no wonder that you can spend the better part of a day wandering around. ✉ *S. Sathorn Rd. 19, Soi Phra Pinit, Sathorn* ☎ *02/286–8185* 🎫 *B50* Ⓜ *Skytrain: Chong Nonsi (10-min walk from station).*

★ Queen Saovabha Memorial Institute
ZOO | FAMILY | The Thai Red Cross established this unusual and fascinating snake farm and toxicology research institute in 1923, and it is well worth a visit. Venom from cobras, pit vipers, and some of the other 56 types of deadly snakes found in Thailand is collected and used to make antidotes for snakebite victims. Venom extraction takes place on weekday mornings at 11. The snake handling show and photo op is at 2:30 on weekdays and 11 on weekends and holidays. A few displays can be viewed any time, but photo op is the big draw. ✉ *1871 Rama IV Rd., Pathumwan* ☎ *02/252–0161, 02/252–0167* 🌐 *www.saovabha.com/en/snakefarm_service.asp* 🎫 *B200* Ⓜ *Subway: Silom; Skytrain: Sala Daeng.*

Restaurants

Silom has Bangkok's widest selection of restaurants, many in hotels, on the upper floors of skyscrapers, or around Patpong. You'll find everything from authentic, humble northern Thai food to elaborate, wallet-busting international cuisine.

Baan Khanitha & Gallery
$$ | THAI | This is one of the places—and they can be hard to find—that balances an upmarket feel with fairly authentic Thai cuisine. The basics are done well here, from *chu chee goong nang* (curried river shrimp) to mango with sticky rice. **Known for:** local artwork; wide menu; mango sticky rice. 💲 *Average main: B300* ✉ *69 S. Sathorn Rd., Silom* ☎ *02/2675–4200* 🌐 *www.baan-khanitha.com* Ⓜ *Skytrain: Saphan Taksin.*

Baan Klang Nam 2
$$$ | THAI | If you cruise the Chao Phraya River at night, you might end up gazing upon the clapboard house this restaurant occupies, wishing you were among the crowd dining at this most romantic spot. The place is less touristy than others of its type, most of which are inside big hotels—there's also another branch on Rama III Road at 288 Soi 14, but this one has more atmosphere. **Known for:** white-teak traditional house; authentic Thai cuisine; seafood dishes like steamed fish and spicy fried crab. 💲 *Average main: B390* ✉ *762/7 Bangkok Sq., Rama III Rd., Bangkok* ✥ *Just south of Silom* ☎ *02/682–7180* Ⓜ *Skytrain: Chong Nonsi, then taxi.*

Ban Chiang
$ | THAI | This old wooden house is an oasis in the concrete city; the decor is turn-of-the-20th-century Bangkok, with antique prints and old photographs adorning the walls. Ban Chiang is a Thai restaurant popular with the foreigner and tourist set, so your food won't come spicy unless you request it that way but despite this caveat, the dishes are otherwise prepared true to form. **Known for:** sea bass cooked in various ways; good desserts like banana fritters and coconut ice cream; comfortable outdoor seating. 💲 *Average main: B175* ✉ *14 Soi Srivieng, Surasak Rd., Bang Rak* ✥ *Just north of Sathorn Rd.* ☎ *02/236–7045, 02/266–6994* 🌐 *www.banchiangrestaurant.com* Ⓜ *Skytrain: Surasak.*

Banana Leaf
$ | THAI | If you need to recuperate from Silom Road shopping, head up to the fourth floor of the Silom Complex at Banana Leaf for wonderful cheap eats

Continued on page 119

BANGKOK STREET FOOD

by Robin Goldstein & Alexis Herschkowitsch

In Thailand a good rule of thumb is, the less you pay for food, the better it is. And the food offered by street vendors is very cheap and very good. At any hour, day or night, Thais crowd around sidewalk carts and stalls, slurping noodles or devouring fiery *som tam* (green papaya salad) all for just pennies.

The cooks at street stalls are Thailand's true culinary giants.

If you only eat at upscale restaurants geared to foreigners, you'll miss out on the chili, fish sauce, and bright herbal flavors that define Thai cuisine. Even if you're picky, consider trying simple noodle dishes and skewered meats.

A typical meal costs between B20 and B50 (you pay when you get your food), and most stalls have a few tables and chairs where you can eat.

Street food in Bangkok.

Vendors don't adhere to meal times, nor are different foods served for breakfast, lunch, or dinner, as Thais often eat multiple snacks throughout the day rather than full meals. It's OK to combine foods from more than one cart; vendors won't mind, especially if they're selling something like a curried stew that comes in a plastic bag with no utensils. Find a different stall that offers plates and cutlery, order rice, and add your curry to the mix. Enjoy!

SOM TAM

Thai chefs use contrasting flavors to create balance in their cuisine. The popular green papaya salad is a good example, with dried shrimp, tart lime, salty fish sauce, crunchy peanuts, and long thin slices of green papaya. Pair it with sticky rice for a refreshing treat on a hot day.

SOUR Lime adds a welcome tartness to salads and other dishes, counteracting sweetness.

SPICY Thais like it hot, sometimes using more than 10 fiery chili peppers per dish.

SALTY Instead of salt, Thais often use fish sauce and fermented shrimp paste, which have more nuanced flavors.

BITTER Roasted peanuts add a pleasant bitterness and crunch.

SWEET Palm sugar, a dark brown, natural, aromatic sweetener—will make you wonder why you've been using refined sugar all your life.

STAYING HEALTHY

Sanitary standards in Thailand are far higher than those in many developing countries. By taking a few precautions, you can safely enjoy this wonderful cuisine.

- Avoid tap water. It's the bacteria in the water supply that causes most problems. The water on the table at stalls and restaurants is almost always purified, but stick with bottled water to play it safe.
- Lots of flies are never a good sign. Enough said.
- Know your stomach. Freshly cooked, hot food is least likely to contain bacteria. Steer clear of raw foods and fruits that cannot be peeled if you know you're sensitive.
- Use common sense when selecting a street vendor or a restaurant. Crowds mean high turnover, which translates into fresher food.

Fruit from Chatusak Market, Bangkok.

WHAT SHOULD I ORDER?

Locals will probably be eating the cart's specialty, so if you're not sure what to order, don't be afraid to point. The following are a few common and delicious dishes you'll find in Bangkok.

LARB Another refreshing and flavorful shredded salad, larb (pronounced lahb) consists of ground meat or fish, lime, fish sauce, and a generous helping of aromatic kaffir lime leaves.

PAD Noodles come in many varieties at street carts, and vendors add their own twists. Noodle soups with meat or innards, though traditionally Chinese or Vietnamese, are common in Bangkok, as are ***pad khee mao*** (drunken noodles) with vegetables, shellfish, or meat, wok-singed and served without broth. Another popular dish is ***pad khee mao***—decadently big rice noodles with river prawns and basil.

TOM YUM This delicious and aromatic water-based soup—flavored with fish sauce, lemongrass, kaffir lime leaves, and vegetables—is a local favorite. ***Tom yum goong,*** with shrimp, is a popular variation.

YANG Thais love these marinated meat sticks, grilled over charcoal. Pork is usually the tastiest.

Larb.

Pad Thai.

Tom yum.

WILL IT BE TOO SPICY?

Because most Thai cooks tone things down for foreigners, the biggest battle can sometimes be getting enough heat in your food. To be sure that your dish is spicy, ask for it ***phet phet*** (spicy); if you want it mild, request ***mai phet*** (less spicy). If you get a bite that's too spicy, water won't help—eat a bite of rice or something sweet to counteract the heat.

Food on sale at Damnoen Saduak floating market.

WHAT ARE ALL THE CONDIMENTS FOR?

At some street stalls, particularly soup and noodle shops, you'll be offered an array of seasonings and herbs to add to your dish: chilies marinated in salty fish sauce or soaking in oil; fresh herbs like mint, cilantro, and Thai basil; crunchy bits of toasted rice, peanuts, or fried onions; and lime wedges. Although it's a good idea to taste things you don't recognize so you don't over-flavor your meal, our advice is to pile it on!

Though it has a bad rap, the flavor enhancer MSG is sometimes used at street stalls and restaurants in Thailand. You can ask for food without it *(mai sai phong chu rat)* if it doesn't agree with you. You may also see MSG, a crystal that looks like white sugar, in a little jar on your table, along with sugar, chili paste, and fish sauce.

Two varieties of Thai basil.

YOU WANT ME TO EAT WHAT?

Pan-fried, seasoned insects such as ants, grasshoppers, and cockroaches, are popular snacks in Thailand. A plastic bag full of these crunchy delicacies will cost you about B20 or 50¢. To try your hand at insect-eating, start small. Little guys like ants are the most palatable, since they really just taste like whatever they've been flavored with (lime or chili, for example). Cockroaches have a higher squeamish factor: You have to pull the legs and the wings off the larger ones. And stay away from the silkworm cocoons, which do not taste any better than they sound.

At fruit stalls in Bangkok you may find the durian, a husk-covered fruit famous for its unpleasant smell. In fact the scent, which is a bit like spicy body odor, is so overpowering that some Thai hotels don't let you keep durians in your room. But don't judge the durian by its smell alone: Many love the fruit's pudding-like texture and intense tropical flavor, which is similar to passion fruit. Buy one at a fruit stand, ask the seller to cut it open, and taste its yellow flesh for yourself.

(above) Deep fried bugs (actual size). (below) Durian.

Thought for Food

The first term you should file away is "aroi," which means delicious. You'll no doubt use that one again and again, whether you're dining at food stalls or upscale restaurants. When someone asks "Aroi mai?" that's your cue to practice your Thai—most likely your answer will be a resounding "aroi mak" (It's very delicious).

Another useful word is "Kaw," which simply means "Could I have ...?" However, the most important phrase to remember may be "Gin ped dai mai?" or "Can you eat spicy food?" Answer this one wrong and you might have a five-alarm fire in your mouth. You can answer with a basic "dai" (can), "mai dai" (cannot), or "dai nit noi" (a little). Most restaurants will tone down dishes for foreigners, but if you're visiting a food stall or if you're nervous, you can specify that you would like your food "mai ped" (not spicy), "ped nit noi khrup/kah" (a little spicy), or if you have very resilient taste buds, "ped ped" (very spicy). Don't be surprised if the latter request is met with some laughter—and if all Thai eyes are on you when you take your first bite. Remember, water won't put out the fire; you'll need to eat something sweet or oily, or drink beer or milk.

Essentials

Check bin khrup/kah: the check, please.

Gin jay: vegetarian.

Kaw eek noi khrup/kah: more, please!

Ped mai? Is it spicy?

Kaw glub baan khrup/kah: take away

Beverages

Thai iced tea (*cha yen*) is Thai black tea mixed with cinnamon, vanilla, star anise, often food coloring, and sometimes other spices. It's usually served cold, but you might see a hot version being enjoyed at the end of a meal. It's very sweet. Use caution when buying from food stalls that are working off a block of ice—though made with purified water, the ice is not always kept clean in transportation and storage.

plain water: nam plao

soda water: nam soda

tea: nam charr

iced coffee: ga-fare-yen

whisky: wis-gee

vodka: what gaa

a sweet drink brewed from lemon-grass: nam takrai

How do you like it?

Pad king: stir-fried with ginger.

Pad ped: stir-fried hot and spicy.

Ping: grilled (use phao instead when referring to seafood).

Thom: boiled.

Tawd: deep fried.

Desserts

Ka nom: dessert

Ka nom krog: coconut pudding

Kao niao ma muang: mango with sticky rice

Kao larm: rice based dessert cooked in coconut milk

Gluay bping: grilled bananas

(although there's a B400 minimum to pay by credit card). The mall atmosphere might turn off some, but friendly service and an extensive menu of Thai classics and seafood dishes make up for it. **Known for:** river prawns with glass noodles; good vegetarian options; close to Skytrain station direct link. *Average main: B150* *Silom Complex, 191 Silom Rd., 4th fl., Silom* *Near Skytrain station's south exit* *02/231–3124* *www.bananaleafthailand.com* *Skytrain: Sala Daeng.*

★ Breeze

$$$$ | **MODERN ASIAN** | Practically in the clouds at the State Tower, this ultrahip eatery has a futuristic design that may leave you feeling transported to 2060—especially at night on the outdoor Sky Bridge and in the dining room glowing purple neon. Pan-Asian cuisine creations culminate in chef Sam Pang's tasting menu priced at B4,500, but you can also order à la carte. **Known for:** incredible views from the 51st and 52nd floors; luxurious flourishes like caviar selection; high-profile guests. *Average main: B1,500* *State Tower, 1055 Silom Rd., 52nd fl., Bang Rak* *02/624–9555* *www.lebua.com/breeze* *No lunch* *Skytrain: Saphan Taksin.*

Celadon

$$$$ | **THAI** | Lotus ponds reflect the city's beautiful evening lights at this romantic restaurant. The upmarket Thai food is good, with elegant touches that cater to locals as well as foreigners. **Known for:** regional dishes like khao soi and southern-style yellow curry; several vegetarian options; seafood specialties like grilled river prawns. *Average main: B500* *Sukhothai Hotel, 13/3 S. Sathorn Rd., Sathorn* *02/344–8888* *www.sukhothai.com* *Subway: Lumphini.*

Ciao

$$$$ | **ITALIAN** | A riverside location with pleasant breezes and great views provides a relaxed setting for Ciao's classic Italian fare. From bruschetta to focaccia, everything on the menu is made with fine and fresh ingredients, meats and cheeses imported from Italy, and plenty of attention to detail; top-notch wines also complement the elegant food and surroundings. **Known for:** homemade pastas and risottos; oven-fired pizzas; great setting for romance. *Average main: B1,420* *Mandarin Oriental, 48 Oriental Ave., Bang Rak* *02/659–9000* *www.mandarinoriental.com* *No lunch* *Skytrain: Saphan Taksin, then hotel shuttle boat.*

Eat Me

$$$$ | **INTERNATIONAL** | This Aussie establishment is both a high-end eatery and art space where temporary exhibits from H Gallery provide quite a funky atmosphere. The international fusion menu is also reflected by a staff well mixed between foreigners and Thais, including mixologist Buntanes "Pop" Direkrittikul who's been generating buzz for his creative Thai-inspired cocktails using ingredients like toasted rice, shallots, and chili paste. **Known for:** young hip crowd; Thai-inspired cocktail tastings; premium Australian meats. *Average main: B800* *Soi Pipat 2, Silom* *Off Convent Rd.* *02/238–0931* *www.eatmerestaurant.com* *No lunch* *Subway: Silom; Skytrain: Sala Daeng.*

Hai Som Tam Convent

$ | **THAI** | A good sign of quality, this restaurant is packed with Thais sharing tables filled with northeastern favorites like grilled chicken, spicy papaya salad, and savory minced pork. The open-air dining area can be hot, it's often crowded and noisy, and the staff don't speak much English, so you'll need to pick and point from the menu—but that's part of the fun. **Known for:** properly spicy Thai food; no air-conditioning; cheap yet satisfying eats. *Average main: B80* *2/4 Convent, Soi 5, Silom* *Off Silom Rd.* *02/631–0216* *No credit cards* *Closed Sun.* *Subway: Silom; Skytrain: Sala Daeng.*

Harmonique

$$ | **THAI** | This small house near the river is filled with Thai antiques, chests scattered with bric-a-brac, and more relaxing clutter, as though you're dining at a relative's house. The staff is very good at helping indecisive diners choose from the brief menu, and although the restaurant has become more touristy over the years, it also retains a loyal and regular local clientele. **Known for:** terrace and dining room seating; unusual Thai dishes like hoa mouk (fish curry in a banana leaf); excellent curries. *Average main: B250 22 Charoen Krung (New Rd.), Soi 34, Bang Rak 02/237–8175, 02/630–6270 Closed Sun. Skytrain: Saphan Taksin.*

Himali Cha Cha

$$ | **INDIAN** | Cha Cha, who cooked for Indian Prime Minister Jawaharlal Nehru, died in 1996, but his recipes live on and are prepared with equal ability by his son Kovit. Typical Indian-themed decor and a longstanding menu of traditional dishes as well as intriguing daily specials make this restaurant an oldie but a goodie, with two other locations in Bangkok also available. **Known for:** famous tandoori chicken; northern Indian specialties; garlic naan and cheese naan. *Average main: B300 1229/11 Charoen Krung (New Rd.), Bang Rak 02/235–1569, 02/630–6358 www.himalichacha.com Skytrain: Saphan Taksin.*

Home Cuisine Islamic Restaurant

$ | **INDIAN** | This simple family restaurant serves plenty of Thai-Muslim dishes, but it's most famous for the *khao mok gai* (chicken biryani), a spicy rice dish that's served here with pickled eggplant and a side dish of sweet yogurt sauce. The restaurant is a 15-minute walk from the Saphan Taksin Skytrain station. **Known for:** halal food; some of Bangkok's best biryani; mutton biryani that's less well known but equally delicious as the chicken biryani. *Average main: B120 185 Charoen Krung, Soi 36, Bang Rak Near the French embassy 02/234–7911 No credit cards No lunch Sun. Skytrain: Saphan Taksin.*

The House on Sathorn

$$$$ | **TURKISH** | Turkish chef Fatik Tutak's reimagined mezes are full of surprises, elegantly served in the courtyard and dining room of a century-old colonial mansion next to the W Bangkok. Unusual ingredients like bone marrow, seasonal products bolstering a constantly changing tasting menu (starting at 11 courses for B2,800), and fun platings like pure ice bowls make for a fun gourmand's evening out. **Known for:** Bangkok's only Turkish fine-dining establishment; signature manti dish dedicated to the chef's mother; historic building that was formerly the Russian embassy. *Average main: B2,800 W Bangkok, 106 N. Sathorn Rd., Silom, Bang Rak 02/344–4000 www.thehouseonsathorn.com Skytrain: Chong Nonsi.*

Issaya Siamese Club

$$$$ | **THAI** | An upscale and much-raved-about Thai restaurant, Issaya both surprises and charms with its delightfully laid-back atmosphere, set in a tropical garden peppered with colorful bean bags during dry season. The dining room is cozy with big couches and lots of antique touches, coupled with fun platings and garnishes and impeccable service. **Known for:** dishes inspired by celeb chef Ian Kittichai's childhood; good cocktails; the beloved banana blossom and heart of palm salad. *Average main: B800 Sri Aksorn, Soi 4, Chua Ploeng Rd., Sathorn 02/6729–0401 www.issaya.com Subway: Lumphini, then taxi.*

Le Du

$$$$ | **THAI** | At this modern Thai restaurant, helmed by chef Thitid "Ton" Tassanakajohn, you're likely to try something new in a tasting menu—maybe a crunchy ant larvae topping or a charcoal-grilled pork jowl curry. Sleek minimalist surrounds put the focus on the food and drink, and seeing as the chef is also a

sommelier, wine pairings perfectly complement each course. **Known for:** young, trendy crowd; creative Thai dishes like a deconstructed pad kra pao; fresh regional products including free-range chicken. *Average main: B1,690 ✉ 399/3 Silom 7 Alley, Bang Rak ☎ 09/2919–9969 www.ledubkk.com Closed Sun. Ⓜ Skytrain: Chong Nonsi.*

★ Le Normandie

$$$$ | **FRENCH** | Atop the Mandarin Oriental, this legendary French restaurant excites with impressive views of the Chao Phraya and remarkable food. Chef Arnaud Dunand regularly imports high-quality ingredients from his home region of Savoy for dishes that taste classically of the old country yet with a haute personal touch—tasting menus are of good value compared to à la carte, with the three-course lunch priced at B1,800. **Known for:** French Alps–inspired cuisine like the signature roasted pigeon; winner of major culinary awards; formal dress code. *Average main: B2,300 ✉ Mandarin Oriental, 48 Oriental Ave., Bang Rak ☎ 02/659–9000 www.mandarinoriental.com Closed Sun. Jacket required Ⓜ Skytrain: Saphan Taksin, then hotel shuttle boat.*

★ Lek Seafood

$$ | **THAI** | This unassuming storefront beneath an overpass is the sort of establishment that brings international foodies flocking to Bangkok. The interior here is nothing special, with poor lighting and bluish walls, but you'll barely notice or care with the lively buzz of the local Thai clientele, expert preparations with balanced flavors, and reasonable prices compared to many other seafood joints. **Known for:** beloved by locals; no-frills dining; specialties like the curry crab and cockles. *Average main: B300 ✉ 156 Narathiwat Ratchanakharin Rd., Soi 3, Bang Rak ✣ Below Skytrain station ☎ 02/636–6460 Closed Sun. No lunch Ⓜ Skytrain: Chong Nonsi.*

★ Mezzaluna

$$$$ | **FUSION** | Mezzaluna is a blockbuster restaurant for a couple of reasons: dramatic views of Bangkok from the soaring State Tower and a truly magical menu from the French-trained chef Ryuki Kawasaki. The seven-course menu features organic ingredients and deeply personal touches, such as the mind-blowing signature dish—buttery-soft Wagyu beef paired with sake, both from the chef's home in Japan. **Known for:** award-winning cuisine; fine French ingredients like Brittany blue lobster and foie gras; excellent wine and sake pairings. *Average main: B6,500 ✉ State Tower, 1055 Silom Rd., 65th fl., Bang Rak ☎ 02/624–9555 www.lebua.com Closed Mon. No lunch Ⓜ Skytrain: Saphan Taksin.*

Nahm

$$$$ | **THAI** | Started by master chef David Thompson, who won accolades for his Thai eatery in London, the distinguished Nahm changed hands to chef Pim Techamuanvivit in 2018. Her cuisine marries the traditionalist concept of Nahm—where Thompson turned heads with recipes from ancient cookbooks—and the labor-intensive approach of Techamuanvivit's first restaurant, San Francisco's Kin Khao, for an upscale yet authentic Thai cuisine. **Known for:** carefully selected wines; à la carte options as well as a tasting menu; little-known regional dishes like the blue swimmer crab curry. *Average main: B600 ✉ Metropolitan Hotel, 27 S. Sathorn Rd., Sathorn ☎ 02/625–3333 www.comohotels.com/metropolitanbangkok/dining/nahm No lunch weekends Ⓜ Subway: Lumphini.*

★ Pen

$$$$ | **THAI** | This restaurant has little in the way of atmosphere, but seafood aficionados still brave the traffic up to Yannawa in order to splurge. Pen is expensive by Thai restaurant standards, but it's still a bargain compared to most hotel restaurants for charcoal-grilled seafood and a range of classic Thai fare. **Known for:** specialties

like deep-fried parrot fish with shallots; local favorite; no-frills dining. *Average main: B420 ✉ 25 Chan Rd., Chong Nonsi, Bangkok ✣ Just south of Silom ☎ 02/287–2907, 02/286–7061 Ⓜ Skytrain: Chong Nonsi, then taxi.*

Prachak

$ | **CHINESE** | This little place with bare walls and tile floor is beloved by locals for its soft juicy *pet* (roast duck) and *moo daeng* (red pork). Getting here early is a good idea—by 6 pm there's often little duck left—and allow yourself time to find the entrance, which is quite easy to miss on the busy Charoen Krung road. **Known for:** wonton noodle soup; popular with Thai families; open for over a century. *Average main: B80 ✉ Bang Rak Market, 1415 Charoen Krung (New Rd.), Bang Rak ☎ 02/234–3755 🌐 www.prachakrestaurant.com ▭ No credit cards Ⓜ Skytrain: Saphan Taksin.*

Saffron

$$$$ | **THAI** | The menu at Saffron, mixing creative modern Thai with more classic dishes, is just as exciting as the stunning views from the 52nd floor of the Banyan Tree Bangkok. If you don't fancy dinner, stop by the adjoining bar on the balcony for a cocktail or some street food–inspired snacks—the comfy seating, cool breeze, and vistas are superb. **Known for:** traditional Thai favorites like banana blossom salad; rare ingredients like Tasmanian salmon in the signature yum pla salad; lots of smaller bites available. *Average main: B550 ✉ Banyan Tree Bangkok, 21/100 S. Sathorn Rd., Sathorn ☎ 02/679–1200 🌐 www.banyantree.com/en/bangkok ⏲ No lunch Ⓜ Subway: Lumphini.*

Salathip

$$$$ | **THAI** | On a veranda facing the Chao Phraya River, this restaurant has a setting that practically guarantees a romantic evening—book an outside table so you can enjoy the breeze. Although the food may not have as many chilies as locals would like, the Thai standards are represented on the menu, with à la carte and set menus of seven or eight Thai favorites. **Known for:** stunning river views; traditional Thai music; seafood specialties like the Phuket lobster. *Average main: B425 ✉ Shangri-La Hotel, 89 Wat Suan Plu, Charoen Krung (New Rd.), Bang Rak ☎ 02/236–7777 🌐 www.shangri-la.com/bangkok/shangrila/dining/restaurants/salathip ⏲ No lunch Ⓜ Skytrain: Saphan Taksin.*

★ Sühring

$$$$ | **GERMAN** | This fine-dining restaurant from twin chefs Thomas and Matthew Sühring has evolved German cuisine past the stereotypes of schnitzel and sauerkraut. The brothers, who can be seen working together in a sleek open kitchen every night, serve tasting menus inspired by their childhood in East Berlin—it's no wonder Sühring is one of Bangkok's trendiest restaurants. **Known for:** multiple fine-dining awards; modern interpretations of German classics; outstanding German wine list. *Average main: B3,600 ✉ 10 Yen Akat, Soi 3, Bangkok ☎ 02/2287–1799 🌐 restaurantsuhring.com Ⓜ Subway: Lumphini, then taxi.*

Tawandang German Brewery

$$$ | **ECLECTIC** | From the outside, Tawandang looks like a big barrel representing the 40,000 liters of lager and other beers brewed here every month. With such an active brewery, you might think food would be an afterthought, especially considering the cheesy entertainment such as comedy drag and Thai traditional dancing, but the kitchen actually turns out decent Thai food, with some German and Chinese fare thrown in. **Known for:** Thailand's first microbrewery; decent pub grub; popular for large groups. *Average main: B350 ✉ 462/61 Rama III Rd., Bangkok ☎ 02/678–1114 🌐 www.tawandang.co.th ⏲ No lunch Ⓜ Skytrain: Chong Nonsi, then taxi.*

Vertigo

$$$$ | **SEAFOOD** | You'll feel on top of the world at this classy 61st-floor space, one

of the loftiest open-air restaurants anywhere. The international menu focuses on grilled seafood prepared with flair, and the service is friendly, but as with most of Bangkok's rooftop restaurants, you're paying for the sky-high setting, not the food—you might just prefer to come for a sunset drink to enjoy the stupendous views. **Known for:** à la carte and set menus available; frequent closures due to high winds; good for romantic dates. *Average main: B1,250 ✉ Banyan Tree Bangkok, 21/100 S. Sathorn Rd., 61st fl., Sathorn ☎ 02/679–1200 ⊕ www.banyantree.com/en/bangkok ⊗ No lunch Ⓜ Subway: Lumphini; Skytrain: Sala Daeng.*

★ Zanotti

$$$$ | **ITALIAN** | Everything about this Italian restaurant is top drawer, from the elegant white tablecloths to attentive service and an extensive menu focusing on the regional cuisines of Piedmont and Tuscany. There is something for every palate to indulge in, including pizza, pasta, fish, and steak, as well as Italian wine by the bottle, glass, or carafe from an unusually broad list. **Known for:** the traditional osso buco served with gremolata and saffron risotto; bargain prixe-fixe lunch menu; lively atmosphere. *Average main: B600 ✉ Saladaeng Colonnade Condominium, 21/2 Saladaeng Rd., Silom ☎ 02/636–0002, 02/636–0266 ⊕ www.zanotti-ristorante.com Ⓜ Skytrain: Sala Daeng.*

Hotels

Banyan Tree Bangkok

$$$ | **HOTEL** | After checking in on the ground floor, you soar up to your room at this 60-story hotel—the light-filled suites in the impossibly slender tower all have sweeping city views. **Pros:** wonderful views; cozy rooms; feel on top of the world. **Cons:** not near public transportation; expensive rates; long waits for elevator. *Rooms from: B5,500 ✉ 21/100 S. Sathorn Rd., Sathorn ☎ 02/679–1200 ⊕ www.banyantree.com/bangkok 327 rooms No meals Ⓜ Subway: Lumphini.*

★ COMO Metropolitan Bangkok

$$$$ | **HOTEL** | A modern aesthetic and a trendy focus on healthy living truly sets this hotel apart from the competition. **Pros:** excellent dining on-site; free yoga classes and nice outdoor pool; high environmental and sustainability standards. **Cons:** has declined in popularity; not on river; high prices. *Rooms from: B6,500 ✉ 27 S. Sathorn, Sathorn ☎ 02/625–3333 ⊕ www.comohotels.com/metropolitanbangkok 160 rooms, 9 suites Free breakfast Ⓜ Subway: Lumphini; Skytrain: Sala Daeng or Chong Nonsi.*

La Residence

$ | **HOTEL** | You'd expect to find this charming little hotel on Paris's Left Bank—the rooms are small but comfortable, and each is individually decorated with an unerring eye for detail. **Pros:** cozy, elegant atmosphere; quiet surroundings; plenty of charm. **Cons:** not as cheap as it once was; rooms a bit small; traffic can be noisy. *Rooms from: B1,800 ✉ 173/8–9 Surawong Rd., Bang Rak ☎ 02/233–3301 ⊕ www.laresidencebangkok.com 29 rooms, 7 suites Free breakfast Ⓜ Skytrain: Chong Nonsi.*

Ma Hotel

$$ | **HOTEL** | The expansive marble lobby is your first clue that this hotel is head and shoulders above others in its price range. **Pros:** good value; friendly staff; short walk from river. **Cons:** pool is indoors; popular with tour groups; high traffic on Surawong Road. *Rooms from: B2,500 ✉ 412 Surawong Rd., Si Phraya, Bang Rak ☎ 02/234–5070 ⊕ www.mahotelbangkok.com 243 rooms Free breakfast Ⓜ Skytrain: Surasak.*

★ Mandarin Oriental Bangkok

$$$$ | **HOTEL** | With a rich history dating back to 1879, the Mandarin is one of Bangkok's most prestigious hotels. **Pros:** excellent staff; butler service in all rooms; outstanding pool. **Cons:** popular for private functions; can be very crowded; free Wi-Fi requires fan club sign-up. *Rooms from: B20,250 ✉ 48 Oriental Ave., Bang Rak ☎ 02/659–9000 🌐 www.mandarinoriental.com/bangkok 347 rooms, 35 suites Free breakfast Ⓜ Oriental.*

Montien

$$ | **HOTEL** | This hotel within stumbling distance of Patpong has been well maintained since it was built in 1970, playing up its old-fashioned aesthetic. **Pros:** regal decor; lots of space; tucked away from traffic on Surawong Road. **Cons:** not the most modern hotel; popular with tour groups; party clientele. *Rooms from: B3,200 ✉ 54 Surawong Rd., Silom ☎ 02/233–7060 🌐 www.montien.com/bangkok 475 rooms No meals Ⓜ Subway: Silom; Skytrain: Sala Daeng.*

Narai Hotel

$$ | **HOTEL** | Dating back to 1969, this is one of Bangkok's older hotels, but it's well kept up and conveniently located by the business district on Silom Road. **Pros:** fun neighborhood; short walk to river; good value for proximity to business district. **Cons:** unexciting pool and decor; long walk to Skytrain; heavy traffic on Silom Road. *Rooms from: B3,200 ✉ 222 Silom Rd., Silom ☎ 02/237–0100 🌐 www.naraihotel.co.th 475 rooms Free breakfast Ⓜ Skytrain: Chong Nonsi.*

Royal Orchid Sheraton Hotel and Towers

$$$ | **HOTEL** | Of the luxury hotels along the riverfront, this 28-story palace is most popular with tour groups. **Pros:** nice river views; comfortable beds; good prices for a river hotel. **Cons:** often busy with groups; tired decor; far from public transportation unless you use boat shuttle. *Rooms from: B6,000 ✉ 2 Charoen Krung Rd., Soi 30 (Captain Bush La.), Bang Rak ☎ 02/266–0123 🌐 www.royalorchidsheraton.com 726 rooms, 26 suites No meals Ⓜ Skytrain: Saphan Taksin.*

★ Shangri-La Hotel Bangkok

$$$$ | **HOTEL** | One of Bangkok's most prestigious riverfront properties, the Shangri-La rivals even the more famous Mandarin Oriental. **Pros:** breathtaking lobby; gorgeous pool and terrace; private balconies available. **Cons:** older wing not as nice as newer area; slightly impersonal feel; buffet breakfast costs extra. *Rooms from: B7,000 ✉ 89 Soi Wat Suan Plu, Charoen Krung (New Rd.), Bang Rak ☎ 02/236–7777 🌐 www.shangri-la.com/bangkok 802 rooms, 66 suites No meals Ⓜ Skytrain: Saphan Taksin.*

Siam Heritage

$$ | **HOTEL** | The family that runs the Siam Heritage has created a classy boutique hotel with a purpose—to preserve and promote Thai heritage. **Pros:** reasonably priced; family run; cool Thai decor. **Cons:** not on river; rooms a bit small; very small pool. *Rooms from: B2,500 ✉ 115/1 Surawong Rd., Bang Rak ☎ 02/353–6166 🌐 www.thesiamheritage.com 73 rooms Free breakfast Ⓜ Subway: Silom; Skytrain: Sala Daeng.*

★ Sofitel So Bangkok

$$$$ | **HOTEL** | An architectural gem, this elegant hotel is designed around the five elements of water, earth, wood, metal, and fire: the "earth" rooms, for example, resemble blue caves, and "water" rooms come with bathtubs overlooking the Bangkok skyline. **Pros:** fantastic location; superior service; free computers for in-room use. **Cons:** not all rooms have park views; expensive; can get very busy. *Rooms from: B9,100 ✉ 2 N. Sathorn Rd., Sathorn ☎ 02/624–0000 🌐 www.sofitel-so-bangkok.com 238 rooms No meals Ⓜ Subway: Lumphini.*

The Sukhothai Bangkok

$$$$ | **HOTEL** | On 6 landscaped acres near Sathorn Road, The Sukhothai has numerous courtyards that make the hustle and bustle of Bangkok seem worlds away. **Pros:** beautiful decor in suites; spacious grounds; great on-site restaurants. **Cons:**

expensive rates; not all rooms have courtyard views; far walk to the main street. *Rooms from: B12,700* ✉ *13/3 S. Sathorn Rd., Sathorn* ☎ *02/344–8888* 🌐 *www.sukhothai.com* *210 rooms* *No meals* Ⓜ *Subway: Lumphini.*

★ Tower Club at Lebua

$$$$ | **HOTEL** | With beautiful rooftop venues and abundant flair, the ultraluxurious Tower Club section of Lebua has spacious rooms with stunning upper-floor views and prices to match. **Pros:** stunning panorama; use of Tower Lounge; spacious rooms. **Cons:** sky-high rates; popular with see-and-be-seen crowd; long wait for the elevators. *Rooms from: B8,000* ✉ *1055 Silom Rd., Silom* ☎ *02/624–9999* 🌐 *www.lebua.com/tower-club* *221 rooms* *Free breakfast* Ⓜ *Skytrain: Saphan Taksin.*

Triple Two Silom

$$$ | **HOTEL** | The trendy sister property of the adjacent Narai Hotel has spacious rooms with wood floors and modern fittings in the standard hip colors these days: deep brown, cream, black, and red. **Pros:** tasteful decor; friendly and helpful staff; extra facilities at Narai. **Cons:** some rooms can be noisy; not a great option for kids; heavy traffic on Silom Road. *Rooms from: B4,300* ✉ *222 Silom Rd., Silom* ☎ *02/627–2222* 🌐 *www.tripletwosilom.com* *75 rooms* *Free breakfast* Ⓜ *Skytrain: Chong Nonsi.*

W Bangkok

$$$$ | **HOTEL** | From gigantic sparkly muay Thai boxing gloves on room beds to a swimming pool with an underwater sound system and twinkly LED lights, the high-flying W is loaded with snazzy design and high-tech touches. **Pros:** great central location; 24-hour pool and fitness center; happening on-site bars and restaurants. **Cons:** views not great; Woo Bar next to check-in area; often occupied with events. *Rooms from: B9,000* ✉ *106 N. Sathorn Rd., Silom* ☎ *02/344–4000* 🌐 *www.whotels.com/bangkok* *403 rooms* *No meals.*

Wall Street Inn

$ | **HOTEL** | Most of the guests at this hotel on Surawong Road are from Japan, perhaps because of the many Japanese businesses in the immediate area, but its location near Lumphini Park, Patpong's night market, and Silom Road makes it an appealing option for anyone. **Pros:** happening location; very affordable deluxe rooms; traditional Thai massage available. **Cons:** boring room decor; proximity to nightlife can mean noise; standard rooms are windowless. *Rooms from: B55* ✉ *Surawong Rd., 37/20–24 Soi Surawong Plaza, Silom* ☎ *02/233–4144, 02/233–4164* 🌐 *www.wallstreetinnhotel.com* *63 rooms* *Free breakfast* Ⓜ *Subway: Silom; Skytrain: Sala Daeng.*

Nightlife

Many of the best rooftop bars and upscale lounges are in Silom's high-rise towers and in fashionable spots along the Chao Phraya River. Here's where you'll also find the notorious Patpong red-light district and the Silom Soi 4 gay bars.

BARS AND PUBS

Distil

BARS/PUBS | Thai A-listers have made Distil, on the 64th floor of one of Bangkok's tallest buildings, their stomping ground. It's done up in chic black, coffee, and slate tones. A full-time sommelier is on hand to take care of your wine desires, and you can order a Hangovertini, created one floor down at the Sky Bar for the Hollywood film *Hangover II.* ✉ *Lebua at State Tower, 1055 Silom Rd., 64th fl., Bang Rak* ☎ *02/624–9555* 🌐 *www.lebua.com/distil* Ⓜ *Skytrain: Saphan Taksin.*

★ Moon Bar

BARS/PUBS | The views are staggering at the Banyan Tree Bangkok's 61st-floor alfresco bar. The cost of cocktails ranges from B400 to B680, but for the vistas alone they're worth the splurge. Come a bit before sunset—the bar opens at 5—to get the best view from the

The view is spectacular from Bangkok's famous Sky Bar, in one of the city's tallest buildings.

low-slung seating, and don't forget your camera. If the weather is clear, you can stargaze using the bar's telescope. If the weather's bad at all, the place will be closed. ✉ *Banyan Tree Bangkok, 21/100 S. Sathorn Rd., Sathorn* ☎ *02/679–1200* 🌐 *www.banyantree.com/en/thailand/bangkok/dining/vertigo* Ⓜ *Subway: Lumphini.*

Park Society

BARS/PUBS | The sophisticated rooftop bar adjoining the same-named restaurant has marvelous skyline views and the finest perspective on vast Lumphini Park. Watch the sunset colors while downing a martini or glass of wine from the globe-trotting selection. If you're in a romantic mood, inquire about the private cabanas, complete with butlers, upstairs in the Hi So section. ✉ *Sofitel So Bangkok, 2 N. Sathorn Rd., Sathorn* ☎ *02/624–0000* 🌐 *www.so-sofitel-bangkok.com/wine-dine/park-society* Ⓜ *Subway: Lumphini.*

★ Sky Bar

BARS/PUBS | There's nothing else quite like this bar on the 63rd floor of one of Bangkok's tallest buildings. Head toward the pyramidlike structure emitting eerie blue light at the far end of the restaurant and check out the head-spinning views. The place's most famous concoction, the Hangovertini, was made famous by the Hollywood film *(Hangover II)*shot here. ✉ *Lebua at State Tower, 1055 Silom Rd., 63rd fl., Bang Rak* ☎ *02/624–9555* 🌐 *www.lebua.com/sky-bar* Ⓜ *Skytrain: Saphan Taksin.*

GAY BARS

Silom Soi 2 and Silom Soi 4 are the center of Bangkok's gay scene, with every establishment from restaurants to bars to clubs all catering to a gay clientele.

Balcony

BARS/PUBS | Sometimes the party spills out onto the street at this bar that overlooks the crowds along Soi 4. Balcony has a friendly staff and one of the best happy hours on the soi. ✉ *86–88 Silom,*

Soi 4, Bang Rak ☎ 02/235–5891 ⊕ www.balconypub.com Ⓜ Subway: Silom; Skytrain: Sala Daeng.

DJ Station

BARS/PUBS | A young crowd packs this snappy-looking bar to bask in the "fun, lust, and joy" (or so the website says). The B300 cover charge on weekends includes two drinks, while B150 on weekdays includes one. ✉ *8/6–8 Silom, Soi 2, Silom ☎ 02/266–4029 ⊕ www.dj-station.com Ⓜ Subway: Silom; Skytrain: Sala Daeng.*

Telephone

BARS/PUBS | Bangkok's most venerable gay bar, the pub-style Telephone is hopping every night of the week. The telephones are on the table so you can chat up your neighbors. The staff is friendly and knowledgeable about the neighborhood. ✉ *114/1 Silom, Soi 4, Bang Rak ☎ 02/234–3279 ⊕ www.telephone-pub.com Ⓜ Subway: Silom; Skytrain: Sala Daeng.*

JAZZ BARS

Bamboo Bar

MUSIC CLUBS | This legendary watering hole hosts international musicians playing easy-on-the-ears jazz. Expensive-looking animal print–upholstered furniture and dark wood create an upscale yet cozy space for enjoying Thai-inspired cocktails at the same time. ✉ *Mandarin Oriental, 48 Oriental Ave., Bang Rak ☎ 02/659–9000 ⊕ www.mandarinoriental.com/bangkok/chao-phraya-river/fine-dining/bars/the-bamboo-bar Ⓜ Skytrain: Saphan Taksin.*

★ Smalls

MUSIC CLUBS | The impresario behind the late Q Bar opened this Parisian-style space that feels more Berlin or New York—or Paris—than Bangkok. There's an open-air rooftop hangout and the second floor is sceney, but downstairs is the place to be, if only to check out the French antiques and the traditional absinthe spigot. Jazz performances take place on the ground floor on Wednesdays and eclectic DJs spin all other evenings. The last Thursday of every month there's Vietnamese pho. ✉ *186/3 Suan Phlu, Soi 1, Sathorn ✣ Down Suan Phlu from Sathorn intersection, on right ☎ 095/585–1398 Ⓜ Subway: Lumphini.*

★ Teens of Thailand

BARS/PUBS | Hidden behind an antiquated Indian-style door in Chinatown, the gin bar Teens of Thailand has helped kick off a renaissance of trendy cocktail bars and art galleries in the area. Choose from a list of different gins and tonics for your perfect poison; otherwise the chalkboard cocktail specials change daily. ✉ *76 Charoen Krung Rd. (Soi Nana), Bang Rak ☎ 09/6846–0506.*

Performing Arts

THEATER AND DANCE

Sala Rim Naam

DANCE | **FAMILY** | Across from the Mandarin Oriental, Sala Rim Naam stages a beautiful dance show nightly at 7:45, accompanied by a touristy dinner. ✉ *Mandarin Oriental, 48 Oriental Ave., Bangkok ☎ 02/659–9000 ⊕ www.mandarinoriental.com/bangkok Ⓜ Skytrain: Saphan Taksin.*

★ Silom Village

DANCE | **FAMILY** | This place appeals mostly to foreigners, but it also draws Thais. The block-size complex, open daily from 11 to 11:30, presents classical dance performances and has a restaurant that serves all the Thai favorites. ✉ *286 Silom Rd., Silom ☎ 02/234–4448 ⊕ www.silomvillage.co.th Ⓜ Subway: Silom; Skytrain: Sala Daeng.*

Shopping

CLOTHING AND FABRICS

Jim Thompson Thai Silk Company

CLOTHING | The shops of the pioneering company are prime places to buy silk by the yard and as ready-made clothes. The

Bangkok's Contemporary Art Scene 

In aging commercial pockets around Chinatown, abandoned shophouses tucked away in hidden back alleys are being reborn as cool spaces for urban art, documentary photography, and all kinds of eye candy.

JAM

JAM is a gallery, design office, bar and restaurant all rolled into one. It's incredibly stylish, with a rotating glass door and iron framing retaining the industrial feel of the space's former life as a factory. Art exhibitions, live music performances, and other events take place throughout the week. 🌐 *www.facebook.com/TheJamFactoryBangkok*

Speedy Grandma

Located in an old shophouse, you'll find a special focus on pop and urban artwork here. Gallery owner Unchalee "Lee" Anantawat is a university art professor known for discovering and supporting local talent. The gallery only opens for events—check Facebook for updates. 🌐 *www.facebook.com/SpeedyGrandma*

Maison Close

A tattoo shop, bar, and gallery Maison Close's racy exhibitions push the boundaries between art and pornography. Signature cocktails made with ya dong, or Thai moonshine, and red and black walls filled with curios between showcased works, combine for memorable evenings in old Bangkok. 🌐 *www.facebook.com/maisonclosebkk*

TCDC

Opened by the Thai government in 2005, the Thailand Creative Design Centre or TCDC, spotlights designers and entrepreneurs of diverse creative stripes. To get a full taste of what's happening around Silom and Bangrak, join one of the Centre's lively gallery crawls. 🌐 *www.facebook.com/tcdc.thailand*

MoCA

Opened in 2012, the Museum of Contemporary Art, or MOCA, houses six floors of Thai modern art and is Thailand's largest privately funded museum, with the works coming from the personal collection of billionaire mogul Boonchai Bencharongkul. 🌐 *www.facebook.com/MOCA.BKK*

BACC

The Bangkok Arts & Culture Centre, or BACC, is the most well-known contemporary art gallery in the city, holding diverse exhibitions in a sprawling space. Be sure to stop by Icedea when you visit, to sample tasty ice cream treats that are fashioned into beautiful works of art. 🌐 *www.facebook.com/baccpage*

The Old Guard

The old guard of contemporary art galleries still props up the scene with prestigious showings in more central areas such as Sukhumvit and Silom. Since 2002, H Gallery (🌐 *www.facebook.com/hgallerybangkok*) has presented solo exhibitions by renowned Asian artists. Nearby, the Kathmandu Photo Gallery (🌐 *www.facebook.com/kathmanduphotogallery*), founded by photographer Manit Sriwanichpoom, hosts exhibitions that tell moving, deeply personal stories from around the world.

prices are high, but the staff members are knowledgeable. In addition to this Bang Rak shop there are numerous other locations throughout the city, including at the Mandarin Oriental, The Peninsula, and the Central Chitlom shopping center. ✉ *9 Surawong Rd., Bang Rak* ☎ *02/632–8100* 🌐 *www.jimthompson.com* Ⓜ *Subway: Silom; Skytrain: Sala Daeng.*

LEATHER

Chao Phaya Bootery

SHOES/LUGGAGE/LEATHER GOODS | You can get custom-made cowboy boots for around $200 here. The shop also stocks a large inventory of ready-made leather shoes, boots, and accessories. ✉ *141 Sukhumvit, Soi 11, Sukhumvit* ☎ *02/253–5400* ⏲ *Closed Sun.* Ⓜ *Skytrain: Nana.*

Siam Leather Goods

SHOES/LUGGAGE/LEATHER GOODS | This shop is a good stop for shoes and jackets, along with pants, skirts, and purses, belts, and other accessories. ✉ *River City Shopping Complex, 23 Charoen Krung (New Rd.), Bang Rak* ☎ *02/237–0077* 🌐 *www.siamleathergoods.com* Ⓜ *Skytrain: Saphan Taksin.*

MARKETS

Patpong

OUTDOOR/FLEA/GREEN MARKETS | Bangkok's oldest red-light district, once frequented by U.S. troops stationed during the Vietnam War, is these days also known for a night market with fake Rolex watches and designer handbags for sale. Be wary of pickpockets, as it gets very crowded here. ✉ *Silom Rd., Soi 2, Silom* Ⓜ *Subway: Silom; Skytrain: Sala Daeng.*

PORCELAIN, CERAMICS, AND CELADON

Thai Benjarong

CERAMICS/GLASSWARE | This massive ceramics shop has a huge inventory and will make to order dining sets, bowls, and vases. ✉ *River City Shopping Complex, 23 Charoen Krung (New Rd.), 3rd fl., Bang Rak* ☎ *02/639–0716, 08/9646–1028* 🌐 *www.thaibenjarong.com* Ⓜ *Skytrain: Saphan Taksin.*

PRECIOUS METALS

Lin Silvercraft

HOUSEHOLD ITEMS/FURNITURE | Among all the knickknacks stacked from floor to ceiling, this shop has some of the most finely crafted silver cutlery in town. ✉ *3 Charoen Krung (New Rd.), Soi 38, Bang Rak* ☎ *02/234–2391* 🌐 *www.linjewelers.com* Ⓜ *Skytrain: Saphan Taksin.*

Siam Bronze Factory

JEWELRY/ACCESSORIES | For quality works in bronze, try this showroom near the Mandarin Oriental. ✉ *1250 Charoen Krung (New Rd.), Bang Rak* ☎ *08/9885–8898, 02/237–1534* 🌐 *siambronze.com* Ⓜ *Skytrain: Saphan Taksin.*

SPAS

Away Spa

SPA/BEAUTY | The flashy spa at W Bangkok has a variety of treatments to soothe after long hours of travel, like the detoxifying Drain Away massage. ✉ *W Bangkok, 106 N. Sathorn Rd., Silom, Silom* ☎ *02/344–4160* 🌐 *www.marriott.com/hotels/hotel-information/fitness-spa-services/bkkwb-w-bangkok/* Ⓜ *Skytrain: Chong Nonsi.*

The Oriental Spa

SPA/BEAUTY | A gentle massage in genteel surroundings is what you'll get at the spa at the historic Mandarian Oriental hotel, considered by some to be the best in Bangkok. Amid the wood-panel sophistication you can treat yourself to facials, wraps, and massage. The signature treatments run two hours and will leave you feeling exquisitely pampered. ✉ *Mandarin Oriental, 48 Oriental Ave., Bang Rak* ☎ *02/659–9000* 🌐 *www.mandarinoriental.com/bangkok/chao-phraya-river/luxury-spa* Ⓜ *Skytrain: Saphan Taksin.*

Silom Bodyworks

SPA/BEAUTY | The decor is simple and rather old-fashioned at this spa, but the massages and other treatments are done well and are reasonably priced—a

90-minute Thai massage with a hot compress is B500. ✉ *1035-1035/1 Silom 21, Silom Rd., Bang Rak* ☎ *02/234–5543* 🌐 *www.silombodyworks.com* Ⓜ *Skytrain: Saphan Taksin.*

Sukhumvit

 Restaurants

Sukhumvit is Bangkok's hippest area for dining and going out. Consequently, many of the restaurants here have more style than substance, but there's good food to be had, and the area of Thong Lor has evolved into a food lover's paradise.

★ Appia

$$$ | **ITALIAN** | A food critic turned restaurateur and the son of a Roman butcher teamed up to create this homey trattoria. Jarrett Wrisley, best known for the Bangkok street-food parlor Soul Food Mahanakorn, and his business partner, Paolo Vitaletti, a five-star chef whose dad toiled in a storied Roman meat market, run this small cozy space for which reservations are highly advisable. **Known for:** handmade pastas; slow-roasted meats like fresh-off-the-rotisserie porchetta; affordable Italian wine list. $ *Average main: B400* ✉ *20/4 Sukhumvit, Soi 31, Sukhumvit* ☎ *02/261–2056* 🌐 *www.appia-bangkok.com* ⏲ *No lunch Tues.–Sat.* 💳 *No credit cards* Ⓜ *Skytrain: Phrom Phong.*

★ Bo.lan

$$$$ | **THAI** | Named after its two owners, a Thai-Western couple, Bo.lan consistently appears on lists of Thailand's and Asia's best restaurants for its modern interpretations of Thai cuisine. Located in a renovated old house just off Sukhumvit, the restaurant is striving to eventually have a zero-carbon footprint—the owners grow their own vegetables, recycle organic waste, and purify their groundwater. **Known for:** fresh seasonal dishes; no à la carte—tasting menus only; good for vegetarians. $ *Average main: B2,680* ✉ *24 Sukhumvit, Soi 53, Sukhumvit* ☎ *02/260–2962* 🌐 *www.bolan.co.th* ⏲ *No lunch Tues.–Fri. Closed Mon.* Ⓜ *Skytrain: Thong Lor.*

Cabbages & Condoms

$$ | **THAI** | This popular place raises funds for the Population and Community Development Association (PDA), a sex education/AIDS prevention organization. The food, geared to foreign tastes, is competently prepared but what you'll come for is quirky decor, with fairy lights and condom-decorated mannequins contrasting traditional teakwood. **Known for:** free condoms instead of after-dinner mints; unconventional gift shop; beautiful outdoor seating. $ *Average main: B300* ✉ *10 Sukhumvit, Soi 12, Sukhumvit* ☎ *02/229–4610* 🌐 *www.cabbagesandcondoms.com* Ⓜ *Subway: Sukhumvit; Skytrain: Asok.*

The Commons

$$$ | **INTERNATIONAL** | It's easy to laze all afternoon at The Commons, a lofty community mall known for its gourmet food stands, restaurants, and comfortable open-air seating. You'll see groups dining on smorgasbords at single tables, with cuisines from Thai to Mexican, as well as dishes like fried chicken and waffles, artisanal sandwiches, and more—but plenty of people simply grab an iced coffee and sit on their laptops, too. **Known for:** stands from popular Bangkok restaurants like Daniel Thaiger, Peppina, and Soul Food 55; good brunch and coffee at Roast; yoga studio and retail shops on second floor. $ *Average main: B350* ✉ *335 (Thong Lor 17) Sukhumvit, Soi 55, Thong Lor* ☎ *02/712–5400* 🌐 *www.thecommonsbkk.com* ⏲ *Opening hrs of vendors vary* Ⓜ *Skytrain: Thong Lor.*

Doo Rae

$$ | **KOREAN** | Many authentic Korean restaurants do business in Sukhumvit Plaza, but even with three stories of tables, there's often a wait day or night at Doo Rae. Go for the do-it-yourself barbecue

Muay Thai, the Sport of Kings

Muay Thai is believed to be more than 2,000 years old. It's been practiced by kings and was used to defend the country. It's so important to Thai culture that until the 1920s muay Thai instruction was part of the country's public school curriculum.

Techniques: Developed with the battlefield in mind, muay Thai moves mimic the weapons of ancient combat. Punching combinations, similar to modern-day boxing, turn the fists into spears that jab relentlessly at an opponent. The roundhouse kick—delivered to the thigh, ribs, or head—turns the shinbone into a devastating striking surface. Elbow strikes to the face and strong knees to the abdomen mimic the motion of a battle-ax. Finally, strong front kicks, using the ball of the foot to jab at the abdomen, thigh, or face, mimic an array of weapons.

Rules: Professional bouts have five three-minute rounds, with a two-minute rest period between rounds. Fights are judged using a point system, with judges awarding rounds to each fighter, but not all rounds are given equal weight—the later rounds are more important, as judges view fights as "marathons," with the winner being the fighter who's fared best throughout the entire match. The winner is determined by majority decision. Of course, a fight can also end decisively with a knockout or a technical knockout (wherein a fighter is conscious, but too injured to continue).

Rituals: The "dance" you see before each match is called the *ram muay* or *wai kru* (these terms are often used interchangeably, though the wai kru really refers to the homage paid to the *kru* or trainer). The ram muay serves to honor the fighter's supporters and his god, as well as to help him warm up, relax, and focus. Both fighters walk around the ring with one arm on the top rope to seal out bad spirits, pausing at each corner to say a short prayer. They then kneel in the center of the ring facing the direction of their birthplace and go through a set of specific movements, often incorporating aspects of the *Ramakien*. Fighters wear several good-luck charms, including armbands (*kruang rang*) and a headpiece (*mongkron*). Live musicians speed up or slow down the music to the tempo of the fight.

Lumpinee Boxing Stadium. The stadium, which debuted in 2014 after moving north of the city from Lumphini Park, hosts muay Thai matches on Tuesday, Friday, and Saturday, starting at around 6:30 pm. ✉ *6 Ramintra Rd., Anusawaree, Bang Khen, Bangkok* ✣ *About 10 km (6½ miles) south of Don Mueang airport* ☎ *02/522–6843 stadium, 02/282–3141 office* 🌐 *www.lumpineemuaythai.com* 🎫 *B1,000–B2,000* Ⓜ *Subway: Chatuchak Park, then taxi from either; Skytrain: Mo Chit.*

Ratchadamnoen Stadium. The sprawling Ratchadamnoen Stadium presents muay Thai bouts on Monday, Wednesday, Thursday, and Sunday from 6:30 pm to 10 pm. Ringside seats for most matches cost about B2,000. ✉ *1 Ratchadamnoen Nok Rd., Pom Prap Sattru Phai, Banglamphu* ☎ *02/281–4205* 🎫 *B1,000–B2,000.*

grilling, with *bulgogi* (thin slices of beef in a tasty marinade) and fresh veggies, as well as sake or soju, a rice-based drink similar to vodka but with a lower alcohol content. **Known for:** substantial kimchi and tofu stews; complimentary side dishes; location in a mall known as Bangkok's Korean Town. *Average main: B300 ✉ 212/15 Sukhumvit Plaza, Soi 12, Sukhumvit ☎ 02/653–3815 Ⓜ Subway: Sukhumvit; Skytrain: Asok.*

55 Pochana

$ | **THAI** | You wouldn't expect much by looking at this nondescript restaurant on Sukhumvit Road from the outside, but locals have been packing it night after night for years. The place, which started out as a late night khao tom rice soup eatery, has expanded to having one of the most extensive and tastiest Thai-Chinese menus in town. **Known for:** classic Thai dishes like tom yum soup; signature dishes like aw suan (oyster and egg soufflé) and dok krajon ("little flower" salad); open late until 4:30 am. *Average main: B150 ✉ 1087–1093 Sukhumvit Rd., Thong Lor ✣ 100 meters (110 yds) east of the corner of Sukhumvit 55 ☎ 02/391–2021 No credit cards No lunch.*

★ Isao

$$$ | **SUSHI** | Bangkok has hundreds of Japanese restaurants, but only Isao has a line out the door 365 nights a year thanks to the most creative sushi rolls west of California. The owner studied under the chef at the revered Green Tea in Chicago, and the repeat clientele attests to the widespread enthusiasm for his culinary flights of fancy in sleek modern surrounds. **Known for:** caterpillar-shaped sushi roll with shrimp and tempura; reasonable prices; reservations not accepted. *Average main: B350 ✉ 5 Sukhumvit, Soi 31, Sukhumvit ☎ 02/258–0645 🌐 www.isaotaste.com Ⓜ Skytrain: Phrom Phong.*

Je Ngor's Kitchen

$$ | **THAI** | Locals adore this Thai eatery for various stir-fried seafood dishes, loaded with fried garlic, pepper, and fragrant curry, as well as reasonably priced lunch set menus and a smattering of Chinese dishes to choose from, too. The decor is homey but attractive, with warm colors and lots of space, making the Sukhumvit location of this popular chain the comfiest and most convenient. **Known for:** special menu items like stir-fried rock lobster and braised sea cucumber; hot pot soups; traditional Thai desserts. *Average main: B250 ✉ 68/2 Sukhumvit, Soi 20, Sukhumvit ☎ 02/258–8008 🌐 www.jengor-seafoods.com Ⓜ Skytrain: Phrom Phong.*

Kuppa

$$$ | **CAFÉ** | This light-and-airy space maintains the aura of its former life as a warehouse, but it's certainly more chic than shabby these days, with polished metal and blond wood adding a hip counterpoint to cement floors. Kuppa serves traditional Thai fare as well as many international dishes, and it has a dedicated following for its coffee, roasted on the premises. **Known for:** popular for weekend brunch; coffee roasted on-site; small portions. *Average main: B350 ✉ 39 Sukhumvit Rd., Soi 16, Sukhumvit ☎ 02/663–0450, 02/258–0194 🌐 www.kuppa.co.th Ⓜ Subway: Sukhumvit; Skytrain: Asok.*

Le Dalat

$$ | **VIETNAMESE** | **FAMILY** | Classy Le Dalat is a favorite with Bangkok residents, serving royal Vietnamese cuisine in a former private home set among lovely gardens. The several intimate dining rooms have nostalgic design touches, such as vintage paintings and black-and-white photos, wicker seats with colorful pillows, and fine china tableware. **Known for:** seafood dishes like the Hanoi-style fried fish with dill; reservations recommended; quiet, somewhat hidden location. *Average main: B250 ✉ 57 Soi Prasarnmitr, Sukhumvit, Soi 23, Sukhumvit ☎ 02/259–9593 🌐 www.ledalatbkk.com Ⓜ Subway: Sukhumvit; Skytrain: Asok.*

★ The Local

$$$ | THAI | The emphasis at this traditional Thai restaurant in a century-old house is on fresh seasonal ingredients and hard-to-find regional delicacies, with a regular menu but also a smaller one of specials that is consistently changing. The Local's decor, outdoor terrace, wood floors, and antiques and old photos make for a pleasant setting. **Known for:** separate vegetarian menu; tom yum martinis and dragonfruit mojitos; popular with tourists. *Average main: B320 32 Sukhumvit, Soi 23, Sukhumvit 02/664–0664 www.thelocalthaicuisine.com Subway: Sukhumvit; Skytrain: Asok.*

My Choice

$$ | THAI | FAMILY | My Choice might be located quite far off the main Sukhumvit drag into Soi 38, but it's very popular among Thais with a taste for their grandmothers' traditional recipes. Natural light, modern wood furniture, and leafy plants create a warm and inviting atmosphere, but when the weather is cool, diners prefer to sit outside. **Known for:** popular for family dining; the ped aob (whole roasted duck); traditional recipes. *Average main: B250 5 Sukhumvit, Soi 36, Sukhumvit 02/258–6174, 02/259–9470 Skytrain: Thong Lo.*

★ Peppina

$$$ | PIZZA | Hands down Bangkok's best pizzeria, warmly industrial-looking Peppina is booked solid on most nights (although there are other locations in malls, too). Chef Paolo Vitaletti of Appia trattoria fame is behind this restaurant, where attention to detail includes wood firing, special dough that's left to rise overnight, and fresh buffalo mozzarella and other ingredients imported from Italy. **Known for:** inventive antipasti; gourmet pizza; extensive drink list. *Average main: B390 27/1 Sukhumvit, Soi 31, Sukhumvit 02/119–7677 www.peppinabkk.com.*

Seafood Market

$$$$ | SEAFOOD | The seafood at this 1,500-seat, garishly fluorescent-lit establishment is way overpriced (plus you pay a charge for the cooking), and the atmosphere is extremely touristy, but the place is always packed and it makes for a fun night out. As in a supermarket, you take a small cart and choose from an array of seafood—crabs, prawns, lobsters, clams, oysters, and fish—which chefs then cook how you prefer. **Known for:** fresh quality of seafood; cheesy decor; the motto: "If it swims, we have it!". *Average main: B450 89 Sukhumvit, Soi 24, Sukhumvit ↔ Closer to Rama IV Rd.; take taxi down Sukhumvit 24 02/261–2071 www.seafood.co.th Skytrain: Phrom Phong.*

★ Soul Food Mahanakorn

$$ | THAI | Launched by food critic Jarrett Wrisley, this gem of a restaurant and bar is in a converted Chinese shophouse in trendy Thong Lor and is usually packed to the rafters. It's no surprise, as the place serves some of the city's best Thai food, with double-pour drinks that are every bit as good as the food. **Known for:** popular with Thais and foreigners; house-smoked duck dishes; locally inspired cocktails like Lycheegrass Collins or Lo-So Mojito. *Average main: B250 56/10 Sukhumvit, Soi 55, Thong Lor 02/714–7708 www.soulfoodmahanakorn.com No lunch Skytrain: Thong Lor.*

★ Supanniga Eating Room

$$ | THAI | Thanaruek Laoraowirodge, a successful restaurateur in New York City and Bangkok, has earned high praise for this cozy shophouse venue that specializes in regional dishes based on the recipes of his grandmother. The au courant cocktails go well with an eclectic menu, and Supanniga now has two other locations in Sathorn and Tha Thien plus an evening dinner cruise to its name. **Known for:** charcoal-grilled meats; variations of nam prik (traditional spicy sauces served with vegetables); street-food dishes like fried rice and noodles. *Average main:*

Dinner Cruises

Though they're definitely touristy, dinner cruises on the Chao Phraya River are worth considering. They're a great way to see the city at night, although the food is often subpar. You might even want to skip the dinner, just have drinks, and dine at a real Thai restaurant afterward. Two-hour cruises on modern boats or refurbished rice barges include a buffet or set-menu dinner, and often feature live music and sometimes a traditional dance show. Many companies also offer a less expensive lunch cruise, though the heat can make these a little unpleasant. In general it's wise to reserve a few days in advance, and reservations are a must for some of the more popular dinner cruises.

Horizon. The buffet dinner cruise aboard the *Horizon*, with Thai and international cuisine, departs each evening at 7:30 pm. ✉ *Shangri-La Hotel, 89 Soi Wat Suan Plu, Charoen Krung (New Rd.), Bang Rak* ☎ *02/236–7777* 🌐 *http://www.shangri-la.com/bangkok/shangrila/dining/restaurants/horizon-cruise* ⏲ *No lunch* Ⓜ *Skytrain: Saphan Taksin.*

Manohra Dining Cruise. The most beautiful dining boat on the river departs on both breakfast and dinner cruises, with the former serving international items and the latter 10 courses of Thai cuisine. The vessel is smaller than most of its peers, with less space to walk around. ✉ *Anantara Bangkok Riverside Hotel, 257/1–3 Charoen Nakhorn, Thonburi* ☎ *02/476–0022* 🌐 *www.manohracruises.com* Ⓜ *Skytrain: Saphan Taksin, then hotel boat.*

Supanigga Cruise. The newest dinner cruise in Bangkok serves Thai food a cut above the rest—dishes from the popular authentic Thai restaurant Supanigga Eating Room. The six-course dinner menu lasts about two hours; there are also 45-minute Champagne and cocktail cruises. ✉ *160/11 Sukhumvit 55, Sukhumvit* ☎ *02/714–7608, 09/7238–8284* 🌐 *www.supannigacruise.com* ⏲ *No lunch* Ⓜ *Skytrain: Thong Lor.*

Yok Yor. Departing each evening at 8 pm, the *Yok Yor* is a little like a floating restaurant. The boat ride costs B200, and the food is ordered à la carte as opposed to a set menu, making this different from most of Bangkok's dinner cruises. ✉ *885 Somdet Chao Phraya 17, Klong San* ☎ *02/863–0565* 🌐 *www.yokyor.co.th* 💳 *No credit cards* ⏲ *No lunch.*

B210 ✉ *160/11 Sukhumvit, Soi 55, Thong Lor* ✥ *Between Thong Lor Soi 6 and 8* ☎ *02/714–7608* 🌐 *www.supannigaeating-room.com* Ⓜ *Skytrain: Thong Lor.*

Hotels

★ The Cabochon Hotel

$$$$ | HOTEL | A colonial-style boutique hotel with small and large suites and a few multibedroom residences, the Cabochon is a period piece out of 1920s Shanghai. **Pros:** colonial-style property with period decor; antiques-filled rooms; rooftop pool. **Cons:** restaurant food is not special; expensive; must book well in advance. $ *Rooms from: B6,100* ✉ *14/29 Sukhumvit, Soi 45, Sukhumvit* ☎ *02/259–2871, 02/259–2872* 🌐 *cabochonhotel.com* *8 rooms* 🍽 *Free breakfast* Ⓜ *Skytrain: Phrom Phong and Thong Lor.*

The Davis Bangkok

$$ | HOTEL | The Davis has a main building and another one two doors down with a separate lobby and reception area but no matter where you end up, the rooms are comfortable and classy. **Pros:** individually decorated rooms; beautiful pool area; quiet location. **Cons:** not close to public transit; uninteresting view from rooms; separate buildings can be confusing. *Rooms from: B2,700* *80 Sukhumvit, Soi 24, Sukhumvit* *02/260–8000* *www.davisbangkok.net* *247 rooms, 2 villas* *Free breakfast* *Skytrain: Phrom Phong.*

The Landmark Bangkok
$$$ | **HOTEL** | The generous use of polished wood in the reception area may suggest a grand European hotel, but The Landmark is surprisingly modern. **Pros:** modern amenities; discount packages frequently available; good for business travelers. **Cons:** may be too formal for families; some rooms noisy; close to red-light district. *Rooms from: B4,600* *138 Sukhumvit Rd., Sukhumvit* *02/254–0404* *www.landmarkbangkok.com* *450 rooms* *No meals* *Skytrain: Nana.*

★ Marriott Hotel Sukhumvit
$$$ | **HOTEL** | This snazzy urban-design property brings five-star luxury to the Thong Lor area where it is set apart from Sukhumvit's main hotel zone, occupying its area's tallest building, affording patrons of Octave, the swank rooftop bar, 360-degree city views. **Pros:** great views; nice outdoor pool; close to trendy Thong Lor restaurants and bars. **Cons:** not in the heart of the city; away from tourist attractions; horrible rush-hour traffic. *Rooms from: B5,200* *2 Sukhumvit, Soi 57, Thong Lor* *02/797–0000* *www.marriott.com/hotels/travel/bkkms-bangkok-marriott-hotel-sukhumvit* *295 rooms and suites* *Free breakfast* *Skytrain: Thong Lor.*

Pullman Bangkok Grande Sukhumvit
$$$ | **HOTEL** | A futuristic facade of soaring glass and odd angles sets the tone at this upscale lodging located conveniently in the heart of Sukhumvit. **Pros:** centrally located; interesting exterior architecture; attentive service. **Cons:** many business travelers; bathrooms lack privacy; design somewhat dated. *Rooms from: B5,500* *30 Sukhumvit, Soi 21, Sukhumvit* *02/204–4000* *www.pullmanbangkokgrandesukhumvit.com* *325 rooms* *No meals* *Subway: Sukhumvit; Skytrain: Asok.*

Sheraton Grande Sukhumvit
$$$$ | **HOTEL** | The Sheraton soars 33 floors above the noisy city streets, and the upper-floor suites get tons of natural light. **Pros:** close to fun nightlife; near public transportation; impressive views from most rooms. **Cons:** somewhat impersonal due to size; pricey; expensive for area. *Rooms from: B9,000* *250 Sukhumvit Rd., Sukhumvit* *02/649–8888* *www.sheratongrandesukhumvit.com* *420 rooms, 36 suites* *No meals* *Subway: Sukhumvit; Skytrain: Asok.*

The Westin Grande Sukhumvit
$$$$ | **HOTEL** | Fancy with sleek surfaces and neon lighting, the Westin is very convenient to Sukhumvit shopping and nightlife—it's just out the front door. **Pros:** near Skytrain and subway; close to nightlife; comfortable beds. **Cons:** on-site restaurants not great; overpriced compared to nearby options; dated design. *Rooms from: B7,400* *259 Sukhumvit Rd., Sukhumvit* *02/207–8000* *www.westingrandesukhumvit.com* *362 rooms, 31 suites* *No meals* *Subway: Sukhumvit; Skytrain: Asok.*

Nightlife

There's an incredible mix of bars and clubs around Sukhumvit. Lower Sukhumvit (Asok and Nana) is where you'll find the Nana Plaza and Soi Cowboy red-light districts. Farther east, the neighborhoods of Thong Lor and Ekkamai are *the* places where lots of young Thais and foreigners are partying, from buzzy nightclubs to speakeasy-style cocktail bars.

BARS AND PUBS

Above Eleven

BARS/PUBS | This rooftop bar on the 33nd floor of the Frasier Suites Sukhumvit offers sweeping views of the city in sophisticated surrounds. Order a pisco sour and some Japanese-Peruvian snacks, like ceviche and sushi, and enjoy the DJ's beats. ✉ *Frasier Suites Sukhumvit, 38/8 Sukhumvit, Soi 11, 33nd fl., Sukhumvit* ☎ *02/038–5111* 🌐 *www.aboveeleven.com* Ⓜ *Skytrain: Nana.*

The Bar Upstairs

BARS/PUBS | This alcove covered in greenery aims to transport guests straight to the south of France. Duck away from all the neon on Sukhumvit 11 for a glass of wine with some charcuterie and cheese, surrounded by leafy plants and wood furnishings. ✉ *33/30 Sukhumvit, Soi 11, Sukhumvit* ✣ *On top of Brasserie Cordonnier* ☎ *02/821–5110* 🌐 *www.upstairsbkk.com* Ⓜ *Skytrain: Nana.*

Craft Bangkok

BREWPUBS/BEER GARDENS | Boutique beer lovers flock to this hip outdoor spot where all the brews are 100% craft. Bottles include U.S. craft favorites like Rogue, Anderson Valley, and Deschutes, but there are Czech, Scandinavian, and Japanese entries as well. On Friday nights the DJ plays any and all requests from guests. A second branch is located at 981 Silom Road. ✉ *16 Sukhumvit, Soi 23, Sukhumvit* ✣ *About 200 meters (655 feet) up Soi 23 on right* ☎ *02/661–3220* 🌐 *www.craftbangkok.com* Ⓜ *Subway: Sukhumvit; Skytrain: Asok.*

J. Boroski

BARS/PUBS | There is no cocktail menu at this hidden speakeasy from legendary Bangkok mixologist Joseph Boroski. Simply tell the bartender what you're in the mood for, something special will be made with dashes of rare ingredients. ✉ *Thong Lor Soi 9 (Sukhumvit 55), Thong Lor* ✣ *At the end of the alley on the right* ☎ *02/712–6025* 🌐 *www.sipslowly.com/jboroski-1* Ⓜ *Skytrain: Thong Lor.*

Mikkeller Bangkok

BREWPUBS/BEER GARDENS | The craft-beer gypsy brewers from Denmark opened up shop in Bangkok at this hideaway in a residential garden home. Around 30 brews are on tap, many of them experimental and avant-garde specimens found only at the world's few Mikkeller branches. The garden is a fine spot to relax in, and there is also a bottle shop and a popular fine-dining restaurant. ✉ *26 Ekkamai, Soi 10, Yaek 2, Watthana* ✣ *Hidden off Soi 10 (call or check website map)* ☎ *02/381–9891* 🌐 *www.mikkellerbangkok.com* Ⓜ *Skytrain: Ekkamai.*

★ Octave

BARS/PUBS | This downtown rooftop bar atop the Bangkok Marriott Hotel Sukhumvit offers 360-degree panoramas, with reasonable drink prices compared to other rooftop bars. More trendy bars and restaurants are just a hop away in Thong Lor. Reservations are a good idea. ✉ *Bangkok Marriott Hotel Sukhumvit, 2 Sukhumvit, Soi 57, Thong Lor* ☎ *02/797–0000* 🌐 *www.marriott.com/hotel-restaurants/bkkms-bangkok-marriott-hotel-sukhumvit* Ⓜ *Skytrain: Thong Lor.*

Oskar Bistro

BARS/PUBS | On any night of the week, Oskar is full of a well-mixed Thai and foreign crowd enjoying good cocktails, wood-fired pizzas, and more satisfying international bites. You can't miss it for the electronic beats spilling out onto the street, and eclectic DJs are regularly brought in to spin. ✉ *24 Sukhumvit, Soi 11, Sukhumvit* ☎ *09/7289–4410* 🌐 *www.oskar-bistro.com* Ⓜ *Skytrain: Nana.*

Royal Oak Pub

BARS/PUBS | With many different brews on tap and in bottles, this very British pub is a place for serious beer drinkers. Activities to keep you entertained include a quiz on Wednesday and ladies' specials on Thursday ✉ *595/10–11 Sukhumvit, Soi 33, Sukhumvit* ☎ *02/662–1652* 🌐 *www.royaloakthailand.com* Ⓜ *Skytrain: Phrom Phong.*

TaladNath

BARS/PUBS | You'll find this funky cocktail bar on a dead-end soi of Thong Lor, where well-known Thai mixologist Nath Arjhan creates drinks inspired by his travels and his native land. The decor is inspired by the local street food culture, with plastic chairs, neon lights, and cocktails being prepared on an upcycled cart. ✉ *160/5 Thonglor, Soi 6 (Sukhumvit 55), Thong Lor* ☎ *08/4553–7706* Ⓜ *Skytrain: Thong Lor.*

DANCE CLUBS

★ Beam

DANCE CLUBS | Beam's home to Asia's first "body kinetic" dance floor, shaking vibrations into dancer's feet during live techno and deep house gigs. The futuristic decor and throbbing lights fit perfectly with the progressive underground beats of DJs from Bangkok and abroad. ✉ *72 Courtyard, 72 Sukhumvit, Soi 55, 1st fl., Thong Lor* ☎ *02/392–7750* 🌐 *www.beamclub.com* Ⓜ *Skytrain: Thong Lor.*

Glow

DANCE CLUBS | An underground dance club playing only cutting-edge electronic music, Glow lights up Sukhumvit with a revolving lineup of local and international DJs. You'll find a trendy mix of expats and locals here enjoying the top-notch sound system and an excellent vodka selection. ✉ *96/4–5 Sukhumvit, Soi 23, Sukhumvit* ☎ *02/261–3007* Ⓜ *Subway: Sukhumvit; Skytrain: Asok.*

★ Havana Social

DANCE CLUBS | The entrance to this secret salsa lair is located behind a fake telephone booth in a dark unsuspecting alley across from the Frasier Suites Sukhumvit. Inside you'll find a trendy crowd shimmying to Afro-Cuban beats, sipping Cubra Libres on leather couches and smoking in the cigar lounge, harking back to Havana before the revolution. Make sure to call ahead to receive the entry password. ✉ *41/3 Sukhumvit, Soi 11, Sukhumvit* ✣ *Down the alley across from Frasier Suites Sukhumvit* ☎ *06/1450–3750* Ⓜ *Skytrain: Nana.*

Sing Sing Theater

DANCE CLUBS | This stylish nightclub challenges reality for the 1930s Shanghai underground, covered in wrought-iron corners, red lighting, and lanterns. DJs spin upbeat electronic music, beckoning some to squeeze onto the compact dance floor and others to lounge at tables and by the bar. ✉ *Sukhumvit Rd., Soi 45, Sukhumvit* ☎ *06/3225–1331* 🌐 *www.singsingbangkok.com* ☞ *Closed Mon.* Ⓜ *Skytrain: Phrom Pong.*

 Shopping

CLOTHING AND FABRICS

Raja Fashions

CLOTHING | Photographs here show former heads of state proudly modeling their new suits made by Raja Fashions. Raja has a reputation for tailoring some of the finest men's and women's fashions in Bangkok. ✉ *160/1 Sukhumvit, Sukhumvit* ✣ *Between Soi 6 and 8* ☎ *02/253–8379* 🌐 *www.rajasfashions.com* ⏲ *Closed Sun.* Ⓜ *Subway: Sukhumvit; Skytrain: Nana.*

SHOPPING CENTERS

Emporium

SHOPPING CENTERS/MALLS | One of the first malls in Bangkok, this glitzy place has a little sales area on the sixth floor full of beautiful silks, incense, and glassware, all reasonably priced. The mall was renovated and expanded to include EmQuartier, which opened in 2015, spreading a development called EM District with exclusive high-end shops and fine dining on both sides of Sukhumvit. ✉ *622 Sukhumvit Rd., Sukhumvit* ✣ *Between Sois 24 and 26* ☎ *02/269–1000* 🌐 *www.theemdistrict.com* Ⓜ *Skytrain: Phrom Phong.*

Terminal 21

SHOPPING CENTERS/MALLS | The levels at this upscale mall represent different parts of the world. There's a San Francisco section, for instance, complete with cable

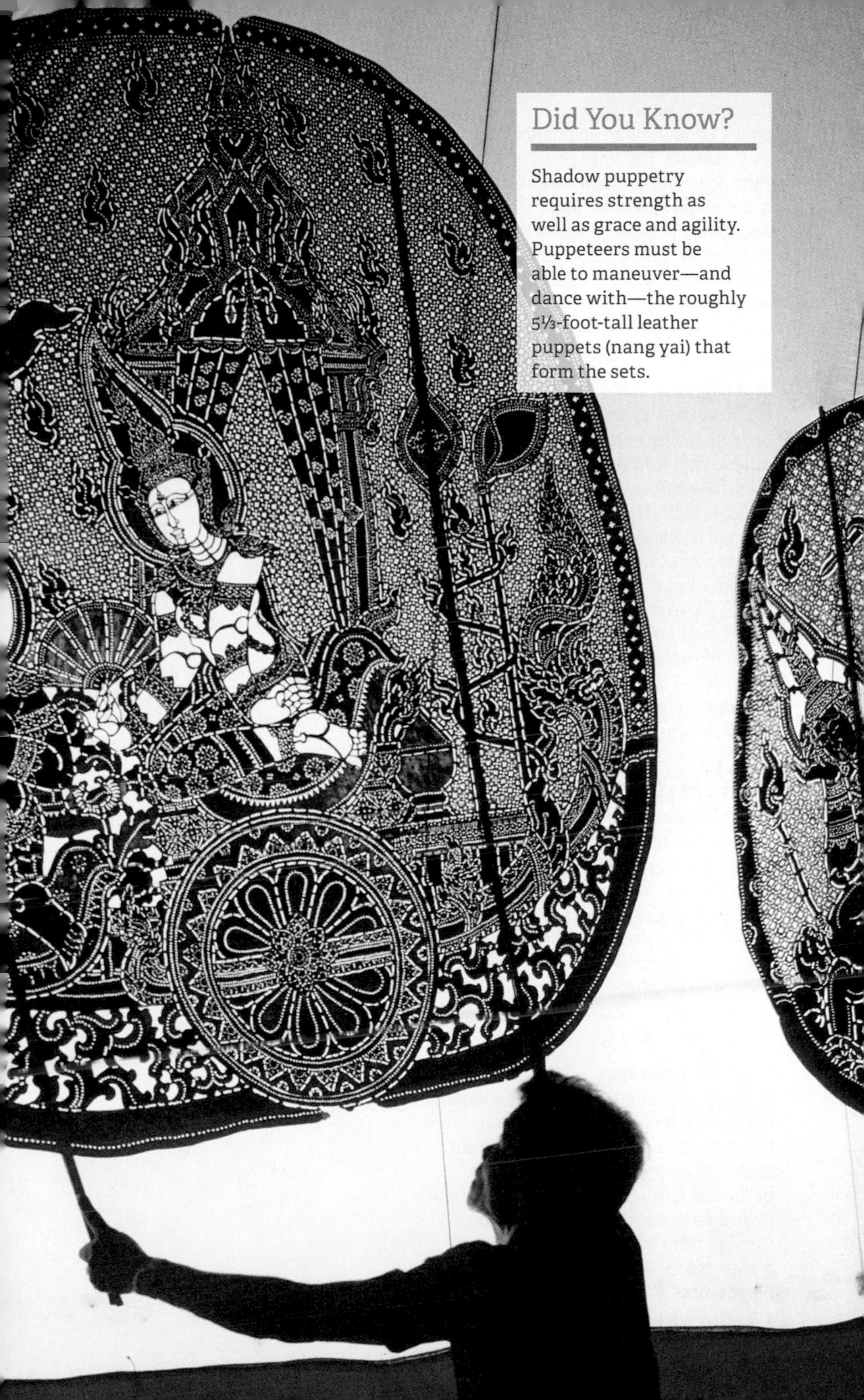

Did You Know?

Shadow puppetry requires strength as well as grace and agility. Puppeteers must be able to maneuver—and dance with—the roughly 5⅓-foot-tall leather puppets (nang yai) that form the sets.

cars and a miniature Golden Gate Bridge, plus a London floor, an Istanbul, and many others. The food court on the top floor is one of Bangkok's best, and there is a multiplex cinema, and many shops and restaurants to hang out in. ✉ *2,88 Sukhumvit, Soi 19, Sukhumvit* ✣ *At Asok Montri Rd.* ☎ *02/108–0888* 🌐 *www.terminal21.co.th* ☞ *Daily 10–10* Ⓜ *Subway: Sukhumvit, Skytrain: Asok.*

SPAS

★ Health Land Spa

SPA/BEAUTY | This spa chain is known for its high-quality massages at reasonable prices, with a 120-minute traditional Thai massage costing B600. There are multiple locations around Bangkok, but the one at Asok is easy to get to by Skytrain or subway. Appointments book up fast, so call ahead. ✉ *55/5 Sukhumvit 21 Rd. (Asoke), Sukhumvit* ✣ *Walk down Sukhumvit 19 and take your first right; from Sukhumvit 21 your first left.* ☎ *02/261–1110, 08/6378–6771* 🌐 *www.healthlandspa.com* Ⓜ *Subway: Sukhumvit; Skytrain: Asok.*

Oasis Spa

SPA/BEAUTY | The treatments at Oasis Spa take place in a Thai-style house. Among the inventive treatments are a coffee, honey, and yogurt body scrub and soothing aloe and lavender body wraps. A second branch at Sukhumvit, Soi 31, is just as lovely, and both offer free transportation from the Skytrain station Phrom Phong. ✉ *88 Sukhumvit, Soi 51, Sukhumvit* ☎ *02/262–2122* 🌐 *www.oasisspa.net* Ⓜ *Skytrain: Thong Lo.*

Yunomori Onsen Spa

SPA/BEAUTY | Bangkok's first Japanese hot spring, this traditional bathhouse has first-class spa treatments. There's even real spring water, thousands of gallons of it, trucked up from the famed Raksawarin Hot Springs in Ranong. Choose from among several pools, from a toasty hot tub down to a cold plunge pool. ✉ *A-Square 120/5, Sukhumvit, Soi 26, Sukhumvit* ✣ *Take a taxi down Sukhumvit, Soi 26 to A-Square* ☎ *02/259–5778* 🌐 *www.yunomorionsen.com* Ⓜ *Skytrain: Phrom Phong.*

Suvarnabhumi Airport

Although too far south of the city to be a logical base of operations while visiting Bangkok, the area around the airport can be a convenient option given the number of Bangkok flights that depart or arrive in the middle of the night.

Hotels

Novotel Suvarnabhumi Airport

$$$$ | **HOTEL** | This stunning hotel near Bangkok's main airport rents rooms in four-hour blocks, a boon during lengthy layovers. **Pros:** no set check-in time; five minutes from airport via free shuttle service; restaurants, spa, gym, and pool. **Cons:** far from town; big and impersonal; plane noise. $ *Rooms from: B8,000* ✉ *Moo 1 Nongprue Bang Phli, Samut Prakan* ☎ *02/131–1111* 🌐 *www.novotel.com* *612 rooms* 🍽 *No meals.*

Chapter 4

AROUND BANGKOK

Updated by
Barbara Woolsey

Sights ★★★★☆ Restaurants ★★★☆☆ Hotels ★★★☆☆ Shopping ★★★☆☆ Nightlife ★☆☆☆☆

WELCOME TO AROUND BANGKOK

TOP REASONS TO GO

★ **Heading into the Wild:** A huge expanse of untouched jungle surrounds Kanchanaburi, a launchpad for trekking and river rafting.

★ **Floating Markets:** This area has more floating markets than anywhere else in Thailand. The most famous is at Damnoen Saduak, the region's sole market that still operates daily.

★ **Seeing Old Siam:** History awaits outside Bangkok at a Neolithic site, the remains of a Khmer temple (Muang Singh Historical Park in Kanchanaburi), and in Nakhon Pathom, Thailand's oldest seat of Buddhist learning.

★ **Bridge on the River Kwai:** For a glimpse of more recent history, visit the remnants of the "Death Railway" in Kanchanaburi and walk across the bridge made famous by the movie The Bridge on the River Kwai.

★ **River Views in Ayutthaya:** This city, an easy day trip from Bangkok, combines great river views with an island full of fascinating wats.

1 Muang Boran. See replicas of Thailand's most important architectural sites.

2 Damnoen Saduak. Home to the most popular floating market in the region.

3 Samut Songkram. A good base when exploring villages on the canal network.

4 Nakhon Pathom. A diverse city on Myanmar's doorstep.

5 Pretchaburi. These temples and royal summer palaces are best enjoyed on an overnight trip.

6 Kanchanaburi. The site of the famous Bridge on the River Kwai.

7 Greater Kanchanaburi Province. The main access point to the large national parks of western Thailand.

8 Sangklaburi. A diverse city on Myanmar's doorstep.

9 Ayutthaya. Once one of the country's most important cities.

10 Bang Pa-In. Famous for its 18th century Royal Palace and topiary gardens.

11 Lopburi. Best known for its monkey-infested temples.

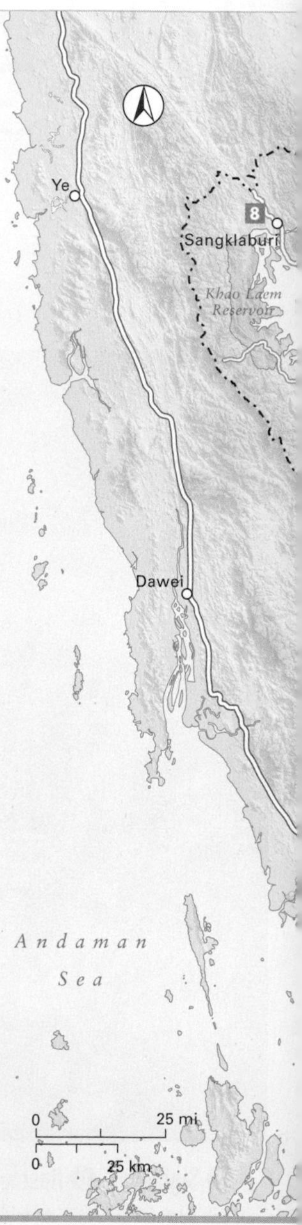

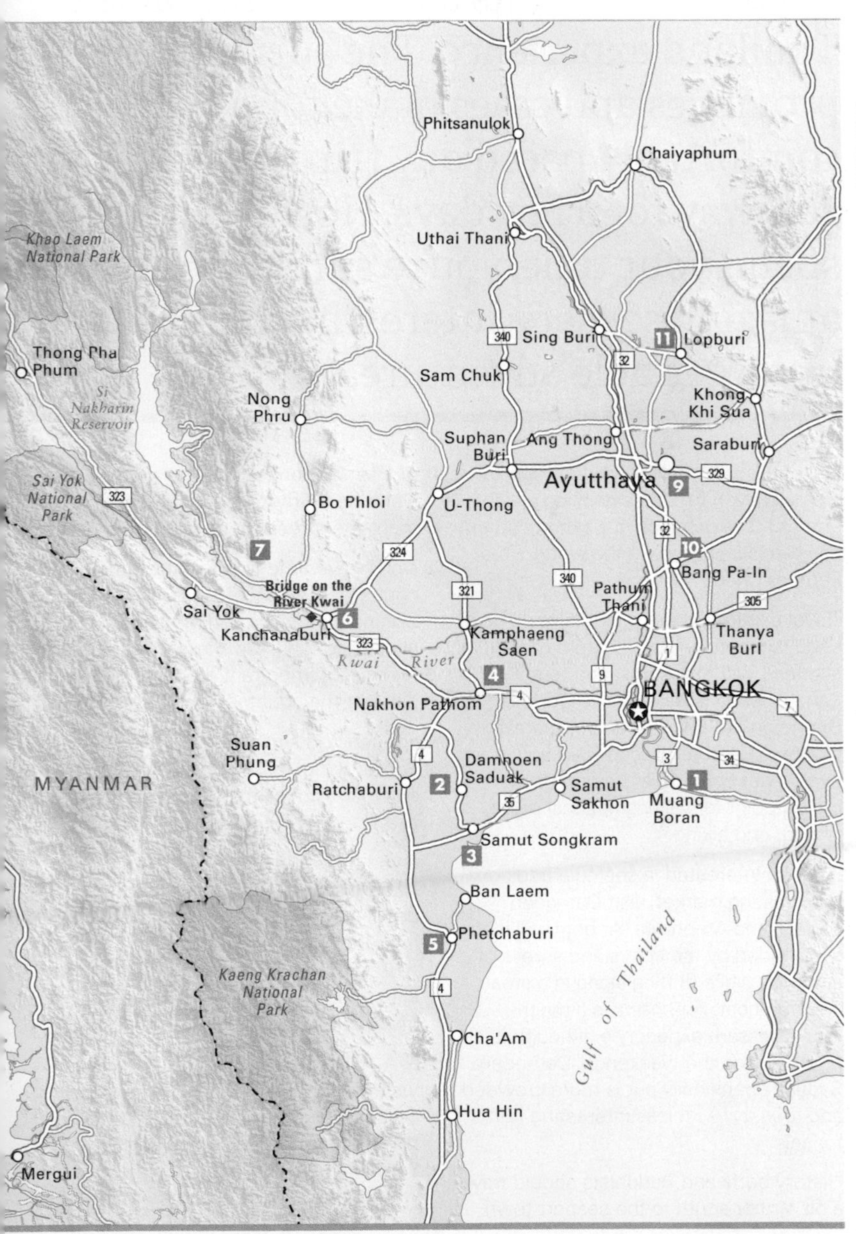

Phitsanulok
Chaiyaphum
Uthai Thani
Khao Laem National Park
Thong Pha Phum
Si Nakharin Reservoir
Sai Yok National Park
340
Sing Buri
11
Lopburi
32
Sam Chuk
Nong Phru
Khong Khi Sua
Suphan Buri
Ang Thong
Saraburi
Ayutthaya
9
329
323
Bo Phloi
U-Thong
7
324
32
10
Bang Pa-In
340
321
Bridge on the River Kwai
Pathum Thani
305
Sai Yok
6
Kanchanaburi
Kamphaeng Saen
Thanya Buri
323
Kwai River
1
4
9
BANGKOK
Nakhon Pathom
4
7
Suan Phung
4
Damnoen Saduak
3
34
MYANMAR
Ratchaburi
2
Samut Sakhon
1
Muang Boran
35
Samut Songkram
3
Ban Laem
Gulf of Thailand
5
Phetchaburi
Kaeng Krachan National Park
4
Cha'Am
Hua Hin
Mergui

Escaping the congestion and chaos of Bangkok is quite simple, and a must for anyone who wants a truly memorable Thailand experience. The surrounding provinces and cities make for a comfortably paced day trip, or an easy getaway for a few days. However you spend your time, you're sure to encounter amazing scenery, interesting culture, and unforgettable adventure.

Only 50 km (31 miles) west of Bangkok is a small haven for those seeking enlightenment. The province of Nakhon Pathom has the tallest stupa in the world, Phra Pathom Chedi.

Travel a little farther west and you'll be in Kanchanaburi, with its mixture of tranquil scenery, war museums, and temples. Kanchanaburi is most known for the Bridge on the River Kwai, but there's plenty to keep you occupied. If you're an explorer at heart, this is a great starting-off point for visiting national parks, rafting, and hiking.

If you're interested in seeing a traditional Thai floating market, visit Damnoen Saduak and Amphawa. At both you'll be surrounded by the colors and smells of a market while drifting along in a small, wooden boat. Amphawa is a much more pleasant experience although it is only open on the weekends. Damnoen Saduak opens daily but is more crowded and touristy, with less interesting items for sale.

History buffs and Buddhists should travel a bit farther south to the seaport town of Phetchaburi for its wats and palaces. Don't be frightened of the monkeys that roam the streets here.

Don't have time to travel the entire country? The peaceful grounds of Muang Boran, an outdoor park-museum, is shaped roughly like Thailand and displays replicas of important monuments from all parts of the country.

For seafood served Thai-style, head to Samut Songkram, where you'll be able to eat your fill of clams and other fruit of the sea along the Gulf of Thailand.

If you have more time, check out Sangklaburi. Thai, Mon, Karen, and Bangladeshi communities flourish in this city near the Myanmar border. Many people who venture to Sangklaburi go on trekking tours and visit the Thai border town of Three Pagodas Pass.

MAJOR REGIONS

Visitors to Bangkok usually allow time for **day trips from Bangkok** to visit Thailand's famous floating markets at **Damnoen Saduak** and **Muang Boran,** a huge park with replicas of the country's landmarks.

To the west of Bangkok is **Nakhon Pathom,** keeper of Thailand's biggest stupa. **Phetchaburi,** a small seaport town, has many interesting temples and a few royal summer palaces.

Kanchanaburi Province is home to the city of **Kanchanaburi,** two hours west of Bangkok, and its interesting and sometimes moving World War II historic sites, among them the Bridge on the River Kwai. If you're not in a hurry to get back to Bangkok, you can continue your exploration of **Greater Kanchanaburi Province,** with day trips to 13th-century Khmer ruins and two national parks containing waterfalls.

The **Ayutthaya and its environs** region encompasses an important historical journey that traces Thailand's cultural developments from Buddhist art and architecture to modern government and language. **Ayutthaya** with its UNESCO World Heritage Site gets the most attention, drawing day-trippers from Bangkok, but a visit to **Lopburi**, with its Khmer temples and French-influenced Phra Narai Ratchaniwet, lends additional historical context to the museums and ransacked ruins found at Ayutthaya's historical park and the 18th-century Royal Palace in nearby **Bang Pa-In.**

Planning

WHEN TO GO

On weekends and national holidays, particularly during the mid-April Buddhist New Year water festival, Kanchanaburi and the restaurants at Samut Songkram are packed with Thais. In high season (from November to March) the floating market in Damnoen Saduak has more tourists than vendors. The waterfalls of Kanchanaburi Province are at their best during or just after the rainy season (from June to November). The fossil shells in Don Hoi Lod in Samut Songkram are best seen in dry season or at low tide in rainy season. See the fireflies in Ampawa between May and October.

PLANNING YOUR TIME

You can take in all the highlights north and west of Bangkok in about a week. Three or four days are enough to experience the top Kanchanaburi Province sights, starting with the serene River Kwai and the town of Kanchanaburi. From there you can take day trips to explore the waterfalls and other natural wonders. Historic Ayutthaya, a drive of little more than an hour from downtown Bangkok (depending on traffic), is an easy day trip, as are Lopburi and the floating market at Damnoen Saduak.

GETTING HERE AND AROUND

BUS TRAVEL

Most buses depart from Bangkok's Southern Bus Terminal; tickets are sold on a first-come, first-served basis, but service is so frequent that it's seldom a problem finding an empty seat.

CAR TRAVEL

Distances from Bangkok are short enough to drive, though it's more relaxing to hire a car and driver.

TAXI AND SONGTHAEW TRAVEL

Taking one of Bangkok's air-conditioned taxis is a good way to access sights, particularly those in Nakhon Pathom, Samut Songkram, and Muang Boran. Estimate around B500 per hour, with the final amount dependent upon your bargaining skills. Standard rates for trips outside Bangkok, implemented by the Ministry of Transport, are displayed in many, though not all, taxis and if available should be used as a starting point for any negotiations.

Outside Bangkok, *songthaews* (pickups with wooden benches in the truck bed) are often the closest thing to taxis.

HEALTH AND SAFETY

The region is generally safe, and the towns mentioned *in this chapter* have hospitals. Take normal precautions and keep valuables on your person at all times when traveling by bus or train. Too-good-to-be-true deals—particularly involving gems—are *always* a rip-off. On a more amusing note, the monkeys of Phetchaburi are cute but cunning, and may relieve you of your possessions, especially food.

MONEY MATTERS

Generally speaking, finding banks and ATMs isn't difficult, especially in towns. Most main bank branches close at 4 pm, with many smaller branches, often located in shopping malls and department stores, remaining open into the evening and on weekends. Remember that the farther out from civilization you travel, the fewer ATMs you'll find. Don't expect to withdraw money outside a national park or in a tribal village. It's probably best if before leaving Bangkok you exchange the money you think you'll require.

RESTAURANTS

The areas around Bangkok allow you to sample both regional and non-Thai ethnic foods. Kanchanaburi and Sangklaburi have Mon, Karen, Bangladeshi, and Burmese communities serving their own specialties. A must-try is *laphae to,* a Burmese salad of nuts and fermented tea leaves. In Nakhon Pathom try the excellent rice-based dessert *khao larm.* Phetchaburi is famous for its desserts and for *khao chae,* chilled rice soaked in herb-infused water.

HOTELS

An overnight stay is essential in Sangklaburi and highly recommended in Kanchanaburi and Phetchaburi. Stay in Damnoen Saduak the night before you visit the floating market to avoid an early-morning bus ride.

Luxury accommodations are more common in most provincial towns, but be prepared to stay at a resort on the outskirts if you want to sample the very best. It's best to book ahead on weekends and national holidays in Kanchanaburi.

What It Costs In Baht

	$	$$	$$$	$$$$
RESTAURANTS	under B200	B200–B300	B301–B400	over B400
HOTELS	under B2,000	B2,000–B4,000	B4,001–B6,000	over B6,000

TOURS

Asian Trails

GUIDED TOURS | It's easy to travel in the areas around Bangkok on your own, but this company organizes trips to the floating markets, as well as trekking trips, homestays, and bicycle tours. ✉ *SG Tower, 161/1 Soi Mahadlek Luang 3, Rajdamri Rd., 9th fl., Pathumwan* ☎ *02/626–2000* 🌐 *www.asiantrails.travel* 🎫 *From B2,600.*

Diethelm Travel

GUIDED TOURS | Ayutthaya and the Damnoen Saduak floating market are among the stops on this outfit's three-day Ayutthaya & Maeklong tour, led by an English-speaking guide. The all-inclusive fee covers lodging, meals, and entrance and boat fees. One-day excursions to the floating market and other attractions are also available. ☎ *02/660–7000* 🌐 *www.diethelmtravel.com/Thailand* 🎫 *From B16,100 per person; call for shorter trips' pricing.*

Muang Boran

20 km (12 miles) southeast of Bangkok.

An easy and popular day trip from Bangkok, Muang Boran provides a captivating introduction to Thailand's architectural and cultural highlights via replicas and reconstructions.

GETTING HERE AND AROUND

BUS TRAVEL

The best bus choice from Bangkok to Muang Boran (two hours; B30) is the air-conditioned Bus 511, which leaves every half hour from Bangkok's Southern Bus Terminal; take it to the end of the line at Pak Nam. You can also catch this bus on Sukhumvit Road. Transfer to Songthaew 36 (B10), which goes to the entrance of Muang Boran.

CAR TRAVEL

Driving to Muang Boran requires engaging Bangkok's heavy and unpredictable traffic. Take the Samrong–Samut Prakan expressway and turn left at the Samut Prakan intersection onto Old Sukhumvit Road. Muang Boran is well signposted on the left at Km 33. The trip should take less than two hours.

Sights

Muang Boran (*Ancient City*)

ARTS VENUE | An outdoor museum with more than 100 replicas and reconstructions of Thailand's most important architectural sites, monuments, and palaces, this park is shaped like the country, and the attractions are placed roughly in their correct geographical position. A "traditional Thai village" on the grounds sells crafts, but the experience is surprisingly untouristy. The park stretches over 320 acres, and takes about four hours to cover by car. Or you can rent a bicycle at the entrance for B50. Small outdoor cafés throughout the grounds serve decent Thai food. ✉ *296/1 Sukhumvit Rd., Bangpoo, Samut Prakan* ☎ *02/7091–6448* 🌐 *www.ancientcitygroup.net/ancientsiam/en* 🎫 *B700.*

Damnoen Saduak

109 km (68 miles) southwest of Bangkok.

The image of this frenetic market of floating vendors selling all sorts of raw and prepared food is so evocative that it has become an ad agency favorite. Though the market can feel touristy, a visit here is a memorable way to experience a Thai tradition.

GETTING HERE AND AROUND

Getting to Damnoen Saduak can be tricky. It's probably best to join one of the tours offered at most hotels and guesthouses.

Canary Travel Thailand

GUIDED TOURS | Kanchanaburi and the floating market at Damnoen Saduak are among the destinations on sightseeing and package tours booked by this agency that specializes in western Thailand. Canary Travel does online and phone bookings, will arrange a pick up from your hotel in Bangkok, and offers several multiday stay packages. ✉ *10 Tani Rd., Banglamphu, Taladyod, Pranakorn, Bangkok* ✣ *Khao San Rd.* ☎ *02/629–1687* 🌐 *www.canarytravelthailand.com* 🎫 *From B450.*

BUS TRAVEL

Buses to Damnoen Saduak (from two to three hours; B73) leave Bangkok's Southern Bus Terminal every 20 minutes starting at 5 am. From the station in Damnoen Saduak, walk or take a songthaew along the canal for 1½ km (1 mile) to the floating market. Buses also run from Nakhon Pathom and Samut Songkram.

CAR TRAVEL

Take Route 4 (Phetkasem Road) and turn left at Km 80. Continue for 25 km (16 miles) along the Bang Phae–Damnoen Saduak Road. The drive from Samut Songkram to Damnoen Saduak, along Route 325, is pleasant, particularly if you go via Amphawa. The entire trip takes two hours.

Sights

Damnoen Saduak floating market

MARKET | A colorful market of produce and other foods sold by vendors on small boats, Damnoen Saduak is an icon of Thai tourism. Often overrun with visitors, the market comes off a bit like a Disney World exhibit and bears only passing resemblance to the authentic commercial life of this canal-strewn corner of Thailand. On the other hand, even though it feels like a theatrical production, this is one of the few opportunities to witness a fading Thai tradition, and some of the food—including noodle soup, seafood dishes, grilled meats, mango ice cream, coconut pancakes, and fried bananas—is quite tasty. The best way to enjoy the market is to hire a boat and come early. The area only becomes more crowded as the day progresses and ever more tour groups arrive. ✣ *Off Rte. 325, 109 km (68 miles) southwest of Bangkok.*

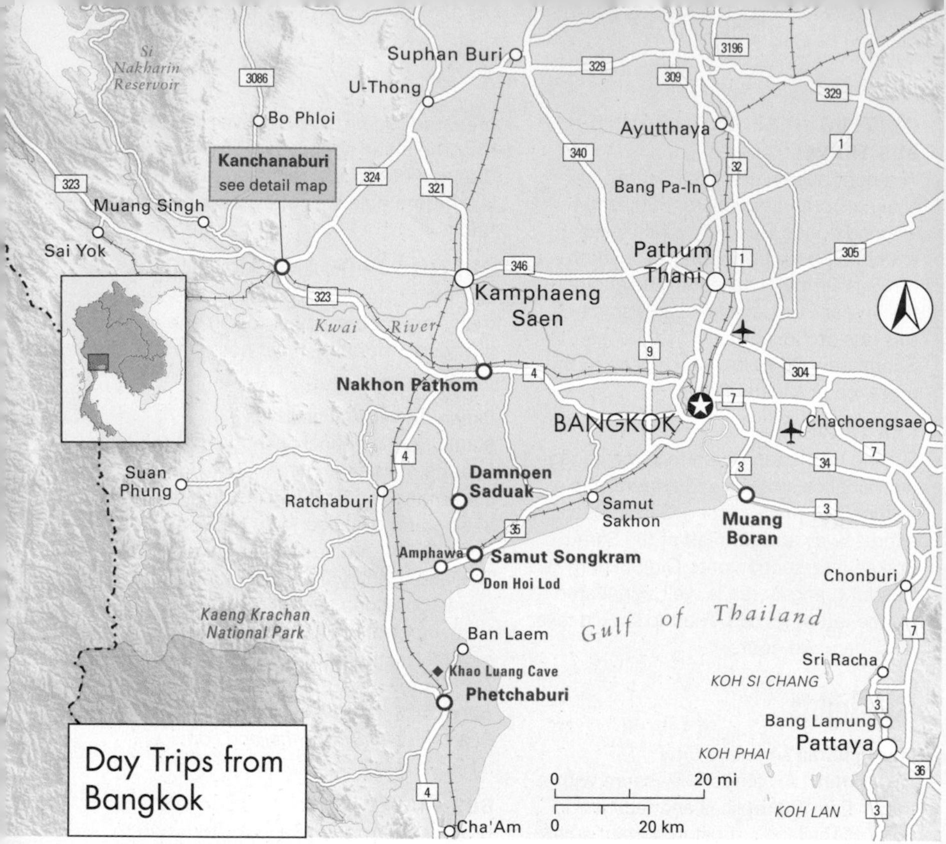

Hotels

Baan Sukchoke Country Resort
$ | **RESORT** | The small wooden bungalows surrounding a pond are a bit rickety, but they're clean and comfortable. **Pros:** countryside atmosphere; helpful staff; one of limited options near floating market. **Cons:** aging facilities; a bit out of town; not within walking distance of floating market. $ *Rooms from: B450* ✉ *103 Moo 5, T. Thanat* ☎ *032/254301* ▭ *No credit cards* *40 rooms* *No meals.*

Samut Songkram

72 km (45 miles) south of Bangkok.

The provincial town of Samut Songkram has little to recommend it, but the many nearby attractions make this an enjoyable day trip from Bangkok. There are terrific seafood restaurants along the waterfront at Don Hoi Lod; the area is also a good base for exploring some of the surrounding villages on the canal network, such as Amphawa, with its small floating market.

GETTING HERE AND AROUND

BUS TRAVEL

Buses depart from Bangkok's Southern Bus Terminal for Samut Songkram (1½ hours; B50) every hour from 3 am to 6:30 pm. Bus 996 can drop you off at Amphawa.

CAR TRAVEL

Route 35, the main road south to Samut Songkram (one hour), is mainly a two-lane highway that can be slow going if there's heavy traffic. Add an extra half hour to all trip times for possible delays.

SONGTHAEW TRAVEL

In town there are frequent songthaews to Don Hoi Lod and returning from Amphawa (10 minutes; up to B20). Drivers stop taking passengers at 5 pm.

HEALTH

EMERGENCY CONTACTS Mae Khlong Song Hospital ✉ *198/1 Ratrasit Rd.* ☎ *034/715001.*

SAFETY AND PRECAUTIONS

Amphawa can be crowded, especially during holidays. Keep a careful eye on your possessions. Make sure you keep an eye on the time if you are taking a songthaew from Don Hoi Lod to Amphawa.

Sights

Amphawa

TOWN | FAMILY | The charming village of Amphawa, 10 km (7 miles) by songthaew from Samuk Songkram, has a **floating market** similar to, but smaller than, the one in Damnoen Saduak—it is also touristy but less in-your-face about it with characterful cafés and boutiques, and because of this is often preferred. The market opens on Friday evening from 3 to 9, and Saturday and Sunday from 11 to 9. The food market in the street adjacent to the canal starts at around 1 pm. Featured in a Thai movie, popular **fireflies tours** allow you to enjoy both the market and the beautiful insect-lighted trees. The bugs are best seen from May to October and in the waning moon. The hour-long tours usually run every half hour from 6 to 9 pm. You can arrange a tour directly at the pier (B600 for a boat) or through your hotel (around B70 per person). Unless you have private transportation, you'll have to spend the night in Amphawa, but there are some lovely options. The last bus back to Bangkok is in the early evening. ✉ *Samut Songkram* 🎫 *Free.*

Don Hoi Lod

BODY OF WATER | FAMILY | On weekends Thai families flock to the village of Don Hoi Lod, about 3 km (2 miles) south of Samut Songkram, to feast on clams and other seafood dishes at tree-shaded restaurants and local fresh market at the mouth of the Mae Khlong River. The village is named after a local clam with a tubular shell, the fossilized remains of which are found on the riverbanks. The best times to view the fossils are March and April, when the water is low. The rest of the year you can also see the fossils in the early morning and in the evening at low tide. ✉ *Samut Songkram* ✣ *Off Rte. 35.*

Restaurants

Kunpao

$ | SEAFOOD | FAMILY | Among the last in a long row of seafood places in Don Hoi Lod, this restaurant on wooden stilts is usually packed with Thai families who come to enjoy the gentle breeze and seafood dishes. Try to get one of the few sit-on-the-floor tables directly above the water, and let your feet dangle down. **Known for:** dishes made with fresh local seafood like fried sea bass and horseshoe crab egg spicy salad; children's playground; busy on weekends and holidays. *Average main: B120* *1/3 Moo 4, Tambon Bang Pakong, Amphoe Mueang* *034/723703, 08/1941–0376* *www.thailandseafoods.com.*

Hotels

★ House of Passion

$$ | B&B/INN | This cozy boutique hotel is filled with character—rooms and suites feature four-poster beds, upcycled furniture and wood floors, with some duplexes also available. **Pros:** modern accommodation near floating market; free bicycles; romantic vibe good for couples. **Cons:** expensive weekend rates; not within walking distance of floating market; mismatched furniture not everyone's taste. *Rooms from: B2,500* *62 Moo 7, Bang Chang, Amphawa* *08/613–7838* *24 rooms, 4 suites* *Free breakfast.*

Thanicha Healthy Resort

$ | RESORT | In an old wooden house close to the market, this boutique hotel by the main canal is a perfect weekend escape from Bangkok. **Pros:** nice café and restaurant in front; free Wi-Fi in hotel; right next to floating market. **Cons:** busier and more expensive on weekends; car park often full; only basic amenities. *Rooms from: B1,590* *261 T. Ampawa A., Amphawa* *034/751942, 06/2324–2914* *www.thanicha.com* *25 rooms* *Free breakfast.*

Nakhon Pathom

56 km (35 miles) west of Bangkok.

Reputed to be Thailand's oldest city (it's thought to date from 150 BC), Nakhon Pathom was once the center of the Dvaravati kingdom, an affiliation of Mon city-states between the 6th and the 11th century. The region's first center of Buddhist learning, established about a millennium ago, it's home to the Buddhist monument Phra Pathom Chedi.

GETTING HERE AND AROUND

BUS TRAVEL

Buses depart from Bangkok's Southern Bus Terminal for Nakhon Pathom (one hour; B46) every hour from 5:30 am to 8 pm.

CAR TRAVEL

Driving west from Bangkok, allow an hour to get to Nakhon Pathom on Route 4.

TRAIN TRAVEL

From Bangkok, 10 trains a day run at regular intervals to Nakhon Pathom (1½ hours; from B14 to B20). Some of the Nakhon Pathom trains continue on to Phetchaburi (four hours; from B94 to B114) and points farther south. Trains to Kanchanaburi also stop in Nakhon Pathom.

Sights

Phra Pathom Chedi

RELIGIOUS SITE | The tallest stupa in the world, Phra Pathom Chedi tops out at 417 feet. Erected in the 6th century, the site's first chedi was destroyed in a Burmese attack in 1057. Surrounding the chedi is one of Thailand's most important temples, which contains the ashes of King Rama VI.

The terraces around the temple complex are full of fascinating statuary, including Chinese figures, a large reclining Buddha, and an unusual Buddha seated in a chair. By walking around the inner circle surrounding the chedi, you can see novice monks in their classrooms through arched stone doorways. Traditional dances are sometimes performed in front of the temple, and during Loi Krathong, a festival in November that celebrates the end of the rainy season, a fair is set up in the adjacent park. *Khwa T. Phrapathom Chedi Rd.* ✣ *Off Phetkasem Rd.* *B60.*

Phra Pathom Chedi National Museum

MUSEUM | Next to Phra Pathom Chedi is the Phra Pathom Chedi National

Continued on page 156

THAI MARKETS

by Hana Borrowman

For an authentic Thai shopping experience, forget air-conditioned malls and head to the traditional markets, or *talaats*. Take a deep breath and prepare for an intoxicating medley of colors, sounds, smells, and tastes.

Entrepreneurs set up shop wherever there's an open space—roadsides, footbridges, and bustling waterways. You'll find all sorts of intriguing items: caramelized crickets and still-wriggling eels; "potency" potions made from pigs' feet; fierce-looking hand weapons like elegant samurai swords and knife-edged brass knuckles; temple offerings; plastic toys; and clothing.

Markets are an integral part of Thai life. Locals stop by for a meal from their favorite food vendor or to sit at a coffee stall, gossiping or discussing politics. Whole families take part: You might see an old woman bargaining with a customer at a hardware stall while her grandchild sleeps in a makeshift hammock strung up beneath the table.

Damnoen Saduak's floating market.

GREAT FINDS

Low prices make impulse buys almost irresistible. Here are a few things to keep your eyes out for while you shop.

Housewares. You'll find metal "monks' bowls" like those used for alms-collection, cushions, wicker baskets, carved tables, and ornate daybeds. Polished coconut-shell spoons and wooden salad servers are more practical if you're not up for shipping home your wares. Small wooden bowls and utensils start at around B150.

Memorabilia. Toy *tuk-tuks* (three-wheeled cabs) made from old tin cans, sequined elephants sewn onto cushion covers, satin Muay Thai boxer shorts, wooden frogs that croak—all make great and inexpensive souvenirs, and most Thai markets have them in droves.

Jewelry. Throughout the country, hill-tribe women sell beautiful silver and beaded jewelry. Silver bangles start at B250 and chunky silver rings with semiprecious stones like opal and mother-of-pearl are B350 and up. You'll also find "precious" gemstones and crystals, but you're better off making serious purchases at reputable shops in Bangkok.

Silk. Thailand is famous for its bright, beautiful silks. Raw Thai silk has a relatively coarse texture and a matte finish; it's good value, and wonderful for curtains and upholstery. You'll also find bolts of less expensive shimmering satins, and ready-made items like pajamas, purses, and scarves.

Prices vary enormously—depending on quality and weight—from B100 to upwards of B700 a meter. To test for authenticity, hold the fabric up to the light: If it's pure silk, the color changes, but fake silk shines a uniformly whitish tone. You can also ask for a swatch to burn—pure fibers crumble to ash, while synthetics curl or melt.

Clothes. Markets have tons of clothing: the ubiquitous Thai fisherman pants; factory seconds from The Gap; knockoff designer jeans; and, invariably, frilly underwear. But some of Thailand's edgiest designers are touting more modern apparel at markets as well. It's hard to say whether these up-and-comers are following catwalk trends or vice-versa. Bangkok fashion houses like **Sretsis** (feminine dresses; 🌐 www.sretsis.com) and **Greyhound** (casual, unisex urbanwear; 🌐 www.greyhound.co.th) are good places to scope out styles beforehand. Prices vary greatly—a cheaply made suit could cost as little as B1,000, while an expertly tailored, high-quality version might be B20,000 or more. But it's difficult to determine quality unless you're experienced.

FLOATING MARKETS

Sunday morning at Damnoen Saduak.

Floating markets date from Bangkok's "Venice of the East" era in the 19th century, when canal-side residents didn't have to go to market—the market came to them. Many waterways have been filled in to create roads, so there are only a handful of floating markets left. These survivors have a nostalgic appeal, with vendors in straw hats peddling produce, flowers, snacks, and crafts against a backdrop of stilt houses and riverbanks.

Thailand's original floating market in Damnoen Saduak (⇨ *above*) is very famous, but it's also crowded and overpriced. Still, you can get a taste of the old river life here, in addition to lots of touristy souvenirs. If you visit, try to stay nearby so that you can arrive near dawn; the market is open from 6 AM till noon, but by 9 it's usually swarming with sightseers.

The Amphawa Floating market near Samut Songkram, set on a leafy waterway dotted with temples and traditional Thai homes, is less crowded and more authentic.

LOGISTICS

Many hotels and guesthouses can arrange a longtail boat and an oarsman for you. You can also just head to the pier, though it's a good idea to ask your hotel what going rates are first. Private boats start at around B500 an hour, but oarsmen may try to charge much more. Haggle hard, and don't get in a boat before you've agreed on price and duration. If you join a group of locals in a boat, you'll often pay a set rate per person.

Longtail boat.

SHOPPING KNOW-HOW

Most markets begin to stir around dawn, and morning is the best time to visit—it's not too hot, and most Thais do their marketing early in the day, so you'll get to watch all the local action. Avoid rainy days: The scene loses a lot of its allure when everything's covered in plastic sheets.

Flower market in Bangkok.

SHOPPING TIPS

■ Check prices at less touristy spots—Chinatown, Pratunam Market, and MBK in Bangkok—to get a sense of cost.

■ Keep money and valuables like cell phones tucked away.

■ Avoid tuk-tuk drivers who offer you a shopping tour. They'll pressure you to drop a lot of cash at their friends' stalls.

■ Look for the One Tambon One Product (OTOP) government stamp on market goods. A tambon is a subdistrict—there are over 7,000 in the country, and one handmade, locally sourced product is selected from each.

■ Steer clear of exotic animal products, such as lizard skins, ivory, tortoiseshell, and anything made of tiger. These products may come from endangered animals; if so, it's illegal to leave Thailand with them or bring them into the U.S. If not illegal, they may be counterfeit.

■ Only buy antiques at reputable shops; real Thai antiques cannot be exported without a license, which good shops provide. Most so-called antiques at markets are knockoffs.

■ Thai markets are full of counterfeits—DVDs, computer software, and designer clothes and accessories. In addition to being illegal, these items vary in quality, so examine the products and your conscience carefully before you buy.

Straw hats for sale.

HOW TO BARGAIN

Thais love theatrical bargaining, and it's customary to haggle over nearly everything. Here are some tips for getting a fair price. The most important thing is to have fun!

DO

■ Decide about how much you're willing to pay before you start bargaining.

■ Let the vendor set the opening price. This is the standard etiquette; vendors who make you go first may be trying to take you for a ride. Vendors who don't speak English may type their price into a calculator, and you can respond in kind.

■ Come equipped with a few Thai phrases, such as "How much is this?" "A discount?" and "Expensive!"

■ Bargain quietly, and if possible, when the vendor is alone. Vendors are unlikely to give big discounts in front of an audience.

■ Be polite, no matter what. Confidence and charming persistence are winning tactics in Thailand—not hostility.

■ Honor your lowest bid if it's accepted.

DON'T

■ Don't lose your temper or raise your voice. These are big no-no's in the land of smiles.

■ Don't hesitate to aim low. Your opening counteroffer should be around 50% or 60% of the vendor's price, and you can expect to settle for 10% to 30% off the initial price. If you're buying more than one item, shoot for a bigger discount.

■ Don't be afraid to walk away. Often the vendor will call you back with a lower price.

■ Don't get too caught up in negotiating. It's OK to back down if you really want something.

■ Don't bargain for food—prices are fixed.

Woman displaying Thai silk.

Museum, which contains Dvaravati artifacts such as images of the Buddha, stone carvings, and stuccos from the 6th to the 11th century. ✉ *Khwa T. Phrapathom Chedi Rd., Samut Songkram* 🎫 *Free.*

Sampran Riverside

GARDEN | FAMILY | Roses are just a part of this complex where herbs, bananas, and various flowers, including orchids, flourish. Within the complex are traditional houses where guests can participate in activities such as garland and pottery making. The park, popular with Thai families, has restaurants and a nice hotel with rooms starting at B2,300. ✉ *Km 32, Pet Kasem Rd., Samut Songkram* ☎ *034/322544* 🌐 *www.sampranriverside.com* 🎫 *From B40 per activity.*

Sanam Chandra Palace

CASTLE/PALACE | While still a prince, the future King Rama VI commissioned this palace, completed in 1911, that's notable architecturally for its French and British flourishes. The surrounding park, which includes ponds and broad lawns, is a lovely place to relax. English signs and translations provide information and guidance around the grounds. ✉ *Samut Songkram* ✣ *Follow Petchkasem Rd. 2½ km (1½ miles) west from Phra Pathom Chedi* 🎫 *Free.*

Phetchaburi

132 km (82 miles) south of Bangkok.

This small seaport town with many wats once linked the old Thai capitals of Sukhothai and Ayutthaya with trade routes on the South China Sea and Indian Ocean. Phetchaburi is famous for *khao chae,* a chilled rice dish with sweetmeats once favored by royals that has become a summer tradition in posh Bangkok hotels. You can find it around the day market on Phanit Charoen Road—look for people eating at stalls from small silver bowls—along with *khanom jeen thotman* (noodles with curried fish cake). The city was also a royal retreat during the reigns of Rama IV and Rama V (1851–1910) and has two palaces open to the public. Phetchaburi's wats are within or easily accessible on foot from the town center, particularly along Matayawong, Pongsuriya, and Phrasong roads. ■ **TIP→ Steer clear of the gangs of monkeys on the streets and around Khao Wang, especially with food in your hands.**

GETTING HERE AND AROUND

BIKE TRAVEL

A bike or a motorbike rented at Rabieng Guesthouse (B120 per day for a bike, from B150 per day for a motorbike) is a good way to get around town.

BUS TRAVEL

Phetchaburi-bound vans depart Bangkok's Mo Chit Bus Terminal (two hours; B200) every 30 minutes from 5 am to 9 pm. The bus lets you off at the side of the road near Big C supermarket, near a songtaew stop where you can hop on for B10. There is also a motorcycle taxi stand there with a few drivers who will be happy to help you—this is probably the easiest option. This area doesn't have many English speakers, so be patient.

CAR TRAVEL

If you're driving, take Route 35, the main road south from Bangkok, then continue on Route 4 to Phetchaburi Province. The trip takes 90 minutes. On the way back to Bangkok, there are two alternatives. Follow signs to Samut Songkram for the shorter trip along Route 35.

TRAIN TRAVEL

All trains to southern Thailand stop at Phetchaburi (three hours; from B94 to B114). The train station is north of Phetchaburi on Rot Fai Road. You can hire motorbikes taxis or tuk-tuks from the train or bus station to get to sights or downtown.

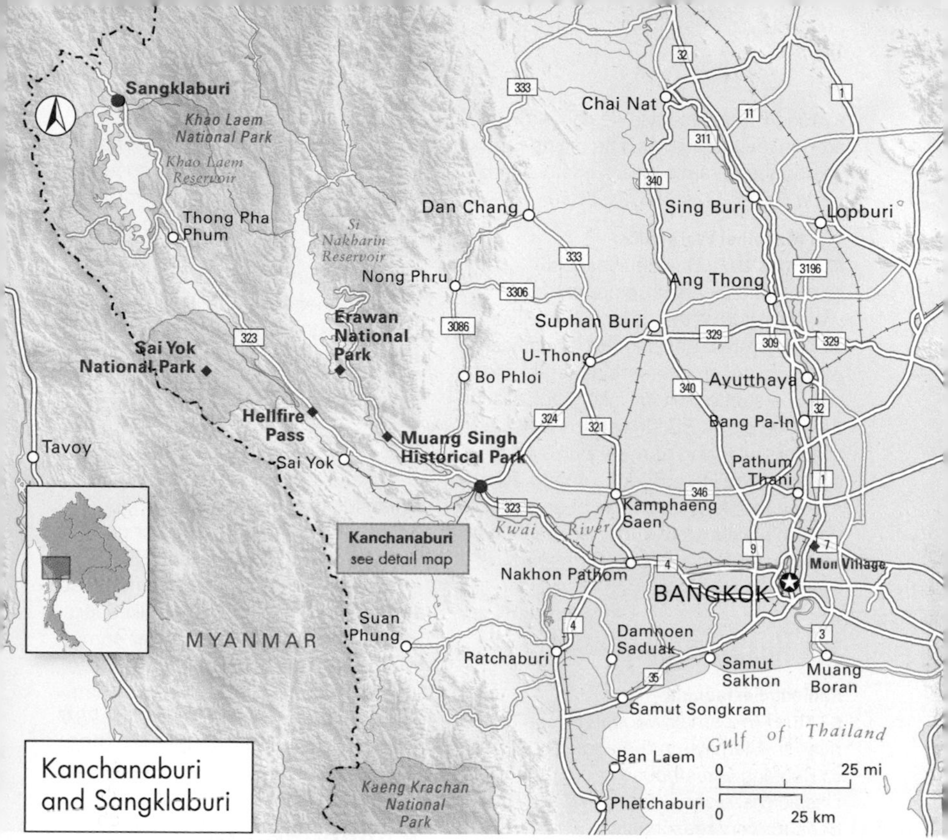

Kanchanaburi and Sangklaburi

Sights

Khao Luang Cave

CAVE | Studded with stalactites, this cave overflows with images of the Buddha, among them a 10-meter-long reclining one. Most were put in place by kings Rama IV and Rama V. For a donation of B20 or so to pay for the electricity, a nun will light up the rear of the cave for you. It is about a kilometer's walk from the entrance, but a shuttle service is provided for B15. **■TIP➔ The cave is best appreciated on a clear morning, between 9 and 10, when the sun shines in and reflects off the brass iconography.** ✉ *Phetchaburi* ✥ *Off Rot Fai Rd., 5 km (3 miles) north of Phra Nakhon* 🎫 *Free.*

Phra Nakhon Khiri Historical Park (*Khao Wang*)

NATIONAL/STATE PARK | On a forested hillside at the edge of Phetchaburi, the park includes one of King Rama IV's palaces and a series of temples and shrines. Many of these are set high on the hilltop and have good views. Monkeys are a major shoplifting hazard around the gift shops at the foot of the hill. Cable-car rides to the top and back are included in the admission price. ✉ *Phetchaburi* ✥ *Off Phetkasem Rd., east of Rte. 4* ☎ *032/428539, 032/425600* 🎫 *B200.*

Phra Ram Ratchaniwet

HOUSE | Intended as a rainy-season retreat by King Rama V and started in 1910, the palace was eventually completed by King Rama VI in 1916. Phra Ram Ratchaniwet was modeled on a palace of Germany's Kaiser Wilhelm and consequently has a grand European-style design with art-nouveau flourishes. The dining room has ornate ceramic tiles. ✉ *Ratchadamnoen Rd.* ☎ *032/428083* 🎫 *B50.*

Wat Mahathat Worawihan

RELIGIOUS SITE | This 800-year-old Khmer-influenced structure on the western side of the Phetchaburi River is a royal temple. Besides the magnificent architecture, an interesting feature of this wat is a subtle political joke. Look around the base of the Buddha statue outside the chapel. A ring of monkeylike Atlases supports the large Buddha image, except for one monkey which has been replaced with the likeness of a former Thai prime minister. ✉ *Bandai-it and Damnoen Kasem Rds.* 🎫 *Free.*

Restaurants

Rabieng Restaurant

$ | THAI | In a small wooden house by the river, this family-run restaurant attached to Rabieng Guesthouse serves many classic Thai dishes and a few Western ones for very reasonable prices. It opens early at 8 am but is one of just a few places in the area that stays open after sunset (until midnight daily). **Known for:** friendly service; traditional Thai dishes like spicy banana-blossom salad and the stuffed chicken with pandanus leaves; river views. $ *Average main: B100* ✉ *1 Shesrain Rd.* ☎ *032/425707* ▭ *No credit cards.*

Hotels

Rabieng Guesthouse

$ | B&B/INN | In a cluster of dark-wood plank buildings, these basic rooms are just big enough for beds. **Pros:** restaurant overlooking the river; walking distance to bus terminal; attentive staff. **Cons:** thin walls next to noisy road; shared bathrooms; small rooms. $ *Rooms from: B250* ✉ *1 Shesrain Rd.* ☎ *032/425707* ▭ *No credit cards* *8 rooms with shared bath* 🍽 *No meals.*

Royal Diamond Hotel

$ | HOTEL | About 3 km (2 miles) northwest of town, the Royal Diamond is one of Phetchaburi's few choices for those seeking a hotel instead of a guesthouse. **Pros:** close to Phra Nakhon Khiri Historical Park; clean and comfortable; rooms rather spacious. **Cons:** out of town; most rooms have no views; not modern. $ *Rooms from: B1,090* ✉ *555 Moo 1, Phetkasem Rd., Ban Rai Som* ☎ *032/411061 up to 70* 🌐 *www.royaldiamondhotel.com* *58 rooms* 🍽 *Free breakfast.*

White Monkey Guesthouse

$ | B&B/INN | One of the newer guesthouses in Petchaburi, White Monkey is simply decorated but cozy nonetheless. **Pros:** modern facilities; free bikes for guests; centrally located. **Cons:** some rooms with shared bath; limited occupancy; rooms accessible only by sets of stairs. $ *Rooms from: B900* ✉ *78/7 Khlong Krachang Rd.* ☎ *09/325–3885, 032/400187* *12 rooms* 🍽 *No meals.*

Kanchanaburi

140 km (87 miles) west of Bangkok.

Kanchanaburi is laid out along the Mae Khlong and Kwai Yai rivers. Several museums and war cemeteries document the building of the Thailand-Burma Railway during World War II and the high cost paid in death and suffering. A visit to some of these attractions will put into context the city's top one, the Bridge on the River Kwai.

GETTING HERE AND AROUND

BUS TRAVEL

Air-conditioned buses headed to Kanchanaburi leave from Bangkok's Southern Bus Terminal (two hours; B85) every 20 minutes from 5 am to 10:30 pm. Buses also leave eight times a day from Bangkok's Mo Chit Northern Bus Terminal (three hours; B115).

Kanchanaburi

Sights

1 Bridge on the River Kwai .. **A2**
2 Chong-Kai War Cemetery ... **B5**
3 JEATH War Museum **A2**
4 Kanchanaburi War Cemetery ... **C2**
5 Thailand-Burma Railway Centre **C2**
6 Wat Tham Khao Pun ... **B5**

Restaurants

1 Blue Rice ... **B2**
2 Kanchanaburi Night Market **C2**
3 Keeree Tara **A1**
4 River Kwai Floating Restaurant.. **B2**

Hotels

1 Apple Retreat and Guest-house........ **B2**
2 Felix River Kwai Resort **A1**
3 Pavilion Rim Kwai Resort **A1**
4 River Kwai Village Hotel......... **A1**
5 Sam's House **B2**
6 Smiley Frog Guesthouse. **B2**

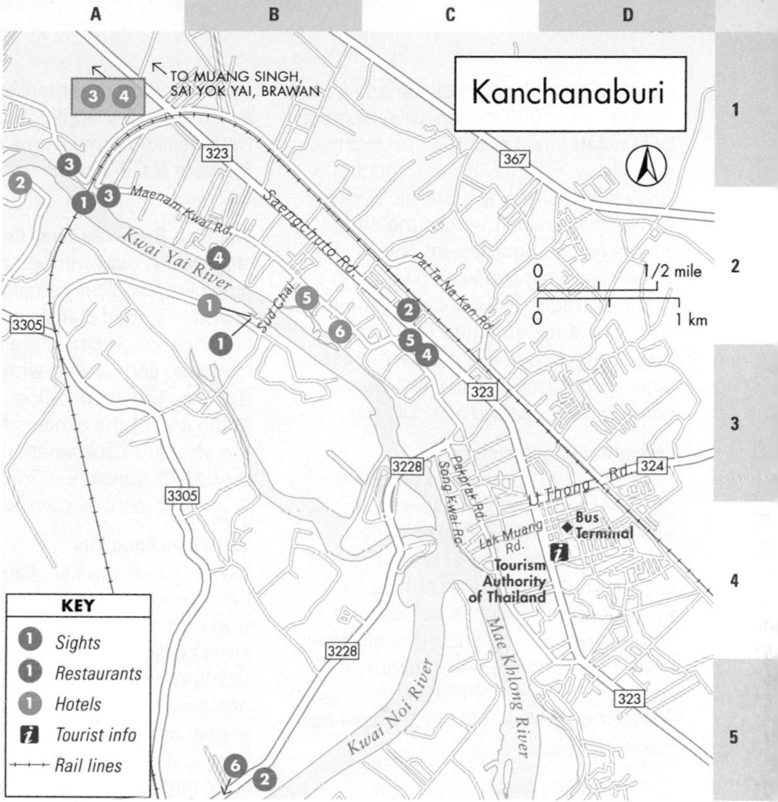

KEY

Sights
Restaurants
Hotels
Tourist info
Rail lines

TO MUANG SINGH, SAI YOK YAI, BRAWAN

Maenam Kwai Rd.
Saengchuto Rd.
Kwai Yai River
Pat Ta Na Kan Rd.
Sud Chai
U Thong Rd.
Pakprak Rd.
Song Kwai Rd.
Lak Muang Rd.
Bus Terminal
Tourism Authority of Thailand
Mae Khlong River
Kwai Noi River

0 1/2 mile
0 1 km

CAR TRAVEL

Allow two hours to reach Kanchanaburi along Route 4. The first half is on a busy truck route that continues to southern Thailand, but the second half is more pleasant, through agricultural land. The road to Kanchanaburi passes through Nakhon Pathom.

TAXI AND SONGTHAEW TRAVEL

In town, options for getting around include pedicabs and motorcycles with sidecars. Songthaews are better for longer forays out of town and can be flagged down. The few tuk-tuks and taxis are harder to find. Drivers are notorious for hiking up prices for tourists, so bring your best bargaining face.

TRAIN TRAVEL

Two Kanchanaburi-bound trains (three hours; B100) leave every day from Bangkok Noi Railway Station, on the Thonburi side of the Chao Phraya River.

VISITOR AND TOUR INFORMATION

CONTACT Tourism Authority of Thailand (*TAT*) ✉ *325 Saengchuto Rd.* ☎ *034/511200* 🌐 *www.tourismthailand.org.*

Sights

★ Bridge on the River Kwai

BRIDGE/TUNNEL | Kanchanaburi is most famous as the location of this bridge, a section of the Thailand-Burma Railway immortalized in director David Lean's epic 1957 film *The Bridge on the River Kwai.* During World War II, the Japanese, with whom Thailand sided, forced about 16,000 prisoners of war and from 50,000 to 100,000 civilian slave laborers from neighboring countries to construct the railway, a supply route through the jungles of Thailand and Burma. Sure-footed visitors can walk across the bridge, whose arched portions are original. In December a big fair takes place with a sound-and-light show depicting the Allied bombing of the structure late in the war. Next to the bridge is a plaza with restaurants and souvenir shops. ✉ *Maenamkwai and New Zealand Rds.* 🎫 *Free.*

Chong-Kai War Cemetery

CEMETERY | The serene and simple resting place of many of the soldiers forced to work on the Thailand-Burma Railway has neatly organized rows of grave markers. On the grounds of a former hospital for prisoners of war, the cemetery is a little out of the way, and therefore rarely visited. To get here, hire a tuk-tuk or moto-taxi for about B60. ✉ *Kanchanaburi* ✣ *West side of river, 3 km (2 miles) from town* 🎫 *Free.*

JEATH War Museum

MUSEUM | The letters in the first part of its name an acronym for Japan, England, America, Australia, Thailand, and Holland, this museum sits a little more than 2 km (1 mile) downriver from the Bridge on the River Kwai. The museum, founded in 1977 by a monk from the adjoining Wat Chaichumpol, is housed in a replica of the bamboo huts that were used to hold prisoners of war. On display are railway spikes, aerial photographs, newspaper clippings, and original sketches by ex-prisoners depicting their living conditions. ✉ *Wat Chaichumpol, Bantai* ☎ *034/515263* 🎫 *B30.*

Kanchanaburi War Cemetery

CEMETERY | Next to noisy Saengchuto Road, this cemetery has row upon row of neatly laid-out graves: 6,982 Australian, British, and Dutch prisoners of war are laid to rest here. The remains of the American POWs were returned to the United States during the Eisenhower administration. A remembrance ceremony is held every April 25th, Australia and New Zealand Army Corps Day. ✉ *Saengchuto Rd.* ✣ *Across from train station* 🎫 *Free.*

Thailand-Burma Railway Centre

MUSEUM | A walk through the center's nine chronologically arranged galleries provides a good overview of the railway's history. Though small, the center is well designed and packed with informative displays. The second-floor coffee shop at the end of the exhibits has a view of the adjacent Kanchanaburi War Cemetery. ✉ *73 Jaokannun Rd.* ☎ *034/512721* 🌐 *www.tbrconline.com* 🎫 *B140.*

Wat Tham Khao Pun

CAVE | One of the Kanchanaburi area's best cave-temples, the wat displays Buddhist and Hindu statues and figurines amid stalagmites and stalactites. During World War II the Japanese used the cave complex as storerooms. A local may appear at the small shrine outside the cave and offer to direct you, but you can walk through the cave by yourself. Paying a donation to enter the cave is voluntary. ✉ *Kanchanaburi* ✣ *Rte. 3228, west side of river, 1½ km (1 mile) southwest of Chong-Kai War Cemetery* 🎫 *Free.*

Restaurants

Blue Rice Restaurant

$ | **THAI** | This quiet garden restaurant is decked out in wood with lots of local flourishes, from the thatched roof to the colorful woven tablecloths and settings. The signature dish, massaman curry, is popular with the backpacker crowd—thick, mildly spiced, and made with heaps of palm sugar, it's a good balm for stomachs struggling with chili overdose. **Known for:** authentic spicy dishes; cooking classes; accommodations also available. 💲 *Average main: B120* ✉ *153/4 Sutjai Bridge, Moo 4, Thamakhan Muang* ☎ *034/512017, 062/324–5879*

🌐 *www.applenoikanchanaburi.com/our-apples-restaurants/.*

Kanchanaburi Night Market

$ | **THAI** | For cheap eats, the market opens early in the evening with dozens of vendors selling Thai soups, rice dishes, satays, and other delights. The blended frozen fruit drinks are particularly good. **Known for:** good variety; cheap meals. *Average main: B40* *Saengchuto Rd.* *Next to train station* *No credit cards.*

Keeree Tara

$ | **THAI** | With a great view of the River Kwai Bridge from its terraces and lots of lush greenery, this floating restaurant has a sophisticated yet comfortable feel. It caters mostly to Thais, so the food can be quite spicy—if you can't handle it, ask the waiter to tone the heat down (say "*mai phet*"). **Known for:** popular with locals; authentic Thai dishes; great fish and curries. *Average main: B150* *43/1 River Kwai Rd.* *034/513855.*

River Kwai Floating Restaurant

$ | **SEAFOOD** | Follow the crowds to this open-air floating restaurant in the shadow of the railway bridge, where the offering includes aromatic Thai favorites and seafood freshly caught in the Kwai Yai and Kwai Noi rivers. The chefs tone down the food considerably for foreigners, so if you want yours spicy, you'll have to say so. **Known for:** popular with tourists; close to attractions; local delicacies like a fish called yeesok. *Average main: B130* *425 Maenamkwai Rd.* *Beside River Kwai Bridge* *034/512595* *No credit cards.*

Hotels

Apple Retreat and Guesthouse

$ | **RESORT** | **FAMILY** | At this longtime favorite, choose between guesthouse rooms set around a central courtyard and simple, comfortable rooms in a two-story building on the opposite side of the river. **Pros:** good restaurant; knowledgeable owners; tours and cooking classes available. **Cons:** can fill quickly in high season; simple decor; long walk to attractions. *Rooms from: B990* *153/4 Moo 4, Thamakhan Muang* *034/512017, 081/948–4646* *www.applenoi-kanchanaburi.com* *16 rooms* *No meals.*

Felix River Kwai Resort

$$ | **RESORT** | **FAMILY** | Kanchanaburi's first luxury hotel has faded somewhat, but it's still a good value. **Pros:** right by the famous bridge; wonderful tropical garden; good for families. **Cons:** taxi required for trips to city center; aging decor; inconsistent Wi-Fi. *Rooms from: B3,450* *9/1 Moo 3, Tambon Thamakham* *034/551–00023, 02/634–4111 reservations center* *www.felix-riverkwai.co.th* *255 rooms* *Free breakfast.*

Pavilion Rim Kwai Resort Kanchanaburi

$ | **RESORT** | Wealthy Bangkok residents who want to retreat into the country without giving up creature comforts head to this resort near the Erawan Waterfall. **Pros:** some rooms have great views; huge pool; pretty garden. **Cons:** far from town, a bit outdated; restaurants are not very good. *Rooms from: B1,600* *79/2 Moo 4, Km 9, Ladya-Erawan Rd., Tambon Wangdong* *034/513800* *www.pavilionhotels.com/rimkwai* *194 rooms* *Free breakfast.*

River Kwai Village Hotel

$$ | **RESORT** | Most of the simple rooms in this jungle hideaway in the River Kwai Valley are in single-story log cabins, but more adventurous types can opt for "raftels"—rooms on rafts floating in the river. **Pros:** jungle location; river views; hot spring on-site. **Cons:** very far from town; no nighttime entertainment; dated. *Rooms from: B3,400* *72/12 Moo 4, Tambon Thasaso* *083/242–1120, 02/251–7828 in Bangkok* *www.riverkwaivillage.com* *249 rooms, 26 raftels* *Free breakfast.*

Sam's House

$ | **RESORT** | A popular launching pad for treks, Sam's House has a trio of air-conditioned floating rooms that are nice, if a little cramped, as well as less expensive rooms set away from the river. **Pros:** some rooms have nice river views; can arrange tours; well priced. **Cons:** more expensive than other budget options; lots of mosquitoes; books up fast. *Rooms from: B600* *14/2 River Kwai Rd.* *034/515956* *www.samsguesthouse.com* *No credit cards* *31 rooms* *No meals.*

Smiley Frog Guesthouse

$ | **B&B/INN** | Popular with backpackers, the bungalow rooms here are small and spartan. **Pros:** cheap single rooms; nice garden with hammocks; clean. **Cons:** staff lacks warmth; restaurant has no view; some rooms need renovation. *Rooms from: B100* *28 Soi China, at River Kwai Rd.* *034/514579* *www.guesthouse-343.business.site* *55 rooms, 14 with shared bath* *No meals.*

Activities

RAFTING

Daylong rafting trips on the Kwai Yai or Mae Khlong rivers allow you to venture far into the jungle. The mammoth rafts, which resemble houseboats, are often divided into separate sections for eating, sleeping, and sunbathing. **TIP→ Be careful when taking a dip—the currents can sometimes suck a swimmer down.** Rates start at about B450. Longer trips are also available.

TREKKING

Jungle treks of one to four days are possible all over the region. They typically include bamboo rafting, visits to Karen villages, sampling local food, and sometimes a cultural performance. Stick to tour companies with Tourism Authority of Thailand licenses, which will be prominently displayed on the premises.

Good Times Travel

TOUR—SPORTS | A reputable agency with a good track record, Good Times offers all the usual highlights, including national parks, rafting, caves, and Karen village stays. The agency's day trips and multiday excursions depart from Kanchanaburi or Bangkok; the price per person depends on the size of your group. *63/1 River Kwai Rd.* *034/915484, 08/1913–7758* *www.good-times-travel.com* *From B2,450 per person (2 participants).*

Shopping

Blue sapphires from the Bo Phloi mines, 45 km (28 miles) north of Kanchanaburi Town, are for sale at many shops and stalls in the plaza near the bridge. The price is determined by the size and color of the stone, and, as usual, your bargaining skills. You'll do best when there are few tourists around and business is slow. Stick to stalls with licenses.

Greater Kanchanaburi Province

The third-largest province in Thailand, Kanchanaburi has scenic jungles, rivers, waterfalls, and mountains, especially near Sangklaburi, as you approach the Myanmar border. For centuries it was a favorite invasion route into Siam for the Burmese. Today it is home to Karen and Mon communities, whose villages can be visited.

GETTING HERE AND AROUND

The region is easily accessible by car. Roads 323 and 3199 take you to the main sights. It's also quite easy to travel around by public transportation, although package tours can be helpful if you have limited time. Reaching less-popular sights, such as Muang Singh Historical Park, is complicated if you don't have private transportation. Consider hiring a songthaew (around B750 for half a day). Public buses from Kanchanaburi leave the bus station, or from Saengchuto Road, close to the guesthouse area on River Kwai Road. There's also a private minibus office near the main bus station; minibuses go to many places in the province but are more expensive than public buses and fill up quickly. Sai Yok Noi National Park is accessible by train.

Sights

★ Erawan National Park

NATIONAL/STATE PARK | Some of Kanchanaburi Province's most spectacular scenery can be found in this park. The main attraction, **Erawan Waterfall,** has seven tiers; the topmost supposedly resembles the mythical three-headed elephant (Erawan) belonging to the Hindu god Indra. Getting to the top requires a steep 2-km (1-mile) hike. Comfortable footwear is essential for the two-hour trek, and don't forget to bring water. You can swim at each level of the waterfall (levels two through five are the most popular). The first tier has a small café, and there are several others near the visitor center. There are also eight-person bungalows costing from B800 to B2,400—the ones nearest the waterfall are quieter.

Five caves are among the massive park's other highlights. One of the caves, **Ta Duang,** has wall paintings, and another, **Ruea,** has prehistoric coffins. The caves are much farther away and are accessed via a different road. About 2 km (1 mile) from the park is Erawan Village; songthaews (B500 to B600) leave from its market and travel to the park entrance and the caves. Erawan-bound Bus 8170 leaves Kanchanaburi's bus station every 50 minutes; the trip takes 90 minutes. ✉ *Erawan National Park, Kanchanaburi* ☎ *034/574222, 034/574234* 🌐 *www.dnp.go.th* 🎫 *B300.*

★ Hellfire Pass

MUSEUM | The museum at Hellfire Pass is a moving memorial to the Allied prisoners of war who built the River Kwai railway, 12,399 of whom died in the process. Along with a film and exhibits, there's a 4½-km (3-mile) walk along a section of the railway, including the notorious Hellfire Pass, one of the most grueling sections to build. The pass got its name from the fire lanterns that flickered on the mountain walls as the men worked through the night. Many people do the walk in the early morning, before the museum opens and before it gets too hot. Allow 2½ hours round-trip for the walk. Take plenty of water and snacks; there's a small shack near the museum that sells drinks, but not much food. The pass can be busy on weekends (when an average of 500 people a day visit). Bus 8203 (two hours) makes the trip to the museum. The last bus back to Kanchanaburi is at 4 pm. The drive by car takes about an hour. ✉ *Rte. 323, Km 66, Kanchanaburi* ☎ *034/919605* 🌐 *www.dva.gov.au/about-dva/publications/commemorations-and-war-graves/hellfire-pass-memorial* 🎫 *Free.*

Muang Singh Historical Park

NATIONAL/STATE PARK | King Chulalongkorn reportedly discovered this 13th- to 14th-century Khmer settlement while traveling along the Kwai Noi River. The restored remains of the city range from mere foundations to a largely intact, well-preserved monument and building complex. There are also examples of Khmer statues and pottery and a prehistoric burial site. You can navigate the expansive grounds with the aid of taped commentary in English, Thai, or French, available at the park's entrance. Bicycle rentals cost around B20 per hour. If you don't want to make the 45-minute drive from Kanchanaburi, take the train to Tha Kilen Station (one hour; B15); the park is a 1-km (½-mile) walk west. There are lodgings and a small café on the grounds.

⊠ *Tha Kilen* ☏ *034/670–2645* 🌐 *www.muangsinghp.com* 🎫 *B100.*

Sai Yok National Park

NATIONAL/STATE PARK | The national park's main attraction is **Sai Yok Yai waterfall,** which flows into the Kwai Noi River. The waterfall, an easy walk from the visitor center, is single tier and not nearly as spectacular as Erawan's. More unique are the **bat caves,** 2 km (1 mile) past the waterfall. They are the only place you can see the thumb-size Kitti's hog-nosed bat, the world's smallest mammal. Rent flashlights at the visitor center. Other caves worth visiting include Tham Wang Badan and Lawa Cave.

This part of the park has several options for accommodations, all without electricity. The private raft houses on the Kwai Noi River are the more scenic choices. The accommodations near the waterfall have inexpensive restaurants that are more pleasant than the food stalls near the visitor center.

Driving here from Bangkok or Kanchanaburi you'll pass **Sai Yok Noi waterfall,** also within the park's boundaries. Despite being taller than Sai Yok Yai, Sai Yok Noi has less water, but there's enough to swim in from June to November, when the area is often packed with Thai families on weekends. ⊠ *Park headquarters, Rte. 323, Km 97, Sai Yok* ☏ *034/686024* 🌐 *www.dnp.go.th* 🎫 *B300.*

Sangklaburi

203 km (126 miles) northwest of Kanchanaburi.

This sleepy town sits on a large lake created by the Khao Laem Dam. There was once a Mon village here, but when the dam was built in 1983 it was almost completely covered by water. (Some parts, including a temple, are still visible beneath the surface.) The Mon people were relocated to a village on the shore opposite Sangklaburi.

Due to its proximity to Myanmar's border, Sangklaburi is also home to Karen and Bangladeshi communities, whose residents you'll spot in the town's small night market. Jungle trekking and visits to Karen villages are popular activities for visitors.

GETTING HERE AND AROUND

BUS TRAVEL

Air-conditioned buses from Bangkok's Northern Bus Terminal leave for Sangklaburi four times a day (6½ hours; B330). The last direct Bangkok-bound bus leaves Sangklaburi early in the afternoon. Air-conditioned buses from Kanchanaburi (three hours) leave hourly between 7:30 am and 4:30 pm. Guesthouses are accessible by motorcycle taxi (B10) or songthaew (B60) from the station.

CAR TRAVEL

The 2½- to 3-hour drive from Kanchanaburi, on well-paved Route 323, passes fields of pomelo, corn, and banana palms. Myanmar's mist-shrouded mountains are in the distance.

MOTORCYCLE TAXI TRAVEL

Motorcycle taxis (B10–B20) are the favored way to get around this sprawling provincial town. For longer trips, ask your hotel to arrange car transport.

Sights

Mon Village

TOWN | To make way for Khao Laem Dam, a village settled a half century ago by Mon people from Myanmar was relocated to the shore opposite Sangklaburi. The village has a temple with Indian and Burmese influences and a bronze-color pyramid chedi that's beautifully illuminated at night. A dry-goods market in the village sells Chinese and Burmese clothes and trinkets, with Mon dishes available at nearby food stalls. Get here

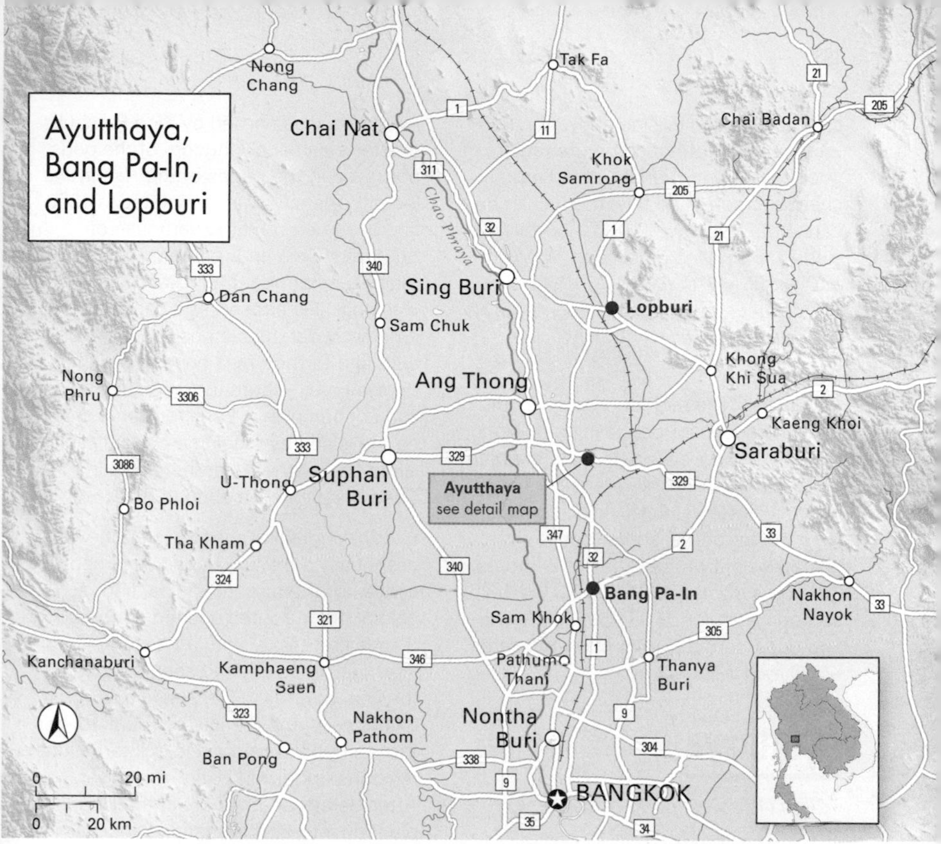

Ayutthaya, Bang Pa-In, and Lopburi

by car or boat, or walk across Thailand's longest wooden bridge.

Restaurants

Six or seven guesthouses are on the lakeside road, all with views of the wooden bridge and the Mon village. They all have restaurants, and most offer Burmese and Mon food such as *haeng leh curry* (a country dish made of whatever ingredients are on hand, but often including pork) and the coconut-and-noodle dish *kao sawy,* usually made with chicken. The temple's lights shimmer on the water at night. Other than watching this mesmerizing image, nightlife here consists of a karaoke bar and a noodle soup stall at the market that sells beer and local whiskey until 2 am.

Burmese Inn Restaurant

$ | **THAI** | This terrace restaurant, covered in classic Thai wood furniture, is nestled in a little garden overlooking the wooden bridge and the lake. You can order local fish dishes, Thai and Burmese specialties, as well as salads, sandwiches, and Western-style breakfasts. **Known for:** Burmese specialties like laphae to (salad of nuts, beans, and fermented tea leaves); nice views; restaurant of Burmese Inn guesthouse. *Average main: B70* *Burmese Inn, 52/3 Moo 3, Tambon Nongloo* *034/595146* *www.burmese-inn.com/en/restaurant* *No credit cards.*

Hotels

Burmese Inn

$ | **B&B/INN** | These homey bungalows, run by an Austrian and his Thai wife, sit on a flower-filled hillside above the lake. **Pros:** lots of information on the region; good restaurant; friendly staff. **Cons:** cheapest rooms are tiny; rooms can be dark; not perfectly clean. $ *Rooms from: B600* ✉ *52/3 Moo 3, Tambon Nongloo* ☎ *034/595146, 086/168–1801* 🌐 *www.burmese-inn.com/en* *19 rooms* 🍴 *No meals.*

P Guest House

$ | **B&B/INN** | The stone bungalows here sit in a stepped garden leading down to the lake. **Pros:** wooden deck for sunbathing and swimming; all rooms are very clean; nice views. **Cons:** no air-conditioning in most rooms; some rooms with shared bath; front desk is not 24 hours. $ *Rooms from: B400* ✉ *81/2 Moo 1, Tambon Nongloo* ☎ *034/595061* 🌐 *www.p-guesthouse.com* 💳 *No credit cards* *35 rooms* 🍴 *No meals.*

Ayutthaya

72 km (45 miles) north of Bangkok.

★ A UNESCO World Heritage Site, carefully preserved Ayutthaya provides a fascinating snapshot of ancient Siam. Scattered ruins testify to the kingdom's brutal demise at the hands of the Burmese in 1767, while broad thoroughfares preserve a sense of its former greatness. Although the modern town is on the eastern bank of the Pa Sak, most of the temples are on an island. An exception is Wat Yai Chai Mongkol, a short tuk-tuk ride away. Ayutthaya is best appreciated in a historical context, and a visit to the Historical Study Center is a must for first-time visitors.

Certain sites are guaranteed to take your breath away—Wat Phra Si Sanphet, Wat Yai Chai Mongkol, Wat Phra Mahathat, and Wat Ratchaburana, to name a few. Aside from the temples, Ayutthaya's friendly guesthouses, welcoming people, and floating restaurants make for a refreshing change from Bangkok.

Ayutthaya was named by King Ramatibodi after a mythical kingdom of the gods portrayed in the pages of the *Ramayana* legend. The city was completed in 1350 and became both a powerhouse of Southeast Asia and reputedly one of the region's most beautiful royal capitals. It was originally chosen as a capital for its eminently defensible position, lying on an island formed by a bend of the Chao Phraya River, where it meets the Pa Sak and Lopburi rivers. Early residents created the island by digging a curving canal along the northern perimeter, linking the Chao Phraya to the Lopburi River.

Ayutthaya quickly changed from being essentially a military base to an important center for the arts, medicine, and technology. Trade routes opened up following Siam's first treaty with a Western nation (Portugal, in 1516), and soon afterward the Dutch, English, Japanese and, most influentially, the French, accelerated Ayutthaya's rise to importance in international relations under King Narai the Great. After Narai's death in 1688, the kingdom plunged into internal conflict and was laid waste by Burmese invading forces in 1767.

GETTING HERE AND AROUND

BUS TRAVEL

Hourly buses to Ayutthaya (1½ hours) leave Bangkok's Mo Chit Northern Bus Terminal between 6 am and 7 pm. Tickets cost B50 for the 1½-hour trip.

CAR TRAVEL

Driving to Ayutthaya from Bangkok is an easy day trip once you're beyond the congestion of the big city. Kanchanaphisek Road, Bangkok's outer ring road, is the best route, costing around B130 in tolls. Following this road will bring you to Bang Pa-In—a good opportunity to visit the Royal Palace before continuing to Ayutthaya.

TAXI AND TUK-TUK TRAVEL

All forms of local transport are available from samlors to songthaews, but the brightly colored tuk-tuks are most popular. Tuk-tuks can be hired for an hour for about B300 or the day for about B1,200 to B1,500 and make easier work of Ayutthaya's historical sites. Though the island site of the Old City is quite compact, don't be tempted to tour it on foot; hire a tuk-tuk (about B600 for an afternoon) or a three-wheel bicycle cab (about B500). You can also rent a bicycle for about B50 a day. Nong Nine restaurant directly across from the train station is a good place to grab a bicycle or motorbike as soon as you arrive (✉ *Ho Rattanachai* ☎ *081/9464–005*).

TRAIN TRAVEL

The Northeastern Line, which heads all the way up to Isan, has frequent service from Bangkok to Ayutthaya. Beginning at 4:30 am, trains depart about every 40 minutes from Bangkok's Hua Lamphong Station, arriving in Ayutthaya 80 minutes later.

MONEY MATTERS

ATMs and exchange services are abundant on Naresuan Road in Ayutthaya and in Lopburi on Ratchadamnoen Road.

TIMING

Ayutthaya can be visited on a day trip from Bangkok, but the city really warrants a longer stay. Besides the temple ruins there are many other attractions—such as boat tips on the Chao Praya River. Ayutthaya is an excellent base for exploring the surrounding region.

VISITOR AND TOUR INFORMATION

CONTACT Tourist Authority of Thailand (TAT) ✉ *108/22 Moo 4, Si Sanphet Rd.* ☎ *035/246–0767* 🌐 *www.tourismthailand.org.*

Sights

Chao Sam Phraya National Museum

MUSEUM | This museum on spacious grounds in the center of the Old City was opened by the king and queen of Thailand in 1961. Its many exhibits include Buddhist sculpture from the Dvaravati, Lopburi, Ayutthayan, and U-Thong periods. Also on display is a jewel-encrusted sword with which one Ayutthayan prince killed his brother in an elephant-back duel. ✉ *Rotchana Rd.* ↔ *At Si San Phet Rd.* ☎ *035/241587* 🎫 *B150.*

Viharn Phra Mongkol Bopitr

RELIGIOUS SITE | When this temple's roof collapsed in 1767, one of Thailand's biggest and most revered bronze Buddha images was revealed. It lay here uncovered for almost 200 years before a huge modern viharn was built in 1951. Historians have dated the image back to 1538. ✉ *Off Naresuan Rd.* 🎫 *Free.*

Wat Phanan Choeng

RELIGIOUS SITE | This bustling temple complex on the banks of the Lopburi River is an interesting diversion from the dormant ruins that dominate Ayutthaya. A short B3 ferry ride across the river sets the scene for its dramatic origins. The temple was built in 1324 (26 years before Ayutthaya's rise to power) by a U-Thong king in atonement for the death of his fiancée. Instead of bringing his bride, a Chinese princess, into the city himself, the king arranged an escort for her. Distraught at what she interpreted to be a lackluster welcome, the princess threw herself into the river (at the site of the current temple) and drowned. ✉ *Ayutthaya* ↔ *East of the Old City* 🎫 *Free.*

★ Wat Phra Mahathat

RELIGIOUS SITE | Building began on this royal monastery in 1374 and was completed during the reign of King Ramesuan (1388–95). The tree-shaded, parklike grounds, a pleasant place to linger, contain what's left of the monastery's 140-foot prang. The brick Khmer-style

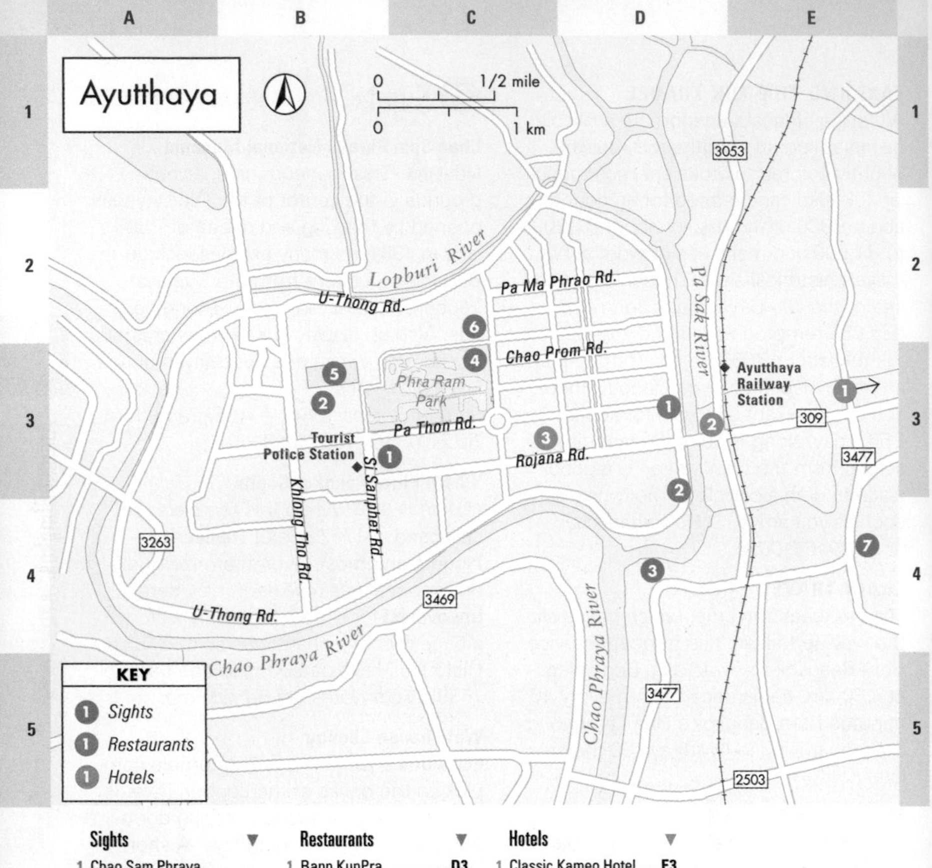

Sights

1 Chao Sam Phraya National Museum....... **B3**
2 Viharn Phra Mongkol Bopitr **B3**
3 Wat Phanan Choeng ... **D4**
4 Wat Phra Mahathat **C3**
5 Wat Phra Si Sanphet... **B3**
6 Wat Ratchaburana **C2**
7 Wat Yai Chai Mongkhon................ **E4**

Restaurants

1 Bann KunPra **D3**
2 Pae Krung Kao **D3**

Hotels

1 Classic Kameo Hotel **E3**
2 Krungsri River Hotel.... **D3**
3 Luang Chumni Village ... **C3**

prang, which collapsed twice between 1610 and 1628, and again in the early 20th century, barely reflects its former glory. Partially in ruins, the prang is said to contain relics of the Lord Buddha. It and the beheaded Buddhas that remain in Wat Phra Mahathat are a result of the Burmese sacking of the temple in 1767. ✉ *Sois Naresuan and Chikun* 🎫 *B50.*

Wat Phra Si Sanphet

RELIGIOUS SITE | The royal family worshipped at this wat, Ayutthaya's largest temple. The 14th-century structure lost its 50-foot Buddha in 1767, when the invading Burmese melted it down for its 374 pounds of gold. The trio of chedis survived and are the best existing examples of Ayutthaya architecture; enshrining the ashes of several kings, they stand as eternal memories of a golden age. If the design looks familiar, it's because Wat Phra Si Sanphet was the model for Wat Phra Keo at the Grand Palace in Bangkok. Beyond the monuments you can find a grassy field where the Royal Palace once stood. The foundation is all that remains of the palace that was home to 33 kings. ✉ *Naresuan Rd.* 🎫 *B50.*

Wat Ratchaburana

RELIGIOUS SITE | Across from Wat Phra Mahathat stands Wat Ratchaburana, whose Khmer-style prang dominates the skyline. King Borommaracha II (Chao Sam Phraya) built this temple in 1424 to commemorate the death of his two older brothers, whose duel for the throne ironically left him as king. Their relics, including their swords, were buried in a crypt under the prang's base, which was looted in 1957. Arrests were made, however, and the retrieved treasures can now be seen in the Chao Sam Phraya National Museum. ✉ *Sois Naresuan and Chikun* 🎫 *B50.*

Wat Yai Chai Mongkol

RELIGIOUS SITE | King Naresuan constructed the enormous chedi at Wat Yai Chai Mongkol, the largest in Ayutthaya, after defeating the Burmese crown prince during a battle atop elephants in 1593. A recent painting of the battle is one of the temple's highlights. The complex, parts of which date to 1357, was totally restored in 1982. Linger a while to pay your respects to the huge reclining Buddha, or climb to the top for a spectacular view. The site closes at 5 pm, but you can enter after that if the gates are left open, as they often are. The view at sunset is beautiful, and you'll completely escape the crowds. ✉ *Ayutthaya* ✣ *Off Rte. 3477, 1 km (½ mile) south of Rte. 309* 🎫 *B20.*

Restaurants

Bann KunPra

$ | **THAI** | Handsome locally fired floor tiles are among the original features of the century-old teak home this atmospheric old restaurant occupies. Step onto the riverside terrace and you could be in Venice—the waterway throbs with life, with tiny tugs pulling impossibly large barges loaded with rice, and a small jetty where guests get picked up for a dinner cruise. **Known for:** nice views; guest rooms above restaurant; seafood dishes. 💲 *Average main: B150* ✉ *48 Moo 3, Huarattanachai U-Thong Rd.* ☎ *035/241978.*

Pae Krung Kao

$ | **THAI** | An appealing mélange of local flora and traditional Thai decor greets patrons as they enter this charming bar and restaurant on the bank of the Pa Sak River. The visual delights continue in the low-ceilinged dining areas, which are packed with collectibles, from old bottles to timepieces, and half the restaurant sits on a pontoon floating on the water. **Known for:** traditional Thai food; closes early at 9 pm; opens early at 10 am. 💲 *Average main: B150* ✉ *4 Moo 2, U-Thong Rd.* ☎ *035/241555.*

Hotels

A stay in Ayutthaya allows you to wander among the ruins at night, a romantic experience indeed. Most tourists leave

Did You Know

Wat Phanan Choeng's central Buddha statue is surrounded by hundreds of small Buddha figures, which sit in niches along the temple walls. Each figure honors someone who has made a substantial donation to the temple.

Ayutthaya by 4 pm, but those who remain are treated to a less hectic and more genuine version of Thai hospitality. This is particularly the case at the small-scale guesthouses along the waterfront, some in historic, beautifully restored timber-built homes. These lodgings often provide far better value than Ayutthaya's older, more established hotels, which look impressive from afar but often have rooms of questionable or no taste and lack a personal touch.

★ Classic Kameo Hotel

$$ | HOTEL | FAMILY | This hotel's contemporary fittings are in contrast to Ayutthaya's ancient vibes, but the rooms are clean and comfortable with firm beds and nice bathrooms. **Pros:** close to tourist sights; modern design; good facilities like hot tub, pool, and gym. **Cons:** not traditional like other Ayutthaya accommodations; some rooms without nice views; on the expensive side. *Rooms from: B2,500 ✉ 210–211, 148 Moo 5, Rojana Rd. ☎ 035/212535 ⊕ www.kameocollection.com ⇨ 208 rooms ǀ◎ǀ Free breakfast.*

Krungsri River Hotel

$ | HOTEL | A refreshingly cool and spacious marble-floor lobby distinguishes this luxury hotel. **Pros:** near the train station; river views; spacious suites. **Cons:** dated decor in some rooms; on the expensive side; not all rooms have views. *Rooms from: B1,950 ✉ 27/2 Moo 11, Rojana Rd. ☎ 035/244333 ⊕ www.krungsririver.com ⇨ 206 rooms ǀ◎ǀ Free breakfast.*

Luang Chumni Village

$ | HOTEL | This warren of six snug teak rooms is one of the most popular lodgings in town, so booking well ahead is essential. **Pros:** serene atmosphere; lots of polished teak; tropical gardens. **Cons:** some guests may miss an en suite bathroom; books up fast; front desk not 24 hours. *Rooms from: B1,200 ✉ 2/4 Rojana Rd. ☎ 035/322990 ⊕ www.luangchumnivillage.com ⇨ 6 rooms ǀ◎ǀ Free breakfast.*

Bang Pa-In

20 km (12 miles) south of Ayutthaya.

This village, a popular stopping point between Bangkok and Ayutthaya, has a few architectural sites of note: a Thai palace, a European-style temple, and a Chinese pagoda, all grouped around a lake and open fields with bushes trimmed in the shapes of various animals. Most visitors spend about two hours at the palaces and topiary gardens before heading for Ayutthaya, though if the weather's not too hot you might be tempted to linger longer on the banks of Bang Pa-In's calm lake.

GETTING HERE AND AROUND

BUS TRAVEL

Buses regularly leave from Bangkok's Northern Bus Terminal to Bang Pa-In Bus Station, less than half a mile from the palace. Fares are about B50 for an air-conditioned bus. From Ayutthaya, buses leave from the station on Naresuan Road.

CAR TRAVEL

Once you get out of Bangkok's labyrinthine roads, it's also easy to get to Bang Pa-In by car. Get on Route 1 (Phahonyothin Road) to Route 32. It's a 30-minute drive here from Ayutthaya along Route 32.

SONGTHAEW TRAVEL

Songthaews travel regularly between the bus stations in Bang Pa-In and Ayutthaya.

TAXI TRAVEL

One-way taxi fares from Bangkok to Bang Pa-In should be about B800 (depending on your starting point), but be sure that the driver agrees to a fare before departing, or you may be charged more upon arrival.

TRAIN TRAVEL

Trains from Bangkok's Hua Lamphong Station take an hour to get to Bang Pa-In Station, where you can catch a tuk-tuk or songthaew to the palace. The train fares, which are generally less than B70, vary by class of travel.

Sights

Royal Palace

CASTLE/PALACE | Bang Pa-In's extravagant Royal Palace sits amid well-tended gardens. The original structure, built by King Prusat on the banks of the Pa Sak River, was used by the Ayutthaya kings until the Burmese invasion of 1767. After being neglected for 80 years, it was rebuilt during the reign of Rama IV and became the summer palace of King Rama V.

King Rama V was interested in European architecture, and many influences are evident here. The most beautiful building, however, is the **Aisawan Thippaya,** a Thai pavilion that seems to float on a small lake. China also fascinated the two rulers, and **Phra Thinang Warophat Phiman,** nicknamed the Peking Palace, is a replica of a Chinese imperial court palace. It was built from materials custom-made in China—a gift from Chinese Thais eager to win the king's favor. It contains a collection of exquisite jade and Ming porcelain.

Don't forget to visit the Buddhist temple built in best British neo-Gothic style, **Wat Nivet Thamaprawat,** which even has a fine steeple, buttresses, a belfry, and stained-glass windows. ✉ *Bang Pa-in* ☎ *035/261548* 🎫 *B100.*

Shopping

Bang Sai Folk Arts and Craft Centre

CRAFTS | The center was set up by Queen Sirikit in 1982 to train farming families to make traditional crafts for extra income. Workers regularly demonstrate their technique, and a small souvenir shop provides the chance to buy the fruits of their labors. The center holds an annual fair at the end of January. ✉ *Bang Pa-in* ✣ *Off Rte. 3442, 24 km (14½ miles) south of Bang Pa-In* ☎ *035/366252* 🎫 *B100.*

Lopburi

75 km (47 miles) north of Ayutthaya, 150 km (94 miles) north of Bangkok.

Lopburi is off the beaten track for most tourists, and those who do come here are generally outnumbered by the city's monkey population. Some foreigners show up on their way to or from Ayutthaya, but few stay overnight. The rarity of foreigners may explain why locals are so friendly and eager to show you their town—and to practice their English. Samlors are available, but most of Lopburi's attractions are within easy walking distance of downtown and the train station.

One of Thailand's oldest cities, Lopburi has been inhabited since the 4th century. After the 6th century its influence grew under the Dvaravati rulers, who dominated northern Thailand until the Khmers swept in from the east. From the beginning of the 10th century until the middle of the 13th, when the new Thai kingdom drove them out, the Khmers used Lopburi as their provincial capital. During the Sukhothai and early Ayutthaya periods, the city's importance declined until, in 1664, King Narai made it his second capital to escape the heat and humidity of Ayutthaya. He employed French architects to build his palace; consequently, Lopburi is a strange mixture of Khmer, Thai, and Western architecture. Lopburi is a day trip from Bangkok or Ayutthaya. Its sights can be covered in a few hours. There are few comfortable overnight accommodations.

GETTING HERE AND AROUND

BUS TRAVEL

Buses to Lopburi leave Bangkok's Mo Chit Northern Bus Terminal (Mo Chit) about every 20 minutes between 6 am and 7 pm. Tickets for the three-hour journey start at around B120 for air-conditioned buses. Lopburi is an hour and a half from Ayutthaya on the green

Bus 607 from Ayutthaya's bus terminal. Lopburi's bus station is about 6 km (3½ miles) from town, making it necessary to take a tuk-tuk or songthaew into town.

CAR TRAVEL
If you're driving from Bangkok, take Route 1 (Phahonyothin) north via Saluburi. The trip will take up to two hours.

TRAIN TRAVEL
The Northeastern train line has frequent service from Bangkok. Three morning and two afternoon trains depart for the three-hour trip from Bangkok's Hua Lamphong Station. Trains back to Bangkok run in the early and late afternoon. Advance tickets aren't necessary. Fares for air-conditioned cars on the express train cost about B350. Lopburi's station is downtown near the historic sites and lodgings on Na Phra Kan Road.

VISITOR AND TOUR INFORMATION
CONTACT Tourist Authority of Thailand (TAT)
28/9 Narai Maharach Rd., City Center *036/770–0967* *www.tourismthailand.org.*

Sights

Phra Narai Ratchaniwet
CASTLE/PALACE | This palace's well-preserved buildings, completed between 1665 and 1677, have been converted into museums. Surrounding the buildings are castellated walls and triumphal archways grand enough to admit an entourage mounted on elephants. The most elaborate structure is the Dusit Mahaprasat Hall, built by King Narai to receive foreign ambassadors. The roof is gone, but you can spot the mixture of architectural styles: the square doors are Thai and the domed arches are Western. North of Phra Narai Ratchaniwet is the restored Wat Sao Thong Thong. *Ratchadamneon Rd.* *036/411458* *B150* *Closed Mon. and Tues.*

Monkey Business

Lopburi has an unusually large monkey population. The monkeys cluster around the monuments, particularly Phra Prang Sam Yot. Each November the Lopburi Inn organizes a monkey banquet, in which a grand buffet is laid out for the monkeys and much of the town's population comes out to watch them feast.

Phra Prang Sam Yot
RELIGIOUS SITE | Lopburi's most famous landmark is this Khmer shrine whose three prangs symbolize the sacred triad of Brahma, Vishnu, and Shiva. King Narai converted the shrine into a Buddhist temple, and a stucco image of the Buddha sits serenely before the central prang. The most memorable aspect of the monument is its hundreds of resident monkeys, including mothers and nursing babies, wizened old males, and aggressive youngsters. Hold tight to your possessions, as the monkeys steal everything from city maps to digital cameras. Most tourists wind up having a blast with the monkeys, though. Approach them and stand still for a minute, and you'll soon have monkeys all over your head, shoulders, and just about everywhere else—a perfect photo op. *Vichayen Rd.* *B30* *Closed Mon. and Tues.*

Vichayen House
HOUSE | Built for King Louis XIV of France's personal representative, De Chaumont, Vichayen House was later occupied by King Narai's infamous Greek minister, Constantine Phaulkon, whose political schemes eventually resulted in the ouster of all Westerners from Thailand. When King Narai was dying in 1668, his army commander, Phra Phetracha,

seized power and beheaded Phaulkon. ✉ *Vichayen Rd.* 🎫 *B50* ⏲ *Closed Mon. and Tues.*

Wat Phra Si Rattana Mahathat

RELIGIOUS SITE | Built by the Khmers, this wat underwent so many restorations during the Sukhothai and Ayutthaya periods that it's difficult to discern the three original Khmer prangs—only the central one is intact. Several Sukhothai- and Ayutthaya-style chedis sit within the compound. ✉ *Na Phra Karn Rd.* 🎫 *B50* ⏲ *Closed Mon. and Tues.*

Bualuang Restaurant

$ | **THAI** | This is the sort of local restaurant that you shouldn't miss on your travels in Thailand, a place to relax and feast on true regional specialties and good seafood after sightseeing under the hot sun. There are also multicourse Chinese-style set meals for six or more people. **Known for:** charcoal-grilled fish, including cotton fish and snakehead; seafood dishes like steamed blue crab and mussels hot pot; friendly service. [$] *Average main: B100* ✉ *46/1 Moo 3* ☎ *036/413009, 036/422669.*

Lopburi Inn Resort

$ | **RESORT** | This monkey-themed retreat is the best value in Lopburi, with stylish rooms decorated in a modern Thai style, a generous buffet breakfast, and a good range of facilities including a pleasant pool. **Pros:** pool; Wi-Fi access; gym. **Cons:** far from main sights; decor in rooms not modern; monkey theme on the tacky side. [$] *Rooms from: B990* ✉ *17/1–2 Ratchadamnoen Rd.* ☎ *036/614790, 036/420777* 🌐 *www.lopburiinnresort.com* *76 rooms* 🍽 *Free breakfast.*

Noom Guesthouse

$ | **B&B/INN** | The seven rooms at this comfortable city-center guesthouse are basically furnished but are more than adequate, and the bathrooms are well appointed. **Pros:** central location; good restaurant; close to attractions. **Cons:** street noise can be heard in rooms; on-street parking; no decorating scheme. [$] *Rooms from: B250* ✉ *15/17 Phayakamjad Rd., City Center* ☎ *036/427693, 089/104–1811* 🌐 *www.noomguesthouse.com* *7 rooms* 🍽 *No meals.*

Chapter 5

THE GULF COAST BEACHES

Updated by
Andrew Parks

Sights ★★★★☆ | Restaurants ★★★☆☆ | Hotels ★★★★☆ | Shopping ★☆☆☆☆ | Nightlife ★★★★☆

WELCOME TO THE GULF COAST BEACHES

TOP REASONS TO GO

★ **Sunset at Hua Hin:** Take a stroll down the wide beaches at Hua Hin for unbeatable views of the setting sun—the same ones the king and queen of Thailand have enjoyed from their nearby palace.

★ **Relaxing Quick Getaway:** Bangkok weekenders flock to Cha-am to enjoy the sun, surf, seafood, and inexpensive accommodations. Off all the beaches a quick hop from Bangkok, this is by far the most laid-back.

★ **Island Diving:** A divers' heaven, the small island of Koh Tao has escaped the worst excesses of tourist development. Divers also flock to even tinier Koh Nang Yuan.

★ **Midnight Revelry:** Thirteen times a year as many as 10,000 locals and visitors descend on the island of Koh Phangan for a late-night, full-moon beachfront bacchanal.

★ **Dramatic Koh Samui:** A drive around the dramatic rocky coastline of Thailand's third-largest island takes you from one eye-popping view to another.

1 **Pattaya.** Seedy but great water sports.

2 **Koh Samet.** Famous for its sugary beaches.

3 **Chanthaburi.** A popular stop for its Gem Market and French architecture.

4 **Koh Chang.** The beaches are picturesque and the jungle verdant.

5 **Cha-am.** This affordable beach getaway has retained its sleepy charm.

6 **Hua Hin.** A small city with long beaches, busy markets, and summer guests including Thai Royals.

7 **Takiab Beach.** An escape from Hua Hin with luxury hotels and uncrowded beaches.

8 **Chumphon.** A gateway to the south with beaches and birdwatching.

9 **Surat Thani.** A great night market and a national park with the most beautiful forest in Thailand.

10 **Koh Samui.** Perfect beaches, turquoise waters, and perfect weather.

11 **Koh Phangan.** Famous for its full moon parties.

12 **Koh Tao.** Known for excellent diving sites right off shore.

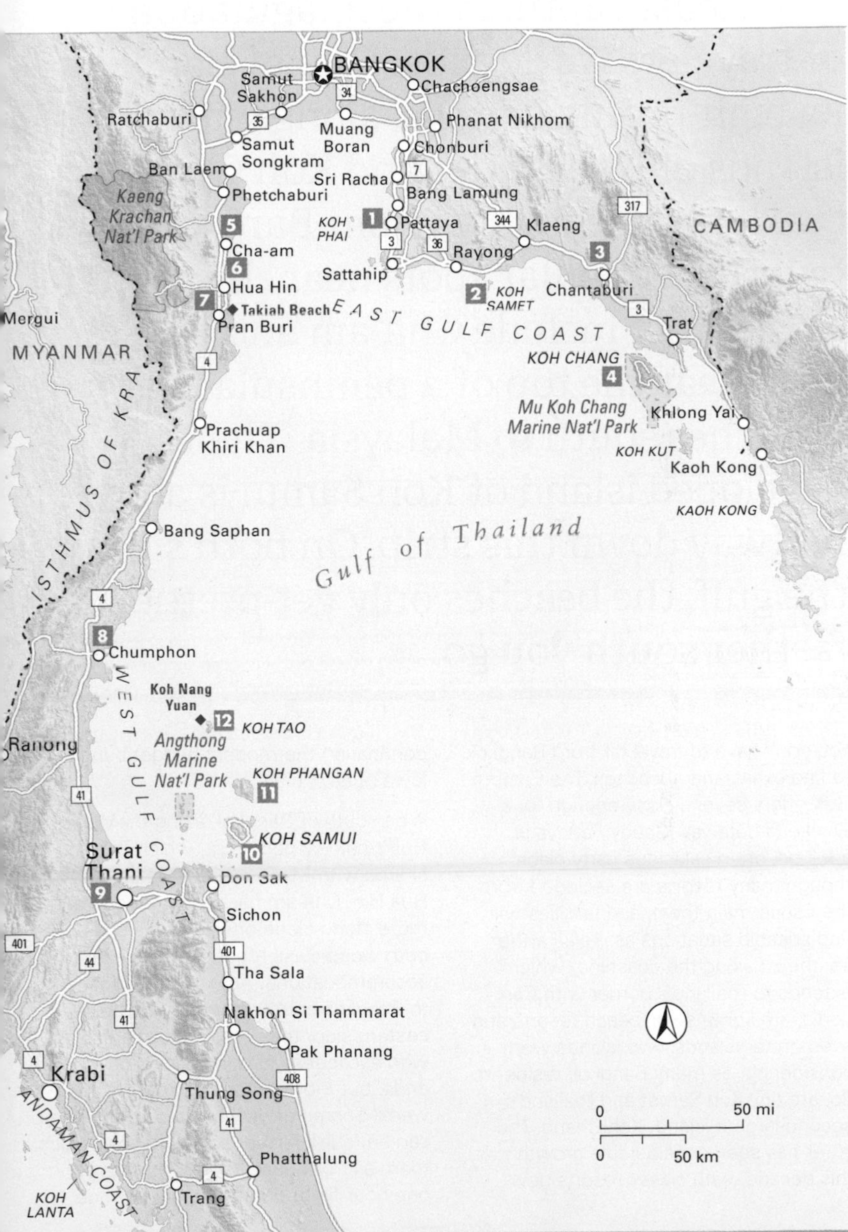

BANGKOK
Samut Sakhon
Chachoengsae
Ratchaburi
Muang Boran
Phanat Nikhom
Samut Songkram
Chonburi
Ban Laem
Sri Racha
Phetchaburi
Bang Lamung
Kaeng Krachan Nat'l Park
KOH PHAI
Pattaya
Klaeng
CAMBODIA
Cha-am
Rayong
Sattahip
Chantaburi
Hua Hin
KOH SAMET
Takiab Beach
EAST GULF COAST
Mergui
Pran Buri
Trat
MYANMAR
KOH CHANG
Mu Koh Chang Marine Nat'l Park
Khlong Yai
Prachuap Khiri Khan
KOH KUT
Kaoh Kong
KAOH KONG
ISTHMUS OF KRA
Bang Saphan
Gulf of Thailand
Chumphon
WEST GULF COAST
Koh Nang Yuan
KOH TAO
Ranong
Angthong Marine Nat'l Park
KOH PHANGAN
KOH SAMUI
Surat Thani
Don Sak
Sichon
Tha Sala
Nakhon Si Thammarat
Pak Phanang
Krabi
Thung Song
ANDAMAN COAST
Phatthalung
KOH LANTA
Trang
0 50 mi
0 50 km

With its white sandy beaches, crystal-blue water, and laid-back lifestyle, the Gulf Coast captures the imaginations of travelers worldwide. East of Bangkok lie high-profile Pattaya, along with the islands of Koh Samet and Koh Chang, two longtime escape-from-Bangkok favorites. Popular spots near the capital to the west include Cha-am and Hua Hin, both near the top of a peninsula that stretches south to Malaysia. The very developed island of Koh Samui is about halfway down this strip. On both sides of the gulf, the beaches only get prettier the farther south you go.

You don't have to travel far from Bangkok to find exhilarating beaches. The Eastern Gulf offers several close enough for a weekend getaway. Gaudy Pattaya is a full-on, often salacious party place, though many resorts are secluded from the risqué main town, and families will find suitable situations as well. Farther southeast along the coastline, which extends to Thailand's border with Cambodia, are some swell beach resorts and even better islands. Two islands worth considering, as many Bangkok residents do, are tiny Koh Samet and Thailand's second-largest island, Koh Chang. The latter has seen considerable growth this decade, with classy resorts now dominating the modest budget bungalows of days past.

A bit south of Bangkok along the Western Gulf's narrow peninsula, which Thailand shares with Myanmar, lie Cha-am and Hua Hin. Cha-am has bigger resorts and more stand-alone ones; Hua Hin has both world-class resorts and less fancy accommodations. As with their close-to-Bangkok counterparts on the gulf's eastern side, these two cities can fill up with escapees from the capital on weekends, but they're less busy during the week. Scores of beaches worth exploring can be found farther south. You can reach them all from Surat Thani, which is a one-hour flight or an 11-hour train ride from Bangkok. Northeast of Surat Thani is the very developed island of Koh Samui, popular in part because daily flights from Bangkok make it so easy to access.

MAJOR REGIONS

The **Eastern Gulf** has long been a favorite escape from the heat and humidity of Bangkok. Its proximity to the capital means that weekend trips are possible, which in turn means that the area is overrun with sunseekers during long or holiday weekends. In-the-know visitors skip overdeveloped and seedy Pattaya and head farther east where you will find some splendid islands, among them **Koh Samet**, a longtime favorite of Bangkok residents. **Chanthanaburi** and its Gem Market is a popular stop on the way to **Koh Chang**, farther east, which has experienced considerable expansion in recent years.

South of Bangkok lies the **Western Gulf** coast, hundreds of miles of shoreline where resort towns are the exception rather than the rule. About three hours south of Bangkok are the laid-back beaches of **Cha-am** and **Hua Hin**. Bangkok residents have traveled to Hua Hin since the 1920s, when King Rama VII built a palace here. Where royalty goes, high society inevitably follows, but despite the attention the city received, Hua Hin was spared the pitfalls of rapid development. Directly to the south of Hua Hin, **Takiab Beach** is where well-off Thais go to avoid the well-off scene of Hua Hin while **Chumphon** is the gateway to the south, with trains and buses connecting here for Bangkok to the north and **Surat Thani** and Phuket to the south. As the former capital of an ancient Siamese kingdom and the center of its civilization, Surat Thani developed its own artistic and architectural style. In modern times it has remained an important commercial and historic Thai city, and the province is home to one of the most pristine tropical forests in Thailand, Khao Sok National Park. Nevertheless, most travelers know Surat Thani only as a departure point for the islands off its coast.

Though very developed, **Koh Samui,** the most popular destination on the Western Gulf isn't too frenzied. The island's beaches are gorgeous, the weather's often perfect, and the mood is laid back. After a few days exploring the island's many beaches and sights, travelers seeking more adventure take advantage of easy **side trips from Koh Samui. Koh Phangan** is a two-hour ferry ride from Koh Samui and is famous for its beautiful beaches and full moon parties while **Koh Tao,** a tiny island north of Koh Phangan, is a sought-after diving getaway.

Planning

WHEN TO GO

The best time to visit the Gulf Coast is between December and March, when the seas are mostly calm and the skies generally clear. On the Eastern Gulf, Pattaya and Koh Samet are year-round destinations. Many places in Koh Chang and nearby Islands used to close down during the rainy season but no more. The big car ferries continue to run on a limited schedule during the rainy season, and most resorts and hotels stay open, offering cheaper rates. On the Western Gulf, Cha-am and Hua Hin are busy year-round. Flying to Koh Samui is still convenient in low season, and the island and its neighbors are beautiful even with cloudiness and rain.

PLANNING YOUR TIME

Disparate and geographically far apart, the many beaches along the Gulf of Thailand would take nearly a month just to survey. With Bangkok serving as the urban divider, most travelers choose either the gulf's east or west coast to explore, and then concentrate on one or at most a few places. Except for divers and hikers, this region is largely about relaxing and taking your time. Where you end up and how long you stay depend on what you're looking for. It only takes a day, for instance, to figure out what wild Pattaya is all about, but if this is your thing you could spend a fun week or two here. Ditto for genteel Koh Samet or developed, but not too hyper, Koh Chang. As with their east-coast counterparts, the west-coast beaches would take about two weeks to explore even superficially. Both Cha-am and Hua Hin, the closest of the major west-coast beaches to Bangkok, become very crowded on weekends and holidays; if you can arrange to visit at other times, you'll have a mellower experience. The farther south you go from Hua Hin, the less you need to worry about when you visit, except during major holidays or, in the case of Koh Phangan, the full moon party that takes place every four weeks.

GETTING HERE AND AROUND

AIR TRAVEL

Relatively inexpensive flights depart daily from Bangkok for all the major beach destinations: Surat Thani, Trat, Koh Samui, and Pattaya. It's generally cheaper to fly to Surat Thani, mostly because the government owns the airport. There are some flights from Chiang Mai to the beaches. Thai Airways and Bangkok Airways have regular flights, as do the budget carriers AirAsia and Nok Air. All the airports in this region are small and much easier to deal with than Bangkok's Suvarnabhumi.

BOAT AND FERRY TRAVEL

Boats depart from the mainland to the islands from Chumphon and Surat Thani. High-speed catamarans, regular passenger ferries, and "slow boats," which are car ferries, make these trips. The main boat operators are Lomprayah, Seatran, Songserm, and Raja.

■ **TIP→ Don't take the chance of traveling on rickety or overcrowded boats. Because of lax safety standards, dangerously crowded boats are all too common. Ensure that life jackets are available and that the crew takes safety seriously. Responsible companies—and there are many—keep safety concerns front and center.**

CONTACTS Lomprayah ☎ *02/629–0011, 02/629–2570 in Bangkok, 077/420121 in Samui, 077/951129 on Koh Tao* 🌐 *www.lomprayah.com.* **Raja Ferry** ☎ *02/2768–2112, 092/2473–4235* 🌐 *www.rajaferryport.com.* **Seatran Ferry** ☎ *077/950559* 🌐 *www.seatranferry.com.*

BUS TRAVEL

Buses travel regularly between Bangkok and all major destinations in southern Thailand. Bus service within the south is also good. ■ **TIP→ Public buses have a better reputation than private bus companies, on which travelers often report thefts from luggage compartments and other annoyances.**

CAR TRAVEL

Eastern Gulf resorts are fairly close to Bangkok, so driving is a possibility. The worst part is getting out of Bangkok. On the Western Gulf, it's a long, exhausting drive farther south to Chumphon, Surat Thani, or Krabi. It may be cheaper, safer, and more convenient to hire a car and driver. This is best done while in Bangkok; your hotel can make arrangements.

MOTORCYCLE TRAVEL

Scooters may seem like a fun way to explore the islands and beaches, but think twice before renting one. Every year hundreds of foreigners are killed or injured in accidents along the Gulf Coast. The consequences of even a minor wreck can be dire if you're only wearing shorts and flip-flops. If you've never driven a motorcycle before, this is not the time to learn.

SONGTHAEW, TAXI, AND TUK-TUK TRAVEL

Most areas of the south have everything from samlors to tuk-tuks to songthaews. "Metered" taxis can be found in the larger towns and on Samui. Drivers don't actually run the meters, however, and are unscrupulous bargainers.

TRAIN TRAVEL

One daily train departs Bangkok's Hua Lamphong Station for Sri Racha and Pattaya; there's more frequent service to Hua Hin, Chumphon, and Surat Thani. In general, bus travel is a better way to go in southern Thailand.

HEALTH AND SAFETY

Malaria is very rare but not unheard of in Thailand's southeast. Health authorities have done a great job controlling mosquitoes in and around the southern resorts, but you'll still need a good supply of repellent.

Be careful at the beach, as the sun is stronger than you think. Wear a hat and plenty of sunscreen. Protective clothing while diving or snorkeling is a good idea, as accidentally brushing against or stepping on coral can be painful. Keep an eye out for sea urchins and even more dangerous creatures like jellyfish, especially during the monsoon season. If you are stung, seek medical attention immediately.

Strong undertows often develop during monsoon season, especially along the west coast. Pay attention to posted warnings and listen if locals tell you not to swim.

Condoms are available in southern Thailand; not all brands are equally reliable, so it may be simpler to bring any you'll need.

Take the same safety precautions you would in any other location. When traveling to isolated spots, let someone know where you are going and how long you expect to be away, and be aware of strangers you encounter along the way. Though rare, serious incidents involving tourists have taken place on the southern gulf islands, including two murders and the suspicious deaths of several others.

MONEY MATTERS

Banks and ATMs are numerous, but it's always a good idea to carry some extra cash. Places on remote islands often don't accept credit cards. Some add a small service charge, typically 3%, when you pay with a credit card.

RESTAURANTS

Dining options in the beach regions vary from exclusive and expensive resort restaurants to wooden shacks that seem moments from toppling over. On Koh Chang and Koh Samet "dining rooms" are set up each night on the beach. Pattaya, Hua Hin, and Samui have the widest range of restaurants, from fast-food chains to five-star restaurants.

HOTELS

There's something for everyone in this region, from luxurious retreats to simple thatch huts on the beach. Many places combine the two experiences by offering fancy bungalows. Rates fluctuate widely: in holiday periods they can more than double. Always double-check your rate when you book. In general, prices are lower than what you'd pay in Bangkok, but higher than in other parts of the country.

What It Costs In Baht

	$	$$	$$$	$$$$
RESTAURANTS	under B200	B200–B300	B301–B400	over B400
HOTELS	under B2,000	B2,000–B4,000	B4,001–B6,000	over B6,000

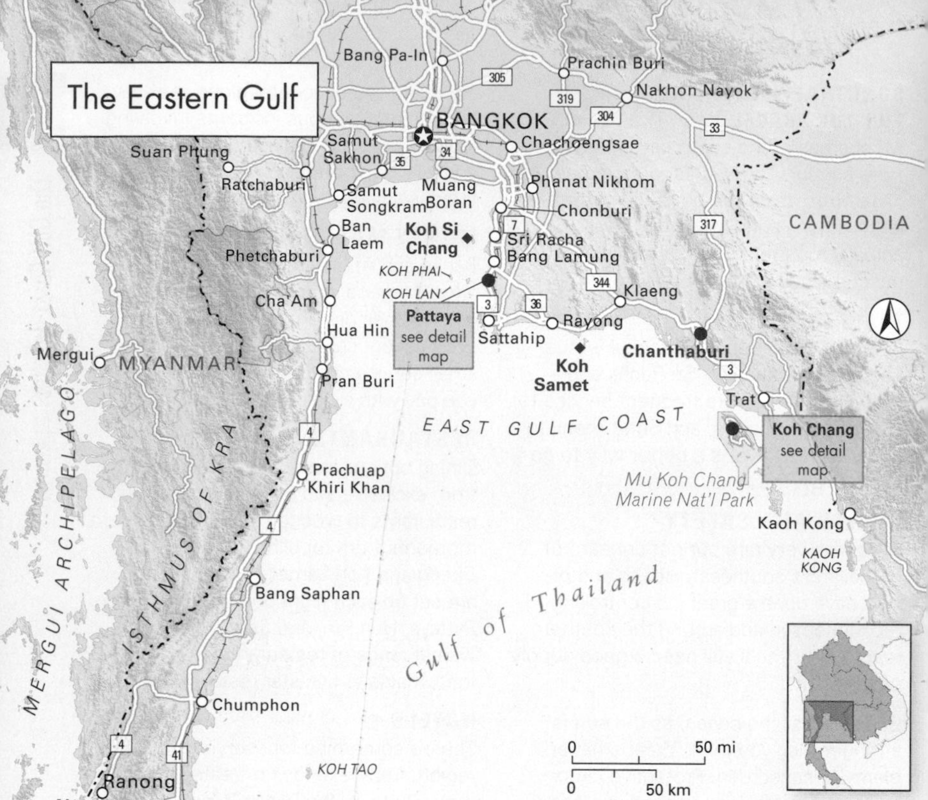

Pattaya

147 km (88 miles) southeast of Bangkok.

Pattaya's proponents boast that their city has finally emerged as a legitimate upscale beach destination. This is partly true: recent years have seen the opening of chic restaurants and more family-friendly attractions. Still, Pattaya remains a city as divided as ever between sand and sex—and the emphasis still falls clearly on the latter. ■ **TIP→ If you're averse to encountering live sex shows and smut shops at every turn, avoid Pattaya. Commercial sex is not just a reality here: it is the lifeblood of the city.**

Pattaya was not always like this. Until the end of the 1950s it was a fishing village with an unspoiled natural harbor. Even after affluent Bangkok residents discovered the area, it remained small and tranquil. Then came the Vietnam War, with thousands of American soldiers stationed at nearby air and naval bases. They piled into Pattaya, and the resort grew with the unrestrained fervor of any boomtown. But the boom eventually went bust. Pattaya was nearly abandoned, but its proximity to Bangkok and the beauty of the natural harbor ensured that it didn't crumble completely.

In the late 1990s, after much talk and government planning, Pattaya started regaining popularity. Two expressways were finished, making the trip from Bangkok even easier. Now that Bangkok's international airport is located on the southeast side of the capital, it is even more convenient to visit Pattaya.

Curving Beach Road, with palm trees on the beach side and modern resort hotels on the other, traces the arc of Pattaya Bay in the heart of the city. Bars, clubs, and open-air cafés proliferate on the pedestrian streets by the old pier. South of here lies Jomtien, an agreeable, if somewhat overdeveloped, beach. The bay's northern part is Pattaya's quietest, most easygoing section. Pattaya's big water-sports industry caters to jet-skiers, paragliders, and even water-skiers.

GETTING HERE AND AROUND

Buses to Pattaya leave from Bangkok's Eastern Bus Terminal on Sukhumvit at least every hour daily. The journey takes about an hour and a half, and fares are cheap—usually around B120. You can also drive from Bangkok, and many rental companies vie for your business. One of the cheapest available is Thai Rent a Car. A number of taxi and limousine services are available, including Pattaya4leisure.

CONTACTS Pattaya4leisure *www.pattaya4leisure.com.* **Thai Rent A Car** *1647 www.thairentacar.com.*

SAFETY AND PRECAUTIONS

Pattaya is a city built on prostitution, and it has all the trappings that go with the seedy atmosphere generated by the sex trade. Street thefts do happen, and thefts from hotels are not unheard of. Take sensible precautions with valuables, always use hotel safes, and avoid late-night strolls down dark streets. Tourist police are on duty, and in recent years they've been joined by tourist police volunteers—expat residents acting as liaisons with the regular police units.

VISITOR AND TOUR INFORMATION

CONTACT Tourism Authority of Thailand *609 Moo 10, Pratamnak Rd. 038/427667, 038/428750 www.tourismthailand.org.*

Sights

Sanctuary of Truth

BUILDING | A wealthy businessman started building this massive teak structure in 1981, and it's still not finished. The aim of the sanctuary, whose intricate carvings blend modern and traditional styles, is to make a statement about the balance of different cultures. The waterfront setting north of Pattaya is pleasant. *206/2 Moo 5, Naklua Rd., Bang Lamung 038/367229, 038/367230 www.sanctuaryoftruth.com B500.*

Beaches

Jomtien Beach

BEACH—SIGHT | Pattaya Beach's quieter neighbor to the south, Jomtien Beach is less gaudy, less crowded, and a bit less expensive. The white sand, cleaner water, and cordoned-off swimming areas are also draws. Shaded areas with deck chairs cover large sections of the beach, and vendors sell food and drink at inflated prices. Water sports play a dominant role here; you can rent Jet Skis, paragliders, and speedboats up and down the beach. Jomtien is home to a few windsurfing schools. **Amenities:** food and drink. **Best for:** swimming; windsurfing. *Moo 12.*

Koh Lan

BEACH—SIGHT | From Pattaya Bay, speedboats take just 15 minutes to reach the island of Koh Lan. The beaches have white sand, and the water is cleaner than at Pattaya Beach. Koh Lan gets busy by midday, so arrive early if you want peace and quiet. The waters are crowded with speedboats and other motorized craft—some speedboat operators are reckless, so be cautious when swimming. Food and drink vendors wander among the shaded deck chairs, although the prices are steep. Ferries leave South Pattaya Pier daily from 10 am to 6:30 pm; a ride costs B50. Speedboats can be hired for

B2,200. **Amenities:** food and drink. **Best for:** partiers; swimming. ✉ *Koh Lan.*

Pattaya Beach

BEACH—SIGHT | The city's namesake beach is slightly murky, but its sand is golden and fine, and safe swimming areas have been added in recent years. You can rent shaded deck chairs by the hour, and food vendors and trinket merchants wander up and down the beach. The bay is usually crowded with small boats, Jet Skis, and other diversions. Parallel to the shore, Pattaya Beach Road has a landscaped walkway that separates the beach from the restaurants, shopping malls, and resorts on the opposite side. **Amenities:** food and drink. **Best for:** walking. ✉ *Pattaya Beach Rd.*

Restaurants

Much of Pattaya feels like Little America, with McDonald's, Burger King, and KFC next to each other in the Royal Gardens Plaza mall, and other familiar names nearby. But Pattaya has access to just-picked produce and seafood fresh from the gulf, so you'll have no trouble finding worthwhile local cuisine. Fancier, if not necessarily better, restaurants can be a refuge from the noise and crowds at the simple beachside places.

The Bay

$$$ | ITALIAN | Once home to a flashy Italian restaurant, this sleek, modern restaurant overlooking the Dusit Thani resort's expansive pool and shimmering Pattaya Bay is now offering an "international skewers" concept with a wide variety of Chinese, Thai, and Western takes on grilled meat, seafood, and vegetables on skewers. **Known for:** Pattaya Bay views; an all-inclusive Saturday night buffet; seafood skewers. *$ Average main: B400* ✉ *Dusit Thani Pattaya, 240/2 Pattaya Beach Rd.* ☎ *038/425611* 🌐 *www.dusit.com* ⏲ *Closed Sun.*

Bruno's

$$$$ | SWISS | This restaurant and wine bar has built a good reputation among the expat community for its Euro-centric cuisine. The set B450 lunch menu is a bargain, and the à la carte dinner menu includes interesting options such as squid ink noodles with lobster ragout. **Known for:** walk-in wine cellar; imported beef, lamb, and veal from Australia; international cuisine with a fine-dining feel. *$ Average main: B500* ✉ *306/63 Chateau Dale Plaza, Thappraya Rd.* ☎ *038/119586, 038/119587* 🌐 *www.brunos-pattaya.com.*

Flare

$$$$ | ECLECTIC | The vibe at this discreet, sophisticated spot—one of Pattaya's best—is intimate and romantic. The mainly modern Thai food includes classics like amazing *massaman* beef and red curry dishes, but the chefs also prepare grilled meats and seafood and baked fish. **Known for:** high-caliber cooking; attentive service; lengthy wine list. *$ Average main: B500* ✉ *Pattaya Hilton Hotel, 333/101 Moo 9, Level 15* ☎ *038/253000* 🌐 *www3.hilton.com/en/hotels/thailand/hilton-pattaya-BKKHPHI/dining/index.html* ⏲ *No lunch.*

Indian By Nature

$$$ | INDIAN | Regulars pack the room at this elegant Indian restaurant, which honors Pattaya's bountiful seafood supply with such dishes as a comforting fish curry and a crab masala special that's an absolute must when it's available. Service is attentive but never overbearing, living up to the awards this local favorite has earned since it opened in 2004. **Known for:** a drink trolley devoted to gin; private dining for special occasions; excellent dessert menu. *$ Average main: B400* ✉ *306/64-68 Thapraya Rd.* ☎ *038/364656* 🌐 *www.indian-by-nature.com* ⏲ *No lunch.*

Mantra

$$$$ | INTERNATIONAL | This enormous, ultramodern restaurant is one of Pattaya's most talked-about eateries. With a menu that devotes entire pages to everything from Italian to Indian food, Mantra covers a lot of culinary ground, making it a popular something-for-everyone spot. **Known for:** not one, but seven open kitchens; several unique seating options; familiar mains like brick-oven pizza and seared Wagyu beef. *Average main: B600 ✉ Amari Ocean Pattaya, Pattaya Beach Rd. ☎ 038/429591 🌐 www.mantra-pattaya.com ⏲ No lunch Mon.–Sat.*

Moom Aroi

$$ | **SEAFOOD** | For a different side of Pattaya, head north of the city to this beautiful, romantic seafood restaurant that sits right on the waterfront. The almost exclusively Thai clientele enjoys hand-picked lobster, tiger prawns, crab, oysters, and fish amid shimmering pools, palm trees, and sweeping bay views. **Known for:** point-and-smile ordering; fresh seafood tanks; reasonable prices considering the quality of the food. *Average main: B200 ✉ 83/4 Na Klua Rd. ☎ 038/223252.*

Nang Nual

$$ | **SEAFOOD** | At the southern end of Pattaya Beach Road is one of the city's best places for seafood. A huge array of freshly caught fish is laid out on blocks of ice at the entrance; point to what you want, explain how you'd like it cooked (most people prefer grilled), and ask for some fried rice on the side for a flawless meal. **Known for:** picture menus for indecisive diners; plump steaks for the non-seafood crowd; terrace dining overlooking the ocean. *Average main: B200 ✉ 214–10 S. Pattaya Beach Rd. ☎ 038/428177.*

Vientiane Restaurant

$$ | **ASIAN** | Named after the capital of Laos, this eatery serves satisfying cuisine from that Southeast Asia staple, as well as dependable Western, Thai, and Chinese dishes. The kitchen isn't afraid to cook spicy food for tourist types, so tell your server if you'd like them to go light on the chilies. **Known for:** Pattaya's best papaya salad; gai yang (roast chicken) with sticky rice; authentic recipes. *Average main: B200 ✉ 68 Moo 10 South Pattaya, Bang Lamung ☎ 038/411298.*

Hotels

Only Bangkok beats Pattaya in number of hotel rooms. For seclusion, you'll have to stay at one of the high-end places.

★ Amari Ocean Pattaya

$$$ | **HOTEL** | Step into the modern, open-air lobby here, and you'll immediately be transported to a tropical paradise worlds away from Pattaya's hectic streets. **Pros:** luxurious tower rooms; superb customer service; prime beachside location. **Cons:** not all rooms have great views; building looks imposing; ongoing renovations. *Rooms from: B4,250 ✉ 240 Pattaya Beach Rd. ☎ 038/418418 🌐 www.amari.com/ocean-pattaya 527 rooms Free breakfast.*

Dusit Thani Pattaya

$$$ | **RESORT** | At the northern end of Pattaya Beach, this sprawling hotel has superb bay views and several pools, including one with a swim-up bar. **Pros:** calm amid Pattaya's chaos; many rooms have private balconies with great views; immaculate grounds. **Cons:** rudimentary service; can feel large and impersonal; a short songthaew ride from Pattaya's main attractions. *Rooms from: B6,000 ✉ 240/2 Pattaya Beach Rd. ☎ 038/425611 🌐 www.dusit.com/dusitthani/pattaya/ 457 rooms Free breakfast.*

Hilton Pattaya

$$$ | **HOTEL** | In the middle of the beach yet convenient to much of Pattaya—especially the shopping mall it looms over—the Hilton serves up business-class luxury. **Pros:** central location; outstanding restaurants; bay-facing business suites. **Cons:** unimaginative room decor; noise from nearby bars; beginning to show its age. *Rooms from: B5,700 ✉ 333/101 Moo 9, Nong*

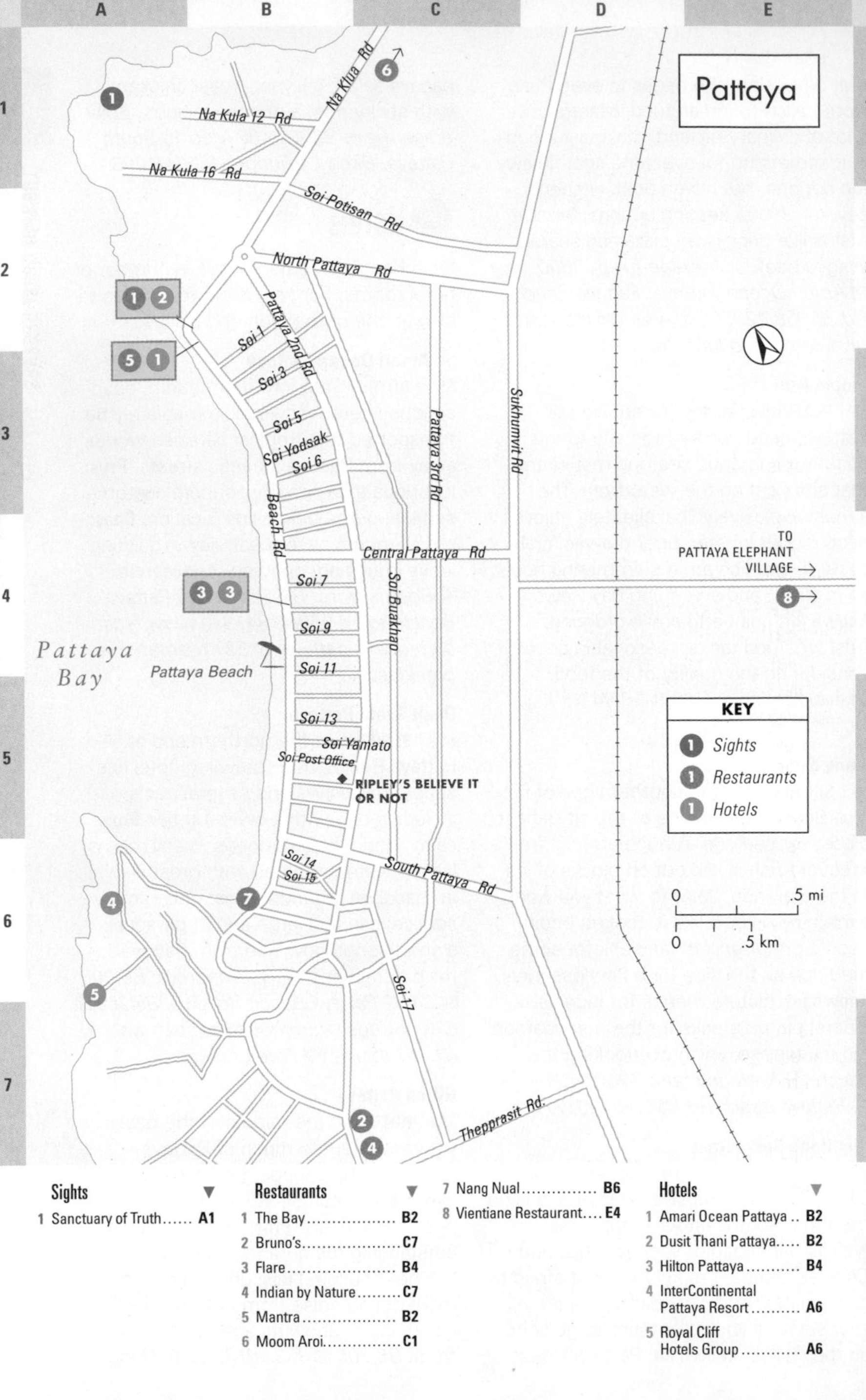

Pattaya
A
B
C
D
E
1
2
3
4
5
6
7
Na Klua Rd
Na Kula 12 Rd
Na Kula 16 Rd
Soi Potisan Rd
North Pattaya Rd
Pattaya 2nd Rd
Soi 1
Soi 3
Soi 5
Soi Yodsak
Soi 6
Beach Rd
Pattaya 3rd Rd
Sukhumvit Rd
Central Pattaya Rd
Soi 7
Soi Buakhao
Soi 9
Soi 11
Soi 13
Soi Yamato
Soi Post Office
RIPLEY'S BELIEVE IT OR NOT
Soi 14
Soi 15
South Pattaya Rd
Soi 17
Thepprasit Rd.
Pattaya Bay
Pattaya Beach
TO PATTAYA ELEPHANT VILLAGE
KEY
Sights
Restaurants
Hotels
0
.5 mi
0
.5 km
Sights
1 Sanctuary of Truth...... A1
Restaurants
1 The Bay.................. B2
2 Bruno's................... C7
3 Flare...................... B4
4 Indian by Nature......... C7
5 Mantra.................. B2
6 Moom Aroi............... C1
7 Nang Nual.............. B6
8 Vientiane Restaurant.... E4
Hotels
1 Amari Ocean Pattaya .. B2
2 Dusit Thani Pattaya..... B2
3 Hilton Pattaya B4
4 InterContinental Pattaya Resort.......... A6
5 Royal Cliff Hotels Group A6

Prue, Banglamung, Pattaya Beach Rd. ☎ 038/253000 🌐 www.hilton.com/pattaya ⇨ 321 rooms 🍽 Free breakfast.

★ InterContinental Pattaya Resort
$$$$ | HOTEL | Now rebranded under the InterContinental banner, this spectacular resort builds on its reputation as a beloved Sheraton property with a paradisiacal village of newly renovated rooms, private cabanas, and shade-providing palm trees. **Pros:** unbeatable setting; the region's most luxurious spa; three lagoon-like swimming pools. **Cons:** rooms small for price; still undergoing renovations; breakfast is rather basic. *$ Rooms from: B6,175 ✉ 437 Phra Tamnak Rd., 1½ km (1 mile) south of town ☎ 038/259888 🌐 www.pattaya.intercontinental.com/ ⇨ 156 rooms 🍽 Free breakfast.*

Royal Cliff Hotels Group
$$$ | RESORT | High on a bluff about 1½ km (1 mile) south of town, this four-hotel ensemble, a Thai institution, is known far and wide for its gulf views, setting, and staggering size. **Pros:** attractive Thai decor; beautiful views; several picturesque pools. **Cons:** tricky to get to beach; so-so dining; out-of-town location *$ Rooms from: B4,600 ✉ 353 Phra Tamnak Rd. ☎ 038/250421, 02/294–7272 🌐 www.royalcliff.com ⇨ 1128 rooms 🍽 Free breakfast.*

Nightlife

Nightlife in Pattaya centers on the sex trade. Scattered throughout town (though mostly concentrated on Sai Song) are hundreds of beer bars—low-key places whose hostesses merely want to keep customers buying drinks. Raunchier go-go bars are mostly found on the southern end of town. Pattaya's, and perhaps Thailand's, most shockingly in-your-face red-light district is on Soi 6, about a block in from the beach. Whether you find it intriguing or beyond the pale, the street is a sight to behold, with hundreds of prostitutes lined up shoulder-to-shoulder at all hours, spilling out of bars and storefronts and catcalling to every male passerby. Gay bars are in the sois between Pattaya Beach Road and Pattaya 2 Road called Pattayaland.

■ TIP→ Generally, the only bars in town that are somewhat removed from the commercial sex trade are in pricey hotels.

Below we've listed a few alternatives to the red-light district scene.

Latitude
BARS/PUBS | At this hotel bar you'll get a great view of the sunset over the Gulf of Thailand—through plate-glass windows or, better yet, alfresco—while sipping wines or well-crafted cocktails, perhaps accompanied by tapas. There's a small library adjacent to the wine bar. *✉ InterContinental Pattaya Resort, 437 Phra Tamnak Rd. ☎ 038/259888 🌐 www.pattaya.intercontinental.com/.*

Mantra
BARS/PUBS | The see-and-be-seen spot for business executives and visiting jet-setters, Mantra is as popular for drinks as it is for food. Don't miss a secluded table surrounded by ornate curtains. *✉ Amari Ocean Pattaya, Pattaya Beach Rd. ☎ 038/429591 🌐 www.mantra-pattaya.com/.*

Mulligan's Pub and Restaurant
BARS/PUBS | Antique Irish liquor posters adorn the walls of this pub that's as authentically Irish as it gets in Pattaya. Sports play a central role, with large flat-screen TVs showing all manner of events. The staff is friendly and well trained. *✉ Central Festival Pattaya Beach, 333/99 Moo 9 Beach Rd. ☎ 038/043388.*

Tiffany
CABARET | This world-renowned, award-winning extravaganza has been entertaining curious locals and ecstatic travelers for more than 40 years now. It's famous throughout Southeast Asia

for being one of the first cabaret shows to feature transgender performers—setting the stage for similar performances throughout Thailand. ✉ *464 Moo 9, Pattaya 2 Rd.* ☎ *038/421711* 🌐 *www.tiffany-show.co.th.*

Activities

Pattaya Beach is the spot for water sports. Waterskiing starts at B1,500 for 30 minutes, jet-skiing costs B1,000 for 30 minutes, and parasailing runs B500 for 15 minutes. Big inflatable bananas, yet another thing to dodge when you're in the water, hold five people and are towed behind a speedboat. They go for B1,000 or more for 30 minutes. For windsurfing, head to Jomtien Beach. **■TIP→ Beware of a common scam among shady jet ski vendors who try to charge for preexisting damage. Before heading out, inspect the equipment and take pictures of any dings, dents, or scratches.**

Koh Samet

30 minutes by passenger ferry from Ban Phe, which is 223 km (139 miles) southeast of Bangkok.

Koh Samet's beautiful beaches are a hit with Thais and Bangkok expats, especially on weekends. Although newer resort areas beckon, Koh Samet remains popular with laid-back travelers who just want to sunbathe and read on the beach. There are no high-rises, and just one rutted road for songthaews.

GETTING HERE AND AROUND

Koh Samet is a 30-minute passenger ferry ride—costing between B100 and B200 depending on destination—from one of three piers in the small village of Ban Phe, a 90-minute minibus ride east of Pattaya. Ferries to Koh Samet dock at Na Duan on the north shore and An Vong Duan on the eastern shore. The islands' beaches are an easy walk from either village.

Sights

Koh Samet National Park

NATIONAL/STATE PARK | The government has been unable—or unwilling—to control development on some parts of Koh Samet despite its protected status as a national marine park, but its fine sand and smooth water is still serene and beautiful in many places. Development is greatest in the village and northern beaches. Other irritants involve Jet Skis, which can be heard roaring away in some places. Trash is also an increasingly vexing issue. All the beaches have licensed ladies offering one- and two-hour Thai massages, which generally cost B100 an hour not including tip. ✈ *30-min ferry ride from Ban Phe* 🎫 *B200.*

Beaches

Ao Kiu

BEACH—SIGHT | On the southern end of Koh Samet, this beautiful and secluded beach has crystal-blue waters and fine white sand that lend the strand a picture-postcard feel. If you're looking to relax, Ao Kiu is an ideal choice. **Amenities:** food and drink. **Best for:** solitude. ✉ *Koh Samet.*

Ao Vong Duan

BEACH—SIGHT | This beautiful shoreline of a half-moon bay is packed with resorts and restaurants, so food and drink are never far away. Ao Vong Duan is the epicenter of water sports on Koh Samet, with Jet Skis and speedboats operating from the beach. The white sands and crystal-blue waters make the beach worth a visit, and the beaches of Ao Cho to the north and Ao Thian to the south are an enjoyable five-minute stroll away. **Amenities:** food and drink; water sports. **Best for:** sunrise; walking. ✉ *Koh Samet.*

Haad Sai Kaew

BEACH—SIGHT | This beach on Koh Samet's northeastern edge is the island's longest and busiest one. The sand is white and the water is clear, though in the rainy season the sea does get a little rough. A few boats operate from the beach, but Haad Sai Kaew is a better place to relax than the crowded beaches of Pattaya. All manner of food and drink is available from the nearby resorts and restaurants. **Amenities:** food and drink; water sports. **Best for:** partiers. ✉ *Beach Rd.*

Nanai Beach

BEACH—SIGHT | One of the few sandy stretches on Koh Samet's southern shore, this is among the island's quieter options. The beach is beautiful, and its views include the mainland. **Amenities:** none. **Best for:** solitude; walking. ✉ *Koh Samet.*

Hotels

The island has many bungalows and cottages with, and less frequently these days, without electricity. *Although the resorts below have good restaurants, you'll have a more memorable experience at one of the delicious seafood joints that set up along the beach each afternoon.*

Paradee Resort

$$$$ | **RESORT** | For serious luxury away from the fray, head to this Ao Kiew resort at the island's far southern reaches. **Pros:** beautiful grounds; more secluded than most Samet resorts; private pools. **Cons:** very pricey; may feel isolated; not good for families. 💲 *Rooms from: B12,120* ✉ *76 Moo 4, Rayong* ☎ *038/6442846* 🌐 *www.samedresorts.com/paradee/* *40 bungalows* 🍴 *No meals.*

Samed Cliff Resort

$$ | **RESORT** | This resort's bungalows are simply furnished, but they're clean and comfortable and have the requisite amenities, including hot water and air-conditioning. **Pros:** beachside dining and grills; on scenic stretch of beach; white sand. **Cons:** rooms look dated; few creature comforts; busy at night. 💲 *Rooms from: B3,100* ✉ *Noi Na Beach* ☎ *016/457115, 02/635–0800 in Bangkok* 🌐 *www.samedcliff.com* *38 bungalows* 🍴 *No meals.*

Vongdeuan Resort

$$ | **RESORT** | This resort has the best bungalows on Ao Vong Duan Beach, and is near much of the island's activity. **Pros:** near all the action; fun atmosphere; reasonable bungalow rates. **Cons:** not everything has air-conditioning; could use sprucing up; noisy from nearby boats. 💲 *Rooms from: B2,800* ✉ *22/2 Moo 4* ☎ *038/651777, 095/535–7555* 🌐 *www.vrsamed.com/en/home-en/* *45 bungalows* 🍴 *Free breakfast.*

Chanthaburi

100 km (62 miles) east of Rayong, 180 km (108 miles) east of Pattaya.

Chanthaburi has played a big role in Thai history. It was here that the man who would become King Taksin gathered and prepared his troops to retake Ayutthaya from the Burmese after they sacked the capital of Siam in 1767. The King Taksin Shrine, shaped like a house-size helmet from that era, is on the north end of town. The French occupied the city from 1893 to 1905, and you can spot some architecture from that era along the river. Gems and jewelry form an important part of the town's modern economy, and you will see plenty of evidence of the gem trade in and around town. Most visitors stop here on the way to Koh Chang, attracted by either gem shopping or the fruit season in May and June.

Continued on page 196

Thailand's Beaches

Thailand is a beach-lover's paradise, with nearly 2,000 miles of coastline divided between two stunning shores. Whether you're looking for an exclusive resort, a tranquil beach town, an island with great rock-climbing, or a secluded cove, you can find the right atmosphere on the Andaman or the Gulf coast.

by Martin Young

With so many beaches to choose from, deciding where to go can be overwhelming. What time of year you're traveling helps narrow things down, since the two coasts have different monsoon seasons. In general, the Andaman Coast has bigger waves and better water clarity, although the Gulf Coast has some great snorkeling and diving spots too, particularly around the islands. On both coasts there are windy spots ideal for wind- and kite-surfing, and peaceful bays that beckon swimmers and sunbathers.

Sea temperature averages near a luxurious 80 degrees on both coasts, and almost all beaches are sandy; Andaman beaches tend to have more powdery sand, while Gulf sand is a bit grainier. Developed beaches on both coasts offer tons of activities like sailing, fishing, and rock climbing.

Ao Nang beach, Krabi.

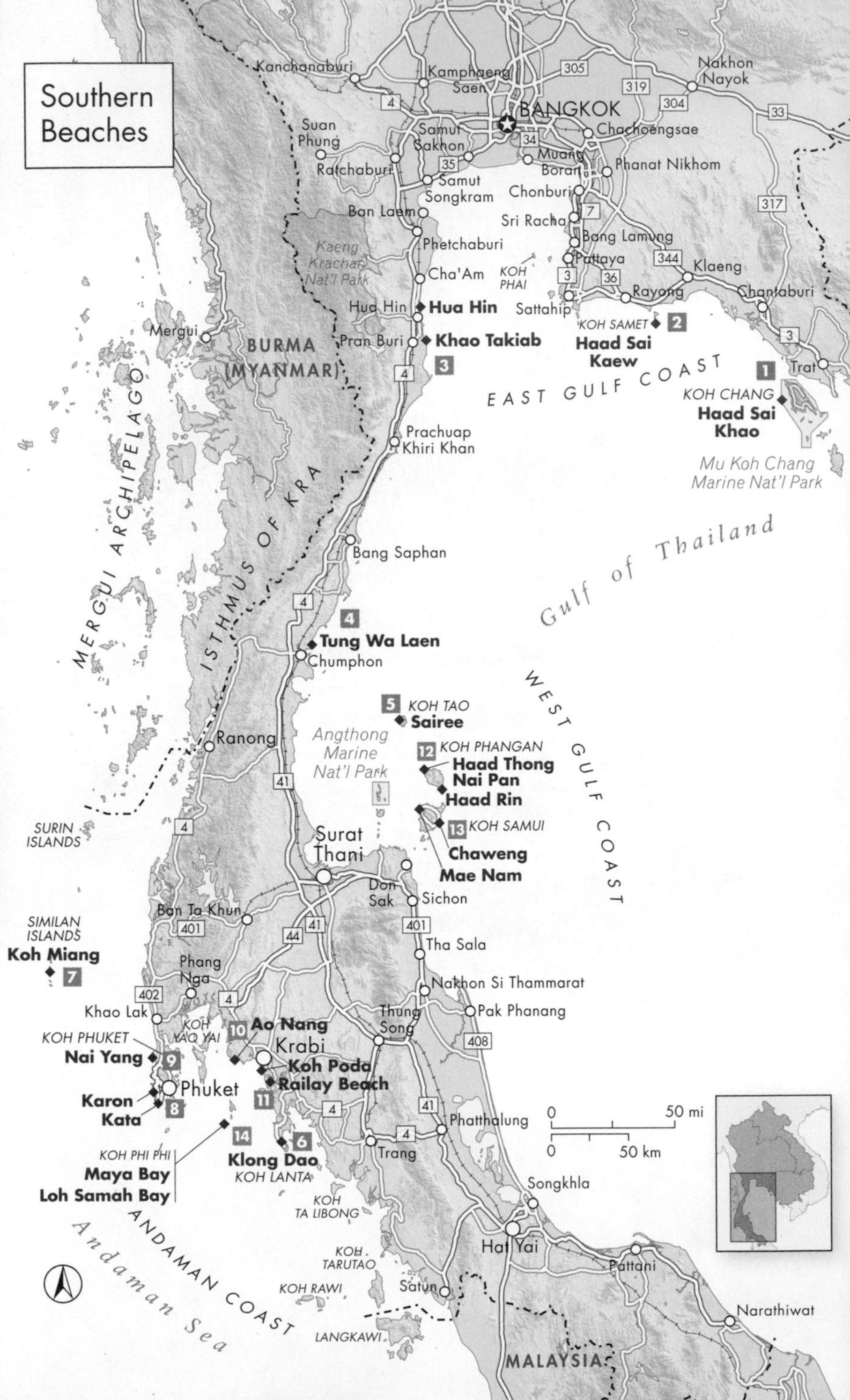
Southern Beaches
Kanchanaburi
Kamphaeng Saen
BANGKOK
Nakhon Nayok
Suan Phung
Samut Sakhon
Chachoengsae
Muang Boran
Ratchaburi
Phanat Nikhom
Samut Songkram
Chonburi
Ban Laem
Sri Racha
Bang Lamung
Phetchaburi
Kaeng Krachan Nat'l Park
Pattaya
Cha'Am
KOH PHAI
Klaeng
Rayong
Chantaburi
Hua Hin
Hua Hin
Sattahip
KOH SAMET
2
Haad Sai Kaew
Mergui
BURMA (MYANMAR)
Pran Buri
Khao Takiab
3
Trat
1
EAST GULF COAST
KOH CHANG
Haad Sai Khao
Prachuap Khiri Khan
Mu Koh Chang Marine Nat'l Park
MERGUI ARCHIPELAGO
ISTHMUS OF KRA
Bang Saphan
Gulf of Thailand
4
Tung Wa Laen
Chumphon
WEST GULF COAST
5
KOH TAO
Sairee
Angthong Marine Nat'l Park
Ranong
12
KOH PHANGAN
Haad Thong Nai Pan
Haad Rin
13
KOH SAMUI
SURIN ISLANDS
Surat Thani
Chaweng
Mae Nam
Don Sak
Sichon
Ban Ta Khun
SIMILAN ISLANDS
Koh Miang
7
Tha Sala
Phang Nga
Nakhon Si Thammarat
Khao Lak
KOH YAO YAI
Pak Phanang
KOH PHUKET
10
Ao Nang
Thung Song
Krabi
Nai Yang
9
Koh Poda
Railay Beach
Phuket
Karon
Kata
8
11
Phatthalung
14
6
Trang
KOH PHI PHI
Maya Bay
Loh Samah Bay
Klong Dao
KOH LANTA
0
50 mi
0
50 km
Songkhla
KOH TA LIBONG
ANDAMAN COAST
Andaman Sea
Hat Yai
KOH TARUTAO
Pattani
KOH RAWI
Satun
Narathiwat
LANGKAWI
MALAYSIA
4
41
44
401
402
408
305
319
304
33
34
35
317
7
344
36
3

TOP SPOTS

(left) Kata beach, Phuket (right) Maya Bay, famous from the Hollywood film *The Beach*.

1 On mountainous **Koh Chang**, hillside meets powdery white sand and calm, clear water at **Haad Sai Khao.**

2 **Koh Samet** is famous for its sugary beaches and crystal-clear water; there's room for everyone on **Haad Sai Kaew,** the island's longest beach.

3 Water sports enthusiasts like **Hua Hin's** wide, sandy beach. Just south, **Khao Takiab's** longer, wider beach is more popular with locals, but gets busy on weekends and holidays.

4 Kitesurfers love long, quiet **Tung Wa Laen** beach for its winds and shallow water.

5 **Koh Tao's** most developed beach, **Sairee**, is the place to learn to dive and has gorgeous sunsets.

6 Laid-back **Klong Dao** on **Koh Lanta** has long expanses of palm-fringed white sand and azure water.

7 The clear water around the nine **Similan Islands** is Thailand's best underwater playground. **Koh Miang** has some basic bungalows and tranquil white-sand beaches.

8 On **Phuket,** neighboring beaches **Karon** and **Kata** have killer sunsets, great waves, and plenty of daytime and nighttime activities.

9 **Nai Yang,** a tranquil, curving beach on northern **Phuket,** is a pretty place to relax.

10 **Ao Nang** has a nice strip of shops and restaurants and stunning views of the islands in Phanga Bay from its beach. Boats to **Koh Poda**—a small island with white coral sand, hidden coves, and jaw-dropping views—leave from here.

11 **Railay Beach** peninsula has limestone cliffs, knockout views, and crystal-clear water.

12 Backpackers flock to **Haad Rin** for **Koh Phangan's** famous full-moon parties. To get away from the crowds, head north to **Haad Thong Nai Pan**, a beautiful horseshoe bay on **Phangan's** more remote east coast.

13 **Chaweng, Koh Samui's** busiest beach, has gently sloping white sand, clear water, and vibrant nightlife. On the north coast, less developed **Mae Nam** beach is a natural beauty.

14 On **Koh Phi Phi,** breathtaking **Maya Bay,** closes periodically as it gets very crowded; small but beautiful **Loh Samah Bay** on the other side of the island is less hectic.

KEY

- Diving
- Fishing
- Kayaking
- Land Sports
- Sailing
- Snorkeling
- Surfing

BEACH FINDER

BEACH	NATURAL BEAUTY	DESERTED	PARTY SCENE	THAI CULTURE	RESORTS	BUNGALOWS	GOLF	SNORKELING/ DIVING	SURFING	KITEBOARDING/ WINDSURFING	ACCESSIBILITY
EASTERN GULF											
Pattaya	□		■		□	□		□	□	■	■
Koh Samet	■	■		□		□					□
Koh Chang	□		□		□	■		■			□
Koh Si Chang	□	□		□		□					□
WESTERN GULF											
Cha-am	□	□		■		□		□	□	□	■
Hua Hin	■		■	□	□	□		□	□	□	■
Takiab Beach	□	□		□	□	□		■	□	■	■
Koh Samui	■	□	□	□	■	□	□	□	□	□	■
Koh Phangan	■	□	□	□		■		□	□	□	□
Koh Tao	■	□	□	□	□	■		■	□	□	□
KOH PHUKET											
Mai Khao Beach	□	■		□	■	□	□	□			■
Nai Yang Beach	□	■		□	■	□	□				■
Nai Thon & Layan Beaches	□	■		□	■	□	□	□			■
Bang Thao Beach	□	■	□	□	■	□	□	□		■	□
Pansea, Surin & Laem Beaches	□	□		□	□	□	□				□
Kamala Beach	■	□	□	□	□	□	□	□			□
Patong	■		■	□	■	■	□	□		□	■
Karon Beach	■	□	□	□	■	■	□				□
Kata Beach	□	□	■	□	■	■	□	□	■	□	□
Nai Harn	□	■		■	□	□	□				□
Chalong		■		■			□				□
ANDAMAN COAST											
Phang Nga Bay	■		■					■			
Koh Yao	□	■		□	□	□		■			
Khao Lak	■		□	□	□	□	□	■			□
Similan Islands	■	□		□		□		■			
Surin Islands	■	□		□		□		■			
Ao Nang	□		■	□	■	■		■	□		□
Nang Cape/Railay Beach	■	□	■	□	■	■		■			
Koh Phi Phi	■	□	■		■	■		■			
Koh Lanta	□	□	□		■	■	□	□			□

KEY: □ = Available ■ = Exceptional

GOOD TO KNOW

WHAT SHOULD I WEAR?

On most beaches, bikinis, Speedos, and other swimwear are all perfectly OK. But wear *something*—going topless or nude is generally not acceptable. Women should exercise some caution on remote beaches where skimpy attire might attract unwanted attention from locals.

Once you leave the beach, throw on a cover up or a sarong. Unbuttoned shirts are fine, but sitting at a restaurant or walking through town in only your bathing suit is tacky, though you'll see other travelers doing it. Some areas have a Muslim majority, and too much exposed skin is frowned upon.

Beachside dining on Khao Lak.

WHAT TO EXPECT

Eating & Drinking: most popular beaches have a number of bars and restaurants.

Restrooms: few beaches have public facilities, so buy a drink at a restaurant and use theirs.

Rentals & Guides: You can arrange rentals and guides once you arrive. A dive trip costs B2,000 to B3,000 per person; snorkeling gear starts at about B300 a day; a surfboard or a board and kite is B1,000 to B1,500 a day; and a jet-ski rental runs around B500 for 15 minutes.

Hawkers: Vendors selling fruit, drinks, sarongs, and souvenirs can become a nuisance, but a firm "No, thank you" and a smile is the only required response.

Beach chairs: The chairs you'll see at many beaches are for rent; if you plop down in one, someone will usually appear to collect your baht.

WHAT TO WATCH OUT FOR

- **The tropical sun.** Wear strong sunscreen. Drink lots of water. Enough said.
- **Undertows** are a danger, and most beaces lack lifeguards.
- **Jellyfish** are a problem at certain times of year, usually before the rainy season. If you are stung, apply vinegar to the sting—beachside restaurants will probably have some. ("Jellyfish sting" in Thai is *maeng ga-proon fai*, but the locals will probably understand your sign language.)
- **Nefarious characters,** including prostitutes and drug dealers, may approach you, particularly in Patong and Pattaya. As with hawkers, a firm "No, thank you" should send them on their way.

BEACH VOCABULARY

Here are a few words help you decipher Thai beach names.

Ao means "bay."
Haad means "beach."
Koh means "island."
Talay means "sea."

GETTING HERE AND AROUND

Buses make the 90-minute journey from Rayong and Ban Phe. There's also a bus from Bangkok's Eastern Bus Terminal that takes from four to five hours.

Sights

Cathedral of Immaculate Conception

RELIGIOUS SITE | Chanthaburi's French influence is evident in its dual-spired Catholic cathedral, across the river from the center of town. Christian Vietnamese who migrated to the area erected the first church on this site in 1711, and the cathedral has been rebuilt four times since. The present Gothic-inspired structure was completed in the early 1900s when the city was under French control. The best time to visit is during the morning market, when local foods, fruits, and desserts are sold on the grounds. ⊠ *110 Moo 5, Chanthanimit Rd.* ✣ *Past eastern end of Sichan Rd., take footbridge across Chanthaburi River* 🎟 *Free.*

Gem Market

MARKET | Chanthaburi's gem mines are mostly closed, but the Gem Market, in the center of town, still attracts traders. You can often see them sorting through rubies and sapphires and making deals worth hundreds of thousands of baht. The market, an assortment of tables and stalls, takes place on Friday and Saturday along Sichan Road and various alleys off and near it. ⊠ *Sichan Rd.* 🎟 *Free.*

Koh Chang

1 hour by ferry from Laem Ngop, which is 15 km (9 miles) southwest of Trat; Trat is 400 km (250 miles) southeast of Bangkok.

Koh Chang, or Elephant Island, is the largest and most developed of the 52-island archipelago that became Mu Koh Chang National Park in 1982. Most of the 30-km-long (18-mile-long) island is mountainous—there are only a few small beaches and only nine villages, some accessible only by boat. Beautiful, albeit somewhat inaccessible, rain forest covers a large portion of this little paradise, making it ideal for those wanting more than just sun and sand. But the island is also a good bet for seaside relaxation: the beaches are picturesque and lack the overheated party scene of Pattaya. As the tourism industry grows on Koh Chang, mid-level resorts are becoming more common than expensive upscale establishments. Resorts are also being built on some of the other islands in the national park, including Koh Mak. **■ TIP→ Every beach on Koh Chang has something being built or renovated. Before you book your hotel, make sure there is no major construction project going on nearby.**

GETTING HERE AND AROUND

To get to Koh Chang you must first get to Trat, 96 km (60 miles) southeast of Chanthaburi. The easiest way is to take one of Bangkok Airways' daily flights. There are also air-conditioned buses from Bangkok's Eastern and Northern bus terminals; the trip takes a bit more than five hours and costs about B270.

BOAT TRAVEL

Take a ferry from one of three piers in Trat (Laem Ngop, Center Point, or Ao Thammachat) to one of two piers on Koh Chang. The trip takes a little more than half an hour, and the fare is roughly B140 round-trip.

SONGTHAEW TRAVEL

Once you're on the island, songthaews are the easiest way to get around. They cost between B30 and B50 per ride, or more if you venture toward the eastern part of the island.

SAFETY AND PRECAUTIONS

Koh Chang is becoming a bustling resort island, and though the crime rate is still very low, thieves do strike. Keep your valuables secured and use hotel safes.

During monsoon season, from June to October, take particular care when swimming. Currents can be deceptive, creating dangerous riptides that make swimming dangerous. Warning signs have been installed, but the beaches still lack lifeguards.

VISITOR AND TOUR INFORMATION

CONTACT Tourism Authority of Thailand
✉ *100 Moo 1, Trat* ✣ *Near Laem Ngop pier* ☎ *039/597255, 039/597259.*

Sights

Mu Koh Chang National Park

ISLAND | This 52-island marine national park covers all of Koh Chang. It's mostly mountainous, and there are only a few beaches, the best of them along the western shore. Haad Sai Khao (White Sand Beach) is the farthest north and the most developed. A few miles south is the more serene Haad Khlong Phrao, a long, curving stretch of pale golden sand. Nearby Haad Kai Bae is a mix of sand and pebbles. Still farther south is Haad Ta Nam (Lonely Beach), which is perhaps the most picturesque of all. But it's also the smallest one and therefore more crowded. In the southwest corner of the island is the fishing village Bang Bao, with restaurants, dive shops, and cheap bungalows. The east coast is beautiful, but it's mostly rugged rain forest, and beaches are in short supply. ✉ *Koh Chang* ✣ *Take Koh Chang Ferry (30 mins) from Trat.*

Beaches

Haad Kai Bae

BEACH—SIGHT | Its mix of pebbles and sand makes Kai Bae less popular than nearby strands, but this beach provides the best, and safest, swimming on Koh Chang. Quiet and relaxed, still enjoying a sleepy feel, Kai Bae has only a few restaurants and resorts. **Amenities:** food and drink. **Best for:** solitude; swimming. ✉ *Haad Kai Bae.*

Haad Khlong Phrao

BEACH—SIGHT | A quieter option than Sai Kaew's main beach, Khlong Phrao is an arc of golden sand leading down to placid waters. Scattered around the beach are a few high-end resorts and restaurants. The shallow waters discourage boaters, but also don't invite much swimming. **Amenities:** food and drink. **Best for:** walking. ✉ *Haad Khlong Phrao.*

Haad Sai Khao

BEACH—SIGHT | With numerous resorts and some great restaurants, Koh Chang's busiest beach is ideal for those seeking a bustling atmosphere. The beach remains free from deck chair vendors, but a few hawkers wander through during the day. Especially during the rainy season, between June and October, severe riptides can occur, and swimming can be unsafe for extended periods. **Amenities:** food and drink. **Best for:** partiers. ✉ *Haad Sai Khao.*

Haad Ta Nam (*Lonely Beach*)

BEACH—SIGHT | Koh Chang's hangout for the backpacker set has murky, sometimes rough water that's not ideal for swimming, but the vibe is cool. Though the beach itself is strewn with rocks, the hammock-lined bars draw patrons seeking a bit of spiritual enlightenment, cheap drinks, or both. Despite its name, beautiful Lonely Beach can get crowded. **Amenities:** food and drink. **Best for:** partiers. ✉ *Haad Ta Nam.*

Restaurants

Blues Blues

$ | **THAI** | Hidden in plain sight on the way to an elephant camp and waterfall is this family-run Thai restaurant that brings a love of food, art (one of the owners is a multimedia artist and the decor reflects this), and music together under one canopy. Keep it classic with curries, stir-fries, or stuffed omelets—all fairly priced and full of flavor. **Known for:** open-air dining; unique decor; simple yet satisfying local

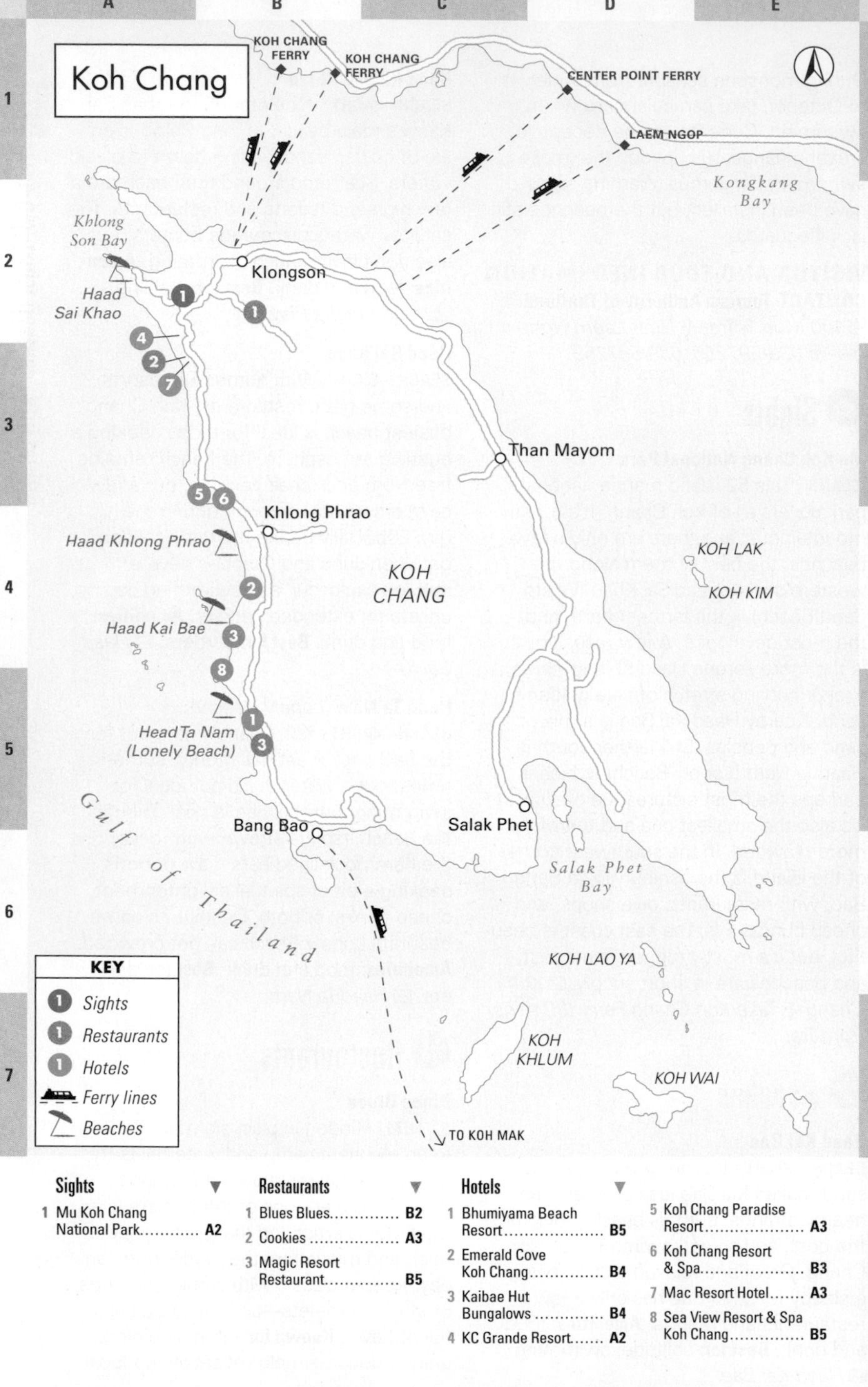

Sights

1 Mu Koh Chang National Park........... **A2**

Restaurants

1 Blues Blues............. **B2**
2 Cookies.................. **A3**
3 Magic Resort Restaurant.............. **B5**

Hotels

1 Bhumiyama Beach Resort.................... **B5**
2 Emerald Cove Koh Chang............... **B4**
3 Kaibae Hut Bungalows.............. **B4**
4 KC Grande Resort....... **A2**
5 Koh Chang Paradise Resort.................... **A3**
6 Koh Chang Resort & Spa.................... **B3**
7 Mac Resort Hotel....... **A3**
8 Sea View Resort & Spa Koh Chang.............. **B5**

dishes. $ *Average main: B100 ✉ Klong Son ☎ 087/144–6412 ▭ No credit cards.*

Cookies

$ | **ECLECTIC** | The best feature of Cookies Hotel is its delightful beachfront restaurant, where the Thai food is consistently good and inexpensive. The *tom yum talay* (hot-and-sour seafood soup) could be hotter, but it's definitely a standout. **Known for:** banana shakes and pancakes; reasonable bungalow rates; perfect spot to watch the sunset on White Sand Beach. $ *Average main: B150 ✉ Cookies Hotel, 7/2 Moo 4, Haad Sai Khao ☎ 039/551107 🌐 www.cookieskohchang.com.*

Magic Resort Restaurant

$ | **SEAFOOD** | A refreshing breeze cools the open-air dining area of this low-key resort that has good views of the coastline and the surrounding high hills. Sitting over the water, the restaurant is in a rather worn-down wooden structure, but the trade-off is very good seafood. **Known for:** breakfast all day; fairly priced Western food; spicy crab. $ *Average main: B150 ✉ 34 Moo 4, Haad Khlong Phrao ☎ 039/557074.*

Hotels

Bhumiyama Beach Resort

$$ | **RESORT** | These two-story bungalows set in a tropical garden have a modern look and a luxurious feel, with white walls and much polished wood. **Pros:** good deal; interesting decor; next to Lonely Beach. **Cons:** slightly claustrophobic feel; some rooms lack sea views; breakfast is very basic. $ *Rooms from: B3,271 ✉ 99/1 Moo 4, Lonely Beach ☎ 02/236–5064 🌐 www.bhumiyama.com 🛏 43 rooms 🍽 Free breakfast.*

★ Emerald Cove Koh Chang

$$$ | **RESORT** | Koh Chang's top hotel lives up to its five-star reputation with spacious and tastefully decorated rooms with hardwood floors and private balconies. **Pros:** classy accommodations; high level of service; plenty of sun beds. **Cons:** expensive rates; unexciting dining; a little isolated. $ *Rooms from: B4,699 ✉ 88/8 Moo 4, Tambol, Haad Khlong Phrao ☎ 039/552000, 089/236–5064 in Bangkok 🌐 www.emeraldcovekohchang.com 🛏 165 rooms 🍽 Free breakfast.*

Kaibae Hut Bungalows

$ | **RESORT** | There are many strings of bungalows on Kai Bae Beach, but this property is the most established and reliable. **Pros:** attentive staff; central location; stable Wi-Fi. **Cons:** beach is far from some rooms; some bungalows could use upgrading; nearby bar can be noisy at night. $ *Rooms from: B1,500 ✉ 10/3 Moo 4, Kai Bae Beach ☎ 039/557142, 086/063–2876, 081/862–8426 🌐 www.kaibaehutresort.com/ ▭ No credit cards 🛏 54 rooms 🍽 Free breakfast.*

KC Grande Resort

$$$ | **RESORT** | The bungalows here range from fan-cooled huts to spacious, amenities-laden suites; some of the best accommodations are right on the beach. **Pros:** beautiful location; bungalows feel very private; lots of variety at breakfast. **Cons:** atmosphere may feel stuffy; least expensive rooms not so desirable; could use an upgrade in some areas. $ *Rooms from: B4,480 ✉ 1/1 Moo 4, White Sand Beach ☎ 039/552111, 02/539–5424 in Bangkok 🌐 www.kckohchang.com ▭ No credit cards 🛏 61 bungalows 🍽 No meals.*

Koh Chang Paradise Resort

$$ | **RESORT** | With all the amenities of a big-city hotel, these spacious bungalows have private porches for enjoying the breeze. **Pros:** swim-up bar; lovely beachside location; fire show a few nights a week. **Cons:** not luxurious; subpar food; superior bungalows suffer from street noise. $ *Rooms from: B3,600 ✉ 39/4 Moo 4, Haad Khlong Phrao ☎ 039/551100, 039/551101 🌐 www.kohchangparadise.com 🛏 69 bungalows 🍽 Free breakfast.*

Koh Mak, an island just south of Koh Chang, is known for its spectacular sunsets.

Koh Chang Resort & Spa

$ | **RESORT** | On the edge of the bay, this self-contained complex was one of Koh Chang's first major developments. **Pros:** good for couples; nice spa; good value. **Cons:** dated room decor; disappointing food; poor Wi-Fi connection. *Rooms from: B1,900* *39 Moo 4* *086/302–6064, 086/301–0770* *www.kohchangresortandspa.com* *145 rooms* *Free breakfast.*

Mac Resort Hotel

$ | **RESORT** | An ocean-view room with a hot tub and private balcony—or if not that, a poolside beachfront bungalow—is the way to go at the Mac. This is a friendly place, and there's a nightly barbecue on the beach. **Pros:** reasonable rates; generally cool guests; wide range of accommodations. **Cons:** not fancy; noise from nearby nightclub; food is unremarkable. *Rooms from: B1,500* *7/3 Moo 4, Sai Khao Beach* *039/551124, 01/864–6463* *www.macresortkohchang.com/en/* *25 rooms* *Free breakfast.*

Sea View Resort & Spa Koh Chang

$$ | **RESORT** | At the far end of the beach, this resort is quieter than most at Kai Bae. Choose between bungalows a stone's throw from the surf or rooms in a building looming over the strand. **Pros:** private beach access; well-manicured grounds; breakfast comes with beautiful views. **Cons:** removed from action; limited food options; steep hill setting. *Rooms from: B3,600* *63 Moo 4* *039/552888, 039/552800* *www.seaviewkohchang.com* *74 rooms, 2 suites* *Free breakfast.*

Activities

HIKING AND TREKKING

Hiking trips, particularly to some of the island's waterfalls, are popular. It's a good idea to hire a guide if you plan to venture farther than one of the well-traveled routes, as good maps of the mostly jungle terrain are hard to come by.

Ban Kwan Chang

TOUR—SPORTS | On the northern end of the island, this outfit conducts elephant treks endorsed by the Asian Elephant Foundation, so you can trust that the animals are treated humanely. Half-day tours (from 8:30 to noon; B1500 per person) include a bathing and feeding session and a 90-minute journey into the jungle, as well as transportation from your hotel. There are also shorter treks that cost B850. Most hotels can arrange trips for you. ✉ *22/16 Moo 4* ☎ *081/919–3995.*

SCUBA DIVING AND SNORKELING

Scuba diving, including PADI-certified courses, is readily available. Divers report that the fish are smaller than in other parts of Thailand, but the coral is better. Prices run from B3,500 for an introductory dive to more than B20,000 for dive-master certification. Snorkeling off a boat costs as little as B900 a day. Snorkelers usually just tag along on dive boats, but boat snorkeling excursions also take place.

Chang Diving Center

SCUBA DIVING | Snorkeling trips in the shallow parts of this company's dive sites are offered here for B950, along with scuba courses that cover all sorts of skill sets and special interests. ✉ *21/17 Moo 4, Klong Praw Beach* ☎ *039/611273* 🌐 *www.changdiving.com/.*

Scuba Dawgs

SCUBA DIVING | Experienced divers are encouraged to book a shipwreck trip with this courteous and professional company. They also organize daily snorkeling trips (B900) and host a wide array of educational classes, from refresher courses to advanced open-water techniques. ✉ *114/1 Bang Bao Pier Tambon* ☎ *083/469–6964* 🌐 *www.scuba-dawgs.com/.*

Thai Fun

SCUBA DIVING | This outfit's 10-hour, 15-island tour of the marine park includes a buffet lunch, excursions to two or more islands, and two snorkeling stops. The cost is around B1,400. ☎ *06/141–7498* 🌐 *www.thaifun-kohchang.com/.*

Cha-am

163 km (101 miles) south of Bangkok, 40 km (25 miles) from Petchaburi.

It may not be the most picturesque seaside town, but Cha-am does offer an authentic Thai-style beach experience. The pier at the north end of Cha-am Beach is the center of this small quiet town. Its main street, Ruamchit Beach Road, passes by a tree-lined strip of beach on one side and restaurants, bars, guesthouses, and hotels on the other. Fresh seafood is available at small cafés along this road, where there are also stalls selling trays of deep-fried squid, shrimp, and tiny crab for around B25. Cha-am retains its sleepy charm, and those searching for peace and quiet may find their niche here.

GETTING HERE AND AROUND

Buses leave Bangkok's Southern Bus Terminal every 30 minutes between 6:30 am and 7 pm; the 2½-hour trip costs around B150. Once you're here, tuk-tuks are the best way to get around.

VISITOR AND TOUR INFORMATION

CONTACT Tourism Authority of Thailand ✉ *Petchkasem Rd.* ☎ *032/471005, 032/471502* 🌐 *www.tourismthailand.org.*

 Beaches

Cha-am Beach

BEACH—SIGHT | At Cha-am's broad town beach you can often see Bangkok families gathered at umbrella-covered tables for all-day meals, stocking up on fresh fruit and seafood and cold beer from wandering vendors. The beach's sand, though, is fairly dark and dirty. Most visitors head to one of the all-inclusive resorts farther away, where the sand is prettier and the water better for swimming. **Amenities:** food and drink; parking; toilets. **Best for:** walking. ✉ *Ruamchit Beach Rd.*

Restaurants

Poom Restaurant

$ | **SEAFOOD** | The steady stream of locals is one clue that the seafood here ranks among the town's best. Try the charcoal-grilled whole fish, large prawns, crab, and squid—all fresh and accompanied by a delicious chili sauce. **Known for:** ample portions; sea-view terrace; devoted Thai clientele. *Average main: B120* ✉ *274/1 Ruamchit Rd.* ☎ *032/471036.*

Hotels

Regent Beach Cha-am

$$ | **RESORT** | Taking a swim couldn't be easier than at this resort with its quartet of pools amid dozens of bungalows facing the beach. **Pros:** pretty layout; fun nightlife; solid food options. **Cons:** unpredictable availability; remote location; lack of air-conditioning. *Rooms from: B2,900* ✉ *849/21 Cha-am Beach* ☎ *032/451240, 02/251–0305 in Bangkok* *www.regent-chaam.com* *660 rooms* *Free breakfast.*

Sabaya Jungle Resort

$$ | **RESORT** | Whether relaxing in your room or sipping a cup of tea in the common area, you'll feel at home in this attractive resort. **Pros:** nice spa; cool rooms; breathtaking location. **Cons:** not on the beach; unexciting pool; small bungalows. *Rooms from: B2,000* ✉ *304/7 Nong Chaeng Rd.* ☎ *032/470716, 032/470717* *www.sabayaresort.com/* *16 bungalows* *Free breakfast.*

Hua Hin

66 km (41 miles) from Cha-am, 189 km (118 miles) south of Bangkok.

The golden sands near the small seaside city of Hua Hin have long attracted Bangkok's rich and famous. The most renowned visitors are the king and queen of Thailand, who now use the Klai Kangwol Palace north of Hua Hin town as their primary residence. The palace was completed in 1928 by King Rama VII, who gave it the name Klai Kangwol, which means "Far From Worries."

Hua Hin is a year-round destination. Weekends and Thai public holidays are times to avoid, when the Bangkok set floods the city—prices rise and the streets become noticeably busier.

GETTING HERE AND AROUND

The bus is the most convenient way to get here from Bangkok. Buses depart hourly from the Southern Bus Terminal; the trip takes three hours and costs about B200. Minivans (B280) head here from Bangkok's Khao San Road or Victory Monument and are generally faster than buses, though some operators try to squeeze in too many passengers.

BUS CONTACT Hua Hin ✉ *1991/20 Phet Kasem Rd.*

SAFETY AND PRECAUTIONS

Hua Hin has witnessed an expat boom in recent years, and along with high-rise condos has come inevitable influx of less desirable elements. Pickpockets sometimes operate in town, and some hotel-room theft has occurred. These incidents are few and far between, however.

Overall the town is safe, as you would expect for a place that hosts the king and queen of Thailand, and the police are in full evidence day and night. Always engage a registered tuk-tuk driver (easy to spot because they will display their credentials) if you are going some distance.

Khao Sam Roi Yod National Park

You'll pass rice fields, sugar palms, pineapple plantations, and crab farms as you make your way to this park south of Hua Hin, the gloriously named "300 Peaks." It has two main trails and is a great place to spot wildlife, especially monitor lizards and barking deer. With a little luck you might even see the adorable dusky langur, a monkey known for the white circles around its eyes. About a kilometer (½ mile) from the park's headquarters is Khao Daeng Hill, which is worth a hike up to the viewpoint, especially at sunrise. Another 16 km (10 miles) from the headquarters is Haad Laem Sala, a white-sand beach. Near the beach is Phraya Nakhon Cave, once visited by King Rama V. The cave has an opening in its roof where sunlight shines through for a beautiful effect. If you don't have a car or haven't hired one, you'll have to take a bus to the Pranburi District in Prachuab Kiri Khan Province. From here you take a songthaew to the park.

Sights

Chatchai Street Market

MARKET | This long-established market is a favorite with locals and tourists. Residents come during the day to purchase meats, seafood, and produce; after 5 pm you'll find everything from jewelry and clothing to toys and artworks. The evening market also has interesting eats, including Thai *kanom* (sweets), exotic fruits, barbecued meats, and traditional Thai dishes. ✉ *Dechanuchit St.*

Beaches

Hua Hin Beach

BEACH—SIGHT | Hua Hin's namesake beach is the nicest of those along this part of the coast, but it's also the most popular. Though not as stunning as other Thai beaches, it's a wide, 7-km-long (4½-mile-long) boulevard of golden sand. Vendors hawk food and drink nonstop, but you can escape this parade by booking a relaxing beach massage or taking a horseback ride to less populated sections. Water sports can be arranged at various points. It can get rough and the sea isn't clear, but you can definitely swim here. **Amenities:** food and drink; water sports. **Best for:** walking. ✉ *Hua Hin* ✣ *Off Petchkasem Rd.*

Restaurants

Buffalo Bill's at Fisherman's Wharf

$$ | **SEAFOOD** | This surf-and-turf restaurant takes pride in using the best of the region's produce and seafood. Try the beer-battered fish-and-chips served in traditional newspaper wrapping, or start your day with the best eggs Benedict in town. **Known for:** Sunday roast specials; spicy Thai food if you don't want Western fare, reputable guest rooms. $ *Average main: B250* ✉ *8 Chomsin Rd.* ☎ *08/0727–4710* 🌐 *www.buffalobillshuahin.com.*

★ Koti

$$ | **SEAFOOD** | A longtime local favorite for Thai-style seafood, Koti has a no-nonsense decor and a packed dining room that attests to the flavor of dishes like *hor mok talay* (steamed seafood curry). The large menu includes such crowd-pleasers as fried fish with garlic and pepper. **Known for:** prime night market location; bustling atmosphere; open kitchen.

$ Average main: B200 ✉ 61/1 Petchkasem Rd. ☎ 032/511252 ▭ No credit cards ⏲ No lunch.

Orchids Restaurant

$$ | **FRENCH FUSION** | The chefs at this Thai-French restaurant acknowledge its Asian influences while relying mainly on French technique. Prawns might come, for instance, Thai-style in a curry with fresh coriander in coconut milk or with echoes of France in a vermouth sauce. **Known for:** steak and seafood; locally grown organic vegetables; understated decor with traditional Thai flourishes. *$ Average main: B250 ✉ Fulay Hotel, 110/1 Naresdamri Rd. ☎ 032/513670 ⊕ www.fulayhuahin.com ▭ No credit cards.*

Saeng Thai

$ | **SEAFOOD** | Popular with Thais (always a good sign), Saeng Thai serves everything from grilled prawns with bean noodles to fried grouper with chili and tamarind juice. Now in a new larger inland location that's a step up from its original ramshackle setting. **Known for:** eclectic seafood dishes; huge prawns; private air-conditioned rooms. *$ Average main: B150 ✉ 8/3 Naebkehardt Rd. ☎ 032/530343.*

Hotels

Anantara

$$$ | **RESORT** | Surrounded by a 10-foot-tall terra-cotta wall, this beach resort looks like an ancient Thai village. **Pros:** lots of elephants; inspiring setting; many activities. **Cons:** verges on stuffy; expensive rates; service can be inconsistent. *$ Rooms from: B5,000 ✉ 43/1 Phetkasem Beach Rd. ☎ 032/520250 ⊕ www.anantara.com ⇨ 187 rooms 🍴 Free breakfast.*

★ Centara Grand Beach Resort and Villas

$$$ | **HOTEL** | Even if you don't stay at this local landmark, its old-world charm makes it worth a visit. **Pros:** tricked-out topiaries; cool atmosphere; fantastic ocean views on the second floor. **Cons:** pricey; not a party destination; service is slipping a little. *$ Rooms from: B5,300 ✉ 1 Damnernkasem Rd. ☎ 032/512021 up to 38, 02/541–1125 in Bangkok ⊕ www.centarahotelsresorts.com ⇨ 207 rooms, 30 suites 🍴 No meals.*

★ Chiva-Som

$$$$ | **HOTEL** | One of the best spa resorts in the region—and possibly the world—Chiva-Som has tasteful and comfortable rooms accented with natural woods. **Pros:** unique spa program; high level of service; great variety of activities and services. **Cons:** not for partiers; expensive; must book at least three nights. *$ Rooms from: B64,000 ✉ 73/4 Petchkasem Rd. ☎ 032/536536 ⊕ www.chivasom.com ⇨ 57 rooms 🍴 No meals.*

★ Dusit Thani Hua Hin Hotel

$$$ | **RESORT** | The spacious lobby at this hotel between Hua Hin and Cha-am serves as a lounge for afternoon tea and evening cocktails, sipped to the soft melodies of traditional Thai music. **Pros:** beachfront setting; traditional architecture; lots of amenities; friendly bilingual staff. **Cons:** need a car (or taxi) to get around; some rooms need freshening up. *$ Rooms from: B4,600 ✉ 1349 Petchkasem Rd., Cha-am ☎ 032/520009, 02/636–3333 in Bangkok ⊕ www.dusit.com/dusitthani/huahin ⇨ 300 rooms 🍴 Free breakfast.*

Evason Hideaway and Evason Hua Hin Resort

$$ | **RESORT** | These neighboring properties are set on a quiet beach in Pranburi, about 20 minutes south of Hua Hin. The newer Hideaway resort has villas and suites, all of which have private plunge pools and outdoor tubs, along with lounging areas with umbrella-shaded daybeds. **Pros:** supercomfortable accommodations; access to double the amenities; lots of activities. **Cons:** out of the way; too quiet for some; not-so-great beach. *$ Rooms from: B3,700 ✉ 9/22 Moo 5 Paknampran,*

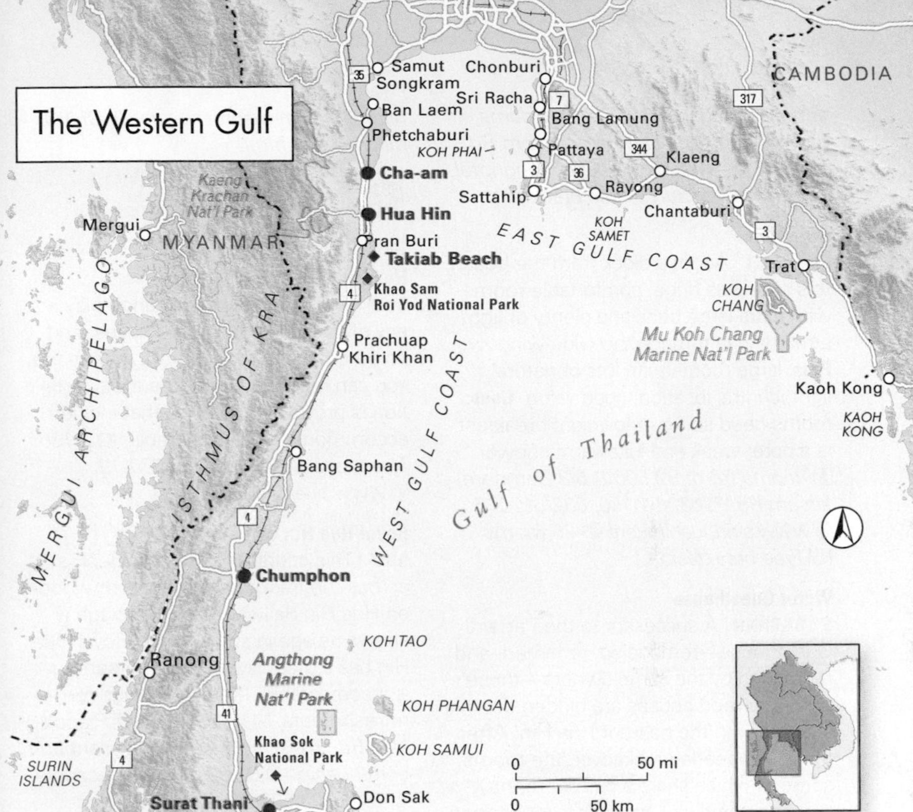

Pran Buri ☎ *032/618200 Hideaway, 032/632111 resort* ⊕ *www.sixsenses.com/Evason-Hua-Hin* ⇨ *Hideaway: 17 suites, 38 villas; Resort: 185 rooms, 40 villas* 🍴 *Free breakfast.*

Fulay Guesthouse

$ | **B&B/INN** | On a pier that juts out over the water, this guesthouse is unlike any other in Hua Hin. The Cape Cod–blue planks of the pier match the color of the trim around the whitewashed walls. **Pros:** hard to beat the price; cool location; sounds of the sea. **Cons:** questionable decor; some rooms lack air-conditioning; thin walls. $ *Rooms from: B550* ✉ *110/1 Naresdamri Rd.* ☎ *032/513145, 032/513670* ⊕ *www.fulayhuahin.net* ▭ *No credit cards* ⇨ *14 rooms* 🍴 *Free breakfast.*

Hilton Hua Hin Resort and Spa

$$$$ | **HOTEL** | In the liveliest part of town, the Hilton is perfect for fun-and-sun enthusiasts who want to be close to the action. **Pros:** central location; rooms with great views; high-tech touches. **Cons:** narrow road leading to the hotel; too much foot traffic; could use a fresh coat of paint. $ *Rooms from: B6,500* ✉ *33 Naresdamri Rd.* ☎ *032/512888* ⊕ *www.hua-hin.hilton.com* ⇨ *296 rooms* 🍴 *Free breakfast.*

Jed Pee Nong Hotel

$ | **HOTEL** | On one of the main streets leading to the public entrance to Hua Hin Beach, Jed Pee Nong has bungalows clustered around a swimming pool and standard rooms in a high-rise building. **Pros:** reasonable rates; prime location by the beach; kept nice and clean. **Cons:** nothing fancy; lots of nearby foot traffic; lacking in amenities. *$ Rooms from: B1,700 ✉ 17 Damnernkasem Rd. ☎ 032/512381 🌐 www.jedpeenonghotel.com/ 40 rooms 🍴 Free breakfast.*

Sirin Hotel

$$ | HOTEL | About a block from the beach, this hotel has huge, comfortable rooms with extra-large beds and plenty of light streaming in through the wide windows. **Pros:** large rooms with lots of natural light; central location; good value. **Cons:** rooms need some renovation; breakfast is a bore; weak and lukewarm shower. *$ Rooms from: B2,500 ✉ 6/3 Damnernkasem Rd. ☎ 032/511150, 032/512045 🌐 www.sirinhuahin.com 25 rooms 🍴 Free breakfast.*

Victor Guesthouse

$ | B&B/INN | A successor to the Pattana Guesthouse—remodeled, renamed, and rebranded by the same owners—these two teakwood houses are hidden down a small alley in the heart of Hua Hin. After the much-needed makeover, the rooms, some of which share a bathroom, now feel bright and airy. **Pros:** ideal for budget travelers; cute for what it is; central location. **Cons:** no adjacent beach; sounds from adjacent rooms easily heard; brick-like bedding. *$ Rooms from: B490 ✉ 60 Naresdamri Rd. ☎ 032/511564 🌐 www.victor-hotel-huahin.com/ No credit cards 13 rooms 🍴 No meals.*

Nightlife

Hua Hin Brewing Company

BREWPUBS/BEER GARDENS | Local bands energetically perform Thai and Western pop-rock music here nightly. Although this isn't a true brewpub (the beers are made in Bangkok), the selection is good, and you can try a sampler of three tasty beers. The outdoor patio offers a full multicultural dining menu and is a prime spot to people-watch. *✉ Hilton Hua Hin Resort and Spa, 33 Naresdamri Rd. ☎ 032/512888 🌐 www3.hilton.com/en/hotels/thailand/hilton-hua-hin-resort-and-spa-HHQHIHI/dining/index.html.*

Activities

GOLF

Hua Hin Golf Tours

GOLF | This company can arrange play at any of the area's 10 or so courses, and no surcharge is added to the greens fee. You can rent clubs, and free transportation is provided. Packages that include accommodations are available. *✉ 2/136 Naebkehardt Road ☎ 032/530119 🌐 www.huahingolf.com.*

Royal Hua Hin Golf Course

GOLF | This course, the area's oldest, sits across the tracks from the quaint wooden Hua Hin Railway Station. Though it shows its age in some spots, Royal Hua Hin has a great layout, and the setting is incomparable. There's a lounge for refreshments. *✉ Hua Hin ✣ Off Prapokklao Rd. ☎ 032/512475 🌐 www.santiburi.com/huahin/ B2,500, includes caddie 18 holes, 6678 yards, par 72.*

Takiab Beach

4 km (2½ miles) south of Hua Hin.

Directly to the south of Hua Hin, Khao Takiab is a good alternative for people who wish to avoid Hua Hin's busier scene. Takiab is favored by well-off Thais who prefer Takiab's exclusivity to Hua Hin's touristy atmosphere, and you can find many upscale condos and small luxury hotels here. The beach itself is wide and long, but the water is murky and shallow and not very suitable for swimming.

GETTING HERE AND AROUND

To get to Takiab, flag down a songthaew (B20) on Petchkasem Road in Hua Hin. You can also hire a horse and trot down the coast.

Beaches

Khao Takiab Beach

BEACH—SIGHT | Sunbathing is the ideal activity at Khao Tokiab, especially during low tide, when the golden, sandy strand is flat and dry. Jet-skiing, banana boating, and other water-sports activities are available here, all the more enjoyable than in Hua Hin because the beach and water are less crowded. A granite headland also named Khao Takiab separates the beach's northern and southern sections. On the headland's northern side, there's a tall standing image of the Buddha. You can hike to the top of the hill, where you'll find a small Buddhist monastery and several restaurants with excellent views. **Amenities:** food and drink; water sports. **Best for:** walking. ✉ *Nong Kae* ✣ *South of Hua Hin Beach.*

Restaurants

Supatra-by-the-Sea

$ | **THAI** | On the northern side of the Khao Takiab headland, this restaurant has outdoor seating with views of the nearby standing Buddha. Entrées are mainly seafood, such as prawn soup with a deep-fried green omelet, although other Thai dishes and vegetarian options are also available. **Known for:** exquisitely designed dining room; inventive beachside cocktails; extensive menu. [$] *Average main: B150* ✉ *122/63 Takiab Rd., Nong Kae* ☎ *032/655–3312* 🌐 *www.supatrabythesea.com/.*

Hotels

Chom View Hotel

$$ | **HOTEL** | **FAMILY** | This serene hotel is on the beach but with easy access to the rest of Hua Hin. The accommodations range from clean and simple standard rooms to expansive sea-view duplexes. **Pros:** family-friendly; steps away from the sea; modern decor. **Cons:** can feel isolated; unreliable Wi-Fi; sad breakfast spread. [$] *Rooms from: B2,900* ✉ *93 Soi Huatanon 23, Nongkae, Hua Hin* ✣ *Off Petkasem Rd.* ☎ *032/655–2925* 🌐 *www.chomviewhotel.com* *134 rooms* *Free breakfast* *No credit cards.*

Kaban Tamor Resort

$$ | **HOTEL** | The rooms at this resort are tucked inside two-story structures that were designed to resemble seashells but actually look more like mushrooms. **Pros:** easy beach access; cute rooms; laid-back location. **Cons:** tacky exterior; very oriented to Thai customers; feels a little isolated. [$] *Rooms from: B2,200* ✉ *122/43–57 Takiab Beach, Nong Kae* ☎ *032/655041* 🌐 *www.kabantamor.com* *23 rooms* *No meals.*

Chumphon

400 km (240 miles) south of Bangkok, 211 km (131 miles) south of Hua Hin.

Chumphon is regarded as the gateway to the south, because trains and buses connect to Bangkok to the north, to Surat Thani and Phuket to the south, and to Ranong to the southwest. Ferries to Koh Tao dock at Pak Nam at the mouth of the Chumphon River, 11 km (7 miles) southeast of town. Most of the city's boat services run a free shuttle to the docks.

GETTING HERE AND AROUND

Buses leave regularly from Bangkok's Southern Terminal. The journey takes between six and nine hours; most buses leave at night, so you'll arrive early in the morning, and tickets are between B300 and B600. Though buses are cheaper and more reliable, the *Southern Line* train from Bangkok's Hualamphong Station stops here. In Chumphon proper, tuk-tuks are a ubiquitous and easy way to get around.

Khao Sok National Park

A landscape of tall mountains, lush greenery, and small streams, this 161,000-acre park contains the most beautiful forest in Thailand. The diverse and rare wildlife that thrives here includes gaurs, bantengs, sambar deer, bears, Malayan tapirs, macaques, gibbons, mouse deer, and porcupines. Khao Sok is also one of the few places to see a rafflesia, the world's largest flower, and rare bird species such as hornbills live here. Hiking, boat rides, and night safaris are some of the activities that take place in the park. Rain is inevitable in Khao Sok, as the weather is influenced by monsoon winds from both the northeast and west—the best and driest time to visit is between December and April. Both the national park and some private resorts offer various types of lodging, but don't expect too much. Only very basic accommodations can be found in the park. There is additional private accommodation outside the park, most notably an oddly shaped tree-house accommodation 1 km (½ mile) before the park's entrance. The bus ride (B80) from the station in Surat Thani to the park takes about 2½ hours. The TAT office in Surat Thani has information about the park. A few hours by bus south of Surat Thani you'll discover a different landscape of tall mountain ranges covered with lush greenery and small streams.

SAFETY AND PRECAUTIONS

Theft sometimes occurs on overnight private buses traveling between Bangkok and Chumphon. Never leave valuables in luggage that's out of view.

Beaches

Thung Wua Laen Beach

BEACH—SIGHT | Small islands that make up one of the world's strangest bird sanctuaries dot the horizon of this excellent 3-km (2-mile) stretch of curving white-yellow sand. Vast flocks of swifts breed on the islands, and their nests are harvested, not without controversy, for the bird's-nest soup served in Chinese restaurants throughout Southeast Asia. It's such a lucrative business that the concessionaires patrol their properties with armed guards. But all is calm and serene on the beach, which is just north of Chumphon. To get here, catch a songthaew on the street across from the bus station. **Amenities:** food and drink. **Best for:** solitude. ✉ *Chumphon.*

Hotels

Chumphon Cabana Beach Resort

$ | **HOTEL** | This resort at the southern end of Thung Wua Laen Beach is a great place to stay if you plan to make brief visits to Koh Samui and other nearby islands. **Pros:** home base for island-hopping; also a diving center; not as touristry. **Cons:** you won't be fawned over; rooms nothing special; rustic and rough around the edges. *Rooms from: B1,650* ✉ *69 Moo 8 Thung Wua Laen Beach* ☎ *077/560245* *www.chumphoncabanaresort.com/* *73 rooms* *No meals.*

Marokot Hotel

$ | **HOTEL** | Lodging options are few in Chumphon, but this centrally located hotel has comfortable rooms and provides a reasonable level of service. **Pros:** inexpensive; centrally located; newly renovated rooms. **Cons:** some rooms lack air-conditioning; few amenities; breakfast is basic. *Rooms from: B990* ✉ *102–112 Taweesinka Rd.* ☎ *077/502999, 086/478–6377* *www.morakothotel.com*

No credit cards 130 rooms Free breakfast.

Surat Thani

193 km (120 miles) south of Chumphon, 685 km (425 miles) south of Bangkok.

Surat Thani is where you board the boats bound for Koh Samui. Though not particularly attractive, Surat Thani has a few culturally interesting sights that make it a good destination for those easily bored by the beach, and the mountains and greenery of Khao Sok National Park are a few hours away by bus. There are also some good restaurants and a handsome hotel.

GETTING HERE AND AROUND

You can get here from Bangkok by bus or train, but flying is the most efficient way to arrive. Thai Air Asia often has low fares. Bus trips from Bangkok's Southern Bus Terminal take about 10 hours and cost from B400 to B800. There's also an overnight train here from Bangkok's Hua Lamphong Station.

VISITOR AND TOUR INFORMATION

CONTACT Tourism Authority of Thailand *5 Talat Mai Rd.* *077/281828* *www.tourismthailand.org.*

Sights

San Chao Night Market

MARKET | Every night the sleepy downtown turns into an electrifying street fair centered around the San Chao Night Market, which is illuminated by the lights of numerous food stalls and shop carts. The market is popular with tourists and locals, especially for the tasty seafood meals on offer. *Surat Thani* *Alley off Na Muang Rd.*

Hotels

Wang Tai Hotel

$ | **HOTEL** | This modern high-rise offers everything you need for a Surat Thani stopover as you prepare for your onward journey. **Pros:** tasty food; handy location; great views. **Cons:** the rooms are tatty; doesn't feel particularly Thai; far from city center. *Rooms from: B1,250* *1 Talad Mai Rd.* *077/283020, 077/281007* *www.wangtaisurat.com/* *230 rooms* *Free breakfast.*

Koh Samui

20 km (12 miles) by boat east of Don Sak.

★ Koh Samui is the most popular tourist destination on the Western Gulf coast, which isn't surprising, considering the island's gorgeous beaches, perfect weather, and sparkling blue, almost turquoise, water. Koh Samui has seen rapid development since the 1990s, and you'll encounter hotels in all price ranges.

Koh Samui is half the size of Phuket, so you could easily drive around it in a day. But Koh Samui is best appreciated by those who take a slower, more casual approach. Most people come for the sun and sea, so they head straight to their hotel and rarely venture beyond its beach. But it's worth exploring beyond your lodging. Every beach has its own character, and you might find the perfect one for you.

One beach many visitors find to their liking is Chawaeng. On Koh Samui's east coast, this stretch of glistening white sand is divided into two main sections—Chawaeng Yai (*yai* means "big") and Chawaeng Noi (*noi* means "little"). You'll find the greatest variety of hotels, restaurants, and bars here. Despite the crowds, Chawaeng is no Pattaya or Patong—the mood is very laid-back. A rocky headland separates Chawaeng

Lamai Beach, whose clear water and long stretch of sand were the first place on the island to attract developers. More budget accommodations are available here than in Chawaeng, and there are some happening nightclubs.

On the west coast of Koh Samui, Na Thon is the island's primary port and the spot where ferries arrive from the mainland. It's home to the island's governmental offices, including the Tourism Authority of Thailand, and there are banks, foreign-exchange booths, travel agents, shops, restaurants, and cafés by the ferry pier. A few places rent rooms, but there's really no reason to stay here—nicer accommodations can be found a short songthaew ride away.

To the north and east of Na Thon lie a few beaches worthy of exploration. Laem Yai, 5 km (3 miles) north, has great seafood. East of here, a small headland separates two low-key communities on the northern shore, Mae Nam and Bophut Beach. Mae Nam is also the departure point for boats bound for Koh Phangan and Koh Tao *(see Side Trips from Koh Samui, below)*. Just south of the Samui's northeastern tip you'll find sandy Choengmon Beach, a good area for swimming that's not overdeveloped.

GETTING HERE AND AROUND

AIR TRAVEL

Bangkok Airways offers multiple daily flights from Bangkok, and Thai Airways has a morning and an evening flight. At around $200, the hour-long flight is a bit pricier than other flights within Thailand, mainly because the airport is owned by Bangkok Airways and not, as in most cases in Thailand, by the government.

BOAT TRAVEL

From Surat Thani's Donsak Pier, ferries leave every couple of hours for Koh Samui's Na Thon Pier on the west coast; the trip takes roughly two hours. Tour operators in Surat Thani and Koh Samui have information on the ferry schedules, or you can also just head to the pier. Expect to pay around B250 for the trip.

CAR AND TAXI TRAVEL

Koh Samui is a delight to explore, and it's one of the few destinations where having a car can come in really handy. A drive along the coastal road will provide one beautiful view after another; the interior of the island isn't as scenic. Budget and Hertz have counters at the Koh Samui airport, and National has its counter in downtown Koh Samui. Thai Rent a Car has a counter near the airport, and the company will deliver your car to you when you land. TA Car Rental is a reputable local company based on Samui.

Taxis don't always meet incoming flights at the airport in Koh Samui, but they can easily be called.

RENTAL CONTACTS Car4You Samui ✉ *42/15 Moo 4 Bophut* ☎ *086/476–8031* 🌐 *www.samui4ucarrent.com/*.

SAFETY AND PRECAUTIONS

Samui is a safe place. Crime rarely affects visitors, but there are the odd reports of thefts from hotel rooms and late-night robberies. Take sensible precautions, though, and your risk will be minimal.

The greatest safety issue for visitors involves ones with no experience who rent motorcycles and don't wear helmets. Additionally, some roads are hazardous, and there are reckless drivers who take advantage of lax law enforcement.

VISITOR INFORMATION

CONTACTS Tourism Authority of Thailand ✉ *Na Thon* ☎ *077/421281* 🌐 *www.tourismthailand.org*.

Sights

Coral Buddha

PUBLIC ART | About 4 km (2½ miles) from Lamai, at the small Chinese fishing village of Baan Hua Thanon, the road that forks inland toward Na Thon leads to the Coral Buddha, a small temple complex built on a natural rock formation carved by years of erosion. One of Samui's most serene and least touristy spots, the Coral Buddha provides a glimpse of a more fundamental, traditional world of Buddhism less apparent at brasher, more high-profile destinations. ✉ *Ban Hua Thanon.*

Koh Fan

ISLAND | Off the northeastern tip of Koh Samui is Koh Fan (not to be confused with Koh Fan Noi), a little island with a huge Buddha image covered in moss. The island is best visited at sunset, when the light off the water shows the statue at its best. ✉ *Koh Samui.*

Koh Fan Noi

BEACH—SIGHT | Just offshore at Choengmon Beach is Koh Fan Noi, a little island with a narrow strip of sandy beach. The waters are shallow enough to wade to the island. Despite the hectic pace of development on Samui, the beautiful beach here remains nearly deserted. ✉ *Choeng Mon Beach.*

Na Muang

BODY OF WATER | On the inland road to Na Thon lies the village of Baan Thurian, famous for its durian trees. A track to the right climbs up into jungle-clad hills to the island's best waterfall, Na Muang. The 105-foot falls are spectacular—especially just after the rainy season—as they tumble from a limestone cliff into a small pool. You are cooled by the spray and warmed by the sun. For a thrill, swim through the curtain of falling water; you can sit on a ledge at the back to catch your breath. ✉ *Ban Huai Thurian.*

Beaches

Bophut Beach

BEACH—SIGHT | Quaint and romantic Bophut has a devoted following of return visitors who enjoy its quiet vibe. This north-shore beach is narrow, but more than wide enough for sunbathing. The water is like glass, making it good for swimming, though it's deep enough to be unsuitable for young children. Bophut has a bit of nightlife. Central Bophut, known to everyone as Fisherman's Village, has a beachside strip of old houses that have been converted into restaurants, bars, and boutiques. **Amenities:** food and drink. **Best for:** swimming. ✉ *Tambon Bophut.*

Chawaeng Noi Beach

BEACH—SIGHT | The smaller and less developed of the east-coast beaches adjoining Chawaeng town, Chawaeng Noi lacks the charms and spectacular golden curve of its bigger brother, Chawaeng Yai. It's quieter and more relaxed, though, and there are nearby resorts where you can grab a snack. **Amenities:** food and drink; water sports. **Best for:** solitude. ✉ *Chaweng Noi Beach.*

Chawaeng Yai Beach

BEACH—SIGHT | Travelers in search of sun and fun flock here, especially during high season. The northern half of this beautiful east-coast beach is a hit with backpackers because it's lined with budget lodgings. The southern half, more popular with the package tourists, is lined with high-end resorts. Chawaeng Yai is a great swimming beach. The fine sand is brilliant white, and the waters are clear and usually calm. During the day, tourists pack in and the water buzzes with Jet Skis and banana boats. At night the streets come alive as shops, bars, and restaurants vie for your vacation allowance. **Amenities:** food and drink; water sports. **Best for:** swimming. ✉ *Chaweng Noi Beach.*

Choengmon Beach

BEACH—SIGHT | A mellow spot on Samui's northeastern coast, this beach is blessed with crystal-clear water. Choengmon was once pitched as the island's next big thing. There's hardly a boom, but a few

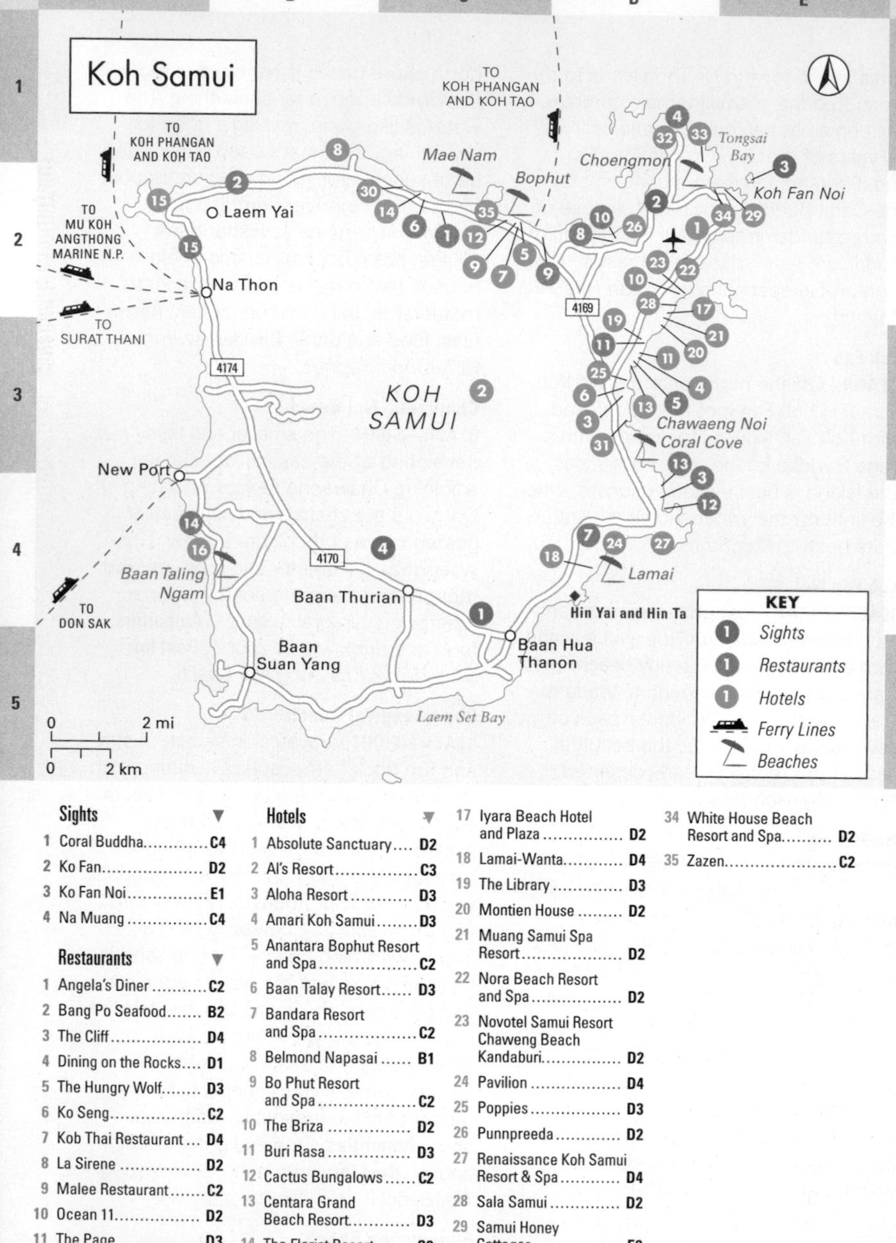

Sights

1 Coral Buddha............ **C4**
2 Ko Fan.................... **D2**
3 Ko Fan Noi................ **E1**
4 Na Muang **C4**

Restaurants

1 Angela's Diner **C2**
2 Bang Po Seafood....... **B2**
3 The Cliff.................. **D4**
4 Dining on the Rocks.... **D1**
5 The Hungry Wolf........ **D3**
6 Ko Seng.................... **C2**
7 Kob Thai Restaurant ... **D4**
8 La Sirene **D2**
9 Malee Restaurant....... **C2**
10 Ocean 11................. **D2**
11 The Page **D3**
12 Tarua Samui Seafood.. **D4**
13 Vikasa Life Cafe **D4**
14 The Virgin Coast........ **A4**
15 Whan Tok................ **A2**

Hotels

1 Absolute Sanctuary.... **D2**
2 Al's Resort................ **C3**
3 Aloha Resort **D3**
4 Amari Koh Samui........ **D3**
5 Anantara Bophut Resort and Spa.................. **C2**
6 Baan Talay Resort...... **D3**
7 Bandara Resort and Spa.................. **C2**
8 Belmond Napasai **B1**
9 Bo Phut Resort and Spa.................. **C2**
10 The Briza **D2**
11 Buri Rasa **D3**
12 Cactus Bungalows...... **C2**
13 Centara Grand Beach Resort........... **D3**
14 The Florist Resort........ **C2**
15 Four Seasons Koh Samui.............. **A2**
16 InterContinental Samui Baan Taling Ngam Resort.................... **A4**
17 Iyara Beach Hotel and Plaza **D2**
18 Lamai-Wanta............ **D4**
19 The Library **D3**
20 Montien House **D2**
21 Muang Samui Spa Resort................... **D2**
22 Nora Beach Resort and Spa................. **D2**
23 Novotel Samui Resort Chaweng Beach Kandaburi............... **D2**
24 Pavilion **D4**
25 Poppies................... **D3**
26 Punnpreeda............. **D2**
27 Renaissance Koh Samui Resort & Spa........... **D4**
28 Sala Samui **D2**
29 Samui Honey Cottages................. **E2**
30 Santiburi Resort and Spa.................. **C2**
31 Sheraton Samui Resort.................... **D3**
32 Six Senses Samui **D1**
33 Tongsai Bay **D1**
34 White House Beach Resort and Spa.......... **D2**
35 Zazen...................... **C2**

guesthouses, a handful of luxury resorts, and some restaurants are scattered along the wide shore. The sand is firm and strewn with pebbles and shells, but the beach is adequate for sunbathing, and there's an interesting rock formation at one end. A few of its food options are right on the beach. **Amenities:** food and drink; water sports. **Best for:** swimming. ✉ *Choeng Mon Beach.*

Lamai Beach

BEACH—SIGHT | Popular Lamai lacks the glistening white sand of Chawaeng Beach, but its water is clear and the beach is ideal for swimming. The steeply shelved shoreline might be too much for kids, though. Numerous bars and restaurants line the beach, emphasizing that Lamai is mostly for young people looking to party. Almost every visitor to Koh Samui makes a pilgrimage to the point marking the southern end of Lamai Beach to see two rocks, named Hin Yai (Grandmother Rock) and Hin Ta (Grandfather Rock). Erosion has shaped the rocks to resemble weathered and wrinkled private parts. It's nature at its most whimsical. Laem Set Bay, a small rocky cape on the southeastern tip of the island, is just south of Lamai. It's a good 3 km (2 miles) off the main road, so it's hard to reach without your own car. Head here to escape the hustle and bustle of Samui. **Amenities:** food and drink; water sports. **Best for:** partiers; swimming. ✉ *Ban Lamai.*

Mae Nam Beach

BEACH—SIGHT | The long, curving beach at Mae Nam has coarse, golden sand shaded by tall coconut trees. It's one of the island's more unspoiled beaches—inexpensive guesthouses and a few luxurious resorts share the 5-km (3-mile) strand. Quiet both day and night, this north shore beach has little nightlife and only a scattering of restaurants. The shallow waters are suitable for swimming, and several water-sports companies operate in the area. **Amenities:** food and drink; water sports. **Best for:** swimming. ✉ *Mae Nam Beach.*

Restaurants

CHAWAENG

The Hungry Wolf

$$ | **EUROPEAN** | A pair of fine-dining vets from Poland are behind this cutting-edge café, which leans heavily on crowd-pleasing Western food made with quality ingredients. They were at first known for their beef-tongue burgers, which were a tough sell to a casual beach crowd, but a gourmet Wagyu option made with foi gras, truffle mayo, and red onion jam is now the attention-grabber. **Known for:** homemade pizza, bread, and pasta; high-end techniques without the pretense; wide vegan menu. *Average main: B300* ✉ *17/46 Moo 3* ☎ *095/257–4080* *No credit cards.*

The Page

$$$$ | **THAI** | Stick to the fun and interesting cocktails at the Library's popular restaurant—it claims to make 101 different kinds—not the so-so wine list, and after a few sips you'll feel as hip as the surroundings. The menu is mostly Thai, featuring "old kingdom" takes on traditional favorites like prawns with garlic and pepper, and sea bass with chili and basil. **Known for:** smartly designed surroundings; "tea by the sea" afternoon service; Wagyu beef. *Average main: B500* ✉ *14/1 Moo 2, Chaweng Noi Beach* ☎ *077/422767* *www.thelibrarysamui.com/the-page/.*

Tarua Samui Seafood

$$ | **SEAFOOD** | The view is definitely what you come here for—high up on a mountain, the restaurant juts out above a rocky beach and turquoise waters—but the food is also memorable. Check the seafood tank as you walk in; you might spy something you can't resist. **Known for:** seafood you hand-select; Thai-Chinese techniques; plump grilled prawns with garlic or curry. *Average main: B250*

Koh Samui's accessibility and beautiful beaches make it a popular destination year-round.

✉ *210/9 Moo 4, Chaweng Noi Beach* ☎ *077/960635* ▭ *No credit cards.*

Vikasa Life Cafe

$$ | **VEGETARIAN** | Organic vegetables take center stage at this collaboration between a couple of acclaimed chefs from Paris and Berlin. Begin your day with a freshly packed jar of chia pudding, a superfood bowl, or a chili-spiked Thai Greens smoothie, and come back later for an encyclopedic array of clean eats. **Known for:** dawn-to-dusk deliciousness; rarely seen raw food; LA-caliber light dishes. $ *Average main: B300* ✉ *211 Bontji Moo 4* ☎ *077/422232* 🌐 *www.vikasayoga.com/the-place/life-cafe/.*

LAMAI

The Cliff

$$$$ | **MEDITERRANEAN** | Halfway along the road from Chawaeng to Lamai, the Cliff perches on a big boulder overlooking the sea. You can have lunch or dinner inside a spartan dining room or out on a scenic terrace. **Known for:** reservation-worthy views; cooler-than-thou cocktails and solid wine selection; locally caught seafood. $ *Average main: B500* ✉ *124/2 Samui Ring Rd., Lamai Beach* ☎ *077/448508* 🌐 *www.thecliffsamui.com.*

Kob Thai Restaurant

$$ | **THAI** | While everything on the à la carte menu at this well-run Lamai restaurant is excellent, the real draw here is its multicourse meals. The "full discovery" tasting for two costs a little more than B1000 and includes three starters, one meat dish, a couple of seafood classics, steamed rice, and two kinds of dessert. **Known for:** prideful service; a serene tropical setting; authentic Thai food. $ *Average main: B200* ✉ *101/18 Moo 3* ☎ *082/534–9325* 🌐 *www.restaurantsnapshot.com/Kob_Thai_Restaurant/.*

BAAN TALING NGAM

The Virgin Coast

$$$$ | **SEAFOOD** | Thai fusion cuisine and a relaxing tropical setting await guests at this reincarnation of the popular Five Islands restaurant. Now in a slightly

different location and renamed the Virgin Coast, the restaurant offers the same laid-back charm, superlative service, and high-quality cooking. **Known for:** seafood dishes with a Western twist; two-person "Kantok" tasting menu; locally sourced ingredients. *Average main: B500 Ban Taling Ngam 089/499–6334 www.thevirgincoastsamui.com No credit cards.*

MAE NAM

Angela's Diner

$ | **CAFÉ** | On the main road running through Mae Nam, the diner formerly known as Angela's Cafe & Bakery serves salads and sandwiches, both traditional and inventive. Among the latter, the "Hot Bandana" is a tasty vegetarian sandwich baked inside a bread bowl and wrapped in a bandana. **Known for:** British standards like bangers and mash; imported meat and cheese; a ridiculous amount of bread and baked goods. *Average main: B100 64/29 Samui Ring Rd., Mae Nam Beach 077/427396 No credit cards.*

Bang Po Seafood

$ | **SEAFOOD** | Mere feet from lapping waves, this shack serves the freshest seafood at the best of prices. The jarringly purple baby-octopus soup and the sour curry with whole fish are two great options. **Known for:** sandy beach setting; truly authentic tom yum; a sea urchin salad that doesn't break the bank. *Average main: B100 56/4 Moo 6, Mae Nam Beach 077/420010 No credit cards.*

Ko Seng

$ | **SEAFOOD** | This two-story seafood restaurant has been feeding Mae Nam residents for decades. Its most famous dish, stir-fried crab with black pepper, is highly recommended. **Known for:** low prices; rotating catch-of-the-day specials; house-grown organic vegetables. *Average main: B80 95 Soi Kohseng, Mae Nam Beach 077/425365 No credit cards.*

Whan Tok

$ | **SEAFOOD** | Perched on the water, this family-owned joint is filled with locals who come for the seafood. Finding the place is half the fun; the sign out front has no writing in English, so if you're coming by cab, ask someone at your hotel to write out the name in Thai. **Known for:** massive prawns; bold seafood broth; inexpensive dishes. *Average main: B80 37/1 Moo 5, Mae Nam Beach 081/597–3171 No credit cards.*

BOPHUT

La Sirene

$$ | **FRENCH** | For elegant French cooking, try this small waterfront bistro whose owner moved here from Nice. The three-course tasting menu might include such delicacies as a shark with pineapple entrée, along with a salad and dessert. **Known for:** à la carte options like shrimp in cognac sauce; several Thai staples, including a glass noodle salad with seafood; delightful waterfront seating on its deck. *Average main: B240 65/1 Bophut Beach, Tambon Bophut 077/425301, 081/797–3499 www.lasirenebophut.com/restaurant.html.*

Ocean 11

$$$$ | **SEAFOOD** | This restaurant's unapologetically Western menu attracts Americans and Europeans. Soft-shell crab on arugula and white snapper baked in a banana leaf provide a refreshing change of pace from Thai-centric fare. **Known for:** inviting beachside atmosphere; penne with prawns; a particularly lavish rack of lamb. *Average main: B660 23 Moo 4, Tambon Bophut 089/813–5715, 089/123–2364 www.o11s.com.*

Malee Restaurant

$ | **THAI** | Noodle soup is the name of the game at this no-frills eatery just a few steps from Samui's main Fisherman's Village market. A "big set" costs B199 and contains enough tom yum to feed two or three people; steer clear of the totally

Mu Koh Angthong

This archipelago of 42 islands covers some 102 square km (40 square miles) and lies 35 km (22 miles) northwest of Koh Samui. The seven main islands are Wua Talap Island (which houses the national park's headquarters), Phaluai Island, Mae Koh Island, Sam Sao Island, Hin Dap Island, Nai Phut Island, and Phai Luak Island. The islands contain limestone mountains, strangely shaped caves, and emerald-green lakes and ponds. Most tourists visit on a one-day trip, which can be arranged from Koh Samui. Prices vary depending on the tour (some offer kayaking around several islands, and others take you out on small speedboats for snorkeling or cave tours). The park is open year-round, although the seas can be rough and the water less clear during the monsoon season, between October and December.

unnecessary deep-fried cheese appetizer, though. **Known for:** seafood with chili paste special; clear and dry noodle soup; small bites like pork balls and deep-fried dumplings. *$ Average main: B100 ✉ Bo Put ☎ 092/207–2848 ▭ No credit cards.*

CHOENGMON

Dining on the Rocks

$$$ | **INTERNATIONAL** | Arranged on several terraces, the tables here all have panoramic sea views; arrive before sunset to get the full effect. In addition to à la carte entrées and apps like iced *tom yum* gazpacho with oysters, this Six Senses' staple offers a wide range of revelatory set menus that start at B2800 (or B2600 if you're vegetarian). **Known for:** thoughtful vegan and vegetarian options; progressive wine pairings; the island's most ambitious tasting menus. *$ Average main: B400 ✉ Six Senses Samui, 9/10 Moo 5, Baan Plai Laem, Tambon Bophut ☎ 077/245678 ⊕ www.sixsenses.com/resorts/samui/dining.*

Hotels

CHAWAENG

Al's Resort

$$ | **RESORT** | The newer deluxe villas at this resort are fashionably Thai, with art on the walls, outdoor showers, and wooden bed frames, trims, and desks. **Pros:** trendy place; hip crowd; even the older rooms are stylish. **Cons:** older rooms not as nice; not ideal for families; contrived decor. *$ Rooms from: B3,550 ✉ 200 Moo 2, Chaweng Noi Beach ☎ 077/300561 ⊕ www.alsresortsamui.com ⇆ 43 rooms 🍽 Free breakfast.*

Amari Koh Samui

$$$ | **RESORT** | This luxurious resort faces a beach where the water's too shallow for swimming—which can be an advantage, as it keeps the crowds away. **Pros:** local touches to the rooms; lovely views; on the beach. **Cons:** inconsistent service; overrun with raucous families; garden wing can't compete with the beach one. *$ Rooms from: B4,400 ✉ 14/3 Chaweng Beach, Chaweng Noi Beach ☎ 077/300–3069, 077/915250 ⊕ www.amari.com/koh-samui/ ⇆ 187 rooms 🍽 Free breakfast.*

Baan Talay Resort

$$ | **RESORT** | Bungalows huddled around a shimmering pool are the focal point at Baan Talay, but the real reasons to stay here are the few huts just a stone's throw from the beach. **Pros:** close to beach; quieter side of Chaweng; clean and comfortable rooms. **Cons:** outdated

decor; noise from nearby road; forgettable breakfast. $ *Rooms from: B3,900* ✉ *17/36 Moo 3 Chawaeng Beach Rd., Chaweng Noi Beach* ☎ *077/413555* 🌐 *www.baantalay.com* *54 rooms* *Free breakfast.*

The Briza

$$$ | **RESORT** | Rather than attempt yet another iteration of Thai design, this resort opted for what can best be described as a fusion of Indian and Chinese styles for its villas. **Pros:** unique style; luxurious, secluded, and exclusive; deck chairs double as massage beds. **Cons:** very expensive; not the life of the party; breakfast is a bore. $ *Rooms from: B5,500* ✉ *173/22 Moo 2, Chawaeng Beach* ☎ *077/231997* 🌐 *www.thebriza.com* *57 villas* *Free breakfast.*

Buri Rasa

$$$ | **RESORT** | One of many hotels along a happening stretch of Chawaeng Beach, Buri Rasa blends in well with the party scene yet manages to retain a semblance of a relaxing getaway feel. **Pros:** chill vibe; fun pool; great design. **Cons:** on party stretch of beach; some foot traffic; noisy club next door. $ *Rooms from: B5,600* ✉ *11/2 Moo 2, Chaweng Noi Beach* ☎ *077/956055* 🌐 *www.burirasa.com* *32 rooms* *Free breakfast.*

Centara Grand Beach Resort

$$$$ | **RESORT** | This spacious resort has more amenities than any other resort on Chawaeng Beach. **Pros:** plenty of activities; good for families; cordoned-off swimming area keeps Jet Skis away. **Cons:** may feel big and impersonal; you pay a lot for what you get; poorly maintained in parts. $ *Rooms from: B8,200* ✉ *38/2 Samui Ring Rd., South Chaweng Beach* ☎ *077/230500* 🌐 *www.centarahotelsresorts.com/centaragrand/csbr/* *208 rooms* *Free breakfast.*

Iyara Beach Hotel and Plaza

$$ | **RESORT** | A getaway for young urbanites who don't want to give up the luxuries of home, this complex includes a maze of boutiques, including Lacoste and Bossini. **Pros:** good deal; close to many activities; luxurious rooms. **Cons:** feels a bit hectic; many rooms lack views; Wi-Fi is wonky. $ *Rooms from: B3,065* ✉ *90/13–16 Chawaeng Beach, Chaweng Noi Beach* ☎ *077/231629* 🌐 *www.iyarabeachhotelandplaza.com* *78 rooms* *Free breakfast.*

The Library

$$$$ | **RESORT** | This place is worth a visit for its amusingly hip decor alone; check out the white figures reading books on the lawn, inviting you to lounge as well. **Pros:** very stylish; cool, young crowd; 20 private spaces. **Cons:** pricey; not ideal if you're looking for quiet; not suited to families. $ *Rooms from: B12,500* ✉ *14/1 Moo 2 Chawaeng Beach, Chaweng Noi Beach* ☎ *077/422767* 🌐 *www.thelibrary.co.th* *26 rooms* *Free breakfast.*

Montien House

$$ | **RESORT** | Two rows of charming bungalows line the path leading to the beach at this comfortable little resort. **Pros:** cute rooms; attentive staff and management; close to Chaweng without the chaos. **Cons:** not much pizzazz; lacks creature comforts; average food. $ *Rooms from: B3,250* ✉ *5 Moo 2, Chaweng Noi Beach* ☎ *077/422169* 🌐 *www.montienhouse.com* *60 rooms* *Free breakfast.*

Muang Samui Spa Resort

$$$$ | **RESORT** | At this tranquil resort, a meandering garden path with small bridges and stepping-stones crosses a flowing, fish-filled stream. **Pros:** different sense of style; well-kept grounds; Thai cooking classes. **Cons:** feels sprawling; expensive; some rooms in need of renovation. $ *Rooms from: B15,000* ✉ *13/1 Moo 2, Chaweng Noi Beach* ☎ *077/429700* 🌐 *www.muangsamui.com* *53 suites* *Free breakfast.*

Nora Beach Resort and Spa

$$$ | **RESORT** | A big plus of this hotel is that about two dozen rooms have sea views and many overlook the pool, so

you're almost guaranteed an aquatic perspective. **Pros:** comfortable surroundings; spacious bathrooms; brisk Wi-Fi. **Cons:** unexciting furnishings; not cheap; lack of sun beds. *Rooms from: B5,000* *222 Moo 2 Chawaeng Beach, North Chaweng Beach* *077/413999, 077/429400* *www.norabeachresort.com* *113 rooms* *Free breakfast.*

★ Poppies

$$$$ | **RESORT** | Dozens of cheerful employees are on hand to attend to your every need at this romantic beachfront resort on the quiet southern end of Chawaeng Beach. **Pros:** snappy service; immediate area not too crazy; restaurant is as remarkable as the resort itself. **Cons:** a little staid; not cheap; long walk from busiest stretch of Chaweng Beach. *Rooms from: B8,500* *28/1 Moo 3, South Chaweng Beach* *077/422419* *www.poppiessamui.com* *24 cottages* *No meals.*

Sheraton Samui Resort

$$$$ | **RESORT** | A landscaped terrace leads down to a private beach at this resort on the less crowded southern end of Chawaeng Noi. If you want to do more than catch rays, this is the place for you—the Sheraton offers every kind of beach activity imaginable. **Pros:** great views from pool terrace; good beachside restaurant; lots of beach activities. **Cons:** may be too quiet for some people; downhill walk to beach; no elevator. *Rooms from: B6,900* *86 Moo 3, Chawaeng Noi Beach, Chaweng Noi Beach* *077/422020* *www.sheratonsamui.com* *141 rooms* *Free breakfast.*

LAMAI

Aloha Resort

$$ | **RESORT** | All the rooms at this oceanfront resort have private terraces or balconies that face in the general direction of the beach. **Pros:** can accommodate larger groups; reasonable price; family-friendly. **Cons:** some rooms not so nice; outdated decor; small beach. *Rooms from: B3,000* *128 Moo 3 Lamai Beach, Ban Lamai* *077/424014* *www.alohasamui.com* *74 rooms* *Free breakfast.*

Lamai-Wanta

$$ | **RESORT** | These incredibly spartan rooms are kept immaculately clean—perhaps not surprising, given that the owners are a nurse-and-doctor couple. **Pros:** photogenic pool; beautiful beach; well-kept grounds. **Cons:** blah decor; breakfast gets boring quick; pesky geckos. *Rooms from: B2,600* *124/264 Moo 3, T. Maret Lamai Beach, Ban Lamai* *077/424550* *www.lamaiwanta.com* *50 rooms* *Free breakfast.*

Pavilion

$$$$ | **RESORT** | This amiable place offers a little respite from the downtown hustle and bustle. **Pros:** near reputable bars and restaurants; hot tubs in some rooms; convenient beach location without the chaos. **Cons:** can get expensive; not the most modern hotel; common areas aren't as nice as the rooms. *Rooms from: B6,400* *124/24 Lamai Beach, Ban Lamai* *077/424030* *www.pavilionsamui.com* *70 rooms* *Free breakfast.*

Renaissance Koh Samui Resort & Spa

$$$ | **RESORT** | At the far northern end of Lamai, the Renaissance sits on its own secluded beach—two small beaches to be exact. **Pros:** sprawling grounds; high-end feel; the epitome of a private getaway. **Cons:** isolated location; pricey; road to hotel is rough. *Rooms from: B4,700* *208/1 Moo 4, T. Maret, Lamai Beach* *077/429300* *www.marriott.com/hotels/travel/usmbr-renaissance-koh-samui-resort-and-spa/* *78 rooms* *No meals.*

BAAN TALING NGAM

InterContinental Samui Baan Taling Ngam Resort

$$$$ | **RESORT** | The name means "home on a beautiful bank," but that doesn't come close to summing up the stunning

location of this luxurious hotel. **Pros:** beautiful views; plenty of activities; perfect jumping-off point for Marine Park. **Cons:** can't lounge on narrow beach; somewhat isolated; not quite five-star service. *Rooms from: B8,000 295 Moo 3 Taling Ngam Beach, Ban Taling Ngam 077/429100, 02/656–0440 for reservations www.samui.intercontinental.com 70 rooms Free breakfast.*

MAE NAM AND LAEM YAI

Belmond Napasai

$$$$ | **RESORT** | If you book a beachfront room here you can enjoy views of both the sky *and* sea from your outdoor terrace, room, or bathtub. **Pros:** great views; superb staff; stable Wi-Fi speed. **Cons:** pricey; some rooms starting to show their age; food and drinks not as good as some other resorts. *Rooms from: B10,500 65/10 Baan Tai, Mae Nam Beach 077/429200 www.napasai.com 69 rooms Free breakfast.*

The Florist Resort

$ | **RESORT** | This guesthouse is tiny but in a cute and cozy way. **Pros:** good bang for your buck; easy beach access; seafront room has perfect view of Koh Phangan. **Cons:** lacks the comfort of some megachains; staff not so attentive; old wing has aging furniture and slightly musty smell. *Rooms from: B1,300 190 Moo 1, Tambon Maenam, Mae Nam Beach 086/313–7725 www.floristresort.com 32 rooms Free breakfast.*

★ Four Seasons Koh Samui

$$$$ | **RESORT** | This is easily one of the most spectacular hotels in the world. **Pros:** ultimate luxury and relaxation; cool room design; excellent food on-site. **Cons:** might break the bank; golf carts necessary to get around; can feel isolated. *Rooms from: B28,900 219 Moo 5, Angthong, Laem Yai 077/243000 www.fourseasons.com/kohsamui 74 villas No meals.*

★ Santiburi Resort and Spa

$$$$ | **RESORT** | The villas on this beachfront estate have the feel of a billionaire's holiday hideaway; accordingly, this is one of the most expensive lodgings on the island. **Pros:** on a private beach; elegant rooms; fantastic Thai food. **Cons:** not ideal for families; decor beginning to look dated; some villas are more private than others. *Rooms from: B19,000 12/12 Samui Ring Rd., Mae Nam Beach 077/425031 www.santiburis-amui.com/ 71 villas and suites Free breakfast.*

BOPHUT

Absolute Sanctuary

$$$ | **RESORT** | If you're on vacation to detox, this is the spot—and if you aren't, well, it probably isn't. **Pros:** prime yoga facilities; unique concept; terrific massage treatments. **Cons:** no fun if you're not detoxing; doesn't quite live up to its star rating; lacks the luxe feel of other properties. *Rooms from: B4,300 88 Moo 5, Tambol, Tambon Bophut 077/601190 www.absolutesanctuary.com 38 rooms Free breakfast.*

Anantara Bophut Resort and Spa

$$$$ | **RESORT** | Anantara captures the essence of Samui: coconut trees dot the grounds, monkey statues and sculptures decorate the interior, and, of course, there's a beautiful beach. **Pros:** decent dining; pretty place; prime vantage points. **Cons:** feels quite big, not for young party crowd; cleanliness is inconsistent. *Rooms from: B10,000 99/9 Bophut Bay, Bophut Beach 077/428300 www.anantara.com/en/bophut-koh-samui 106 rooms Free breakfast.*

Bandara Resort and Spa

$$$ | **RESORT** | Bandara gets high marks for its location on the nicest stretch of Bophut Beach. **Pros:** ideal location; attentive staff; Fisherman's Village is a short walk away. **Cons:** pool not inviting; decor lost its luster; deluxe rooms aren't that deluxe. *Rooms from: B4,250*

✉ *178/2 Moo 1, Tambol, Tambon Bophut* ☎ *077/245795* 🌐 *www.bandarasamui.com* 🛏 *151 rooms* 🍴 *Free breakfast.*

Bo Phut Resort and Spa
$$$$ | **RESORT** | Not every beach hotel that claims to be a "resort and spa" measures up, which is why the massages, scrubs, and herbal steam therapies here are such a pleasant surprise. **Pros:** spectacular spa; nice restaurant; rather calm. **Cons:** a bit overpriced; not the most happening location; sand around here is rough. 💲 *Rooms from: B8,100* ✉ *12/12 Moo 1, Tambon Bophut* ☎ *077/245776* 🌐 *www.bophutresort.com* 🛏 *61 rooms* 🍴 *Free breakfast.*

Cactus Bungalows
$ | **RESORT** | This laid-back place caters mostly to the budget backpacker crowd. **Pros:** interesting decor; good vibes; peace and quiet. **Cons:** some rooms lack air-conditioning; not luxurious; poorly maintained. 💲 *Rooms from: B800* ✉ *175/7 Moo 1, Tambon Bophut* ☎ *077/245565* 🌐 *www.cactus-bungalow.com* 🛏 *14 rooms* 🍴 *No meals.*

Punnpreeda
$ | **RESORT** | Although it doesn't quite achieve the effortless cool it's striving for, Punnpreeda is still a fine place to stay. **Pros:** fun atmosphere; convenient shuttle; near the Big Buddha and Wat Plai Laem. **Cons:** not ideal for families; a taxi ride away from Koh Samui's main drag; trying a little too hard. 💲 *Rooms from: B1,302* ✉ *199 Moo 1, Bang Rak Beach, Tambon Bophut* ☎ *077/950558, 083/803–9222* 🌐 *www.punnpreeda.com/* 🛏 *25 rooms* 🍴 *Free breakfast.*

Zazen
$$$$ | **RESORT** | Minimalist Japanese style makes this hotel a refreshing change of pace, especially if you've been in Thailand for a while. **Pros:** on a nice stretch of sand; great atmosphere; first-rate spa. **Cons:** expensive; not a party destination; beach itself is small. 💲 *Rooms from: B7,000* ✉ *177 Moo 1, Tambon Bophut* ☎ *077/425085* 🌐 *www.samuizazen.com* 🛏 *35 rooms* 🍴 *Free breakfast.*

CHOENGMON

Novotel Samui Resort Chaweng Beach Kandaburi
$$ | **RESORT** | Vaguely Balinese in design, this classy boutique hotel makes use of dark woods—often as a stunning contrast against stark white or shimmering gold. **Pros:** aesthetically pleasing; shuttle bus to center of town; family-friendly. **Cons:** most rooms lack beach views; service is indifferent; air conditioners don't always work. 💲 *Rooms from: B3,800* ✉ *20 Moo 2, Choeng Mon Beach* ☎ *077/428888* 🌐 *www.novotel-samui-resort-chaweng.com/* 🛏 *183 rooms* 🍴 *Free breakfast.*

Sala Samui
$$$$ | **RESORT** | Bright, nearly all-white rooms open onto private courtyards on one side and curtain-enclosed bathrooms on the other. **Pros:** lots of privacy; good dining options; nice pool. **Cons:** could use some improvements considering the cost; beach views aren't the best; water is cloudy and for wading, not swimming. 💲 *Rooms from: B11,000* ✉ *10/9 Moo 5, Baan Plai Laem, Tambon Bophut* ☎ *077/245888* 🌐 *www.salahospitality.com/samui/* 🛏 *69 rooms* 🍴 *Free breakfast.*

Samui Honey Cottages
$$ | **RESORT** | The cottages at this small resort on one of the island's quieter beaches have glass sliding doors and peaked roofs, and bathrooms have showers with glass ceilings. **Pros:** well located; welcoming staff; free kayaks. **Cons:** not that special; no real nightlife; simple breakfast. 💲 *Rooms from: B3,000* ✉ *24/34 Moo 5, Choeng Mon Beach* ☎ *083/646–4188* 🌐 *www.samuihoney.com* 🛏 *20 rooms* 🍴 *Free breakfast.*

★ Six Senses Samui
$$$$ | **RESORT** | From the moment that you're introduced to your private butler, you'll realize that this is not just another

high-end resort—you're about to embark on an amazing experience. **Pros:** butler service; excellent restaurant; 30-meter infinity pool on the cliff. **Cons:** expensive; sprawling property difficult to navigate; location can feel isolated. *Rooms from: B10,500 ✉ 9/10 Moo 5, Baan Plai Laem, Tambon Bophut ☎ 077/245678 ⊕ www.sixsenses.com/resorts/samui/destination ⇨ 66 villas 🍴 Free breakfast.*

Tongsai Bay

$$$$ | **RESORT** | The owners of this splendid all-suites resort managed to build it without sacrificing even one of the tropical trees that give the place a refreshing sense of utter seclusion. **Pros:** beautiful exterior and interior; luxurious bungalows; romantic setting. **Cons:** beach so-so for lounging; staff could be more attentive; lots of walking and stairs if you have mobility issues. *Rooms from: B8,500 ✉ 84 Tongsai Bay, Choeng Mon Beach ☎ 077/913–7509 ⊕ www.tongsai-bay.co.th ⇨ 83 suites 🍴 Free breakfast.*

White House Beach Resort and Spa

$ | **RESORT** | Step back in time as you pass under the Khmer-style stone facade and enter the classic lobby, which is filled with giant Chinese vases, Persian carpets, and classic Lanna art. **Pros:** quiet location on beach; old-world opulence; gardens are lush and lovely. **Cons:** some rooms need renovating; could be cleaner; moldy smell in some rooms. *Rooms from: B1,500 ✉ 59/3 Moo 5, Choeng Mon Beach ☎ 077/332048 ⊕ www.samuithewhitehouse.com ⇨ 43 rooms 🍴 Free breakfast.*

Nightlife

You'll find the most nighttime action in central Lamai and on Chawaeng's Soi Green Mango—a looping street chock-ablock with beer bars and nightclubs of all sizes.

Ark Bar

BARS/PUBS | One of Samui's original nightlife venues on the beach, the Ark throws a free barbecue every Wednesday around sunset. *✉ 159/75 Moo 2, Chaweng Noi Beach ☎ 077/961333 ⊕ www.ark-bar.com.*

Bees Knees Brewpub

BREWPUBS/BEER GARDENS | Belgium-sourced barley and wheat gets put to good use at this local take on Thai craft beer brewpub. British and German-style brews are light on alcohol and big on taste, encouraging serious hop heads and thirsty tourists to pull up a stool and stay a while. *✉ 83/3 Moo 2, Bophut ☎ 085/537–2498 ⊕ www.samuibrew.pub/.*

Islander Pub & Restaurant

BARS/PUBS | The many large-screen TVs at this popular place broadcast Thai, Australian, and Malaysian programs—lots of sports—and there are pool competitions and quiz nights. *✉ 166/79 Chawaeng Beach Rd., Central Chaweng ☎ 077/230836.*

Reggae Pub

BARS/PUBS | A must if you're a reggae fan, this longtime favorite with several bars and dance floors has a nonstop party atmosphere. *✉ Chawaeng Lakeside Rd., Chaweng Noi Beach ☎ 077/422331.*

Activities

Canopy Adventures

ZIP LINING | For a bird's-eye view of the jungle, zip-line through the air on 330 yards of wire strung among six tree houses. This outfit also arranges fun expeditions to waterfalls. *✉ Koh Samui ☎ 077/300340, 087/046–7307 ⊕ www.canopyadventuresthailand.com 🎫 B3,250.*

Santiburi Samui Country Club

GOLF | The Santiburi Resort has a driving range and a beautiful 18-hole course that incorporates the natural terrain of the Samui mountains to create a challenging multilevel golfing experience. You can play 9 holes for half the full-course greens fee. ✉ *Koh Samui* ☎ *077/421700* 🌐 *www.santiburisamui.com/experiences/golf/* 💳 *B5,600 (B3,350 for early-bird tee time before 7 am)* ⛳ *18 holes, 6930 yards, par 72.*

Shopping

SPAS

Tamarind Springs Forest Spa

SPA—SIGHT | Koh Samui has a few top-end spas, as well as several in the luxury hotels, but the island's ultimate spa experience is at Tamarind Springs. Many different treatments are available, from hot-oil massages to herbal rubs to the Over the Top massage package, which lasts 2½ hours. The spa employs the latest treatment methods, including the use of Tibetan singing bowls. The plunge pools, hot tubs, and tearoom are built harmoniously into Tamarind's boulder-strewn hillside. ✉ *205/7 Thong Takian, Lamai Beach* ☎ *077/424221* 🌐 *www.tamarindsprings.com.*

Side Trips from Koh Samui

Koh Phangan

12 km (7 miles) by boat north of Koh Samui.

As Koh Samui developed into an international hot spot, travelers looking for a more laid-back scene headed for Koh Phangan. Decades ago, the few wanderers who arrived here stayed in fishermen's houses or slung hammocks on the beach. Investors bought up beach property with plans for sprawling resorts, but before commercial development marred too much of the island, the allure of Koh Tao's crystalline waters starting drawing away a lot of the attention.

Haad Rin Town has many good restaurants, shops, and bars. It's densely built up, and not very quiet, but full of fun. The town is sandwiched between the beaches of Haad Rin West and Haad Rin East.

While Haad Rin boomed as a result of its world-famous full moon party, most of Koh Phangan's smaller beaches continued to develop, but at a much slower pace. For now, most of Koh Phangan remains a destination for backpackers looking for beautiful beaches with budget accommodations, and hippies (old-school and nouveau) searching for chilled-out beaches and alternative retreats.

Boats from the mainland drop passengers off at the main pier in Thong Sala. It's an uninteresting town, but there are taxis that can shuttle you around the island.

If you want to find the beach that most appeals to you, take a longtail boat (a simple motorized vessel named for its shape) around the island—the trip takes a full day and stops in many places along the way, including Haad Rin. Close to Haad Rin are Haad Sarikantang, Haad Yuan, and Haad Thien: good choices for those interested in going to the full moon party, but who want to stay on a nicer, more relaxing beach.

If you aren't here for the full moon party, head up the east coast to quieter Haad Thong Nai Pan, or even farther afield. One of the island's most remote beaches—and the most beautiful—is Haad Kuat, which has gorgeous white sand and simple accommodations. Haad Salad and Haad Yao, on the northwest coast, are similarly remote beaches for those looking for relaxation.

GETTING HERE AND AROUND

The best way to get here is by ferry from Koh Samui, or from Surat Thani via Koh Samui. Boats depart hourly from Surat Thani's Donsak Pier for Na Thon Pier on Koh Samui; the price includes the hour-long bus ride from Surat Thani's airport

Koh Phangan's beaches are popular with travelers looking for a tranquil getaway.

to the pier. After the 2½-hour voyage to Samui, passengers must disembark and catch a second boat to Koh Phangan's Thong Sala Pier, a 30-minute journey. Seatran boats depart from Koh Samui for Koh Phangan daily at 8 am and 1:30 pm. Return travel from Koh Phangan to Koh Samui is at 10:30 am and 4:30 pm.

If you take a Songserm ferry instead, you won't have to switch boats on Samui; however, Songserm makes the Surat Thani–Koh Samui–Koh Phangan run only once a day, leaving Surat Thani at 8 am and returning from Koh Phangan at 12:30 pm.

There are a number of ways to travel between Koh Phangan and either Koh Samui or Koh Tao—Lomphrayah and Seatran boats are the best options. Boats to and from Koh Tao take from 2 to 2½ hours.

Even though most beaches are accessible via songthaew pickup trucks, the island's twisting roads make it easier and safer to beach-hop via boat. It is unwise to travel around Koh Phangan on a motorcycle: the roads are not safe, and accidents involving motorcycles are a far too regular occurrence.

SAFETY AND PRECAUTIONS

Koh Phangan has become famous for its full moon parties and for numerous other parties associated with the moon's waxing and waning. These events attract as many as 10,000 revelers, and the criminal element knows this. Break-ins are a problem. Thieves assume you're out partying, so don't leave valuables in your room.

The biggest problem is drugs, which are treated very seriously by Thai authorities. There are all-too-frequent stories of travelers who have been arrested, either for purchasing or consuming, so expect harsh treatment if you're caught.

TIMING

The Full Moon Party, probably the biggest draw to the island, happens 13 times a year on Haad Rin East. If you want some peace and quiet, consult your lunar calendar. At other times the island is a tranquil place.

Beaches

★ Haad Kuat (*Bottle Beach*)
BEACH—SIGHT | With a quarter mile of fine white sand, this isolated beach on the island's north coast is a sunbather's paradise. The vibe is decidedly young and funky, and there are several places to grab a decent meal. Get here by songthaew from Thong Sala Pier, or by longtail boat from nearby Thong Nai Pan. Haad Kuat might be more difficult to reach than other beaches, but it's one of Koh Phangan's best and definitely worth the effort. **Amenities:** food and drink; water sports. **Best for:** partiers. ⊠ *Haad Kuat.*

Haad Rin
BEACH—SIGHT | If you are looking for the party, then head to Haad Rin. The beach is divided into two parts, Haad Rin West and Haad Rin East, each with its own personality. Haad Rin West has swimmable water, but you needn't settle for this beach when Haad Rin East is only a short walk away. Beautiful Haad Rin East is lined with bungalows and bars, although the water isn't nearly as pristine as at the more-remote beaches. Every four weeks, Haad Rin East gets seriously crowded when throngs of young people gather on the beach for an all-night full moon party. **Amenities:** food and drink. **Best for:** partiers; swimming. ⊠ *Haad Rin.*

Haad Sarikantang
BEACH—SIGHT | Just south of Haad Rin, this smaller strand is close to the party yet relatively peaceful. Also known as Leela Beach, Haad Sarikantang has picturesque palms, fine white sand, and clear blue water. Resorts and restaurants surround the beach. **Amenities:** food and drink. **Best for:** swimming. ⊠ *Haad Sarikantang.*

Haad Thien
BEACH—SIGHT | A small strip north of the party beaches at Haad Rin, this is an ideal choice for those seeking relaxation and smaller crowds. The sand is a fine yellow and the waters are shallow and clear. A few resort hotels and several good restaurants do business on the waterfront or near the beach. **Amenities:** food and drink; water sports. **Best for:** swimming. ⊠ *Haad Thien.*

Haad Thong Nai Pan
BEACH—SIGHT | On a horseshoe bay at the island's northern end, Haad Thong Nai Pan is split into two. The northern part is the most beautiful, with stunning golden sands set around crystal-blue waters. The seas are usually calm, but swimming can be rough when the monsoon rains sweep in. Guesthouses and mid-range resorts surround the beach. Food and drink are available from the nearby restaurants. **Amenities:** food and drink; water sports. **Best for:** swimming. ⊠ *Haad Thong Nai Pan.*

Haad Yuan
BEACH—SIGHT | A 10-minute boat ride from Haad Rin, small beautiful Haad Yuan is worlds away. Extremely quiet most of the time, the beach is wide and clean, with fine sand and crystal-blue waters. The rocky outcrop at one end makes a fine photo backdrop. The swimming is good here, but the water occasionally gets rough. **Amenities:** food and drink. **Best for:** swimming. ⊠ *Haad Yuan.*

Restaurants

Haad Rin has the most restaurants, but you'll find plenty of simple seafood restaurants on other beaches as well.

Lucky Crab Restaurant
$$$ | **SEAFOOD** | As if striving to please every last one of the island's international visitors, this fun restaurant serves entrées from around the world. The specialty, though, is grilled seafood, prepared with one of 12 sauces; select your

fish and sauce, then enjoy the breeze from the ceiling fans while you await your food. **Known for:** hot pan special of sizzling seafood; wide menu, covering all the culinary bases; grilled fish. *Average main: B350 ✉ 94/18 Haad Rin W, Haad Rin ☎ 077/375125, 077/375498 No credit cards.*

Nira's Home Bakery

$ | **CAFÉ** | The alluring scent of fresh baked goods immediately delights all who enter this funky place. The owner, who picked up his baking skills while living and working in Germany, opened Nira's in the mid-1980s, before the island even had electricity. **Known for:** homemade lasagna; fresh, fresh juices; gourmet sandwiches. *Average main: B80 ✉ 74/10 Moo 1, Thong Sala, Haad Rin ☎ 081/535–5215 No credit cards.*

Hotels

HAAD RIN

Buri Beach Resort

$ | **RESORT** | What you get at this Haad Rin West property is a standard hotel room, complete with modern amenities and touches of Thai style, including art on the walls. **Pros:** feels new; nice views; well maintained. **Cons:** a bit generic; room decor could be nicer; lacks island-getaway feel. *Rooms from: B1,299 ✉ 120/1 Moo 6, Haad Rin, Haad Rin ☎ 077/961877 www.buri-beach-phangan.com/ 106 rooms Free breakfast.*

Cocohut Resort

$$ | **RESORT** | This resort is on mellow Haad Sarikantang, a five-minute walk from Haad Rin West. **Pros:** good deal; cute quarters; right by the beach. **Cons:** not so scenic; not the best swimming beach; staff can seem brusque. *Rooms from: B3,000 ✉ 130/20 Leela Beach, Haad Sarikantang ☎ 077/375368 www.cocohut.com 100 rooms Free breakfast.*

Phangan Bayshore Resort

$$ | **RESORT** | On Haad Rin East near the action but away from the crowds, this was one of the island's original resorts. **Pros:** close to the party; good value; spacious layout. **Cons:** some rooms need renovation; modern huts lack personality; food is unremarkable. *Rooms from: B2,600 ✉ 141 Moo 6, Haad Rin, Haad Rin ☎ 077/375227 www.phanganbayshore.com 71 rooms Free breakfast.*

Sarikantang

$$ | **RESORT** | On Haad Sarikantang, this small resort is a short walk from the festive atmosphere at Haad Rin. The nicer accommodations have outdoor showers and baths, hot water, air-conditioning, and hammocks, while some of the wooden bungalows have only the most basic amenities. **Pros:** ample ocean views; friendly staff; picture-perfect location. **Cons:** could be more central; least expensive rooms not comfortable; beach is private but rocky. *Rooms from: B2,600 ✉ 129/3 Leela Beach, Haad Sarikantang ☎ 077/375055, 086/789–9541 www.sarikantang.com 47 rooms Free breakfast.*

Seaview Sunrise

$ | **RESORT** | These simple wooden huts directly on the beach at the "quieter" northern end of Haad Rin East are the best deal in the area—for the best location. **Pros:** good deal; extremely low-key vibe; can arrange transportation. **Cons:** not near the action; some rooms lack air-conditioning; as basic as it gets. *Rooms from: B700 ✉ 134 Moo 6, Haad Rin East, Haad Rin ☎ 077/375160 www.seaviewsunrise.com No credit cards 40 rooms No meals.*

HAAD YUAN

Barcelona Resort

$ | **RESORT** | For very few baht you get a private cottage on Haad Yuan with doors on two walls that unfold to reveal a wraparound deck. **Pros:** low price; fun experience; step above simple bungalows. **Cons:** no air-conditioning; few amenities; main resort is a taxi boat ride away. *Rooms from: B400 Haad Yuan Beach 077/375113 www.imagealchemy.org/sites/barcelona No credit cards 35 rooms Free breakfast.*

HAAD THONG NAI PAN

Dolphin Bungalows

$ | **RESORT** | These are the perfect beach bungalows, built entirely of wood with shuttered windows and hammocks slung on the decks. **Pros:** lush grounds; cool crowd; decent food. **Cons:** not beachfront; few creature comforts; breakfast not included. *Rooms from: B600 61 Moo 5, Haad Thong Nai Pan 077/445135 No credit cards 20 rooms No meals.*

Longtail Beach Resort

$ | **RESORT** | The bungalows and restaurant at this well-landscaped resort in northern Koh Phangan are built of wood, thatch, and bamboo in traditional southern Thai style. **Pros:** close to the beach; inexpensive; local touches to the rooms and resort. **Cons:** small pool; full of families; few amenities. *Rooms from: B1,250 2/5 Moo 5, Thong Nai Pan Yai Beach, Haad Thong Nai Pan 77/445018 www.longtailbeachresort.com 22 bungalows No meals.*

Panviman Resort

$$$ | **RESORT** | The big attractions at this cheerful resort on Koh Phangan's northern coast are its two restaurants: one is a circular dining area that's open to the ocean breezes; the other is a seaside terrace. **Pros:** good for families; shuttle service back to Bangkok; gorgeous, well-maintained grounds. **Cons:** high rates; not near interesting nightlife; fairly remote. *Rooms from: B5,200 22/1 Moo 5, Thong Nai Pan Noi Bay, Haad Thong Nai Pan 077/445–1019, 02/4594–7057 www.panvimanresort-kohphangan.com/ 104 rooms Free breakfast.*

HAAD KUAT

Smile Bungalows

$ | **RESORT** | Of the guesthouses on northern Koh Phangan's Haad Kuat, this one on the beach's western end is the best. **Pros:** duplexes have dramatic views; personable staff; white sand and turquoise waters. **Cons:** no air-conditioning; lacks amenities; hard to get here. *Rooms from: B550 74/9 Moo 7, Haad Kuat 085/429–4995 www.smilebungalows.com No credit cards 25 rooms No meals.*

Nightlife

Haad Rin East is lined with bars and clubs—music pumps and drinks pour from dusk until dawn, seven days a week, 365 days a year. All this culminates in a huge beach party with tens of thousands of revelers every full moon (or the night after, if the full moon lands on a major Buddhist holiday). Check out *www.fullmoonparty-thailand.com* for details.

Koh Tao

47 km (29 miles) by boat north of Koh Phangan.

★ In just a few decades, the tiny island of Koh Tao has evolved from a sleepy backwater to a sought-after diving getaway, with lodgings that range from basic bungalows to luxurious resorts. The peace and quiet may have disappeared from the main beaches, with a strong, backpacker-oriented, party scene in the island's two main areas. Along with cheap drinks, the bars, pubs, and clubs in each offer all manner of pub crawls and late-night shenanigans. This said, the primary reason to come here remains the underwater world. Koh Tao is an excellent place to get your scuba certification. Many operators don't have pools, so the initial dives must be done in the shallow,

Koh Tao – meaning 'Turtle Island' – lives up to its name, being the scuba diving destination of choice in Thailand.

crystal-clear ocean water. Advanced divers will appreciate the great visibility, decent amount of coral, and exotic and plentiful marine life.

GETTING HERE AND AROUND

Getting to Koh Tao is easy—it's on the scheduled ferry routes out of Koh Phangan and Koh Samui, and several boats a day make the trip from Chumphon on the mainland. Catamarans take 1½ hours, high-speed Seatran vessels take 2 hours, and regular ferry service takes 6.

Lomprayah Catamaran has 1¾-hour trips between Koh Samui and Koh Tao for B500 twice daily, at 7 am and 5 pm. In addition, speedboats leave at 8:30 am from Bophut Pier on the north side of Koh Samui, taking snorkelers on day trips to the island and its neighbor, Koh Nang Yuan.

CONTACTS Lomprayah High Speed Catamaran 🌐 *www.lomprayah.com.*

Sights

Koh Nang Yuan

ISLAND | The three small islands of Koh Nang Yuan lie close to Koh Tao. At high tide the islands, separated by shallow, translucent water, look like the endpoints of an obtuse triangle. At low tide the receding water exposes two narrow sandbars that connect the outer islands, which contain bungalows for overnight stays, to the central island, which has a lodge, a restaurant and beach bar, and a coffee shop. The islands are privately owned by the Nangyuan Island Dive Resort, and all visitors who wish to set foot on Koh Nang Yuan must shell out a B100 fee. Although many visitors opt to pay, others simply dock offshore to snorkel and dive the gorgeous waters surrounding the islands. To get here from Koh Tao, you can kayak from Sairee Beach or hire a longtail boat (B200 round-trip from Sairee) to ferry you here. The trip takes about 15 minutes—it works best to arrange your return with the

Diving and Snorkeling Responsibly

Decades of visitors scuba diving on Thailand's islands and reefs have had far greater negative effects on marine life than any tsunami. All divers need to be aware of, and consequently minimize, their impact on the environment.

Touch nothing, stand only on sand: As fascinating as something you see may be, resist the urge to handle it, and never stand on anything that isn't sand. Coral is extremely fragile, urchins are as painful as they look, and although sharks may be no threat to divers, you can appreciate the foolishness of grabbing one's tail. Other dangers to both you and the environment are less obvious: eels live within holes in rocks and reef; turtles are reptiles that require air to breathe, and even some dive instructors are guilty of "hitching a ride" on them, causing the turtles to expend precious air. Furthermore, don't feed fish human food.

Secure diving equipment, maintain level buoyancy: Divers should make sure equipment is securely fastened or stored, so that no items are lost or scrape against coral. Divers should also maintain level buoyancy to prevent inadvertent brushes with coral, as well as to save air. Snorkelers who need to remove their masks should pull them down around their necks rather than up on their foreheads. Masks can fall off and quickly sink, and a mask on the forehead is considered a symbol of distress.

Check your pockets, no butts: Minimize underwater pollution when snorkeling by checking your pockets before jumping into the water. Conscientious divers can clip a stuff sack to their BCDs to pocket random trash they encounter. Lastly, if you smoke, don't flick cigarette butts into the water.

Protect yourself and nature: Sunscreen is a must anytime you are exposed to Thailand's tropical sun. Snorkeling unprotected is a guaranteed skin disaster (and painful obstacle to the rest of your holiday); however, sunblock, when dissolving into the water from hundreds of visitors each day, is bound to take its toll on the marine environment. You can limit the amount of sunscreen you must slather on by covering your back with a Lycra rash guard or a short- or long-sleeved shirt while snorkeling.

Follow the credo, "Leave only footprints, take only memories." Try to minimize your impact on this ecosystem in which you are only a visitor.

same operator. While you are visiting, be sure to slip up to the viewpoint on the southern island to snap photos guaranteed to make your friends back home jealous. **■ TIP→ The islands are busy throughout the day; it's best to visit early in the morning or late in the afternoon.** ✉ *Koh Tao* ✣ *15-min longtail ride from Koh Tao* 🌐 *www.nangyuan.com* 🎫 *B100.*

Beaches

Chalok Baan Kao Beach

BEACH—SIGHT | A peaceful strand on Koh Tao's southern shore, Chalok Baan Kao has a relaxed, friendly vibe. The beach itself lacks the crystal-blue water and golden sands of other beaches in the region, but it's reasonably good for swimming. Budget accommodations surround the beach. **Amenities:** food and drink. **Best for:** solitude; swimming. ✉ *Koh Tao.*

Sairee Beach

BEACH—SIGHT | Palm trees at crescent-shaped Sairee, Koh Tao's most popular beach, arch over the aquamarine water as if yearning to sip from the sea. Along the thin sliver of golden sand sit rustic, traditional wooden beach huts with bohemian youths lounging in hammocks, novice divers practicing in seaside pools, and European students sampling cocktails at basic beach bars. On the far northern end of the beach, a few resorts nestle amid manicured landscapes. Sairee faces west, making it great for watching the sunset and for kayaking to Koh Nang Yuan. **Amenities:** food and drink; water sports. **Best for:** partiers. ✉ *Koh Tao.*

Restaurants

The Gallery

$$ | **THAI** | Combining fine dining and photography, this restaurant-gallery serves delicate interpretations of southern Thai classics—fish dishes, curries, grilled seafood, and the like. The service is first-rate, the atmosphere relaxed and romantic. **Known for:** fine art meets fine dining; "Trust the chef" menu; lavish wine list. $ *Average main: B300* ✉ *10/29 Moo 1, Sairee Village* ☎ *077/456547* 🌐 *www.thegallerykohtao.com.*

Taste of Home

$$ | **INTERNATIONAL** | At first glance this simple open-air eatery seems like it's nothing special, but pleasant surprises await those who sample its eclectic international fare. The portions are generous—order the Wiener schnitzel, and you'll be amazed it even fits on the plate—and the welcome even more so. **Known for:** reasonable prices; authentic German food; friendly owner. $ *Average main: B200* ✉ *Sairee Beach* ✣ *East Sairee, opposite the Yellow Hotel* ☎ *086/012–0727* ▭ *No credit cards.*

Hotels

Black Tip Dive Resort

$ | **RESORT** | This Tanote Bay resort makes a perfect base for snorkeling because of the colorful coral, interesting fish, and small reef sharks that cruise around at sunset. **Pros:** great for divers; transportation around island easily arranged; close to beach. **Cons:** far from action; some rooms lack hot water or private bathrooms; closed during low season. $ *Rooms from: B800* ✉ *40/6 Tanote Bay* ☎ *077/456867* 🌐 *www.blacktipresort.com/* *25 bungalows* 🍽 *No meals.*

★ Charm Churee Villa

$$ | **RESORT** | Whether you opt to stay in one of the uniquely designed tropical villas, a deluxe room, or a (very) basic bungalow, you'll enjoy a tiny corner of heaven on the private beach at Jansom Bay. Rooms and thatched-roof villas are built into the landscape, constructed on or around massive boulders and trees, and situated to maximize exposure to the magnificent views of Sairee Beach. **Pros:** private beach; sweeping views; snorkeling can be spectacular. **Cons:** isolated; feels spread out; staff is very lax. $ *Rooms from: B3,600* ✉ *30/1 Moo 2, Jansom Bay* ☎ *077/456–3934, 081/424–5252* 🌐 *www.charmchureevilla.com* *40 rooms* 🍽 *Free breakfast.*

Chintakiri Resort

$$ | **RESORT** | Set against a mountain backdrop and surrounded by a lush garden, this resort close to Sairee Beach has 19 wooden bungalows with spectacular views of the turquoise ocean. **Pros:** spectacular views; eco-friendly; small pool. **Cons:** long uphill access to the resort; breakfast is basic; difficult for anyone with mobility issues. $ *Rooms from: B2,900* ✉ *19/59–77 Moo 3, Chalok Baan Kao* ☎ *077/456391* 🌐 *www.chintakiriresort.com* *19 bungalows* 🍽 *Free breakfast* ▭ *No credit cards.*

Koh Tao Cabana

$$$ | **RESORT** | On the far northern end of Sairee Beach, this is one of Koh Tao's few boutique resorts. **Pros:** attractive decor; stylish resort; locally sourced ingredients at restaurant. **Cons:** so-so food; some rooms lack easy beach access; poor Wi-Fi. *Rooms from: B4,500 ✉ 16 Moo 1, Baan Haad Sai Ree, Sairee Beach ☎ 02/621–7890, 089/698–2266 ⊕ www.kohtaocabana.com 33 villas and cottages Free breakfast.*

Koh Tao Coral Grand Resort

$$ | **RESORT** | On the quieter northern end of Sairee Beach, this resort is a good place to get your scuba certification. **Pros:** feels peaceful; lots of amenities; lush grounds. **Cons:** can be noisy; some foot traffic; not a lot happening around here. *Rooms from: B3,300 ✉ 15/4 Moo 1, Sairee Beach ☎ 077/456431 ⊕ www.kohtaocoral.com 42 rooms Free breakfast.*

★ The Place Luxury Boutique Villas

$$$$ | **RESORT** | A total escape that provides serious pampering, this resort nestles on the hillside above Sairee Beach. **Pros:** private infinity pool with each villa; award-winning accommodations; stunning views out to sea. **Cons:** a bit of a hike up to the highest villas; may be too isolated for some; breakfast not included. *Rooms from: B9,000 ✉ 15/4 Moo 2, Sairee Beach ☎ 087/887–5066 ⊕ www.theplacekohtao.com 9 villas No meals No credit cards.*

Chapter 6

PHUKET AND THE ANDAMAN COAST

Updated by
Simon Ostheimer

Sights	Restaurants	Hotels	Shopping	Nightlife
★★★★☆	★★★☆☆	★★★★☆	★☆☆☆☆	★★★☆☆

WELCOME TO PHUKET AND THE ANDAMAN COAST

TOP REASONS TO GO

★ **Sunsets at Railay Beach:** The sunsets here are unbeatable, however you choose to view them—floating in a kayak, strolling along the sand, or lounging in a beachfront bungalow.

★ **Kayaking Phang Nga Bay:** Phang Nga Bay's maze of islands is ideal for gliding alongside towering cliffs.

★ **Discovering Koh Lanta:** This has become an artsy, laid-back destination for travelers in the know, with long sandy beaches studded with tiny bars, and glorious sunsets.

★ **Camping at Koh Similan:** This gorgeous national park has a handful of tents for rent. Hire a longtail boat to do some snorkeling while you're here.

★ **Exploring Koh Phi Phi:** The jewel of Phang Nga Bay cannot be truly appreciated from one beach. Make day trips aboard a longtail boat: quieter Loh Samah Bay is magical.

★ **Walking Phuket Old Town:** Stroll through historic roads filled with century-old shophouses, and savor the unique atmosphere and markets of the Old Town.

1 **Phuket Town.** Phuket still has beautiful beaches where you can escape the crowds.

2 **Khao Phra Taew National Park.** The last virgin rain forest in Phuket.

3 **Mai Khao Beach.** A prime destination for snorkeling and diving.

4 **Nai Yang Beach.** One of the most relaxed beaches on Phuket.

5 **Nai Thon and Layan Beaches.** A tropical rain forest means more wildlife than nightlife.

6 **Bang Thao Beach.** A favorite of those seeking a more refined pace.

7 **Pansea, Surin, and Laem Sing.** Three picturesque beaches locally known as "Millionaires' Mile."

8 **Kamala Beach.** A good base with reasonably priced accommodations that attract longer-stay visitors.

9 **Patong.** Overdeveloped but a nice beach and lively nightlife.

10 **Karon Beach.** Quality restaurants, bars, and cheerful shops.

11 **Kata Beach.** Beautiful beaches and a chill vibe.

12 **Nai Harn.** Authentic restaurants and viewpoints such as the Promthep Cape.

13 **Cape Yamu.** An isolated cape on Phuket's eastern side.

14 **Chalong.** Access to snorkeling, diving, and parasailing trips.

15 **Phang Nga Bay National Marine Park.** Draws thousands of day-trippers from Phuket.

16 **Khao Lak.** Peaceful with a National Park and uncrowded beaches.

17 **Koh Yao.** A pair of peaceful, unspoiled islands.

18 **Similan Islands.** Rare marine life and spectacular, unspoiled beaches.

19 **Surin Islands.** Five unspoiled islands popular with divers and fishermen.

20 **Krabi.** A friendly town and gateway to the nearby islands.

21 **Ao Nang.** A convenient base for exploring nearby islands and beaches.

22 **Nang Cape.** Four interconnected beaches surrounded by skyscraping cliffs.

23 **Koh Lanta.** Beautiful beaches and a charming Old Town.

24 **Koh Phi Phi.** Overdeveloped but still stunning beaches.

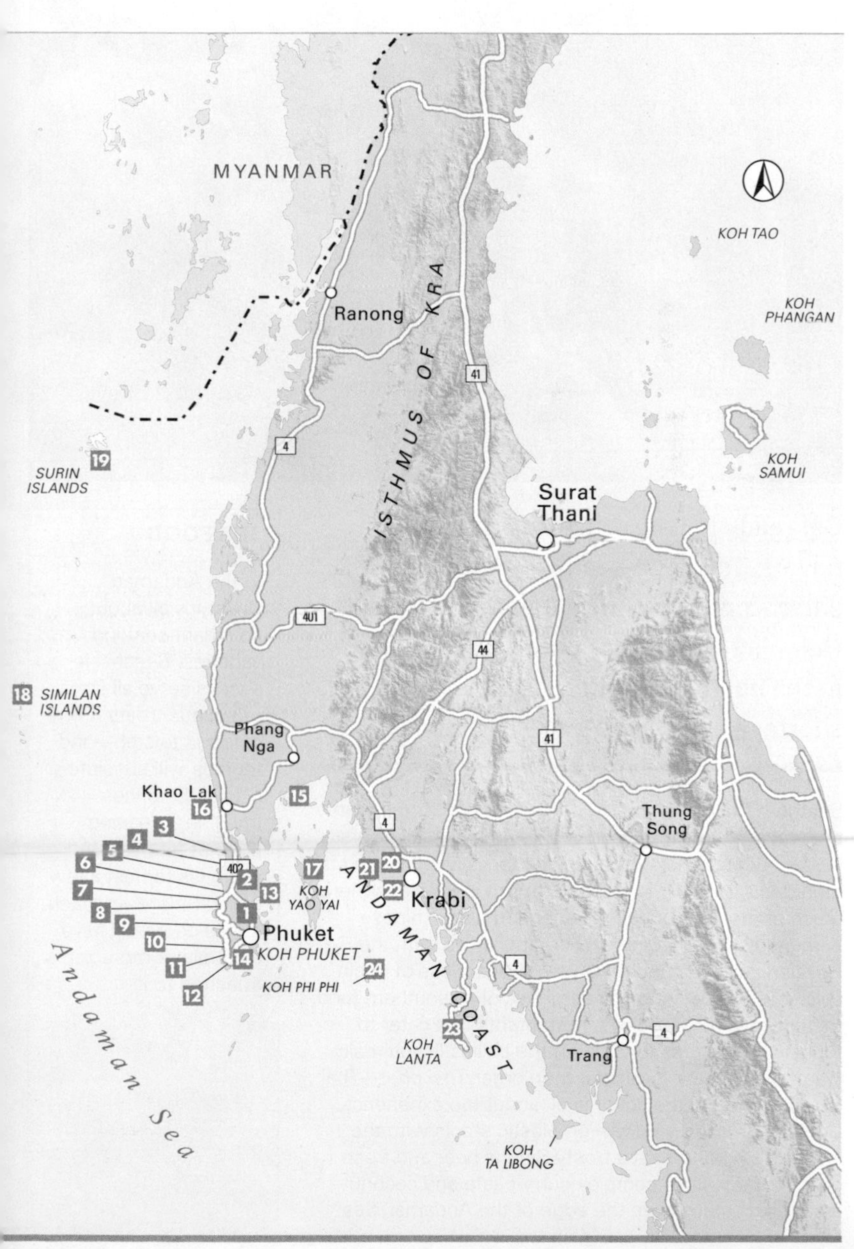
MYANMAR
KOH TAO
Ranong
ISTHMUS OF KRA
KOH PHANGAN
41
4
KOH SAMUI
19
SURIN ISLANDS
Surat Thani
4U1
44
18
SIMILAN ISLANDS
Phang Nga
41
Khao Lak
16
15
4
Thung Song
3
4
5
6
402
2
21
20
7
13
KOH YAO YAI
17
22
Krabi
8
1
9
Phuket
10
KOH PHUKET
14
ANDAMAN COAST
11
24
KOH PHI PHI
4
12
23
KOH LANTA
4
Trang
Andaman Sea
KOH TA LIBONG

EATING AND DRINKING WELL IN SOUTHERN THAILAND

Get ready for the south's distinctive flavors. Turmeric, peanuts, bird's-eye chili, and coconut milk are a few ingredients that play larger roles here than they do in the north. And, of course, there's no shortage of delectable fresh seafood.

Southern Thailand has a larger Muslim population than the rest of the country, and you'll find this halal diversity in southern cuisine, which was historically influenced by ethnic Malays living farther south. But in Phuket, where much of the population is descended from Chinese immigrants, you'll also discover similarities with the Hokkien cuisine found in Penang. Regardless of origin, spiciness is a defining characteristic of all southern food, though as in other regions, restaurants that cater to tourists sometimes tone down the chilies (if you really want to eat as the locals do, then order *Thai phet*—Thai spicy). A meal in the south is all about the experience. Don't be afraid to sit down on plastic stools with the locals. It's hard to beat a frosty Singha beer and fresh crab married with a complex curry paste and coconut cream, just steps from the edge of the Andaman Sea.

SEAFOOD

In the Andaman Coast it's all about abundant seafood varieties. Beachside shacks serve all sorts of aquatic treats, from octopus to crab—and foodies will absolutely love the prices. Imagine a heaping plate of fresh, grilled sea bass for just a few dollars; that same dish stateside would have a couple of more zeros attached to it.

GAENG MASSAMAN

A Muslim dish by origin (its name is derived from Musulman, an older version of the word "Muslim"), massaman curry has a distinct flavor that's somewhat reminiscent of Malay and Indian cuisine. It's not usually a spicy dish, but star anise and cinnamon add a big burst of flavor and peanuts an even bigger crunch. Usually made with beef, coconut milk softens everything, and the result is a soupy and comforting curry.

GAENG SOM

Known as sour curry, this local favorite is usually spicy as well as tart. It's made with fish sauce instead of coconut milk, and the flavor can take some getting used to. It's typically made with fish (*gaeng som pla*) and green vegetables, such as cabbage and beans. Sour curry is runnier than coconut-milk curries—more like a sauce—and tends to acquire a greenish hue from all the vegetables it contains.

KHAO MOK KAI

This simple but delicious chicken-and-rice dish is a Thai version of Indian chicken *biryani,* which means "fried" or "roasted." Chicken—which is usually on the bone—lies under a fragrant mound of rice, which owes its bright yellow color to a liberal amount of turmeric. Though turmeric often shows up in Indian cuisine, this is one of its few cameos in southern Thailand food. Deep-fried shallots add another element of textural complexity.

BOO PAHT PONG KAREE

Curry-powder crab is not a traditional, soupy curry: instead whole crab is fried in a mixture of curry powder and other spices. The piquant curry is a perfect counterpoint to the sweet crabmeat. Coconut milk is often used to moisten the mix and moderate the spiciness. You'll find other kinds of seafood prepared this way in the south, but crab is particularly tasty.

PLA

Whole fish such as *garoupa* (grouper) is often on the menu in the south, and is so much more flavorful than fillets. Garlic and chilies are common seasonings, and the skin is usually cooked until it's deliciously crispy. It may be spicy, but whole fish is definitely a treat you don't get to enjoy too often stateside. You can also find steamed versions and less spicy seasonings like ginger.

For its amazing setting, variety, and charm, Phuket has consistently been voted as one of the world's favorite tourist destinations, both for budget travelers and those seeking sumptuous luxury. Though it has its share of overdevelopment issues, the island has many beautiful beaches and a dazzling array of restaurants, hotels, activities, and nightlife. Once you leave Phuket and head for the Andaman Coast, though, the attractions become even more spectacular. The coastline delivers spectacular limestones karsts, secluded islands with crystal waters, and miles of unspoiled beaches.

Phuket is the busy hub of the southwestern coast, with daily flights from Bangkok and around the world landing in its airport and boats to scenic but often packed Ko Phi Phi, Krabi, and the dreamy Similan and Surin islands departing daily from its docks. Beyond Phuket, the secrets of this magical coastline begin to reveal itself. Krabi has powdery white sand and magnificent limestone cliffs shooting straight up out of emerald waters that have become popular with all levels of rock-climbing enthusiasts. Railay Beach is especially sought out by adventurers who enjoy acrobatics and climbing. Nearby the Phang Nga National Park attracts nature lovers because of its world-renowned postcard-perfect locations, such as Koh Phing Kan, known as James Bond Island. Ko Phi Phi is a prime destination for snorkeling and diving (you may actually see more divers than fish in some waters as it gets incredibly busy in high season), along with being a mainstay of the easygoing backpacker tourist circuit. Koh Lanta has developed its own scene and attracts visitors who like fewer crowds and more offbeat individuality—as reflected in some of its quirky shops and restaurants; it combines lovely beaches with colorful villages where you will meet interesting locals and expats who differ from those in other parts of the Andaman Coast. Ao Nang has become very popular over the years, and numerous resorts have sprung up near its popular beaches and shops to cater to all tastes and budgets.

A note of caution: don't take the chance of getting on rickety or overcrowded boats. Speedboats can often be hired to travel the ferry routes. Ensure that life jackets are available and that the crew takes safety seriously.

MAJOR REGIONS

Phuket is the hub of the southwestern coast, with daily flights from Bangkok and around the world landing in its airport and boats to Koh Phi Phi, Koh Lanta, and the Similan and Surin islands departing from its docks. Though it's got its share of overdevelopment issues, Phuket still has beautiful beaches where you can escape the crowds. **Phuket Town** is in the center of the island and is one of the more culturally interesting places with its Old Chinese quarter and one of the island's revered landmarks, the Big Buddha. **Khao Phra Taew National Park** in the north of the Island is worth a visit for Tonsai Waterfall and a wander through a real tropical rain forest. On the northwest coast of Phuket, **Mai Khao Beach**, part of Sirinat National Park, is mostly undeveloped and a haven for leatherback turtles. Mai Khao connects to **Nai Yang Beach** to its south to form Phuket's longest stretch of sand. Nai Yang is quieter than most of Phuket's beaches, with just a small string of beachside restaurants and bars. **Nai Thon and Layan beaches** exude a calm vibe attracting more wildlife than nightlife. **Bang Thao Beach**, once the site of a tin mine, attracts an affluent clientele with its upscale accommodations, eateries, and golf courses. The picturesque beaches of **Pansea, Surin, and Laem Sing** are where Phuket's wealthy set call home and you can also find high-end resorts. **Kamala Beach** is a good base for exploring the island and its affordable accommodation options attract a laid-back, long-term visitor. About 8 miles west of Phuket Town, **Patong** is a thriving, beach-resort community with a lively nightlife scene, shopping, good Thai food, and watersports making it a hotspot for weekending Bangkokians and international tourists. Just south of Patong, **Karon Beach** caters to Patong's spillover. Farther southwest of Phuket Town, **Kata Beach** offers stunning white-sand beaches with turquoise waters that are a big draw for surfers. Less busy **Nai Harn** is a local hotspot but visitors throng here at sunset for the views from Phromthep Cape. The isolated headland at **Cape Yamu,** on Phuket's east side, hosts some of the island's most exclusive properties. Just 7 miles south of Phuket Town, **Chalong** is a working port and a good spot for chartering boats and booking diving or snorkeling trips to nearby islands. You'll also find Wat Chalong, the largest and most famous of Phuket's Buddhist temples.

The Andaman Coast stretches from Ranong Province, bordering Myanmar (Burma) to the north, to Satun Province, flanking Malaysia to the south. Along this shore are hundreds of islands and thousands of beaches. Because of their proximity to Phuket, Phang Nga and Krabi provinces are the two most appealing destinations on the Andaman Coast. **Phang Nga Bay National Marine Park** is Phang Nga's most heralded attraction, drawing thousands of day-trippers from Phuket. There are dozens of little islands to explore, as well as offshore caves and startling karst formations rising out of the sea. Most visitors make an obligatory stop at Phing Kan Island, made famous by the James Bond movie *The Man with the Golden Gun.* **Khao Lak's** Khao Lak Lamru National Park attracts nature lovers, while the beaches along this coast draw beachgoers who want a vibe more tranquil than Phuket has to offer. Travelers looking for even greater seclusion head to the **Koh Yao** Islands, which have cultural tours and homestays that provide insight into southern Thai lifestyles. The **Similan Islands** and **Surin Islands** national parks are well known to scuba divers for their crystalline waters and abundant marine life. You can camp or stay in a national park bungalow on either of the islands; no commercial lodging is available in either park. Many divers opt to stay on live-aboard ships departing from Phuket or Khao Lak. **Krabi** lies to the east of Phuket. Its capital, Krabi Town, sits on the northeastern shore of Phuket Bay. Once a favorite harbor for smugglers bringing in alcohol and tobacco from Malaysia, the town has been transformed into a gateway to the nearby islands. **Ao Nang**, a short distance from Krabi Town, has evolved into a busy little beach town. Ao Nang and nearby Noppharat Thara exist simply to cater to tourists, with restaurants and shopping for every taste. Ao Nang is a more convenient base of operations than Krabi Town for exploring nearby islands and beaches. Longtail boats and ferries depart from Ao Nang for **Nang Cape, Koh Lanta, Koh Phi Phi,** and the multitude of smaller islands in eastern Phang Nga Bay.

Planning

WHEN TO GO

The peak season on the Andaman Coast is November through April. The monsoon season is May through October, during which high seas can make boat travel unwise and beaches unsafe for swimming (a number of tourist deaths are registered each year in the treacherous monsoon waters) though hotel prices are considerably lower.

PLANNING YOUR TIME

Visitors to Phuket and the Andaman Coast can find a new activity every day; you could spend weeks in this region and still not do the same thing twice. It has great tourism infrastructure. Children and families will find plenty to do and see, as will singles and couples.

GETTING HERE AND AROUND

AIR TRAVEL

There are daily, relatively inexpensive flights from Bangkok to the major beach destinations in the south: Phuket and Krabi, though air travel to Koh Samui is pricey (try Surat Thai on the mainland instead). There are also some flights from Chiang Mai to the beaches, including on Thai Smile, Bangkok Airways, and Air Asia. If you're flexible with your dates, you can find some ridiculously cheap fares. Keep in mind that planes fill up fast during the high season, and the lowest fares are mostly available if booked weeks or months in advance. *(See Air Travel in Travel Smart Thailand).* All the airports in this region are small and much easier to deal with than Bangkok's Suvarnabhumi, though Phuket can get busy with its growing number of international destinations.

BUS TRAVEL

Buses travel regularly between Bangkok and all major destinations on the Andaman Coast. There's also good bus service within the south. Many Bangkok travel agents charge three times the price for bus tickets, and organize a long, exhausting, and convoluted trip with various stops to the main bus stations. It's best to visit the bus station under your own steam and buy your ticket either in advance or on the day; you will save both time and money. Buses leave from Bangkok's Southern Bus Terminal, generally in the late afternoon and evening. The trip to Phuket takes from 12 to 14 hours, depending on the bus and road conditions. You'll need to go to either a travel agent or to the bus station to check exact times and purchase tickets in advance, especially for VIP buses. Costs run from B500 for a large 32-seat air-conditioned bus to around B1,000 for a 24-seat air-conditioned VIP bus. Most long-haul VIP buses travel overnight, but day trips are recommended, as Thailand's highways grow even more dangerous at night. There are buses from Phuket to almost every major destination in southern Thailand. This includes, but is not limited to: Surat Thani, Krabi, Trang, Hat Yai, Satun, Phang Nga, and the ferry crossing to Koh Samui. You can check departure times at your hotel or the centrally located bus station just east of Montri Road, two blocks north of Phang Nga Road in Phuket Town. **■ TIP→ Private buses are less reputable than public buses.**

CAR TRAVEL

You can take Highway 4 from Thonburi in Bangkok all the way to the bridge at the north end of Phuket Island, where it turns into Highway 402. It's a long, exhausting, and not particularly recommended, drive, but once you're out of the capital all you have to do is follow the compass due south. For the scenic route, follow Highway 4 to Chumphon, where it jogs west and south and follows the Andaman Sea coast to Phuket Island. Phuket Town is 862 km (517 miles) from Bangkok; bus companies make the trip in 13 to 15 hours. *(See Car Travel in Travel Smart Thailand.)*

MOTORCYCLE TRAVEL

Cheap and readily available, scooters are probably the easiest hassle-free (park anywhere) way to get around and discover all sites and beaches, but think twice before renting one. Accidents are not uncommon on Phuket, Koh Lanta, or in Krabi, as the Thais tend to speed, many tourists drink and drive, and helmets are often shunned. If you've never driven a motorcycle before, this is not the time or place to learn. A somewhat safer, if expensive option could be to hire a tuk-tuk.

SONGTHAEW, TAXI, AND TUK-TUK TRAVEL

Most areas of the south have a variety of motorized taxi services from samlors to tuk-tuks to songthaews. Some "metered" taxis can be found in most of the region now, but they usually don't run their meters, preferring to set a price at the start of the trip. Alternatively, popular Southeast Asian taxi app Grab (a local version of Uber) has arrived locally. It makes it much easier to book a vehicle, though the prices may not be much cheaper.

TRAIN TRAVEL

Bangkok is connected to Sri Racha and Pattaya via one daily train; there are more frequent trains to Hua Hin, Chumphon, and Surat Thani. There are regular express trains to Surat Thani, the closest station to Phuket (albeit still a distance away), which leave Bangkok's Hua Lamphong Station. From Surat Thani you can take a bus to Phuket. Express trains from Bangkok's Hua Lamphong railway station stop at Surat Thani on their way south. The journey takes 12 hours or so; if you leave Bangkok at 3 pm, you'll arrive at a dark train station in Surat Thani at around 3 am. *(See Train Travel in Travel Smart Thailand.)* Bus services or flights, though, are generally considered to be a far better way to get to the Andaman Coast.

HEALTH AND SAFETY

Malaria and dengue fever are rare but not unheard of in Thailand's southwest. Health authorities have done a great job controlling mosquitoes in the more urban areas, but you'll still need a good supply of repellent. Wear long-sleeve shirts and long pants at dusk to reduce the chances of dengue.

As with any developed resort locations, the dangers and annoyances usually involve petty theft. Phuket has its fair share of crime, usually items being stolen from hotel rooms or pickpockets operating in the entertainment areas. Especially watch out for motorcycle "snatch" theives, and ensure that your valuables are secured at all times. Brawls caused by too much liquor and sun can also be a problem. There are many bars and pubs here, and many tend to overindulge. The police do patrol tourist areas, but violence does occasionally break out.

Be careful at the beach, as the sun is stronger than you think. Wear a hat, plenty of sunscreen, and anti-UV clothing. Protective footwear while diving or snorkeling is a good idea, as accidentally stepping on coral or sea urchins can be painful. Keep an eye out for dangerous creatures like jellyfish, especially during the monsoon season. If you are stung, seek medical attention immediately.

Strong undertows often develop during monsoon season, especially along the west coast. Pay attention to posted warnings, only swim in designated areas where marked, and listen if locals tell you not to swim.

MONEY MATTERS

Banks and ATMs are everywhere, and can always be found outside the numerous 7-Eleven and Family Mart convenience stores, but it's still always a good idea to carry some extra cash. There have also been cases of stand-alone ATMs being hacked, so try to use ones directly attached to banks where possible. Remote islands do not widely accept credit cards but have many eager currency exchangers. Some places add a small service charge, typically 3%, when you pay with a credit card.

RESTAURANTS

Restaurants of all sorts are available in the beach regions, from exclusive (and usually expensive) resort eateries to wooden shacks that seem like they're about to fall over, though a government-mandated beach clean-up project in Phuket led to many disappearing. On Koh Lanta food stalls pop up just before dusk on the beaches, where in the daytime there's only sand and sunbathers. Phuket has the widest range of restaurants, from the fast-food giants of America (with some Thai adaptations on their menus) to beach huts to five-star Western-style restaurants, while Khao Lak in Phang Nga and Ao Nang in Krabi also has a great many dining spots to choose from.

HOTELS

Hotel prices in beach areas are generally lower than what you'd pay in Bangkok (Phuket excluded) but higher than in other parts of the country. There are budget bungalows and guesthouses everywhere, though if you haven't booked ahead in high season you may end up in a questionable room with just a humble fan. At the other end of the spectrum are upscale resorts that run more than $1,000-plus a night—though they are some of the most luxurious resorts in the world.

Many places combine the two experiences by offering pricey luxury bungalows. Rates fluctuate widely—in holiday periods they can be more than double. Always double-check your rate when you book.

What It Costs In Baht

	$	$$	$$$	$$$$
RESTAURANTS				
	under B200	B200–B300	B301–B400	over B400
HOTELS				
	under B2,000	B2,000–B4,000	B4,001–B6,000	over B6,000

Phuket Town

862 km (539 miles) south of Bangkok.

Increasingly popular with tourists, Phuket Town, the provincial capital, is one of the more culturally interesting places on the island to spend half a day. About one-third of the island's population lives here, and the town is an intriguing mix of old Sino-Colonial architecture and the influences of the ethnic Chinese, Malays, and Thais that inhabit it. The old shophouses around Thalang Road make it especially good for a stroll, filled as they are with a variety of antiques shops, art studios, and trendy cafés. Besides Thalang, the major thoroughfares are Ratsada, Phuket, Dibuk, and Ranong roads. Ratsada connects Phuket Road to Ranong Road, where there's an aromatic local market filled with fruits, vegetables, spices, and meats, though its at the weekly Sunday Walking Street, when Thalang Road is closed to traffic and fills with food stalls, handicraft sellers, and musical performers, when the area really comes alive.

GETTING HERE AND AROUND

Phuket Town is in the southeast of the island. Taxis, tuk-tuks, motorcycles, and local buses will take you from here to the west-coast beaches and to the airport. Expect to pay approximately B500 to travel from the town to the airport or Patong via taxi—a little more to most other southern and northern beaches. The price will depend on your negotiation techniques. The best place to pick up transport is at the bus station in the center of town. Ranong Road also has a songthaew terminal, where minibuses depart for the most popular beaches every half hour. The fare is B30 to B100.

VISITOR INFORMATION AND TOURS

As the saying goes, you can't throw a stone in Phuket without hitting a tour operator. Nearly all of them are selling the same package tours and renting the same cars and motorcycles, so feel free to comparison shop and haggle over prices. Common half-day sightseeing tours include visits to Wat Chalong, Rawai Beach, Phromthep Cape, and Khao Rang.

In general, be wary of what tour operators tell you; they are in business to sell you a trip to the beach, not to tell you how to get there on your own. If you feel you have been ripped off, note the offender's name and other info and report him to the local Tourism Authority of Thailand (TAT) office. Also let the manager at your hotel know, so he or she can steer other tourists clear.

TOURS

Dive Asia

SPECIAL-INTEREST | Based on Kata Beach, Dive Asia is a PADI-certified instructor and operator that's been in business for more than two decades. They do a multitude of day trips to different dive sites and snorkeling spots. ✉ *Kata Beach* ☎ *076/330598* 🌐 *www.diveasia.com* 🎫 *From B3,400.*

John Gray's Sea Canoe

ECOTOURISM | This company is known internationally for ecotourism trips, including awesome canoeing through Phang Nga Bay. Look for their flyers at travel agencies. Various tours are offered, from day trips to longer overnight stays. ✉ *Phuket* ☎ *076/254505* 🌐 *www.johngray-seacanoe.com* 🎫 *From B3,950.*

Thailand Divers

GUIDED TOURS | Day trips by boat, snorkeling, and a broad range of diving courses are offered by this well-organized, friendly, and highly professional agency. ✉ *Patong* ☎ *076/344155* 🌐 *www.thailand-divers.com* 🎫 *From B2,000.*

Tourism Authority of Thailand

SELF-GUIDED | The efficient Tourism Authority of Thailand in Phuket Town provides up-to-date maps, and brochures, as well as thorough information about local excursions. ✉ *Phuket* ☎ *076/212213* 🌐 *www.tourismthailand.org.*

Sights

Big Buddha

RELIGIOUS SITE | The Big Buddha is one of the island's most revered landmarks. The huge, white-marble Buddha image sits on top of the Nakkerd Hills between Chalong and Kata. It is 45 meters high, and the site offers the best 360-degree views of the island. Take the road from Phuket's main artery—it's a must-visit island destination. ✉ *Phuket.*

Khao Rang

VIEWPOINT | If you want to get your bearings, there's a fine view of Phuket Town, the island's interior, and even the 45-meter-high Big Buddha from atop Khao Rang, a hill north of town. From the town's center, take either Ranong or Thalang Road west and turn north on Khaw Sim Bee Road. Follow the winding, ascending, forested road. There are a few restaurants and a picnic area once you reach the top, where you can relax after soaking in the vista from the large viewing platform next to a tower (which you can't ascend). ✉ *Northwest, Phuket.*

Siam Niramit

SOUND/LIGHT SHOW | **FAMILY** | Costing B2.5 billion to construct, this huge entertainment park contains a cultural village, complete with boats, games, and traditional crafts, and an indoor theater where Thai history is told through dance, performance, and song. The main show starts nightly at 8:30 pm, so make sure you arrive early to wander among the stalls. ☎ *076/335–000* 🌐 *www.siamniramit.com* 🎫 *Tickets from B1,500.*

Thalang National Museum

MUSEUM | **FAMILY** | The National Museum, opposite the Heroine's Monument, has an engaging exhibition of the island's culture and history, including its encounter with the Burmese and their defeat by the island's two heroines. The building itself gives a glimpse into local culture, with its attractive architecture and design. The halls each show a different period of local and wider Thai history. ✉ *Srisoonthorn, Phuket* ✣ *12 km (7 miles) north of Phuket Town* ☎ *076/311426* 🎫 *B100.*

Restaurants

Bookhemian

$ | **THAI** | If there's one place that sums up the gentrification of the Old Town—a wonderful collection of 100 year-old shophouses—it's this bohemian-chic café. As the name suggests, it's also home to a design bookshop, as well as an exhibition arts space, and an upstairs film room, where indie flicks are played from time to time. **Known for:** homemade brownies and freshly ground coffee; collection of design books; bohemian atmosphere. 💲 *Average main: B115* ✉ *61 Thalang Rd., Phuket* ☎ *98/090–0657.*

Chino Café Gallery

$ | **CAFÉ** | Coffee lovers will immediately yearn for a cup upon entering, as the air carries the smell of freshly ground espresso. The loveliest aspect of this café is its natural wood decor, which gives it a New Age trendy aesthetic. **Known for:** handmade souvenirs; freshly ground coffee; natural wood decor. 💲 *Average main: B115* ✉ *4 Thalang Rd., Taladyai Muang, Phuket* ☎ *081/979–6190* 💳 *No credit cards.*

Kopi de Phuket

$ | **CAFÉ** | For a good cup of coffee, try this artsy store, which sells funky designer souvenirs and serves traditional Thai food and international snacks, sandwiches, desserts, and shakes. It opens daily at 9:30 am. **Known for:** southern Thai snacks;

Than Bokkharani

Between Krabi and Phang Nga is this forested park, which has several emerald-green ponds surrounded by tropical foliage, including wild gardenia and apocynaceae. The pools are filled with refreshing cool water, fed by a mountain spring 4 km (2½ miles) away. The largest pond is 130 feet by 100 feet, deep and suitable for swimming. The pools are best visited in the dry season, as they get quite murky when it rains. From Krabi: take Hwy. 4 to Ao Luek, then turn onto Rte. 4039.

designer souvenirs; baked garlic butter prawns. *$ Average main: B150 ✉ Phuket Rd., Phuket ☎ 076/212225 🌐 www.kopidephuket.com ▭ No credit cards.*

★ Kopitiam by Wilai

$ | **THAI** | The walls of this unique restaurant-café in the heart of the architecturally quaint Sino-Colonial Old Town are lined with vintage black-and-white images of Phuket, which pretty much reflect the kind of food served here—old-school Thai-Chinese fare. Signature dishes are inspired by secret recipes of owner Wiwan's mother (who also owns the popular Wilai restaurant nearby) and grandmother, and often include Chinese medicinal ingredients from her uncle's herbal shop next door. **Known for:** old-world charm; traditional treats; bak kut teh soup. *$ Average main: B160 ✉ 18 Thalang Rd., Phuket ☎ 083/606–9776 ▭ No credit cards ⏲ Closed Sun.*

★ Raya Restaurant

$ | **THAI** | In the heart of Phuket Old Town, this beloved restaurant is in a historical Sino-Thai mansion, built in the early 20th century by a rich tin mining family. The charming decor is traditional Thai, with a nod to colonial influences, and the atmosphere is as much part of the experience as the outstanding food. **Known for:** historic surroundings; yellow crab curry; family antiques. *$ Average main: B160 ✉ 48/1 New Debuk Rd., Phuket ☎ 076/218155 ▭ No credit cards.*

★ Suay

$$ | **ASIAN FUSION** | With his restaurant Suay—Thai for "beautiful"—chef Noi put Thai fusion cuisine on the map in Phuket, combining his local family heritage with an upbringing in Germany, and in the process, creating one of the island's most-talked-about dining destinations. It was only meant to be temporary, helping his sister open a small eatery in the then-quiet Old Town, but after they transformed an old wooden house into a culinary hot spot, he stuck around to turn the business into a culinary empire, spanning TV appearances, a catering business, cooking school, and a second branch in the chi-chi area of Cherngtalay. **Known for:** tom yum spaghetti; German desserts; celebrity chef. *$ Average main: B200 ✉ 50/2 Takuapa Rd, Phuket ☎ 87/888–6990 🌐 www.suayrestaurant.com.*

Tu Kab Khao

$$ | **THAI** | Located in one of the Old Town's most impressive mansions, this stylish eatery pays homage to classic home-cooked Phuket dishes—hence the name, which translates as "food cupboard." Pay attention to your dining neighbors, as the local cusine draws Thai celebrities from as far away as Bangkok. **Known for:** celebrity guests; Phuket specialties; stylish decor. *$ Average main: B200 ✉ 8 Phangnga Rd., Phuket ☎ 076/608888.*

Tunk Ka Cafe

$ | **THAI** | A favorite haunt of local businessfolk and dating couples, Tunk Ka Cafe is nestled in a jungle setting atop of the biggest hill in Phuket Town. Serving up proper Thai food made from fresh local ingredients, the views are marvelous, especially at sunset, and more than justify the tuk-tuk drive up. **Known for:** Old Town views; Ruby Red dessert; romantic setting. *$ Average main: B180 ✉ Phuket ⊕ Top of Rang Hill ☎ 076/211500, 082/412–2131 ▭ No credit cards.*

Hotels

Casa Blanca

$$ | **B&B/INN** | The best among a string of boutique B&Bs in the charming Sino-Colonial Old Town, Casa Blanca is comprised of 17 tasteful rooms with cream walls and wooden floors, and either garden courtyard views or a small balcony looking out onto the street. **Pros:** good location; small swimming pool; historic building with lots of charm. **Cons:** breakfast not included; hot water access erratic; far from the beach. *$ Rooms*

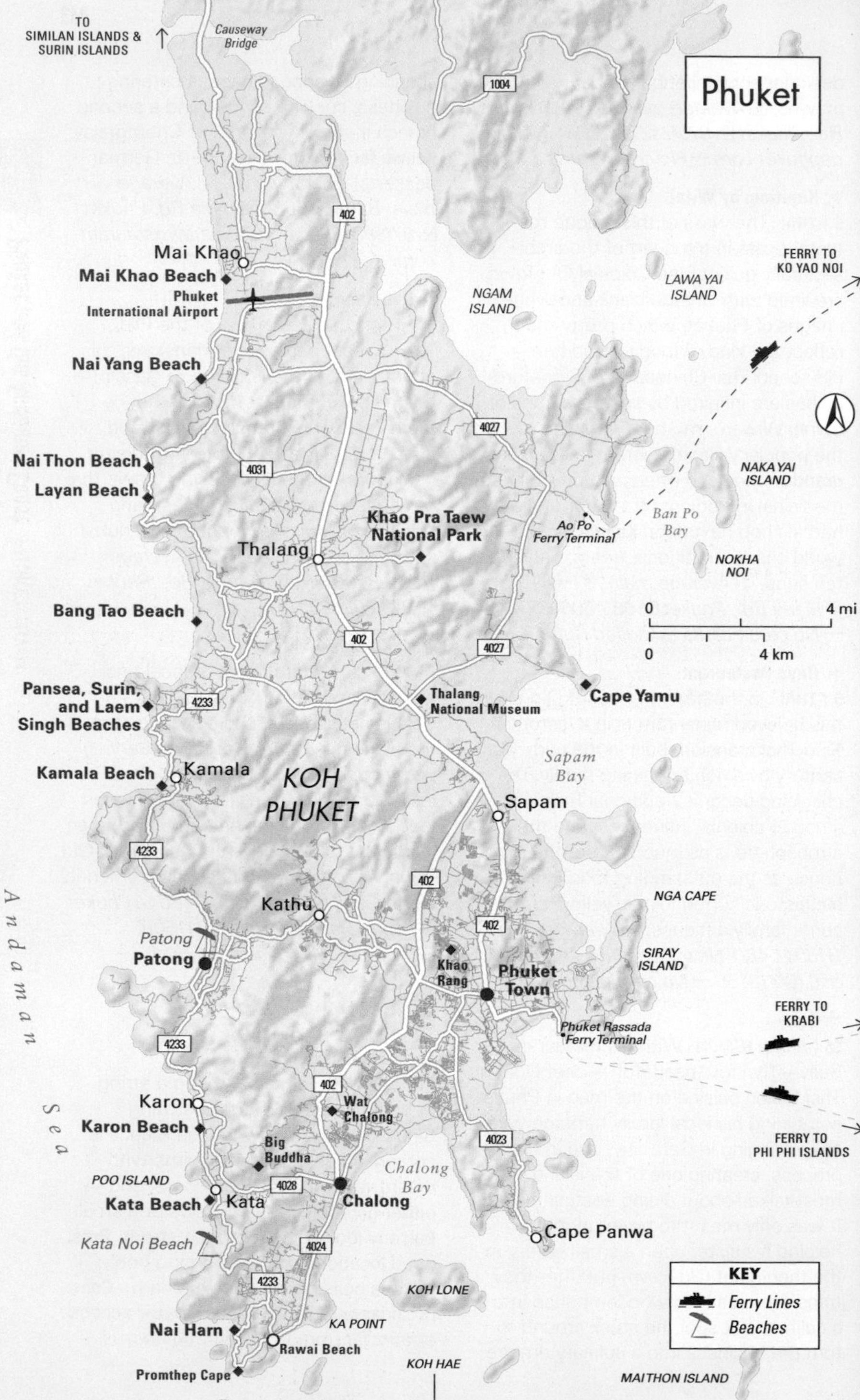

Phuket
TO SIMILAN ISLANDS & SURIN ISLANDS
Causeway Bridge
1004
402
Mai Khao
Mai Khao Beach
Phuket International Airport
Nai Yang Beach
Nai Thon Beach
Layan Beach
4031
4027
NGAM ISLAND
LAWA YAI ISLAND
FERRY TO KO YAO NOI
NAKA YAI ISLAND
Khao Pra Taew National Park
Thalang
Ao Po Ferry Terminal
Ban Po Bay
NOKHA NOI
0 4 mi
0 4 km
Bang Tao Beach
Cape Yamu
Pansea, Surin, and Laem Singh Beaches
4233
Thalang National Museum
Sapam Bay
Kamala Beach
Kamala
KOH PHUKET
Sapam
NGA CAPE
Andaman Sea
Kathu
Patong
SIRAY ISLAND
Khao Rang
Phuket Town
FERRY TO KRABI
Phuket Rassada Ferry Terminal
Karon
Karon Beach
Wat Chalong
Big Buddha
4023
FERRY TO PHI PHI ISLANDS
POO ISLAND
4028
Chalong Bay
Kata Beach
Kata
Chalong
Kata Noi Beach
4024
Cape Panwa
KOH LONE
KA POINT
Nai Harn
Rawai Beach
Promthep Cape
KOH HAE
MAI THON ISLAND
KEY
Ferry Lines
Beaches

from: B2,000 ✉ 26 Phuket Rd., Talat Yai, Phuket ☎ 076/219019 🌐 www.casablancaphuket.com ▭ No credit cards 🛏 17 rooms 🍽 No meals.

Metropole

$ | **HOTEL** | The grand old Metropole—the town's first luxury hotel—has a shuttle service to the closest beaches, so you can stay in town and commute to the sea. **Pros:** shuttle service to beaches; decent food; reasonable rates. **Cons:** busy with large tour groups; a little run-down; impersonal. *$ Rooms from: B1,000 ✉ 1 Montri Rd., Phuket ☎ 076/215050, 076/214020 🌐 www.metropolephuket.com 🛏 26 rooms 🍽 No meals.*

Pearl Hotel

$ | **HOTEL** | For a less expensive option, this is a comfortable, convenient hotel in the center of Phuket Town, though it's a little tired around the edges. **Pros:** convenient location; shuttle service; great live music. **Cons:** needs renovation; basic; can be noisy. *$ Rooms from: B1,300 ✉ 42 Montri Rd., Phuket ☎ 076/211044 🌐 www.pearlhotel.co.th 🛏 212 rooms 🍽 No meals.*

Royal Phuket City Hotel

$$ | **HOTEL** | This is arguably Phuket Town's best address, with rooms that are spacious and contemporary. **Pros:** large rooms; good gym; conference center. **Cons:** some rooms lack views; in-room Wi-Fi is extra; a little short on personality. *$ Rooms from: B2,300 ✉ 154 Phang Nga Rd., Phuket, Phuket ☎ 076/233333 🌐 www.royalphuketcity.com 🛏 251 rooms 🍽 No meals.*

Sino House

$$ | **HOTEL** | This much-needed recent addition to Phuket Town provides a pleasant option from the larger, often less charming hotels in the area. **Pros:** central; 50% discount for the spa for all guests; basic kitchenette. **Cons:** poor English; noisy air-conditioning; dull views. *$ Rooms from: B2,000 ✉ 1 Montree Rd., Talad Yai, Phuket ☎ 076/232494 up to 95 🌐 www.sinohousephuket.com ▭ No credit cards 🛏 57 rooms 🍽 No meals.*

Thalang 37 Guesthouse

$ | **B&B/INN** | This inexpensive guesthouse in a lovely building is becoming ever more popular with backpackers, offering both basic fan-cooled rooms and some air-conditioned ones in an old building. **Pros:** cheap; good views from roof; good location in Old Town. **Cons:** street-side rooms can be noisy; clean but a little worn. *$ Rooms from: B600 ✉ 37 Thalang Rd., Phuket ☎ 076/214225 🌐 www.thalangguesthouse.com ▭ No credit cards 🛏 13 rooms 🍽 Free breakfast.*

Nightlife

★ Z1mplex

BARS/PUBS | Despite being possibly Thailand's coolest cocktail bar (outside of Bangkok), Z1mplex goes surprisingly under the radar. Perhaps that's to do with the out-of-the-way location down the quiet end of Phangnga Road in Phuket Town, that it's only open from 8 pm to midnight, or that it's not a place to spend the whole night. Whatever the reason, this place has to be on your go-to list as couple co-owners Tom and Nann serve up shots that resemble science experiments—kaleidoscopic drinks with names like Ultimate Unrealm, Parallel Universe, and Aztec Jellyfish. *✉ 156/48 Phangnga Rd, Phuket ☎ 84/003–6664.*

Khao Pra Taew National Park

19 km (12 miles) north of Phuket Town.

Located in the north of the island, Khao Pra Taew is the last virgin rain forest in Phuket. You can take a hike through the park (8 km) or just take a walk up to the beautiful Tonsai waterfall. The Gibbon Rehabilitation Project is on the other side of the park, close to Bang Pae waterfall.

The Gibbon Rehabilitation Project

Just inside Khao Pra Taew National Park, between a hillside jungle and a gurgling stream, dozens of gibbons swing from branch to branch, filling the forest with boisterous hooting.

It seems like a happy sign of jungle life, but something is wrong with this picture. These animals are not roaming around free; instead, they live in cages near the park entrance as part of the Gibbon Rehabilitation Project. Most of these small apes were poached from jungles around Thailand and kept as pets or zoo and bar amusements. They were forced to perform shows, do tricks, drink beer, or get their pictures taken with tourists before they were rescued by this project. As a branch of the Wild Animal Rescue Foundation of Thailand, the center aims to rehabilitate the gibbons in their natural habitat, with the intention of releasing the animals into the wild (though some animals that were abused will never be able to live freely again).

The center holds more than 60 gibbons. They're kept in large cages, away from visitors. The idea is to purge them of their familiarity with people, although visitors can hear them in the distance and glimpse their playful leaps through the trees. All gibbons are named, and their life stories are posted at the center for tourists to read: Lamut and Pai Mei were working as tourist attractions at Patong Beach before their rescue. A baby, called Bam-Bam, was found in a cardboard box at a roadside. Saul, a young blond male, is missing a patch of fur, which researchers think could be the result of bullets that grazed him when his mother was shot.

When new gibbons arrive at the center they get a complete medical checkup, including tests for HIV, hepatitis, and tuberculosis. It costs $700 a year to treat, feed, and house each animal, and although the center sits within the national park, it receives none of the $5 entrance fee. In fact, the center receives no funding from the Thai government—it survives on donations alone. For B1,500, the price of a good night out in Patong, visitors can "adopt" a gibbon for a year. If you're unable to make it out to the center, the website of the Gibbon Rehabilitation Project (🌐 *www.gibbonproject.org*) has information on how to adopt a gibbon or make a donation.

—Karen Coates

Although small, this animal charity center does worthy work rehabilitating captured gibbons to the wild.

GETTING HERE AND AROUND

You can take a taxi, tuk-tuk, or motorcycle here from any of the island's beaches or from Phuket Town. The cost depends on distance—a taxi from Phuket Town would be about B400, a tuk-tuk a little more. If you're driving, take Highway 4027, watch the signs, and turn west toward Bang Pae Waterfall and the Gibbon Rehabilitation Center.

Sights

Thailand's islands have several national parks, and this one is home to Phuket's last remaining virgin forest and populations of endangered animals. The park has two easily accessible waterfalls. The Gibbon Rehabilitation Center, which works to protect the primates and educate visitors about them, is part of the park.

You'll have to pay the standard foreigner's fee to enter the park: B200 (Thais pay B40). To access **Tonsai Waterfall** on the other side of the park, follow the signs and turn east off Highway 402. Here you can find two trails (600 meters and 2 km [1 mile]), through rich, tropical, evergreen forest. Expect buckets of rain in the monsoon season. Gibbons, civets, macaques, mouse deer, wild boar, lemurs, and loris live in the park, but spotting one would be a rare and impressive feat.

The park advertises the good deeds of the Gibbon Center, and indeed it's a worthy cause. (What they don't tell you is that the center, which sits near the parking lot at Bang Pae, receives none of your entrance fee.) After visiting the center, follow the paved trail along the waterfall. It's a relatively easy hike, quite lush in the rainy season. Both park entrances have bathrooms, parking lots, and food stalls. If you plan to visit both waterfalls, make sure you get entrance tickets at your first stop—they're good for both sites.

Mai Khao Beach

37 km (23 miles) northwest of Phuket Town.

On the northwest coast of Phuket, this 11-km-long beach is still undeveloped by Phuket standards, as it is part of the Sirinat National Park. The only significant constructions along it are a smattering of resorts and Phuket International Airport near Nai Yang Beach. The sand here is possibly the coarsest of any on Phuket, but it is practically deserted most of the time

Mai Khao Beach

BEACH—SIGHT | This is Phuket's northernmost beach, still a haven for leatherback turtles that lay their eggs here between November and February. It is a rare event, but it does happen sometimes. You can pop into the Marriott Resort for a bite at their beach club, or visit the next-door Sirinath Marine National Park (established to protect the turtles) here. Mai Khao connects with Nai Yang Beach to form Phuket's longest stretch of sand, and is ideal for long walks or a jog. It's dangerous to swim during the monsoons. **Amenities:** food and drink. **Best for:** solitude; sunset; walking. ✉ *Phuket.*

★ J. W. Marriott Resort & Spa

$$$ | **RESORT** | Far from the crowds, this secluded resort offers the longest stretch of sand on the island and has spotlessly clean, luxurious rooms with impeccable classic Thai design. **Pros:** long and quiet beach; Thai-style rooms; a wide range of amenities. **Cons:** may be too isolated for some; surf sometimes too rough for swimming. *$ Rooms from: B4,400* ✉ *231 Moo 3, Mai Khao, Phuket* ☎ *076/338000* 🌐 *www.marriott.com/HKTJW* *265 rooms* *Free breakfast.*

Nai Yang Beach

34 km (20 miles) northwest of Phuket Town.

Smaller than its northerly neighbor, and one of the most relaxed beaches on Phuket, Nai Yang attracts a local and expat crowd. Parts of the beach are inside Sirinath National Park, which helps to preserve the beach from the worst excesses of Phuket development. There is a good selection of places to stay, and folks head here if they want isolation and a calm atmosphere.

GETTING HERE AND AROUND

Nai Yang Beach is accessible from Highway 4027, the main road running through the island. Taxis, tuk-tuks, and motorcycles will take you to and from other parts of the island. ■ **TIP→ Transport is often difficult to find on the road through Nai Yang Beach.** Your hotel may be able to help arrange transportation.

Beaches

Nai Yang Beach

BEACH—SIGHT | Nai Yang Beach is really a continuation south of Mai Khao, making a long stretch of sand good for a jog or swimming in the dry season. Casuarina trees line the gently curving shore offering shade. It's a far quieter beach than most, with a strip of trees and a small string of beachside restaurants and bars, tour guides, tailors, and shops. Fishing boats anchor nearby, making for picture-perfect sunrises and sunsets. **Amenities:** food and drink. **Best for:** snorkeling; sunrise; sunset; swimming. ⊠ *Nai Yang Beach Rd., Phuket* ✣ *Near airport.*

Hotels

You can find tasty, fresh seafood at Nai Yang's beachside restaurants.

★ The Slate

$$$ | **HOTEL** | **FAMILY** | Phuket's tin-mining history is the inspiration for The Slate, and the resort—the wild creation of famous American resort designer Bill Bensley—features interesting collectibles from the Na-Rarong family mines, with a design-conscious decor that blends funky postindustrial (concrete features strongly) with a hint of Thai rustic luxury. **Pros:** great breakfast; unique decor; good spa. **Cons:** staff can be unhelpful; some rooms affected by noise from nearby beach bar; lots of mosquitoes. ⓢ *Rooms from: B4,300* ⊠ *Nai Yang Beach and National Park, 116 Moo 1, Phuket* ☎ *076/327006, 076/327015* ⊕ *www.theslatephuket.com* ▭ *No credit cards* ⇨ *177 rooms* 🍽 *No meals.*

Nai Thon and Layan Beaches

30 km (18½ miles) northwest of Phuket Town.

It's one of the smallest beaches on the island, and the tropical rain forest that acts as a natural barrier keeps many visitors away, but this beach exudes a calm and relaxed vibe. There are a few resorts on the beach, but they are unobtrusive and you can easily feel alone when wandering along the wide, sandy expanse.

GETTING HERE AND AROUND

Nai Thon and Layan beaches are easily accessible from all parts of Phuket Island. Taxis, tuk-tuks, and motorcycles will gladly ferry you to and from these quiet beaches.

Beaches

Nai Thon and Layan Beaches

BEACH—SIGHT | A few miles north of Bang Thao Bay, follow a smaller highway off the main routes (4030 and 4031) along a scenic coastline reminiscent of California's Pacific Coast Highway. These beaches are good for swimming and snorkeling in the dry season. Layan is a wildlife hot spot, as the lake behind the beach attracts lots of wildfowl. Nai Thon is 1-km long and still has few accommodations. **Amenities:** food and drink. **Best for:** snorkeling; swimming; walking. ⊠ *Phuket.*

Hotels

The Pavilions

$$$$ | **RESORT** | Many resorts claim that they're set up so that you never have to leave your villa, but the Pavilions really means it. **Pros:** fabulous views from the bar; great amenities; real sense of privacy. **Cons:** a bit isolated; no children under 14. ⓢ *Rooms from: B9,000* ⊠ *31/1 Moo 6, Cherngtalay, Thalang* ☎ *076/317600, 091/621–4841 in Bangkok* www.pavilions-resorts.com 30 villas *All-inclusive.*

Trisara

$$$$ | **RESORT** | Opulence is the standard at the Trisara resort; rooms feature a variety of Thai wooden art pieces, silk throw pillows on the divans, and 32-inch plasma TVs hidden in the walls. **Pros:** beautiful Thai decor; golf course; subtle and professional service. **Cons:** often fully booked; pricey. *Rooms from: B21,000* *60/1 Moo 6, Srisoonthorn Rd., Cherngtalay, Phuket* *076/310100, 076/310355* *www.trisara.com* *42 rooms* *No meals.*

Bang Tao Beach

22 km (14 miles) northwest of Phuket Town.

Dotted with resorts and villas along its 4-mile stretch, Bang Tao beach is a favorite of those seeking a more refined pace than that of the more popular and developed Phuket beaches. The waters here are shallow and there is a good depth of beach to wander along.

Once the site of a tin mine, Bang Tao Beach (a resort area collectively called Laguna Phuket) now glistens with the more precious metals worn by its affluent visitors. Due to the ingenuity of developer Ho Kwon Ping and his family, this area was built nearly 20 years ago in a spot so damaged from mining that most thought it beyond repair. Now it's recovered enough to support an array of accommodations, eateries, and golf courses set around the lagoons.

The Laguna Beach Resort has been instrumental in showcasing this part of Phuket and has picked up an enviable international reputation. It holds a famous international triathlon each year, and also hosts many other events throughout the year. Nevertheless, as anywhere on the island, some of the older resorts are showing signs of age and tropical-weather damage, despite frequent renovations.

GETTING HERE AND AROUND

Bang Tao Beach is accessible from Highway 4027. Taxis, tuk-tuks, and motorcycles can all take you to and from the beach. Getting away from the beach is sometimes a little difficult, but if you wait on the beach road a taxi or another form of transport will materialize eventually. If you get stuck, ask for help at one of the resorts. There's a free shuttle service between the resorts along the shore.

 Beaches

Bang Tao Beach

BEACH—SIGHT | The beach itself is a long stretch (4 miles) of white sand, with vendors offering a variety of sports equipment rental, inexpensive seafood, beach massages, and cocktails. The beach is good for swimming in the hot season, the lagoon for kayaking anytime. The atmosphere is relaxed, making this a beach well suited to young families. **Amenities:** food and drink; showers; toilets; water sports. **Best for:** sunset, swimming; walking. *Bang Tao, Soi Ao Bangtao, Cherng Talay.*

 Restaurants

Catch Beach Club

$$$$ | **FUSION** | Although now just one among many superb venues, Catch remains the standard-bearer for beach clubs on the island. In its former location on Surin Beach, this gleaming white, St. Tropez-style lounge drew Phuket's rich—and occasionally famous—with its DJ beats, imported Champagne and fine-dining tapas. **Known for:** wood-fired pizza; beachside tapas; DJ. *Average main: B3,500* *12/88 Moo 2, Cherng Talay* *65/348–2017* *www.catchbeachclub.com.*

Seafood

$ | **SEAFOOD** | The friendly ladies at this popular street-side shanty serve made-to-order seafood, noodles, and stir-fries. Every meal comes with a bowl of aromatic cardamom soup, which can be a great tonic. **Known for:** free cardamom soup; made-to-order cuisine; authentic flavors. *Average main: B100 Phuket About 5 km (3 miles) east of resort. Look for small sign on left side of road that reads "Seafood." If you reach mosque, you've gone too far No credit cards.*

Hotels

Allamanda Laguna Phuket

$ | **RESORT** | Unlike the other resorts in the area, this property sits on the lagoon instead of the beach, and therefore offers lower rates; you definitely get more bang for your buck here. **Pros:** good choice of rooms with different amenities; shuttle boat service; relaxing setting. **Cons:** away from the beach; not ideal for families; can get busy. *Rooms from: B1,200 29 Moo 4, Srisoonthorn Rd., Cherngtalay, Phuket 076/362700 www.allamandaphuket.com 131 suites Free breakfast.*

Andaman Bangtao Bay Resort

$ | **RESORT** | **FAMILY** | Don't expect opulence, but this small, friendly, and beautifully situated resort offers clean, comfortable rooms only 20 meters from the beach, with nice en suite bathrooms, air-conditioning, and satellite TV, details of traditional Thai decor, and beachfront patios. **Pros:** nice location; friendly service; good restaurant. **Cons:** beach is not that great; pool very small; a little pricey for what you get. *Rooms from: B1,900 82/9 Moo 3, Cherngtalay 076/270246, 081/599–7889 www.andamanbangtaobayresort.com No credit cards 8 rooms Free breakfast.*

★ **Banyan Tree Phuket**

$$$$ | **RESORT** | **FAMILY** | Of the quintet of resorts on Laguna Beach, this is the most exclusive—and expensive. **Pros:** peaceful setting; great spa; children's programs. **Cons:** pricey; resort is huge. *Rooms from: B12,000 33 Moo 4, Srisoonthorn Rd., Cherngtalay, Amphur Talang, Phuket 076/372400 www.banyantree.com 123 villas Free breakfast.*

Sunwing Bangtao Beach

$$ | **RESORT** | **FAMILY** | Families keep coming back to this resort, as it really has it all for kids of every age, keeping them busy with numerous facilities and well-organized daily activities, babysitting services, discos, and shows. **Pros:** safe, fun environment for kids; two restaurants have varied, interesting menus; resort shop sells all the essentials. **Cons:** somewhat remote from shops or restaurants; poolside can be chaotic. *Rooms from: B3,500 22 Moo 2, Chueng Thalay, Phuket 076/314263 up to 65 www.sunwingphuket.com No credit cards 283 rooms Free breakfast.*

Pansea, Surin, and Laem Singh Beaches

21 km (12 miles) northwest of Phuket Town.

If you want luxury accommodations, then look no further than these three picturesque beaches on Phuket's west coast. Many of the island's rich set have houses here (it's known locally as Millionaires' Mile), sprinkled among high-end resorts. The sand is white and the waters are crystal clear, but the scene here has remained pretty quiet.

GETTING HERE AND AROUND

The beaches are accessible from Highway 4027. Taxis, tuk-tuks, and motorcycles can all take you to and from the beach. A taxi to or from Phuket Town should cost approximately B550 to B700; expect to pay a little more for a tuk-tuk.

Beaches

Laem Singh Beach

BEACH—SIGHT | Laem Singh is a lovely little beach off the beaten path but well worth the 10-minute trek down a rocky track. This minor inconvenience means that in contrast to the majority of Phuket's beaches, this is quiet and uncluttered. It's just off the winding coastal road between Kamala and Surin. Luckily there are a couple of food stalls, so you don't need to haul refreshments down with you. **Amenities:** food and drink; parking (B30); toilets. **Best for:** solitude; swimming. ✉ *Laem Sing Beach* ✣ *Just off the road from Kamala-Surin.*

Surin Beach

BEACH—SIGHT | This is a peaceful, long stretch of sandy beach that gets busy on the weekends, as it is popular with local Thais and expatriates. There are grassy areas shaded by pine trees that make good spots to take refuge from the midday sun. Best avoided during the rainy season, as the seas can get rough, and there are some strong, dangerous currents. Tasty treats can be bought from local vendors working the beach. **Amenities:** food and drink; toilets. **Best for:** snorkeling; swimming; walking. ✉ *Surin Beach* ✣ *Go through Kamala and continue past Laem Singh Beach. Take sharp left turn down to beach when you reach the three-way junction. It's a 25-min drive north from Patong.*

Hotels

★ Amanpuri Resort

$$$$ | **RESORT** | You'd be hard-pressed to find a more sparklingly dignified hotel in Thailand—nor one quite as expensive (The nightly rate for the largest of the villas is more than $8,000!). **Pros:** private beach; great sunsets; multi-award-winning. **Cons:** too isolated for some; service can be apathetic at times. $ *Rooms from: B21,000* ✉ *Pansea Beach, Cherngtalay, Thalang, Phuket* ☎ *076/324333* 🌐 *www.amanpuri.com* *40 pavilions, 31 villas* 🍴 *Free breakfast.*

Surin Bay Inn

$ | **B&B/INN** | For reasonably priced accommodations near Surin Beach (only a few minutes' walk away), try this small hotel. **Pros:** nice restaurant; great rooms for moderate price; particularly helpful staff. **Cons:** not on beach; no elevator; only top-floor rooms have good views. $ *Rooms from: B1,100* ✉ *106/11 Surin Beach, Surin Beach* ☎ *076/271601* *12 rooms* 🍴 *Free breakfast.*

The Surin Phuket

$$$$ | **RESORT** | Almost completely concealed by a grove of coconut palms, this resort has more than 100 thatched-roof cottages overlooking a quiet beach. **Pros:** great location; private beach. **Cons:** layout a little confusing; long walk (uphill) from the beach to top villas; isolated. $ *Rooms from: B6,200* ✉ *118 Moo 3, Cherngtalay, Phuket* ☎ *076/621580 up to 82* 🌐 *www.thesurinphuket.com* *103 chalets* 🍴 *Free breakfast.*

Kamala Beach

18 km (11 miles) west of Phuket Town.

Unlike the more upscale enclaves to the north, Kamala Beach has some reasonably priced accommodations that attract longer-stay visitors, and is a good launchpad for the rest of the island, as it retains its calm and quiet. Better get there soon however, as the large resorts are beginning to move in.

GETTING HERE AND AROUND

A taxi from Phuket Town or Patong Beach will cost about B500.

Kamala Beach is quieter and less touristy than neighboring Patong, and attracts a more laid-back crowd. The beach is quite small, but has a distinct feel to it, with mangrove trees and blue water.

Kamala Beach

BEACH—SIGHT | Kamala Beach is unremarkable but endearing, particularly to pensioners who return here year after year for the beach's more reserved ambience. Kamala can get cramped during the day and offers numerous accommodation and dining options, but if you're staying, don't expect a lively nightlife. **Amenities:** food and drink; water sports. **Best for:** swimming. ✉ *Phuket.*

Baan Chaba

$ | **RESORT** | If you're looking for a bungalow or hotel on the beach, you'll find several options at the north end of Kamala (none of which have views of the beach, and some of which are absurdly priced). **Pros:** spacious bungalows; reasonable rates. **Cons:** not beachfront; lacks amenities. *Rooms from: B1,000 ✉ 95/3 Moo 3, Kamala Beach, Kathu, Phuket ☎ 076/279158 🌐 www.baanchaba.com No credit cards 8 bungalows No meals.*

★ Keemala

$$$$ | **RESORT** | Upon arrival, you hear the legend of four mythical island clans: Earth, Wanderer, Sky, and Nest, whose backstories have inspired the stylish fantasy of dangling, thatched tree houses, and pod-shaped chambers set atop wooden perches, all tucked into the slopes of a serene jungle valley close to the shores of Kamala Beach. **Pros:** innovative theme; health-focused cuisine; unique lodgings. **Cons:** not on the beach; steep inclines to walk; too quirky for some. *Rooms from: B26,000 ✉ 10/88 Moo 6, Nakasud Rd. ☎ 076/358777 🌐 keemala.com 38 rooms Free breakfast.*

PapaCrab Boutique Guesthouse

$ | **B&B/INN** | This small, friendly, family-run boutique guesthouse is in a quiet spot near the town. **Pros:** excellent price for what is offered; good service; just off the beach. **Cons:** not great views; patchy Wi-Fi; no landline in rooms. *Rooms from: B950 ✉ 93/5 Moo 3 ☎ 084/744–0482 🌐 phuketpapacrab.com No credit cards 10 rooms No meals.*

Patong

13 km (8 miles) west of Phuket Town.

You'd hardly believe it today, but Patong was once the island's most remote beach, completely cut off by the surrounding mountains and only accessible by boat. Today it's a thriving, thronged, beach-resort community frequented mainly by international visitors. Though overdeveloped, its convenience and compact size makes Patong a great place for new visitors to Thailand looking for a nice beach with characteristic Thai experiences, like *muay Thai* (Thai boxing), street shopping, and authentic Thai food, as well as familiar facilities, like Starbucks, sushi bars, shopping malls, and chain hotels.

The beachfront has long been a congested mishmash of high-end hotels and restaurants, patrolled by hawkers and beach vendors. The sidewalk is clearer since the Thai army intervened to try and force out the overabundance of illegal businesses; however, things are still not perfect. You can stroll along several miles of boutiques, Western restaurants and bars, ice-cream parlors, and upscale nightlife venues, interspersed with traditional Thai market stalls selling food, cheap T-shirts, and knockoff goods. The lively nightlife scene remains a big draw for many tourists, but the sheer variety of restaurants, hotels, and entertainment on offer ensures Patong's popularity with a wide variety of visitors.

GETTING HERE AND AROUND

Every street, hotel, and shop in Patong seems to have a ready team of taxis, tuk-tuks, and motorcycles whose drivers are all more than happy to ferry you around. Just pick your vehicle of choice and bargain hard. Tuk-tuks to Phuket Town should cost approximately B500; to Karon will be B400; and to Kamala is around B300. It can be a little frustrating to get to the beach during morning rush hour, because the road from Phuket Town is often congested.

Beaches

Patong Beach

BEACH—SIGHT | Once cluttered with beach umbrellas, Patong Beach now has some room for both sunbathing and playing soccer or Frisbee on the beach. Every conceivable beach activity from wakeboarding to jet skiing to parasailing is available. Patong became so popular because of its picture-perfect paradisical nature, and now its popularity has caused some degradation of the environment, particularly noticeable when the monsoon rains wash the grime off the street and onto the beach. **Amenities:** food and drink; showers; toilets; water sports. **Best for:** partiers; sunset; swimming; walking. ✉ *Thaweewong Rd., Phuket.*

Restaurants

Baan Rim Pa

$$$$ | **THAI** | On a large terrace that clings to a cliff at the north end of Patong Beach, this restaurant has some tables set back from the edge, but you'll then miss the gorgeous ocean views. The food is among the best Phuket has to offer. **Known for:** cliff-side dining; sunset views; tourist-friendly fare. $ *Average main: B1,450* ✉ *223 Prabaramee Rd., Kalim Beach* ☎ *076/340789* 🌐 *www.baanrimpa.com.*

Da Maurizio

$$$$ | **ITALIAN** | An Italian bar-ristorante is the last in the trio of Patong's cliff restaurants. Dining is just above a secluded beach. **Known for:** fine-dining Italian cuisine; wood-burning oven; beach views. $ *Average main: B1,000* ✉ *223/2 Kalim Rd., Patong* ☎ *076/344079* 🌐 *www.baanrimpa.com/italian-restaurant/.*

Sam's Steaks & Grill

$$$$ | **STEAKHOUSE** | In the Holiday Inn Resort, this stylish restaurant serves prime cuts of imported beef prepared with notable French flair. The lively, popular restaurant serves elegantly presented, delectable meals in a calming atmosphere, away from the madding crowds on Patong's busy streets. **Known for:** quality cuts; sophisticated atmosphere; romantic evenings. $ *Average main: B950* ✉ *52 Thaweewong Rd.* ☎ *076/370200* ▬ *No credit cards.*

Hotels

Avantika

$$$$ | **HOTEL** | The south end of Patong is a little quieter than the rest, and several "boutique" hotels have sprung up in recent years, and this one, across the road from the beach, has some elegant rooms. **Pros:** refreshing sea views from some rooms; next to beach; laid-back vibe. **Cons:** pricey; unremarkable; small pool. $ *Rooms from: B12,300* ✉ *4/1 Thaweewong Rd.* ☎ *076/292801 to 05* 🌐 *www.avantika-phuket.com* ⇨ *31 rooms.*

FunDee Boutique Hotel

$ | **HOTEL** | In the heart of Patong and close to all the action, the boutique FunDee is a good budget option for this bustling locale. **Pros:** central but quiet location; Wi-Fi; good service. **Cons:** bit of a trek to the beach (10 minutes); only one elevator; no views. $ *Rooms from: B600* ✉ *232/3-4 Phung Muang Sai Gor Rd., Patong Kathu* ☎ *076/366780* 🌐 *www.*

fundee.co.th ⊟ *No credit cards* ⇨ *36 rooms* 🍽 *No meals.*

Holiday Inn Resort Phuket

$$ | **RESORT** | **FAMILY** | This is no ordinary Holiday Inn: this stylish, modern hotel exudes the kind of sophistication that most people would never imagine possible from a Holiday Inn or from Patong in general. **Pros:** central location; children's programs; next to beach. **Cons:** family atmosphere not ideal for everyone; large complex. $ *Rooms from: B3,400* ✉ *52 Thaweewong Rd., Patong Beach* ☎ *076/349991 up to 92, 076/370200* 🌐 *www.phuket.holidayinnresorts.com* ⇨ *405 rooms* 🍽 *Free breakfast.*

Impiana Resort Patong

$$ | **RESORT** | This hotel's chief attraction is its unbeatable location, right in the middle of the city yet facing the beach. **Pros:** beachfront spa; good restaurant and bar; best location in Patong. **Cons:** busy beach road traffic; check for rooms with a view; beach fills up. $ *Rooms from: B3,500* ✉ *41 Taweewong Rd.* ☎ *076/340138* 🌐 *phukethotels.impiana.com.my* ⇨ *68 rooms* 🍽 *No meals.*

Red Planet Phuket Hotel

$ | **HOTEL** | This convenient, practical hotel is new to the scene and has a great location. **Pros:** immaculate; cheap; great modern amenities. **Cons:** no pool. $ *Rooms from: B700* ✉ *56 Raj, Uthit 200 Pee Rd., Karon Beach* ✥ *Opposite Patong Post Office* ☎ *26/135888* 🌐 *www.redplanethotels.com* ⇨ *60 rooms* 🍽 *No meals* ⊟ *No credit cards.*

★ Rosewood Phuket

$$$$ | **RESORT** | **FAMILY** | On an island filled with luxury resorts, the Rosewood sets itself apart, literally, with its 600-meter secluded beach and expansive private pavilions and villas, instead of standard rooms or suites. **Pros:** private beach; luxury spa; only villas and pavilions. **Cons:** long walk to town; few local restaurants; pricey lodgings. $ *Rooms from: B25,500* ✉ *88/28 Muen-Ngern Rd* ☎ *076/356888* 🌐 *rosewoodhotels.com/en/phuket* ⇨ *71 pavilions and villas.*

Nightlife

The vast majority of tourists only venture as far as Bangla Road, a walking street that is more like a carnival than something disturbingly sleazy. Children pose for photos with flamboyant and friendly ladyboys; honeymooning couples people-watch from numerous beer bars along the traffic-free promenade; and everyone else simply strolls the strip, some stopping to dance or play Connect Four, Jenga, or a curiously popular nail-hammering game with friendly Thai hostesses.

There are also regularly scheduled *muay Thai* fights at the arena on the corner of Bangla and Rat-U-Thit Songroipee roads.

The Boat Bar Disco & Cabaret

BARS/PUBS | With numerous male staff, two dance performances every night, and live DJ sessions, this gay-friendly bar attracts huge crowds for fun, late-night parties. ✉ *Paradise Complex, 125/20 Rat-U-Thit Rd.* ☎ *076/342206.*

Simon Cabaret

THEMED ENTERTAINMENT | With the varied nightlife in Patong, it's no surprise to find a sensational drag show here. The famous Simon Cabaret treats you to a beautifully costumed and choreographed show. There are two shows daily, at 7:30 and 9:30. ✉ *8 Sirirach Rd.* ☎ *076/342011.*

Thaweewong Road

MUSIC CLUBS | Patong has a reputation for its happening nightlife, and the seedy side of it is easily avoidable. Some of the more tasteful nightlife venues are found along **Thaweewong Road**, including live music bars, expat pubs, and folks picking up a to-go drink from 7-Eleven and sitting on the beach. ✉ *Thaweewong Rd.*

Whitebox Restaurant & Bar

BARS/PUBS | Let's face it, in Patong it can be difficult to come by a sophisticated spot to enjoy a drink. Whitebox, designed in a white, contemporary, minimalist style, is a restaurant serving fusion Thai-European food that generally looks better than it tastes, but its rooftop bar, offering creative cocktails and tapas paired with open sea views, fits the bill. The rooftop bar opens from August to May. ✉ *245/7 Prabaramee Rd.* ☎ *076/346271* 🌐 *www.whitebox.co.th.*

Karon Beach

20 km (12 miles) southwest of Phuket Town.

Just south of Patong lie Karon Beach and its smaller northern counterpart, Karon Noi. Bunches of hotels, restaurants, tailors, dive operators, and gift shops line the main beach strip to serve the influx of tourists, though Karon is also home to a small community of local artists, who live and work in a cluster of huts and galleries.

GETTING HERE AND AROUND

Taxis, tuk-tuks, and motorcycles take you to and from Karon Beach. A taxi costs about B400 for the 5-km (3-mile) ride to Patong; a tuk-tuk is about B300.

Sights

Getting your bearings is easy in Karon. There's a small village just off the traffic circle to your left as you enter town from Patong. For the glut of resorts, continue your journey down the beach road. You can also find quality restaurants, bars, and cheerful shops, as well as the beautiful long beach.

Dino Park Mini Golf

SPORTS—SIGHT | **FAMILY** | The Flintstones-style buildings along the road in central Karon village belong to Dino Park Mini Golf. Street-side are a dinosaur-themed bar and restaurant, but the real fun is inside: 18 holes of miniature golf, featuring a swamp, a lava cave, and a real live Tyrannosaurus Rex (Well, the kids will think so!). Afterward, grab a bite at the restaurant and get your orders taken by Fred and Wilma. ✉ *Karon Beach* ☎ *076/330625* 🌐 *www.dinopark.com* 🎫 *B240.*

Karon Beach

BEACH—SIGHT | It's impossible not to be tempted by this long stretch of white sand and good dry-season swimming (it's great for running year-round). You will find that the beach is more open than most in Phuket—there are no trees covering the beach and precious little shade. The beach is also strewn with a few rocks; however, on the whole, it is a beautiful, clean, and open space that will appeal to those looking to get away from the more frantic pace of Patong. **Amenities:** food and drink; showers; water sports. **Best for:** snorkeling; sunset; swimming; walking. ✉ *Karon Beach.*

Restaurants

El Gaucho Steakhouse

$$$$ | **BRAZILIAN** | Churrasco (Brazilian grilled meat) is the specialty at the Movenpick resort's restaurant, with sunset views that make dining here a genuinely delightful experience. There's a soothing orange-and-red theme running through El Gaucho that the setting sun only serves to magnify. **Known for:** Brazilian barbecue; beach views; large interior. 💲 *Average main: B900* ✉ *Karon Beach Sq., Movenpick Resort, 509 Patak Rd.* 🌐 *www.moevenpick-hotels.com/en/asia/thailand/phuket/resort-phuket-karon-beach/restaurants/restaurants/el-gaucho/* 💳 *No credit cards.*

★ On the Rock

$$$ | **ECLECTIC** | Built, you guessed it, on a rock overlooking Karon Beach, this restaurant has great views of the water. Seafood is the specialty, but well-made Italian and traditional Thai dishes are also on the menu. **Known for:** rocky location; local seafood; beachside

A Festival for Health and Purity

Phuket's most important festival is its annual Vegetarian Festival, held in late September or early October. According to local legend, it started in 1825 when a traveling Chinese opera group fell ill in the mining village of Kathu. The Taoist group feared that their illnesses were the result of their failure to pay proper respects to the nine Emperor Gods. After sticking to a strict vegetarian diet to honor these gods, they quickly recovered. This made quite an impression on the local villagers, and the island has celebrated a nine-day festival for good health ever since. The many devotees, who wear white, abstain from eating meat, drinking alcohol, and having sex. Along with detoxing the body, the festival is meant to renew the soul—not killing animals for food is supposed to calm and purify the spirit.

The festival involves numerous temple ceremonies, parades, and fireworks. But what most fascinates visitors are the tests of faith, including fire walking and climbing ladders made of sharp blades, and the grisly body-piercing rituals. Some devotees become mediums for warrior spirits, known as *mah song*, going into trances and mutilating their bodies to ward off demons and bring the whole community good luck. These mediums pierce their bodies (tongues and cheeks are popular choices) with all sorts of things from swords to bicycle spokes to guns (gas pumps have even been seen on occasion). Supposedly, the presence of the spirits within them keeps them from feeling any pain.

The events are centered on the island's 40 or so Chinese shrines and temples. Processions are held daily from morning until midafternoon, all finishing at the seaside Kiew Teng Heng temple on the Saphan Hin Peninsula. The Tourism Authority of Thailand office in Phuket Town can provide a list of all activities and their locations, as does local newspaper *The Phuket News*. Note that you might want to invest in earplugs—it's believed that the louder the fireworks, the more evil spirits they'll scare away.

tables. *Average main: B350* *47 Karon Rd.* *South end of Karon Beach* *076/330625, 076/330493 up to 95* *www.marinaphuket.com/restaurants.html.*

Hotels

Fantasy Hill Bungalows

$ | **B&B/INN** | Standing on a hill between the two beach areas of Kata and Karon, these well-situated accommodations are a great value. **Pros:** garden courtyard; balconies; good location. **Cons:** few amenities; not all rooms have air-conditioning; breakfast is extra. *Rooms from: B400* *8/1 Karon Rd.* *076/330106* *fantasyhill@hotmail.com* *No credit cards* *18 rooms, 6 bungalows* *No meals.*

In On the Beach

$ | **HOTEL** | This place way at the north end of Karon is literally on the beach, with great sea views from many of the rooms, which are decorated in a modern, functional style. **Pros:** beach location; quiet; nice swimming pool. **Cons:** slightly removed from center of town; ground-floor rooms lack some privacy; noisy air-conditioning. *Rooms from: B1,750* *Moo 1, Patak Rd.* *076/398220 up to 24* *www.karon-inonthebeach.com* *30 rooms* *Free breakfast.*

Le Meridien

$$ | **RESORT** | **FAMILY** | Between Patong and Karon Beach, this sprawling resort has more bars, cafés, and restaurants than in many small towns, while the range of outdoor diversions—everything from tennis to waterskiing—means you never have to leave the property. **Pros:** large swimming pool; excellent activities; private beach. **Cons:** too big for some; not all rooms have a view. *Rooms from: B3,750 ✉ 29 Soi Karon Nui, Tambon Karon, Amphur Muang ☎ 076/370100 🌐 www.lemeridienphuketbeachresort.com 470 rooms 🍴 Free breakfast.*

Marina Phuket Resort

$$$$ | **RESORT** | This surprisingly quiet option has luxury cottages that stretch over the lush hillside that separates Karon from Kata Beach—those higher on the hill are the quietest. **Pros:** good location; private beach and nice pool; free airport shuttle. **Cons:** difference in amenities between rooms; pool closes after sunset; no hotel loungers on beach. *Rooms from: B7,500 ✉ 47 Karon Rd. ☎ 076/330493 to 95, 076/330625 🌐 www.marinaphuket.com 89 rooms 🍴 Free breakfast.*

Movenpick Resort and Spa

$$$ | **RESORT** | **FAMILY** | This resort takes great pride in its service levels, with polite, knowledgeable, and informative staff; live Thai music greets you as you enter an expansive lobby lavishly decorated with Thai art. **Pros:** beachfront location; amazing facilities; close to Karon Town. **Cons:** slight package-tour feel; old structure; large complex. *Rooms from: B4,500 ✉ 509 Patak Rd., Karon Beach ☎ 076/396139 🌐 www.moevenpick-hotels.com 175 rooms 159 suites 🍴 Free breakfast.*

Phuket Orchid Resort

$ | **RESORT** | **FAMILY** | This resort is slightly inland, but the beach is a short walk away, and the lack of a beachfront brings the rates down considerably (which makes it very popular). **Pros:** interesting design influences including Khmer and Chinese; great pool; budget. **Cons:** not on beach; only partly renovated. *Rooms from: B1,500 ✉ 34 Luang Pohchuan Rd., Karon Muang ☎ 076/396519 🌐 www.katagroup.com 525 rooms 🍴 Free breakfast.*

Kata Beach

22 km (13 miles) southwest of Phuket Town.

Popular for its stunning white-sand beach with turquoise waters, and especially appealing to families for its serene ambience, Kata Beach is made up of its southern part, where numerous resorts are located, and its central part, which is a stone's throw from Karon to the north. There's plenty to see and do besides relaxing and taking in the beautiful landscape. Surfing is one of the main draws to Kata, from May to October, which brings with it a lively nightlife scene and a thriving restaurant base. This is a family destination as well, mainly because Kata lacks the in-your-face bar scene of Patong, and has a greater variety of restaurants and shopping than its neighbor, Karon, to the north.

GETTING HERE AND AROUND

Taxis, tuk-tuks, and motorcycles all vie for your attention to take you to and from Kata Beach. Expect to pay B500 into Phuket Town or B400 into Patong by taxi, and about B50 more for a tuk-tuk.

Walking around Kata is easy—just follow the beach road from north to south. Kata Yai is the main beach and located near the main shopping street of Thai Na. To the south, Kata Noi is almost exclusively taken up with the long and expensive Katathani Phuket Beach Resort. This is a public beach (as all beaches in Thailand are), so be sure to exercise your beach rights and soak up some sun on delightfully quiet Kata Noi if you're in the area.

Kata Beach

BEACH—SIGHT | Of the three most popular beaches on the west coast of Phuket, this is the calmest of the lot. A shady sidewalk runs the length of the beach. Club Med dominates a large hunk of the beachfront, keeping the development frenzy to the southern end. There's also a committed group of regulars here who surf the small local breaks. This is one of the calmer beach scenes in Phuket, and so is especially good for families. **Amenities:** food and drink; water sports. **Best for:** sunset; surfing; swimming; windsurfing. ✉ *Pakbang Rd., Laem Sai.*

Hotels

The Boathouse Phuket

$$$$ | **RESORT** | Following an extensive makeover, this landmark resort—one of Phuket's oldest—is once again the belle of the ball. **Pros:** excellent restaurant; cooking class available; good wine selection. **Cons:** swimming pool area a bit on the small side. *Rooms from: B8,700 ✉ 182 Koktanode Rd. ☎ 076/330015 www.boathousephuket.com 33 rooms, 6 villas Free breakfast.*

Katathani Phuket Beach Resort

$$ | **RESORT** | **FAMILY** | This long, sprawling lodge fronts most of the Kata Noi Beach. **Pros:** peaceful beach location; six swimming pools and another four for children; spacious, well-kept grounds. **Cons:** large and rather impersonal touch; the food is average; in-room Wi-Fi extra charge. *Rooms from: B3,400 ✉ 14 Kata Noi Rd., Karon, Muang, Phuket ☎ 076/330124 up to 26 www.katathani.com 479 rooms No meals.*

Sawasdee Village

$$ | **RESORT** | A few minutes' walk from Kata Beach, this resort comprises a spacious garden with four large swimming pools, lush greenery, beautiful stone-carved fountains, and a complex of villas and rooms designed and decorated in a Thai–Moroccan style. **Pros:** attentive staff; good dining. **Cons:** 10 minutes from Kata Beach; rooms on the small side; mosquitoes. *Rooms from: B4,000 ✉ 38 Katekwan Rd. ☎ 076/330870 up to 71 www.phuketsawasdee.com No credit cards 40 rooms Free breakfast.*

Nai Harn

18 km (11 miles) southwest of Phuket Town.

Less busy than other nearby beaches and more popular among locals, Nai Harn offers a small but interesting choice of accommodations and nearby attractions, such as Nai Harn Lake and viewpoints such as the Promthep Cape, as well as simple but authentic restaurants.

GETTING HERE AND AROUND

This is the southernmost beach on Phuket. You can get here from Phuket Town or along the coastal road through Kata, Karon, and Patong. Taxis, tuk-tuks, and motorcycles will all take you to and from Nai Harn; a taxi to or from Phuket Town should be about B550, and it costs B800 to get to the airport.

Sights

Nai Harn

BEACH—SIGHT | South of Kata Beach the road cuts inland across the hills before it drops into yet another beautiful bay, Nai Harn. On the north side of the bay is the gleaming-white Nai Harn resort, beyond which lies the tiny bay of Ao Sane. But the main attraction is Nai Harn Beach itself, with plenty of surf to play in, and a favorite anchorage for yachts. ✉ *Nai Harn.*

Promthep Cape

VIEWPOINT | From the top of the cliff at Promthep Cape, the southernmost point on Phuket, you're treated to a fantastic, panoramic view of Nai Harn Bay, the coastline, and a few outlying islands.

At sunset you can share the view with swarms of others who pour forth from tour buses to view the same sight. If you're driving, arrive early so you get a parking spot. There's a lighthouse atop the point, as well as a collection of elephant statues where locals go to pray for good fortune. ✉ *Nai Harn.*

Rawai Beach

BEACH—SIGHT | Not far from Chalong is Rawai Beach. Though its not a beach to relax on, the pier makes for a pleasant early-evening walk. Longtails depart from here for offshore islands, and numerous decent Thai restaurants line the seafront. ✉ *Karon Beach.*

Restaurants

Promthep Cape Restaurant

$ | **THAI** | Although it doesn't look like much from the Promthep Cape parking lot, views from the tables out back are hard to beat. Just slightly down the hill from the lighthouse, this place enjoys unobstructed perspectives of the cape and coastline. Plus you get lower prices and better views than at most other places on the island that play up their panoramas. **Known for:** secluded setting; proximity to lighthouse; fresh seafood. *Average main: B180* ✉ *94/6 Moo 6, Rawai Beach* ☎ *076/288656, 076/288084* 🌐 *www.phuketdir.com/phromthepcaperest.*

Hotels

The Nai Harn

$$$$ | **HOTEL** | Once known as the Royal Phuket Yacht Club, this legacy resort has welcomed celebrity guests such as Roger Moore and Prince Albert of Monaco. **Pros:** modern Thai furnishings; great views; on a lovely beach. **Cons:** isolated location; no direct access to beach; long way from airport. *Rooms from: B7,000* ✉ *Nai Harn Beach, Phuket 23/3 Moo 1, Vises Rd.* ☎ *076/380200* 🌐 *www.thenaiharn.com* *No credit cards* *64 rooms, 25 suites* *No meals.*

Cape Yamu

21km (13 miles) east of Phuket Town.

The headland at Yamu is an isolated part of Phuket and, because of the isolation, is particularly quiet and exclusive. There is no beach here, but the rocky point hosts some of Phuket's most exclusive properties. Boats at the jetty whisk travelers off to beach spots on Phuket and nearby islands. There are a few local villages and several high-end gated communities.

GETTING HERE AND AROUND

This is an isolated cape on Phuket's eastern side. You can get here from Phuket Town or along the main arterial roads from Phuket Airport or any of Phuket's main destinations. Taxis are the best choice to get here, but minivans serve the destination from the airport; a taxi to or from Phuket Town should be about B700; from Patong it will cost about B800, and it costs B800 to get to the airport.

Restaurants

★ Breeze at Cape Yamu

$$$$ | **INTERNATIONAL** | Situated on top of the cape, overlooking the isolated bay, Breeze is a strong contender for the finest restaurant in this part of Phuket. The sea breeze (hence the name) blows gently through the open dining area, giving it a romantic and natural atmosphere. **Known for:** hilltop location; open-air dining; changing menu. *Average main: B750* ✉ *Laem Yamu, Phuket* ✣ *Atop the farthest part of the cape, just outside the Point Yamu hotel* ☎ *81/271–2320* 🌐 *www.breezecapeyamu.com* *No credit cards.*

Hotels

★ COMO Point Yamu

$$$$ | HOTEL | FAMILY | From the moment you enter the vast, open lobby, the care that has gone into the intricate design of this stunningly situated hotel is apparent. **Pros:** playful minimalist design; luxury rooms, most with plunge pools; service levels are extraordinary. **Cons:** isolated. *Rooms from: B10,500* *225 Moo 7, Paklok, Talang, Thalang* *076/360100* *www.comohotels.com* *106 rooms* *Free breakfast.*

★ Thanyapura Health & Sports Resort

$$ | HOTEL | Unusual in its concept and style, Thanyapura is a paradise for sporty people of all ages and levels as well as professional athletes (including Olympic gold medalists and Formula One drivers), who regularly come here from around the world to train in a pristine, relaxing environment with pacifying mountain views. **Pros:** highly professional staff; unbeatable sports facilities; excellent spa. **Cons:** remote location; quiet from 10 pm; a bit of a mishmash between hotel and sports resort. *Rooms from: B3,250* *120/1 Moo 7 Thepkasattri Rd., Thepkasattri, Thalang* *076/336000* *www.thanyapura.com* *No credit cards* *77 rooms at sports hotel, 38 rooms at retreat* *Free breakfast.*

Chalong

11 km (7 miles) south of Phuket Town.

The waters in horseshoe-shaped Chalong Bay are usually calm, as the entrance is guarded by the twin isles of Koh Lone and Koh Hae. It's not a scenic stop in itself—it's more of a working port than a beach. The reason to come is to see Wat Chalong. From the jetty you can charter boats or book one-day or half-day trips to Koh Hae, Koh Lone, and other nearby islands for snorkeling, diving, parasailing, and other activities (B750 to B1,600).

Ao Chalong is a wide-open bay that is most frequently used as a jumping-off point for surrounding islands. Head for the pier where you can catch ferries to nearby islands. One road takes you from the northern end to the southern end of the bay.

GETTING HERE AND AROUND

Chalong Bay is an easy 11-km (7-mile) ride from Phuket Town. Taxis, tuk-tuks, and motorcycles will all take you here.

Sights

Wat Chalong

RELIGIOUS SITE | Not far from Chalong Bay you can find Wat Chalong, the largest and most famous of Phuket's Buddhist temples. Notable for its steeple-shaped roof, it enshrines gilt statues of two revered monks who helped quell an 1876 Chinese rebellion. They're wrapped in brilliant saffron robes. Wats are generally open during daylight hours, and you can show up at 5 pm to see the resident monks pray. It's also home to the annual Chalong Temple Fair, held every February. *Chaofa Rd. (West).*

Restaurants

Kan Eang at Pier

$$ | SEAFOOD | Grab a palm-shaded table next to the seawall and order some delicious grilled fish. Be sure that your waiter understands whether you want yours served *phet* (spicy hot) or *mai phet* (not spicy). **Known for:** ocean views; fresh seafood; next to Chalong Pier. *Average main: B200* *44/1 Viset Rd.* *076/381212.*

Hotels

★ Sri Panwa

$$$$ | RESORT | Perfectly situated on a lush headland, this beautifully designed resort has a cool, contemporary vibe that makes it popular with visiting celebrities seeking luxurious seclusion. **Pros:**

stunning, 360-degree ocean views; truly exceptional service from young, friendly staff; one of the world's best rooftop bars. **Cons:** gradient might be tricky for those with mobility problems. [$] *Rooms from: B28,000* ✉ *88 Moo 8, Sakdidej Rd., Vichit, Muang* ☎ *076/371000* 🌐 *www.sripanwa.com* 🛏 *52 villas* 🍴 *No meals.*

Phang Nga Bay National Marine Park

100 km (62 miles) north of Phuket, 93 km (56 miles) northwest of Krabi.

The looming limestone karsts are the most spectacular feature of Phang Nga Bay, made famous in movies and a thousand picture postcards.

GETTING HERE AND AROUND

Many travel agencies in Phuket offer half-day tours of the area, and this is the way most travelers see the park. Another option is to take a bus heading north from Phuket Town (B120) to one of two inlets near the town of Phang Nga, where you can hire a longtail boat and explore at your own pace, but unless you speak Thai or are intrepid, this is likely to be more of a hassle than it's worth. At the western inlet, you can rent a boat for about B1,800 for two hours. The second inlet sees fewer foreign tourists, so the prices are better—about B1,200 for three hours. The bay can also be explored via tour boat, speedboat, or sea canoe. Most tourists don't arrive from Phuket until 11 am, so if you get into the bay earlier, you can explore it in solitude. To get an early start, you may want to stay overnight in the area. Be sure to take time to appreciate the sunsets, which are particularly beautiful on the island of **Koh Mak.**

Sights

From stunning monoliths that rise from the sea to the secluded, crystal-clear bays, Phang Nga Bay is a must-see for any nature lover. The only way to visit is by boat. Tours (B1,000 to B3,000) can be arranged through your hotel or resort if you're staying in the area.

There are several key sights around Phang Nga Bay. The island of **Koh Panyi** has a Muslim fishing village consisting of houses built on stilts. Restaurants are no bargain, tripling their prices for tourists. **Koh Phing Kan,** now known locally as James Bond Island, is a popular tour destination. The island of **Koh Tapu** resembles a nail driven into the sea. **Kao Kien** has overhanging cliffs covered with primitive paintings of elephants, fish, and crabs. Many are thought to be at least 3,500 years old.

James Bond Island

ISLAND | Named for tourist purposes after the 1974 Bond film *The Man with the Golden Gun* starring Roger Moore as 007, and traditionally known as Koh Phing Kan, this natural attraction has unfortunately fallen victim to greedy tour operators and merchants, losing the beauty that made it famous. Visiting this island (with a stopover often not longer than half an hour) usually involves a day trip that involves stops to the equally jaded Koh Panyi island, known for its charming Muslim gypsy fishing village, a lunch break, and other stops such as to the Monkey Caves. The water in this zone is visibly polluted, the landscape can easily be beat by a multitude of other stunning landscapes around Thailand's south, and the throng of other tourists can be as buzzy for some as unbearable for others. ✉ *Phang Nga.*

Koh Panyi

BOAT TOURS | The island of Koh Panyi has a Muslim fishing village with houses built on stilts. The whole village backs onto a looming limestone cliff, giving it some protection from Mother Nature. The village is an interesting study in marine sustainability, but it does have the feel of a tourist trap—quirky floating soccer pitch aside. Restaurants are no bargain, tripling their prices for tourists. ✉ *Phang Nga.*

Tham Lot Cave

CAVE | Tham Lot is a large, limestone, stalactite-studded cave that has an opening large enough for boats to pass through. It can be explored by canoe or an inflatable boat, floating along seawater to enjoy the sight of impressive stalactites and stalagmites, some as long as 100 meters. No guide required. ✉ *Tarnboke Koranee National Park, Ao Luk District, Phang Nga.*

★ Wat Tham Cave

CAVE | The Buddha Cave, or fully named in Thai as Wat Tham Suwan Khuha, is a large, impressive cavern with a temple gate, filled with a broad and beautiful variety of Buddha statues placed in various spots, inspiring tourists to stop and relax wherever feels right to them. It's mostly known for its giant gold statue of a reclining Buddha, before which a stage is set where faithful visitors can light incense and pray under his gaze. Before or after your uphill walk through the cave, you may get to meet the many gray monkeys jumping down from the top of the hill and ropy trees to be fed, so have some peanuts, bananas, or coconut handy if you want to interact with them. There are several tourist stalls around selling snacks and other items such as jewelry and souvenirs. ✉ *6 miles outside Phang Nga, Phang Nga.*

Hotels

★ Aleenta Phuket Resort & Spa

$$$$ | **RESORT** | Stylish design, a romantic atmosphere, and a beautiful beach contribute to the Aleenta experience. **Pros:** great sunset views from some suites; quiet, relaxing location. **Cons:** fills up early in high season; not all rooms have sea views. *Rooms from: B6,300* ✉ *33 Moo 5, Khokkloy, Phang Nga, Phang Nga* ☎ *066/2514–8112* 🌐 *www.aleenta.com* *15 suites and villas* *Free breakfast.*

Ao Phang Nga National Park

$ | **B&B/INN** | In addition to the camping grounds (where you can rent tents), the park has a few well-built bungalows within its grounds. **Pros:** excellent location; good base for exploring the area; decent service. **Cons:** some rooms are basic; lack of amenities; often booked up. *Rooms from: B100* ✉ *80 Ban Tha Dan, Koh Panyi, Phang Nga* ☎ *025/620760 for reservations* *No credit cards* *15 bungalows.*

Golden Buddha Beach Resort

$$$$ | **RESORT** | **FAMILY** | This eco-resort has its own stunning 10-km (6-mile) beach where the endangered giant leatherback turtle nests, beautiful beachfront and beach-adjacent homes, a spa offering a relaxing range of treatments, yoga classes (it's a prime yoga retreat destination), and a desert-island feel. **Pros:** wonderful beach; helpful, friendly staff; ideal for nature lovers. **Cons:** no kitchen in-house; remote; no air-conditioning. *Rooms from: B9,800* ✉ *131 Moo 2, Ko Phra Thong* ☎ *081/919–5228* 🌐 *www.goldenbuddharesort.com* *No credit cards* *25 homes* *No meals.*

Koh Yao

30 mins by boat from Bangrong Pier, Phuket, or 45 mins by boat from Chaofa Pier, Krabi.

Koh Yao Noi is the most developed of this pair of islands, Noi (little) and Yai (large), but it is still worlds away from the development on Phuket and other parts of the Andaman. The focus of the island is nature, and activities such as eco-projects, kayaking, snorkeling, and diving are the primary focus of travelers who venture to the shores.

Did You Know?

The limestone formations off Railay Beach—called karsts—are the result of a collision between mainland Asia and India about 30 million years ago, which forced limestone deposits to rise from the ocean floor.

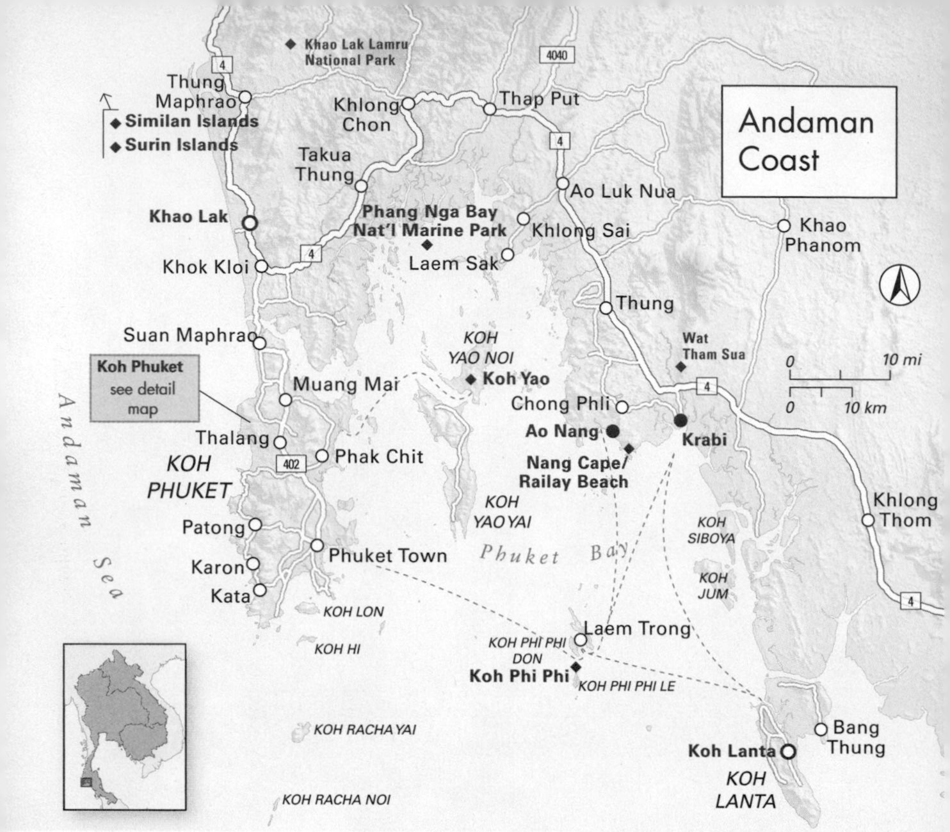

GETTING HERE AND AROUND

Public ferry is the easiest, most scenic, and cheapest way to get to and from Koh Yao Noi. Most of the tourist developments can be found on Koh Yao Noi. Ferries from Bang Rong Pier to the north of Phuket leave regularly throughout the day and cost B150 per person. You can also travel from Chaofa Pier in Krabi for B160.

Sights

Koh Yao Yai and Koh Yao Noi are the two large islands in the center of Phang Nga Bay. Both are quiet, peaceful places, fringed with sandy beaches and clear water.

A visit to Koh Yao will allow you to experience the local culture and customs while exploring the beauty of the islands (kayaks and mountain bikes are popular transportation options). The Ecotourism Club provides homestays if you really want the full experience of the islands; otherwise, most resorts provide day tours or information for self-guided exploration.

Koh Yao Noi Ecotourism Club

BOAT TOURS | Most inhabitants of the islands still make their living by traditional means such as fishing, rubber tapping, and batik painting. Considering their size and proximity to Phuket and Krabi, it's surprising how little development these islands have seen. During the 1990s many tourists began to discover the islands and the impact was negative. To reduce the impact on the land and their culture, the villagers residing on Koh Yao organized the Koh Yao Noi Ecotourism Club to regulate growth on the islands.

They've certainly been successful—they even picked up an award for tourism development sponsored by Conservation International. ✉ *Phuket.*

 Hotels

Koh Yao Homestay

$$$$ | **B&B/INN** | Organized by a community of Koh Yao residents who invite tourists to experience their way of life, the community provides visitors with lodging in their own homes, meals (consisting primarily of fish caught by village fishermen), and knowledge about local customs. **Pros:** up-close cultural experience; ecotourism at its best; well organized. **Cons:** homestay accommodations don't suit everyone; usually very basic. $ *Rooms from: B6,500* ✉ *Baan Laem Sai, Koh Yao Noi, Phang Nga* ☎ *089/9703384* 🌐 *www.kohyao-homestay.com* 💳 *No credit cards* 🛏 *10 rooms* 🍽 *All-inclusive.*

★ **Koyao Island Resort**

$$$$ | **RESORT** | Koyao Island Resort has one of the best views among beach resorts in Thailand; from east-facing Haad Pa Sai you can take in a panoramic vista of a string of magnificent islands. **Pros:** captivating views of nearby islands; attentive service; many activities. **Cons:** not family oriented; open air can make you more mosquito accessible; beach itself could be better. $ *Rooms from: B6,500* ✉ *24/2 Koh Yao Noi, Phang Nga* ☎ *076/597474 up to 76* 🌐 *www.koyao.com* 🛏 *15 villas* 🍽 *Free breakfast.*

Khao Lak

80 km (50 miles) north of Phuket.

Khao Lak is a place to go to if you want a relaxed, low-key holiday. It just cuts the right side of developed to offer all the amenities you might want, without the overdevelopment characteristic of much of the Andaman coastline.

GETTING HERE AND AROUND

VIP and first-class buses leave for Khao Lak from Bangkok's Southern Bus Terminal each evening around 6 or 7 pm. The journey takes at least 12 hours. There's also regular bus service here from other beach areas. The journey to Phuket takes about two hours and costs around B200 (by taxi expect to pay anywhere between B1,600 and B2,000). There's no direct bus from Phuket to Khao Lak, but you can take a local bus bound for Ranong, Surat Thani, or Kuraburi and ask to get dropped off in Khao Lak.

The usual array of motorcycles, songthaews, and taxis will shuttle you around the area.

Sights

Khao Lak Beach

BEACH—SIGHT | Khao Lak Beach proper lies to the south of the national park, and most resorts and dive operators purporting to hail from Khao Lak actually line the coasts of Nang Thong, Bang Niang, Khuk Khak, and Bang Sak beaches to the north. As a result of Khao Lak's booming popularity, many properties stay open during the low season; however, Khao Lak is best visited near or during the high and dry season (November to May) when you can be sure that all businesses are in full operation. **Amenities:** food and drink; showers; toilets; water sports. **Best for:** sunset; surfing; swimming; walking. ✉ *Thanon Phet Kasem.*

Khao Lak Lamru National Marine Park

NATIONAL/STATE PARK | Khao Lak Lamru National Marine Park's rolling green hills and abundant wildlife are a primary attraction. The park grounds cover more than 325 square km (125 square miles) from the sea to the mountains, including a secluded sandy beach and several waterfalls. The park preserves some pristine tropical evergreen forest that is often supplanted in the south by fruit and rubber trees. Wildlife includes wild pigs, barking deer, macaques, and reticulated pythons. Walking trails lead to waterfalls with swimmable pools. Three rudimentary cabins are available for overnight stays, as are tent rentals for visitors who do not have their own. The park headquarters, on the road from Khao Lak Beach to Khao Lak town, provides information about exploring or staying in the park. ☎ *025/794842, 025/578–0529 National Park Division in Bangkok* 🌐 *www.dnp.go.th.*

Restaurants

Hill Tribes Restaurant

$ | **THAI** | Allow your taste buds to celebrate this loving tribute to northern Thai cuisine. The chefs here specialize in seafood and fish dishes made according to traditional recipes from the northern hill tribes folk, which provide a pleasant change from southern fare. **Known for:** northern Thai cuisine; hill tribe decor; mango sticky rice. *Average main: B145* ✉ *13/22 Phetchkasem Rd., Bangniang* ☎ *086/283–0933* 🌐 *www.hilltribe-restaurant.com* *No credit cards.*

Smile

$$ | **THAI** | **FAMILY** | Showing a special awareness to diners with food allergies and diabetes and offering a menu especially designed for vegetarians and vegans, this successful restaurant serves delicious Thai curries, a wonderful choice of appetizers, and salads and stir-fries made with an interesting French twist. **Known for:** vegan options; Thai curries; French twist. *Average main: B200* ✉ *29/31 Phetkasem Rd., Phangnga, Phang Nga* ☎ *083/391–2600* *No credit cards.*

Smoh Ruer Restaurant

$ | **THAI** | A few minutes' tuk-tuk ride north from the busy part of town, Smoh Ruer is a high-end (in food, not price) local eatery occasionally chanced upon by a few lucky travelers. There's nothing chancy about the food, however. **Known for:** wild-boar red curry; quality menu; relaxed atmosphere. *Average main: B160* ✉ *12/2 Moo 6, T. Khukkak* ☎ *089/288–9889, 089/875–9018* *No credit cards.*

Hotels

Baan Krating

$ | **RESORT** | Occupying a wonderful spot on a cliff above a beach, this boutique resort boasts a beautiful view and a path down to the shore that travels within Khao Lak Lamru National Marine Park. **Pros:** relaxed atmosphere; captivating views; clean rooms. **Cons:** spartan accommodations; slightly worn; a bit of a trek to beach. *Rooms from: B1,100* ✉ *28 Khao Lak, Takuapa, Phang Nga* ☎ *076/485188 up to 89* 🌐 *www.baankrating.com* *24 cottages* *No meals.*

Centara Seaview Resort Khao Lak

$ | **RESORT** | **FAMILY** | The octagonal villas with high ceilings, four-poster beds, and whirlpool tubs epitomize the luxury available to guests. **Pros:** tiered pool; luxurious feel; friendly staff. **Cons:** not the best views; somewhat costly; beach not ideal. *Rooms from: B1,700* ✉ *18/1 Moo 7, Petchkasem Rd., Khuk Khak* ☎ *076/429800* 🌐 *www.centarahotels-resorts.com* *No credit cards* *197 rooms* *Free breakfast.*

Green Beach Resort

$ | **RESORT** | Standard clapboard bungalows have wooden floors, rattan walls, and bamboo furniture. **Pros:** inexpensive; beachfront. **Cons:** slightly tacky exterior; bland feeling. *Rooms from: B1,600* ✉ *13/51 Moo 7, Haad Nangtong, Khuk Khak* ☎ *076/420046* 🌐 *www.khaolak-greenbeachresort.com* *Closed May–Nov.* *40 bungalows* *No meals.*

★ **La Flora Resort & Spa**

$$$ | **RESORT** | This is a lovely, service-oriented boutique resort where rooms are fashionably decorated in a modern Asian aesthetic, and most have balconies or daybeds. **Pros:** tasteful, spacious rooms;

Tropical forest meets powdery white sand on the Similan Islands.

stunning villas; lovely beach with deep waters. **Cons:** families may find it a little isolated; dining is not outstanding; rooftop bar understaffed. *Rooms from: B4,400* *59/1 Moo 5, Khuk Khak, Phang Nga* *076/428000, 026/798828* *www.laflораresort.com* *125 rooms, 13 villas* *Free breakfast.*

Mukdara Beach Resort
$$ | RESORT | This sumptuous resort has been designed in classical Thai style, with a great deal of emphasis on wood and traditional craftsmanship. **Pros:** villas on beach; tasteful Thai furnishings; luxurious. **Cons:** large resort, so not intimate; layout of some rooms is odd. *Rooms from: B2,800* *26/14 Moo 7, Thanon Khuk Khak, Takuapa, Phang Nga* *076/429999* *www.mukdarabeach.com* *70 rooms, 64 villas, 7 suites* *Free breakfast.*

Nang Thong Bay Resort
$ | RESORT | The majority of rooms here are surprisingly inexpensive cottages that face the beach and are surrounded by well-maintained gardens. **Pros:** good value; well located; new pool. **Cons:** disappointing restaurant; service a little amiss. *Rooms from: B1,000* *13/5 Moo 7, Thanon Khuk Khak, Takuapa, Phang Nga* *076/485000 up to 89* *www.nangthong.com* *82 rooms* *No meals.*

The Sarojin
$$$$ | RESORT | This exquisite boutique resort's smaller size makes it more intimate and exclusive than nearby megaresorts. **Pros:** intimate and exclusive; cooking classes; unique aesthetics. **Cons:** price a bit higher than at comparable resorts. *Rooms from: B7,150* *60 Moo 2, Khuk Khak, Takuapa, Phang Nga* *076/427900 up to 07* *www.sarojin.com* *56 rooms* *No meals.*

Similan Islands

70 km (45 miles) or 1½ hours by boat from Thaplamu Pier.

★ The Similan Islands are synonymous with two things: beautiful, unspoiled beaches and diving in crystal-blue waters. There are nine islands in this archipelago, each with its own number and name. Huge boulders adorn the white, sandy beaches and beneath the waters lies some of the world's best diving.

GETTING HERE AND AROUND

BOAT TRAVEL

Speedboats to Similan National Park leave from Thap Lamu Pier in the Tai Muang District just south of Khao Lak Beach at 8:30 am when the park is open to the public (November to May). Once you reach Koh Similan, motorboats will take you to other islands for between B250 and B600, depending on distance.

You can also take a private tour boat from Thap Lamu Pier for around B2,000 per person. The tour boat departs from Thap Lamu at 8 am daily and returns at 2 pm. Direct tickets, booked through the national parks, cost B2,000; however, private tours are a better value.

Sights

Koh Miang

NATIONAL/STATE PARK | Koh Miang, where the park headquarters is located, has bungalows with 24-hour electricity and even some with air-conditioning; some bungalows have ocean views as well. Beachside camping is also available on Koh Miang (the park rents out roomy tents, large enough to stand in, which have two camping cots). Koh Similan has no bungalows, but has the same large tents for rent, as well as an area for visitors to set up their own tents. If you choose to visit the island to stay at the park, expect to pay B2,500 to B3,000 for a round-trip boat transfer. Once on the island, you can hire a longtail boat to explore the other islands. **■ TIP→ The park is extremely popular with Thais, so book well in advance if you're planning a visit during a Thai holiday. The islands are more enjoyable, and more explorable, if visited midweek.** The park entrance fee is B500 per visit. Note that the islands are normally closed to visitors from mid-May until early November. ☎ *076/595045 for campsite reservations, 02/562–0760 for bungalow reservations* 🌐 *www.dnp.go.th.*

Mu Koh Similan

ISLAND | The Mu (group) Koh Similan National Marine Park consists of the nine Similan Islands, as well as Koh Tachai and Koh Bon, which are farther north. The diving around the Similan Islands is world-class, with visibility of up to 120 feet; abundant blue, green, and purple coral; and rare marine life, such as the whale shark, the world's largest fish. In addition to sparkling, crystal-clear water, the Similan Islands also have ultrafine, powdery white-sand beaches and lush tropical forests. The National Park Service allows visitors to stay on the beaches of Koh Miang (Island 4) and Koh Similan (Island 8). **■ TIP→ If you plan to dive, contact a dive operator in Phuket or Khao Lak; there are no dive shops on the islands, though snorkeling gear is available for rent from the ranger stations..**

Surin Islands

60 km (37 miles) or 2 hrs by boat from Kuraburi Pier.

Sixty kilometers (37 miles) off the west coast of Phang Nga, the five Surin Islands are special for their diving and fishing. The national park status has stopped all development here, and this is a strong draw for tourists to come and see an unspoiled part of Thailand. There is a community of "sea gypsies" or *moken* (as they identify themselves) living here, who have become a slight tourist attraction in themselves.

GETTING HERE AND AROUND

Khuraburi Pier, north of Khao Lak Beach, is the departure point for boats to the Surin Islands and can be reached by any bus going to or from Ranong (about B200 from Phuket or Krabi). Songthaews will take you to the pier, approximately 9 km (5½ miles) out of town. Expect to pay B1,000 and up for boat trips to the various islands. Negotiating prices is not really an option here. An easier option is to book a trip through your resort. They will arrange your transportation to Khuraburi and your boat ticket.

 Sights

On the Surin Islands the visibility and diversity of marine life is spectacular, and this is arguably the most unspoiled Thai island retreat, owing to its remote location and low number of visitors. Note that the park is normally closed during the rainy season (June to November).

Mu Koh Surin National Marine Park

ISLAND | Mu Koh Surin National Marine Park or the Surin Islands is a remote island paradise practically unknown to anyone other than adventurous scuba divers and Thais. Five islands make up the national park, each with sea turtles, varieties of sharks, and plentiful coral. If you get tired of sun and sea, there are several hiking trails that lead to waterfalls and a sea-gypsy village. ✉ *Phang Nga.*

 Hotels

Koh Surin Nua

$$ | **RENTAL** | There are 10 recently built, comfortable, fan-cooled, wooden huts on Koh Surin Nua, and tent camping is allowed at a site that has decent facilities, including toilets and showers. *Rooms from: B2,000* ☎ *02/562–0760 inquiries and bungalow reservations, 076/491378* 🌐 *www.dnp.go.th* 💳 *No credit cards* 🛏 *10 bungalows* 🍽 *No meals.*

Krabi

814 km (506 miles) south of Bangkok, 180 km (117 miles) southeast of Phuket, 43 km (27 miles) by boat east of Koh Phi Phi.

Krabi is a major travel hub in southern Thailand. Where once travelers would breeze through without stopping to enjoy the atmosphere, they're increasingly making it a destination, with international flights to the province's airport on the rise. There are a few good restaurants in Krabi Town, though Ao Nang has a better variety, and there's excellent seafood at the night markets (try the fish cakes with sweet chili sauce), which also sells clothes, accessories, and souvenirs.

GETTING HERE AND AROUND

AIR TRAVEL

Flying is the easiest way to get here from Bangkok. Thai Airways, Bangkok Airways, and Air Asia all have daily flights to Krabi International Airport. One-way prices from Bangkok range from B1,000 to B3,500; the flight takes about an hour.

The airport is a 20-minute ride from Krabi Town, and there are taxis (B400) and minibuses (B150) waiting outside the airport. These vehicles can also take you to other nearby (and not-so-nearby) beach areas. Minivans don't leave until they're full, which can happen quickly or after a long wait. Your best bet is to check in with the minivans first to make sure you get a seat if one is about to depart—if not, you can opt for a taxi. Another, more recent transport addition, is the regular bus service to and from Krabi Town. The bus departs hourly (B100) from 6 am and runs throughout the day until 10 pm.

BUS AND SONGTHAEW TRAVEL

Buses from Bangkok to Krabi leave from Bangkok's Southern Bus Terminal and take at least 12 hours. VIP and first-class buses leave once every evening around 6 or 7 pm. Public buses leave Krabi for Bangkok at 8 am and 4 and 5:30 pm.

First-class buses travel between Phuket and Krabi (a three-hour journey) every hour. Getting around town or to Ao Nang is best done by songthaew. You can find songthaews at the corner of Maharat Soi 4 and Pruksa Uthit Road.

Bus and boat combination tickets are available from Krabi to Koh Samui and Koh Phangan.

There are a few bus terminals in Krabi, but if you don't arrive at the pier, songthaews can take you there; if you've purchased a combination ticket, this transfer is included.

CAR TRAVEL

The airport has Avis, National, and Budget rental counters. Prices start at about B1,500 per day; for a little more, you can also rent a four-wheel-drive jeep in town.

SAFETY AND PRECAUTIONS

Krabi is a sleepy, laid-back town with little crime and few annoyances, but taking routine precautions with your valuables is always a good idea. People drive annoyingly fast, so take care when crossing the road, especially at the major junctions.

VISITOR INFORMATION

Krabi has its own small Tourism Authority of Thailand (TAT) offices, where you can pick up maps and brochures, as well as information about local excursions. Tour operators and your hotel's tour desk are also good sources of information.

CONTACTS Krabi Tourist Information Center
✉ *Uttarakit Rd.* ☎ *075/622163.*

Sights

Wat Tham Sua

RELIGIOUS SITE | Just 3 km (2 miles, or 10 minutes' drive) from Krabi Town is Wat Tham Sua, with its giant Buddha statue and scenic surrounding landscapes. Built in 1976 as a monastery and meditation retreat, Wat Tham Sua is both respected by the local population and popular with tourists. Locals come to participate in Buddhist rituals, while most tourists come to climb the 1,277 steps to panoramic views of the cliffs, Krabi Town, Krabi River, and the Panom Benja mountain range. There's also a cave with many chambers, which can be fun to explore, though it's not terribly attractive. A really large tree grows outside the entrance. The wat is between Krabi Town and the airport. ✉ *, Tambon Muang Chum ✣ 4 km (2½ miles) after Wachiralongkorn Dam.*

Restaurants

Carnivore Steak and Grill

$$ | INTERNATIONAL | As the name suggests, meat lovers can find high-quality imported cuts served with delicious sauces and sides at this well-known restaurant. Fish lovers can also be satisfied here, with fresh lobster bisque, perfectly grilled tuna steak, or white snapper in butter-and-garlic-cream sauce. **Known for:** imported steaks; smart service; lively atmosphere. $ *Average main: B230* ✉ *127 Moo 3* ☎ *075/661061* 🌐 *www.carnivore-thailand.com* ▭ *No credit cards.*

Chao Fa Pier Street Food Stalls

$ | THAI | Looking for local quality food at a low price? This strip of street-side food stalls serves everything from simple fried rice and papaya salad to more sophisticated southern delicacies such as *kanom jeen* (rice noodles topped with whatever sauces and vegetables you want). **Known for:** southern delicacies; kanom jeen noodles; carnival atmosphere. $ *Average main: B60* ✉ *Chao Fa Pier, Khong Kha Rd.* ▭ *No credit cards.*

Frog and Catfish

$ | SEAFOOD | At the Frog and Catfish you can try some regional specialties that are not that easy to come across. Located in the small village of Din Daeang Noi, the restaurant serves great seafood (try the fresh crab spring rolls) as well as delicious curries. **Known for:** out-of-the-way location; fantastic seafood;

knowledgeable owner. *Average main: B175 76 Moo 6, Din Daeng Noi 084/773–0301 www.frogandcatfish-krabi.com No credit cards.*

★ Marina Villa

$$ | **SEAFOOD** | Opened in 2011, this restaurant sits on the banks of Krabi River on a picturesque marina and specializes in thoughtfully presented Thai seafood dishes. It's a favorite for well-to-do Krabi locals. **Known for:** Hawaiian shirt–wearing waiters; riverside location; mussels with garlic. *Average main: B300 Krabi Marina Next to yacht club 075/611635, 086/276–8556 No credit cards.*

Relax Coffee and Restaurant

$ | **CAFÉ** | The menu at this street-side café includes more than 10 different breakfast platters; a number of sandwiches, such as chicken satay, served on homemade freshly baked brown bread, baguette, or ciabatta; many Thai dishes, including 10 different barracuda plates, and, not surprisingly, a huge variety of coffee drinks, like raspberry latte frappés. It's in the heart of the hotel district and caters mainly to foreigners. **Known for:** breakfast platters; range of coffees; close to hotels. *Average main: B100 7/4 Chaofa Rd. 075/611570 No credit cards Closed 2nd and 4th Fri. of each month.*

Ruen Pae

$ | **SEAFOOD** | This massive floating restaurant aboard a large, flat barge serves Thai standards, with an emphasis on seafood dishes. It's at the Chao Fa Pier beside the night market. **Known for:** floating dining; close to night market; popular on weekends. *Average main: B100 Ut-tarkit Rd. 076/611956, 075/611148 No credit cards Closed Mon.*

Hotels

City Hotel

$ | **HOTEL** | At what is perhaps the oldest and largest hotel in Krabi, rooms in the old wing are simple but clean, and come with air-conditioning or fans; rooms in the new wing are more modern but unexceptional. **Pros:** central location; cheap rooms; free Wi-Fi. **Cons:** basic; only rooms in the new wing worth staying in; old wing needs renovation. *Rooms from: B850 15/2-4 Soi 10, Maharat Rd. 075/621280 to 1 No credit cards www.citykrabi.com 124 rooms.*

Hometel

$ | **HOTEL** | A solid budget choice, this little family-run hotel is a great base for those using Krabi as a stepping-stone to the tropical islands beyond. **Pros:** central; speedy, free Wi-Fi; good restaurant. **Cons:** book well in advance; not enough natural light in the rooms; some rooms are small. *Rooms from: B500 7 Maharaj Rd., Soi 10, Pak Nam 075/622301 No credit cards 10 rooms No meals.*

Krabi River Hotel

$ | **HOTEL** | Not to everyone's taste because it's so basic, the Krabi River Hotel is at the marina (earmarked for major development), and is a good budget option for Krabi. **Pros:** pleasant riverside location; some rooms have lovely views; free Wi-Fi. **Cons:** off the main drag; rooms at the back are small and have no views; breakfast not included. *Rooms from: B600 73/1 Kongkha Rd. 075/612321 No credit cards 20 rooms No meals.*

Ao Nang

20 km (12 miles) from Krabi Town.

In the daytime, Ao Nang is busy with visitors flowing to and from beaches. In the evening storefronts light up the sidewalk and open-air restaurants provide excellent places to kick back with a beer and watch the crowd go by. For a more romantic atmosphere, head to the half dozen seafood restaurants atop a pier extending from the bend in Liab Chai

Haad Road in between Ao Nang and Noppharat Thara beaches. During the day longtail boats depart from Ao Nang for the more spectacular beaches and waters of Hong, Poda, Gai, Lanta, and the Phi Phi Islands, as well as nearby Railay Beach. Less adventurous types can find nicer sand and better water for swimming on the far eastern end of the beach or at Noppharat Thara Beach National Park to the west.

GETTING HERE AND AROUND

Buses from Bangkok headed to Krabi stop here. If you fly into Krabi, it takes about 45 minutes to Ao Nang in a taxi. Songthaews travel between Ao Nang and Krabi Town regularly. The fare shouldn't be more than B80; you can find them on the main road, displaying Krabi–Ao Nang signs. A taxi from the airport will cost you considerably more—usually the minimum fare is B650.

Beaches

Klong Muang

BEACH—SIGHT | Farther north are the beaches of Klong Muang and Tubkaak, isolated, beautiful stretches of sand with amazing views of the limestone karst islands on the horizon. The beaches are largely occupied by upmarket resorts such as the Sheraton and The Tubkaak, and none of the amenities come free. **Amenities:** food and drink; toilet; water sports. **Best for:** solitude; sunset; walking. ✉ *Krabi.*

Laem Son Beach

BEACH—SIGHT | A narrow river pier delineates the western edge of Noppharat Thara National Park. Here you can catch boats departing from the pier to Railay, Phi Phi, and Lanta, or simply cross to the other side and enjoy the unspoiled natural beauty of Laem Son Beach. There are a few cheap beachside bungalows to stay at. **Amenities:** none. **Best for:** solitude; sunset; swimming; walking. ✉ *Krabi.*

Noppharat Thara Beach

BEACH—SIGHT | Noppharat Thara Beach is a 15-minute walk from central Ao Nang. Since the renovated walking path was extended from Ao Nang in 2004, a mish-mash of development followed (even though it's supposedly part of the national park). The beach is still pleasant but many of the trees have been uprooted to make way for resorts. **Amenities:** food and drink. **Best for:** swimming; walking. ✉ *96 Moo 3, Nopphara Thara, Krabi.*

Restaurants

Ao Nang Cuisine

$ | **THAI** | The tender chicken satay (curry chicken skewers), an otherwise ordinary dish, is skillfully prepared at this traditional restaurant, with a side of spicy peanut sauce. More elaborate Thai dishes are available for tourists who are tired of street-side barbecued seafood. **Known for:** chicken satay; excellent value; large portions. 💲 *Average main: B100* ✉ *245/4 Liab Chai Haad Rd., Krabi* ☎ *075/695399.*

Krua Thara

$ | **SEAFOOD** | There are two positive signs at this restaurant before you even try the food—locals hanging out, and the fish and seafood that will end up on your plate are on display in tanks in all their variety. You'll find every kind of fresh catch prepared using lots of local herbs and spices at this friendly, colorful place. **Known for:** popular with locals; seafood displays; friendly atmosphere. 💲 *Average main: B115* ✉ *82 Moo 5, Nopparat Thara Rd., Krabi* ☎ *075/637361* ▭ *No credit cards.*

Lae Lay Grill

$$ | **SEAFOOD** | The seafood here is perfectly cooked and artfully presented, but what makes Lae Lay Grill special is its location. The restaurant is on a terrace on a hill overlooking Ao Nang and the sea, which makes it a highly romantic spot from sunset on, but also lovely during the day. **Known for:** hillside location;

van pickup; seafood dishes. *Average main: B200 89 Moo 3 075/661588 www.laelaygrill.com No credit cards.*

Hotels

Alisea Boutique Hotel
$ | **HOTEL** | Whitewashed walls and red, ceramic-tile floors contribute to the Moroccan design at Alisea. **Pros:** polite, helpful staff; good facilities for the price. **Cons:** whitewash needs to be reapplied; staff can be apathetic. *Rooms from: B1,750 125 Moo 3 075/638000, 02/801–0760 in Bangkok www.alisthailand.com 34 rooms Free breakfast.*

Anyavee Ao Nang Bay Resort
$ | **RESORT** | The resort is a cluster of four-story buildings in Thai design, including northern-style peaked roofs. **Pros:** good selection of facilities; great location for nature lovers. **Cons:** a bit removed from beach; exterior needs some renovation. *Rooms from: B1,900 31/3 Liab Chai Haad Rd. 075/695051 up to 54 www.anyavee.com 71 rooms Free breakfast.*

The Cliff
$ | **RESORT** | You can get a great view of the cliff that inspired the hotel's name as soon as you step into the lobby. **Pros:** atmospheric design; stunning location; good Wi-Fi connection. **Cons:** not on beach; some rooms are very stuffy. *Rooms from: B1,750 85/2 Liab Chai Haad Rd. 075/638117 up to 18 www.thecliffkrabi.com 20 rooms, 1 suite Free breakfast.*

Dusit Thani Krabi Beach Resort
$$$ | **RESORT** | **FAMILY** | The resort is built around an expansive mangrove forest, and there's a wide, sandy beach on the premises. **Pros:** beachfront location; great amenities; stylish. **Cons:** location may disappoint beach purists—water isn't crystal clear; Wi-Fi connection only in reception area; a little worn in places. *Rooms from: B5,000 155 Klong Muang Beach, Nongtalay, Krabi 075/628000 246 rooms, 6 suites Free breakfast.*

Emerald Bungalow
$ | **B&B/INN** | On isolated Laem Son Beach, this family-run resort offers genuine Thai hospitality. **Pros:** close to national park; relaxed atmosphere; decent restaurant. **Cons:** a bit pricey for basic lodgings; too remote for some. *Rooms from: B1,400 Noppharat Thara Beach, Krabi 081/892–1072, 081/956–2566 www.the-emerald-bungalow-resortkrabi.com No credit cards 36 rooms No meals.*

J Mansion
$ | **HOTEL** | Top-floor rooms peek out over surrounding buildings for a nice view of the sea. **Pros:** large rooms; good views from top floor; friendly staff. **Cons:** slow Internet connection; very basic. *Rooms from: B1,000 23/3 Moo 2 075/637878 www.jmansionaonang.com/accommodation.htm 21 rooms No meals.*

Krabi Resort
$$ | **RESORT** | The only beachfront bungalows in Ao Nang Town, the best swimming is here as well as a seaside park with plenty of benches positioned for gazing at the sea. **Pros:** great location; lots of facilities for the price. **Cons:** breakfast buffet can be a little stale and bland. *Rooms from: B2,400 232 Liab Chai Haad Rd. 075/637030 up to 35, 02/208–9165 in Bangkok www.krabiresort.net 130 rooms, 2 suites Free breakfast.*

Phra Nang Inn
$ | **B&B/INN** | The resort has a wonderfully kooky vibe—you might find headboards decorated with bright paintings of seashells and fish in the Coconut Wing, and a few pieces of furniture might look like they're made from tree branches in the Betel-nut Wing. **Pros:** airport shuttle available; central location. **Cons:** decor not for everyone. *Rooms from: B1,400 119 Liab Chai Haad Rd. 075/637130*

🌐 *www.vacationvillage.co.th/phrananginn* ⇨ *74 rooms* 🍽 *Free breakfast.*

The Small, Krabi

$$ | HOTEL | This sleek boutique hotel stands quietly in one of the busier parts of Ao Nang, offering proximity to shopping, dining, drinking, and swimming at the Noppharatthara and Ao Nang beaches on either side. **Pros:** cleanliness and attention to detail; great location; short walk to beach. **Cons:** no big pool; having a TV in the bathroom is not to everyone's taste. 💲 *Rooms from: B2,000* ✉ *167 Moo 3, Tambon, Amphur Muang* ☎ *075/661590* 🌐 *www.thesmallhotel-group.com/krabi/* ▭ *No credit cards* ⇨ *38 rooms* 🍽 *No meals.*

Srisuksant Resort

$$ | HOTEL | FAMILY | On the eastern end of Noppharat Thara, Srisuksant is a short walk from Ao Nang's shops and directly across from the beach. **Pros:** nice pools; well set up for kids and families; friendly staff. **Cons:** a little overwhelming for couples without kids. 💲 *Rooms from: B2,000* ✉ *145 Noppharat, Thara Beach* ☎ *075/638002 up to 04* 🌐 *www.srisuksantresort.com* ⇨ *66 rooms* 🍽 *Free breakfast.*

The Tubkaak Boutique Resort

$$$$ | RESORT | Each of the elegant wooden buildings here resembles a *kor lae*, a traditional southern Thai fishing boat. **Pros:** relaxed environment; beach location; great pool area. **Cons:** disappointing restaurant; rooms are small. 💲 *Rooms from: B7,500* ✉ *123 Taab Kaak Beach, Nongtalay* ☎ *075/628400* 🌐 *www.tubkaakresort.com* ⇨ *44 rooms, 2 suites* 🍽 *No meals.*

Nightlife

The Last Fisherman

BARS/PUBS | The last—and most scenic—social spot on the end of Ao Nang Beach is where you should have your frosty drink just before sunset, although it's open for lunch as well. If you're peckish in the early afternoon or at night, a plain surf-and-turf, barbecue buffet, salads, and gooey desserts are on the menu. ✉ *266 Moo 2* ☎ *075/637968.*

Nang Cape/Railay Beach

15 mins by longtail boat east of Ao Nang.

Be careful not to strain your neck admiring the skyscraping cliffs as your longtail boat delivers you to Nang Cape. Here four interconnected beaches are collectively referred to as Railay Beach; the isolated beaches of Tonsai, Phra Nang, East Railay, and West Railay, only accessible by boat, are sandy oases surrounded by impressive verdant, vertical cliffs. The sand on these beaches is talcum-powder white and soft, the water is crystalline, and the crowd is an offbeat blend of bohemian travelers, rock climbers, and fitness enthusiasts.

GETTING HERE AND AROUND

Longtails will ferry you here from Ao Nang. Prices vary depending on time of day and which beach you're headed to, but expect to pay around B100 or B120 each way. Prices can rise dramatically in the evening, so leave early to save money.

Beaches

Nang Cape/Railay Beach

BEACH—SIGHT | The four beaches that make up Railay Beach are connected by walking paths, and each has its own attractions. Tonsai Beach, with a pebble-strewn shore and shallow, rocky water, caters to budget travelers and rock climbers. West Railay has powdery white sand, shallow but swimmable water, gorgeous sunset views, and many kayaks for hire. East Railay, a mangrove-lined shore unsuitable for beach or water activities, draws rock-climbing enthusiasts, as well as younger travelers looking for late-night drinks and loud music. Phra Nang

Beach, one of the nicest beaches in all Krabi, is ideal for swimming, sunbathing, and rock-climbing. **Amenities:** food and drink; toilets; water sports. **Best for:** snorkeling; sunset; swimming. ✉ *Railay Beach.*

 Restaurants

There are plenty of bars and restaurants along the beaches. Most restaurants serve standard Thai and Western fare—no gourmet renditions *yet.* As you move away from the beach, you'll find less expensive and more atmospheric places, including some climber hangouts where trainings and socializing with fellow climbers take place.

Hotels

Bhu Nga Thani Resort and Spa
$$ | **RESORT** | Located on the quieter Railay East Beach, the lovely infinity pool and a popular spa make this a good option for those staying at Railay, though East Beach faces out onto a mangrove swamp, and there is better swimming to be had at Tonsai or West Beach. **Pros:** most rooms have ocean views; bars and restaurants nearby; resort arranges excursions. **Cons:** 10-minute walk from boat drop; not on a swimming beach; food can be hit or miss. $ *Rooms from: B4,000* ✉ *Railay East Beach, 479 Moo 2, Railay Beach* ☎ *075/819451 up to 04* 🌐 *www.bhungathani.com* ▭ *No credit cards* ⇨ *60 rooms* 🍽 *No meals.*

Koh Jum Lodge
$$$ | **B&B/INN** | On the island of Koh Jum, in Phang Nga Bay between Krabi, Phi Phi, and Koh Lanta, Koh Jum Lodge has rooms in 20 wooden cottages designed in traditional Thai architectural style. **Pros:** traditional Thai design; helpful management and staff; stunning sunset over the Phi Phi Islands. **Cons:** a bit isolated from resort towns; difficult to access in off-peak season; food and drinks pricey. $ *Rooms from: B4,500* ✉ *286 Moo 3, Koh Siboya, Nua Klong, Krabi, Railay Beach* ☎ *075/618275, 089/921–1621* 🌐 *www.kohjumlodge.com* ⇨ *20 bungalows* 🍽 *Free breakfast.*

Railay Bay Resort and Spa
$$ | **RESORT** | Great Thai food ($$) and a beachside patio and bar from which you can watch the sunset are a few good reasons to visit Railay Bay Resort and Spa. Basic cottages and rooms in a row of modern two-story buildings are suitable reasons to lodge here, also. **Pros:** alluring views; central location; decent food. **Cons:** staff may not speak great English; pricey spa; patchy Wi-Fi. $ *Rooms from: B3,500* ✉ *145 Moo 2, Railay West Beach, Railay Beach* ☎ *075/622998 up to 99* 🌐 *www.railaybayresort.com* ⇨ *140 rooms, 10 suites* 🍽 *Free breakfast.*

Railay Garden View
$ | **B&B/INN** | Among the best of the less expensive options on Railay, this place offers clean bungalows in a garden setting, and a great location near the beach. **Pros:** complimentary breakfast; good restaurant; free Wi-Fi. **Cons:** keep an eye on your belongings; no sea view; noise from longtail boats can get tiring. $ *Rooms from: B750* ✉ *147 Moo 5, Saithai district, Railay Beach* ☎ *085/888–5143, 084/295–1112* 🌐 *www.railaygardenview.com/en/* ▭ *No credit cards* ⇨ *10 rooms* 🍽 *Free breakfast.*

Railay Phutawan Resort
$$ | **RESORT** | From practically everywhere you stand in this resort, you can enjoy overwhelming vistas of the bay and climber-covered limestone cliffs. **Pros:** inexpensive; stunning views; good food. **Cons:** no advance booking; lacking facilities; an uphill trek to get there. $ *Rooms from: B2,000* ✉ *Moo 1, Railay East Beach, Krabi, Railay Beach* ☎ *075/621731* 🌐 *www.railayphutawan.com* ▭ *No credit cards* ⇨ *20 bungalows* 🍽 *Free breakfast.*

Railay Princess Resort and Spa
$ | **HOTEL** | Thai-style lamps and silk throw pillows on the beds and sofas are colorful

touches at this quiet retreat midway between East and West Railay beaches. **Pros:** quiet location; good value; tasteful details. **Cons:** not on beach; furniture looks cheap. *$ Rooms from: B1,900 ✉ 145/1 Moo 2, Railay Beach, Ao Nang, Railay Beach ☎ 075/819401 up to 03, 075/819407 up to 09 🌐 www.krabi-railay-princess.com 59 rooms No meals.*

★ Railei Beach Club

$$ | RENTAL | FAMILY | Each of the 24 privately owned homes here is individually named and designed, giving each its own unique character. **Pros:** great choice of accommodations and prices; good location; sunsets. **Cons:** fills up early in high season; some staff can be aloof; bring your own beach towels. *$ Rooms from: B2,000 ✉ 200 Moo 2, Railay West Beach ☎ 075/622582, 086/685–9359 🌐 www.raileibeachclub.com 24 houses No meals.*

Rayavadee Resort

$$$$ | RESORT | Scattered across 26 landscaped acres, this magnificent resort is set in coconut groves with white-sand beaches on three sides. **Pros:** great dining variety; intricate room design; plenty of facilities. **Cons:** notably nonecological use of wood; beach very busy during the day; during low tide boat access is challenging. *$ Rooms from: B12,000 ✉ 214 Moo 2, Tambol Ao Nang, Krabi ☎ 075/620740 up to 43 🌐 www.rayavadee.com 98 rooms, 5 suites Free breakfast.*

Activities

ROCK CLIMBING

Climbers discovered the cliffs around Nang Cape in the late 1980s. The mostly vertical cliffs rising up out of the sea were, and certainly are, a dream come true for hard-core climbers. Today anyone daring enough can learn to scale the face of a rock (and to jump off it) in one of the most beautiful destinations in the world. There are 500 to 600 established climbing routes. Notable feats include the Tonsai Beach overhang and Thaiwand Wall, where climbers must use lanterns to pass through a cave and then rappel down from the top. Beginners can learn some skills through half-day or full-day courses for fixed rates of B1,200 or B2,000, respectively. Most climbing organizations are found on East Railay. Slightly less adventurous, or more spendthrift, types can try the free climb to "the lagoon." The lagoon itself isn't all that impressive, but the view from the top is spectacular. The trailhead for the fairly arduous climb up the occasionally near-vertical mud, rock, vine, and fixed-rope ascent is along the path to Phra Nang Beach, immediately across from the gazebo. Watch out for monkeys!

King Climbers

CLIMBING/MOUNTAINEERING | All the guides here are accredited by the ACGA and have a minimum of five years' climbing experience. *✉ East Railey, Railay Beach ☎ 075/637125 🌐 www.railay.com.*

Tex Rock Climbing

CLIMBING/MOUNTAINEERING | Half-day to three-day climbing courses can be arranged here. *✉ East Railey, Railay Beach ☎ 075/631509.*

Koh Lanta

70 km (42 miles) south of Krabi Town.

Long beaches, crystal-clear water, and a laid-back natural environment are Koh Lanta's main attractions. Although "discovered" by international travelers in the early 2000s, Koh Lanta remains fairly quiet. Early development resulted in the construction of hundreds of budget bungalows and several swanky resorts along the west coast of Lanta Yai (Lanta Noi's coast is less suitable for development); however, as one of the largest islands in Thailand, Lanta was able to absorb the "boom" and therefore remains relatively uncluttered. In addition, Lanta is approximately 70 km (44 miles) south of Krabi

Town, far enough outside established tourist circuits that visitor arrivals have increased a little more slowly than at other Krabi and Phang Nga beaches and islands.

Most smaller resorts are closed during the low season (May through October). Nevertheless, some do open in late October and remain open until mid-May—during these (slightly) off times, the weather is still generally good, and you can find that the rates are much lower and the beaches much less crowded.

GETTING HERE AND AROUND

Krabi's airport is about two hours from Koh Lanta by taxi (B2,300 to B3,000) or minibus (B350). Minibuses depart from Krabi Town and Ao Nang, not the airport. There's no direct bus service from Bangkok to Koh Lanta; you'll have to take the bus to Trang or Krabi and then continue on in a minivan (songthaews will take you from the bus station to the minivans bound for Koh Lanta). There are two short (15 minutes) Ro-Ro ferries crossings between the mainland and Lanta catering specifically to those coming by car or bus. There's one direct passenger ferry every morning from Krabi at 11:30 am; it costs B400. A bridge built in 2016 now connects Koh Lanta Yai and Lanta Noi, but a ferry is still required to reach the Krabi mainland.

One main road runs along the island that will take you to all major resorts. Pickup trucks masquerading as taxis and motorcycles with sidecars will take you wherever you want to go. Negotiate hard for good fares; prices start at about B60 for a short ride of 1 km (½ mile).

SAFETY AND PRECAUTIONS

Lanta is one of Thailand's quieter islands, not because it lacks a tourism infrastructure but because the traditional way of life is strong here. Like on Koh Yao Yai off Phuket, the majority of inhabitants here are Muslim, and this guides much of the island's development. The girly bars, the loud late-night discos, and the hectic frenzy of a drinking culture are largely absent. This means that there's a low crime rate, even for Thailand, though precautions should still be taken.

 Beaches

Klong Dao Beach and Phra Ae Beach, both on Lanta Yai's west coast, are the most developed. If you head south, you'll reach calmer Klong Nin Beach and southern Lanta's quiet, scenic coves. Southern Lanta beaches consist of several widely dispersed small coves and beaches ending at Klong Chak National Park. Immediately south of Klong Nin the road suddenly becomes well paved (much smoother than the road from Long Beach to Klong Nin), making the southern beaches accessible by road as well as by taxi boat. The nicest of the southern beaches is Bakantiang Beach, a beautiful one to visit on the way to the national park.

Bakantiang (Kantiang) Beach

BEACH—SIGHT | The last beach before the national park on the southern tip of Koh Lanta, the crescent-shaped Kantiang Beach is small but truly stunning. The fine white sands are favored by travelers in the know, or expat residents who want to get away from the busier beaches. The village that backs the beach is the friendliest on the island, and there are a few food stalls and roadside cafés that serve some of the tastiest food on Koh Lanta. **Amenities:** food and drink; showers; toilets. **Best for:** snorkeling; sunset; swimming. ✣ *Last stop on main road heading south, before national park.*

Klong Dao Beach

BEACH—SIGHT | FAMILY | Klong Dao Beach is a 2-km-long (1-mile-long) beach on the northern coast of Lanta Yai, the larger of the two islands that comprise Koh Lanta. Most resorts along Klong Dao are larger facilities catering to families and couples looking for a quiet environment. The water is shallow but swimmable, and at low tide the firm, exposed sand is ideal for long jogs on the beach. **Amenities:** food and drink; toilets. **Best for:** sunset; swimming; walking. ⊕ *To right of Lanta's main road, first beach after port town Saladan.*

Klong Nin Beach

BEACH—SIGHT | Klong Nin Beach, approximately 30 minutes south of Long Beach by car or boat, is one of the larger, nicer beaches toward the southern end of Lanta Yai. Klong Nin is less developed and more tranquil than Long Beach. A typical day on Klong Nin can be a long walk on the silky soft sand interrupted by occasional dips in the sea, a spectacular sunset, a seaside massage, and a candlelight barbecue beneath a canopy of stars. Central Klong Nin is the best for swimming, as rocks punctuate the rest of the shoreline. Kayaks are available from some resorts, and longtail boat taxis are for hire along the sea. Most resorts here rent motorbikes as well, as the road to the south is much smoother than the road from Long Beach. **Amenities:** food and drink; toilets. **Best for:** solitude; sunset; swimming; walking. ⊕ *To right of Lanta's main road from Saladan, after intersection for Old Town and Southern Lanta.*

Phra Ae Beach

BEACH—SIGHT | Long and wide, Phra Ae Beach (aka Long Beach) is Lanta Yai's main tourist destination. The sand is soft and fine, perfect for both sunbathing and long walks. The water is less shallow than at other Lanta beaches, and therefore more suitable for diving in and having a swim. Nevertheless, kayaks, catamarans, and other water activities, while available, are not as ubiquitous as on other islands. Although most lodging consists of simple budget resorts, the beachfront does have several three- and four-star accommodations. Along the beach and on the main road are many restaurants, bars, Internet cafés, and dive operators. **Amenities:** food and drink; showers; toilets; water sports. **Best for:** sunset; swimming; walking. ⊕ *Second beach to right of Lanta's main road from port town Saladan.*

Restaurants

KLONG DAO

Fat Monkey (Ling Uan)

$$ | **EUROPEAN** | Two kitchens, and two cuisines—Thai and Western. Fat Monkey serves an extensive range of Thai dishes but is best known and loved for its large, juicy burgers. **Known for:** juicy burgers; ice-cream cocktails; chilled atmosphere. *$ Average main: B200 ✉ Klong Dao Rd., Saladan ⊕ Center of Klong Dao Beach ☎ 087/886–5017 ▭ No credit cards ⊙ Closed Mon.*

★ Time for Lime

$$ | **THAI** | Time for Lime is a large, open-air kitchen-restaurant right off the beach, where you can learn to cook fresh, seasonal, and creative Thai food (with Chinese, Malaysian, and Indian twists), under fun, expert instruction. Their excellent classes include a valuable theoretical introduction to Thai food and a five-hour option, during which you will prepare, and learn to beautifully present, your own feast. **Known for:** cooking classes; animal charity support; changing menus. *$ Average main: B200 ✉ 72/2 Klong Dao Beach, Lanta Yai, Saladan ☎ 075/684590, 089/967–5017 ⊕ www.timeforlime.net ▭ No credit cards.*

OLD TOWN

Caoutchouc

$ | **THAI** | At the end of a small dirt road, and barely above sea level, is Caoutchouc, run by its French owner and his chef partner. The café-restaurant is in a wooden, traditional house with high ceilings from which colorful Chinese lanterns hang, swaying in the sea breeze. **Known for:** sea gypsy chef; in-season fare; traditional setting. *$ Average main:*

B145 ✉ Moo 1, Old Town ☎ 075/697060, 084/629–0704 ▭ No credit cards.

Shanti Shanti

$ | **FRENCH** | This large beach hut stands on the sand looking out to the ocean, and serves crepes with homemade French jam, cocktails, ice cream, and coffees to accompany the lovely view, as well as having a small shop selling clothes and accessories. Owner Fafa is a young French artist (his works decorate the café and are on sale) who traveled broadly in India before settling in Koh Lanta, where he creates decorative pieces made from things he finds in his natural environment. **Known for:** homemade jam; arty souvenirs; unique ice-creams. *$ Average main: B150 ✉ Klong Nin, Old Town ☎ 083/748–9527 ▭ No credit cards ⏲ Closed Tues.*

PHRA AE

★ Cook Kai

$ | **THAI** | From the outside, this place appears to be a standard, wooden Thai beach restaurant, but the creative cooking elevates it out of the ordinary. Sizzling "hotpan" dishes of seafood in coconut cream, stir-fried morning glory, and sweet-and-sour shrimp are succulent. **Known for:** creative cooking; sizzling seafood; extensive menu. *$ Average main: B115 ✉ Moo 6, Klong Nin Beach ☎ 081/606–3015 🌐 www.cook-kai.com ▭ No credit cards.*

Lap Royet

$ | **THAI** | Thai street food is a class of its own, and you will find it absolutely everywhere you turn, though some eateries are definitely more refined than others. This extremely casual roadside restaurant serves 100% authentic, basic, and cheap food that locals seem to relish. **Known for:** superb street food; Isaan catfish; casual setting. *$ Average main: B50 ✉ Klong Dao Rd. ✣ Toward northern end of Klong Dao Beach ☎ No phone ▭ No credit cards.*

The Red Snapper

$$ | **THAI** | Serving Thai and European fusion food in an atmospheric garden setting, with a compact menu that creative chef Ed Qarré renews every six weeks, Red Snapper, unsurprisingly, has become one of the island's most happening restaurants. If you're hungry order one of their large platters, or opt for a wonderful selection of tapas dishes if your palate is yearning for adventure; the eponymous red snapper is always succulent and fresh. **Known for:** garden setting; succulent red snapper; inspired cocktails. *$ Average main: B250 ✉ 176 Moo 2 ☎ 078/856965 🌐 www.redsnapper-lanta.com ▭ No credit cards.*

Tides

$$ | **THAI** | This high-profile restaurant in Layana Resort and Spa welcomes outside visitors for a romantic and sophisticated dinner. Set on a polished seafront terrace, Tides serves specials of the day such as grilled giant prawns, as well as more traditional Thai dishes like green curry, and a selection of international classics with a sophisticated spin. **Known for:** giant grilled prawns; sophisticated setting; excellent wine list. *$ Average main: B250 ✉ 272 Moo 3, Saladan, Phra Ae Beach ☎ 075/607100 🌐 www.layanaresort.com ▭ No credit cards.*

KLONG NIN

★ Otto Bar & Grill

$ | **INTERNATIONAL** | This is one of the most popular old-time bars in Koh Lanta, mostly owing to its vibrant owner, Otto, a been-there, done-that, mature rocker-hippie whose joie de vivre remains charmingly intact. The bar and grill stands right on the beach and is open all day, serving delicious cocktails made with exotic fruits, and a variety of barbecued meats (burgers have a following) and salads, made by its British chef. **Known for:** rocker-hippie owner; beachside location; superb burgers. *$ Average main: B130 ✉ Klong Nin Beach ▭ No credit cards.*

Roi Thai

$ | **INTERNATIONAL** | With tables facing out to the horizon, and fresh, flavorsome seafood and fish barbecues, this is an idyllic beach dinner location. The simple yet charming restaurant prides itself on its fresh ingredients, quality meats, and authentic dishes prepared without the addition of MSG or other flavor enhancers (that are unfortunately used all too often in Thailand today). **Known for:** beach setting; cooking classes; laidback vibe. *Average main: B100 ✉ 75/1 Moo 6, Klong Nin Beach ☎ 083/636–0470 No credit cards.*

SOUTHERN LANTA

Drunken Sailors

$ | **AMERICAN** | **FAMILY** | Drunken Sailors is a friendly, laid-back meeting point for tech-savvy travelers (free Wi-Fi), young families, trendy locals, and expats. The Thai-American owners effortlessly create a sense of ease; beanbags and hammocks that are occupied throughout the day attest to this. **Known for:** chilled vibe; backpacker popularity; tuna wasabi subs. *Average main: B100 ✉ 116 Moo 5, Koh Lanta Yai, Kantiang Bay ☎ 075/665076 No credit cards.*

Phad Thai Rock n' Roll

$ | **THAI** | Everything is in the name at this tiny roadside eatery, where you can try fresh, authentic, and delicious pad Thai made with shrimp, chicken, vegetables, or all of the above, by the talented rock musician–owner. Meet musicians, sip a delicious, healthy, and creative smoothie, and watch the world go by. **Known for:** authentic pad Thai; musician owner; regular gigs. *Average main: B70 ✉ 92 Moo 5, Kantiang Bay ☎ 080/784–8729 No credit cards.*

Hotels

KLONG DAO

Costa Lanta

$$$ | **RESORT** | The coolest thing about Costa Lanta is the room design; each room at this trendy boutique resort is a convertible box, so if you're too hot you can open up the "walls" and allow the breeze to blow through. **Pros:** quiet, green location; art deco design; innovative housing. **Cons:** not great value; not on best beach. *Rooms from: B4,250 ✉ 212 Klong Dao Beach, Lanta Yai ☎ 075/618092, 075/668186 www.costalanta.com 22 rooms Free breakfast.*

Southern Lanta

$ | **RESORT** | **FAMILY** | With a fun slide plunging into a big pool and several two-bedroom villas (each with large multibed rooms), Southern Lanta is understandably popular with families. **Pros:** family-friendly; good location; pleasant restaurant. **Cons:** needs redecoration; pool crowds easily; limited views. *Rooms from: B1,000 ✉ 105 Klong Dao Beach, Lanta Yai ☎ 075/684175 up to 77 www.southernlanta.com 100 bungalows Free breakfast.*

Twin Lotus Resort and Spa

$$$ | **RESORT** | This resort is as much an architectural and interior-design exhibition as it is a sophisticated and tranquil retreat. **Pros:** quality dining; appealing in-room facilities; stunning location. **Cons:** may be too quiet for families; service can be slack. *Rooms from: B4,200 ✉ 199 Moo 1, Klong Dao Beach, Koh Lanta Yai ☎ 075/560–7000, 02/361–1946 up to 49 in Bangkok www.twinlotusresort.com 81 rooms No meals.*

PHRA AE

Best House

$ | **B&B/INN** | The Best House lobby, an inviting high-ceilinged room with comfortable chairs, white tile floors, and wooden beams, offers a good sense of what you can expect from the accommodations. **Pros:** inexpensive; near the beach; friendly service. **Cons:** rooms are basic; no pool; no in-room amenities. *Rooms from: B1,000 ✉ 5/1 Moo 3, Phra Ae Beach, Lanta Yai ☎ 075/684560, 084/464–1500* www.besthouselantaguesthouse.com No credit cards Closed Apr.–Oct. 30 rooms No meals.

Lanta Sand Resort and Spa

$ | RESORT | Large ponds with water lilies and spraying fountains cover the grounds of Lanta Sand Resort and Spa. Aged-brick paths meander from villa to pool to spa, where aromatic candles burn, illuminating Thai silk tapestries. **Pros:** spacious rooms; romantic; near beach. **Cons:** far from any town; noisy air-conditioning in some rooms; prices too high for what's on offer. *Rooms from: B1,750* *279 Moo 3, Phra Ae Beach, Lanta Yai* *075/684633, 089/724–2682* *www.lantasand.com* *78 rooms* *No meals.*

★ Layana Resort and Spa

$$$$ | RESORT | Guests repeatedly return to the Layana for a real sense of pampering, understated luxury, and a relaxed, peaceful environment. **Pros:** varied breakfast buffet includes healthy juice bar; many activities organized in-house; lovely beach. **Cons:** strictly no children; some bungalows lack sea views; not for party animals. *Rooms from: B7,500* *272 Moo 3, Saladan, Phra Ae Beach, Koh Lanta* *075/607100, 02/713–2313 in Bangkok* *www.layanaresort.com* *50 rooms* *Free breakfast.*

Nakara Long Beach Resort

$$ | RESORT | If you're staying in a resort on a beautiful, white-sand beach with crystal-clear, blue water, you should treat yourself to a room with a view. **Pros:** friendly staff; great views. **Cons:** bland design; free Wi-Fi only in lobby. *Rooms from: B3,700* *172 Moo 3, Phra Ae Beach, Saladan* *075/684198* *www.lantalongbeach.com* *41 cottages* *Free breakfast.*

Somewhere Else

$ | B&B/INN | FAMILY | If you like your huts to be of progressive design, go Somewhere Else—the six octagonal rooms in the front of the clearing are particularly cool, with fold-down windows, wooden floors, and loose-pebble bathroom floors. **Pros:** very friendly and helpful staff; wonderful beach location; nice restaurant. **Cons:** no hot water; no TV. *Rooms from: B900* *253 Moo 3, Phra Ae Beach, Lanta Yai* *091/536–0858, 089/731–1312* *No credit cards* *Closed June–Sept.* *16 rooms* *No meals.*

KLONG NIN

Lanta Miami Resort

$ | B&B/INN | The affordable, beachside bungalows at the Lanta Miami are clean, spacious, and with big beds, and have nicely sized, tiled bathrooms. **Pros:** great location; comfortable; nice pool. **Cons:** some rooms lack hot water; staff can be unaccommodating; rooms without sea views are a bit stuffy. *Rooms from: B1,000* *13 Moo 6, Klong Nin Beach, Lanta Yai* *075/662559* *No credit cards* *Closed June–Sept.* *26 rooms* *Free breakfast.*

Lanta Paradise Beach Resort

$ | RESORT | It's a short walk along the beach to the best swimming spot, but the sand gets so hot you'll be glad to have the pool outside your room. **Pros:** prime location; impressive Western food at restaurant; nice views. **Cons:** not the best value; very basic rooms; lack of amenities. *Rooms from: B1,100* *67 Moo 6, Klong Nin Beach, Lanta Yai* *075/662569, 089/473–3279* *www.lantaparadisebeachresort.com* *No credit cards* *Closed June–Sept.* *34 rooms* *Free breakfast.*

Rawi Warin Resort and Spa

$$ | RESORT | FAMILY | This enormous, lively resort with luxuriously outfitted rooms and high-tech amenities stretches gracefully across an entire hillside along the road from Klong Khong Beach to Klong Nin. The resort features, among many other things, a 24-seat minitheater, a music room, a video game room, a dive shop, and a beautiful private beach. **Pros:** many amenities; helpful staff; family-friendly. **Cons:** not great value;

beach is rocky; activities are limited. *Rooms from: B4,000* ✉ *139 Moo 8, Lanta Yai Island, Krabi* ☎ *026/643490 up to 48, 02/434–5526 in Bangkok* 🌐 *www.rawiwarin.com* *185 rooms* *Free breakfast.*

SriLanta

$$ | **RESORT** | One of the first upscale resorts in the area to market the "less is more" philosophy, SriLanta remains an island getaway for edgy urbanites. **Pros:** great in-room amenities; yoga classes; nice pool. **Cons:** staff a bit standoffish; attention to detail is slack; no sea views. *Rooms from: B2,200* ✉ *111 Moo 6, Klong Nin Beach, Lanta Yai* ☎ *075/697288* 🌐 *www.srilanta.com* *49 rooms, 3 suites.*

SOUTHERN LANTA

Mango House

$$ | **HOTEL** | In the laid-back and increasingly trendy Old Town, or Sri Raya, Mango House is a home away from home, with three seafront suites and three villas, all in Chinese-style wooden houses that stand on stilts over the water. **Pros:** welcoming atmosphere; comfortable rooms; a great base for exploring the Old Town. **Cons:** private property next to rooms is shabby; no air-conditioning. *Rooms from: B2,500* ✉ *45 Sriraya Rd., Moo 2, Old Town* ☎ *089/948–6836* 🌐 *www.mangohouses.com* *No credit cards* *6 rooms.*

Narima Bungalow Resort

$$ | **B&B/INN** | With almost all its bungalows overlooking a refreshing view of Koh Ha and with relaxing balconies where you can sway in a hammock or kick back in a palm-straw rocking chair, Narima definitely generates a sense of calm. **Pros:** spanning views; pleasant hosts; professional dive school. **Cons:** rocky beach; bathrooms are rough around the edges; restaurant could be better. *Rooms from: B3,937* ✉ *98 Moo 5, Klong Nin Beach, Lanta Yai* ☎ *075/662668, 075/662670* 🌐 *www.narima-lanta.com* *32 rooms.*

★ Pimalai Resort and Spa

$$$$ | **RESORT** | Pimalai's mantra is "peace, serenity, and solitude," explaining why royalty and celebrities regularly favor the elegant resort, which offers seductive yet unpretentious luxury in a place where the rain forest meets the sea, fronting a stunning beach. **Pros:** gorgeous Andaman beach with crystal-clear water; beautiful location and architecture; friendly, helpful management and staff; uniquely luxurious setting. **Cons:** prices also exclusive; fills up fast. *Rooms from: B7,000* ✉ *99 Moo 5, Bakantiang Beach, Lanta Yai* ☎ *075/607999* 🌐 *www.pimalai.com* *72 rooms, 7 suites, 40 private villas* *No meals.*

Nightlife

Bob Bar

$ | **BARS/PUBS** | A living tribute to reggae, colorful owner Bob welcomes his adoring clientele with a big smile, cold beer, and friendly banter in this laid-back, popular bar. ✉ *Klong Dao, Ban Koh Lanta.*

The Frog Wine Cellar and Restaurant

$ | **BARS/PUBS** | In Saladan port town near the pier, this wine bar with an atmospheric garden setting offers a nice change of scene for those interested in sampling wines and accompanying appetizers. They have labels from 12 countries. ✉ *295/19 Moo 3, Klong Dao Beach* 🌐 *www.thefroglanta.com.*

Funky Monkey

$ | **BARS/PUBS** | Designed to look like the inside of a jungle, this roadside bar-club is the venue for live gigs that get locals, expats, and tourists dancing together until the late hours. Outside, benches offer respite from blaring music and a place to snack from nearby street food stalls. Not as fun on nights when there isn't a live performance. ✉ *Klong Dao Rd., Koh Lanta.*

Did You Know?

Koh Phi Phi is actually six islands, though only the largest, Phi Phi Don, is inhabited. Phi Phi Leh is home to the famous Maya Bay; the other islands are really just large limestone outcroppings.

Activities

Diving, snorkeling, hiking, and elephant trekking are a few activities available on Koh Lanta and the nearby islands.

Diving Koh Lanta

DIVING/SNORKELING | Diving and snorkeling activities are available on Koh Lanta and the nearby islands. Trips can be arranged through dive and tour operators, though most people choose to book through their own resort. Popular nearby dive sites are **Koh Ha** and **Koh Rok,** off Koh Lanta. ✉ *Koh Lanta.*

Emerald Cave

BOAT TOURS | A boat trip to the famous **Emerald Cave** on **Koh Mook** is a worthwhile experience. Swim and snorkel through a dark water cave to an idyllic lagoon, though get here early to avoid the flotilla of boats taking others to do the same thing. ✉ *Koh Lanta.*

Koh Phi Phi

48 km (30 miles) or 90 mins by boat southeast of Phuket Town, 42 km (26 miles) or 2 hrs by boat southwest of Krabi.

The Phi Phi Islands consist of six islands. The largest, Phi Phi Don, is shaped like a butterfly: the "wings," covered by limestone mountains, are connected by a flat 2-km (1-mile) narrow body featuring two opposing sandy beaches. Phi Phi Don is the only inhabited island.

The islands of Koh Phi Phi were once idyllic retreats, with secret silver-sand coves, unspoiled stretches of shoreline, and limestone cliffs dropping precipitously into the sea. After it was portrayed in the film *The Beach* (2000), Phi Phi became a hot (overcrowded) property. The beaches on Phi Phi are still stunning and are some of the most accessible in Thailand, though the famed Maya Bay is closed to tourists from time to time to allow it to recover from the crowds. Luxury resorts have spread themselves across the sands here and a multitude of restaurants, bars, and smaller guesthouses fill the demand for lodging. Many of the budget accommodations that dominated the island for years have upgraded their facilities (and their prices) in a hit-and-miss process of development—some have achieved grandeur, or class, others are tacky and overpriced for what they offer. It appears that unchecked development is the norm. The buildings are creeping higher each year, and the resorts have generally become more high-end; but beware, the terms *resort* and *deluxe* are used liberally, so do not rely too much on impressions created by artful photographs in websites.

The tsunami of 2004 has not had any lasting impact and, if you were unaware that such a catastrophe had taken place, you would think it was a beautiful island under a lot of development, rather than one that was destroyed and has been rebuilt. The popularity of the Phi Phi Islands stems from the outstanding scuba diving; leopard sharks, turtles, and seahorses are some species still frequenting popular reefs.

As Phi Phi becomes more developed, people have been forced away from the center of Ao Dalerm Beach. Other beaches have been discovered and now bear the brunt of growing tourist numbers on the island. Long Beach has become popular but still retains its charm.

GETTING HERE AND AROUND

Ferries depart from Ratsada Pier on Phuket five times daily and reach Phi Phi Don two hours later. PP Cruiser also takes two hours to reach Phi Phi Don, but departs from Phuket's Makham Pier. A one-way ticket is B650, and a round-trip ticket is B1,000. Ferries traveling to Phuket from Ao Nang or Koh Lanta stop at Koh Phi Phi in the high season (November to April) as well. From Krabi, boats depart four times each day and

Tsunami Memorials

On the eastern end of Loh Dalam Beach is the Phi Phi Tsunami Memorial Park, a tiny garden with a small plaque listing some of the names of those who lost their lives in the 2004 tsunami. Several benches have been dedicated to the memory of others lost in the disaster. The memorial is a little sad, because it seems so small in relation to the devastation that claimed 5,395 lives. Regardless, it is a nice little park, and looking out across the beach and sea, one cannot help but be moved.

Another memorial, this one underwater, is 66 feet deep, off the coast of Monkey Beach. The granite memorial consists of three pyramid-shaped plaques arranged in the shape of an equilateral triangle; the plaques are the exact number of centimeters apart as the number of victims taken by the sea. The bases of the pyramids contain philosophical quotations, and the three markers symbolize the elements of land, water, and air in which humans must learn to live in balance. In the center of the triangle rests a single granite stand that describes the tsunami's occurrence. In addition, 2,874 (the number of missing persons) centimeters from the memorial is a traditional Thai sala made from tsunami debris. It is the first underwater memorial monument on Earth.

cost B650. A few years ago local authorities implemented a B20 "clean up" tax, collected upon arrival at the dock. It's not clear, however, how this money is being used, as there have been no immediately apparent improvements to the island's environment.

Beaches

Laem Tong Beach

BEACH—SIGHT | Accessible by boat only, Laem Tong Beach is more secluded than some of the other Phi Phi beaches. The turquoise waters are warm and the beach is bordered by jungle. All this gives Laem Tong more of a tropical-island-paradise feel than other busier Phi Phi beaches. Perfect for couples who want an intimate and romantic location. ■ **TIP→ Local fishermen can bring you here and take you to other nearby destinations on their longtail boats for less money than organized trips.** **Amenities:** food and drink; toilets. **Best for:** snorkeling; sunrise; swimming. ✉ *Northern Phi Phi.*

Loh Dalum Beach

BEACH—SIGHT | On the other side of the Phi Phi Don Island from Tonsai Village, Loh Dalum has all the hallmarks of a tropical paradise: clear emerald waters, views onto the beautiful bay, white sandy beach. Nevertheless, it is touristy, busy, and noisy—an unfortunate symptom of Phi Phi's popularity. Beach bars put on spectacular fire shows at night, and the partying lasts well into the early hours. Swimming is best at high tide. **Amenities:** food and drink; showers; toilets; water sports. **Best for:** partiers; swimming. ✉ *Koh Phi Phi Don.*

Long Beach

BEACH—SIGHT | Long Beach, a few minutes' longtail boat ride from Tonsai, affords visitors a calmer and more relaxing experience away from the madding crowds. The white sands are almost silky underfoot and there are gorgeous views of Phi Phi Leh. Day-trippers often only stay for a dip and lunch, so the rest of the time it's pretty peaceful. **Amenities:** food and drink; toilets. **Best for:**

Longtail Day Trips

A popular day trip from Phi Phi Don is a visit to nearby Phi Phi Lae via longtail or speedboat. The first stop is Viking Cave, a vast cavern of limestone pillars covered with crude drawings. Most boats continue on for an afternoon in **Maya Bay,** aka "The Beach" (though note the government has taken to closing Maya Bay periodically to allow the area's nature to recover from mass tourism). If you don't mind throngs of crowds (the snorkelers practically outnumber the fish), Maya Bay is a spectacular site. If you get a really early jump on everyone, cruise into a bay and leave first tracks along the powdery sand beach; otherwise, head to **Loh Samah Bay,** on the opposite side of the island. Loh Samah Bay may, in fact, be the better option. Though smaller, it is as beautiful as Maya Bay but receives less attention. Alternatively, you can take a 45-minute trip by longtail boat to circular **Bamboo Island**, with a superb beach around it. The underwater colors of the fish and the coral are brilliant

snorkeling; swimming. ✉ *Long Beach, Koh Phi Phi.*

Tonsai Beach

BEACH—SIGHT | This is not a place for the fainthearted; it is crowded, noisy, and not the cleanest. The best time to visit is in the early morning when most of the young revelers are sleeping off the excesses of the previous night. **Amenities:** showers; toilets; water sports. **Best for:** partiers. ✉ *Ton Sai, Koh Phi Phi.*

Restaurants

Chao Koh Restaurant

$$ | **SEAFOOD** | As you stroll Tonsai's walking path, you'll surely notice the catch of the day on display in front of Chao Koh Restaurant (opposite the Chao Koh Resort). Kingfish, swordfish, and barracuda, grilled with garlic and butter, white wine, or marsala sauce, and served with rice or a baked potato, is a mere B250. **Known for:** grilled barracuda; popular with day-trippers; seafood display. *$ Average main: B230* ✉ *Tongsai Bay* ☎ *075/620800* ▭ *No credit cards.*

Ciao Bella

$ | **ITALIAN** | It's hardly a local haunt in Napoli or Rome, but for Phi Phi, this offers a tasty rendition of basic Italian cuisine to be enjoyed in a candlelighted seaside setting under the moon. Their pizza and focaccia comes from a wood-fired oven, and inventive pasta dishes and classic appetizers such as bruschetta, caprese salad, and prosciutto di Parma round out the menu. **Known for:** simple Italian cuisine; candlelit setting; wood-fired oven. *$ Average main: B145* ✉ *9 Koh Phi Phi Muu, Loh Dalum Beach* ☎ *081/894–1246* ▭ *No credit cards.*

Hippies Bar

$$ | **MIDDLE EASTERN** | On the eastern end of Tonsai Beach, Hippies serves a mixture of international food, from burgers and steaks to pasta and pizza. The staff at both the restaurant and seaside bar are friendly. **Known for:** international cuisine; beach views. *$ Average main: B200* ✉ *Tonsai Beach* ▭ *No credit cards.*

Phi Phi Bakery

$ | **CAFÉ** | Craving fresh-baked doughnuts, Danish, croissants, mouthwatering eggs Benedict, porridge, or real coffee rather than the vile instant stuff? Check out the family-run Phi Phi Bakery, which serves American, continental, and Thai breakfast and brunch specials and freshly baked pastries (the cinnamon buns are especially good). **Known for:** fresh baked goods; Thai brunch specials; family atmosphere. *$ Average main: B150 ✉ 97 Moo 7, Tonsai Village ☎ 075/601017 ▭ No credit cards.*

Hotels

Arayaburi Resort

$$ | **RESORT** | The rooms here are modern and clean, and all have tile floors, which keeps the resort looking fresh. **Pros:** private beach; quiet away from the noise of Tonsai; great views out to sea. **Cons:** sometimes slippery access when it rains. *$ Rooms from: B2,200 ✉ 69 Laem Hin Beach ☎ 076/281360 🌐 www.arayaburi-phiphi.com 38 rooms No meals.*

Bay View Resort

$$ | **RESORT** | Every bungalow here has a large deck with a great view of both Phi Phi Lae and Tonsai Bay. The rooms are old with hardwood floors. **Pros:** quiet location; great views; breakfast included. **Cons:** removed from main village; not on best beach. *$ Rooms from: B2,200 ✉ 69 Laem Hin Beach ☎ 076/281360 up to 64 🌐 www.phiphibayview.com 109 bungalows Free breakfast.*

Chao Koh Phi Phi Lodge

$ | **B&B/INN** | Chao Koh Phi Phi Lodge is a collection of unfortunately lime-green, basic but comfortable bungalows near Tonsai Bay. There's a great swimming pool, and the resort features family-size suites. **Pros:** budget accommodations; short walk from the beach; nice pool. **Cons:** bungalows have gaudy exteriors; very basic standards; somewhat pricey for what you get. *$ Rooms from: B1,760 ✉ Tonsai Bay ☎ 075/620800 🌐 www.chaokohresort.com 44 bungalows Free breakfast.*

★ Holiday Inn Resort

$$ | **RESORT** | The Holiday Inn couldn't have a better location—it's on more than 50 acres of tropical gardens along a beach with only three other resorts, which has gorgeous blue water with a sandy sea floor, where you can swim and snorkel year-round. **Pros:** secluded, private beach; attentive staff. **Cons:** set away from the main part of Koh Phi Phi. *$ Rooms from: B3,600 ✉ Laem Tong Beach ☎ 075/627300 🌐 www.phiphi.holidayinn.com 130 bungalows Free breakfast.*

Paradise Resort

$ | **RESORT** | Despite having undergone renovations and pushing up its prices, this place continues to offer great value for money. **Pros:** budget rooms in idyllic location; clean rooms; great beach massage service. **Cons:** some rooms lack air-conditioning; Wi-Fi at extra charge; may be too quiet for some. *$ Rooms from: B1,700 ✉ Long Beach ☎ 091/968–3982 up to 89 🌐 www.paradiseresort.co.th ▭ No credit cards 25 rooms No meals.*

P. P. Erawan Palms Resort

$$ | **RESORT** | Erawan Palm is a small, comfortable resort in the middle of Laem Tong Beach, next to the sea gypsy village. **Pros:** relaxed resort feel; interesting museum; nice location. **Cons:** boat ride away from main village; decor shows some age. *$ Rooms from: B3,100 ✉ Moo 8, Laem Tong Beach ☎ 075/627500 🌐 www.pperawanpalms.com 18 cottages No meals.*

Phi Phi Island Village Beach Resort

$$$ | **RESORT** | **FAMILY** | At this resort you'll find breezily spacious, thatch-roofed bungalows with sharp, bright, contemporary interiors. **Pros:** stunning location; luxurious pool area; isolation and peace. **Cons:** a little remote; how you get there depends on the tide; staff can be a little lax. *$ Rooms from: B5,000 ✉ 49 Moo 8, Loh Bagao Bay ☎ 075/628900 🌐 www.phiphiislandvillage.com ▭ No credit*

cards ⇆ *144 bungalows, 12 villas* 🍴 *Free breakfast.*

Phi Phi Natural Resort

$$ | **RESORT** | Beautiful sunrise views from the seaside bungalows are this resort's biggest draw. **Pros:** daily boat service to Phuket and Krabi; lovely views at moderate prices. **Cons:** lacks amenities compared to other resorts in price range; remote; can get too busy. $ *Rooms from: B2,200* ✉ *53 Moo 8, Laem Tong Beach* ☎ *075/613000* 🌐 *www.phiphinatural.com* ⇆ *70 rooms* 🍴 *Free breakfast.*

Phi Phi ViewPoint Resort

$ | **RESORT** | On the western hillside overlooking Loh Dalam Bay, Phi Phi ViewPoint Resort was the sole survivor of the 2004 tsunami that devastated the resorts on this beautiful beach. **Pros:** good location overlooking bay. **Cons:** some huts are basic for the price. $ *Rooms from: B1,900* ✉ *107 Loh Dalam Bay* ☎ *075/618111* 🌐 *www.phiphiviewpoint.com* ⇆ *54 huts, 1 suite.*

Phi Phi Villa Resort

$$ | **RESORT** | Large thatch-covered huts in a natural setting give Phi Phi Villa a relaxing island feeling quite different from bustling Tonsai Bay, a short walk away. **Pros:** budget prices; close to the action; yoga. **Cons:** noise from nearby bars; rocky beach not great for swimming. $ *Rooms from: B2,200* ✉ *Tonsai Bay* ☎ *075/601100* 🌐 *www.phiphivillaresort.com* ⇆ *55 bungalows* 🍴 *Free breakfast.*

★ Zeavola

$$$$ | **RESORT** | This resort takes its name from a flower, the name of which translates in Thai to "love of the sea," which certainly is fitting, as the water off the powdery white-sand Laem Tong Beach is simply stunning. **Pros:** stunning beach location; tasteful design; private. **Cons:** doubled service charge on food. $ *Rooms from: B8,600* ✉ *11 Moo 8, Laem Tong, Koh Phi Phi* ☎ *075/627000* 🌐 *www.zeavola.com* ⇆ *52 villas* 🍴 *Free breakfast.*

Nightlife

Many people come to Phi Phi for two reasons only: to go to Maya Bay during the day, and to party in Tonsai Bay at night. Once you head down the side streets away from the beach there are mazes of bars and clubs competing in stereo wars, filled with young travelers eager to drink and dance the night away. If you like Khao San Road in Bangkok, you will love Tonsai Bay at night. The most popular of these bars, located near the 7-Eleven in the center of "town," is **Reggae Bar.** Along the path running parallel to the sea there are several popular bars, notably **Apache Bar,** which has an impressive "katoey" (drag cabaret) show, and farther to the east are fire shows at the popular beach spot **Hippies Bar.**

Reggae Bar

BARS/PUBS | The boxing ring in the center of the bar draws crowds, eager for some muay Thai action. There are five bars dotted around the complex, keen staff, and a wild atmosphere. The fun gets started when the audience is invited to fight one another in the ring. ✉ *Tonsai Bay.*

Slinky Beach Bar

BARS/PUBS | If you're young, restless, and like to party all night, Slinky is for you. It gathers the wild crowd and regularly hosts theme parties and fire shows. It doesn't get more rowdy and crowded than this on Koh Phi Phi. ✉ *Loh Dalum Bay.*

Sunflower Bar

BARS/PUBS | More-remote beaches around the island have more subdued nightlife, primarily centered on resort restaurants and bars. One of the best of these is Sunflower Bar, which is on the eastern end of Loh Dalam Beach, next to the Tsunami Memorial Park. Constructed almost entirely of driftwood or old wooden bungalows, this laid-back beach bar is a great place to enjoy scenic sea views and listen to local reggae bands jamming beneath the stars. ✉ *Loh Dalum Bay.*

Chapter 7

CHIANG MAI

Updated by
Sophie Friedman

Sights ★★★★☆ | Restaurants ★★★★☆ | Hotels ★★★★☆ | Shopping ★★★★☆ | Nightlife ★★★☆☆

WELCOME TO CHIANG MAI

TOP REASONS TO GO

★ **History:** Two excellent museums chronicle Chiang Mai's history, which is vividly on display in the architecture of the Old City.

★ **Temples and Monastery Gardens:** The Old City alone has more than 30 ancient temples, where monks are happy to chat with visitors about the principles of Buddhism and their not-so cloistered lives.

★ **Local Eating:** Chiang Mai's restaurants and street stalls serve the full range of northern Thai cuisine and dishes often cost no more than three dollars.

★ **Views for Miles:** Chiang Mai allows easy access to spectacular mountain scenery, crisscrossed by trekking trails that lead to remote hill tribe villages where visitors are welcome guests. The mountainous region north of the city beckons adventure seekers with actvities like white-water rafting, waterfall swimming, and rock climbing.

Modern Chiang Mai is expanding on all sides, but the Old City is relatively compact. First-time visitors would do well to find accommodations within this square mile of busy roads and quiet lanes containing reminders of the eight centuries Chiang Mai served as a citadel and bulwark against invasion from Burma. A stroll through the backstreets and lanes—known as sois—is one of the top pleasures of a visit. Two ring roads with underpasses keep traffic flowing around the city center.

1 The Old City. An 800-year-old moat surrounds the Old City. Much of the wall that once encircled the city has been restored, and the most important of its five original gates, called Thapae, fronts a broad square where markets and festivals are constantly in full swing. Most of Chiang Mai's principal attractions, including its oldest temples, lie within this square mile and are easily accessible on foot.

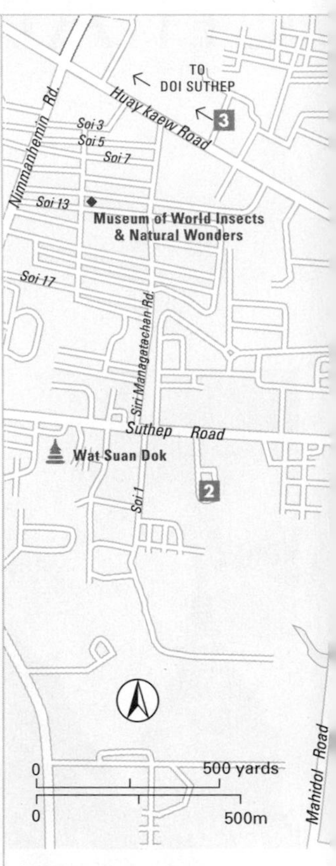

2 Beyond the Old City. The Old City's compact size means that most of Chiang Mai's hotels, guesthouses, restaurants, and commercial premises are located in the areas beyond the moat. Some of the city's liveliest spots are beyond the walls and worth the visit.

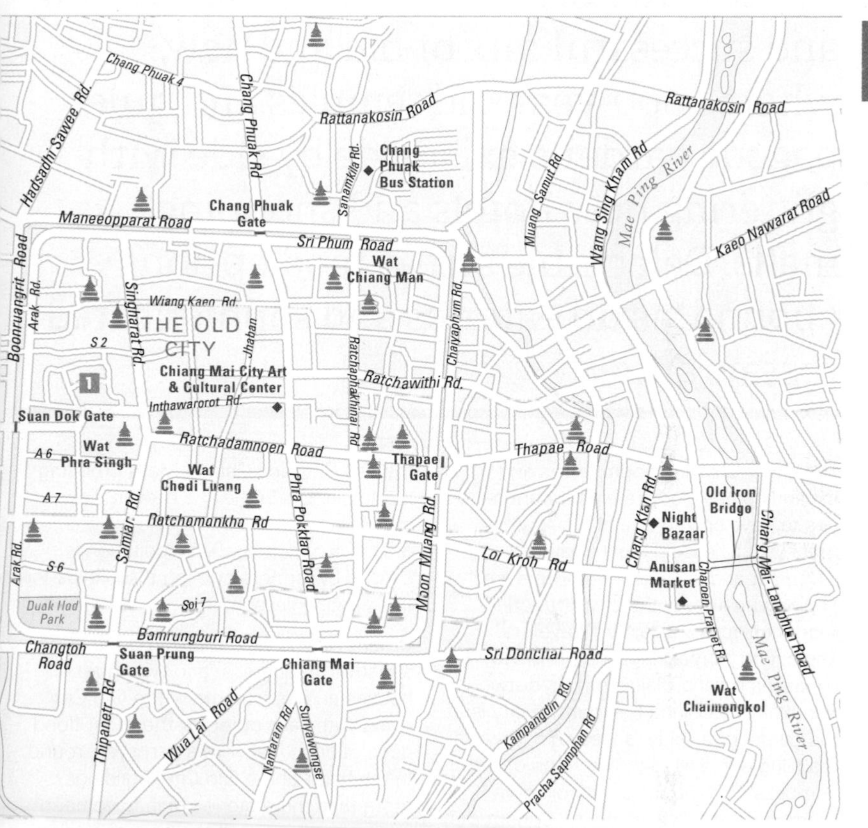

3 Greater Chiang Mai. Two ring roads and a "Super Highway" allow easy access to the rapidly growing residential suburbs and to the mountains that rise east, west, and north of the city. Day trips to the mountains, including Thailand's highest peak, Doi Inthanon, or the city's "guardian mountain," Doi Suthep, can include an action-packed program of elephant washing, white-water rafting, and brief jungle hikes and still leave time for a leisurely evening back in Chiang Mai.

Cosmopolitan Chiang Mai, Thailand's second city, is regarded by many as its rightful, historic capital. It's a fascinating and successful mix of old and new, where 1,000-year-old temples and quiet pagoda gardens exist side by side with glittering new hotels and shopping malls. Delectable street food options abound, as do eateries and sophisticated restaurants.

The city is enjoying boom times and expanding at a giddy rate as it continues to develop into one of Thailand's must-visit cities and a gateway to Myanmar and Laos. Luxury hotels are popping up all over the city, attracting more business and leisure travelers. The country's main highway, Highway 1, bypasses Chiang Mai as it runs between Bangkok and Chiang Rai, but the city is at the center of a spider's web of highways reaching out in all four directions of the compass, with no major city or town more than a day's drive away. Construction on a high-speed rail link with Bangkok begins in 2020, reducing the current 696-km (430-mile), 12-hour journey to less than 4 hours.

First impressions of modern Chiang Mai can be disappointing. The immaculately maintained railroad station and the chaotic bus terminal are in so-so areas, and the drive into the city center is not all that scenic. First-time visitors ask why they can't see the mountains that figure so prominently in the travel brochures. But once you cross the Ping River, Chiang Mai begins to take shape. Enter the Old City, and Chiang Mai's brooding mountain, Doi Suthep, is now in view—except when shrouded in the month of March, when heavy air pollution is caused by farmers burning their fields for the planting season.

Whenever you visit, there's bound to be a festival in progress, and with guesthouses and restaurants in the Old City vying with each other for the most florid decoration, it feels like a party year-round. In the heart of the Old City, buildings more than three stories high have been banned, and many of the streets and sois have been paved with flat, red cobblestones. Strolling these narrow lanes, lingering in the quiet cloisters of a temple, sipping hill tribe coffee at a wayside stall, and fingering local fabrics in one of the many boutiques are among the chief pleasures of a visit to Chiang Mai.

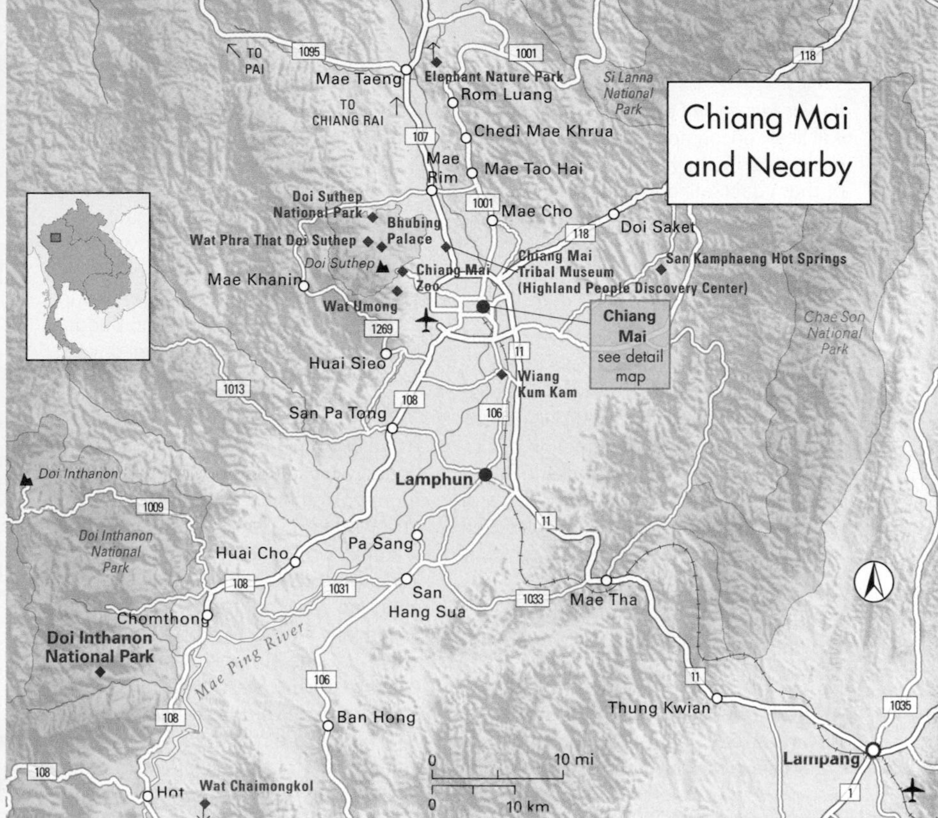

Planning

WHEN TO GO

The best time to visit is during the dry season between November and February, when days are pleasantly sunny and evenings refreshingly cool. From March to June the weather can be uncomfortably hot, and pollution is heavy in March and April. From July to October the monsoon rains drench the city. ■ **TIP→ Pollution has become so bad that travelers with breathing problems are advised to avoid the city in March and April, the hottest months of the year, and should check pollution levels before coming in other months.**

PLANNING YOUR TIME

Most visitors come to Chiang Mai for only a few days, so to sample all the city has to offer, your itinerary will be jam-packed. Be sure to allow a day for exploring the surrounding countryside.

FESTIVALS AND ANNUAL EVENTS

April sees Thailand's New Year, Songkran, known for its water festivals, which can offer a refreshing opportunity to cool off in the scorching heat. Book accommodation months in advance for Songkran and expect to pay high-season rates. Songkran is wild and fun, but Loy Kratong in November, a combination of thanksgiving and prayers for future prosperity, is a quieter occasion. Small boatlike receptacles called *kratong* are launched into the Ping River, surrounding lakes, and even ponds. The simultaneous release of thousands of hot-air lanterns into the night sky above Chiang Mai as part of the celebration, usually around the middle of November, is an awesome sight. Awesome, too, is the annual flower festival in February, at which you will likely encounter exotic shrubs and flowers you've never seen before, many of them decorating the huge floats that wend their way through the city in one of its most spectacular processions.

GETTING HERE AND AROUND

AIR TRAVEL

There are more than 50 flights, most daily, from Bangkok to Chiang Mai (1 hour 10 minutes) ; six daily direct from Phuket (1 hour 50 minutes); and two daily direct from Krabi (1 hour 45 minutes). In peak season flights are heavily booked. Thai Budget airline VietJet flies from BKK and Air Asia and Nok Air from Bangkok's Don Mueang airport.

Chiang Mai International Airport is about 5 km (3 miles) south of the Old City. A taxi ride to the Old City costs B150, a trip in a songthaew about B60.

AIRPORTS AND TRANSFERS Bangkok Airways ☎ *02/706699* 🌐 *www.bangkokair.com.* **Chiang Mai International Airport** 🌐 *www.chiangmaiairportonline.com.* **Thai Airways** ☎ *02/356–1111, 02/545–3691* 🌐 *www.thaiairways.com.*

BUS TRAVEL

VIP buses travel between Bangkok's Northern Bus Terminal and Chiang Mai, stopping at Lampang on the way. For B400 to B850 you get a comfortable 10- to 12-hour ride in a modern, air-conditioned bus with reclining seats, blankets and pillows, TV, onboard refreshments, and lunch or dinner at a motorway stop. **■ TIP→ Sometimes the buses are downright chilly; keep a sweatshirt with you.** You can take cheaper buses, but the faster service and comfort are well worth the few extra baht.

Chiang Mai's Arcade Bus Terminal serves Bangkok, Chiang Rai, Mae Hong Son, and destinations within Chiang Rai Province. Chang Phuak Bus Terminal serves Lamphun, Chiang Dao, Tha Ton, and destinations within Chiang Mai Province.

CAR TRAVEL

The well-paved roads around Chiang Mai are no problem for most drivers—even the mountainous Mae Sa route north of Chiang Mai is perfectly drivable. Nevertheless, if you are not familiar with driving on the left, it may be better to hire a driver. Two major car-rental agencies in Chiang Mai are Avis and Hertz; Budget has a good range of four-wheel-drive vehicles. Motorcycle and scooter rentals shops abound.

Avoid driving in the city during rush hours, which start as early as 7 in the morning and 3 in the afternoon, and pay attention to no-parking restrictions (usually from 9 am to noon and 3 pm to 6 pm). Parking is prohibited on many streets on alternate days, but the explanatory signs are mostly in Thai. Your best bet is to note on which side of the street vehicles are parking. Chiang Mai's traffic police clamp and tow away vehicles parked illegally. Parking lots are numerous and charge as little as B20 for all-day parking.

Hiring a driver with a car is the most convenient way to visit the hard-to-find temples outside the city. This option can be expensive for solo travelers though, and can start at B1,500 ($50) for a half day to B3,000 ($100) for a day trip. It is more affordable to drive yourself or hop in a shared cab. Car-rental agencies also handle car-and-driver hires.

TAXI, TUK-TUK, AND SONGTHAEW TRAVEL

Metered taxis, which can be flagged down on the street, are being introduced gradually in Chiang Mai but are still not as common as tuk-tuks (auto rickshaws) and songthaews (shared rides with bench seating). The basic taxi charge is B30; you'll pay about B100 for a ride across the Old City. Ride-sharing app Grab is very popular and easy to use. Tuk-tuks are generally cheaper than taxis, but you are expected to bargain—offer B20 or so less than the driver demands. The songthaews that trundle around the city on fixed routes are the cheapest form of transportation—from B25 per person if traveling with other people, but more if you hire the whole vehicle. If the driver has to make a detour, you'll be charged an extra B20 or so. Settle on the fare before you get in. To confirm a price just hold up the relevant number of fingers. If you hold up three and your gesture evokes the same response from the driver, you'll be paying B30.

TRAIN TRAVEL

The State Railway links Chiang Mai to Bangkok and points south. As the uninteresting trip from Bangkok takes about 13 hours, overnight sleepers are the best choice. The overnight trains are well maintained and comfortable, with clean sheets on rows of two-tier bunks. **■ TIP→ Spending a few extra baht for a first-class compartment is strongly recommended. In second class you may be kept awake by partying passengers.** Trains for the north depart from Bangkok's Hualamphong Railway Station and arrive in the Chiang Mai Railway Station. First-class fares from Bangkok to Chiang Mai range from B1,650 for a sleeper to B700 or B900 for a day train *(see Train Travel in Travel Smart Thailand)*.

SAFETY AND PRECAUTIONS

Motorcycle accidents are a daily occurrence. Though rentals are easily available, riding a motorbike or scooter is inadvisable unless you have ample experience riding on the left side. If you do ride, cover your skin and wear a good helmet.

Incidents of street crime involving foreign visitors are rare, and when they do occur they are energetically investigated by the police. Nevertheless, the usual precautions should be taken when walking the city streets, and particularly the sois, at night. Leave your valuables in your hotel. If you leave your passport in the hotel, make sure to carry a copy—though you are very unlikely to be stopped, it's required to carry some form of ID. Carry handbags on the side of the sidewalk that's farthest from the street.

RESTAURANTS

All of the city's top hotels serve reasonably good food, but for the best Thai cuisine go to the restaurants in town. The greatest variety—from traditional Thai to Italian—are to be found within the Old City, and Nimmanhaemin Road, about 2 km (1 mile) northwest of downtown, is packed with great places to eat. For street stall fare, get to Anusan Market and the nearby Night Bazaar, the Sunday night market, and Warorot Market.

What It Costs In Baht

	$	$$	$$$	$$$$
RESTAURANTS	under B200	B200–B300	B301–B400	over B400

HOTELS

Soaring tourist numbers—particularly young Chinese visitors with newly acquired wealth and the urge and freedom to travel—have fueled an unprecedented hotel building boom in recent years. Most of the new properties are in the traditional so-called Lanna style, and the most luxurious of them rival hotels in Bangkok. One, the Dhara Dhevi, justly claims to be among Asia's finest. Except for the high season, from December to February, prices are far lower than in the capital. Charming, modestly priced guesthouses and small hotels abound, and some are right on the water.

What It Costs In Baht

	$	$$	$$$	$$$$
HOTELS	under B2,200	B2,200–B4,000	B4,001–B6,000	over B6,000

NIGHTLIFE

Chiang Mai has dozens of places where you can grab a beer or a cocktail, listen to live music, or both. Two centers of action are the Riverside area, where restaurants like the Good View double as bars later in the evening, and Nimmanhaemin Road heading south from Huay Kaew Road. As with elsewhere in Thailand, there are many easy-to-find hostess bars, most notably at the western end of Loi Kroh Road, the southern end of Moon Muang Road, and the Bar Beer Center next to the Top North Hotel on Moon Muang Road.

TOURS AND CLASSES

Every other storefront in Chiang Mai seems to be a tour agency, but professionally run. Pick up a list of agencies approved by the Tourism Authority of Thailand before choosing one (🌐 *www.tourismthailand.org/About-Thailand/About-TAT/TAT-Local-offices*).

Prices vary quite a bit, so shop around, and carefully examine the offerings. Each hotel also has its own travel desk with ties to a tour operator. The prices are often higher, as the hotel adds its own surcharge. If spending time in monasteries makes you wonder about the lives of the monks, or if you find yourself so enthralled by delicious dishes that you want to learn how to prepare them, you're in luck. Chiang Mai has hundreds of schools offering classes in anything from aromatherapy to Zen Buddhism. The city also has dozens of cooking classes—some in the kitchens of guesthouses, others fully accredited schools—teaching the basics of Thai cuisine. Courses cost from B800 to B1,000 a day. *Cooking courses are listed in this chapter under Shopping.* Alternative medicine, cooking, and massage are the other most popular courses, but by no means the most exotic. In three weeks at the Thailand's Elephant Conservation Center near Lampang, you can train to become a fully qualified mahout.

CLASSES

American University Alumni

$ | The alumni group has been offering Thai language courses for more than two decades. Charges vary according to the duration of the course and the number of pupils. ✉ *24 Ratchadamnoen Rd.* ☎ *053/214120, 053/211973* 🌐 *www.learnthaiinchiangmai.com.*

TOUR OPERATORS

Best Tuk Tuk Tours

GUIDED TOURS | **FAMILY** | A Thailand-born American named Paul Collins designs custom tours based on guests' schedules and interests. Fluent in Thai, Paul is a knowledgeable guide to the sights in and around Chiang Mai. ✉ *Chiang Mai* ☎ *084/948–3315* 🌐 *besttuktuktours.wix.com/besttuktuktours* 🎫 *Prices vary based on sights and length of tour.*

Nathlada Boonthueng

GUIDED TOURS | A TAT-registered English-speaking guide with a deep knowledge of the region, Nathlada "Timmy" Boonthueng is one of the best local independent operators. She conducts half-day, full-day, and multiday tours for groups and individuals. ✉ *Chiang Mai* ☎ *081/531–6884* 🌐 *www.chiangmaidestination.com* 🎫 *From B600 for ½-day group tours.*

Tours by Locals

GUIDED TOURS | This worldwide organization pairs travelers with freelance tourism-board-licensed local guides. Hire a personal guide in Chiang Mai for any specific interest or area of focus or choose from more than 15 group tours in and around the city. These range from bird-watching at Doi Inthanon to cycling around the Old City. Prices vary; guides can be contacted directly and group tours booked through the website. ✉ *Chiang Mai* ☎ *866/844–6783* 🌐 *www.toursbylocals.com.*

SpiceRoads Cycle Tours

TOUR—SPORTS | **FAMILY** | Themed cycling tours and holidays of varying durations are the specialty of this very professional Asian-based company. ✉ *1 Moon Muang Rd., Soi 7, Old City* ☎ *053/215837* 🌐 *www.spiceroads.com* 🎫 *From B1,200 for ½-day tour.*

TRAVEL AGENCIES

World Travel Service

From its central office in Bangkok, Thailand's oldest travel agency organizes tours of Chiang Mai and northern Thailand lasting from one to seven days. ✉ *1053 Charoen Krung Rd., Bangrak* ☎ *02/234–4875* 🌐 *www.worldtravelservice.co.th.*

VISITOR INFORMATION

CONTACTS Tourist Authority of Thailand (Chiang Mai) ✉ *105/1 Chiang Mai–Lamphun Rd.* ☎ *053/248604, 053/241466* 🌐 *www.tourismthailand.org/Chiang-Mai.*

The Old City

Covering roughly 2½ square km (1 square mile) and crisscrossed by winding lanes, Chiang Mai's Old City is bounded by remains of the original city wall and a wide, water-filled moat. The compact Old City can be explored easily on foot or by bike. The system of one-way streets can be confusing—though not a problem for pedestrians—but the plan keeps traffic moving quite effectively around the moat, which is crossed by bridges at regular intervals. The moated "one square mile" of the Old City contains 38 of Chiang Mai's temples, including its oldest and most historic ones. The so-called Lanna style of architecture—stepped eaves, dark teak, and gleaming white stucco construction—has been adopted by the owners of boutique hotels in the Old City, where high-rise buildings are banned.

Temple Know-how

Most temple complexes open around 6 am and don't close until 6 or 8 pm, although the hours can be irregular and the doors may be locked for no apparent reason. If that's the case, approach any monk and explain that you'd like to visit. He'll normally open up the temple, and might even chat with you. There's no admission charge at most temples, except at Wat Phra That Doi Suthep (B50 if you take the tram, B30 if you choose to walk) and the viharn (assembly hall) of Wat Phra Singh (B20).

Sights

Chiang Mai City Arts & Cultural Center

MUSEUM | The handsome city museum is housed in a colonnaded palace that was the official administrative headquarters of the last local ruler, Chao (Prince) Inthawichayanon. Around its quiet central courtyard are 15 rooms with exhibits documenting the history of Chiang Mai. In another small, shaded courtyard is a delightful café. The palace was built in 1924 in the exact center of the city, the site of the ancient city pillar that now stands in the compound of nearby Wat Chedi Luang. In front of the museum sit statues of the three kings who founded Chiang Mai. ✉ *Phrapokklao Rd., Old City* ☎ *053/217793, 053/219833* 🎫 *B90; B180 includes admission to Lanna Folklife Museum and Chiang Mai Historical Centre.* ⊗ *Closed Mon.*

★ Wat Chedi Luang

RELIGIOUS SITE | In 1411 King Saen Muang Ma ordered his workers to build a chedi "as high as a dove could fly." He died before the structure was finished, as did the next king. During the reign of the

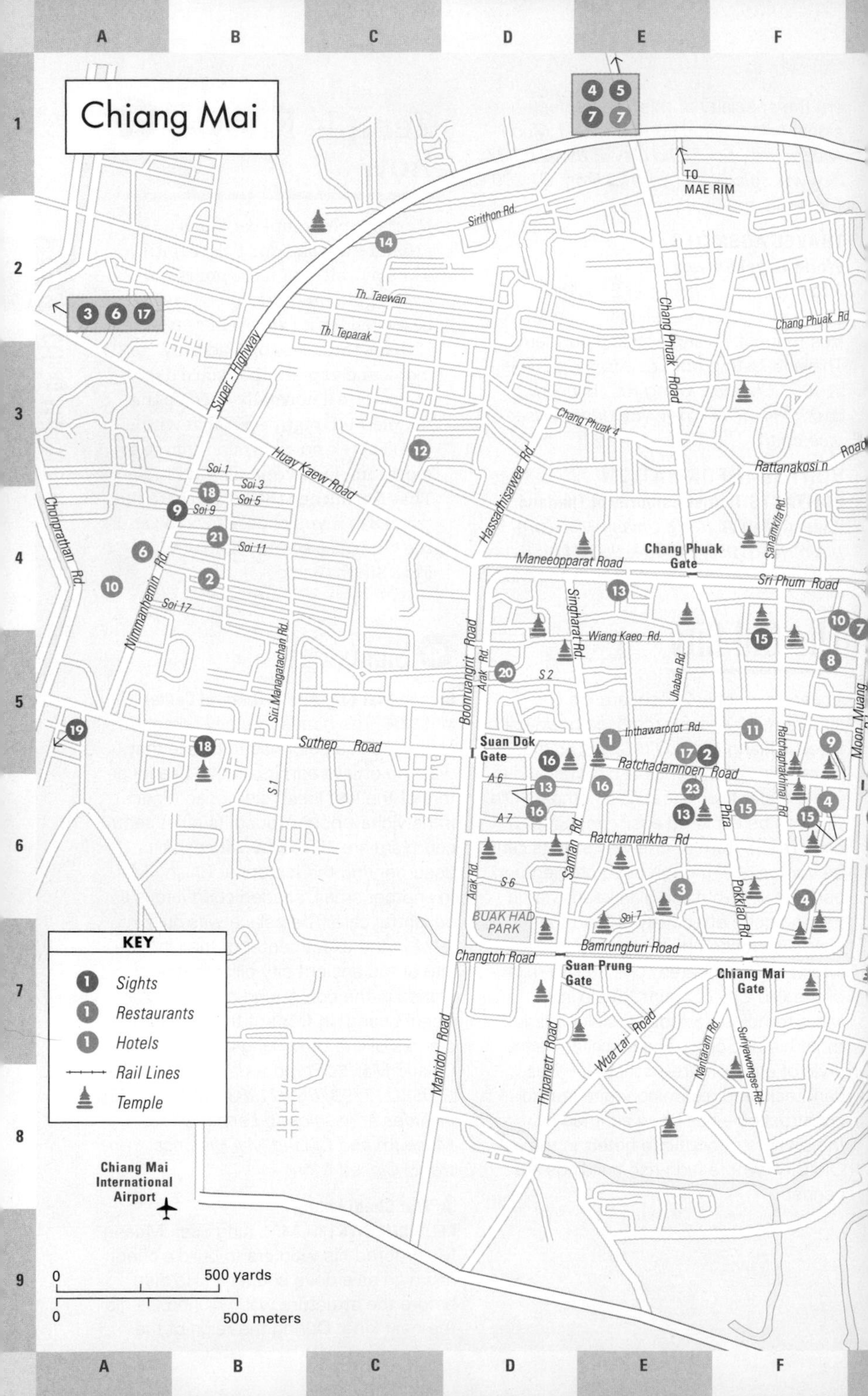
Chiang Mai
KEY
Sights
Restaurants
Hotels
Rail Lines
Temple
Chiang Mai International Airport
0 500 yards
0 500 meters
TO MAE RIM
Sirithon Rd.
Th. Taewan
Th. Teparak
Super - Highway
Huay Kaew Road
Chang Phuak Road
Chang Phuak Rd
Chang Phuak 4
Hassadhisawee Rd.
Rattanakosi n Road
Sanamkila Rd.
Chang Phuak Gate
Maneeopparat Road
Sri Phum Road
Singharat Rd.
Wiang Kaeo Rd.
Jhaban Rd.
Chonprathan Rd.
Nimmanhemin Rd.
Soi 1
Soi 3
Soi 5
Soi 9
Soi 11
Soi 17
Siri Managatachan Rd.
Boonruangrit Road
Arak Rd.
S 2
Suthep Road
Suan Dok Gate
Inthawarorot Rd.
Ratchadamnoen Road
Ratchaphakinai Rd.
Moon Muang
A 6
A 7
S 1
Phra
Ratchamankha Rd
Samlan Rd.
Pokklao Rd.
S 6
Soi 7
BUAK HAD PARK
Bamrungburi Road
Changtoh Road
Suan Prung Gate
Chiang Mai Gate
Mahidol Road
Thipanetr Road
Wua Lai Road
Nantaram Rd.
Suriyawongse Rd.

Sights

1 Bhubing Palace........... I1
2 Chiang Mai City Arts & Cultural Center........... E5
3 Chiang Mai Zoo......... A2
4 Chiang Mai Tribal Museum (Highland People Discovery Museum)..... E1
5 Darapirom Palace....... E1
6 Doi Suthep National Park........... A2
7 Elephant Nature Park... E1
8 Night Market........... H6
9 Nimmanahaemind Road...................... B4
10 Riverside................ H5
11 San Kamphaeng Hot Springs................ I4
12 Wat Chaimongkol......... I1
13 Wat Chedi Luang........ E6
14 Wat Chedi Yot............ I9
15 Wat Chiang Man......... F5
16 Wat Phra Singh......... D5
17 Wat Phra That Doi Suthep............... A2
18 Wat Suan Dok........... B5
19 Wat Umong.............. A5
20 Wiang Kum Kam.......... I9

Restaurants

1 Aroon Rai................ G6
2 Beast Burger............ B4
3 Chez Marco............. G6
4 Dash Teak House........ F6
5 David's Kitchen........... I4
6 Eat is Life................ A4
7 Ginger & Kafe........... G4
8 Graph Table.............. F5
9 Hinlay Curry House..... H5
10 The House Food & Kitchen Bar.................. F4
11 Huen Jai Yong............. I9
12 Huen Muan Jai........... C3
13 Khao Soi Khun Yai....... E4
14 La Terrasse.............. H6
15 Overstand................. F6
16 Rachamankha........... D6
17 Raming Tea House Siam Celadon........... H5
18 Rustic and Blue......... B4
19 River Market............ H6
20 Tikky Cafe................ D5
21 Tong Tem Toh........... B4
22 Whole Earth............ H7
23 Writer's Club & Wine Bar............... E6

Hotels

1 99 The Gallery Hotel..... E5
2 Anantara Chiang Mai Resort & Spa.............. I7
3 Banjai Garden............ E6
4 De Naga.................. F6
5 Dhara Dhevi Chiang Mai............... I6
6 dusitD2 Chiang Mai..... H6
7 Four Seasons Resort Chiang Mai............... E1
8 Galare Guest House.... H6
9 Hotel M Chiang Mai..... F5
10 Kantary Hills............. A4
11 Lamphu House........... F5
12 Ping Nakara Hotel........ I7
13 Rachamankha........... D6
14 Ruen Come In............ C2
15 The 3 Sis Vacation Lodge..................... F6
16 The Sila Boutique Bed & Breakfast......... E6
17 U Chiang Mai............. E5
18 V Lodge.................. G4

Elephants flank the ruined chedi at Wat Chedi Luang.

following king, an earthquake knocked down about a third of the 282-foot spire, and it's now a superb ruin. The parklike grounds contain assembly halls, chapels, a 30-foot-long reclining Buddha, and the ancient pillar. The main assembly hall, a vast, pillared building guarded by two *nagas,* mythical snakes believed to control the irrigation waters in rice fields, was restored in 2008. ✉ *103 Phrapokklao Rd., between Ratchamankha and Ratchadamnoen Rds., Old City* 🎫 *B40.*

Wat Chiang Man

RELIGIOUS SITE | Chiang Mai's oldest monastery, dating from 1296, is typical of northern Thai architecture. It has massive teak pillars inside the bot, and two important images of the Buddha sit in the small building to the right of the main viharn (assembly hall). The Buddha images are supposedly on view only on Sunday, but sometimes the door is unlocked. ✉ *Ratchaphakhinai Rd., 1.5 blocks south of the moat, Old City.*

★ Wat Phra Singh

RELIGIOUS SITE | Chiang Mai's principal monastery was extensively renovated in 2006. In the western section of the Old City, the beautifully decorated wat contains the Phra Singh Buddha, with a serene and benevolent expression that is enhanced by the light filtering in through the tall windows. Also of note are the temple's facades of splendidly carved wood, the elegant teak beams and posts, and the masonry. Don't be surprised if a student monk approaches you to practice his English. ✉ *Phra Singh Rd. and Singharat Rd., Old City* 🎫 *B20.*

Restaurants

★ Dash Teak House

$$ | **THAI** | **FAMILY** | In a beautiful, traditional, two-story teak house with a balcony overlooking a garden, Dash is one of the Old Town's best mid-range restaurants. Guests receive a warm welcome from the Thai mother-son team who returned to Thailand to open the restaurant after living many years in the United States.

Known for: tranquil garden seating; Lanna dishes like gaeng hang lay (pork curry); tasty Western fare for those tired of Thai. Ⓢ *Average main: B300* ✉ *38/2 Moon Muang Rd., Soi 2, Old City* ✥ *One block in from the city wall* ☎ *053/279230* 🌐 *dashteakhouse.com* ▭ *No credit cards.*

Ginger & Kafe

$$$ | **ECLECTIC** | Guests are invited to make themselves comfortable on plump, plush armchairs and sofas and even on large cushions scattered over the polished teak floor at this colorful restaurant, decorated like the home of your kooky bohemian cousin. The cuisine is eclectic, with plenty of Thai offerings as well as mixed Western fare like fish-and-chips. **Known for:** eclectic Thai-boho decor; pretty presentation; zingy cocktails with fresh herbs. Ⓢ *Average main: B375* ✉ *199 Moon Muang Rd., Old City* ☎ *053/287681* 🌐 *www.thehousebygingercm.com.*

Graph Table

$ | **CONTEMPORARY** | The young Thai couple behind the superb Graph Café have followed it up with this stylish yet casual trattoria nearby. The chef, who learned to cook Italian from a Sicilian-born friend, crafts authentic, fresh, handmade pastas and pizzas made to order. **Known for:** coffee with unusual ingredients, like charcoal; thin-crust pizzas; cold brew on tap. Ⓢ *Average main: B120* ✉ *Moon Muang Rd., Soi 6, Old City* ☎ *086/567–3330* ▭ *No credit cards.*

The House Food & Kitchen Bar

$$ | **ECLECTIC** | Trendy locals dig this restaurant, under the same management as, and adjacent to, Ginger & Kafe. The back wall has a blue-and-white-tiled mural of an elephant, traditional Chinese pottery meets Portuguese azulejos, while the banquette seating is topped with colorful throw pillows (you can snap these up in the shop). **Known for:** international cuisine; trendy atmosphere. Ⓢ *Average main: B300* ✉ *199 Moon Muang Rd., Chiang Mai* ☎ *053/287681.*

Khao Soi Khun Yai

$ | **THAI** | The colorful plastic stools and small wooden tables at this open-air *khao soi* joint are packed with a mix of locals and tourists slurping up egg noodles in a curry soup. Get yours with beef, chicken, or pork, each bowl topped with an addictive handful of crunchy noodles. **Known for:** heaping bowls of khao soi; spicy and more moderate khao soi options; fresh-pressed longan juice. Ⓢ *Average main: B50* ✉ *Sri Poom Rd., Soi 8, Chiang Mai* ✥ *Right at the moat, near Wat Kuan Kama. Restaurant is on the left* ☎ *086/712–4314* ⏲ *Closed Sun.* ▭ *No credit cards.*

★ Overstand

$ | **CAFÉ** | **FAMILY** | Owned by a Thai-Aussie couple, this cool little café in the Thapae Gate area serves excellent coffee sourced from local roasters, along with hearty breakfasts and healthy Aussie-style sandwiches and salads made with organic ingredients. The breakfast pizza paired with an iced coconut espresso is a treat for those up early with jet lag. **Known for:** speedy Wi-Fi; Australian iced coffee espresso-ice cream concoction; good vegetarian options. Ⓢ *Average main: B120* ✉ *19/3 Ratchamankha, Soi 2, Old City* ☎ *094/626–8311* 🌐 *www.overstand.co.th/menu* ⏲ *Closed Tues. No dinner* ▭ *No credit cards.*

★ Rachamankha

$$$$ | **THAI** | A meal at the Rachamankha hotel's elegant restaurant is a must whether you're a guest or not. The menu focuses on Lanna, Burmese, and Shan cuisine, a sensible approach given the entwined history of these northern neighbors. **Known for:** romantic courtyard; ample gluten-free items; live Lanna folk music and other entertainment. Ⓢ *Average main: B750* ✉ *6 Ratchamankha, Soi 9, Old City* ☎ *053/904111* 🌐 *www.rachamankha.com.*

Tikky Cafe

$ | **THAI** | **FAMILY** | At rough-hewn wooden tables topped with hill tribe textiles, hungry lunch goers tuck into heaping plates of colorful pan-Thai fare. The refreshing dishes here, like glass noodles with seafood, are loaded with vegetables and in place of white rice a toothsome, nutty purple rice is available (though listed as brown rice, it's a reddish deep purple). **Known for:** pan-Thai fare that skews healthy; fresh fruit shakes; hill tribe textiles on tables and chairs. *Average main: B90 2/2 Arak, Soi 3, Chiang Mai Just across the moat from Wat Pansao 098/796–2182 tikkycafe.restaurantwebexperts.com Closed Sun.*

Writers Club & Wine Bar

$ | **ECLECTIC** | You don't have to be a journalist to dine at Chiang Mai's unofficial press club—the regulars include not only media types but also anyone from artists and eccentric local characters to successful entrepreneurs. Expect the usual classic pan-Thai dishes, including salads, stir-fries, and curries. **Known for:** popular spot; some of the best value wine in Chiang Mai; a respite from the Sunday Market. *Average main: B150 141/3 Ratchadamnoen Rd., Old City 053/814187 No credit cards Closed Sat.*

Hotels

The 3 Sis Vacation Lodge

$$ | **B&B/INN** | A sacred Bhodi tree stands sentinel outside this attractive hotel that looks out directly onto Wat Chedi Luang, one of Chiang Mai's most historic temples. **Pros:** famous Sunday market is right outside; three leading temples within walking distance; 24-hour convenience store next door. **Cons:** breakfast is very limited; Wi-Fi is inconsistent; street noise. *Rooms from: B2,100 150 Phrapokklao Rd., Old City 053/273243 www.the3sis.com 24 rooms Free breakfast.*

99 The Gallery Hotel

$$ | **HOTEL** | Elegant for the price, this mid-range hotel with a fantastic location near the Sunday-night market and other attractions has rooms to suit most budgets. **Pros:** saltwater swimming pool; elegant for the price; fantastic location. **Cons:** many rooms are small; staff doesn't speak much English; beds are hard. *Rooms from: B3,000 99 Intrawarorot Rd., Old City 053/326338 99thegalleryhotel.com 53 rooms and suites Free breakfast No credit cards.*

★ Banjai Garden

$ | **B&B/INN** | A French restaurateur and his Thai wife renovated this sturdy old Chiang Mai residence into a clean and comfortable guesthouse. **Pros:** easy access to bars and restaurants; shaded garden; delightful owners; clean Lanna-style rooms. **Cons:** books up far ahead in high season; some rooms share a bath; some street noise. *Rooms from: B900 43 Phrapokklao Rd., Soi 3, Old City 085/716–1635 www.banjai-garden.com 7 rooms No meals.*

Old City Tour

A good place to start a tour of the Old City is at the Thapae Gate, near the oldest part of Chiang Mai. Heading west on Ratchadamnoen Road and turning north on Ratchaphakhinai Road brings you to Wat Chiang Man, the oldest temple in Chiang Mai. Backtracking down Ratchaphakhinai Road and heading west on Ratchadamnoen Road brings you to Wat Chedi Luang and Wat Phra Singh. Several other worthwhile temples are outside the city walls. Wat Chaimongkol is an easy walk from the Thapae Gate. Tuk-tuk to Wat Suan Dok. Wat Umong is a 30-minute walk from there.

King Saen Muang Ma designed Wat Chedi Luang to house his father's ashes.

De Naga

$$ | **HOTEL** | This Lanna-style boutique hotel is ideally located, with many bars and restaurants nearby. **Pros:** friendly service by English-speaking staff; good restaurant; shady terrace with comfortable garden furniture. **Cons:** nighttime noise from neighboring bars; some bathrooms a bit run down; unreliable Internet. *Rooms from: B3,000 ✉ 21 Soi 2 Ratchamanka, Moon Muang Rd., Old City ☎ 053/209–030 🌐 www.denaga.com 55 rooms Free breakfast.*

Hotel M Chiang Mai

$$ | **HOTEL** | Adjacent to the Thapae Gate and bordering the moat, this refurbished old favorite has a terrace that hums with activity on the weekend. **Pros:** central location; cozy rooms; bright ground-floor café. **Cons:** no pool; traffic noise in rooms facing moat; limited parking. *Rooms from: B2,600 ✉ 2–6 Ratchadamnoen Rd., Chiang Mai ☎ 053/211069 🌐 www.hotelmchiangmai.com 75 rooms Free breakfast.*

Lamphu House

$ | **HOTEL** | An excellent choice for first-time visitors, this Old City budget boutique hotel is a short stroll from Wat Chedi Luang and several other star attractions. **Pros:** near star attractions; balconies; good-size saltwater swimming pool. **Cons:** compact rooms; few amenities; inconsistent service. *Rooms from: B950 ✉ 1 Phrapokklao Rd., Soi 9, Old City ☎ 053/274966 🌐 www.lamphuhousechiangmai.com 41 rooms No meals.*

★ Rachamankha

$$$$ | **HOTEL** | The luxurious rooms at this small hotel on a quiet lane near Wat Phra Singh straddle a series of hushed brick courtyards enclosed by triple-eave Lanna-style buildings. **Pros:** peaceful setting; helpful staff; pool; free parking. **Cons:** service slow and patchy; noisy temple dogs; rooms too spartan for some; children under age 12 not permitted. *Rooms from: B7,800 ✉ 6 Ratchamankha Rd., Soi 9, Chiang Mai ☎ 053/904111 🌐 www.*

rachamankha.com 🛏 *24 rooms* 🍽 *Free breakfast.*

The Sila Boutique Bed & Breakfast
$ | **B&B/INN** | Directly opposite Wat Phra Singh, this small hotel's clean, simple rooms are the ideal base for travelers planning to sightsee all day. **Pros:** central Old City location; very helpful, accommodating staff; good air-conditioning throughout. **Cons:** no elevator; street-facing rooms can be noisy; breakfast is limited. 💲 *Rooms from: B1,800* ✉ *3/11 Samlarn Rd., Chiang Mai* ✥ *Opposite Wat Phra Singh* ☎ *053/273–6589* 🛏 *10 rooms* 🍽 *Free breakfast.*

U Chiang Mai
$$$ | **HOTEL** | A Lanna-style boutique hotel in the exact center of the Old City, the U Chiang Mai was constructed around a century-old teak house, the home of a former governor. **Pros:** 24-hour room rate, so if you arrive at 10 pm, you don't have to leave until 10 pm the next day; prime location in center of town; helpful tour desk. **Cons:** exposed pool that's open to view from most rooms; no parking; high bar and restaurant prices. 💲 *Rooms from: B4,200* ✉ *70 Ratchadamnoen Rd., Old City* ☎ *053/327000* 🌐 *www.uhotels-resorts.com/uchiangmai* 🛏 *79 rooms* 🍽 *Free breakfast.*

V Lodge
$ | **B&B/INN** | Small and intimate, this guesthouse has the feel of a boutique hotel. **Pros:** tasty included breakfast; close to the bar and restaurant scene; helpful owners. **Cons:** no pool; no parking; rooms near reception are quite noisy. 💲 *Rooms from: B1,400* ✉ *13 Chaiyapoom Rd., Soi 1, Old City* ☎ *053/232538* 🌐 *v-lodge.chiangmaihotels365.com/en* 🛏 *15 rooms* 🍽 *Free breakfast.*

Nightlife

BARS

Mixology
BARS/PUBS | The look at this bar on the western edge of the Old City is part industrial, part bric-a-brac shop, but the well-mixed cocktails are au courant, and the crowd is upbeat. The place serves burgers, including pork ones, and other comfort food. A signature libation, the High Flyer, involves bourbon, dark rum, amaretto, vanilla syrup, and bitters. ✉ *61/6 Arak Rd. 4 A, Old City* ✥ *Near Ratchamankha Rd.* ☎ *088/261–3057* ☞ *Closed Mon.*

Namton's House Bar
BARS/PUBS | Brew heads come to this Chiang Mai restaurant-bar for its selection of local and imported craft beers, dozens bottled and 10 on tap. Look for a pale ale from Six Post Meridiem, a Japan-Thai brew, a white ale from Bangkok-based Mahanakhon, and plenty of beers from European and U.S. breweries. ✉ *196/2 Chiangmai-Lamphun Rd, Chiang Mai* ✥ *Opposite the Gymkhana Club* ☎ *086/911–1207.*

Ram Bar
CABARET | The city's most popular gay bar runs a drag show every night from 10 pm, though seats fill up far earlier with a wide mix of travelers and local LGBTQ community members. The costumes are stunning, the dancers' stamina impressive, and the routines a hoot, leaving the audience laughing up a storm. There's no cover charge, drinks are reasonably priced (expect to pay B180 for a local beer), and everyone is welcome. ✉ *48 Charoenprathet Rd., Soi 6, Chiang Mai* ✥ *One block west of the river* ☎ *085/034–5607* 🌐 *www.rambarchiangmai.com.*

Writers Club & Wine Bar
BARS/PUBS | Chiang Mai's unofficial press club is open to anyone who enjoys networking in good company. The decor

Monk Chat

If you're like most people, a visit to Chiang Mai's numerous temples is likely to leave you full of unanswered questions. Head to Wat Suan Dok, Wat Chedi Luang, Wat Pha Khao, or Wat Srisuphan, where help is at hand. The monks and novice monks who reside in the two temples eagerly welcome foreign visitors for chats about the history of their temples, the Buddhist faith, Thai history and culture, or things as benign as what movies they like. Their enthusiasm isn't totally altruistic—they're keen to practice their English.

The talkative monks at Wat Suan Dok are all students of a religious university attached to the temple. Their monk chat is 5:30 to 7:30 pm on Monday, Wednesday, and Friday. At Wat Chedi it's daily, 9 am to 6 pm as they relax under the trees of their parklike compound, although they do step away for breaks. Wat Pha Khao's monk chat is weekends 5 pm to 9 pm, and Wat Srisuphan's is daily 5:30 pm to 7pm. These young monks urge foreign visitors to converse with them about Lanna culture, life in a monastery, or, as one monk put it, "anything at all."

is "eclectic colonial." ✉ *141/3 Ratchadamnoen Rd., Chiang Mai* ☎ *053/814187.*

DANCE CLUBS

Zoe in Yellow

DANCE CLUBS | An unsigned laneway just off Ratchaphakhinai Road in the Old City is a magnet for backpackers and rasta-Thais who gather nightly at the cluster of open-air or open-sided music bars, including Zoe in Yellow. Music tends to be DJs on deck spinning house, EDM, and trance music. Expect inexpensive beer and sugary cocktails. Babylon Bar and Roots Rock Reggae are also popular and will be equally full. The bars close at midnight. ■ **TIP→ The soi (lane) is difficult to find—the entrance is off Ratchaphakinai Road, one block north of Ratvithi Road.** ✉ *40/12 Ratchawithi Rd., east of Ratchaphakhinai Rd., Old City* ☎ *083/989–4925.*

MUSIC

★ North Gate Jazz Co-Op

MUSIC CLUBS | This is the city's most popular bar for jazz music. Doors open at 7 pm and seats on the first floor and mezzanine fill up soon afterwards with a mix of expats, locals, and tourists eager to hear covers of jazz, folk rock, and pop. Tuesdays are jam-session nights, but the place, on the northern edge of the Old City, is packed every night of the week. The bar is super casual—shorts and flip-flops are welcome—and there's no cover, with drinks moderately priced (stick to beer and cider; the cocktails and wine aren't worth the price). ✉ *91/1-2 Sriphum Rd., opposite Chang Phuak Gate, Old City* ☎ *081/765–5246.*

Shopping

COOKING CLASSES

Baan Thai Cookery School

FOOD/CANDY | The classes at this cooking school are among Chiang Mai's best, with lovely, encouraging teachers. A one-day course costs B1,000, including transportation, snacks, and a cookbook to take home; the four-hour evening course is B800. ✉ *9 Prapokklao Rd., Soi 9, Old City* ☎ *053/206388, 053/206315* 🌐 *www.cookinthai.com* ✍ *Reservations essential.*

Chiang Mai Thai Cookery School

FOOD/CANDY | Sompon Nabnian, an internationally recognized TV chef, runs this school, where students learn to make dishes like fish cakes and curries. A one-day beginner's course costs B1,450. The five-day master class costs B6,700. Price includes round-trip transportation. ✉ *47/2 Moon Muang Rd., Old City* ☎ *053/206388* 🌐 *www.thaicookery-school.com.*

Thai Farm Cooking School

FOOD/CANDY | The one-day classes at this popular school run by a genial husband-and-wife team take place at its working farm. Participants visit a food market before heading to the farm, where dishes are prepared and then enjoyed. The B1,500 fee includes transportation to and from lodgings or other points in or near the Old City. ✉ *Office, Moon Muang Rd., Soi 9, Old City* ☎ *081/288–5989, 087/174–9285* 🌐 *www.thaifarmcooking.com.*

PAPER

HQ PaperMaker

BOOKS/STATIONERY | This is the biggest and best paper outlet in Chiang Mai. On its first floor is a gallery whose works include paintings done by elephants at the Elephant Conservation Center near Lampang. ✉ *3/31 Samlan Rd., Chiang Mai* ✣ *Just south of Rachadamnoen Rd.* ☎ *053/814717* 🌐 *www.hqpapermaker.com.*

SPAS

Chiang Mai Women's Correctional Institution (Spa)

SPA/BEAUTY | If you want to do a good deed for Thai society as well as enjoy a great massage, stop by Chiang Mai's women's prison. Female inmates trained in Thai massage are allowed to practice their trade in a room adjoining the prison's shop (where handicrafts from the prison workshops are sold). A two-hour Thai massage costs B200—money well spent in assuring these remarkably cheerful women a solid foundation for life outside the prison walls. After the massage, relax over tea, coffee, or a Thai meal in the neighboring restaurant, also staffed by women prisoners. ✉ *100 Ratvithee Rd., Chiang Mai* ☎ *053/122340.*

Beyond the Old City

Outside the borders of the Old City, Chiang Mai expands into urban sprawl, although there are several worthy sights and a handful of identifiable areas that have preserved or developed some individual style. Shopaholics have to venture outside the enclosing moat and make for the famous Night Market or Nimmanhaemin Road, both a 10-minute tuk-tuk ride away from the city center. Chiang Mai's best and liveliest nighttime scene is to be found on the other side of the city in the Riverside quarter bordering the Ping River.

Sights

Chiang Mai Tribal Museum (Highland People Discovery Museum)

MUSEUM | The varied collection at this museum, more than 1,000 pieces of traditional crafts from the hill tribes living in the region, is one of the finest in the country and includes farming implements, hunting traps, weapons, colorful embroidery, and musical instruments. The museum is off the road to Mae Rim, about 1 km (½ mile) from the National Museum. ✉ *Rama IX Lanna Park, enter on Chotana Rd., Chiang Mai* ☎ *053/210872* 🎫 *Free* ⏲ *Closed weekends.*

Night Market

MARKET | Sandwiched between the Old City and the riverside, this market opens for business around 6 pm. More than 200 stalls—selling fake brands, knickknacks, and some goods worth checking out like pretty handicrafts—line a half-mile section of Chang Klan Road. Some visitors find the scene tacky, commercial, or too much of a zoo, but others visitors find a trip here engaging, if only for the many food purveyors and souvenir opportunities. The area is also a major nighttime entertainment zone. Loi Kroh Road, which bisects the market, is Chiang Mai's (perfectly safe) red-light district. ✉ *Chang Klan Rd., between Thapae and Sri Donchai Rds., Chiang Mai* 🎫 *Free.*

Nimmanhaemin Road

NEIGHBORHOOD | Chiang Mai's version of Bangkok's hip Sukhumvit area is Nimman, a mile-long strip west of the Old City. Cafés, pubs, bars, restaurants, art galleries, boutiques, and trendy One Nimman shopping plaza line this street that's usually packed with students from the nearby Chiang Mai University. Spend time exploring the jumble of side streets off the main drag, where more restaurants, party places, and shops jostle for space. ✉ *Nimmanhaemin Rd., between Huay Kaew and Suthep Rds., Chiang Mai* ✣ *Also accessible via Super Hwy.*

Riverside

NEIGHBORHOOD | Chinese traders originally settled this area 1½ km (1 mile) south of the Old City, and some of their well-preserved homes and commercial premises now house upscale and mid range restaurants, guesthouses and hotels, galleries, boutiques, and antiques shops. Unlike in Bangkok where many of the riverfront spots are full of foreigners, the restaurants, hotels, and bars along the river are enjoyed by Thai couples and families on evenings out. ✉ *Charoen Prathet Rd., at Nawarat Bridge, Chiang Mai.*

Wat Chaimongkol

RELIGIOUS SITE | Although rarely visited, this small temple is well worth the journey. Its little chedi contains holy relics, but its real beauty lies in the serenity of the grounds. Outside the Old City near the Mae Ping River, it has fewer than 20 monks in residence. ✉ *Charoen Prathet Rd., just behind Central Chiang Mai Memorial Hospita, Chiang Mai.*

Wat Chedi Yot

RELIGIOUS SITE | Wat Photharam Maha Viharn is more commonly known as Wat Chedi Yot, or Seven-Spired Monastery. Built in 1455, it's a copy of the Mahabodhi temple in Bodh Gaya, India, where the Buddha is said to have achieved enlightenment. The seven intricately carved spires represent the seven weeks that he subsequently spent there. The sides of the chedi have striking bas-relief sculptures of celestial figures, most of them in poor repair but one bearing a face of hauntingly contemporary beauty. The temple is just off the highway that circles Chiang Mai, but its green lawns and shady corners are strangely still and peaceful. ✉ *Super Hwy., between Huay Kaew and Chang Phuak Rds., Chiang Mai.*

Wat Suan Dok

RELIGIOUS SITE | One of Chiang Mai's largest temples, Wat Suan Dok is said to have been built on the site where bones of Lord Buddha were found. Some of these relics are believed to be inside the chedi; others were transported to Wat Phra That Doi Suthep. At the back of the viharn is the bot housing Phra Chao Kao, a superb bronze Buddha figure cast in 1504. Chiang Mai aristocrats are buried in stupas in the graveyard. ✉ *Suthep Rd., west of the Old City, at Suan Dok Rd., Chiang Mai* 🎫 *Donations welcome.*

Wat Umong

RELIGIOUS SITE | The most unusual temple in Chiang Mai is Wat Umong, dating from 1296 and set within a forest near the airport. According to local lore, a monk named Jam liked to go wandering in the forest. This irritated King Ku Na, who often wanted to consult with the sage. So he could seek advice at any time, the king built this wat for the monk in 1380. Along with the temple, tunnels were constructed and decorated with paintings, fragments of which may still be seen. Beyond the chedi is a pond filled with hungry carp. Throughout the grounds the trees are hung with snippets of wisdom such as "Time unused is the longest time." ■ **TIP→ Within the Old City is a small temple with the same name. For the bigger**

Continued on page 312

SILK-MAKING IN THAILAND

by Dave Stamboulis

According to legend, the Chinese empress His-Ling discovered silk nearly 5,000 years ago when a cocoon fell into her teacup, and she watched it unwind into a fine filament. As China realized the value of these threads, the silk trade was born, spreading through Asia, along what became known as the Silk Road.

For centuries, the Chinese protected the secret of silk production, beheading anyone who tried to take silkworm eggs out of the country. But, eventually, smuggled worms, along with silk-making knowledge, made it to other parts of Asia. As the demand for silk grew, Chinese traders searched for the best climates in which to cultivate worms; historians believe that these traders brought sericulture, or silk-making, to Thailand about 2,000 years ago. Archaeologists have found silk remnants in the ruins of Baan Chiang near Udon Thani.

Though silkworms thrived, the silk business did not take on a large scale in Thailand, because Buddhist Thais were reluctant to kill the silkworms—an unavoidable part of the process. But a few families in Isan did continue to produce silk, using native plants like Palmyra Palm and jackfruit to make natural bleaches and dyes. After World War II, American businessman Jim Thompson discovered Thailand's cottage industry and helped expand it, founding the Thai Silk Company in 1951. Queen Sirikit, King Bhumibol's wife, has also been a long-term supporter of sericulture through her SUPPORT organization, which teaches traditional crafts to rural Thais.

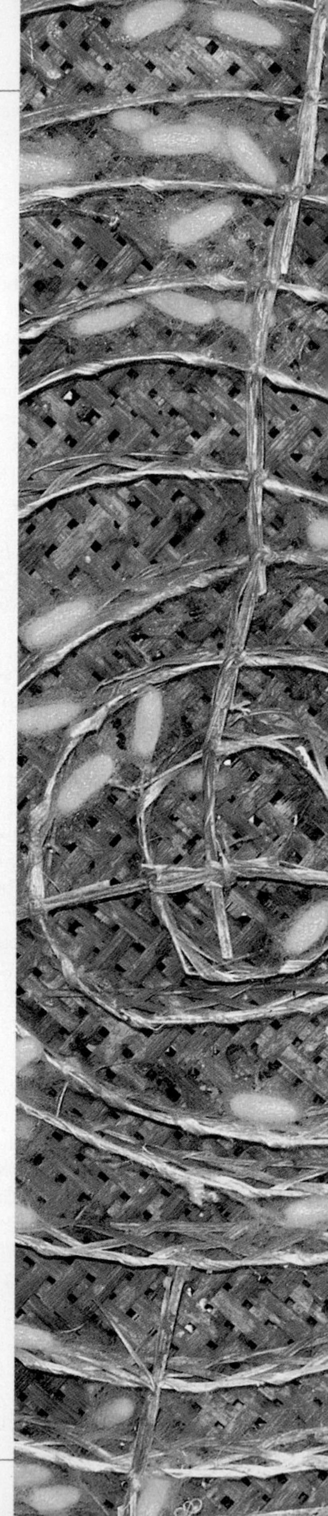

Silk cocoons in the final stage of incubation, Surin.

HOW SILK IS MADE

Adult female bombyx mari.

Female moth laying eggs.

Larvae eating mulberry leaves.

Silkworms are really the caterpillars of bombyx mari, the silk moth. The process begins when a mature female moth lays eggs—about 300 at once. When the eggs hatch 10 days later, the larvae are placed on trays of mulberry leaves, which they devour. After this mulberry binge, when the worms are approximately 7 cm (2.75 in) long, they begin to spin their cocoons. After 36 hours the cocoons are complete.

Before the worms emerge as moths—destroying the cocoons in the process—silk makers boil the cocoons so they can unravel the intact silk filament. The raw silk, which ranges in color from gold to light green, is dried, washed, bleached, and then dyed before being stretched and twisted into strands strong enough for weaving. The course, knotty texture of Thai silk is ideal for hand-weaving on traditional looms—the final step to creating a finished piece of fabric.

Silk cocoons.

Boiling cocoons to remove silk.

DID YOU KNOW?

Thai silk moths reproduce 10 or more times per year—they're much more productive than their Japanese and Korean counterparts, which lay eggs only once annually.

A worm can eat 25,000 times its original weight over a 30-day period, before encasing itself in a single strand of raw silk up to 900 m (3,000 ft) long.

Woman sifting through cocoons.

CHECK IT OUT

In Bangkok, the Naj Collection has an excellent reputation and top quality products, and the Jim Thompson outlets are quite good, as are Shinawatra's.

Naj Collection
42 Convent Rd. (Opposite BNH Hospital), Silom, Bangkok 662/632–1004-6 www.najcollection.com.

Jim Thompson Outlet
9 Surawong Rd., Suriyawong, Bangrak, Bangkok 02/632–8100, 02/234–4900 www.jimthompson.com.

Shinawatra Thai Silk
94 Sukhumvit Soi 23, North Klong Toei, Wattana, Bangkok 02/258-0295-9 www.shinawatrathaisilk.com

Man works a traditional loom.

VARIETIES OF THAI SILK

Most Thai silk is a blend of two different colors, one for the warp (threads that run lengthwise in a loom) and the other for the weft (strands that are woven across the warp.) Smoother silk, made with finer threads, is used for clothing, while rougher fabric is more appropriate for curtains. To make "striped" silk, weavers alternate course and smooth threads. Isan's famous mudmee silk, which is used mainly for clothing, consists of threads that are tie dyed before they are woven into cloth.

Mudmee silk.

SHOPPING TIPS

Appraising silk quality is an art in itself. But there are a few simple ways to be sure you're buying pure, handmade fabric.

- Examine the weave. Hand-woven, authentic silk has small bumps and blemishes—no part of the fabric will look exactly like any other part. Imitation silk has a smooth, flawless surface.
- Hold it up to the light. Imitation silk shines white at any angle, while the color of real silk appears to change.
- Burn a thread. When held to a flame, natural fibers disintegrate into fine ash, while synthetic fabrics melt, smoke, and smell terrible.
- Though this isn't a foolproof method, consider the price. Genuine silk costs five to 10 times more than an imitation or blended fabric. You should expect to pay between B250 and B350 a meter for high-quality, clothing-weight silk. Men's shirts start at B800 but could be more than B2,000; women's scarves run from B350 to B1,500. At Bangkok shops that cater to westerners, you'll pay considerably more, though shops frequented by Thais have comparable prices throughout the country.

Fine Thai silk on bobbins.

Wat Umong, tell your driver you're going to Wat U Mong Thera Jan. ✉ *Off Suthep Rd., past Wat Suan Dok, Chiang Mai.*

Restaurants

Aroon Rai

$ | **THAI** | This simple, open-sided restaurant just outside the city walls has prepared such traditional northern dishes as frogs' legs fried with ginger for more than 30 years. Try the *tabong* (boiled bamboo shoots fried in batter) and *sai ua* (pork sausage with herbs). **Known for:** zesty sai ua (fermented pork sausages); packets of curry mix to go; Cheap and cheerful northern Thai fare. *Ⓢ Average main: B160* ✉ *45 Kotchasarn Rd., Chiang Mai* ☎ *053/276947* ▬ *No credit cards.*

Eat is Life

$$ | **ECLECTIC** | The open kitchen at this small Nimmanhaemin Road restaurant puts out Japanese, Thai, and Continental fare, and though some restaurants fail when trying to do three cuisines at once, Eat is Life succeeds. The food is rich trying to be healthy-ish—grilled chicken with snap peas in a creamy sauce, grilled asparagus, tomatoes, mashed potatoes, and steak—and there's a rainbow-of-salad bar. **Known for:** catering to dietary restrictions; a favorite of trendy locals; delicious salad bar. *Ⓢ Average main: B300* ✉ *Nimmanhaemin Rd., Soi 12, Chiang Mai* ✣ *At Kantary Hills* ☎ *053/217178* 🌐 *eatislife.restaurantwebexperts.com* ⏲ *Closed Sun., Sat. lunch and 2 pm to 5 pm.*

Beast Burger

$$ | **BURGER** | **FAMILY** | If you find yourself craving Western fast food, skip the global franchises and make a beeline for this brilliant restaurant, which grew out of an ultrapopular food truck. Run by two young Thai siblings and open in the evenings until 9:30 or sold out, Beast's burgers are made with premium-quality ingredients and are perfectly cooked. **Known for:** cool crowd; house-made sauces, like Korean ketchup and blue cheese; good value. *Ⓢ Average main: B200* ✉ *14 Nimmanhaemin, Soi 17, Chiang Mai* ☎ *080/124–1414* 🌐 *www.beastburgercafe.com* ⏲ *Closed Sun. and 2 pm–5 pm* ▬ *No credit cards.*

Chez Marco

$$$ | **INTERNATIONAL** | Despite its location in Chiang Mai's "red-light district" (a perfectly safe area), this French restaurant is consistently full of locals and foreigners digging into coq au vin and creamy pâtés. The restaurant, open only evenings and run with Gallic flair by Franco-Japanese chef Marco, began as a modest shophouse, but has doubled in size with the acquisition of neighboring premises, while keeping its tiny, stylishly intimate street terrace. *Ⓢ Average main: B350* ✉ *15/7 Loi Kroh Rd., Chiang Mai* ☎ *053/207032* ⏲ *Closed Sun.*

Hinlay Curry House

$ | **ASIAN** | Tucked away in a corner of a former businessman's mansion, this small, open-sided South Asian restaurant specializes in inexpensive curry dishes from India, Burma, and Thailand. Daily specials, accompanied by two varieties of rice or a selection of Indian breads like pillowy naan, are written on a blackboard. **Known for:** airy, plant-filled dining room; great Indian breads; homemade sorbets and ice creams. *Ⓢ Average main: B120* ✉ *8/1 Na Watket Rd., Soi 1, Wat Ket* ☎ *053/242621* ▬ *No credit cards.*

Huen Muan Jai

$ | **THAI** | On a backstreet in an increasingly cool local neighborhood dotted with cafés and small eateries, this restaurant in a traditional teak house serves authentic Lanna cuisine. Try the *nam prik ong* (tomato, minced-pork dip) served with crispy vegetables, the *larb moo* (a rich minced-pork salad), or the locally revered *gaeng hang lay (pork belly curry).* **Known for:** open-air dining room surrounded by greenery; solid vegetarian options; fried bamboo shoots filled with minced pork. *Ⓢ Average main: B100* ✉ *24 Ratchpruek Rd., Chiang Mai* ☎ *053/404998* 🌐 *www.*

huenmuanjai.com ⏲ Closed Wed. ▭ No credit cards.

La Terrasse

$$ | **FRENCH** | Outside of those in upscale hotels, there are few other restaurants in Chiang Mai where you'll find a good selection of French cheeses. Tucked away on a quiet courtyard off bustling Loi Kroh Road, this unassuming bistro, run by chef-owner Jean Jeacques Thine, keeps it simple but with rich ingredients—butter, foie gras, and cream all make appearances. **Known for:** quiet atmosphere; homemade pâtés. [$] *Average main: ✉ 59/5 Loi Kroh Rd., Chiang Mai ☎ 083/762–6065 🌐 www.laterrassechiangmai.com ▭ No credit cards ⏲ Closed Wed. No lunch.*

Raming Tea House Siam Celadon

$ | **ECLECTIC** | Escape the hustle and bustle of busy Tha Pae Road by stepping into the cool interior of this exquisitely restored century-old Chinese merchant's house. You enter through a showroom of fine celadon pottery and an adjoining courtyard flanked by a shop selling Lanna fabric and the pottery used in the restaurant. **Known for:** pretty home goods in its shop; peaceful garden tables; housemade tea blends. [$] *Average main: B180 ✉ 158 Tha Pae Rd., Chiang Mai ☎ 053/234518 ▭ No credit cards ⏲ No dinner.*

River Market

$$$ | **ECLECTIC** | This handsome Lanna-style restaurant complex sits next to Chiang Mai's historic Iron Bridge, and its spacious outside terrace commands views of the bridge and the Ping River. The chefs prepare the full range of authentic, if pricey, Thai dishes, along with a couple of Continental options, including a cheeseburger. **Known for:** tables overlooking the Ping River; modern twists on pan-Thai fare; high prices to match the setting. [$] *Average main: B310 ✉ 33/12 Charoen Prathet Rd., Chiang Mai ☎ 053/234493 🌐 therivermarket.com/menu ▭ No credit cards.*

Rustic and Blue

$ | **INTERNATIONAL** | **FAMILY** | Part tearoom, part casual eatery, this rustic place, whose furnishings include tables made of recycled wood, focuses on food crafted from fresh organic ingredients sourced from local farmers and artisanal producers. The all-day breakfasts are hugely popular—try the brioche French toast brûlée with fresh fruit—but the tacos and salads, among them a fine one with quinoa and pumpkin, have many fans, too, especially among trendy locals. **Known for:** all-day breakfast; vegan and gluten-free baked goods; housemade ice creams. [$] *Average main: B110 ✉ Nimmanhaemin Rd., Soi 7, Chiang Mai ☎ 086/654–7178 🌐 www.rusticandblue.com ▭ No credit cards.*

Tong Tem Toh

$ | **THAI** | Follow your nose to the street-side barbecue of this cool Lanna restaurant on a busy alley off Nimmanhaemin Road. The casual place is popular with young Thais, who love the great, affordable cuisine and the beer-garden atmosphere. **Known for:** long lines for dinner; you order dishes by number as you wait for a table; northern dishes like larb and sai ou (pork sausages). [$] *Average main: B100 ✉ 11 Nimmanhaemin Rd., Soi 13, Chiang Mai ☎ 053/894701 ▭ No credit cards.*

Whole Earth

$$ | **VEGETARIAN** | On the second floor of an attractive old house, this longtime favorite serves delicious and healthy foods. It's mostly vegetarian fare, but there are a few meat dishes for the carnivorous, such as *gai tahkhrai* (fried chicken with lemon and garlic). **Known for:** catering to vegetarians and gluten-free diners; toned-down flavors for those who don't love spice; good Indian breads, including chapati. [$] *Average main: B250 ✉ 88 Sri Donchai Rd., Chiang Mai ☎ 053/282463.*

Hotels

★ Anantara Chiang Mai Resort & Spa
$$$$ | **HOTEL** | The former grounds of the British Consulate now house this waterfront oasis whose rooms and suites have private terraces overlooking either the Mae Ping River or the verdant gardens. **Pros:** historic setting but contemporary feel; private terraces; faultless service; riverside location; renowned restaurant; immense pool; complimentary smartphone. **Cons:** some find the metallic, rust-colored facade off-putting; water features could be better lighted at night; blackout shades don't fully cover window; when property full, breakfast a bit chaotic. *Rooms from: B10,000* ✉ *123 Charoen Prathet Rd., Chiang Mai* ☎ *053/253333* 🌐 *www.chiang-mai.anantara.com* *84 rooms* *No meals.*

dusitD2 Chiang Mai
$$ | **HOTEL** | Although a bit dated, this overall contemporary hotel makes a complete break from the traditional Lanna style so prevalent in Chiang Mai. Clean lines, brushed-steel-and-glass surfaces, and cubist upholstery set the tone in the interiors, from the airy lobby to the bright rooms, where a wealth of cushions compensates for the somewhat minimalist look. **Pros:** in the thick of the shopping scene; short stroll to Night Bazaar; comfortable mattresses. **Cons:** small pool for the size of the hotel; small rooms; modern style might not appeal to those seeking traditional Thai charm. *Rooms from: B3,500* ✉ *100 Chang Klan Rd., T. Chang Klan, A. Muang, Chiang Mai* ☎ *053/999999* 🌐 *dusitd2chiangmai.dusit.com* *131 rooms* *No meals.*

Galare Guest House
$ | **B&B/INN** | Especially for the price, this guesthouse's location is the envy of many of the city's top hotels; its gardens lead right down to the Mae Ping River and it is a short walk from the Night Bazaar. **Pros:** riverside location; airy terrace restaurant; secluded garden. **Cons:** no pool; many rooms overlook busy parking lot; rooms in need of refresh. *Rooms from: B1,600* ✉ *7 Charoen Prathet Rd., Soi 2, Chiang Mai* ☎ *053/818887* 🌐 *www.galare.com* *35 rooms* *Free breakfast.*

Kantary Hills
$$ | **HOTEL** | **FAMILY** | A showpiece of the Thailand-based Cape & Kantary Hotels collection, this large and stylish complex dominates the glitzy Nimmanhaemin Road district. **Pros:** one-bedroom suites have washing machines; huge selection at breakfast; whirlpool and regular pool. **Cons:** noisy neighborhood; lacks character; gridlock at night. *Rooms from: B3,300* ✉ *44 Nimmanhaemin Rd., Soi 12, Chiang Mai* ☎ *053/222111* 🌐 *www.kantarycollection.com* *152 rooms* *Free breakfast.*

Ping Nakara Hotel
$$$$ | **HOTEL** | It's hard to believe that this stunning riverside property was built in 2009; a masterpiece of colonial-style architecture, it's furnished throughout with exquisite antiques. **Pros:** quiet corners; peaceful setting; garden teatime service; big rooms. **Cons:** drab, main-road neighborhood; some rooms get road noise; so-so restaurant. *Rooms from: B8,000* ✉ *135/9 Charoen Prathet Rd., A. Muang, City Center* ☎ *053/252999* 🌐 *www.pingnakara.com* *19 rooms* *Free breakfast.*

Ruen Come In
$$ | **B&B/INN** | An extremely hospitable (English-speaking) Thai couple runs this two-story teak-timbered hotel whose main building was the family home before the children left the nest. **Pros:** massive rooms; superb food; swimming pool. **Cons:** few facilities; Old City not within walking distance; street and airport noise. *Rooms from: B2,200* ✉ *79/3 Sirithorn Rd., Chiang Mai* ☎ *053/212516* 🌐 *www.ruencomein.com* *13 rooms* *No meals.*

Nightlife

BARS

Wine Connection

WINE BARS—NIGHTLIFE | In reality a retail shop, this well-stocked spot in a shopping plaza has outside bistro tables where customers can sample wines until late. Wine buffs, still a newish breed here, crowd the tables on most evenings. Food can be ordered from a neighboring bistro. ✉ *Nim City Daily, 197 Mahidol Rd., Chiang Mai* ☎ *053/808688* 🌐 *www.wineconnection.co.th.*

DANCE CLUBS

Warm Up

DANCE CLUBS | Young Thais, many students at nearby universities, hit the discos and music bars of the Nimmanhaemin Road area, a major nightlife scene. Visiting ravers under 40 won't feel out of place in haunts like Warm Up, where local bands play Thai pop music and, in between sets, a DJ spins house and EDM. If you don't want to put in earplugs, enjoy a drink at the low-key outdoor tables. ✉ *40 Nimmanhaemin Rd., Chiang Mai* ✣ *One block north of Chiang Mai University* ☎ *053/400677.*

KHANTOKE

Kantoke Palace

THEMED ENTERTAINMENT | At the ever-popular Kantoke Palace, a series of dances that might involve umbrellas, swords, or other props is followed by an audience-participation circle dance. The food is not what you're coming for, though the specialty cocktails aren't bad. ✉ *288/19 Chang Klan Rd., Chiang Mai* ☎ *053/272757* 🌐 *www.kantokepalace.com.*

Old Chiang Mai Cultural Center

THEMED ENTERTAINMENT | This fine ensemble of old-style teak-built houses offers a multicourse dinner accompanied by traditional music and dancing. Grab a seat on the floor to experience the show up close. ✉ *185/3 Wualai Rd., Chiang Mai* ☎ *053/202–9935* 🌐 *www.oldchiangmai.com.*

MUSIC

The Good View

MUSIC CLUBS | Give the food a pass but do grab a drink and a seat at this restaurant on the east bank of the Ping River, which resounds after dark with live rock, jazz, and Motown oldies, played by cover bands. Neighboring Riverside Restaurant & Bar is another good option for a laid-back evening of music. ✉ *13 Charoen Rat Rd., Chiang Mai* ☎ *053/249029* 🌐 *www.goodview.co.th.*

Ploen Ruedee Night Market

GATHERING PLACES | Part–night market, part–outdoor food hall, Ploen Ruedee is a great place to come for a bite, a cold Chang or Singha beer, and to listen to the bands that perform nightly. This is the trendiest of the night markets, with tables made of reclaimed wood, pretty string lights, and a cocktail kiosk. Two-to-three local bands perform nightly, the music ranging from folk to pop to rock. Foodwise you will find stands selling pizza, dumplings, satay, pad Thai, sashimi bowls, crepes, and ice cream. ✉ *Chang Klan Rd. near Thanon Charoen Mueang, Chiang Mai* ✣ *One block north of the Night Bazaar, opposite the mosque.*

Activities

BOATING

Mae Ping River Cruise

BOATING | If you're looking for a low-key river cruise, this is it. The lunch cruise is a languid boat ride with a bowl of *khao soi*at a local farmer's house. The dinner cruise, which is more about the boat ride than the food (though it's not bad), is nightly at 6:30 for 90 minutes. Boats depart from the landing at Wat Chai Mongkol, just downriver from the Iron Bridge, but prices include hotel pickup. ✉ *133 Charoen Prathet Rd., Chiang Mai* ☎ *053/274822* 🌐 *www.maepingriver-cruise.com.*

HORSEBACK RIDING

Pong Horse Park

HORSEBACK RIDING | FAMILY | Half an hour outside the Old City are rolling green hills, dirt trails, and grassy fields through which beginners and experienced riders can gallop. Lessons (45 minutes) are B700 for kids above three and adults. Trail rides are B1,000/hour; a six-hour trek, including lunch, is B,5000. ✉ *119 Moo 1, Chiang Mai* ☎ *081/882–8899.*

THAI BOXING

Kawila Boxing Stadium

BOXING | Friday night is fight night at this popular muay Thai boxing venue whose grittier location attracts a less-touristy crowd than the one at Thapae Stadium. The most-expensive seats are about B600, so it doesn't cost a fortune to get thrillingly close to the action, which generally—but not always—starts at 9 pm. Inquire at your hotel or guesthouse how best to get here; the stadium is away from where most tourists stay, though close to the railway station. ✉ *Kong Sai Rd., Chiang Mai* ✣ *Near San Pa Koy Market* ☎ *081/681–8029.*

Por Silaphai Gym

BOXING | FAMILY | Muay Thai enthusiasts can learn just how to kick, punch, and block at this friendly gym, which runs a two-hour beginners' group session (daily except Sunday 7:30 am to 9:30 am and 4 pm to 6 pm). The B900 price (B700 May through October) includes a free transfer from hotels in the Old City and city center. ✉ *4 Viang Ping Rd., Chiang Mai* ✣ *Off Wiang Ping Rd.* ☎ *082/274–2160* 🌐 *www.silaphaigym.com.*

Thapae Boxing Stadium

BOXING | Professional muay Thai boxing contestants square off every Thursday night at this stadium just outside the Old City's Thapae Gate. Matches start at 8 pm. Tickets cost from B400 to B600. ✉ *1 Moon Muang Rd., Chiang Mai* ✣ *Just south of Thapae Gate* ☎ *081/1648784.*

Five-Star Products

To encourage each *tambon* (community) to make the best use of its special skills, the Thai government set up a program called OTOP, which stands for "One Tambon, One Product." It's been a great success. More than 25,000 community-based artisans and manufacturers have joined the program, and nearly 600 products have been given five-star ratings. About half are food or beverage items, but there are also clothes, housewares and decorations, handicrafts, and souvenirs. Look for the OTOP symbol when you shop.

Shopping

ART

The Gallery

ART GALLERIES | Beautiful traditional Thai paintings, carvings, sculptures, and other artworks are displayed and sold at the fine gallery attached to The Gallery restaurant. ✉ *25–29 Charoen Rat Rd., Chiang Mai* ☎ *053/248–6012* 🌐 *thegallery-restaurant.com/art-gallery.*

Suvannabhumi Art Gallery

ART GALLERIES | Mon art from Myanmar is on permanent display at this gallery run by a charming and knowledgeable Mon art lover named Mar Mar. She mounts regular exhibitions of work by leading and rising Burmese artists. ✉ *116–11 Charoen Rat Rd., Chiang Mai* ☎ *081/031–5309* 🌐 *www.suvannabhumiartgallery.com.*

★ Wattana Art Gallery

ART GALLERIES | The celebrated Thai artist Wattana Wattanapun runs this gallery whose eclectic artworks—textiles and works on paper—represent the full range of Thailand's artistic expression. Gallery staff are welcoming and knowledgeable. ✉ *100/1 Soi Wat Umong, Chiang Mai* ☎ *053/278747, 089/429–1883* 🌐 *www.wwattanapun-art.com.*

HANDICRAFTS

Baan Tawai Village

CRAFTS | Four kilometers (2½ miles) beyond Baan Tawai lies a community of shops dealing in antiques and handicrafts. At workshops you can see teak, mango, rattan, and water hyacinth being worked into attractive and unusual items. If you end up buying a heavy piece of teak furniture, the dealer will arrange for its shipping. ✉ *90 Moo 2 Tambon Baan Tawai, near Hang Dong, Chiang Mai* ☎ *081/882–4882* 🌐 *www.ban-tawai.com.*

Northern Village

CRAFTS | Chiang Mai's largest handicrafts retail outlet has an astounding selection of ceramics, jewelry carvings, and silks and other textiles. ✉ *CentralPlaza Airport Chiangmai, 2 Mahidol Rd., Chiang Mai* ✣ *Near Thipanet Rd.* ☎ *053/999199.*

Thai Tribal Crafts

CRAFTS | Operated by the Baptist Christian Service Foundation, the nonprofit Thai Tribal Crafts has more than 25 years' experience in retailing the products of northern Thailand's hill tribe people. The organization prides itself on its fair trade policy and the authenticity of its products like clothing, accessories, and home goods. They also run weaving classes suitable for beginners, including kids. ✉ *208 Bamrungrat Rd., Chiang Mai* ✣ *Near Kaeo Nawarat Rd.* ☎ *053/241043* 🌐 *www.ttcrafts.co.th.*

JEWELRY

Nova

JEWELRY/ACCESSORIES | This stunning jewelry shop has an attached studio where striking contemporary pieces are created in gold, silver, platinum, and stainless steel. Some pieces incorporate common materials, such as stone and rosewood, into their designs. At the Nova Artlab school you can take jewelry-making workshops lasting from one to five days (from B1,750). ✉ *179 Thapae Rd., Chiang Mai* ☎ *053/273058* 🌐 *www.nova-collection.com.*

Royal Orchid Collection

JEWELRY/ACCESSORIES | A Chiang Mai jewelry specialty features orchid blooms, rose petals, other flowers, leaves, and seeds set in gold and silver. Not to everyone's taste, but certainly unique. The Siam Royal Orchid booth at Northern Village has a spectacular selection. ✉ *94-120 Charoen Muang Rd., Chiang Mai* ✣ *One block from the river* ☎ *053/685–0723* 🌐 *www.royalorchidcollection.com.*

Shiraz

JEWELRY/ACCESSORIES | This small, specialized shop has an unchallenged reputation for reliability, expertise, and good value. If the owner, Mr. Nasser, is behind the counter or at work in his office workroom, you're in luck—you won't find a more knowledgeable gems expert in Chiang Mai. ✉ *170 Thapae Rd., Chiang Mai* ✣ *Near Kampangdin Rd.* ☎ *053/252382* 🌐 *www.shirazjewelrychiangmai.com.*

SPAS

Ban Sabai Village Resort and Spa

SPA/BEAUTY | At this spa you can get your massage in a wooden Thai-style house or a riverside sala. For one treatment of note, the steamed herb massage, soothing herbs are placed on the body. ✉ *210 Moo 0 San Poo Sua, Chiang Mai* ☎ *053/854778 and 79, 082/762–8310* 🌐 *www.bansabaivillage.com.*

Chetawan Thai Traditional Massage School

SPA/BEAUTY | The Chetawan Thai Traditional Massage School is affiliated with Bangkok's famous Wat Po massage school. A 30-minute Thai massage costs B220; a 60-minute oil massage is B400. ✉ *7/1-2 Soi Samut Lana, Chiang Mai* ☎ *053/410360* 🌐 *www.watpomassage.com.*

Oasis Spa

SPA/BEAUTY | Oasis has five locations in Chiang Mai. All offer a full range of massage styles, from Swedish to traditional Thai. The mouthwatering body scrubs include Thai coffee, honey and yogurt, and orange, almond, and honey. ✉ *102 Sirimuangklajan Rd., Chiang Mai* ✥ *At Nimmanhaemin Rd., Soi 17* ☎ *053/920111* 🌐 *www.oasisspa.net/destination/chiang-mai* ✉ *Oasis Spa Lanna, 4 Samlan Rd., Chiang Mai* ☎ *053/920111.*

Thai Massage School Shivagakomarpaj

SPA/BEAUTY | The school, one of Thailand's oldest such establishments, is authorized by the Thai Ministry of Education. A 30-hour, five-day, Level 1 introductory course costs B5,000 (including lunch). ✉ *238/1 Wualai Rd., Chiang Mai* ✥ *Near Thipanet Rd.* ☎ *053/275–085* 🌐 *thaimassageschool.ac.th.*

STREET MARKETS

Kalare Night Bazaar

OUTDOOR/FLEA/GREEN MARKETS | Not to be confused with the Night Bazaar/Night Market, this is in a big entertainment complex on the eastern side of the Night Market on Chang Klan Road (clearly marked). It's packed with boutiques, food and souvenir stalls (and seating), and inexpensive restaurants. Expect regular live music performances, mostly Thai pop bands. ✉ *Chang Klan Rd., Chiang Mai* ✥ *One block north of Loi Kroh Rd.*

★ Night Bazaar

OUTDOOR/FLEA/GREEN MARKETS | The justifiably famous Night Bazaar (also called the Night Market), on Chang Klan Road, is a kind of open-air department store filled with stalls selling everything from inexpensive souvenirs to pricey antiques. In the afternoon and evening, traders set up tented stalls along Chang Klan Road and the adjoining streets. This is a market for tourists; you're expected to bargain, so don't be shy. But remain polite, and don't haggle over tiny sums. ✉ *Chang Klan Rd., Chiang Mai* ✥ *Near Loi Kroh Rd.*

Walking Streets

OUTDOOR/FLEA/GREEN MARKETS | Chiang Mai has two so-called walking streets, closed off to traffic to make way for weekly markets. One is held on **Wualai Road** (the "silver street") on Saturday evening. The other, much larger one, takes up the whole of **Ratchadamnoen Road** and surrounding streets on Sunday. Although the Night Bazaar and Night Market both sell good food and plenty of souvenirs, you will usually find more handicrafts at the walking street markets. ✉ *Chiang Mai.*

TEXTILES

Shinawatra Thai Silk

TEXTILES/SEWING | Silk and other local textiles can be reliably bought at this company's shops, where you can also purchase made-do-order clothing and home-decor items. This is a good place to learn about how silk is made and how the industry has evolved in Thailand. ✉ *18 Huay Kaew Rd., Chiang Mai* ☎ *053/221076* 🌐 *shinawatrathaisilk.co.th* ✉ *Shinawatra Factory, 145/1-2 Chiang Mai-Sankampaeng Rd., Chiang Mai* ☎ *053/221076.*

★ Studio Naenna

TEXTILES/SEWING | Patricia Cheesman has been working with local textiles since 1988 after first encountering them in 1975, when working for the UN in Laos. Today she runs a collective of female weavers, designers, and embroiderers called Weavers for the Evironment (WFE). There's another branch on Nimmanhaemin Road. ✉ *138/8 Soi Chang Khian, Chiang Mai* ☎ *053/226042* 🌐 *www.studio-naenna.com.*

Greater Chiang Mai

Beyond the highway that surrounds Chiang Mai you will find plenty to hold your attention. The most famous sight is Wat Phra That Doi Suthep, the mountaintop temple that overlooks the city. The mountain road that skirts Doi Suthep, winding through the thickly forested Mae

Sa Valley, is lined with tourist attractions for much of the way, from bungee-jumping towers to orchid farms. Several operators have created a network of zip lines through the forest, enabling more adventurous visitors to swing Tarzan-style for more than a mile at treetop level.

Sights

Bhubing Palace

CASTLE/PALACE | The summer residence of the royal family is a serene mansion that shares an exquisitely landscaped park with the more modest mountain retreats of the crown prince and princess. The palace itself cannot be visited, but the gardens are open to the public. Flower enthusiasts swoon at the sight of the roses—among the blooms is a variety created by the king himself. A rough, unpaved road to the left of the palace brings you after 4 km (2½ miles) to a village called Doi Pui Meo, where many of the Hmong women are busy creating finely worked textiles (the songthaew return fare there is B300). On the mountainside above the village are two tiny museums documenting hill tribe life and the opium trade. **■ TIP→ No shorts or short skirts, no bare shoulders.** ✉ *Chiang Mai* ✣ *Off Huay Kaew Rd., 6 km (4 miles) past Wat Phra That Doi Suthep* 🌐 *bhubingpalace.org* 🎫 *Gardens B50* 🕑 *Closed Jan.–Mar.*

Chiang Mai Zoo

ZOO | **FAMILY** | There aren't loads of activities in Chiang Mai that are fun for kids, so this is a good bet if you're traveling with young children. The cages and enclosures of this zoo on the lower slopes of Doi Suthep are spaced out along paths that wind leisurely through shaded woodlands. If the walk seems too strenuous, you can hop on a shuttle that stops at all the sights. The most popular animals are two giant pandas and one cute baby. Koala bears from Australia are also a big attraction—kids are invited to cuddle them. **■ TIP→ The aquarium is within the zoo (additional cost) but is not worth a visit.** ✉ *100 Huay Kaew Rd., Chiang Mai* ☎ *053/221179* 🌐 *www.chiangmai.zoothailand.org/en/index.php* 🎫 *B150; pandas B100 additional; B30 shuttle: B520 aquarium combo ticket.*

Darapirom Palace

HOUSE | This Lanna-style mansion was the last home of Jao Dararasamee, daughter of a late-19th-century ruler of Chiang Mai and the favorite wife of King Chulalongkorn. The low-eaved and galleried building has been restored and furnished with many of the princess's antiques, including clothes she designed herself. It's a living museum of 19th-century Lanna culture and design, and if you've extra time in Chiang Mai, it's worth the 35-minute drive. ✉ *Chiang Mai–Mae Rim Rd., Chiang Mai* 🎫 *B20* 🕑 *Closed Mon. and Sun.*

Doi Suthep National Park

NATIONAL/STATE PARK | **FAMILY** | You don't have to head to the distant mountains to go trekking during your stay in Chiang Mai. Doi Suthep, the 3,542-foot peak that broods over the city, lends its name to a national park with plenty of hiking trails to explore. One of these, a path taken by pilgrims over the centuries preceding the construction of a road, leads up to the gold-spired **Wat Phra That Doi Suthep.** It's a half-day hike from the edge of the city to the temple compound. Set off early to avoid the heat of the midday sun. If it's not a public holiday, you'll probably be alone on the mountain. The trail begins at the entrance of the national park, reached by a five-minute ride in one of the songthaews that wait for passengers at the end of Huay Kaew Road, near the entrance to Chiang Mai Zoo.

An easy hike lasting about 45 minutes brings you to one of Chiang Mai's least known but most charming temples, **Wat Pha Lat.** This modest ensemble of buildings is virtually lost in the forest. Make sure to explore the compound, which has a weathered chedi and a grotto filled with images of the Buddha. After you leave Wat Pha Lat, the path becomes steeper. After another 45 minutes you emerge onto the mountain road, where you can flag down a songthaew if you can't take another step. Otherwise, follow the road for about 200 yards; a break in the forest marks the uphill trail to **Wat Phra That.** Keep a sharp lookout for snakes; they thrive on the mountain, and some of them are highly venomous. ✉ *Huay Kaew Rd., Chiang Mai* ☎ *053/210244* 🌐 *www.thainationalparks.com/doi-suthep-pui-national-park* 🎟 *B200.*

Elephant Nature Park

ZOO | FAMILY | There are several elephant reserves north of Chiang Mai, but there are few where elephants are not ridden. Here more than 30 elephants, including four youngsters, roam freely in the natural enclosure formed by a narrow mountain valley an hour's drive away. Visitors can volunteer to care for the elephants or simply stroll among the elephants, observing them in the river that runs through the park. There are no elephant rides or circuslike shows; Sangduen ("Lek") Chailert, a Ford Foundation laureate who runs the reserve, insists that the animals in her care live as close to nature as possible. Visits, which last a full day, can be arranged online or at the park's Old City office; the rate includes pickup at your Chiang Mai hotel and your return. Longer overnight volunteer packages are also available. ✉ *Old City office, 1 Ratchamankha Rd., Phra Singh, Chiang Mai* ☎ *053/272855, 053/208246* 🌐 *www.elephantnaturepark.org* 🎟 *B2,500.*

San Kamphaeng Hot Springs

HOT SPRINGS | FAMILY | Among northern Thailand's most spectacular hot springs, these include two geysers that shoot water high into the air. The spa complex, set among beautiful flowers, includes an open-air pool and several bathhouses of various sizes. There's a rustic restaurant with a view over the gardens, and small chalets with hot tubs are rented either by the hour (B300) or for the night (B1,000). Tents and sleeping bags can also be rented for B150. The spa is 56 km (35 miles) north of Chiang Mai, beyond the village of San Kamphaeng. Songthaews bound for the spa leave from the riverside flower market in Chiang Mai; be sure to negotiate return transportation. ✉ *Moo 7, Tambon Ban Sahakorn, Mae-On, Chiang Mai* ☎ *053/929077, 053/929099* 🎟 *B100.*

The Mae Sa Valley

This beautiful upland valley winds behind Chiang Mai's Doi Suthep and Doi Pui mountain ranges. A well-paved 100-km (60-mile) loop that begins and ends in Chiang Mai is lined by resorts, country restaurants, hill tribe villages, orchid hothouses, and the Queen Sirikit Botanical Gardens (Darapirom Palace is within 30 minutes' drive). The route follows Highway 1001 north from Chiang Mai, turning left at Mae Rim onto Highway 1096 and then 1269, returning to Chiang Mai from the south on Highway 108.

★ Wat Phra That Doi Suthep

RELIGIOUS SITE | As in so many chapters of Thai history, an elephant is closely involved in the legend surrounding the foundation of the late-14th-century Wat Phra That, northern Thailand's most revered temple and one of only a few enjoying royal patronage. The elephant was dispatched from Chiang Mai carrying religious relics from Wat Suan Dok. Instead of ambling off into the open countryside, it stubbornly climbed up Doi Suthep. When the elephant came to rest at the 3,542-foot summit, the decision was made to establish a temple to contain the relics at that site. Over the centuries the temple compound grew into the glittering assembly of chedis, bots, viharns, and frescoed cloisters you see today. The vast terrace, usually smothered with flowers, commands a breathtaking view of Chiang Mai. Constructing the temple was quite a feat—until 1935 there was no paved road to the temple. Workers and pilgrims alike had to slog through thick jungle. The road was the result of a large-scale community project: individual villages throughout the Chiang Mai region contributed the labor, each laying 1,300-foot sections.

Getting here and around: In Chiang Mai, you can find songthaews at Chang Phuak Gate, the Central Department Store (Huay Kaew Road), and outside Wat Phra Singh to take you on the 30-minute drive to this temple. When you arrive, you are faced with an arduous but exhilarating climb up a broad, 304-step staircase. Flanking it are 16th-century tiled balustrades that take the customary form of nagas, the mythical snakes believed to control irrigation waters. A funicular railway provides a much easier way to the top, but the true pilgrim's path is up the majestic steps. ✉ *Huay Kaew Rd., Chiang Mai* 🎫 *B30; B50 with tram ticket* ☞ *Wheelchair accessible (by elevator).*

Wiang Kum Kam

ARCHAEOLOGICAL SITE | When King Mengrai decided to build his capital on the Ping River, he chose a site a few miles south of present-day Chiang Mai. He selected a low-lying stretch of land, but soon realized the folly of his choice when the river flooded during the rainy seasons. Eight years after establishing Wiang Kum Kam, he moved to higher ground and began work on Chiang Mai. Wiang Kum Kam is now being excavated, and archaeologists have been amazed to uncover a cluster of buildings almost as large as Chiang Mai's Old City. Several agencies run trips to Wiang Kum Kam, with some taking visitors by boat and then horse-drawn carriage. You can book with one, or simply hire a horse and carriage in downtown Chiang Mai (or ask your hotel to; expect to pay around B500 to B650). Horse and carriages hired at the ruins cost B300. ✉ *Chiang Mai* ✣ *4 km (2½ miles) south of Chiang Mai on old Chiang Mai–Lamphun Rd.* 🎫 *Free.*

Restaurants

★ David's Kitchen

$$$$ | **EUROPEAN** | Dress up for this award-winning restaurant owned by a warm and welcoming British-Thai husband-wife front-of-house team and an excellent Thai chef. The three pride themselves on their old-fashioned hospitality, so don't be surprised if one of them greets you at the door and walks you out at the end of the night. **Known for:** crêpes suzette and sticky toffee pudding; curated (if pricey) wine list; rich pastas. [$] *Average main: B650* ✉ *113 Bamrungrad Rd., next to the British Council, Chiang Mai* ☎ *091/068–1744* 🌐 *davidskitchen.co.th* ⏲ *Closed Sun.*

Huen Jai Yong

$ | **THAI** | Ask a Thai chef where to find Chiang Mai's finest and most authentic Lanna food, and you'll likely be directed to this rustic restaurant a 30-minute drive south of the Old City. The place occupies an old timber house and several air-conditioned rooms in a contemporary building that wraps around the back garden. **Known for:** attached shop selling jewelry, textiles, and local honey; big bowls of fermented pork sausage sai ua; cheerful groups of Thai families. [$] *Average main: B80* ✉ *65 Moo 4 San Kamphaeng Rd., Tambon Buak Khang, off Hwy. 1317, Chiang Mai* ☎ *086/671–8710* 💳 *No credit cards.*

Hotels

★ Dhara Dhevi Chiang Mai

$$$$ | **RESORT** | A Thai billionaire turned 60 acres of farmland on the eastern outskirts of Chiang Mai into one of Asia's most extraordinary hotels, re-creating a walled Lanna city surrounded by a moat.

The History of Chiang Mai

Chiang Mai's rich history stretches back more than 700 years to the time when several small tribes, under King Mengrai, banded together to form a new nation called Anachak Lanna Thai. Their first capital was Chiang Rai, but after three decades they moved it to the fertile plains near the Mae Ping River to a site they called Nopburi Si Nakhon Ping Chiang Mai.

The Lanna Thai eventually lost their independence to Ayutthaya and, later, to expansionist Burma. Not until 1774—when the Burmese were finally driven out—did the region revert to the Thai kingdom. After that, the region developed independently of southern Thailand. Even the language is different, marked by a more relaxed tempo. In the last 50 years the city has grown well beyond its original moated city walls, expanding far into the neighboring countryside.

Pros: total seclusion; beautiful grounds; spa treatments. **Cons:** surrounding neighborhood has little activity; navigating the complex can be difficult; it can take 40 minutes to reach the Old City. *Rooms from: B15,000 ✉ 51/4 Chiang Mai–San Kamphaeng Rd., Moo 1, Tambon Tasala, Chiang Mai ☎ 053/888888 www.dharadhevi.com 123 rooms No meals.*

Four Seasons Resort Chiang Mai

$$$$ | RESORT | FAMILY | The magnificent Four Seasons commands 20 acres of tropical countryside above the lush Mae Rim Valley. **Pros:** peaceful mountain setting; idyllic pool; impeccable, attentive service. **Cons:** limited access for those with mobility problems; 40-minute drive from town; rooms and public areas starting to show age. *Rooms from: B23,000 ✉ Mae Rim–Samoeng Old Rd., Chiang Mai ☎ 053/298181, 800/545–4000 in U.S. www.fourseasons.com/chiangmai 98 suites and villas Free breakfast.*

Activities

GOLF

Alpine Golf Resort Chiang Mai

GOLF | This luxurious golf resort has three nine-hole courses across its immaculately maintained green. Morning tee times are most popular because of the heat, so book early. Caddies are well trained and the pro shop stocked with balls, tees, and plenty of clothing—a boon if you've forgotten a hat. *✉ Sankamphaeng Banthi Rd., Chiang Mai ☎ 053/880888 www.alpinegolfresort.com B5,000; B500 caddie; B1,200 club rental; B800 cart rental 18 holes, 7541 yards, par 72.*

Chiangmai Highlands Golf and Spa Resort

GOLF | This comfortable golf resort offers "stay and play" golfing packages with varied accommodation options and extras that include foot massages. The course, designed by Schmidt Curley, opened in 2005. Golfers just starting out can take to the 300-year-old practice range and the two practice putting greens. Its 18th hole, par 5, provides a famously challenging conclusion to a round played here. *✉ 167 Moo 2 Onuar, Mae On, Chiang Mai ☎ 053/261354 www.chiangmai-highlands.com B3,500; B350 caddie; B1,500 club rental; B700 cart rental 18 holes, 7062 yards, par 72.*

ROCK CLIMBING

★ Chiang Mai Rock Climbing Adventures

CLIMBING/MOUNTAINEERING | Enthusiasm and safety standards are both high at CMRCA, which runs caving and rock-climbing excursions for all levels of experience. The guides are passionate about climbing and do everything to make sure guests feels safe, comfortable, and are having a wonderful time. All outings are full-day, and prices vary; the intro-to-climbing day course is B4,995. A day on CMRCA's climbing wall is B250 (shoes B50). **■ TIP→ Kids can be accommodated, but be sure to let CMRCA know in advance.** ✉ *55/3 Ratchapakhinai Rd., Chiang Mai* ☎ *053/207102* 🌐 *www.thailandclimbing.com.*

YOGA

The Yoga Tree

FITNESS/HEALTH CLUBS | No bookings are required for classes at this studio, where beginner classes are held five days a week (B300/class, B1,300/five, B2,500/10). Aspiring yoga teachers can take the 300-hour training course (B2,550). The studio also hosts regular events and workshops throughout the year. ✉ *65/1 Arak Rd., Chiang Mai* ☎ *622/830915* 🌐 *www.theyogatree.com.*

ZIP LINING

Flight of the Gibbon

ZIP LINING | **FAMILY** | Flying Tarzan-style through the jungle of northern Thailand is the ultimate adventure trip for many visitors. Several operators maintain zip lines in stretches of thick forest north of Chiang Mai. Flight of the Gibbon has been established the longest and is reputedly the most reliable. It has more than 7 km (4½ miles) of lines. As you glide along on them, you probably won't see a gibbon, but you'll certainly feel like one. ✉ *Mae Sa Valley Rd., Chiang Mai* ☎ *053/010660* 🌐 *www.flightofthegibbon.com* 🎫 *B4,199.*

Shopping

HANDICRAFTS

Baan Tawai Village

CRAFTS | Four kilometers (2½ miles) beyond Baan Tawai lies a community of shops dealing in antiques and handicrafts. At workshops you can see teak, mango, rattan, and water hyacinth being worked into attractive and unusual items. If you end up buying a heavy piece of teak furniture, the dealer will arrange for its shipping. ✉ *90 Moo 2 Tambon Baan Tawai, near Hang Dong, Chiang Mai* ☎ *081/882–4882* 🌐 *www.ban-tawai.com.*

Umbrella Making Center

CRAFTS | Among the crafts you can find at this large sales outlet in the village of Bo Sang, 10 miles east of Chiang Mai, are hand-painted umbrellas made from lacquered paper and tree bark. Hundreds of these are displayed at the center. The artists here will paint traditional designs on anything from a T-shirt to a suitcase—travelers have discovered that this is a handy way of helping identify their luggage on an airport carousel. ✉ *11/2 Moo 3 Tambon Bo Sang, Chiang Mai* ✥ *On Hwy. 1014 just northeast of Hwy. 1006* ☎ *053/338324.*

Side Trips from Chiang Mai

Doi Inthanon National Park

90 km (54 miles) southwest of Chiang Mai.

GETTING HERE AND AROUND

Although there are minibus services from the nearest village, Chom Tong, to the summit of Doi Inthanon, there is no direct bus route from Chiang Mai. The most convenient way to access the park is either to book a tour with a Chiang Mai operator or hire a car and driver in Chiang Mai for around B3,000 return. If you're driving a rental car (about B2,000 per day), take Highway 108 south (the road to Hot), and after 36 km (22 miles) turn right at Chom Thong onto Road 1099, a sinuous 48-km (30-mile) stretch winding to

Shopping 101

The most popular buys are vibrant hill tribe textiles and products made from textiles, such as handbags and shoes; handicrafts, from handmade paper to pretty parasols (great for the sun); hippie clothes; knockoff bags; and accessories and jewelry.

Antiques

True antiques are hard to find. If you find something you like, examine it very carefully for signs of counterfeiting—new paint or varnish, tooled damage marks—and ask for certificates of provenance and written guarantees that the goods can be returned if proved counterfeit. The Night Bazaar has two floors packed with plenty of nice pieces and trinkets claiming to be "antiques," and most of which are certainly not.

The road south to Hang Dong (take the signposted turn before the airport) is lined with antiques shops. Just outside Hang Dong you'll reach the craft village of Ban Tawai. You could spend an entire morning or afternoon rummaging through its antiques shops and storerooms.

Handicrafts

For two of Chiang Mai's specialties, lacquerware and paper products, take a taxi or songthaew to any of the outlets along San Kamphaeng Road. Large emporiums that line the 10-km (6-mile) stretch sell a wide variety of items. Whole communities here devote themselves to their traditional trades. One community rears silkworms, for instance, providing the raw product for the looms humming in workshops.

Outside the city center, the highways running south and east of Chiang Mai are lined for several miles with workshops stocked with handicrafts of every description. They're a favorite destination for tuk-tuk drivers, who receive a commission on goods bought by their passengers.

For local handicrafts, head to Thapae Road and Loi Kroh Road. Across the Nawarat Bridge, Charoen Rat Road is home to a handful of boutiques selling interesting crafts. Farther afield, along Nimmanhaemin Road, a whole slew of crafts and home goods shops has developed. Start from Soi 1 and work your way south.

Jewelry

Chiang Mai is well known for for its shops selling gems and semiprecious stones. If gold is your passion, make your way to the Chinese district. All the stores that jostle for space at the eastern end of Chang Moi Road are reliable, invariably issuing certificates of authenticity. The city's silver district, Wualai Road, is lined for several hundred yards with shops where you can sometimes see silversmiths at work. ■ **TIP→ If you want trinkets, the Night Market is fine, but it's not the place to find authentic jewelry and gems.**

Textiles

Chiang Mai and textiles, both silk and woven cotton, go hand in hand. Here you can buy products and see them being manufactured. Several companies along San Kamphaeng Road open their workrooms to visitors and explain the process of making fine silk. ■ **TIP→ Factory shops are favorite destinations of package tours, so prices will be higher than in other parts of town or at the Night Market.**

the mountain's summit. ■ **TIP→ The ashes of Chiang Mai's last monarch, King Inthawichayanon, are contained on Road 1099 in a secluded stupa that draws hundreds of thousands of pilgrims annually.**

SAFETY AND PRECAUTIONS

The regular flow of visitors to the mountain ensures that it's a perfectly safe destination, although you should stick to marked paths and forest trails. A guide (obtainable at the national park headquarters) is recommended if you plan a long hike on the thickly forested mountain slopes.

TIMING

Doi Inthanon is a full day's outing from Chiang Mai. Chalets near the national park headquarters are available if you plan to stay overnight. Dawn on the mountain is an unforgettable experience, with the tropical sun slowly penetrating the upland mist against a background of chattering monkeys, barking deer, and birdsong.

Sights

★ Doi Inthanon National Park

NATIONAL/STATE PARK | FAMILY | Doi Inthanon, Thailand's highest mountain (8,464 feet), rises majestically over a national park of staggering beauty. Many have compared the landscape—thick forests of pines, oaks, and laurels—with that of Canada. Only the tropical vegetation on its lower slopes, and the 30 villages that are home to 3,000 Karen and Hmong people, remind you that this is indeed Asia. The reserve is of great interest to nature lovers, especially birders who come to see the 362 species that nest here. Red-and-white rhododendrons run riot, as do plants found nowhere else in Thailand.

Hiking trails penetrate deep into the park, which has some of Thailand's highest and most beautiful waterfalls. The Mae Klang Falls, just past the turnoff to the park, are easily accessible on foot or by vehicle, but the most spectacular are more remote and involve a trek of 4 to 5 km (2½ to 3 miles). The Mae Ya Falls are the country's highest falls, but even more spectacular are the Siribhum Falls, which plunge in two parallel cataracts from a 1,650-foot-high cliff above the Inthanon Royal Research Station. The station's vast nurseries are a gardener's dream, filled with countless varieties of tropical and temperate plants. Rainbow trout—unknown in the warm waters of Southeast Asia—are raised here in tanks fed by cold streams plunging from the mountain's heights, then served at the station's restaurant. The national park office provides maps and guides for trekkers and bird-watchers. Accommodations are available: B1,000 for a two-person chalet, B6,500 for a villa for up to eight people. The park admission fee is collected at a tollbooth at the start of the road to the summit. ✉ *Amphoe Chomtong* ☎ *053/286728, 053/286729* 🌐 *www.thainationalparks.com/doi-inthanon-national-park* 🎫 *B300 per person, plus B30 per car.*

Lamphun

20 km (12 miles) south of Chiang Mai.

Lamphun claims to be the oldest existing city in Thailand (but so does Nakhon Pathom). Originally called Nakhon Hariphunchai, it was founded in AD 660. Its first ruler was a queen, Chamthewi, who has a special place in Thailand's pantheon of powerful female leaders. Two striking statues of her are in the sleepy little town, and one of its wats bears her name. Queen Chamthewi founded the eponymous dynasty, which ruled the region until 1932. Today the compact little city is the capital of Thailand's smallest province and also a textile and silk production center.

Lamphun has two of northern Thailand's most important monasteries, dating back more than 1,000 years. The smallest of them, Wat Chamthewi, holds the remains of the city's fabled 8th-century ruler, Queen Chamthewi. The other, Wat Phra That Hariphunchai, is a walled treasure house of ancient chapels, chedis, and gilded Buddhas.

Several Chiang Mai travel agencies offer day trips to Lamphun, and any hired tour guide will go with you. A vehicle isn't strictly necessary—you can easily take a bus and then walk or take a tuk-tuk around.

Lamphun's Native Fruit

The countryside surrounding Lamphun is blanketed with orchards of longan, aka *lamyai*, a sweet cherry-size fruit with a thin, buff-colored shell. The annual lamyai festival brings the town to a halt in the first week of August with parades, exhibitions, a beauty contest, and copious quantities of lamyai wine. The lamyai-flower honey is reputed to have exceptional healing and aphrodisiacal powers. You can buy lamyai at the market stalls along the 100-yard covered wooden bridge opposite Wat Phra That Hariphunchai.

GETTING HERE AND AROUND

Buses from Chiang Mai to Lampang stop at Lamphun, a 40-minute drive south on Highway 106, a busy but beautiful road shaded by 100-foot-tall rubber trees. The buses leave every 20 to 30 minutes from Chiang Mai's city bus station (Chang Phuek Bus Station, not Arcade) and from a stop next to the Tourism Authority of Thailand office on Chiangmai-Lamphun Road. Blue minibus songthaews also operate a service to Lamphun. They leave from in front of Warorot Market, and you can flag them down anywhere on Chiangmai-Lamphun Road. Fares for all services to Lamphun are about B50. Lamphun has no bus station; buses stop at various points around town, including at the TAT office and outside Wat Hariphunchai.

A couple of slow overnight Bangkok-to-Chiang Mai trains stop at Lamphun, where a *samlor* (pedicab) can take you the 3 km (2 miles) into town for about B30; but unless you're staying in Lamphun or willing to carry around your bags, the bus is more practical.

Lamphun is a compact city, easy to tour on foot, although Wat Chamthewi is on the outskirts and best visited by tuk-tuk or songthaew.

SAFETY AND PRECAUTIONS

Lamphun knows little street crime, although the usual precautions are recommended if walking the city streets at night—leave valuables in your hotel safe or with the management. Women visitors are advised to carry handbags on the side away from the street.

TIMING

One day is sufficient for Lamphun, which is less than an hour's drive from Chiang Mai. The tiny provincial capital has very little nightlife (though that's part of its charm), few restaurants, and only one hotel up to international standards.

Sights

Hariphunchai National Museum
MUSEUM | Just outside Wat Phra That Hariphunchai, the National Museum has a fine selection of Dvaravati-style stuccowork. The collection of Lanna antiques is also impressive. ✉ *Chai Mongkol Rd.* ✥ *At Chiang Mai-Lamphun Rd.* ☎ *053/511186* *B100* *Closed Mon. and Tues.*

Ku Chang
CEMETERY | Lamphun has one of the region's most unusual cemeteries, an elephant's graveyard called Ku Chang. The rounded chedi is said to contain the

remains of Queen Chamthewi's favorite war elephant. ⊠ *38 Soi Ku Chang* ✣ *Enter from Chittawongphan Rangsan.*

★ Wat Chamthewi

RELIGIOUS SITE | About 2 km (1 mile) west of Lamphun's center is Wat Chamthewi, often called the "topless chedi" because the gold that once covered the spire was pillaged sometime during its history. Work began on the monastery in AD 755, and despite a modern viharn added to the side of the complex, it retains an ancient, weathered look. Suwan Chang Kot, to the right of the entrance, is the most famous of the two chedis, built by King Mahantayot to hold the remains of his mother, the legendary Queen Chamthewi. The five-tier sandstone chedi is square; on each tier are Buddha images that get progressively smaller. All are in the 9th-century Dvaravati style, though many have obviously been restored. The other chedi was probably built in the 10th century, though most of what you see today is the doings of King Phaya Sapphasit, who reigned during the 12th century. You'll probably want to take a samlor down the narrow residential street to the complex. This is not an area where samlors generally cruise, so ask the driver to wait for you. ⊠ *Chamadevi Rd.* ✣ *Adjacent to Lamphun Hospital.*

★ Wat Phra That Hariphunchai

RELIGIOUS SITE | The temple complex of the 11th-century Wat Phra That Hariphunchai is dazzling. Through gates guarded by ornamental lions lies a three-tier, sloping-roof viharn, a replica of the original that burned down in 1915. Inside, note the large Chiang Saen–style bronze image of the Buddha and the carved *thammas* (Buddhism's universal principals) to the left of the altar. As you leave the viharn, you pass what is reputedly the largest bronze gong in the world, cast in 1860. The 165-foot Suwana chedi, covered in copper and topped by a golden spire, dates from 847. A century later King Athitayarat, the 32nd ruler of Hariphunchai, added a nine-tier umbrella, gilded with 14 pounds of gold. At the back of the compound—where you can find a shortcut to the center of town—there's another viharn with a standing Buddha, a sala housing four Buddha footprints, and the old museum. ⊠ *Chai Mongkol Rd.* ✣ *At Chiang Mai-Lamphun Rd.* *B40.*

Restaurants

Lamphun Ice Restaurant

$ | **ASIAN** | The name of this restaurant seems to derive from its origins as an ice-cream parlor—and nine flavors are still served. The interior has cozy booths that give the place the feel of a vintage soda fountain. **Known for:** good coffee, hot or iced; ice cream sundaes and banana splits; air-conditioned respite with free Wi-Fi. $ *Average main: B180* ⊠ *Chaimongkol Rd.* ✣ *Opposite southern gate of Wat Phra That Hariphunchai* ☎ *090/891–8708* ⊙ *Closed Fri.*

★ Temple House Lamphun

$$ | **ECLECTIC** | Architect Sing Intrachooto and Chaiyong Rattana-Angkura's airy shophouse-turned-café, art gallery, shop, and guesthouse is the kind of warm, homey space where you'll want to linger all day—a proper gem. The food selection is small but good: pasta, a few sandwiches, and toothsome pastries and cake. **Known for:** rotating art exhibits; hummingbird cake (banana-pineapple spice cake); good coffee. $ *Average main: B200* ⊠ *102 Intharayongyot Rd.* ✣ *Soi Rotkaew near Chiang Mai-Lamphun Rd.* ☎ *065/056–9839* ⊙ *Closed Mon.*

Hotels

PickBaan Hostel & Cafe

$ | **B&B/INN** | A charming and immaculate guesthouse whose ground-floor café is a hub for trendy locals, PickBaan is an excellent base for Lamphun sightseeing. **Pros:** free bikes; excellent coffee; friendly, helpful staff. **Cons:** some may find beds too soft; shared bathrooms; some noise in rooms. $ *Rooms from: B630* ✉ *10 Ratchawong Rd.* ✣ *Near Chiang Mai-Lamphun Rd.* ☎ *082/493–3838* ⇆ *5 rooms* 🍽 *Free breakfast.*

Shopping

Lamphun's silk and other textiles make a visit to this small but charming town worthwhile. Its 91-meter-long (100-yard-long) covered wooden pedestrian bridge is where a handful of vendors set up shop, selling silk, textiles, and local handicrafts, daily from roughly 9 am to 6 pm. The bridge is opposite the main entrance to Wat Phra That Hariphunchai, Inthayongyot Road.

Lampoon Thai Silk

TEXTILES/SEWING | Eight kilometers (5 miles) from Lamphun on the main Lampang highway is one of the area's largest silk businesses, where you can watch women weave at wooden looms. ✉ *8/2 Panangjitawong Rd., Changkong* ☎ *053/510329.*

Lampang

65 km (40 miles) southeast of Lamphun, 91 km (57 miles) southeast of Chiang Mai.

At the end of the 19th century, when Lampang was a thriving center of the teak trade, well-to-do local elders gave the city a genteel look by buying a fleet of English-built carriages and a stable of nimble ponies to pull them through the streets. Until then elephants had been a favored means of transportation—a century ago the number of elephants, employed in the nearby teak forests, nearly matched the city's population. The carriages arrived on the first trains to steam into Lampang's fine railroad station, which still looks much the same as it did back then. More than a century later, the odd sight of horse-drawn carriages still greets visitors to Lampang. The brightly painted, flower-bedecked carriages, driven by hardened types in Stetson hats and cowboy boots, look touristy, but the locals also use them to get around the city, albeit for considerably less than the B10 visitors are usually charged for a short city tour (B200 for a longer tour, or B300 per hour).

Apart from some noteworthy temples and a smattering of fine teak shophouses and private homes, not much else remains of Lampang's prosperous heyday. An ever-dwindling number of sturdy 19th-century teak houses can be found among the maze of concrete. Running parallel to the south bank of the Wang River is a narrow street of ancient shops and homes that once belonged to the Chinese merchants who catered to Lampang's prosperous populace. **■ TIP→ The riverfront promenade is a pleasant place for a stroll; some of the cafés and restaurants along it have terraces overlooking the water.**

GETTING HERE AND AROUND

Lampang Airport, which handles domestic flights, is just west of downtown. Songthaews run to the city center for around B60. Bangkok Airways and Nok Air each have three flights a day from Bangkok.

Buses from Chiang Mai to Lampang, leave every half hour, often more frequently, from Chiang Mai's Arcade Bus Station. You are unlikely to have to wait more than 20 minutes. Expect to pay B40 to B150. The VIP buses that run Bangkok to Chiang Mai also stop in Lampang.

Within Lampang, songthaews are the cheapest way of getting around, though traveling via the city's horse-drawn carriages is delightfully retro. Carriages are at various city stands, outside the old town hall, and outside Wienglakor Hotel and Wiengthong Hotel.

All Bangkok-to-Chiang Mai trains stop at Lampang, where a samlor or tuk-tuk can take you the 3 km (2 miles) into town for about B40. By train Lampang is 2 to 2½ hours from Chiang Mai and 11 to 13 hours from Bangkok depending on which train you choose. First-class fares from Bangkok range from B1,700 for a sleeper to B700 to B900 for a day train.

TOURS

Lampang Holiday Tours
This travel agency arranges tours of the temples and Lampang's old quarter. ✉ *260/17 Chatchai Rd.* ☎ *054/310403* ✉ *lampangholiday@yahoo.co.uk.*

SAFETY AND PRECAUTIONS
Lampang is a famously friendly city, with a sizable expat population, mostly teachers and retirees. Few cases of street crime or theft involve foreigners. The usual precautions are nevertheless advised, particularly if walking on less-busy streets at night—leave valuables in your hotel room.

TIMING
Lampang is worth at least one overnight stay. It has a large selection of comfortable hotels and a few restaurants where a pleasant evening can be spent.

Sights

Wat Phra Kaew Don Tao
RELIGIOUS SITE | Near the banks of the Wang River, this temple is dominated by its tall chedi, built on a rectangular base and topped with a rounded spire. More interesting, however, are the Burmese-style shrine and adjacent Thai-style sala. The 18th-century shrine has a multitier roof. The interior walls are carved and inlaid with colored stones; the ornately engraved ceiling is painted with enamel. The sala, with the traditional three-tier roof and carved-wood pediments, houses a Sukhothai-style reclining Buddha. Legend has it that the sala was once home to the Emerald Buddha, which now resides in Bangkok. In 1436, when King Sam Fang Kaem was transporting the statue from Chiang Rai to Chiang Mai, his elephant reached Lampang and refused to go farther. The Emerald Buddha is said to have remained here for the next 32 years, until the succeeding king managed to get it to Chiang Mai. ✉ *Phra Kaew Rd.* 🎫 *20B.*

★ Wat Phra That Lampang Luang
RELIGIOUS SITE | One of the most venerated temples in the north, Wat Phra That Lampang Luang is also one of the most striking. Surrounded by stout laterite defense walls, the temple, near the village of Ko Khang, has the appearance of a fortress, exactly what it was when the legendary Queen Chamthewi founded her capital here in the 8th century. The Burmese captured it two-and-a-half centuries ago but were ejected by the forces of a Lampang prince—a bullet hole marks the spot where he killed the Burmese commander. The sandy temple compound has much to hold your interest, including a tiny chapel with a hole in the door that creates an amazing, inverted photographic image of the wat's central, gold-covered chedi. The temple's ancient viharn has a beautifully carved wooden facade; note the intricate

Shopping Secrets

Before setting off on a shopping expedition, buy a copy of *Shopping Secrets of Chiang Mai*, a comprehensive 280-page visitors' guide containing in-depth information on virtually everything the city has to offer. It's available in most bookstores. Or page through the local English-language monthlies *Guidelines* (🌐 *guidelineschiangmai.com*) and *Art & Culture Lanna*, available free of charge in most hotels. Both are packed with information and feature local crafts by trustworthy dealers.

decorations around the porticoes. A museum has excellent wood carvings, but its treasure is a small emerald Buddha, which some claim was carved from the same stone as its counterpart in Bangkok. ✉ *Lampang* ✥ *15 km (9 miles) south of Lampang in Koh Kha district.*

Wat Si Chum

RELIGIOUS SITE | Workers from Myanmar were employed in the region's rapidly expanding logging business, and these immigrants left their mark on the city's architecture. Especially well preserved is Wat Sri Chum, a 19th-century Burmese temple. Pay particular attention to the viharn, as the eaves are covered with beautiful carvings. Inside you can find gold-and-black lacquered pillars supporting a carved-wood ceiling. To the right is a bronze Buddha cast in the Burmese style. Red-and-gold panels on the walls depict temple scenes. ✉ *Sukhothai Historical Park, Jarodwititong Rd.* ✥ *Opposite Ramkhamhaeng National Museum* 🎫 *100B.*

Restaurants

Rim Wang

$ | **THAI** | This simple Thai restaurant sits on the banks of the Wang River, 2 km (1 mile) down the main 1034 highway in the village of Ko Kha. Fresh fish is a daily specialty, but try the plump fish cakes or a crispy version of *larb,* a popular minced-pork dish. **Known for:** frills-free seafood; quiet tables in a riverfront restaurant; catch-of-the day river fish. 💲 *Average main: B175* ✉ *Hwy. 1034, Ko Kha* ☎ *054/281104* ▭ *No credit cards.*

Hotels

The Coconut Hotel

$ | **HOTEL** | Ten minutes by tuk-tuk outside downtown Lampang, this pristine hotel has good air-conditioning, comfortable beds, and strong Wi-Fi, and most rooms have balconies. **Pros:** clean, spacious rooms; family rooms available; most rooms have balconies. **Cons:** 30 minutes' walk downtown; noise carries through doors and walls; few choices at breakfast. 💲 *Rooms from: B860* ✉ *124/9, Prabath Rd., Soi 3, Lamphun* ☎ *054/821789* 🌐 *www.thecoconuthotel.com* *50 rooms* 🍽 *Free breakfast.*

Lampang River Lodge

$$ | **RESORT** | Nature lovers are well catered to at this remote lodge, a simple riverside resort isolated in woodland and a 15-minute drive south of Lampang's bright lights. **Pros:** beautifully landscaped grounds; magical riverside bar; ample parking. **Cons:** far from city center; shuttle bus to Lampang infrequent; patchy restaurant service. 💲 *Rooms from: B2,600* ✉ *330 Moo 11, Tambol Chompoo, off Chiang Mai–Lampang Hwy. 11* ☎ *054/336640* 🌐 *www.lampangriverlodge.com* *60 rooms* 🍽 *Free breakfast.*

★ **Riverside Guest House**

$ | **B&B/INN** | Under the same management as the nearby Riverside restaurant, this utterly enchanting place has the same rustic coziness. **Pros:** homey atmosphere; garden hammocks; river views. **Cons:** noisy neighborhood dogs; no restaurant on-site; some rooms share baths. 💲 *Rooms from: B400* ✉ *286 Talad Kao Rd.* ☎ *054/227005* 🌐 *www.theriverside-lampang.com* *7 rooms* 🍽 *No meals.*

Shopping

Lampang is known for its blue, white, and orange pottery, much of it incorporating the image of a cockerel, the city's emblem. The city has a weekend evening street market (Kad Kong Ta), on Talad Kao Road, where vendors sell food and drink, as well as pottery, fabrics, and handicrafts. ■ **TIP→ You can find the best bargains at markets like Thung Kwian Market, a few miles south of the city on the highway to Bangkok, or north of the city on the road to Chiang Mai.**

Thailand's Elephants

The United States has its eagle. Britain acquired the lion. Thailand's symbolic animal is the elephant, which has played an enormous role in the country's history through the ages. It even appeared on the national flag when Thailand was Siam. It's a truly regal gentle giant—white elephants enjoy royal patronage, and several are stabled at the National Elephant Institute's conservation center near Lampang.

But the elephant is also an animal of the people, domesticated some 2,000 years ago to help with the heavy work and logging in the teak forests of northern Thailand. Elephants were in big demand by the European trading companies, who scrambled for rich harvests of teak in the late 19th and early 20th centuries. At one time there were nearly as many elephants in Lampang as people.

Early on, warrior rulers recognized their usefulness in battle, and "Elephants served as the armored tanks of pre-modern Southeast Asian armies," according to the late American historian David K. Wyatt. The director of the mahout training program at the Lampang conservation center believes he is a reincarnation of one of the foot soldiers who ran beside elephants in campaigns against Burmese invaders.

Increasing Threats

Though a few elephants enjoy royal status, most are under threat. The International Union for Conservation of Nature (IUCN) Red List includes Asian elephants as endangered. Ivory poaching, cross-border trade in live elephants, and urban encroachment have reduced Thailand's elephant population from about 100,000 a century ago to just 2,500 today. Despite conservation efforts, even these 2,500 face an uncertain future as mechanization and a 1989 government ban on private logging threw virtually all elephants and their mahouts out of work. Elephants eat roughly 200 kilograms (440 pounds) of food a day, a huge expense for mahouts.

What's a Tourist to Do?

Elephant tourism in Thailand is a contentious issue. With the ban on private logging, mahouts and their elephants have been left with no options for livelihood. The various elephant camps in northern Thailand, sometimes called conservation centers are a response to this. Here tourists can interact with elephants, feeding, bathing, and sometimes riding them. Whether or not these camps are good for elephants is hotly debated. One side argues that without tourism dollars, the mahouts and by proxy their elephants will be destitute. The other says this treatment of elephants is inhumane. Both sides are correct. The best and most considerate (to both sides of the argument) course of action for a visitor is to choose elephant conservation centers that do not allow rides, where elephants do not perform routines, and where elephants—social creatures just like humans—can roam freely and spend time with other elephants. Chiangmai Elephant Land within Doi Inthanon National Park and Happy Elephant Care, near the park and about an hour outside Chiang Mai are good options.

Indra Ceramic

CERAMICS/GLASSWARE | Lampang's biggest pottery outlet is west of the city center on the road to Phrae. You can see the ceramics being made and even paint your own designs. The extensive showrooms feature a ceramic model city. ✉ *382 Vajiravudh Damnoen Rd., Lampang–Phrae Hwy.* ✥ *2 km (1 mile) west of city center* ☎ *054/315591* 🌐 *www.indraceramic.com.*

★ Kad Kong Ta Market

OUTDOOR/FLEA/GREEN MARKETS | The alternately handsome and crumbling colonial-, Burmese- and Chinese-style houses along Old Market Road date to the late 1860s, when British and Burmese teak companies and Chinese traders lived here. Today the street is again a hub of trade, when a market sets up every Saturday and Sunday from 4 to 9 pm. The 1.2-mile market is lined with stalls selling tasty street fare (noodles, summer rolls, satay, sweets, fresh fruit), textiles, contemporary and traditional clothing, artwork, jewelry, and assorted souvenirs. There's always live music which adds to the atmosphere. **■ TIP→ Unlike Chiang Mai markets, this market is not crowded, and you can make your way down the road at a more leisurely pace.** ✉ *Talad Gao Rd.* ✥ *At Tippawan Rd.*

Chapter 8

NORTHERN THAILAND

Updated by
Andrew Parks

Sights	Restaurants	Hotels	Shopping	Nightlife
★★★★☆	★★★★☆	★★★☆☆	★★★★☆	★☆☆☆☆

WELCOME TO NORTHERN THAILAND

TOP REASONS TO GO

★ **Natural Wonders:** Northern Thailand is mountain country. Beyond Chiang Mai, the peaks rise to the borders of Myanmar and Laos, crisscrossed by deep valleys and fast-flowing rivers. National parks welcome hikers and campers to wild areas of outstanding natural beauty and hill tribe villages lost in time. At the southern edge lie the ruins of Sukhothai, a cradle of Siamese civilization.

★ **Shopping:** The region is world famous for its silks, and the night markets of Mae Hong Son and Chiang Rai have an astonishing range of handicrafts, many of them from hill tribe villages.

★ **Eating:** Many people consider northern Thai cuisine the country's tastiest. Excellent restaurants can be found throughout the region, and even the simplest food stall can serve up delicious surprises.

★ **Temples:** The golden spires of thousands of temples dot the region. Each can tell you volumes about Buddhist faith and culture.

1 **Nan.**

2 **Phrae.**

3 **Pai.**

4 **Mae Hong Son.**

5 **Khun Yuam.**

6 **Mae Sariang.**

7 **Chiang Dao.**

8 **Doi Ang Khang.**

9 **Tha Ton.**

10 **Chiang Rai.**

11 **Chiang Saen.**

12 **Ban Sop Ruak.**

13 **Chiang Khong.**

14 **Mae Sai.**

15 **Phitsanulok.**

16 **Sukhothai.**

17 **Si Satchanalai.**

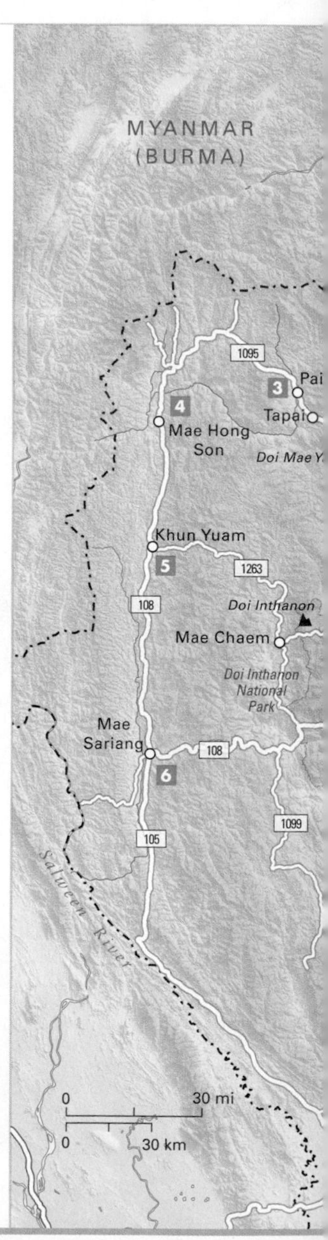

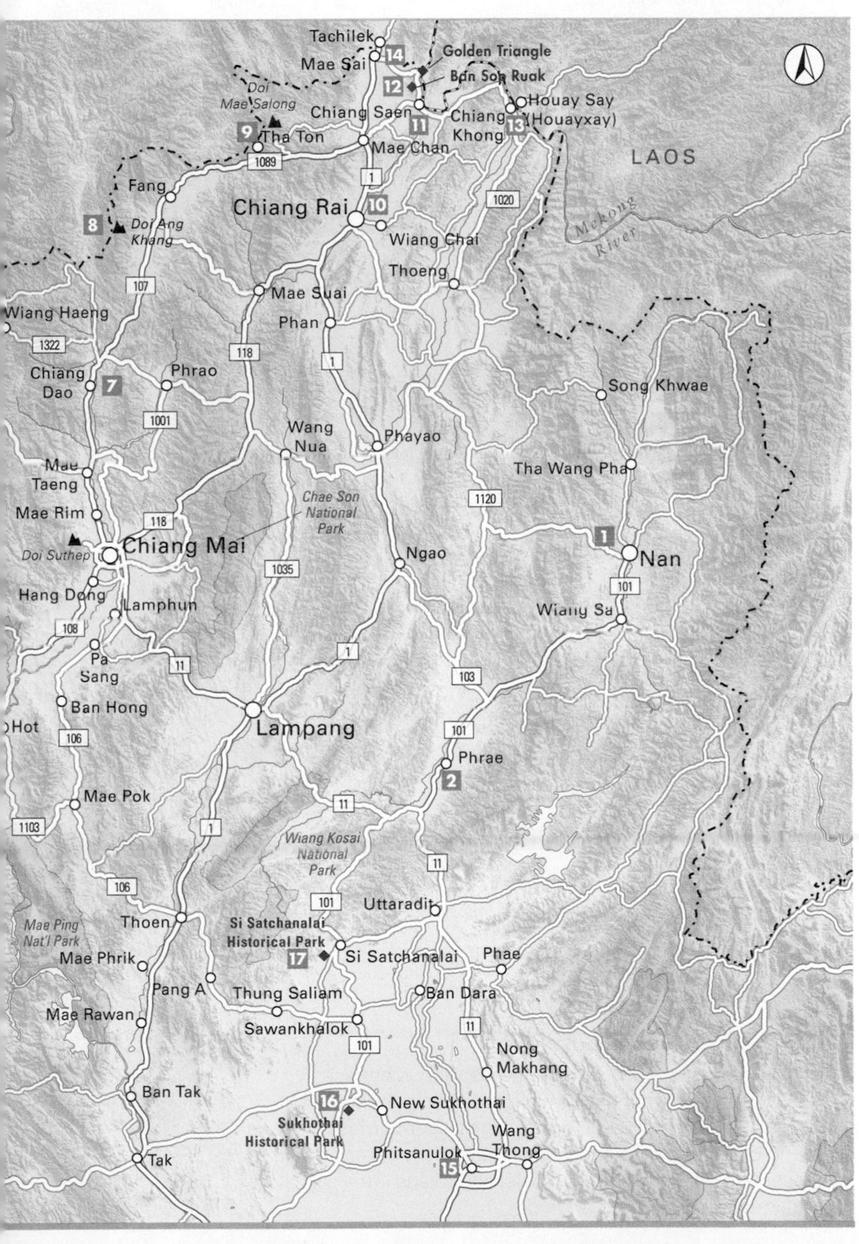
Tachilek
Mae Sai
14
Golden Triangle
Ban Sop Ruak
12
Doi Mae Salong
9
Tha Ton
Chiang Saen
11
Chiang Khong
13
Houay Say (Houayxay)
Mae Chan
1089
LAOS
Fang
1
Chiang Rai
10
1020
8
Doi Ang Khang
Wiang Chai
Mekong River
Thoeng
107
Mae Suai
Wiang Haeng
Phan
1322
118
1
Chiang Dao
7
Phrao
Song Khwae
1001
Wang Nua
Phayao
Mae Taeng
Tha Wang Pha
Mae Rim
Chae Son National Park
1120
118
Doi Suthep
Chiang Mai
1
Nan
Ngao
1035
101
Hang Dong
Lamphun
Wiang Sa
108
Pa Sang
1
11
103
Ban Hong
Hot
Lampang
101
106
Phrae
2
Mae Pok
11
1103
1
Wiang Kosai National Park
11
106
101
Uttaradit
Mae Ping Nat'l Park
Thoen
Si Satchanalai Historical Park
17
Si Satchanalai
Phae
Mae Phrik
Pang A
Thung Saliam
Ban Dara
Mae Rawan
Sawankhalok
11
101
Nong Makhang
Ban Tak
16
New Sukhothai
Sukhothai Historical Park
Wang Thong
Phitsanulok
15
Tak

EATING AND DRINKING WELL IN NORTHERN THAILAND

To most food lovers, Thailand's northern reaches are a culinary hot spot, literally and figuratively. The distinctive Laotian and Burmese influences, as seen in the spicy salads, grilled river fish, and other delicacies prepared here likely resemble no Thai food you've tasted back home. Through rice paddies, across plains, and along the majestic Mekong, a healthy peasant's diet of fresh river fish, sticky rice, sausage, and spicy salads replaces the richer shellfish and coconut curries of Thailand's center and south.

Thailand's expansive north encompasses various ethnicities and immigrant groups, making it hard to pigeonhole the food. Universal, however, are searingly sour curries centering on sharp herbs and spices rather than coconut milk; river fish grilled over open coals; and salads integrating lime and fermented shrimp.

CLEVER COOKING IN NORTHERN THAILAND

The food of the far north is distinctly different from that of the rest of Thailand. In this poorer region of the country, cooks are sometimes inspired by whatever's on hand. Take salted eggs, for example. They're soaked in salt and then pickled, preserving a fragile food in the hot environment and adding another tasty briny element to dishes.

PLA DUK YANG

You'll find grilled river fish throughout the north, and snakehead fish is one of the region's specialties. As opposed to the south, where fish is often deep-fried or curried, here it is usually stuffed with big, long lemongrass skewers and grilled over an open fire, searing the skin. Add the spicy, sour curry that's served atop the fish—and throw in *som tam* salad and sticky rice for good measure—and you've got a quintessential northern meal.

SOM TAM

Som tam, a ragingly hot green papaya salad prepared with a mortar and pestle, originated from the northeastern Isaan region but is popular throughout Thailand. Tease out the differences between three versions: *som tam poo,* integrating black crab shells (a challenging texture, to say the least); *som tam pla,* an Isaan version with salt fish and long bean; and the traditional Thai *som tam,* ground with peanuts and tiny dried and fermented shrimp.

KHAO LAM

On highways, meandering rural roads, and at most markets you'll find women selling tubes of bamboo filled with sticky rice and coconut. The rice is grilled over smoky coals, which adds a woodiness to the rice's rich, sweet, salty flavor. (Slowly peel off the bamboo to eat it.) The rice can be black or white, and sometimes is cooked with minuscule purplish beans. In mango season, *khao neaw ma muang* (mango with sticky rice) is the ultimate salty-sweet dessert.

KHAO SOI

This comforting noodle dish, believed to have Chinese Muslim origins, is ubiquitous in the north. Egg noodles and chicken pieces (generally a leg per serving) swim in a hearty stock fortified by coconut milk, flavored with turmeric and ginger, and topped with deep-fried noodles. Add your own chile paste and lime to taste. Cheap and hearty, it's a street stall favorite in Chiang Mai.

GAENG HANG LAY

Another northern favorite, most likely of Burmese origin, is a rich and complex slow-cooked pork curry (usually pork belly and ribs). It owes its unique flavor to the Indian-influenced use of dried spices such as coriander and cumin seeds, cardamom pods, star anise, and ground nuts (peanuts). It's best served with a side dish of sticky rice that is used to mop up the sauce.

Northern Thailand begins where the flat rice-growing countryside above Bangkok rises north toward the mountains bordering Myanmar and Laos. The vast region is strikingly different, both culturally and geographically, from the south. The north has its own language (Kham Muang), cuisine, traditional beliefs and rituals (many of them animist), and a sturdy architectural style these days called Lanna ("a million rice fields"). The north's distinguishing physical feature, the mountains, contributed to the development of distinctive cultures and subcultures by isolating the mostly rural residents. Even today the daunting terrain is protecting them from too rapid an advance of outside influences.

Although Chiang Mai is the natural capital of northern Thailand it's not the only city in the region deserving inclusion in a Thailand itinerary. Chiang Rai, Chiang Saen, Mae Hong Son, Phrae, and Nan have enough attractions, particularly historic temples, to make at least overnight visits worthwhile. The ancient city of Sukhothai, with its stunning ensemble of temple ruins, is a stand-alone destination in its own right but can be easily integrated into a tour of the north. The mountains and forested uplands that separate these fascinating cities are studded with simple national park lodges and luxury resorts, hot-water spas, elephant camps—the list is endless.

Chiang Rai is a particularly suitable base for exploring the region further—either on treks to the hill tribe villages that dot the mountainsides or on shorter jaunts by elephant. The fast-flowing mountain rivers provide ideal conditions for white-water rafting and canoeing. The truly adventurous may want to head for one of the national parks, which offer overnight accommodations and the services of guides.

From Chiang Rai, circular routes run through the city's upland surroundings and deep into more remote mountains, where descendants of Chinese soldiers who fled after the Communist takeover of their country grow coffee and tea. Nan is tucked away in the mountainous corner bordering Laos, and Myanmar lies just over the nearest range from Mae Hong Son and Mae Sariang. The so-called Mae Hong Son Loop, a spectacular road starting and ending in Chiang Mai, runs through a small market town, Pai, that has developed over the years into a major tourist destination. First discovered by backpackers doing the "Loop," the town's simple guesthouses are now making way for smart resorts designed for Bangkok businesspeople seeking a quiet weekend in the north.

MAJOR REGIONS

A journey through northern Thailand feels like venturing into an entirely different country than what you'll find within the frenzied streets of far-off Bangkok: the landscape, language, architecture, food, and even the people are all quite distinct. Chiang Mai is the area's natural capital and main draw, but Chiang Rai is also developing rapidly. Both cities are not smaller versions of Bangkok, either; they're bustling commercial and cultural centers in their own right. Just beyond each of them rises the mountain range that forms the eastern buttress of the Himalayas. The region's northernmost section borders Myanmar and Laos, and improved land crossings into Laos from here have made forays into that country a popular side trip.

Visitors looking for off-the-beaten-track territory usually head north from Chiang Mai and Chiang Rai to the Golden Triangle or west to Mae Hong Son. Relatively few venture east, toward Laos, but if time permits **Nan and nearby** is a region well worth exploring. At its center, some 70 km (42 miles) from the Laotian border, is **Nan**, the provincial capital and ancient royal residence. The city is very remote; roads to the border end in mountain trails, and there are no frontier crossings, although there are ambitious, long-term plans to run a highway through the mountains to Luang Prabang in Laos. Two roads link Nan with the west and the cities of Chiang Mai, Chiang Rai, and Lampang—they are both modern highways that sweep through some of Thailand's most spectacular scenery, following river valleys, penetrating forests of bamboo and teak, and skirting upland terraces of rice and maize. Hill tribe villages sit on the heights of the surrounding Doi Phu Chi (Phu Chi Mountains), where dozens of waterfalls, mountain river rapids, and revered caves beckon travelers with time on their hands. Here you can find Hmong and Lahu villages untouched by commercialism, and jungle trails where you, your elephant, and mahout beat virgin paths through the thick undergrowth. The southern route from Chiang Mai to Nan passes through the ancient town of **Phrae**, the center of Thailand's richest teak-growing region and a pleasant overnight stop.

Set two or three days aside for traveling Thailand's famous tourist trail **The Mae Hong Son Loop,** which begins and ends in Chiang Mai, winding through spectacular mountain scenery for much of the way. Although the route is named after its principal town, **Mae Hong Son**, the quiet village of **Pai** has become a major destination. The "Loop" route runs from Chiang Mai to Mae Hong Son via Pai if you take the northern route which is considered the most attractive route (about six hours); the southern route (eight hours) is easier to drive and takes you the area's ithrough the mountain village of **Khun Yuam** and the market town of **Mae Sariang.**

The northernmost region of Thailand, **Chiang Rai and the Golden Triangle,** is known mostly for its former role as the center of the opium trade. This fabled area is a beautiful stretch of rolling uplands that conceal remote hill tribe villages and drop down to the broad Mekong, which is backed on its far side by the mountains of Laos. Although some 60 km (37 miles) to the south, **Chiang Rai** is its natural capital, a city equipped with the infrastructure for touring the entire region. Winding your way from Chiang Mai to Chiang Rai will take you past **Chiang Dao**, best known for its astonishing cave complex; **Tha Ton**, a pretty riverside town on the Myanmar border, which has many outdoor activities; and **Doi Ang Khang**, a small, remote settlement—with one fancy resort. The Golden Triangle's apex is the riverside village of **Ban Sop Ruak**, once a bustling center of the opium trade. An archway on the Mekong riverbank at Ban Sop Ruak invites visitors to step symbolically into the Golden Triangle, and a large golden Buddha watches impassively over the river scene. In a nearby valley where poppies once grew stands a huge museum, the Hall of Opium, which describes the history of the worldwide trade in narcotics. If you travel west on a dusty road from Bang Sop Ruak, you find Mae Sai, a Thai-Burmese border town, a popular day trip for its markets and south of Bang Sop Ruak is **Chiang Saen** which sits on the banks of the Mekong and is an embarkation point for river trips to Myanmar, Laos, and China. East of Ban Sop Ruak, the Mekong river town of **Chiang Khong** offers magnificent vistas from the riverside towpath to the hills of Laos across the Mekong.

To history buffs, the soul of the country is to be found in the cities of **Sukhothai and nearby** where architecture and culture evoke Thailand's ancient civilizations. In the valley of the Yom River, protected by a rugged mountain range in the north and richly forested mountains in the south, lies **Sukhothai**. The many ruins here mark the birthplace of the Thai nation and its emergence as a center for Theravada Buddhism. North of Sukhothai 80 km (50 miles) is quieter **Si Satchanalai**, whose historical park contains the remnants of more temples and monuments. Southeast of Sukhothai 60 km (37 miles) is **Phitsanulok**. Despite having fewer reminders of its brief turn centuries ago as the kingdom's capital, this modern provincial administrative seat can make a good base for exploring the area.

Planning

WHEN TO GO

Northern Thailand has three seasons. The region is hottest and driest from February to May. The rainy season is from June to October, with the wettest weather in September. Unpaved roads are often impassable at this time of year. The best time to visit is between November and March, when the days are warm, sunny, and generally cloudless, and the nights are pleasantly cool. (At higher altitudes, it can be quite cold in the evening.) Book hotel accommodations a month or two ahead of the Christmas and New Year holiday periods and the Songkran New Year's celebration, in mid-April.

GETTING HERE AND AROUND

Northern Thailand appears to be a very remote area of Asia, around 700 km (420 miles) from the country's capital, Bangkok, and far from other major centers. In fact, this region—bounded on the north, east, and west by Myanmar and Laos—is easily accessible. Chiang Mai and Chiang Rai are northern Thailand's major centers.

Great Itineraries

To really get a feel for northern Thailand, plan on spending at least a week here.

If You Have 2 Days. Spend your first day exploring the streets of Chiang Mai. On the second day rise early and drive up to Wat Phra That Doi Suthep. In the afternoon, visit Chiang Rai and its mountainous surroundings.

If You Have 5 Days. Begin your stay in the north in Chiang Mai, flying from there to Mae Hong Son, and take a tour of a nearby Karen village. Set out the next day by hired car or bus for Chiang Rai, stopping over for one night at Pai. On the third day, en route for Chiang Rai, you might consider overnighting in Tha Ton or Chiang Dao. On the fourth and fifth days, make a circular tour to Chiang Saen to see its excavated ruins and meet the Mekong River, then to Ban Sop Ruak to visit the magnificent Hall of Opium museum. Finally, head to Mae Sai for a look at Burmese crafts in the busy local markets.

If You Have 7 Days. If you're lucky enough to have a week or more in northern Thailand, you'll have plenty of time to stay a night with a hill tribe family. Treks to these mountain villages can be arranged from Chiang Mai, Chiang Rai, Mae Hong Son, and other communities. Sukhothai, a must-see destination, is a day's journey to the south, so the best way to include it in your itinerary is to return to Chiang Mai and catch a long-distance VIP bus to Sukhothai, where a tour of the well-preserved ruins of ancient Siam's most advanced and most civilized kingdom will take up one day. From Sukhothai, another six-hour bus ride returns you to Bangkok.

AIR TRAVEL

Main cities and towns are linked to Bangkok by frequent and reliable air service. There are dozens of flights a day from Bangkok to Chiang Mai and Chiang Rai, and regular flights from the capital to Mae Hong Son and Nan. Flight schedules to these two towns change with frustrating regularity, so check with your airline or travel agent for the latest information.

BUS TRAVEL

An excellent regional bus service links towns and remote villages via a network of highways. The main north-to-south artery, Highway 1, connects Bangkok with Chiang Rai and the Golden Triangle. Highway 11 branches off for Chiang Mai at Lampang, itself a major transport hub with a long-distance bus terminal, a railroad station, and an airport. From Chiang Mai you can reach the entire region on well-paved roads, with travel times not exceeding eight hours or so. The journey on serpentine mountain roads to Mae Hong Son, however, can be very tiring, requiring a stopover in either the popular resort town of Pai or quieter Mae Sariang. Chiang Rai is a convenient stopover on the road north to the Golden Triangle.

CAR TRAVEL

Driving in Thailand is not for the faint of heart; hiring a car and driver is usually a better option (⇨ *Car Travel in Travel Smart Thailand*). ■ **TIP→ Between Christmas and New Year's Day, the highway between Chiang Mai, Chiang Rai, Pai, and Mae Hong Son may be packed with bumper-to-bumper traffic.**

MOTORCYCLE TRAVEL

Motorcycles are a cheap and popular option for getting around cities and towns. Rental agencies are numerous, and most small hotels have their own. Do not rent a motorcycle unless you are an experienced rider. Tourists are involved in motorcycle accidents on a daily basis.

RESTAURANT AND HOTEL PRICES

What It Costs In Baht			
$	$$	$$$	$$$$
RESTAURANTS			
under B200	B200–B300	B301–B400	over B400
HOTELS			
under B2,000	B2,000–B4,000	B4,001–B6,000	over B6,000

Nan

318 km (198 miles) southeast of Chiang Mai, 270 km (168 miles) southeast of Chiang Rai, 668 km (415 miles) northeast of Bangkok.

Near the border of Laos lies the city of Nan, a provincial capital founded in 1272. According to local legend, Lord Buddha, passing through the Nan Valley, spotted an auspicious site for a temple to be built. By the late 13th century, Nan was brought into Sukhothai's fold, but, largely because of its remoteness, it maintained a fairly independent status until the last few decades.

Nan is rich in teak plantations and fertile valleys that produce rice and superb oranges. The town of Nan itself is small; everything is within walking distance. Daily life centers on the morning and evening markets. The Nan River, which flows past the eastern edge of town, draws visitors at the end of Buddhist Lent, in late October or early November, when traditional boat races are held. Each longtail boat is carved out of a single tree trunk, and at least one capsizes every year, to the delight of the locals. In mid-December Nan honors its famous fruit crop with a special Golden Orange and Red Cross Fair—there's even a Miss Golden Orange contest. It's advisable to book hotels well ahead of time for these events.

Tourist information about Nan Province, Nan itself, and Phrae is handled by the Tourism Authority of Thailand's regional office in Chiang Rai.

GETTING HERE AND AROUND

AIR TRAVEL

Nok Air runs at least a couple of 95-minute flights daily from Bangkok to Nan. Schedules and fares vary with the season. Songthaews meet incoming flights. It costs about B50 for the 3-km (2-mile) drive south into central Nan.

BUS TRAVEL

Several air-conditioned buses leave Bangkok and Chiang Mai daily for Nan, stopping en route at Phrae. The 11-hour journey from Bangkok to Nan costs from B400 to B600; the journey from Chiang Mai to Nan takes 6 hours and costs between B300 and B400. Air-conditioned buses also make the five-hour journey from Lampang to Nan. There's local bus service between Nan and Phrae.

CAR TRAVEL

Hiring a car and driver is the easiest way to get to Nan from Lampang or Chiang Mai. It costs about B1,500 per day.

TAXI AND TUK-TUK TRAVEL

City transport in Nan is provided by tuk-tuks, songthaews, and samlors. All are cheap, and trips within the city should seldom exceed B30.

TRAIN TRAVEL

Nan is not on the railroad route, but a relatively comfortable way of reaching the city from Bangkok is to take the Chiang Mai–bound train and change at Den Chai to a local bus for the remaining 146 km (87 miles) to Nan. The bus stops en route at Phrae.

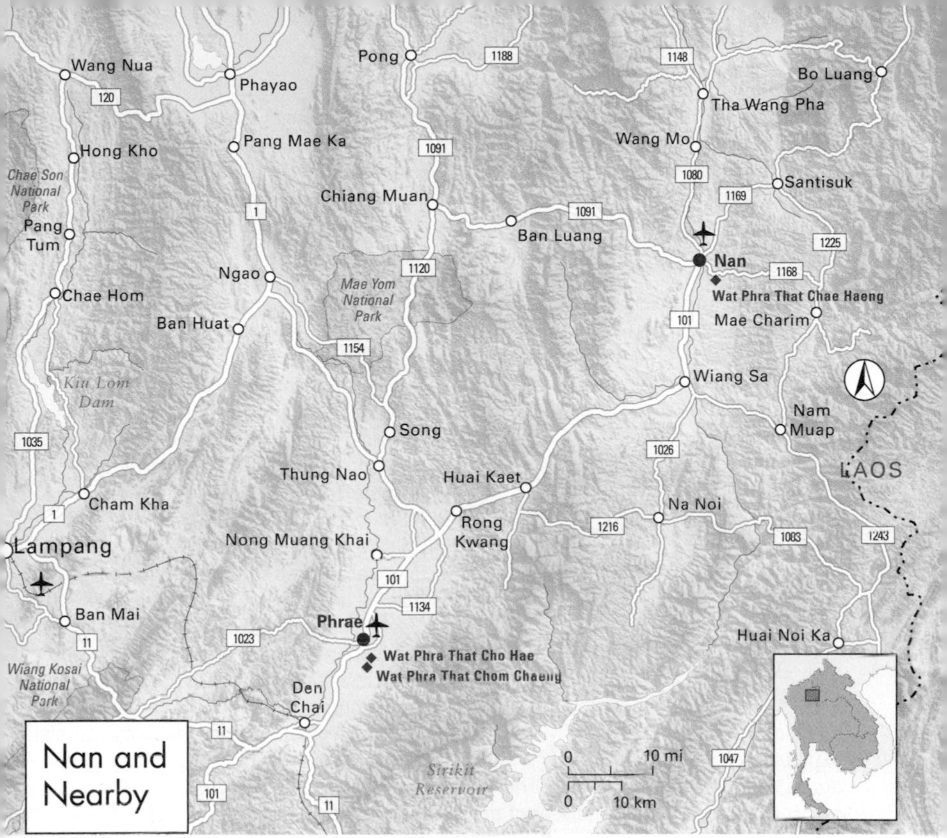

Nan and Nearby

TOURS

Trips range from city tours of Nan and short cycling tours of the region to jungle trekking, elephant riding, and white-water rafting. Nan is the ideal center from which to embark on treks through the nearby mountains, as well as raft and kayak trips along the rivers that cut through them. Khun Chompupach Sirsappuris has run Nan's leading tourist agency, Fhu Travel and Information, for more than 25 years. She speaks fluent English and knows the region like her own backyard.

CONTACTS Fhu Travel ✉ *453/4 Sumondhevaraj Rd.* ☎ *81/287–7209.*

Sights

National Museum

MUSEUM | To get a sense of the region's art, visit the National Museum, which occupies a mansion built in 1923 for the prince who ruled Nan, Chao Suriyapong Pharittadit. The house itself is a work of art, a synthesis of overlapping red roofs, forest-green doors and shutters, and brilliant-white walls. There's a fine array of wood and bronze Buddha statues, musical instruments, ceramics, and other works of Lanna art. The revered black elephant tusk is also an attraction. The tusk, about a meter (3 feet) long, weighs 18 kg (40 pounds). It's actually dark brown in color, but that doesn't detract at all from its special role as a local good-luck charm. ✉ *42 Suriyapong Rd.* ☎ *054/710561* *B100.*

Wat Hua Wiang Tai

RELIGIOUS SITE | Gaudy Wat Hua Wiang Tai has a naga running along the top of the wall and lively murals painted on the viharn's exterior. Small yet spectacular, the rather gaudy Wat Hua Wiang Tai has a splashy naga snake coiled along the edges of its roof and boldly colored murals painted across the viharn's exterior. Swing by in the morning to experience the hustle and flow of a nearby market as well. ⊠ *Sumonthewarat Rd.*

Wat Ming Muang

RELIGIOUS SITE | With its all-white exterior Wat Ming Muang strikes a dramatic pose offset slightly by the exterior's surfeit of intricate carvings (photo ops galore). The wat contains a stone pillar erected at the founding of Nan, some 800 years ago. Don't miss the interior murals, some of which depict life here in days gone by. ⊠ *Suriyaphong Rd.*

Wat Phra That Chae Haeng

RELIGIOUS SITE | This 14th-century wat draws worshippers from all over Thailand, particularly those born in the year of the rabbit; Lanna people believe that traveling to pay respect to the Phra That of their lunar year of birth brings great prosperity. Others are attracted to a hillside location that looks down on the town of Nan and its main river, an iconic reclining Buddha image, and a tall gold chedi said to store a holy Buddha hair that once belonged to King Lithai. ⊠ *Nan* ✣ *4 km (3 miles) southeast of central Nan off Hwy. 1168.*

Wat Phra That Chang Kham

RELIGIOUS SITE | One of Nan's oldest and most historically significant wats, Wat Chang was built at the turn of the 15th century, right across from what is now a National Museum. True to its title, the "elephant temple," its large chedi is propped up by 24 stone pachyderms, protecting the country's largest *ho trai* (scripture library) and a rare solid gold Buddha image from the Sukhothai period. ⊠ *Suriyaphong Rd.*

★ Wat Phumin

RELIGIOUS SITE | Nan has one of the region's most unusual and beautiful temples, Wat Phumin, whose murals alone make a visit to this part of northern Thailand worthwhile. It's an economically constructed temple, combining the main shrine hall and viharn, and qualifies as one of northern Thailand's best examples of folk architecture. To enter, you climb a short flight of steps flanked by two superb *nagas* (mythological snakes), their heads guarding the north entrance and their tails the south. The 16th-century temple was extensively renovated in 1865 and 1873, and at the end of the 19th century murals picturing everyday life were added to the inner walls. Some have a unique historical context—like the French colonial soldiers disembarking at a Mekong River port with their wives in crinolines. A fully rigged merchant ship and a primitive steamboat are portrayed as backdrops to scenes showing colonial soldiers leering at the pretty local girls corralled in a palace courtyard. Even the conventional Buddhist images have a lively originality, ranging from the traumas of hell to the joys of courtly life. The bot's central images are also quite unusual—four Sukhothai Buddhas locked in conflict with the evil Mara. ⊠ *Phakong Rd.*

Restaurants

Ruen Kaew

$$ | **THAI** | The name of this riverside restaurant means Crystal House, which is rather fitting, since it's such a gem. Pass through a profusion of bougainvillea flowers to find a wooden deck overlooking the Nan River, the perfect vantage point for taking in the lush scenery. **Known for:** original takes on Thai food; nightly live music; chicken slathered in honey sauce. [$] *Average main: B240* ⊠ *1/1 Sumondhevaraj Rd.* ☎ *054/710631.*

Suriya Garden

$$ | **THAI** | This substantial restaurant is a larger version of the nearby Ruen Kaew,

with a wooden deck overlooking the Nan River banks and live music every night. Get here early, as it's often full of diners looking for authentic food at fair prices and a prime spot along the water. **Known for:** Chinese-style white bass and pig's trotters; spicy and sour northern Thai notes; a peerless atmosphere. 💲 *Average main: B220* ✉ *9 Sumondhevaraj Rd.* ☎ *054/710687.*

Hotels

Dhevaraj Hotel

$ | **HOTEL** | Built around an attractive interior courtyard, which is lighted for evening dining, the Dhevaraj is a full-service operation within a short walk of all the sights. **Pros:** interior courtyard; central location; large rooms. **Cons:** so-so breakfast; patchy service; dated decor. 💲 *Rooms from: B1,200* ✉ *466 Sumondhevaraj Rd.* ☎ *054/751577* 🌐 *www.dhevarajhotel.com* *160 rooms* *Free breakfast.*

Nan Boutique Hotel

$$ | **HOTEL** | Boutique hotels are rare in rural Thailand, so this small and modern space is very much in a class of its own. **Pros:** free bicycles; busy restaurant with international menu; friendly service. **Cons:** no pool; long walk to town center; rooms with double beds not always available. 💲 *Rooms from: B2,250* ✉ *1/11 Kha Luang Rd.* ☎ *054/775532* 🌐 *tazshotels.com* *32 rooms* *Free breakfast.*

Pukha Nanfa Hotel

$$ | **HOTEL** | Named after the first Nan dynasty, this newly restored two-story number takes its guests on a teak-lined trip back to the early 1900s. **Pros:** centrally located; traditional yet trendy; immaculately maintained. **Cons:** sleepy in the off-season; no elevator; rooms can be rather small. 💲 *Rooms from: B2,600* ✉ *1/11 Khaluang Rd.* ☎ *054/771111* 🌐 *pukhananfahotel.co.th/* *14 rooms* *Free breakfast.*

Phrae

110 km (68 miles) southeast of Lampang, 118 km (73 miles) southwest of Nan.

A market town in a narrow valley well off the beaten path, Phrae is renowned in northern Thailand for its fine teak houses. It's a useful stopover on the 230-km (143-mile) journey from Lampang to Nan, but has little to offer the visitor apart from ruined city walls, some attractive and historic temples, and the sturdy teak buildings that attest to its former importance as a center of the logging industry.

GETTING HERE AND AROUND

The domestic airline Nok Air flies daily between Bangkok and Phrae. The flight takes about 90 minutes. Daily air-conditioned buses from Bangkok and Chiang Mai headed for Nan stop at Phrae. It's a 10-hour journey from Bangkok and a five-hour one from Chiang Mai. Air-conditioned buses travel between Lampang and Phrae (three hours) daily. There's local bus service between Phrae and Nan, an uncomfortable but cheap journey of two to three hours between each center. Hiring a car and driver in Lampang or Chiang Mai is the easiest way to get here, but doing this costs about B3,000 per day.

Sights

Ban Prathap Chai

HOUSE | There are many teak houses to admire all over Phrae, but none match this large one near the city's southern edge. Like many such houses, it's actually a reconstruction of several older houses—in this case nine of them supported on 130 huge centuries-old teak posts. The result is remarkably harmonious. A tour of the rooms open to public view provides a glimpse of bourgeois life in the region. The space between the teak poles on the ground floor of the building is taken up by stalls selling handicrafts, including carved teak. ✉ *Tambon Pa Maet*

✣ *Hwy. 1022, 10 km (6 miles) east of Phrae* 🎫 *B40.*

Wat Chom Sawan

RELIGIOUS SITE | Teak plays a prominent role in this beautiful monastery, which was designed by a Burmese architect and built by migrants from the country's Shan State during King Rama V's reign (1868–1910). The bot and viharn combine to make one giant structure, supported by stilts and housing statues made of marble and bamboo. ✉ *Yantarakitkosol Rd.* ✣ *On northeastern edge of town.*

Wat Luang

RELIGIOUS SITE | Phrae's oldest structure lies within the Old City walls. Although the wat was founded in the 12th century, renovations and expansions completely obscure so much of the original design that the only section visible from that time is a Lanna chedi with primitive elephant statues. A small museum on the grounds contains sacred Buddha images, swords, and texts. ✉ *Kham Lue Rd.*

★ **Wat Phra That Cho Hae**

RELIGIOUS SITE | On a hilltop in Tambon Pa Daeng, this late-12th-century temple is distinguished by its 33-meter-tall (108-foot-tall) golden chedi and breathtaking interior. The chedi is linked to a viharn, a later construction that contains a series of murals depicting scenes from the Buddha's life. The revered Buddha image is said to increase a woman's fertility. Cho Hae is the name given to the cloth woven by the local people, and in the fourth lunar month (June) the chedi is wrapped in this fabric during the annual fair. A fairly steep multitier staircase leads up to the temple. ✉ *Hwy. 1022* ✣ *8 km (5 miles) east of Phrae.*

Wat Phra That Chom Chaeng

RELIGIOUS SITE | In a woodland setting about 2 km (1 mile) east of the more famous Wat Phra That Cho Hae, this smaller wat has a chedi said to contain a strand of Lord Buddha's hair. A large standing Buddha stands watch over the gate, and the grounds contain an enormous reclining Buddha. ✉ *Hwy. 1022* ✣ *10 km (6 miles) east of Phrae.*

Restaurants

Pan Jai

$ | **THAI** | For authentic Lanna cuisine, you can't do better than this simple but superb restaurant. You're automatically served *kanom jin* (Chinese noodles) in basketwork dishes, with a spicy meat sauce, raw and pickled cabbage, and various condiments. **Known for:** relaxed environment; pork dishes. Ⓢ *Average main: B100* ✉ *2 Wira Alley* ☎ *054/620727* 💳 *No credit cards.*

Hotels

Maeyom Palace Hotel

$ | **HOTEL** | This hotel is far from palatial despite its name, but it does have comfortable rooms with Lanna touches like distinctive carvings on the walls. **Pros:** mountain views from some rooms; stable Wi-Fi; close to the bus station. **Cons:** impersonal, chain-hotel atmosphere; traffic noise; dated feel overall. Ⓢ *Rooms from: B1,225* ✉ *181/6 Yantarakitkosol Rd.* ☎ *054/521028* 🌐 *www.maeyompalace.com* 🛏 *104 rooms* 🍽 *Free breakfast.*

Mee Bed and Breakfast

$ | **B&B/INN** | About 10 minutes from Phrae's Old Town area and night market is this clean and contemporary bed-and-breakfast. **Pros:** free bicycle rentals; well-stocked drinks and snacks in the common area; large beds and good water pressure. **Cons:** windowless rooms; brick and concrete can feel a little austere; no elevator. Ⓢ *Rooms from: B800* ✉ *16/5 Rat Damnoen Rd.* ☎ *054/061073* 🛏 *10 rooms* 🍽 *Free breakfast.*

Pai

160 km (99 miles) northwest of Chiang Mai, 110 km (68 miles) east of Mae Hong Son.

Although Pai lies in a flat valley, a 10-minute drive in any direction brings you to a rugged upland terrain with stands of wild teak, groves of towering bamboo, and clusters of palm and banana trees hiding out-of-the-way resorts catering to visitors who seek peace and quiet. At night the surrounding fields and forest seem to enfold the town in a black embrace.
As you enter Pai from the direction of Chiang Mai, you'll pass by the so-called World War II Memorial Bridge, which was stolen from Chiang Mai during the Japanese advance through northern Thailand and rebuilt here to carry heavy armor over the Pai River. When the Japanese left, they neglected to return the bridge to Chiang Mai. Residents of that city are perfectly happy, as they eventually built a much more handsome river crossing.

Exhausted backpackers looking for a stopover along the serpentine road between Chiang Mai and Mae Hong Son discovered Pai in the late 1980s. In 1991 it had seven modest guesthouses and three restaurants; now its frontier-style streets are lined with restaurants and bars of every description, cheap guesthouses and smart hotels, art galleries, and chic coffeehouses, while every class of resort, from back-to-nature to luxury, nestles in the surrounding hills. Thus far, Pai has managed to retain its slightly off-the-beaten-path appeal, but that may change as Bangkok property investors pour money into its infrastructure.

GETTING HERE AND AROUND

BUS TRAVEL

Buses traveling between Mae Hong Son and Chiang Mai stop in Pai. They take four hours for the 120-km (75-mile) journey from Chiang Mai and an additional five hours to cover the 130 km (81 miles) from Pai to Mae Hong Son. Fares for each stretch vary from about B100 to B200. Buses stop in the center of Pai.

CAR TRAVEL

A hired car does the trip from Chiang Mai to Pai one hour faster than the buses, and cuts the journey time from Pai to Mae Hong Son by about the same margin. Cars and four-wheel-drive vehicles can be hired from many companies in Chiang Mai from B1,000 and upward a day. A driver costs about B3,000 per day.

SAFETY AND PRECAUTIONS

Pai had a crime problem, but it was caused by drug-taking young foreign visitors, not the locals. A police crackdown appears to have cleaned up the town, but keep your wits about you when visiting the local bars.

TIMING

Some foreign visitors come to Pai intending to stay a few days and never leave. It's that kind of place. There's not much to do in Pai besides exploring the surrounding countryside by day and partying by night, so if trekking, bike tours, river rafting, and late nights are not your thing, you'll want to get going again after one or two days.

TOURS

Thai Adventure Rafting

This outfit organizes wild-water rafting on the Pai River, as well as sightseeing, elephant riding, mountain biking, and bamboo rafting tours. ✉ *39 Moo 3 Chaisongkram Rd., Tambon Viang Tai, Mae Hong Son* ☎ *053/699111* 🌐 *www.thairafting.com* ☞ *From B1,150 per person for 2 people for ½-day cycling tour.*

Sights

Pai Canyon

CANYON | It's a short if occasionally hair-raising walk from Pai Canyon's' parking lot to a beautiful view of the valley below. Although the staircase to this popular lookout is paved, intrepid hikers can walk at their own risk alongside skinny, unstable trails lined with slippery red sandstone and steep drop-offs. Proper footwear is a must here, so leave the flip-flops and slip-on shoes in your car or hotel room. Also of note in the area: Pam Book Waterfall, which is about a 20-minute drive west on Route 1095, and the nearby Memorial Bridge many pass through on their way to Chiang Mai. ✉ *Hwy. 1095* ✣ *8 km (5 miles) south of Pai.*

Pai Etiquette

Pai has a sizable Muslim population, which is why some of the guesthouses post notices asking foreign visitors to refrain from public displays of affection. Immodest clothing is frowned on, so bikini tops and other revealing garb are definitely out. The music bars close early, meaning that by 1 am the town slumbers beneath the tropical sky. Nevertheless, quiet partying continues behind the shutters of the teak cabins that make up much of the tourist lodgings. This is, after all, backpacker territory.

Restaurants

Cafecito

$ | **MEXICAN** | In an increasingly hip neighborhood on the edge of town, an expat from Colorado serves authentic Mexican food including his own tortillas (flour and corn), salsa, and hot sauce. A nice break from Thai food when the need arises. **Known for:** breakfast all day; coffee that's locally sourced and roasted on-site; smothered and overstuffed burritos. 💲 *Average main: B150* ✉ *258 Moo 8 Vieng Tai* ☎ *088/499–2456* 🌐 *www.cafecitopai.com/* ⏲ *Closed Thurs.* 💳 *No credit cards.*

The Jazz House

$ | **ECLECTIC** | The crowd-pleasing international menu at this friendly café matches the diversity of the live jazz music performed here. Lots of seating and hammocks keep the vibe as laid-back as its regular clientele. **Known for:** everything from pad Thai to pizza; cheap yet tasty cocktails; weekly open mic nights. 💲 *Average main: B150* ✉ *24/1 Chaisongkram Rd., Vieng Tai* ☎ *064/370–0182* 💳 *No credit cards.*

Maya Burger Queen

$ | **BURGER** | After 10 years in Britain, a Pai entrepreneur named Ping returned to her hometown and opened this highly successful burger restaurant. The modest establishment is also the place to share tips with the travelers who gather here nightly. **Known for:** locally sourced beef; freshly cut fries; several vegetarian options, including a sweet-potato-and-pumpkin burger. 💲 *Average main: B150* ✉ *Tedsaban Rd.* ☎ *086/951–5280* 💳 *No credit cards.*

Om Garden Cafe

$ | **ECLECTIC** | Fragrant with incense, this hippie-chic café is set in an idyllic, shaded courtyard garden with mismatched rattan furniture, colorful cushions, sheer curtains, and Buddha statues. The food is healthy, hearty, and wholesome. **Known for:** house-baked cake; fresh juices and fruit shakes; khao soi salad. 💲 *Average main: B175* ✉ *4 Wiang Tai* ☎ *082/4515930* 🌐 *om-garden-cafe.business.site* ⏲ *Closed Mon.* 💳 *No credit cards.*

★ Silhouette

$$ | **MEDITERRANEAN** | Pai's best restaurant serves outstanding Thai-inspired European cuisine, made from fresh, mostly organic, local produce. Panoramic mountain views, the quirky house sense of style, and live jazz music merely add to the pleasure of having a meal here. **Known for:** charcuterie and cheese boards; plentiful small plates; solid wine selection. 💲 *Average main: B250* ✉ *Reverie Siam Resort, 476 Moo 8, Vieng Tai*

☎ 053/699870 🌐 reveriesiam.com ▭ No credit cards.

Hotels

Brook View

$ | **B&B/INN** | The brook babbles right outside your cabin window if you ask for a room with a view at this little resort. **Pros:** near town, but still "away from it all"; ample parking; pretty breakfast gazebo. **Cons:** some cabins are small, with no river view; staff keeps a low profile; uninteresting neighborhood. *Rooms from: B1,500 ✉ 132 Moo 1, Vieng Tai ☎ 081/992–4900 ▭ No credit cards 18 rooms and villas No meals.*

Cave Lodge

$ | **B&B/INN** | The chatter of gibbons wakes you up at this remote mountain lodge between Pai and Mae Hong Son. The cave after which it is named, just a short walk from the lodge, is one of the region's most spectacular caverns, with wall paintings and prehistoric coffins. **Pros:** bread and pastries from the wood-fired oven; tucked away in a tropical forest; Shan herbal sauna on-site. **Cons:** basic rooms and lots of bugs; more than an hour away from Pai and Mae Hong Son; cave tours can be quite challenging for beginners. *Rooms from: B600 ✉ 15 Moo 1, Pang Mapha ☎ 053/617203 🌐 www.cavelodge.com ▭ No credit cards 17 rooms Free breakfast.*

Pai Treehouse Resort

$$ | **RESORT** | The rooms with the best views at this riverside lodging outside Pai are only for the most adventurous travelers—they're in the upper branches of an enormous rain tree. **Pros:** terrace bar-restaurant; fine river views; peaceful location. **Cons:** 20-minute drive from town; popular for seminars; can get crowded. *Rooms from: B2,300 ✉ 90 Moo 2, Tambon Maehee ☎ 081/911–3640 🌐 www.paitreehouse.com 19 rooms No meals.*

Paivimaan Resort

$$ | **HOTEL** | *Vimaan* means "heaven," and this fine resort commands a celestial spot on the banks of the Pai River. **Pros:** family-friendly; close to town center; pleasant and peaceful. **Cons:** villa rooms are small; noise from nearby developments; irksome insects. *Rooms from: B4,000 ✉ 73 Moo 3, Tedsaban Rd. ☎ 053/699403 🌐 www.paivimaan.com 17 rooms Free breakfast.*

★ Reverie Siam Resort

$$$ | **RESORT** | This boutique resort has beautiful rooms decorated with antiques and vintage pieces, and there are two stunning swimming pools. **Pros:** elegant rooms with style to spare; hospitable staff and on-site owners; fantastic low-season rates. **Cons:** pricey in high season; on the edge of town; Wi-Fi can be weak. *Rooms from: B5,000 ✉ 476 Moo 8, Vieng Tai ☎ 053/699870 🌐 reveriesiam.com 20 rooms Free breakfast ▭ No credit cards.*

Nightlife

Jikko Beer

BREWPUBS/BEER GARDENS | The craft beer revolution comes to Pai's main street with a serious bottle selection that pulls its pilsners, IPAs, and strong ales from such popular international breweries as Hitachino Nest, Stone, Deschutes, and Rogue. If hops and heady flavor profiles aren't your thing, Chang's always on tap, keeping the clean lagers flowing as freely as this small bar's lively conversations. *✉ Pai ⊕ Near the end of Pai's main walking street ☎ 081/938–8244.*

Yellow Sun

MUSIC CLUBS | Located right across the street from Burger Queen's busy restaurant is this live-music staple that serves generous drinks and good vibes. Not to mention a pool table, foosball, and free Wi-Fi. *✉ 64 Moo 3, Tadsaban 1 Rd. ☎ 084/992–8765.*

Mae Hong Son

245 km (152 miles) northwest of Chiang Mai via Pai, 368 km (229 miles) via Mae Sariang.

Stressed-out residents of Bangkok and other cities have transformed this remote, mountain-ringed market town into one of northern Thailand's major resort areas. Some handsome hotels now grace the landscape here. Overseas travelers love the town because of its easy access to beautiful countryside.

For a small town, Mae Hong Son has a surprising number of noteworthy temples, many erected by the Burmese. Two of the temples, Wat Chong Kham and Wat Kham Klang, sit on the shore of a placid lake in the center of town, forming a breathtaking ensemble of golden spires. Within a short drive are dozens of villages inhabited by the Karen, the so-called "longneck" people. Fine handicrafts are produced in these hamlets, whose inhabitants trek daily to Mae Hong Son to sell their wares at the lively morning market and along the lakeside promenade.

Although Mae Hong Son offers a welcome cool retreat during the sometimes unbearably hot months of March and April, the mountains can be obscured during that part of the year by the fires farmers set to clear their fields. One of the local names for Mae Hong Son translates as "City of the Three Mists." The other two are refer to the clouds that creep through the valleys in the depths of winter and the gray monsoons of the rainy season.

GETTING HERE AND AROUND

AIR TRAVEL

Bangkok Airways offers one daily 45-minute flight between Chiang Mai and Mae Hong Son. The Mae Hong Son Airport is at the town's northern edge. Songthaews run to the city center for around B50. In March and April, smoke from slash-and-burn fires often causes flight cancellations.

BUS TRAVEL

Chiang Mai's Arcade Bus Terminal serves Mae Hong Son. Several buses depart daily on an eight-hour journey that follows the northern section of the Loop, via Pai. Buses stop in the center of town.

CAR TRAVEL

The most comfortable way to travel the route and enjoy the breathtaking mountain scenery is to let somebody else do the driving. The Loop road brings you here from either direction: the northern route through Pai (six hours) is a more attractive trip; the southern route through Mae Sariang (eight hours) is easier driving.

If you choose to rent a car, you'll probably do it in Chiang Mai, but if needed Avis has an office at Mae Hong Son Airport.

TOURS

A tourist info kiosk with erratic hours stands on the corner of Khunlum Prapas and Chamnansathit roads. An efficient travel agency, Amazing Mae Hong Son, has an office at the airport. In the center of town, Discover Mae Hong Son books day tours of local hill tribe villages.

TRAVEL AGENCIES Mae Hong Son Holidays ☎ *061/310–9789* 🌐 *www.maehongson-holidays.com/.* **Discover Mae Hong Son** ☎ *053/611537.*

Sights

Tham Pla-Namtok Pha Suea National Park
NATIONAL/STATE PARK | FAMILY | About 28 km (17 miles) north of Mae Hong Son on the Pai road, this park has one of the region's strangest sights—a grotto with a dark, cisternlike pool overflowing with fat mountain carp. The pool is fed by a mountain stream that is also full of thrashing fish fighting to get into the cave. Why? Nobody knows. It's a secret that draws thousands of Thai visitors a year. Some see a mystical meaning in

the strange sight. The cave is a pleasant 10-minute stroll from the park's headquarters. ✉ *70 Moo 1 Huay Pa* ☎ *053/619036.*

Wat Chong Kham

RELIGIOUS SITE | A wonderfully self-satisfied Burmese-style Buddha, the cares of the world far from his arched brow, watches over this temple from 1827, which has a fine pulpit carved with incredible precision. It's located on a small lake, right next to the equally important Wat Chong Klang. ✉ *Chamnansathit Rd.*

Wat Chong Klang

RELIGIOUS SITE | Completed in 1871, this striking white-and-gold structure features a rarely seen wicker Buddha, gorgeous stained glass, and teak figurines that depict the various stages of the Lord Buddha's life. It's one of two Burmese temples built on a small lake in the middle of Mae Hong Son—the other being the similarly named Wat Chong Kham. ✉ *Chamnansathit Rd.*

Wat Hua Wiang

RELIGIOUS SITE | Mae Hong Son's most celebrated Buddha image, one of the most revered in northern Thailand, is inside this temple that was built in 1863. Its origins are clear: note the Burmese-style long earlobes, a symbol of the Buddha's omniscience. ✉ *Panishwatana Rd.*

Wat Phra That Doi Kong Mu

RELIGIOUS SITE | On the top of Doi Kong Mu, this temple has a remarkable view, especially at sunset, of the surrounding mountains. The temple's two chedis contain the ashes of two major 19th-century monks, Phra Moggallana (one of the Buddha's closest disciples) and Phaya Singhanat Racha (Mae Hong Son's first governor, who built the building). ✉ *Mae Hong Son* ✣ *2 km (1 mile) west of Mae Hong Son.*

Restaurants

Bai Fern

$ | **THAI** | Mae Hong Son's main thoroughfare, Khunlum Prapas Road, is lined with inexpensive restaurants serving local cuisine, and this is among the best. In the spacious dining room, you eat in typical Thai style amid solid teak columns and beneath whirling fans, while an adjoining café offers free Wi-Fi and strong coffee. **Known for:** pork ribs with pineapple; roast chicken in pandan leaves; steamed whole snakehead fish. *Ⓢ Average main: B150* ✉ *87 Khunlum Prapas Rd.* ☎ *053/611374.*

Little Good Things

$ | **VEGETARIAN** | Affordable vegan fare takes center stage at this family-run café, just a five-minute walk from Wat Chong Klang. Its hand-drawn menu—chef-owner Napat is also an artist—highlights such healthy and hearty dishes as a macrobiotic plate, chickpea omelet, and several different smoothie bowls. **Known for:** all-day breakfast; clean eats; everything under B80. *Ⓢ Average main: B70* ✉ *40 Chamnan Satit Rd.* ☎ *062/274–3805* ⏲ *Closed Tues.* ▭ *No credit cards.*

Hotels

Fern Resort

$$ | **RESORT** | The room rate at Fern is relatively expensive, but it buys unexpected luxury amid the beautiful countryside outside Mae Hong Son. Thirty bungalows in steep-eaved Shan style are scattered over a valley of former rice paddies. **Pros:** regular barbecue nights; fine mountain views; friendly owners. **Cons:** 15-minute drive from town, though there's a shuttle bus; mosquitoes; small bathrooms. *Ⓢ Rooms from: B3,000* ✉ *10 Ban Hua Nam Mae Sakut, Tambon Pha Bong* ☎ *053/686110, 053/686111* 🌐 *www.fernresort.info* *30 rooms* *Free breakfast.*

Imperial Mae Hong Son Resort

$$ | **HOTEL** | Set among mature teak trees, this fine hotel was designed to blend in with the surroundings—bungalows in landscaped gardens have both front and back porches, giving the teak-floored and bamboo-furnished rooms a light-and-airy feel. **Pros:** pleasant walks in the grounds; large rooms; satellite TV. **Cons:** some rooms need refurbishing; long walk from town, though there is shuttle service; insects. *Ⓢ Rooms from: B2,550* ✉ *149 Moo 8, Tambon Pang Moo* ☎ *053/684444* 🌐 *www.imperialmaehongson.com/* *104 rooms* *Free breakfast.*

Rim Nam Klang Doi

$ | **RESORT** | This retreat about 7 km (4 miles) outside Mae Hong Son is an especially good value. **Pros:** helpful tour service; fine local walks; good restaurant. **Cons:** shuttle service to town is erratic; small bathrooms; unreliable plumbing. *Ⓢ Rooms from: B1,020* ✉ *108 Ban Huay Dua* ☎ *053/612142* *39 rooms* *No meals.*

Sunset Views

For a giddy view of Mae Hong Son and the surrounding mountains, take a deep breath and trudge up Doi Kong Mu, a hill on the western edge of town. It's well worth the effort. From here you can see the mountains on the border of Myanmar. The view is particularly lovely at sunset. There's another shade of gold to admire, a flame-surrounded white-marble Buddha in a hilltop temple called Wat Phra That Doi Kong Mu.

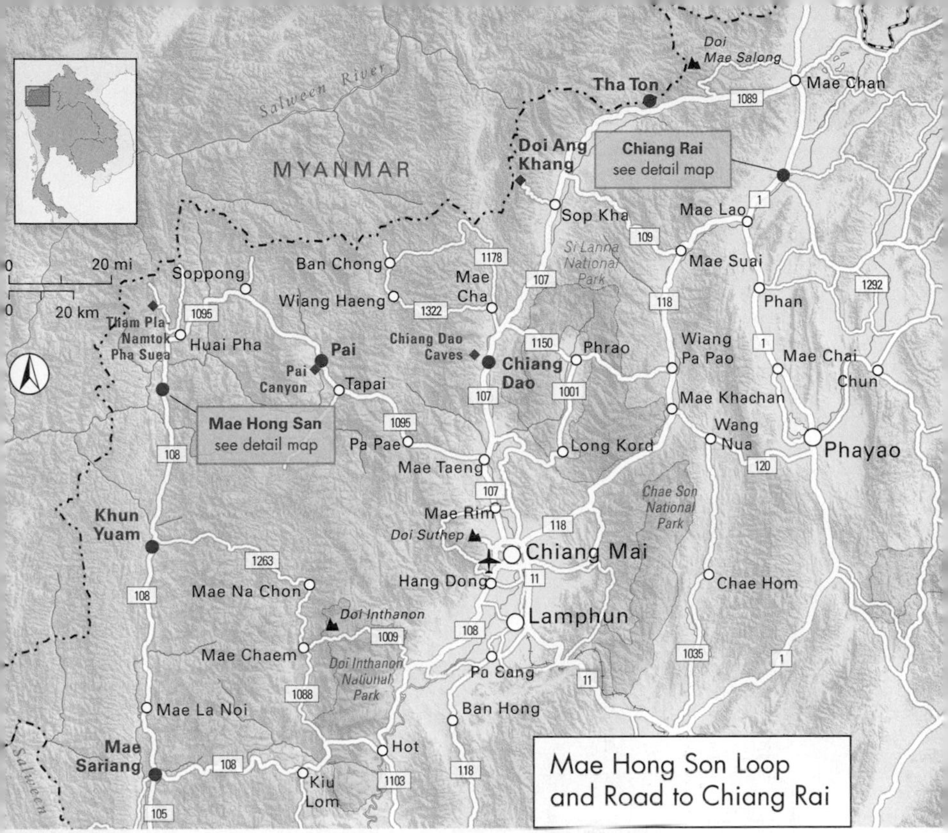

Mae Hong Son Loop and Road to Chiang Rai

Khun Yuam

64 km (40 miles) south of Mae Hong Son, 100 km (62 km) north of Mae Sariang.

In the mountain village of Khun Yuam, along the southern route of the Loop between Mae Hong Son and Mae Sariang, you can find one of the region's most unusual and, for many, most poignant museums, the Thai–Japan Friendship Memorial Hall.

GETTING HERE AND AROUND

Most visitors to Khun Yuam stop here on their southern Loop travels by bus or car along winding mountain roads (so the going can be slow). The village is small and can be covered easily on foot.

TIMING

It only takes an hour or so to tour the town's main attraction, the Thai–Japan Friendship Memorial Hall.

Sights

Thai–Japan Friendship Memorial Hall (*aka World War II Memorial Museum*)
MUSEUM | This museum goes by two different names and commemorates the hundreds of Japanese soldiers who died here during a chaotic retreat from the Allied armies in Burma. Locals took in the dejected and defeated men, and a local historian gathered the belongings they left behind: rifles, uniforms, cooking utensils, personal photographs, and documents. They provide a fascinating glimpse into a little-known chapter of World War II. ✉ *Mae Hong Son Rd.* 🎫 *B40.*

Did You Know?

Though forest still clothes the mountainsides, decades of illegal logging have endangered Thailand's prized old-growth teak trees. These days artisans are turning to alternative woods like bamboo and mango to make ornaments and furnishings.

Hotels

Khun Yuam Resort
$ | **RESORT** | A friendly couple runs this well-appointed property, which offers basic rooms in its main building and larger, more luxurious options in a separate two-story villa. **Pros:** even the grand deluxe rooms are fairly priced; large balconies overlooking the valley below; fast Wi-Fi for the area. **Cons:** 10 minutes outside town; can be hard to find; the drive up to the property is on a dirt road. *$ Rooms from: B800 ✉ 139 Moo 1, Ban Tor Phae ☎ 086/421–3287 10 rooms Free breakfast No credit cards.*

Mae Sariang

175 km (109 miles) southwest of Chiang Mai, 140 km (87 miles) south of Mae Hong Son.

The southern route of the Loop runs through Mae Sariang, a neat little market town that sits beside the Yuam River. With comfortable hotels and a handful of good restaurants, the town makes a good base for trekking in the nearby Salawin National Park or for boat trips on the Salawin River, which borders Myanmar.

GETTING HERE AND AROUND

Buses from Chiang Mai's Chang Phuak bus station take about four hours to reach Mae Sariang. Fares range from B200 to B300. A few songthaews ply the few streets of Mae Sariang, but the town is small and compact, and can be covered easily on foot.

Tours of the border region around Mae Sariang are offered by travel agencies in Mae Hong Son. Two of the leading ones are Amazing Mae Hong Son and Discover Mae Hong Son.

SAFETY AND PRECAUTIONS

Despite its proximity to the sometimes-disputed Myanmar border, Mae Sariang is perfectly safe for visitors. There is little crime, although elementary precautions are advised—leave valuables and large amounts of cash in your hotel safe or with the management.

TIMING

Mae Sariang is a beautiful, laid-back little town. If you're looking for relaxation, a stay of two or three days provides a welcome break on the long Mae Hong Son Loop route.

Sights

Mae Sariang and Nearby
SCENIC DRIVE | Near Mae Sariang the road winds through some of Thailand's most spectacular mountain scenery, with seemingly endless panoramas opening up through gaps in the thick teak forests that line the route. You'll pass hill tribe villages where time seems to have stood still, and Karen women go to market proudly in their traditional dress. Salawin National Park is west of Mae Sariang on Highway 1194, though the road doesn't proceed very far into this beautiful wilderness area that has hiking and biking trails. *✉ Hwy. 108.*

Restaurants

★ **Coriander in Redwood**
$$ | **THAI** | This century-old log trader's home was transformed into a warm, redwood-lined restaurant that serves compelling Thai cuisine and well-executed Western dishes. Tables are also arranged under the trees of a leafy garden for a nice view of the Yuam River. **Known for:** locally sourced beef; ample wine options; date-night setting. *$ Average main: B300 ✉ 12 Moo 2, Langpanich Rd. ☎ 053/683309 🌐 www.riverhousehotel-group.com/coriander-in-redwood.*

Inthira

$ | **THAI** | Family run since Inthira Tansuhaj first opened it in 1964, this Mae Sariang favorite sticks to Thai staples like curries, soups, and stir-fries. English menus are available, and while service can be slow, it's actually quite efficient for an ever-expanding space that now seats up to 300 people. **Known for:** fried river fish; cold bottles of Chang; seasonal specialties like chayote greens, red ant eggs, and giant crickets. *Average main: B100* *170/1 Wiangmai Rd.* *053/681441, 053/681529* *inthira.wordpress.com.*

Hotels

Riverhouse Hotel

$$ | **HOTEL** | Cooling breezes from the Yuam River waft through the open-plan areas of this attractive teak hotel, its rooms a simple but elegant synthesis of white walls, dark woods, and plain cotton drapes. **Pros:** timber-walled bathrooms; homey public lounge area; river views. **Cons:** limited restaurant menu; no nightlife; traffic noise. *Rooms from: B2,300* *77 Langpanich Rd.* *053/621201* *www.riverhousehotelgroup.com/hotel* *No credit cards* *12 rooms* *No meals.*

Riverhouse Resort

$$ | **HOTEL** | The pink facade of this modern hotel might appear to be an incongruous intrusion in this neat little border town, but it hides a smart and comfortable interior. **Pros:** riverside garden; fine views; ample parking. **Cons:** disappointing breakfast; long walk to town center; insects. *Rooms from: B2,700* *6/1 2m Langpanich Rd.* *053/683066* *www.riverhousehotelgroup.com/resort* *No credit cards* *44 rooms* *Free breakfast.*

Chiang Dao

72 km (40 miles) north of Chiang Mai.

The dusty, rather dilapidated village of Chiang Dao has two claims to fame: Thailand's third-highest mountain, 7,500-foot Doi Chiang Dao, which leaps up almost vertically from the valley floor; and the country's most spectacular caves, which penetrate more than 10 km (6 miles) into the massif. If you want to explore more of the mountain, hire a guide.

GETTING HERE AND AROUND

Buses bound for Chiang Dao depart regularly from Chiang Mai's Chang Phuak Bus Terminal. The fare is between B100 and B200, depending on the type of service (express, air-conditioned, etc.). Buses stop on the main road in town.

If you need information about Chiang Dao, the best source is Khun Wicha of the Chiang Dao Nest. The innkeeper knows the town and its attractions so well that she has produced a charming map for visitors.

TIMING

Chiang Dao's famous caves can be explored in a couple of hours, but many visitors are so captivated by the mountain scenery that they stay for a few days. The hike to the top of Chiang Dao mountain takes at least six hours, and most trekkers bivouac overnight at the top.

TOURS

CONTACT Khun Wihataya, Chiang Dao Nest *053/456612* *www.chiangdao.com/nest.*

Sights

Chiang Dao Caves

CAVE | Caves have a mystic hold over Buddhist Thais, so foreign visitors to Chiang Dao's famous caverns find themselves vastly outnumbered by the locals. If you're at all claustrophobic, join a group of Thais to explore the caves, which are thought to penetrate more than 10 km (6 miles) into the small town's guardian mountain, Doi Chiang Dao. The sights in the lighted portion, only a few hundred yards, include spectacular stalagmites and stalactites, along with hundreds of Buddha statues and other votive items placed there by devout Buddhists. If you want to explore past the lighted areas, you can hire a local guide with a lantern for about B100. The mountain itself can be scaled without difficulty in a day, but even just an hour or two of tough walking can bring you to viewpoints with amazing panoramas. ✉ *Chiang Dao* ✣ *About 3 km (2 miles) west of town* ☎ *053/248604* 🎫 *B40.*

Hotels

★ Chiang Dao Nest

$ | **RESORT** | Describing itself as a mini-resort, the Nest consists of two groups of chalets, a mile apart from each other, nestled at the foot of Chiang Dao mountain. **Pros:** total seclusion; great food; bicycles available. **Cons:** dim lighting makes bedtime reading difficult; Western dishes can be pricey, unheated pool water can be cold in winter. [$] *Rooms from: B1,045* ✉ *144/4 Moo 5, Ban Tham* ☎ *053/456612* 🌐 *www.chiangdao.com/nest* 💳 *No credit cards* 🛏 *23 chalets* 🍽 *No meals.*

Rim Doi Resort

$ | **RESORT** | *Rim Doi* means "on the edge of the mountain," so it's fitting that two extraordinary peaks loom over this peaceful little resort near Chiang Dao. After a day exploring the nearby caves or venturing into the mountains, it's just the place to relax and prepare for the journey farther north. **Pros:** pleasant walks on the grounds; well-stocked lake for perch fishing; open-air restaurant. **Cons:** staff has limited English-language skills; rooms could use a refresh; chalet accommodation is very basic. [$] *Rooms from: B850* ✉ *46 Moo 4 Muang Ghay* ☎ *053/375028* 🌐 *www.rimdoiresort.com* 🛏 *40 rooms* 🍽 *No meals.*

Doi Ang Khang

60 km (36 miles) north of Chiang Dao.

Ang means "bowl," and that sums up the mountaintop location of this remote corner of Thailand. A tiny, two-street settlement shares the small valley with the orchards and gardens of a royal agricultural project, which grows temperate fruits and vegetables found nowhere else in Thailand.

GETTING HERE AND AROUND

From Chiang Dao take Highways 1178 and 1340 north to Doi Ang Khang. Local bus services connect the two towns, stopping in the center of Doi Ang Khang.

TIMING

Doi Ang Khang is for nature lovers, who tend to relax for a few days amid its orchards and gardens. It's a long drive from either Chiang Mai or Chiang Rai, so at least an overnight stay is recommended. There's no nightlife, however, and after 9 the small community is wrapped in slumber.

TOURS

Wandering Star and Bens Taxi offer private tours and day trips to Doi Ang Khang.

TRAVEL AGENCY Bens Taxi ☎ *089/853–7527* 🌐 *www.benstaxiserviceandtours.com/.* **Wandering Star Tour** ☎ *053/273602 office, 089/951–8906 mobile* 🌐 *wanderingstarchiangmaitour.com/.*

Sights

Royal Agricultural Station Angkhang (*Doi Ang Khang*)

FARM/RANCH | A project of the royal family, this mountainside facility has both agricultural and political objectives. Developing new and more efficient farming practices is one goal; fruit, tea, and coffee research is another; and a third is to wean northern farmers off opium production. Remote and fascinating, the

Northern Thailand Then and Now

As late as 1939, northern Thailand was a semiautonomous region of Siam, with a history rich in tales of kings, queens, and princes locked in dynastic struggles and wars. The diversity of cultures you find here today is hardly surprising, because the ancestors of today's northern Thai people came from China, and the point where they first crossed the mighty Mekong River, Chiang Saen, became a citadel-kingdom of its own as early as 773. Nearly half a millennium passed before the arrival of a king who was able to unite the citizens of the new realm of Lanna.

That fabled ruler, King Mengrai (1259–1317), established a dynasty that lasted two centuries. Mengrai's first capital was Chiang Rai, but at the end of the 13th century he moved his court south and in 1296 founded a new dynastic city, Chiang Mai. Two friendly rulers, King Ngarm Muang of Phayao and King Rama Kampeng of Sukhothai, helped him in the huge enterprise, and the trio sealed their alliance in blood, drinking from a chalice filled from their slit wrists. A monument outside the city museum in the center of Chiang Mai's Old City commemorates the event. Nearby, another monument marks the spot where King Mengrai died, in 1317, after being struck by lightning in one of the fierce storms that regularly roll down from the neighboring mountains.

Lanna power was weakened by waves of attacks by Burmese and Lao invaders, and for two centuries—from 1556 to the late 1700s—Lanna was virtually a vassal Burmese state. The capital was moved south to Lampang, where Burmese power was finally broken and a new Lanna dynasty, the Chakri, was established under King Rama I.

Chiang Mai, nearby Lamphun (also at the center of Lanna-Burmese struggles), and Lampang are full of reminders of this rich history. Lampang's fortified Wat Lampang Luang commemorates with an ancient bullet hole the spot where the commander of besieging Burmese forces was killed.

To the north is Chiang Rai, a regal capital 30 years before Chiang Mai was built. This quieter, less-developed town is evolving into a base for exploring the country's northernmost reaches. In the far north Chiang Saen, site of the region's first true kingdom, is being excavated, its 1,000-year-old walls slowly taking shape again. Chiang Saen is on the edge of the fabled Golden Triangle. This mountainous region, bordered by Myanmar to the west and Laos to the east, was once ruled by the opium warlord Khun Sa, whose hometown, Ban Sop Ruak, has a magnificent museum that traces the story of the spread of narcotics.

Chiang Mai and Chiang Rai are ideal bases for exploring the hill tribe villages, where people live as they have for centuries. The communities closest to the two cities have been overrun by tourists, but if you strike out on your own with a good map, you may still find some that haven't become theme parks. Most of the villages are bustling crafts centers, where the colorful fabrics you see displayed in Bangkok shop windows take shape before your eyes. The elaborately costumed villagers sell their wares in the night markets of Chiang Mai and Chiang Rai.

station is beloved by bird-watchers for its numerous rare species, and there are many flower gardens. The orchards, gardens, and hothouses are open to the public, and at various times of the year you can buy pears, apples, plums, and peaches harvested on-site. ✉ *Off Hwy. 1249, Angkhang* ✣ *From Chiang Dao, north on Hwy. 1178, east and then north on Hwy. 1340, and north on Hwy. 1249* ☎ *053/969489* 🎫 *B50.*

Hotels

Ang Khang Nature Resort
$$ | **RESORT** | This stylish resort in the mountains near Doi Ang Khang is now part of the Mosaic Collection. **Pros:** pretty gardens; first-rate food at Camellia; open log fire in the lobby in cool season. **Cons:** 2 km (1 mile) from the village center; no nightlife; can be quite chilly. 💲 *Rooms from: B2,200* ✉ *1/1 Moo 5 Baan Koom, Tambon Mae Ngon, Angkhang* ☎ *053/450110* 🌐 *www.mosaic-collection.com/angkhang* 🛏 *74 rooms* 🍽 *No meals.*

Tha Ton

90 km (56 miles) north of Chiang Dao.

North of Chiang Dao lies the pretty resort town of Tha Ton, which sits on the River Kok right across the border from Myanmar. The local temple, Wat Tha Ton, is built on a cliff overlooking the town. From the bridge below boats set off for trips on the River Kok, some of them headed for Chiang Rai, 130 km (81 miles) away.

Tha Ton is a pleasant base for touring this mountainous region. The 1089 and 1130 highways that run north, close to the Myanmar border, pass through villages that are more Chinese than Thai. The largest of these, Mae Salong, is on Highway 1234. Most of the Chinese in the area are descendants of the Nationalist forces who fled their homeland after the Communists' 1949 victory in the civil war that gave birth to the People's Republic of China. Based at first mostly in Burma, the Nationalists arrived in Chiang Rai Province in large numbers in the early 1960s. Many of these families have prospered cultivating tea, coffee, and fruit.

GETTING HERE AND AROUND

Six buses a day leave Chiang Mai's Chang Phuak station for the four-hour journey to Tha Ton. Fares range from B150 to B250. Boats leave Chiang Rai for the four-hour upstream journey to Tha Ton. The single fare is B350.

ESSENTIALS

TIMING

Travelers on the northern route from Chiang Dao to Chiang Rai find it convenient to overnight in Tha Ton, but the town has little to justify a longer stay.

TOURS AND ACTIVITIES

Maekok River Village Resort
For information about Tha Ton and its beautiful surroundings, inquire at this resort, where proprietors Bryan and Rosie Massingham are knowledgeable and helpful hosts. Their travel desk can arrange everything from on-site classes and activities lasting an hour or two to multiday off-site treks for guests and nonguests. ✉ *Tha Ton–Chiang Rai Rd.* ☎ *053/053628* 🌐 *www.maekok-river-village-resort.com.*

Hotels

Mae Salong Flower Hills Resort
$ | **RESORT** | The border hills of Myanmar lie just beyond the grounds of this resort hotel whose timber-built chalets have fine views of tea plantations and the surrounding mountains. **Pros:** authentic Chinese food; ceremonial teatime on the resort terrace; tropical gardens. **Cons:** erratic bathroom plumbing; long walk to village center; no nightlife. 💲 *Rooms from: B1,000* ✉ *779 Moo 1, Doi Mae Salong, Mae Salong* ☎ *053/765–4957, 091/850–6262* 🌐 *www.*

maesalongflowerhills.com ▭ *No credit cards* ⇆ *45 chalets* 🍽 *Free breakfast.*

★ Maekok River Village Resort
$$ | RESORT | FAMILY | This remarkable resort, a combination of hotel and outdoor education center, is in a beautiful Kok River location with sweeping views of the winding waterway, rice paddies, maize fields, orchards, and mountains beyond. **Pros:** friendly and knowledgeable British management; fine open-sided restaurant; snug bar with open fireplace for winter evenings. **Cons:** kids at the education center can be noisy; some rooms are cramped; tour buses call regularly. *$ Rooms from: B3,250* ✉ *333 Moo 4* ☎ *053/053628* 🌐 *www.maekok-river-village-resort.com* ▭ *No credit cards* ⇆ *36 rooms* 🍽 *Free breakfast.*

Chiang Rai

180 km (112 miles) northeast of Chiang Mai, 780 km (485 miles) north of Bangkok.

Chiang Rai attracts more and more visitors each year, and it's easy to see why. Six hill tribes—the Akha, Yao, Meo, Lisu, Lahu, and Karen—all live within Chiang Rai Province. Each has different dialects, customs, handicrafts, and costumes, and all still venerate animist spirits despite their increasing acquaintance with the outside world. You can learn about their cultures and lives at a museum in town, and as in Chiang Mai, they make daily journeys to the markets of Chiang Rai, where you can meet them and enjoy their handiwork. The best of the markets is a night bazaar, just off Phaholyothin Road, which has a cluster of small restaurants and food vendors.

Despite having luxury hotels and sufficient restaurants and bars to keep night owls happy, Chiang Rai comes off as quieter and less flashy than Chiang Mai, and therein many find its charm. It's also a city with far more greenery, a pleasant contrast to Chiang Mai. ■ **TIP→ Climbing to the top of Doi Tong, a modest hill on the northeastern edge of Chiang Rai, is a great way to learn the lay of the land.** From the grounds of the 13th-century Wat Doi Tong, you'll have a fine view of the Mae Kok River and the mountains beyond.

Chiang Rai's Origins

Legend has it that a royal elephant ran away from its patron, the 13th-century king Mengrai, founder of the Lanna kingdom. The beast stopped to rest on the banks of the Mae Kok River. The king regarded this as an auspicious sign, and in 1256 built his capital, Chiang Rai, on the site. Little remains from those heady days: the Emerald Buddha that used to reside in Wat Phra Keo is now in Bangkok's Grand Palace, and a precious Buddha image in the 15th-century Wat Phra Singh has long since disappeared.

GETTING HERE AND AROUND

AIR TRAVEL

Thai Airways has several daily flights from Bangkok to Chiang Rai. Chiang Rai International Airport is 6 km (4 miles) northeast of the city. Incoming flights are met by songthaews and tuk-tuks, whose drivers charge about B50 for the journey to central Chiang Rai.

BOAT AND FERRY TRAVEL

Longtail boats and rafts set off daily from Tha Ton for the 130-km (81-mile) trip downstream to Chiang Rai.

BUS TRAVEL

Chiang Rai is served by buses that leave regularly from Chiang Mai's two terminals. The trip takes from three to four hours and costs between B80 and B200. Buses to Chiang Rai also leave regularly between 8 am and 7:15 pm from Bangkok's Northern Bus Terminal (12 hours; from B600 to B700). Express buses (B180) leave hourly from Chiang Mai's Arcade Terminal.

CAR TRAVEL
Roads are well paved throughout the Golden Triangle, presenting no problem for drivers. The area is bisected by the main north-to-south road, Highway 110, and crisscrossed by good country roads. In Chiang Rai the most prominent car-rental companies are Avis, National, and Budget.

TAXI AND TUK-TUK TRAVEL
Tuk-tuks are the common way of getting around Chiang Rai. A trip across town costs from B40 to B50. Songthaews can also be hailed on the street and hired for trips to outlying areas. The fare inside the city is B15. To go anywhere farther afield is a matter of negotiation.

Travel desks are found in all Chiang Rai hotels and they are generally efficient and reasonably priced.

ESSENTIALS

SAFETY AND PRECAUTIONS
Take the usual urban precautions when visiting Chiang Rai: leave valuables either in your room safe or with the hotel management. Carry only a copy of your passport. The small, ill-lighted lanes around the central market can seem a bit threatening at night, but there's actually little crime.

TIMING
Chiang Rai has few sights of note, so a leisurely walk around town will take at most a few hours. The city makes an ideal base for exploring the surrounding upland countryside and mountains, though, so a stay of at least two or three days is recommended.

TOURS
Chiang Rai is an excellent base from which to set out trekking through the nearby mountains or canoeing and rafting on the region's rivers.

Naming the Golden Triangle

U.S. Assistant Secretary of State Marshall Green coined the term *Golden Triangle* in 1971 during a preview of the historic visit by President Richard Nixon to China. The Nixon administration was concerned about the rise of heroin addiction in the United States and wanted to stem the flow of opium. The greatest source of opium was the wild territory where the Mekong and Ruak rivers formed borders between Thailand, Myanmar, and Laos—the "golden triangle" drawn by Green on the map.

Golden Triangle Tours
GUIDED TOURS | The major hotels in Chiang Rai and the Golden Triangle Resort in Chiang Saen organize minibus tours of the region, and the hotels' travel desks will arrange treks to the hill tribe villages. ✉ *590 Phaholyothin Rd.* ☎ *053/713918, 053/740478* 🌐 *www.goldenchiangrai.com* 🎫 *Check website or call for prices, which vary depending on group size.*

VISITOR INFORMATION
CONTACT Tourist Authority of Thailand (Chiang Rai) ✉ *448/16 Singhaklai Rd.* ☎ *053/744674, 053/717434* 🌐 *www.tourismthailand.org/chiang-rai.*

Sights

Hilltribe Museum & Education Center
MUSEUM | The cultures, ways of life, and crafts of the many hill tribe people that populate the Chiang Rai region are displayed and explained at this exemplary museum in the city center. The museum also supports its own travel service, PDA Tour, which organizes visits to hill tribe villages under the motto "We don't

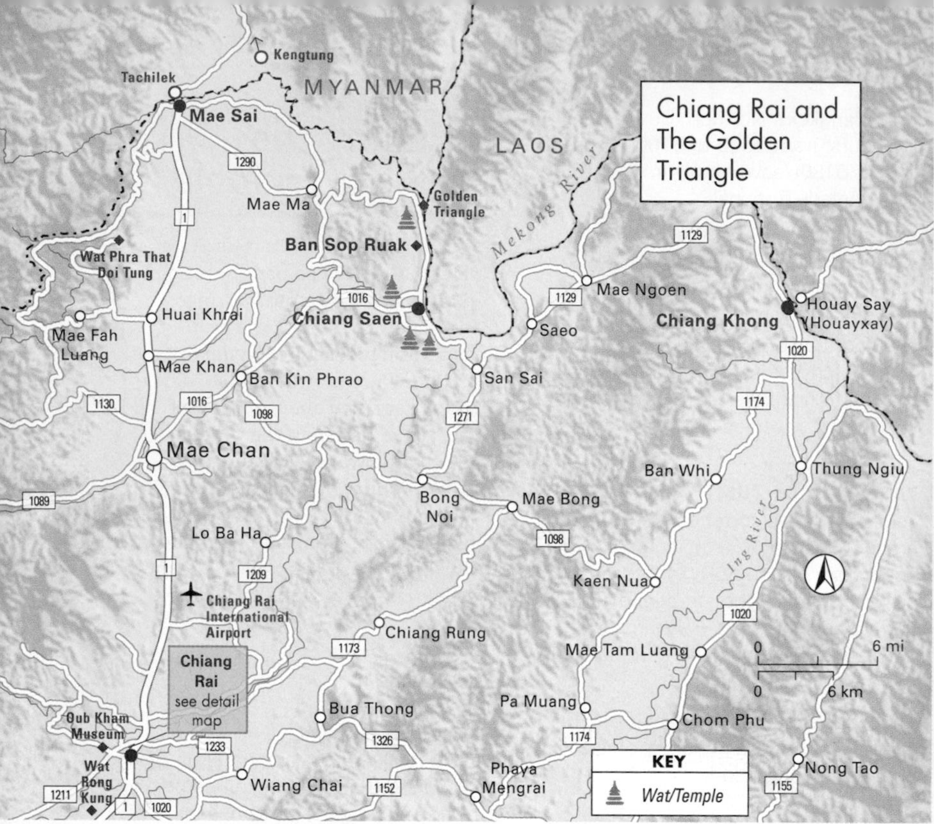

support human zoos!" ✉ *PDA Bldg., 620/25 Thanalai Rd., 3rd fl.* ☎ *053/740088* 🌐 *www.pdacr.org.*

Oub Kham Museum

MUSEUM | Lanna history and culture are vividly chronicled at this jewel of a facility on the outskirts of Chiang Rai. The museum, in an attractive complex of historic buildings, displays several centuries' worth of local artifacts, including the throne and coronation robes of a 16th-century Lanna ruler. ✉ *81/1 Rai Mai Luang Rd.* 🌐 *www.oubkhammuseum.com/* 🎫 *B300.*

Wat Phrathat Doi Tong

RELIGIOUS SITE | Near the summit of Doi Tong, this temple overlooks the Mae Kok River. The ancient pillar that stands here once symbolized the center of the universe for devout Buddhists. The sunset view is worth the trip. ✉ *Winitchaikul Rd.*

Wat Phra Kaew

RELIGIOUS SITE | The Emerald Buddha, which now sits in Thailand's holiest temple, Wat Phra Keo in Bangkok, is said to have been discovered when lightning split the chedi housing it at this similarly named temple at the foot of the Doi Tong in Chiang Rai. A Chinese millionaire financed a jade replica in 1991, and though it's not the real thing, the statuette is still strikingly beautiful. ✉ *19 Trairat Rd.*

Wat Phra Singh

RELIGIOUS SITE | This 14th-century temple is worth visiting for its viharn, distinguished by some remarkably delicate wood carving and for colorful frescoes depicting the life of Lord Buddha. A sacred Indian Bhodhi tree stands in the peaceful temple grounds. ✉ *Singhaklai Rd.*

Mae Salong Nok

Visit this remote mountain village northwest of Chiang Rai, and you could be excused for believing you'd strayed over a couple of borders and into China. The one-street hamlet—the mountainside leaves no room for further expansion—is the home of the descendants of Chinese Nationalist troops who arrived here in the 1960s after spending a dozen or so years in Burma following the Communists' ascension to power in China. The settlers established orchards and tea and coffee plantations that now drape the mountainsides; in December and January, visitors crowd the slopes to admire the cherry blossoms and swaths of sunflowers. Call at any of the numerous tea shops for a pot of refreshing oolong. A local bus service runs from Chiang Rai to Mae Salong (the village's official Thai name is Santikhiri), and most Chiang Rai travel agents offer day tours for about B3,000.

★ Wat Rong Khun

RELIGIOUS SITE | One of Thailand's most astonishing temples, Wat Rong Khun stands like a glistening, sugar-coated wedding cake beside the A-1 Chiang Rai–Bangkok motorway south of Chiang Rai. Popularly called the White Temple because of its lustrous exterior, the extraordinary structure is being built by internationally renowned Thai artist Chalermchai Kositpipat, assisted by a team of more than 40 young artists, craftsmen, and construction workers, as a Buddhist act of winning merit. They have been working on the massive project for 10 years, and Chalermchai doesn't expect it to be finished in his lifetime. The glistening effect comes from thousands of reflective glass mosaics set into the white stucco. Even the fish in the temple's ornamental pool are white Chinese carp. A songthaew ride to the temple from Chiang Rai costs about B50. ✉ *A-1 Chiang Rai–Bangkok motorway* ✣ *13 km (8 miles) south of Chiang Rai* 🎫 *Free.*

Restaurants

Cabbages & Condoms

$$ | THAI | Most of the modest price of your meal at this quirkily named restaurant, one of three in Thailand, goes toward the country's leading nongovernmental organization that specializes in HIV/AIDS education. The cuisine is Thai, geared somewhat to Western tastes. **Known for:** prophylactics as parting gifts; lightly applied chilies; fairly priced Thai food. $ *Average main: B220* ✉ *620/1 Thanalai Rd., City Center* ☎ *053/740657* 🌐 *www.cabbagesandcondoms.net/.*

Chivit Thamma Da

$$ | THAI | Classically trained baker Nattamon Holmberg puts an emphasis on slow and sustainable food at this cozy bistro and café on the Kok River. The prices are a little higher than other restaurants in Chiang Rai, but the quality of its locally sourced ingredients more than make up for it. **Known for:** clean and cold draft lines, featuring a draft beer of the month; a serious tea selection and expansive menu of Thai and Western food; art exhibitions and books you can borrow. $ *Average main: B250* ✉ *179 Moo 2, Rim Kok* ☎ *053/166967* 🌐 *www.chivitthammada.com.*

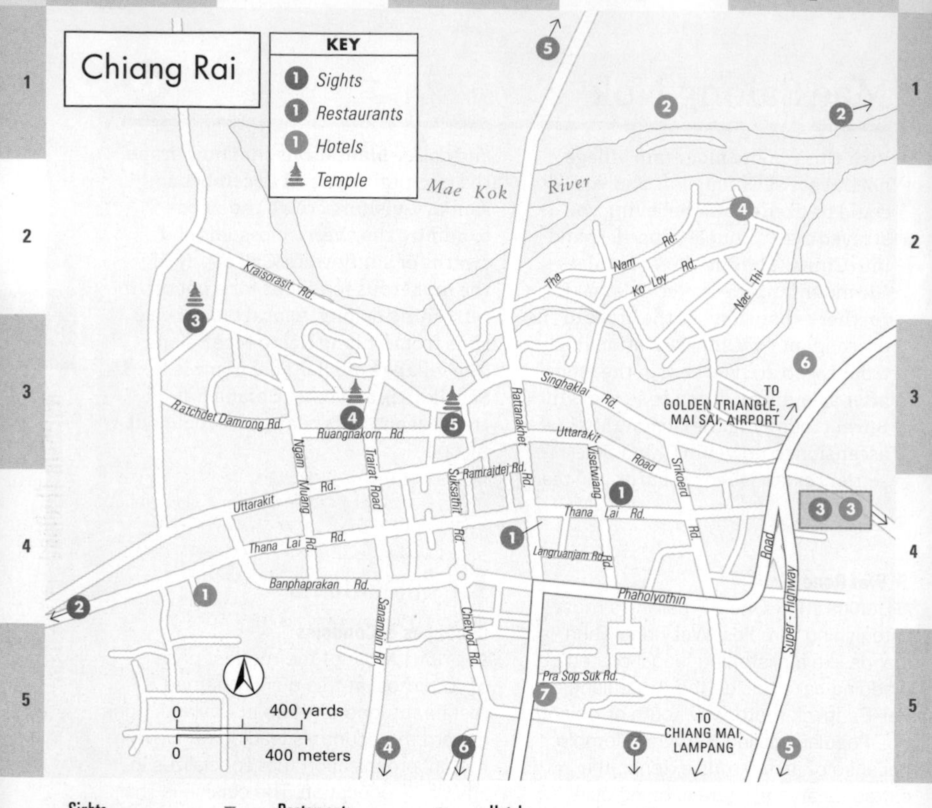

Sights

1 Hilltribe Museum & Education Center **D4**
2 Oub Kham Museum **A4**
3 Wat Phrathat Doi Tong.................. **A3**
4 Wat Phra Kaew......... **B3**
5 Wat Phra Singh **C3**
6 Wat Rong Khun **C5**

Restaurants

1 Cabbages & Condoms.................... **C4**
2 Chivit Thamma Da **E1**
3 Leelawadee **E4**
4 Moommai................. **B5**
5 Give Green Farm House Restaurant................ **C1**
6 Tok Tong **D5**

Hotels

1 Ben Guest House....... **A4**
2 Imperial River House Resort and Spa **D1**
3 Le Meridien............... **E4**
4 The Legend................ **E2**
5 The Mantrini.............. **E5**
6 Rasa Boiutique Hotel.... **E3**
7 Wiang Inn................. **C5**

Give Green Farm House Restaurant

$ | **THAI** | Although it's located right down the street from a major attraction (Thawan Duchanee's "Black House" museum), this family-run business keeps its prices low and its traditional dishes noticeably fresh and delicious. Much of what they make is straight off the Give Green Farm, and operates as a master class in sustainable comfort food. **Known for:** organic without the sticker shock; farm-to-table fare that actually tastes like it; vegetarian options. *Average main: B40 ✉ 300 Moo 13 ☎ 081/090–1805 ▭ No credit cards.*

Leelawadee

$$ | **THAI** | The name of this attractive open-sided restaurant signifies the strongly perfumed frangipani trees that frame its riverside setting. The gargantuan menu embraces Chinese, Thai, and Japanese cuisine, but the specialty is northern Thai food, including fresh fish from the Kok and Mae Kong rivers. **Known for:** frog legs and jellyfish for adventurous eaters; its prime location; big crowds. *Average main: B200 ✉ 58 Moo 19 Kaew Wai Rd. ☎ 053/600–0000, 089/999–8444 ⊕ leelawadeechiangrai.com ▭ No credit cards.*

Moommai

$ | **THAI** | A garden panorama of ceramic dolls and other tiny figurines greets you at this enchanting restaurant, where the tables are distributed among the shrubs and ornamental trees. The locals love the place for its excellent lineup of northern Thai specialties and Chinese-influenced dishes. **Known for:** nightly folk music; laid-back vibes; fantastic Lanna food. *Average main: B150 ✉ 64 Sankhongluang Rd. Moo 16, Tambon Robwiang ☎ 053/716416 ▭ No credit cards.*

Tok Tong

$ | **THAI** | Chinese and northern Thai dishes dominate the extensive menu at this timber-built traditional restaurant in a garden setting on Chiang Rai's main street. The curries can be spicy, so make sure the person taking your order is aware of your tastes. *Average main: B150 ✉ 45/12 Phaholyothin Rd. ☎ 053/756369 ▭ No credit cards.*

Hotels

Ben Guest House

$ | **B&B/INN** | This family-run inn has comfortable, reasonably priced accommodations. **Pros:** friendly staff with deep knowledge of the region; lively evening scene; pool. **Cons:** cheaper rooms are very basic and have thin walls; young clientele can be noisy; 10- to 15-minute walk to town center. *Rooms from: B700 ✉ 351/10 San Khong Noi Soi 4 ☎ 053/716775 ⊕ www.benguesthousechiangrai.com ▭ No credit cards ⇨ 30 rooms ⊙ No meals.*

Imperial River House Resort and Spa

$$ | **RESORT** | A large glass-enclosed lobby—complete with high ceilings and a permanent art gallery—sets the tone at this riverside hotel, leading guests onto an elegant terrace with an infinity pool and dramatic views of Chiang Rai city. **Pros:** spa treatments; tropical gardens and a picturesque swimming pool; near the Blue Temple. **Cons:** far from town; breakfast is nothing special; some decorations are dated. *Rooms from: B3,780 ✉ 482 Moo 4 Mae Kok Rd., Muang ☎ 053/750830 ⊕ www.imperialriverhouse.com ⇨ 36 rooms ⊙ No meals.*

Le Meridien

$$$ | **RESORT** | Large and luxurious, this hotel commands a stretch of the Mae Kok River and views of the northern mountain range. **Pros:** shuttle bus service until 10 pm; special activities like bonfires and yoga; helpful tour desk. **Cons:** shabby neighborhood; slow room service; limited breakfast options. *Rooms from: B5,780 ✉ 221/2 Moo 20 Kwaewai Rd. ☎ 053/603333 ⊕ lemeridienchiangrai.com ⇨ 159 rooms ⊙ Free breakfast.*

Continued on page 373

THAILAND'S HILL TRIBES

Thailand's hill tribes populate the remote, mountainous regions in the north. They welcome visitors, and their villages have become major attractions—some are even dependent on tourist dollars. But other villages, especially those that are harder to reach, have retained an authentic feel; a knowledgeable guide can take you to them.

Hill tribes are descendants of migratory peoples from Myanmar (Burma), Tibet, and China. There are at least 10 tribes living in northern Thailand, and they number a little over half a million, a mere 1% of Thailand's population. The tribes follow forms of ancestral worship and are animists: that is, they believe in a world of spirits that inhabit everything—rivers, forests, homes, and gardens. Historically, some tribes made a living by cultivating poppies for opium, but this practice has mostly died out.

Many tribespeople claim to be victims of official discrimination, and it is indeed often difficult for them to gain full citizenship. Although the Thai government has a program to progressively grant them citizenship, the lack of reliable documentation and the slow workings of the Bangkok bureaucracy are formidable obstacles. However, Thais normally treat hill tribe people with respect; in the Thai language they aren't called "tribes" but Chao Khao, which means "Owners of the Mountains."

Visiting the Chao Khao is a matter of debate. Some of the more accessible villages have become Disneyland-like, with tribespeople, clad in colorful costumes, who are eager to pose in a picture with you—and then collect your baht. In general, the farther afield you go, the more authentic the experience.

Even if you don't visit a village, you'll likely encounter tribespeople selling their crafts at markets in Chiang Mai, Chiang Rai, and Mae Hong Son.

The four tribes you're likely to encounter in northern Thailand are the Karen, Hmong, Akha, and Lisu.

(left) Long neck woman, Chiang Mai; (top) Akha girls wearing ornate headdresses.

KAREN

ORIGINS: Myanmar

POPULATION: 400,000

DID YOU KNOW? The famous "long necks" are actually the Paduang tribe, a subdivision of the Karen.

CRAFTS THEY'RE KNOWN FOR: weaving, beaded jewelry, handmade drums.

The majority of Thailand's hill tribe population is Karen, and there are an estimated 7 million of them living in Myanmar as well. The Karen are the most settled of the tribes, living in permanent villages of well-constructed houses and farming plots of land that leave as much of the forest as possible undisturbed. Though Karen traditionally hold Buddhist and animist beliefs, many communities follow Christianity, which missionaries introduced in colonial Burma.

(top) Karen woman weaving; (bottom) Padaung girls.

LONG NECKS

Traditionally, Paduang women have created the illusion of elongated necks—considered beautiful in their culture—by wrapping brass coils around them. The process begins when a girl is about 5 years old; she will add rings each year. The bands, which can weigh up to 12 lbs, push down on the collarbone, making the neck appear long.

Some human rights groups call the Paduang villages "human zoos" and say that you should not visit because tourism perpetuates the practice of wearing neck coils, which can be harmful. But, most of Thailand's Paduang are refugees who have fled worse conditions in Myanmar, and Thailand's three Paduang villages depend on tourism. Some Paduang women object not to tourism but to the fact that they earn as little as $50 a month from tour operators who profit handsomely. If you go, try to find an operator who treats the Paduang equitably.

HMONG

ORIGINS: China

POPULATION: 80,000

DID YOU KNOW? The Hmong wear elaborate silver lockets to keep their souls firmly locked into their bodies.

CRAFTS THEY'RE KNOWN FOR: needlework, batik, decorative clothing and headdresses.

At the night markets of Chiang Mai and Chiang Rai, you'll recognize Hmong women by their colorful costumes and heavy silver jewelry. There are two divisions of Hmong, White and Blue; White Hmong women wear baggy black pants and blue sashes, while Blue Hmong women wear knee-length pleated skirts. But the divisions "white" and "blue" don't refer to traditional Hmong costumes. "Blue" is a translation of the Hmong word "ntsuab," which also means "dark," a description given to a branch of Hmong whose members once practiced cannibalism. Hmong communities that rejected cannibalism were described as "dlawb," which means "innocent" or "white."

(right) Hmong children.

AKHA

ORIGINS: Tibet

POPULATION: 33,000

DID YOU KNOW? Akha villages are defined by a set of wooden gates, often decorated with charms meant to ward off evil spirits.

CRAFTS THEY'RE KNOWN FOR: silver belt buckles and bracelets, decorative hats and clothing, *saw oo* (fiddles).

The Akha once thrived on opium production, shielded from outside interference by the relative inaccessibility of the remote mountaintop sites they chose for their settlements. Today, all but the most remote communities grow alternative crops, such as rice, beans, and corn. They're a gentle, hospitable people whose women wear elaborate headdresses decorated with silver, beads, and feathers. Akha men wear hollow bracelets containing a silver bead, which they believe keeps them in touch with ancestral spirits.

Akha women wearing traditional headdresses.

LISU

ORIGINS: Tibet
POPULATION: 25,000
DID YOU KNOW? The Lisu pass their history from generation to generation in the form of a song.
CRAFTS THEY'RE KNOWN FOR: silver belt buckles, saw oo, large beaded hats.

Though they're not the most numerous, the businesslike Lisu are the tribe you're most likely to meet on day trips out of Chiang Mai and Chiang Rai. More than any other hill tribe, the Lisu have recognized the earning power of tourism. As tourist buses draw up, women scramble to change from their everyday clothes into the famous multicolored costumes they normally wear only on high days and holidays.

Lisu women.

THE SHAN

Though sometimes referred to as a hill tribe, the Shan, who live predominantly in Myanmar, are actually a large minority (there are an estimated 6 million) who have been fighting for their own state for decades. They have lived in the area for 1,000 years and are believed to be descendents of the Tai people, the original inhabitants of the region. The Shan who reside in Thailand have fled persecution in Myanmar. Unlike the hill tribes, the Shan are predominantly Buddhist. Shan craftspeople make some of the silver jewelry and ornaments you'll find at markets.

Shan women wearing traditional bamboo hats.

VISITING HILL TRIBE COMMUNITIES

(top) Akha woman with children; (bottom) Karen woman.

ETIQUETTE

Hill-tribe people tend to be conservative, so do follow a few simple guidelines on your visit.

- Dress modestly.
- Keep a respectful distance from religious ceremonies or symbols, and don't touch any talismans without asking first.
- Avoid loud or aggressive behavior and public displays of affection.
- Always ask permission before taking a person's picture.

TREKKING

Meeting and staying with tribespeople is one of the main attractions of trekking in northern Thailand. Some day trips include brief stops at villages, which are often little more than theme parks. But if you book a trek of three days or more you're sure to encounter authentic hill tribes living as they have for centuries.

Chao Khao are hospitable to westerners, often organizing spontaneous parties at which home-brewed rice whiskey flows copiously. If you stay overnight, you'll be invited to share the community's simple food and sleep on the floor in one of their basic huts.

Virtually all travel operators offer tours and treks to hill tribe villages. The **Mirror Foundation** (✉ *106 Moo 1, Ban Huay Khom, T. Mae Yao, Chiang Rai,* ☎ *053/737412* 🌐 *www.themirrorfoundation.org*), an NGO that works to improve the lives of hill tribes near Chiang Rai, can arrange culturally respectful tours. The foundation's current projects include bringing volunteer teachers to tribal villages and preventing the exploitation of hill tribe women and children.

■ **TIP→ To avoid being taken to a tourist trap instead of an authentic village, ask the operator to identify the tribes you'll visit and to describe their culture and traditions.** It's a good sign if the operator can answer your questions knowledgeably; the information will also add greatly to the pleasure of your trip.

DAY TRIPS

You can also take daytrips to see hill tribes from Chiang Mai, Chiang Rai, or Mae Hong Son. The villages appear on few maps, so it's not advisable to set out on your own; a guide or driver who knows the region well is a better bet. You can easily hire one for about B1,000 per day; ask the TAT in Chiang Mai or Chiang Rai for recommendations.

Several Chiang Mai operators offer "three country" one-day tours of the Golden Triangle: a boat trip to a Laotian island in the Mekong River; a brief shopping trip to the tax-free Myanmar border town of Tachilek; and a stop at a Thai hill tribe village on the way home. The fare of B800 to B1,000 includes lunch. These tours are likely to feel fairly touristy.

SHOPPING FOR HILL TRIBE CRAFTS

Embroidered textiles at a market near Chiang Mai.

Over the past few decades, the Thai royal family has worked with the government to wean hill tribe farmers off cultivating opium poppies. One initiative has been financing workshops for manufacturing traditional handicrafts, such as basketry, weaving, and woodworking. Some of these royal projects, located near hill tribe villages, offer both employment and on-site training. The workshops also prevent the crafts from dying out and create a market for products that were originally only distributed within the tribal communities.

WORKSHOPS

The Doi Tung mountain, 40 km (25 mile) north of Chiang Rai, is home to 26 hill tribe villages as well as the **Doi Tung Development Project** (☎ *053/767001* 🌐 *www.doitung.org*), a royal project based at the late Queen Mother's former summer palace. The tribes living in the mountain villages produce handicrafts; the project workshops also employ hill tribe craftsmen and women. Both the villages and the project welcome visitors. Daily tours of the project grounds are available for B100; tribespeople sell crafts at a shop and at stalls on the grounds.

Though it's not for the faint of heart, a very curvy 16-km (10-mile) road leads to the top of Doi Tung from the village of Huai Krai, 20 km (12 mile) south of Mae Sai via Highway 101. Local buses and songthaews from Huai Krai will take you here; you can also hire a driver or a guide.

MARKETS & STORES

Although hill tribe crafts are abundant at the night markets in Chiang Mai, Chiang Rai, and Mae Hong Son, serious collectors prefer government-run stores whose products come with certificates of authenticity. Prices are fixed at these stores but are comparable to what you'll pay at markets (upscale hotel boutiques, however, inflate prices substantially). Expect to pay at least B500 for a silver ring or belt buckle and as much as B2,500 for a bracelet or necklace; around B300 for a meter of woven cloth; and B300 to 400 for a simple wooden instrument like a bamboo flute.

★ The Legend

$$$ | **RESORT** | Large, tastefully furnished rooms, vast bathrooms, secluded terraces, an open-air gourmet restaurant, and unrestricted views of the distant mountains make it easy for The Legend to live up to its name. **Pros:** elegant and peaceful; impeccably designed; reliable airport pickup. **Cons:** standard rooms have no bathtubs; city center is a 10-minute drive away; confusing signposting can make it difficult to find your room at night. *Rooms from: B4,410 ✉ 124/15 Kohloy Rd., Amphoe Muang ☎ 053/910400 🌐 www.thelegend-chiangrai.com 79 rooms No meals.*

The Mantrini

$$ | **HOTEL** | Only the tropical vegetation hints that this highly stylish hotel is in Thailand and not a boutique establishment in central Milan or Munich. **Pros:** beautifully designed; shady pool area; friendly staff. **Cons:** drab neighborhood; noisy bars nearby; 15-minute drive to city center. *Rooms from: B2,400 ✉ 292/13 Moo 13 ☎ 053/601555 🌐 www.mantrini.com 63 rooms Free breakfast.*

Rasa Boutique Hotel

$$ | **HOTEL** | Rich hues, warm lighting, and grand Moroccan architectural flourishes set a distinctly exotic tone at this boutique hotel well away from the city center. **Pros:** secluded swimming pool; good restaurant; romantic setting. **Cons:** shabby neighborhood; far from city center; noisy at night. *Rooms from: B3,000 ✉ 789/7 Phaholyothin Rd. ☎ 053/717454 🌐 www.rasaboutiquehotelchiangrai.com 30 rooms No meals.*

Wiang Inn

$$ | **HOTEL** | In the heart of downtown, this sleek, modern hotel is among the best in central Chiang Rai. Spacious rooms are decked out in dark woods and fine fabrics. **Pros:** best facilities of in-city hotels; good restaurant; central location. **Cons:** standard rooms have only single beds; impersonal chain-hotel atmosphere; karaoke can bleed into common areas. *Rooms from: B2,800 ✉ 893 Phaholyothin Rd. ☎ 053/711533 🌐 www.wianginn.com 260 rooms No meals.*

Nightlife

Dinner Late

BARS/PUBS | Walk up a steep set of stairs in the middle of Chiang Rai's main drag and you just might find a tiny rooftop bar that feels like a friend's house. A friend that happens to serve a decent selection of craft beer and fairly priced cocktails, mind you. Get here before 8 pm to save even more with serious happy hour specials that set the tone for a perfect night out. *✉ Phaholyothin Rd. ☎ 087/558–1199.*

Reggae Home & Bar

BARS/PUBS | The laid-back leanings of Chiang Rai are even reflected in its nightlife, with the best example being this relaxed temple to all things reggae. Whether you're playing Jenga with perfect strangers, listening to a live band, or talking to its friendly Rastafarian owner, there's no better way to wind down a night. *✉ 869/39 Thai Viwat Alley ☎ 095/680–0672.*

Activities

BOATING

For something adventurous, catch a bus to the border town of Tha Ton and board a high-powered longtail boat there and ride the rapids 130 km (81 miles) to Chiang Rai. Boats leave from a pier near the town bridge at noon and take about three to four hours to negotiate the bends and rapids of the river, which passes through thick jungle and past remote hill tribe villages. The single fare is B350. For a more leisurely ride to Chiang Rai, board a raft, which takes two days and nights to reach the city, overnighting in hill tribe villages. Fares start at B1,000. ■ **TIP→ Take bottled water and (most important) a hat or umbrella to shade you from the sun.** The best time to make the trip is during October and

November, when the water is still high but the rainy season has passed.

Bamboo Tours

BOATING | ✉ *897 Jed Yod Soi 3* ☎ *086/115–3980* 🌐 *https://www.bambootourschiangrai.com/.*

Coconuts Tours

BOATING | ✉ *1016/2 Jed-Yod Rd.* ☎ *080/677–0375, 091/858–2369* 🌐 *www.coconutstourschiangrai.com/.*

GOLF

Santiburi Country Club

GOLF | Chiang Rai has one of northern Thailand's finest golf courses, the Santiburi Country Club, laid out by the celebrated Robert Trent Jones Jr. The course is set among rolling hills 10 km (6 miles) outside Chiang Rai. The ranch-style clubhouse has an excellent restaurant and coffee shop, and the facilities include a sauna. Visitors are welcome, and clubs, carts, and shoes can be rented. Reservations are required. ✉ *12 Moo 3 Huadoi-Sobpao Rd.* ☎ *053/662–8216* 🌐 *www.santiburi.com/chiangrai/* 🎫 *Weekdays B2,000, weekends B2,500.*

HIKING

Phu Sang National Park

PARK—SPORTS-OUTDOORS | Some 90 km (56 miles) east of Chiang Rai is the region's most beautiful national park, Phu Sang, which has one of Thailand's rarest natural wonders, cascades of hot water. The temperature of the 85-foot-high falls never drops below 33°C (91°F), and a nearby pool is even warmer. The park has some spectacular caves and is crisscrossed by nature trails teeming with bird life. One hour's drive north lies the mountainous border with Laos, straddled by 5,730-foot-high Phu Chee Fah, a favorite destination for trekkers and climbers. You reach Phu Sang National Park via Thoeng, 70 km (43 miles) east of Chiang Rai on Highway 1020. The park rents cabins for B500 a night. Entrance to the park costs B100, and B30 for a vehicle. ✉ *National Hiwy. 1093 Phu Sang* ☎ *054/401099* 🌐 *www.dnp.go.th.*

Shopping

Chiang Rai has a **night market,** on Robviang Nongbua Road, and although it's much smaller than Chiang Mai's, there are many handicrafts and textiles on offer, as well as new additions like Dek Ban Suan's home decor shop El Jardin. A central section of Thanalai Road is closed to traffic on Saturday nights for a "walking street" market, and San Khon Noi Road is made a pedestrian-only area for a Sunday market.

Doy Din Dang Pottery

CERAMICS/GLASSWARE | You'll have to hop in a car or grab a motorbike to get to the serene ceramics studio of Chiang Rai native Somluk Pantiboon, which is located about 12 km north of the city center and also features a café and small exhibition space. Want a closer look at northern Thailand's burgeoning art scene beyond all those cups, bowls, and plates? Stop at the Art Bridge gallery that Pantiboon co-founded on the way back into town. ✉ *Rte. 1* ⊕ *About 6 km north of the airport* ☎ *053/705291* 🌐 *www.dddpottery.com/.*

Chiang Saen

59 km (37 miles) north of Chiang Rai, 239 km (149 miles) northeast of Chiang Mai, 935 km (581 miles) north of Bangkok.

A one-road town on the banks of the Mekong River, Chiang Saen was home to the future King Mengrai, who built a citadel here in the 12th century. Two ancient chedis are all that remain standing to remind the visitor of Chiang Saen's ancient glory, but government-financed excavation is gradually uncovering evidence of the citadel. The ancient flooring and walls that have been exposed are providing tantalizing clues about one of

Doi Tung

If you're traveling north from Chiang Rai on Highway 110, watch for the left-hand turn at Km 32 to Doi Tung. The road winds 42 km (26 miles) to the summit, where an astonishing view opens out over the surrounding countryside. The temple here, Wat Phra That Doi Tung, founded more than a millennium ago, is said to be the repository of some important relics of Lord Buddha, including a collarbone. The shrine attracts pilgrims from as far away as India and China, for whom its huge Chinese Buddha figure is an important symbol of good fortune. On the mountain slopes below the temple is the summer home built for the king's late mother. The fine mansion is closed to the public, but the gardens, an explosion of color in all seasons, are open unless particularly important guests are staying.

the region's first royal palaces. Little of the citadel survived the incursion by the Burmese in 1588, and the remaining fragments were ravaged by fire when the last of the Burmese were ousted in 1786.

The embarkation point for river trips to Myanmar, Laos, and China, Chiang Saen is being developed as a major Mekong River port.

GETTING HERE AND AROUND

Two buses daily run between Chiang Mai's Chang Phuak bus station and Chiang Saen, taking 4½ hours. The fare is about B150; buses stop in the center of town and at the boat piers. Songthaews provide the local transportation. Rides cost B20.

SAFETY AND PRECAUTIONS

Chiang Saen is a river port and something of a smugglers' haven, which keeps the local police busy. Foreign visitors are left alone, though the usual precautions are advised when walking the riverside promenade at night. Leave valuables in your hotel safe or with the hotel or guesthouse management.

TIMING

Chiang Saen is an ideal base from which to explore the Golden Triangle, so plan on staying two or three days—longer if the town's ancient ruins and museum attract your interest.

Sights

National Museum

MUSEUM | Next door to Wat Phra That Luang, the National Museum exhibits artifacts from the Lanna period, as well as some Neolithic discoveries. The museum also has a good collection of carvings and traditional handicrafts from the hill tribes. ✉ *Chiang Saen ✣ Rd. to Chiang Rai, 1 km (½ mile) from town center* ☎ *053/777102* 🌐 *www.virtualmuseum.finearts.go.th/chiangsaen/index.php/en/* 🎫 *B100* ⏲ *Closed Mon. and Tues.*

Wat Pa Sak

RELIGIOUS SITE | The name of this wat, Chiang Saen's oldest chedi, refers to the 300 *ton sak* (teak trees) planted in the surrounding area. The stepped temple, which narrows to a spire, is said to enshrine holy relics brought here in the 1320s, when the city was founded by King Saen Phu. The chedi itself predates that, however; it was built by Phu in 1295, right around the arrival of Lanna's first ruler—and Phu's grandfather—King Mangrai. ✉ *Chiang Saen.*

Wat Phra That Luang

RELIGIOUS SITE | Some scholars attribute this imposing octagonal wat inside Chiang Saen's city walls to its founder and namesake, King Saen Phu (1325–34), though others speculate that it predates him. Regardless of where its roots lie, Wat Phra That Luang is the tallest religious building in the Chiang Rai region, reaching towards the heavens at 88 meters high right next to the National Museum. ✉ *Chiang Saen.*

Hotels

De River Boutique Resort

$ | HOTEL | Most rooms at this small, Lanna-style hotel 1 km (½ mile) east of the National Museum directly overlook the Mekong, with sweeping views across its swirling waters to the hills of Laos on the opposite bank. **Pros:** sunrise from one's private balcony; riverside walks; wonderful views. **Cons:** staff has poor English skills; Ban Sop Ruak a 15-minute drive away; no transportation. *Rooms from: B1,400* ✉ *455 Moo 1 Tambon Wiang* ☎ *053/784488* 🌐 *www.deriverresort.com* *18 rooms* *Free breakfast.*

Viang Yonok

$$ | HOTEL | Although it's not a well-oiled machine like nearby resorts from the Four Seasons and Anantara, this small husband-and-wife-run hotel offers laid-back luxury at a tenth of the price. **Pros:** luxury that doesn't require a bank loan; free kayaks, bikes, and surprisingly strong Wi-Fi; discounts for extended stays. **Cons:** hosts are hospitable but can feel like they're hovering over you; far from other food options; not as lavish as its corporate competitors. *Rooms from: B2,100* ✉ *201 Moo 3, Dtumbon Yonok* ☎ *053/650444, 081/862–8727* 🌐 *www.viangyonok.com* *6 private bungalows* *Free breakfast.*

Ban Sop Ruak

8 km (5 miles) north of Chiang Saen.

Ban Sop Ruak, a village in the heart of the Golden Triangle, was once the domain of the opium warlord Khun Sa. Thai and Burmese troops hounded him out in 1996 and he spent the remaining years until his death in 2007 under house arrest in Yangon, where he lived comfortably in the company of a personal seraglio of four young Shan women. His picaresque reputation still draws those eager to see evidence of the man who once held the region under his thumb.

This simple riverside town has one main street, 1 km (½ mile) in length, that winds along the southern bank of the Mekong River. It's lined with stalls selling souvenirs and textiles from Laos. Waterfront restaurants serve fresh catfish and provide vantage points for watching the evening sun dip over the mountains to the west.

GETTING HERE AND AROUND

Songthaews (about B50) are the only transport service from Chiang Saen to Ban Sop Ruak. A taxi service is operated by Golden Shan Travel (✉ *587 Ban Sop Ruak High St.* ☎ *053/784198*), which also offers tours of the Golden Triangle, Mae Salong, Doi Tung, and hill tribe villages for B3,000 and B3,500.

SAFETY AND PRECAUTIONS

Although Ban Sop Ruak was once the center of the Golden Triangle illegal narcotics trade, it's a law-abiding little town now, and the one main street is perfectly safe, even late at night. Nevertheless, it's advisable to leave valuables in your hotel safe or with the hotel or guesthouse management.

TIMING

Ban Sop Ruak is the Golden Triangle, with enough points of interest to warrant a stay of at least two or three days. The Hall of Opium alone is extensive enough to take up a whole day, and boat trips to Laos beckon.

 Sights

★ Hall of Opium

MUSEUM | The magnificent Hall of Opium is a white stucco, glass, marble, and aluminum building nestled in a valley above the Mekong. The site is so close to former poppy fields that a plan is still being considered to extend the complex to encompass an "open-air" exhibit of a functioning opium plantation. The museum traces the history of the entire drug trade, including a look at how mild stimulants like coffee and tea took hold in the West. It even attempts to give visitors a taste of the "opium experience" by leading them through a long tunnel where atmospheric music wafts between walls bearing phantasmagoric bas-relief scenes. The synthetic smell of opium was originally pumped into the tunnel but the innovation was dropped after official complaints.

It's an arresting introduction to an imaginatively designed and assembled exhibition, which reaches back into the murky history of the opium trade and takes a long look into a potentially darker future. ✉ *Hall of Opium Golden Triangle Park* ☎ *053/784–4446* 🌐 *www.maefahluang.org* 🎫 *B300.*

House of Opium

MUSEUM | Opium is so linked to the history of Ban Sop Ruak that the small town now has two museums devoted to the subject. This smaller one is in the center of town. A commentary in English details the growing, harvesting, and smoking of opium. Many of the exhibits, such as carved teak opium boxes and jade and silver pipes, are fascinating. ✉ *212 Moo 1, Wiang Subdistrict* ☎ *053/784060* 🎫 *B50.*

Imperial Golden Triangle Resort

VIEWPOINT | Even if you don't stay overnight, pay a visit to this sumptuous resort that has the best views over the confluence of the Mae Sai, Ruak, and Mekong rivers. ✉ *222 Ban Sop Ruak* 🌐 *www.imperialhotels.com.*

Longtail excursion boats

TOUR—SIGHT | Longtail excursion boats captained by experienced river men tie up at the Ban Sop Ruak jetty, and the B500 fee covers a 90-minute cruise into the waters of Laos and a stop at a Laotian market. ✉ *Ban Sop Ruak.*

 Restaurants

Mekong Pizza

$ | PIZZA | In a welcome break from all the fancy resort dining options in the Sop Ruak area, crispy thin-crust pizza is topped with traditional and Thai ingredients ranging from pepperoni and Parma ham to a tom yum–tinged seafood and northern-style sausage. Just don't call it fusion food; chef-owner Michael Sullivan is more concerned with keeping it classic while incorporating some of the local flavors he's grown to love since moving here. **Known for:** Ping-Pong; inventive flavor combos and custom pies; a primo location near both opium museums. 💲 *Average main: B189* ✉ *301/5 Rt. 1290* ☎ *083/915–4750* 🌐 *www.mekongpizza.com/* 💳 *No credit cards.*

Sala Mae Nam

$$$ | THAI | Anantara's main breakfast buffet room turns into a reputable Thai restaurant during the lunch and dinner hour, offering northern specialities like *khao soi* (chicken curry with yellow egg noodles), *geang ho* (dry curry pork with toothsome glass noodles and mixed organic vegetables), and a duo of dips made with minced pork and green chilies. Or you could splurge for the B999 tasting, which features such local standards as spicy papaya salad, deep-fried fish cakes, minced pork salad, sticky rice, and grilled chicken satay. **Known for:** surreal elephant spottings; open-air dining; full-bodied flavors. 💲 *Average main: B390* ✉ *229 Moo 1 Weng, Chiang Saen*

☎ 053/784084 🌐 *www.anantara.com/en/golden-triangle-chiang-rai/restaurants/sala-mae-nam.*

★ **Anantara Golden Triangle Elephant Camp & Resort**
$$$$ | **RESORT** | The Anantara is one of the Golden Triangle's greatest hits, a symphony of styles created by Thailand's leading interior designer and architect, Bill Bensley. **Pros:** stunning place to stay; peerless views from nearly every vantage point; service on par with the rest of Anantara's five-star portfolio. **Cons:** access to some rooms involves much stair climbing; isolated from village center; steep bar prices. Ⓢ *Rooms from: B21,930* ✉ *229 Moo 1* ☎ *053/784084, 02/476–0022 in Bangkok* 🌐 *goldentriangle.anantara.com* *110 rooms* *Free breakfast.*

★ **Four Seasons Tented Camp Golden Triangle**
$$$$ | **RESORT** | Elephant lovers, beware—you may never want to leave this pachyderm haven. **Pros:** up-close experiences with humanely treated elephants; interesting regional activities; luxury with a touch of adventure. **Cons:** location might be too remote for some (requires car and boat rides); some tents may not be suitable for guests with mobility issues; the occasional creepy-crawler. Ⓢ *Rooms from: B94,000* ✉ *499 Moo 1 Tambon Wiang, Chiang Saen* ☎ *053/910200* 🌐 *www.fourseasons.com/goldentriangle* *15 tents* *All-inclusive.*

Imperial Golden Triangle Resort
$$ | **HOTEL** | From the superior rooms in this high-eaved, Lanna-style hotel you are treated to magnificent views of three rivers rushing together. **Pros:** spectacular sunsets over the Mekong; excellent travel service; pleasant restaurant terrace. **Cons:** many rooms involve flights of stairs; service staff can be offhand; poor language skills. Ⓢ *Rooms from: B3,025* ✉ *222 Ban Sop Ruak* ☎ *053/784001* 🌐 *www.imperialgoldentriangleresort.com* *73 rooms* *Free breakfast.*

Chiang Khong

64 km (40 miles) east of Ban Sop Ruak, 53 km (33 miles) northeast of Chiang Rai.

This small Mekong River town is gearing up to become a main way station on the planned Asian Highway, and a bridge is being built across the river to the Laotian harbor town of Houay Say (Houayxay). Small skiffs carry people across the Mekong between Chiang Khong and Houay Say, from whose pier daily boats set off for the two-day trip to the World Heritage town of Luang Prabang in Laos. Chiang Khong is a convenient overnight stop before embarking on this excursion.

Chiang Khong has little to attract the visitor apart from the magnificent vistas from the riverside towpath to the hills of Laos across the Mekong. The town's one 300-year-old temple has an interesting Chiang Saen–style chedi but is in need of repair. Textiles from China and Laos can be bought cheaply in Chiang Khong's market.

GETTING HERE AND AROUND

The paved road east out of Chiang Saen parallels the Mekong River for much of the way en route to Chiang Khong and a halfway point commands a magnificent view of the wide river valley far below. A refreshment stall and tables cater to thirsty travelers. Songthaews ply the route for about B100, but you can also hire a speedboat (B500) to go down the river, a thrilling three hours of slipping between the rocks and rapids. Not too many tourists make the journey, especially to villages inhabited by the local Hmong and Yao tribes. The rugged scenery along the Mekong River is actually more dramatic than that of the Golden Triangle.

Ann Tours

TOUR—SIGHT | This outfit headquartered in Vietnam conducts multiday tours in northeastern Thailand. Ann Tours also offers custom itineraries in other parts of Thailand, Laos, Vietnam, and Cambodia. ✉ *166 Moo 8 Saiklang Rd.* ☎ *028/3925–3636* 🌐 *www.anntours.com/thailand/thailand.aspx* *Prices vary depending on group size.*

ESSENTIALS

SAFETY AND PRECAUTIONS

Despite its location on the Laotian border and the occasional arrest of a smuggler or two, Chiang Khong is safe for foreign visitors. Nevertheless, caution is advised when walking the riverside promenade at night—leave valuables and excess cash in your hotel safe or with the management.

TIMING

Chiang Khong is the official border crossing to Laos, and few visitors linger longer than one night, waiting for the Mekong River ferry.

TOURS

Chiang Khong is the embarkation point for the Laotian pier where boats for Luang Prabang are moored. Most Chiang Khong guesthouses have travel desks where tickets for the river cruise to the Laotian World Heritage site can be bought.

The Hub Pub

LOCAL INTEREST | It's backpacker and world-traveler heaven at this hub of three enterprises—a pub, a cycling museum, and a hostel (the Funky Box)—owned by Alan Bate, holder of the Guinness World Record for fastest bicycling trip around the world. A block from the river and the Nam Khong River Side hotel, the Hub Pub is a great place to hang with the ultraconvivial host and other travelers, check out memorabilia from his title-winning 106-day journey, and sip a drink appropriate to the hour. It'll make your day, night, or maybe even both. ✉ *Soi Thetsaban 2* ☎ *093/278–2928* 🌐 *www.funkyboxhostel.com.*

7he Vow

$ | CAFÉ | Much like the trendy cafés that dominate Tokyo's third-wave coffee scene, the menu at this riverside spot is split between pan-Asian staples and Western comfort food like spicy tom yum soup, spaghetti Bolognese, and several kinds of fried chicken. (The "spicy, sour, salty and sweet" version is especially popular.) Also look out for house-made and locally sourced takeway items for the flight back home; 7he Vow's shelves stock everything from tall bottles of wild honey to lightly roasted bags of Thai beans. **Known for:** all-day breakfast; its sister hostel Sleeping Well; Instagrammable desserts. *Average main: B100* ✉ *10/8 Moo 8* ☎ *088/600–0599* *No credit cards.*

Nam Khong Riverside

$ | HOTEL | This hotel edges the south bank of the Mekong River, with most of its clean and comfortable rooms offering unobstructed views to the hills of Laos on the other side. **Pros:** rooftop Thai and European restaurant; helpful travel desk can organize boat trips to Luang Prabang; central location. **Cons:** small bathrooms; drab neighborhood; traffic noise. *Rooms from: B1,000* ✉ *174–176 Moo 8, Wiang Subdistrict* ☎ *053/791796, 053/791801* 🌐 *www.namkhongriverside.com* *40 rooms* *Free breakfast.*

Mae Sai

25 km (16 miles) west of Ban Sop Ruak, 60 km (37 miles) north of Chiang Rai.

From Ban Sop Ruak you can travel west on a dusty road to Mae Sai, a Thai-Burmese border town that straddles the Mae Sai River. The market that nestles next to the border bridge is packed with jewelry stalls, where the careful buyer can find some bargains, including rubies and jade from Myanmar. The cross-border trip is the town's main tourist attraction, though.

GETTING HERE AND AROUND

Buses leave six times daily from Chiang Mai's Chang Phuak bus station for the five-hour journey to Mae Sai. The fare is about B150. Regular bus service also runs between Chiang Rai and Mae Sai (one hour; B50). Around town songthaews are the only means of getting around other than on an organized tour, for which the travel agency Asian Trails is recommended.

ESSENTIALS

SAFETY AND PRECAUTIONS

There are occasional bomb attacks by Burmese anti-regime activists in Tachileik, the Burmese town separated from Mae Sai by only a bridge. Hostilities between Burmese and Thai troops sometimes break out, closing the border. Mae Sai itself is safe for foreign visitors, although it's advisable to leave valuables, excess cash, and passports in your hotel safe or with the management.

TIMING

Mae Sai is essentially a day-trip destination. Many visitors travel from Chiang Mai or Chiang Rai just to shop at the markets in Tachileik.

TOURS

CONTACT Asian Trails ☎ *02/626–2000* 🌐 *www.maekhongtravel.com.*

Sights

Kengtung

TOWN | For $30 (B984) you can get a three-night visa that lets you travel 63 km (39 miles) north to Kengtung, a quaint Burmese town with colonial-era structures built by the British alongside old Buddhist temples. ✉ *Mae Sai.*

Tachileik

TOWN | Foreigners may cross the river to visit Tachileik on a one-day visa ($10, B328) obtainable at the Burmese immigration office at the bridge. The town is a smaller version of Mae Sai, but with a vast tax-free emporium, a busy market, and three casinos packed with Thai gamblers. ✉ *Mae Sai.*

Wat Phra That Doi Wao

VIEWPOINT | For the best view across the river into Myanmar, climb up to Wat Phra That Doi Wao—the 207-step staircase starts behind the Top North Hotel. ✉ *Mae Sai.*

Restaurants

Chan Ka Phak

$ | **THAI** | Set in a lush garden with lots of greenery at the Prince Chakraband Pensiri Centre, this café highlights Princess Maka Chakri Sirindhorn's ongoing efforts to develop organic, disease-resistant crops in northern Thailand. Even something as simple as sautéed morning glory tastes great here as a result—fresh and filling. **Known for:** Chiang Rai's freshest salad bar; don't miss dessert items like kanom krok (coconut cakes) and house-made ice cream; a serene setting full of flowers and fountains. *$ Average main: B70* ✉ *448/16 Singhakhlai Rd.* ☎ *053/733222* ▬ *No credit cards.*

Hotels

Baan Sabai

$ | **HOTEL** | This small guesthouse is in a prime location, right near the Friendship Bridge crossing into Myanmar, a local market, and several street food stalls. **Pros:** large rooms and comfortable beds; friendly staff; central location. **Cons:** no elevators; basic amenities; parking limited. *$ Rooms from: B1,500* ✉ *850*

Moo 10, Tessaban Rd. 8 ☎ 062/031–2233 🌐/ 13 rooms 🍴 Free breakfast 💳 No credit cards.

Easy Maesai Hostel

$ | **HOTEL** | Anyone looking for a solid budget option near the Myanmar border should consider this recent addition to the area. **Pros:** short walk from city center; free bikes; clean and contemporary. **Cons:** fan rooms can get quite hot; shared bathrooms; can be hard to find. *$ Rooms from: B450 ✉ 850/1 Thetsaban 8 Alley, Soi 8 ☎ 086/900–0800 5 rooms 🍴 Free breakfast 💳 No credit cards.*

Mae Sai Guest House

$ | **B&B/INN** | Travelers on a tight budget rank this riverside guesthouse, about 2 km (1 mile) west of the bridge, as the best in Mae Sai. It's certainly among the cheapest. **Pros:** views into Myanmar; riverside walks; friendly staff. **Cons:** rooms are fairly spartan; long walk into town; no parking. *$ Rooms from: B600 ✉ 688 Wiengpangkam ☎ 053/732021 💳 No credit cards 20 bungalows 🍴 No meals.*

The Room

$ | **HOTEL** | This newer property is not right on top of the Myanmar border, but it's much better maintained and more modern looking than many of the other hotel options in the area. **Pros:** close to the bus station, making regional travel easy; quiet, with nice mountain views; good value for the price. **Cons:** about 5 km (3 miles) away from the border; breakfast is nothing special; concrete rooms can feel a little austere. *$ Rooms from: B1,000 ✉ 998 Moo 9 ☎ 093/243–8629 39 rooms 🍴 Free breakfast 💳 No credit cards.*

Shopping

Thais take household goods and consumer products across the river, where Myanmar residents trade them for sandalwood, jade, and rubies. Though you may want to see Myanmar, the prices and quality of the goods will not be better than in Mae Sai.

■ TIP→ Rubies aren't the only red gems here. Mae Sai is also justifiably proud of its sweet strawberries, which ripen in December or January, found at local markets and as far away as Chiang Rai and Chiang Mai.

Mengrai Antique

ANTIQUES/COLLECTIBLES | Near the bridge, this place has a good reputation for selling religious items and rare antiques. *✉ 277 Moo 7, Phaholyothin Rd. ☎ 083/565–1449.*

Phitsanulok

377 km (234 miles) north of Bangkok, 60 km (37 miles) southeast of Sukhothai

For a brief span in the 14th century, after the decline of Sukhothai and before the rise of Ayutthaya, Phitsanulok was the kingdom's capital. Further back in history, it was a Khmer outpost called Song Kwae, though only an ancient monastery remains of that incarnation. This onetime military stronghold has grown away from its roots, leaving only a few reminders like Wat Phra Si Rattana Mahathat and the revered Phra Buddha Chinnarat image. The wat is on Naresuan Road, a major thoroughfare named for the city's most illustrious son, Naresuan the Great, who ruled as King of Ayutthaya from 1590 to 1605.

The current city of Phitsanulok, 5 km (3 miles) from the old site, is a hub of commerce, transportation, and communication with few architectural blessings. It does have two outstanding sights to see, however, Wat Phra Si Rattana Mahathat and the Sgt. Maj. Thawee Folk Museum, an engaging collection of quotidian artifacts. In the evening, tempting food stalls line the promenade along the Nan River. Phitsanulok's mix of attractions and access to outward-bound excursions make it an enjoyable diversion, and its modern hotels make it a comfortable place to spend a night or two while touring Sukhothai region.

GETTING HERE AND AROUND

AIR TRAVEL

Nok Air and Thai AirAsia fly from Bangkok to Phitsanulok, whose airport is 8 km (5 miles) south of town. The flight takes 50 minutes.

AIRPORT Phitsanulok Airport ✣ *8 km (5 miles) south of Phitsanulok, off Hwy. 1064* ☎ *055/378014.*

BUS TRAVEL

Buses to Phitsanulok regularly leave Bangkok's Northern Terminal. Fares on an air-conditioned "VIP" bus start at around B260 for the six-hour trip. The terminal also has buses for travel to and from Chiang Mai via Lampang or via Phrae and Phayao, and to Mae Sot via Tak. Phitsanulok's terminal is downtown, just 1 km (½ mile) from Wat Phra Si Mahatat (known locally as Wat Yai). Inexpensive buses depart Sukhothai for Phitsanulok roughly every hour; the trip takes about 1½ hours.

There's a cheap, cramped, tin-can bus service within Phitsanulok, but you're best off using the open-sided (often cooler and less stuffy) songthaews, motorized samlors, or eco-friendly pedal-powered samlors.

BUS CONTACTS Phitsanulok Bus Station ✉ *834/44–45 Mittaparp Rd.* ☎ *055/242430, 055/242030.*

CAR TRAVEL

A car is a good way to get around the region. Highway 12 from Sukhothai is a long, straight, and reasonably comfortable 59-km (37-mile), one-hour drive. To get to Phitsanulok from Bangkok, take the four-lane Highway 117; the drive from Bangkok takes about 4½ hours. Both Avis and Budget have car-rental desks at the Phitsanulok airport. Economy cars rent for about B1,500 a day; SUVs cost B3,500. Add B1,000 a day for a driver. ■ **TIP→ Make sure to request an English-speaking driver.** Bigger hotels in Phitsanulok offer chauffeur services at similar prices, but are more tour-oriented and generally offer no more than a one-day trip.

SAMLOR AND TAXI TRAVEL

Most of the sights in Phitsanulok are within walking distance, but samlors are easily available. Bargain hard—most trips should cost about B30. Taxis are available for longer trips; you can find a few loitering around the train station.

ESSENTIALS

MONEY MATTERS

There are plenty of ATMs and exchange kiosks in town; Naresuan Road has most of Phitsanulok's banks.

SAFETY AND PRECAUTIONS

Take elementary precautions when visiting Phitsanulok. Leave valuables, unneeded cash, and your passport either in the room safe or with the management.

TIMING

With its historic temples, interesting museums, riverside promenade, and waterfront restaurants, Phitsanulok merits at least an overnight stay.

TOURS AND INFORMATION

The local office of the Tourism Authority of Thailand, TAT, recommends several local travel agents, including Rang Thong Tour.

TRAVEL AGENCY Rang Thong Tour ✉ *55/37 Surasi Commercial Center* ☎ *055/259973.*

VISITOR INFORMATION Tourist Authority of Thailand (TAT) ✉ *209/7–8 Boromtrailokanat Rd., Surasi Trade Center* ☎ *055/252743* 🌐 *www.tourismthailand.org/phitsanulok.*

Sights

Sgt. Maj. Thawee Folk Museum

MUSEUM | This fascinating museum of traditional tools, cooking utensils, animal traps, and handicrafts alone would justify a visit to Phitsanulok. In the early 1980s, Sergeant-Major Khun Thawee traveled to small villages, collecting rapidly disappearing objects of everyday life. He crammed them into a traditional house and barn, and for a decade nothing was properly documented. Visitors stumbled around tiger traps and cooking pots, with little to help them decipher what they were looking at. But Khun Thawee's daughter came to the rescue, and now the marvelous artifacts are systematically laid out, all 10,000 of them. You can now understand the use of everything on display, from the simple wood pipes hunters played to lure their prey, to elaborate rat guillotines. Thawee was honored with two university doctorates for his work in preserving such rare items. He also took over a historic foundry, which casts brass Buddhas and temple bells. The museum is a 15-minute walk south of the railway station, on the east side of the tracks, and the foundry is directly opposite. ✉ *26/138 Wisuttham Rd.* ☎ *055/212749, 055/258715 foundry (phone ahead before visiting)* 🌐 *www.museumthailand.com/Ja_Thawee_Folk_Museum_* 💴 *B100.*

Wat Phra Si Rattana Mahathat

RELIGIOUS SITE | Commonly known as Wat Yai (the Great Temple), this mid-14th century temple developed into a large monastery with typical ornamentation. Particularly noteworthy are the viharn's wooden doors, inlaid with mother-of-pearl in 1756 at the behest of King Boromkot. Behind the viharn is a 100-foot corncob-style prang with a vault containing Buddha relics. Many religious souvenir stands make it hard to gain a good view of the complex, but the *bot,* or chapel, is a fine example of the traditional three-tier roof with low sweeping eaves, designed to diminish the size of the walls, accentuate the nave, and emphasize the image of the Buddha.

Within the viharn is what many consider the world's most beautiful image of the Buddha, Phra Buddha Chinnarat. It was probably cast in the 14th century, during the late Sukhothai period. Its mesmerizing beauty and the mystical powers ascribed to it draw streams of pilgrims—among the most notable of them was the Sukhothai's King Eka Thossarot, who journeyed here in 1631. According to folklore, the king applied with his own hands the gold leaf that covers the Buddha. Many copies of the image have been made, the best-known one residing in Bangkok's Marble Temple. ✉ *Phitsanulok* ✣ *Off Akathodsarod Rd., just north of Hwy. 12 and east of Nan River.*

Restaurants

Phitsanulok has a good range of dining options, from its popular pontoon and riverside restaurants to daytime canteen-style restaurants near the central clock tower on Phayalithai Road. The Muslim restaurants on Pra Ong Dam Road, opposite the town's mosque, are great for curry and roti breakfasts. The night-bazaar promenade along the Nan River contains some basic early-evening places to enjoy the sunset, including the infamous "flying vegetable restaurants," where you can sample the province's famed *pak bung fire dang* (stir-fried morning glory). And the veggies do fly here—when the cooks fling the morning glory to waiters, who deftly catch the food on their plates. Akathodsarod Road near the Topland Hotel is a good bet for late-night noodles.

Boo Bpen Seafood

$ | **SEAFOOD** | Although not on the river, this restaurant has the edge on the competition because of its spacious bench seating and garden atmosphere. House specialties include *gai khua kem* (roasted chicken with salt) and *boo nim* *tort gratium* (crab fried in garlic). **Known for:** barbecue prawns with chili, lime, and fish sauce dip; live bands; fresh seafood. $ *Average main: B150* ✉ *Sanambin Rd.* ☎ *055/211110* ▭ *No credit cards.*

Phae Phu Fa Thai

$$ | **SEAFOOD** | An extensive menu in English makes this teak pontoon eatery on the Nan the most comfortable riverside experience. The emphasis is on fresh seafood—the *pla taptim* (St. Peter's fish, a delicious freshwater variety found everywhere in Thailand), served steamed with a spice lemon-and-lime sauce, is a good choice. **Known for:** packed with locals and tourists; simple yet satisfying seafood; nice views of the river and nearby temple. $ *Average main: B210* ✉ *100/49 Phutabucha Rd.* ☎ *055/242743.*

Hotels

Grand Riverside Hotel

$$ | **HOTEL** | The name is no misnomer—this impressive hotel is very grand indeed. **Pros:** plentiful free parking; shopping mall; nearby market. **Cons:** unreliable Wi-Fi; some rooms beginning to show their age; staff has limited English skills. $ *Rooms from: B2,100* ✉ *59 Praroung Rd.* ☎ *055/248333* 🌐 *www.tgrhotel.com* *79 rooms* 🍽 *Free breakfast.*

Pattara Resort & Spa

$$ | **RESORT** | This luxury hotel is an attractive group of Sukhothai-style chalets built around a palm-fringed tropical lagoon. **Pros:** central yet peaceful location; shady pool area; traditional Thai massage. **Cons:** slow room service; small bathrooms; pesky mosquitoes. $ *Rooms from: B3,230* ✉ *349/40 Chaiyanupap Rd.* ☎ *055/282966* 🌐 *www.pattararesort.com* *64 rooms* 🍽 *Free breakfast.*

Sukhothai

56 km (35 miles) northwest of Phitsanulok, 427 km (265 miles) north of Bangkok, 1 hr by bus from Phitsanulok.

★ Sukhothai, which means "the dawn of happiness," holds a unique place in Thailand's history. Until the 13th century most of Thailand consisted of small vassal states under the thumb of the Khmer Empire based in Angkor Wat. But the Khmers had overextended their reach, allowing the princes of two Thai states to combine forces. In 1238 one of the two princes, Phor Khun Bang Klang Thao, marched on Sukhothai, defeating the Khmer garrison commander in an elephant duel. Installed as the new king of the region, he took the name Sri Indraditya and founded a dynasty that ruled Sukhothai for nearly 150 years. His youngest son became the third king of Sukhothai, Ramkhamhaeng, who ruled from 1279 to 1299. Through military and diplomatic victories, he expanded the kingdom to include most of present-day Thailand and the Malay Peninsula.

By the mid-14th century Sukhothai's power and influence had waned, and Ayutthaya, once its vassal state, became the capital of the Thai kingdom. Sukhothai was gradually abandoned to the jungle, and a new town grew up about 14 km (9 miles) away. A decade-long restoration project costing more than $10 million created 70-square-km (27-square-mile) Sukhothai Historical Park, which contains 193 historic monuments. Sukhothai is busiest during the Loi Krathong festival, which is celebrated in the Historical Park each year on the full moon in November. Its well-orchestrated, three-day light-and-sound show is the highlight. At this time the town's hotels and guesthouses are booked weeks in advance.

New Sukhothai, where all intercity buses arrive, is a quiet town where most inhabitants are in bed by 11 pm. Its many guesthouses are a magnet for tourists coming to see the ruins, and you'll see quite a few *farang* (foreigners), especially young British, German, and American couples, wandering around, drinking at the bars, or browsing the sidewalk food stalls. New Sukhothai's night market is sleepy by the region's standards—don't expect much of an urban cultural experience here. If you've come specifically to visit the Historical Park, seek accommodation at one of the guesthouses or hotels that ring the Old City, rather than making the uncomfortable B50 songthaew or samlor journey there every day from the newer part of town.

GETTING HERE AND AROUND

AIR TRAVEL

Bangkok Airways flies daily from Bangkok to Sukhothai Airport, which is north of town. The airline owns and operates the airport and is its exclusive occupant. You can also fly into Phitsanulok Airport *(see above)*. Served by Nok Air, Thai, and Asian, that airport is 72 km (45 miles) southeast of Sukhothai.

CONTACTS Sukhothai Airport ⊕ *31 km (19 miles) north of Sukhothai, off Hwy. 1195* ☎ *02/134–3960* ⊕ *www.sukhothaiairport.com/.*

BICYCLE TRAVEL

Because the sights are so spread out, the best way to explore the Historical Park is by bicycle; you can rent one for about B40 a day from outlets opposite the entrance.

BUS TRAVEL

Buses to Sukhothai depart from Bangkok's Northern Bus Terminal (Mo Chit) daily from 7 am to 11 pm, leaving roughly every 20 minutes. There are five main companies to choose from, but all charge about the same, most with prices under B300. One company, Win Tours, operates "super VIP" buses that offer comfort and service comparable to business-class air travel. The journey takes about seven hours. Buses from Sukhothai's new bus terminal on the bypass road depart at the same times and for the same prices.

CONTACTS Sukhothai Bus Station ✉ *Bypass Rd.* ⊕ *Off Hwy. 101* ☎ *055/614529.*

CAR TRAVEL

Highway 12 from Phitsanulok leads to Sukhothai and is a long, straight, and reasonably comfortable 59-km (37-mile), one-hour drive. Car rentals are available at Sukhothai Airport. The drive from Bangkok, along the four-lane Highway 117, is about 440 km (273 miles), or roughly seven hours. From Chiang Mai, take the M1 and head to the town of Tak, where Highway 12 branches east to Sukhothai.

SAMLOR AND SONGTHAEW TRAVEL

Sukhothai does not have local buses, and most of the population gets around in souped-up samlors or songthaews.

ESSENTIALS

SAFETY AND PRECAUTIONS

When touring the Historical Park, bring a bottle of water with you—the day will get hotter than you think.

TIMING

At least two days are needed to tour the magnificent Sukhothai Historical Park, and even a glancing survey of the Ramkhamhaeng National Museum's holdings requires an additional morning or afternoon. Depending on your means of transportation, touring the rest of the city could take a few hours or the better part of a day. It's best to tour Sukhothai in the late afternoon to avoid the midday sun and enjoy the late evening's pink-and-orange hues.

If you use Sukhothai as a base for exploring the ruins of Si Satchanalai and the potteries and museum of Sawankhalok, at least an additional two days are mandatory.

TOURS AND INFORMATION

In the Old City the main travel agency is run by the Vitoon guesthouse, whose owner, Kuhn Michael, is a knowledgeable guide who speaks English well. The

Sukhothai declined in power in the 15th century, but its temples and palaces were left intact.

guesthouse has fleets of bicycles and motorbikes and runs a taxi service.

TRAVEL AGENCY Vitoon Guesthouse ✉ *49 Moo 3 Jarodvithithong Rd., Old City* ☎ *055/697045.*

VISITOR INFORMATION Tourism Authority of Thailand Sukhothai Office ✉ *130 Jarodvithithong* ☎ *055/616–2289* 🌐 *www.tourismthailand.org/sukhothai.*

Sights

Ramkhamhaeng National Museum

MUSEUM | The region's most significant artifacts are in Bangkok's National Museum, but the many pieces on display at this fine facility demonstrate the gentle beauty of the Sukhothai era. One of several impressive exhibits reveals how refinements in the use of bronze enabled artisans to create the graceful walking Buddhas. ✉ *Muang Kao Sub-District, Old City* 🎫 *B150.*

Royal Palace

CASTLE/PALACE | Thais imagine Sukhothai's government as a monarchy that served the people, stressing social needs and justice. Slavery was abolished, and people were free to believe in Hinduism and Buddhism (often simultaneously), and to pursue their trades without hindrance. In the 19th century a famous stone inscription of King Ramkhamhaeng was found among the ruins of the palace across from Wat Mahathat. Now in the National Museum in Bangkok, it is sometimes referred to as Thailand's Declaration of Independence. The inscription's best-known quote reads: "This city Sukhothai is good. In the water there are fish, in the field there is rice. The ruler does not levy tax on the people who travel along the road together, leading their oxen on the way to trade and riding their horses on the way to sell. Whoever wants to trade in elephants, so trades. Whoever wants to trade in horses, so trades." ✉ *Old City* 🎫 *B150 (includes all Historical Park sites).*

Wat Chang Lom

RELIGIOUS SITE | Due east of the park is one of Sukhothai's oldest monasteries. Its bell-shape pagoda, thought to have been built in the latter part of the 14th century, is of Sri Lankan influence. The pagoda is perched on a three-tier square base atop damaged elephant buttresses. In front of the chedi are a viharn and solitary pillars; the remains of nine other chedis have been found within this complex. ✉ *Old City* ✣ *2 km (1 mile) east of park entrance, behind Legendha Sukhothai Resort (west of resort, turn north on small lane, cross bridge, and make first right)* 🎫 *B150 (includes all Historical Park sites).*

Wat Mahathat

RELIGIOUS SITE | Sitting amid a tranquil lotus pond, Wat Mahathat is the largest and most beautiful monastery in Sukhothai. Enclosed in the compound are some 200 tightly packed chedis, each containing the funeral ashes of a member of the royal family. Towering above them is a large central chedi, notable for its bulbous, lotus-bud prang. Wrapping around the chedi is a frieze of 111 monks, their hands raised in adoration. Probably built by Sukhothai's first king, Wat Mahathat owes its present form to King Lö Thai, who in 1345 erected the lotus-bud chedi to house two important relics brought back from Sri Lanka by the monk Sisatta. This Sri Lankan–style chedi became the symbol of Sukhothai and classical Sukhothai style. Copies of it were made in the principal cities of its vassal states, signifying a magic circle emanating from Sukhothai, the spiritual and temporal center of the empire. ✉ *Old City* 🎫 *B50.*

Wat Phra Phai Luang

RELIGIOUS SITE | This former Khmer structure, once a Hindu shrine, was converted to a Buddhist temple. Surrounded by a moat, the sanctuary is encircled by three laterite prangs, similar to those at Wat Sri Sawai—the only one that remains intact is decorated with stucco figures. In front of the prangs are the remains of the viharn and a crumbling chedi with a seated Buddha on its pedestal. Facing these structures is the *mondop*, a square structure with a stepped pyramid roof, built to house religious relics. ✉ *Donko Rd., Old City* ✣ *North of Old City walls, opposite Tourist Information Center* 🎫 *B150 (includes all Historical Park sites).*

Wat Saphan Hin

RELIGIOUS SITE | This pretty wat is reached by following a slate pathway and climbing a 200-meter (656-foot) hill. An amazing standing Buddha, nearly 12 meters (40 feet) tall, gazes down on the mere mortals who complete the climb. ✉ *Old City* ✣ *West of Old City walls* 🎫 *Free.*

Wat Sra Sri

RELIGIOUS SITE | This peaceful temple sits on two connected islands within a lotus-filled lake that supplied the monks with water and served as a boundary for the sacred area. A Sri Lankan–style chedi dominates six smaller chedis, and a large stucco seated Buddha looks down a row of columns, past the chedis, and over the lake to the horizon.

Especially wondrous is the walking Buddha beside the Sri Lankan–style chedi. The walking Buddha is a Sukhothai innovation, and the most ethereal of Thailand's artistic styles. The depiction of the Buddha is often a reflection of political authority, and is modeled after the ruler. Under the Khmers, authority was hierarchical, but the kings of Sukhothai represented the ideals of serenity, happiness, and justice. The walking Buddha is the epitome of Sukhothai's art; he appears to be floating in air, neither rooted on Earth nor placed on a pedestal above the reach of the common people. ✉ *Old City* 🎫 *B150 (includes all Historical Park sites).*

Wat Sri Chum

RELIGIOUS SITE | Like many other sanctuaries, Wat Si Chum was originally

Continued on page 396

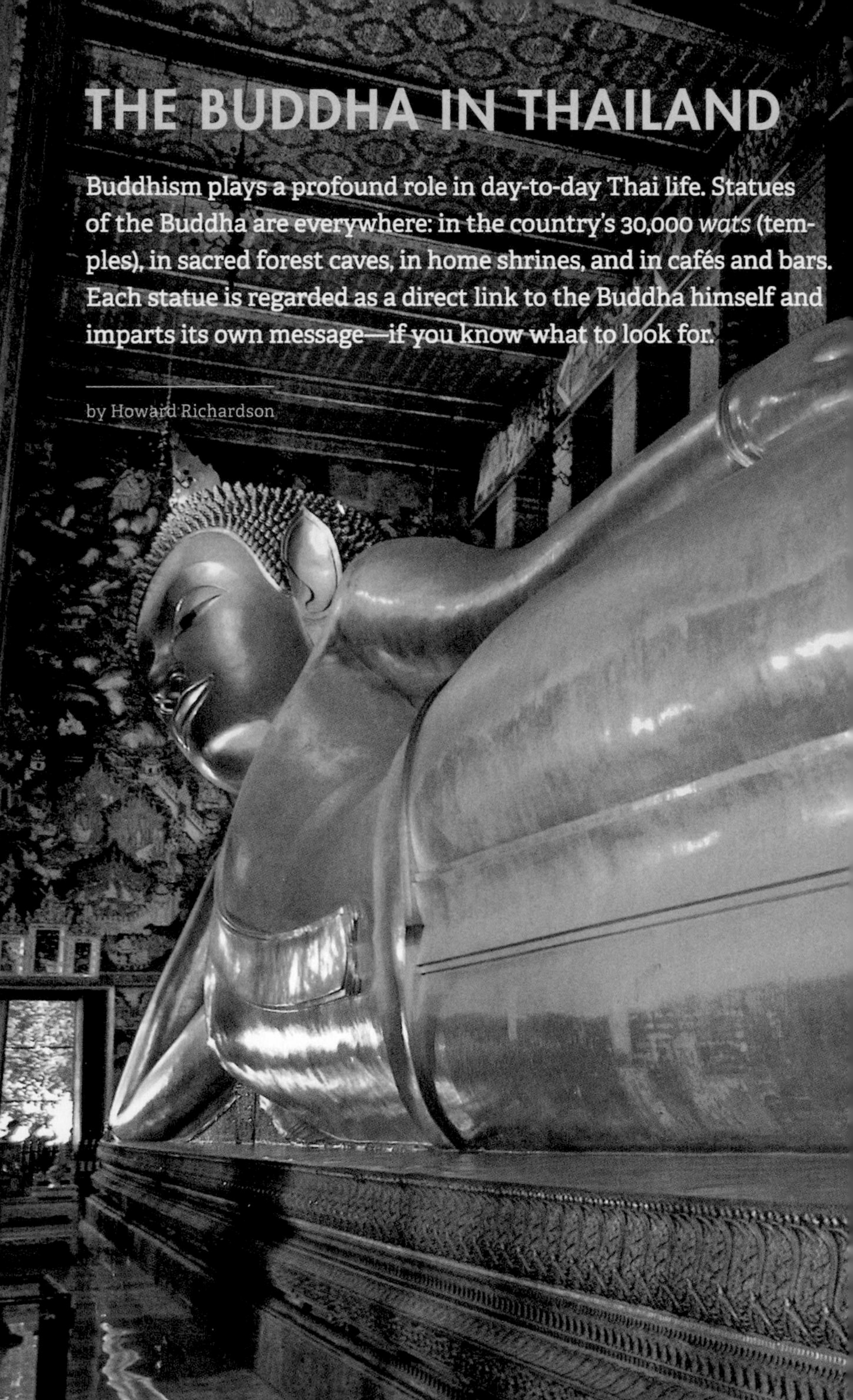

THE BUDDHA IN THAILAND

Buddhism plays a profound role in day-to-day Thai life. Statues of the Buddha are everywhere: in the country's 30,000 *wats* (temples), in sacred forest caves, in home shrines, and in cafés and bars. Each statue is regarded as a direct link to the Buddha himself and imparts its own message—if you know what to look for.

by Howard Richardson

The origins of Buddhism lie in the life of the Indian prince Siddhartha Gautama (563 bc– 483 bc), who became the Buddha (which simply means "awakened"). Statues of the Buddha follow ancient aesthetic rules. The Buddha must be wearing a monastic robe, either covering both shoulders or leaving the right shoulder bare. His body must display sacred marks, or laksanas, such as slender toes and fingers, a full, lion-like chest, and long eyelashes. Many statues also have elongated earlobes, a reminder of the Buddha's original life as a prince, when he wore heavy earrings. Buddha statues are in one of four positions: sitting, standing, walking, or reclining.

Statues of the Buddha have their hands arranged in a mudra or hand position. The mudras, which represent the Buddha's teachings or incidents in his life, were created by his disciples, who used them to enhance their meditation. There are about 100 mudras, but most are variations on six basic forms.

Reclining Buddha, Wat Po, Bangkok.

Detail of Reclining Buddha's head.

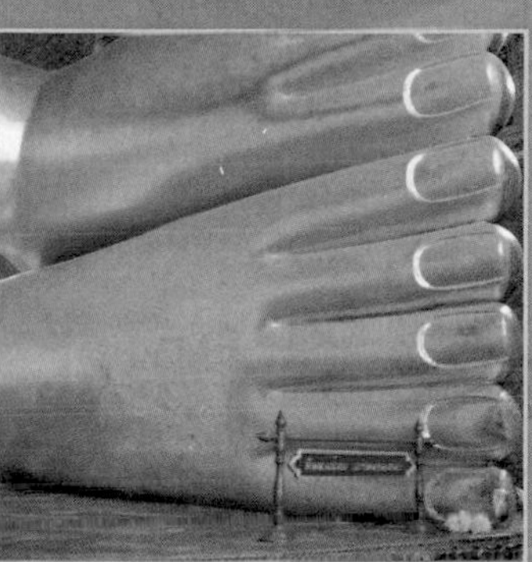

Detail of top of Reclining Buddha's feet.

Detail of bottom of Reclining Buddha's foot.

WHAT THE BUDDHA TAUGHT

Gautama taught that there are three aspects to existence: *dukkha* (suffering), *anicca* (impermanence), and *anatta* (the absence of self). He believed that unfulfilled desire for status, self-worth, and material possessions creates dukkha, but that such desire is pointless because anicca dictates that everything is impermanent and cannot be possessed. Therefore, if we can learn to curb desire and cultivate detachment, we will cease to be unhappy.

The ultimate goal of Buddhism is to reach enlightenment or nirvana, which is basically the cessation of struggle—this happens when you have successfully let go of all desire (and by definition, all suffering). This signals the end to *samsara,* the cycle of reincarnation that Buddhists believe in. Buddhists also believe in karma, a law of cause and effect that suggests that your fate in this life and future lives is determined by your actions. Among the ways to improve your karma—and move toward nirvana—are devoting yourself to spirituality by becoming a monk or a nun, meditating, and *tham boon,* or merit making. Making offerings to the Buddha is one form of tham boon.

Thai painting of monks listening to the Buddha speak at a temple.

THE MIDDLE WAY

Gautama's prescription for ending dukkha is an attitude of moderation towards the material world based on wisdom, morality, and concentration. He broke this threefold approach down further into eight principles, called the Noble Eightfold Path or the Middle Way.

Wisdom:

Right Understanding: to understand dukkha and its causes.

Right Thought: to resist angry or unkind thoughts and acts.

Morality:

Right Speech: to avoid lying, speaking unkindly, or engaging in idle chatter.

Right Action: to refrain from harming or killing others, stealing, and engaging in sexual misconduct.

Right Livelihood: to earn a living peacefully and honestly.

Concentration:

Right Effort: to work towards discipline and kindness, abandoning old, counterproductive habits.

Right Mindfulness: to be aware of your thoughts, words, and actions; to see things as they really are.

Right Concentration: to focus on wholesome thoughts and actions (often while meditating.)

Did You Know?

Burmese invaders damaged many Buddha statues when they sacked Ayutthaya in 1767. The head of one statue became lodged in the roots of a tree at Wat Phra Mahathat, where it remains today.

THE BUDDHA'S POSITIONS

Standing Buddha in saffron robes, Bangkok.

STANDING

The Buddha stands either with his feet together or with one slightly in front of the other. The standing posture is often accompanied by certain hand positions to signify driving away fear or appealing to reason.

⇨ Wat Phra Mahathat, Sukhothai; Wat Benjamabophit, Bangkok.

RECLINING

Many scholars believe that reclining sculptures depict the Buddha dying and simultaneously reaching nirvana. According to another story, the Buddha is showing a proud giant who has refused to bow to him that he can lie down and still make himself appear larger than the giant. The Buddha then took the giant to the heavens and showed him angels that made the Buddha himself appear small, teaching the giant that there are truths beyond the realm of our own experience.

⇨ Wat Po, Bangkok.

Reclining Buddha ornament.

SITTING

Seated Buddhas are the most common. The Buddha can sit in three different postures: adamantine or lotus, with legs crossed and feet resting on opposite thighs; heroic, a half-lotus position with one leg folded over the other; or western, with legs hanging straight down, as if sitting in a chair.

⇨ Wat Suthat, Bangkok (heroic style).

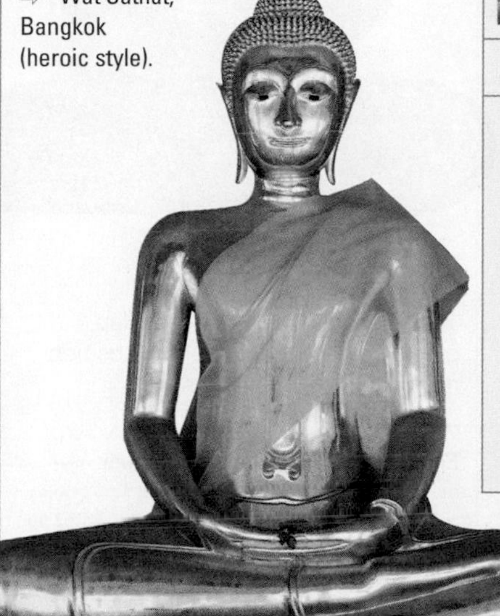

Seated Buddha, Wat Suthat, Bangkok.

THE LAUGHING BUDDHA

The Laughing Buddha, whose large belly and jolly demeanor make him easy to recognize, is a folkloric character based on a 9th century Chinese monk known for his kindness. The Laughing Buddha does not figure into Thai Buddhism but you may see him at temples in Bangkok's Chinatown. And because he represents good fortune and abundance, some Thai shops sell Laughing Buddhas as lucky charms. Laughing Buddha statues often carry sacks full of sweets to give to children.

WALKING

Walking statues represent the Buddha going into the community to spread his teachings. Traditionally, walking Buddhas were constructed in relief. The first walking-Buddha statues were created in Sukhothai, and you can still see a few in the city's ruins.

⇨ Wat Sra Sri, Sukhothai and Wat Phra Phai Luang, Sukhothai.

Walking Buddhas, Wat Phra Mahathat, Sukhothai.

WHAT DO THE BUDDHA'S HANDS MEAN?

SETTING THE WHEEL IN MOTION

In this mudra, the Buddha's thumbs and forefingers join to make a circle, representing the Wheel of Dharma, a symbol for Buddhist law.

⇨ Cloisters of Wat Benjamabophit, Bangkok; Phra Pathom Chedi, Nakhon Pathom.

MEDITATION

The Buddha's hands are in his lap, palms pointing upwards. This position represents a disciplined mind.

⇨ National Museum, Bangkok; Phra Pathom Chedi, Nakhon Pathom.

REASONING

This posture, which signifies the Buddha's preference for reason and peace rather than hasty or thoughtless action, is similar to the absence of fear mudra, but the Buddha's thumb and forefinger are touching to form a circle.

⇨ Cloisters of Wat Benjamabophit, Bangkok; Sukhothai Historical Park.

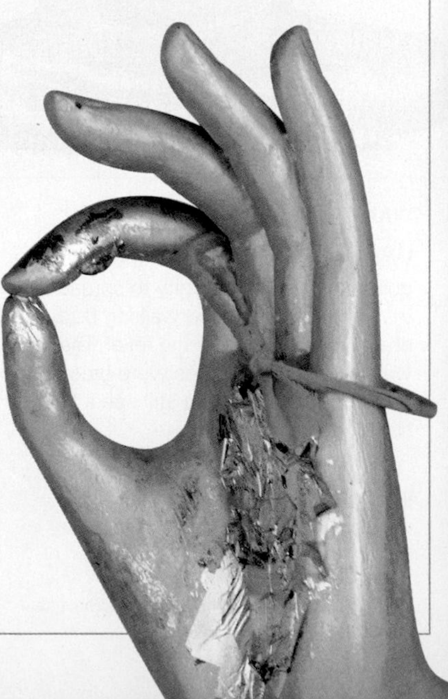

SUBDUING MARA

Mara is a demon who tempted the Buddha with visions of beautiful women. In this posture, the Buddha is renouncing these worldly desires. He sits with his right hand is on his right thigh, fingers pointing down, and his left hand palm-up in his lap.

⇨ **Wat Suthat, Bangkok; Wat Mahathat, Sukhothai; Phra Pathom Chedi, Nakhon Pathom.**

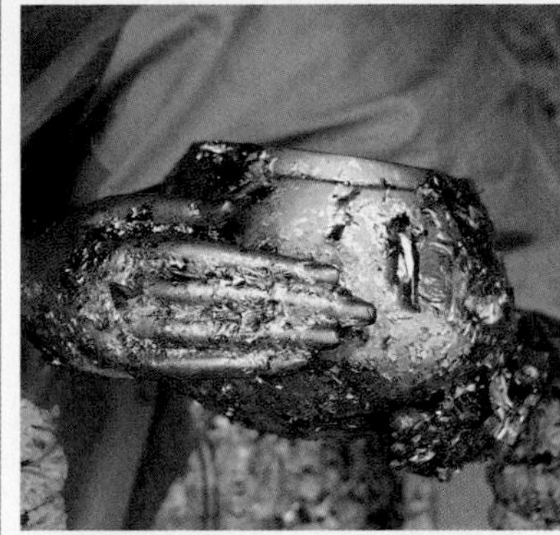

Hand and alms bowl detail; Nakhon Pathom Chedi, Nakon Pathom.

CHARITY

Buddhas using this mudra are usually standing, with their right arm pointing down, palm facing out, to give or receive offerings. In some modern variations, the Buddha is actually holding an alms bowl.

⇨ **National Museum, Bangkok.**

ABSENCE OF FEAR

One or both of the Buddha's arms are bent at the elbow, palms facing out and fingers pointing up (like the international gesture for "Stop!") In this attitude the Buddha is either displaying his own fearlessness or encouraging his followers to be courageous.

⇨ **Cloisters of Wat Benjamabophit, Bangkok.**

surrounded by a moat. The main structure is dominated by a statue of the Buddha in a seated position. The huge but elegant stucco image is one of the largest in Thailand, measuring 11¼ meters (37 feet) from knee to knee. Enter the mondop, a ceremonial structure, through the passage inside the left inner wall. Keep your eyes on the ceiling: more than 50 engraved slabs illustrate scenes from the *Jataka,* which are stories about the previous lives of Lord Buddha. ⊠ *Old City* ✣ *Northwest of Old City walls* 🎫 *B100.*

Wat Sri Sawai

RELIGIOUS SITE | Sukhothai's oldest structure may be this Khmer-style one with three prangs—similar to those found in Lopburi—surrounded by a laterite wall. The many stucco Hindu images and scenes suggest that Sri Sawai was probably first a Hindu temple, later converted to a Buddhist monastery. ⊠ *Old City* 🎫 *B150 (includes all Historical Park sites).*

Wat Traphang Thong Lang

RELIGIOUS SITE | The square mondop of Wat Traphang Thong Lang is the main sanctuary, the outer walls of which contain beautiful stucco figures in niches—some of Sukhothai's finest art. The north side depicts the Buddha returning to preach to his wife. On the west side he preaches to his father and relatives. Note the figures on the south wall, where the story of the Buddha is accompanied by an angel descending from heaven. ⊠ *Sukhothai* ✣ *East of park entrance opposite Ramkhamhaeng museum.*

The Traces of a Nation

The optimism that accompanied the birth of the nation at Sukhothai is reflected in the art and architecture of the period. Strongly influenced by Sri Lankan Buddhism, the monuments left behind by the architects, artisans, and craftsmen of those innovative times had a light, often playful touch. Statues of the Buddha show him as smiling, serene, and confidently walking toward a better future. The iconic image of the walking Buddha originated in Sukhothai. Note also the impossibly graceful elephants portrayed in supporting pillars.

Restaurants

Some of the best food in town can be found at the local food stalls that line the main street before and after the bridge. If you're in the mood for something sweet, look for the stand selling delicious Thai crepes filled with condensed milk, right at the bridge on the city-center side. But it's hard to go wrong almost anywhere in or near the night market or along that street.

Dream Café

$ | **THAI** | While waiting for your meal at this old favorite, feast your eyes on the extraordinary antiques that have filled its weathered space for decades. Everything—the rustic tile floor, the glowing teak tables and chairs, the fine ceramics—comes together in perfect harmony, although its take on Thai food plays it safe, so be sure to ask for things spicy if that's your preference. **Known for:** rustic but romantic guest rooms at the adjacent Cocoon House; stellar ginger salad; crowd-pleasing flavor profiles. [$] *Average main: B150* ⊠ *86/1 Singhawat Rd.* ☎ *094/626–1065.*

Mai Krang Krung

$ | **THAI** | It'd be a shame to leave Sukhothai without actually trying the noodle soup that shares its name, so give its porky, spicy, and chewy flavor profile a shot at this family-run lunch spot. A boutique inside also sells jewelry and silk items, should you still need a souvenir

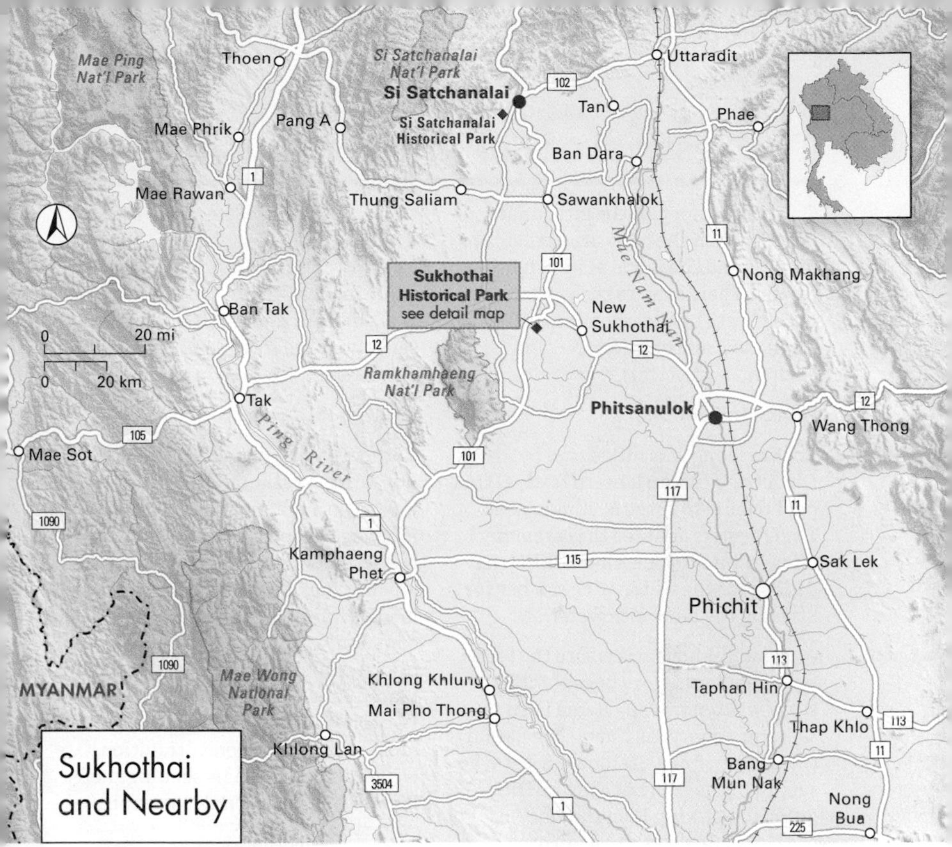

Sukhothai and Nearby

or two. **Known for:** butterfly pea dumplings (chor muang) for dessert; delightful herbal drinks; pad Thai that's nothing like what you've had back home. $ *Average main: B60* ✉ *39 Chodvithithong Rd.* ☎ *055/621882* ▭ *No credit cards.*

Hotels

Ananda Museum Gallery Hotel

$$ | HOTEL | The Ananda has redefined the concept of luxury lodging in Sukhothai; as you might expect from a hotel that is also an art gallery, the rooms are well composed, their design informed by a deep sense of minimalism along with a healthy dose of feng shui. **Pros:** aesthetic surroundings; fine furnishings; elegant Celadon restaurant a destination itself. **Cons:** on a busy highway; taxi fare to town is expensive; some guests may find museumlike stillness unsettling at night. $ *Rooms from: B2,600* ✉ *10 Moo 4, Jarodvithithong Rd., Banlum Muang* ☎ *055/622428* 🌐 *www.ananda-hotel.com* *34 rooms* 🍽 *Free breakfast.*

Boon Lott's Elephant Sanctuary

$$$ | RESORT | FAMILY | Imagine waking near rice fields to an elephant call at sunrise, or hiking beside an entire elephant family as they traverse acres of lush forestland. **Pros:** excellent cause; immersive experience in local culture; 90% of guests are repeat visitors. **Cons:** must book at least six months in advance; not for carnivores, as vegetarian-only meals are served; doesn't accept credit cards despite its high cost. $ *Rooms from: B6,000* ✉ *304 Moo 5, Baan Na Ton Jan, Tambon Baan Tuek* ✣ *5 miles from Sukhothai Airport; Boon Lott's arranges airport transfers, included in cost* 🌐 *www.*

The Festival of Loi Krathong

On the full moon of the 12th lunar month, when the tides are at their highest and the moon at its brightest, the Thais head to the waterways to celebrate Loi Krathong, one of Thailand's most anticipated and enchanting festivals.

Indian Influences

Loi Krathong was influenced by Diwali, the Indian lantern festival that paid tribute to three Brahman gods. Thai farmers adapted the ceremony to offer tribute to Mae Khlong Kha, the goddess of the water, to thank her for blessing the land with water.

Ancient Sukhothai is where the festival's popular history began, with a story written by King Rama IV in 1863. The story concerns Naang Noppamart, the daughter of a Brahman priest who served in the court of King Li-Thai, grandson of King Ramkhamhaeng the Great. She was a woman of exceptional charm and beauty who soon became his queen. She secretly fashioned a *krathong* (a small float used as an offering), setting it alight by candle in accordance with her Brahmanist rites. The king, upon seeing this curious, glimmering offering, embraced its beauty, adapting it for Theravada Buddhism and thus creating the festival of Loi Krathong.

Krathong were traditionally formed by simply cupping banana leaves. Offerings such as dried rice and betel nut were placed at the center along with three incense sticks representing the Brahman gods. Today krathong are more commonly constructed by pinning folded banana leaves to a buoyant base made of a banana tree stem; they're decorated with scented flowers, orange candles (said to represent the Buddhist monkhood), and three incense sticks, whose meaning was changed under Li-Thai to represent the three forms of Buddhist existence.

Modern Meanings

Contemporary young Thai couples "loi" their "krathong" to bind their love in an act almost like that of a marriage proposal, while others use the ceremony more as a way to purge any bad luck or resentments they may be harboring. Loi Krathong also commonly represents the pursuit of material gain, with silent wishes placed for a winning lottery number or two. The festival remains Thailand's most romantic vision of tradition, with millions of Thais sending their hopes floating down the nearest waterway.

Although it's celebrated nationwide, with events centered around cities such as Bangkok, Ayutthaya, Chiang Mai, and Tak, the festival's birthplace of Sukhothai remains the focal point. The Historical Park serves as a kind of Hollywood back lot, with hundreds of costumed students and light, sound, and pyrotechnic engineers preparing for the fanfare of the annual show, which generally happens twice during the evening. With the Historical Park lighted and Wat Mahathat as its stage, the show reenacts the story of Sukhothai and the legend of Loi Krathong. Following this, governors, dignitaries, and other celebrity visitors take part in a spectacular finale that includes sending off the krathong representing the king and queen, and fireworks.

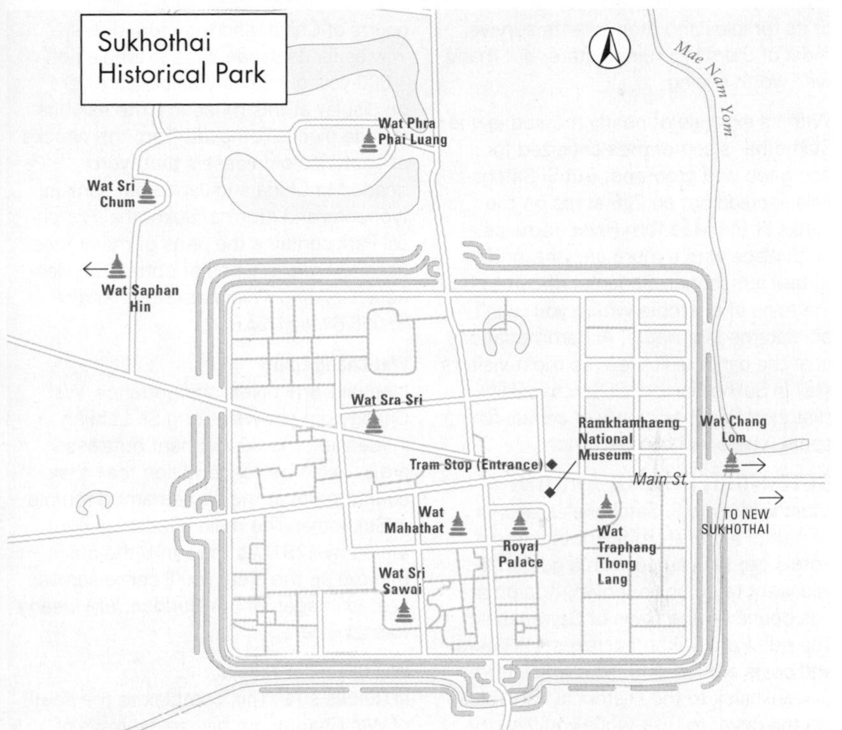

blesele.org *3 cottages* *All-inclusive* *No credit cards.*

★ Legendha

$$ | HOTEL | This attractive resort blends so well with the outskirts of Sukhothai's Historical Park that it could easily pass for a creation of King Ramkhamhaeng himself. **Pros:** welcome fruit basket; friendly, helpful staff; chlorine-free pool. **Cons:** inconvenient location between Historical Park entrance and the new city center; expensive hotel transportation; some rooms need refurbishing. *Rooms from: B3,900* *214 Moo 3, Tambon Muangkao, Old City* *055/697249* *www.legendhasukhothai.com* *62 rooms* *Free breakfast.*

★ Sukhothai Heritage Resort

$$ | RESORT | FAMILY | *Swank* is the word for this luxury resort at just about the midpoint between the historical parks in Sukhothai and Si Satchanalai. **Pros:** gracious service; elegant design; countryside setting. **Cons:** location near Sukhothai Airport may be too remote for some guests; not convenient to historical parks; mosquitoes could be controlled better. *Rooms from: B2,900* *900 Moo 2, Tambon Klongkrajong, Sawankhalok* *055/647567* *www.sukhothaiheritage.com* *68 rooms* *Free breakfast.*

Si Satchanalai

80 km (50 miles) north of Sukhothai.

Si Satchanalai, a sister city to Sukhothai, was governed by a son of Sukhothai's reigning monarch. Despite its secondary position, the city grew to impressive proportions, and the remains of about 200 of its temples and monuments survive, most of them in a ruined state, but many well worth seeing.

With its expanse of neatly mowed lawns, Sukhothai is sometimes criticized for being too well groomed. But Si Satchanalai, spread out on 228 acres on the banks of the Mae Yom River, remains a quiet place with a more ancient, undisturbed atmosphere. It isn't difficult to find the ruins of a temple where you won't be disturbed for hours. Accommodations near the park are limited, so most visitors stay in Sukhothai, but Si Satchanalai Historical Park has plenty of casual dining spots where you can get lunch.

GETTING HERE AND AROUND

Most visitors to Si Satchanalai reach it as part of a tour from Sukhothai (most hotels can set you up with a guide). If you want to go on your own, hop on a bus bound for the town of Sawankhalok. The ride from Sukhothai takes 1½ hours and costs around B40. Take a taxi from Sawankhalok to the Historical Park, asking the driver to wait while you visit the various temples. You can also tour the site by bicycle or on top of an elephant. The Vitoon Guesthouse in Sukhothai also offers day trips to Si Satchanalai and Sawankhalok; it's opposite the entrance to the Sukhothai Historical Park.

TIMING

Si Satchanalai Historical Park is a day's outing from Sukhothai.

TOUR INFORMATION Vitoon Guesthouse
✉ *49 Moo 3 Jarodvittiong Rd., Old City* ☎ *055/697045.*

Sawanworanayok National Museum
MUSEUM | Sukhothai grew wealthy on the fine ceramics it produced from the rich earth around the neighboring town of Sawankhalok. The ceramics were so prized that they were offered as gifts from Sukhothai rulers to the imperial courts of China, and they found their way as far as Japan. Fine examples of 1,000-year-old Sawankhalok wares are on display at this museum. The exhibits include pieces retrieved from the wrecks of centuries-old vessels that were headed to China and Japan but sank in typhoons and storms. Sukhothai Historical Park contains the ruins of many kilns used to fire the types of pottery on view here. ✉ *Wang Phinphat, Sawankhalok* ☎ *055/641571* *B50.*

Wat Chang Lom
RELIGIOUS SITE | Near the entrance, Wat Chang Lom shows strong Sri Lankan influences. The 39 elephant buttresses are in much better condition than their counterparts at the same-named temple in Sukhothai. The main chedi was completed by 1291. As you climb the stairs that run up the side, you'll come across seated images of the Buddha. ✉ *Mueang Kao* *Free.*

Wat Chedi Jet Thaew
RELIGIOUS SITE | This complex to the south of Wat Chang Lom has seven rows of ruined chedis, some with lotus-bud tops that are reminiscent of the larger ones at Sukhothai. The chedis contain the ashes of members of Si Satchanalai's ruling family. ✉ *Si Satchanalai* *B150 (includes admission to entire Historical Park).*

Wat Nang Phya
RELIGIOUS SITE | To the southeast of Wat Chedi Jet Thaew, this temple has well-preserved floral reliefs on its balustrade and stucco reliefs on the viharn wall. ✉ *Si Satchanalai* *B150 (includes admission to entire Historical Park).*

Wat Suan Kaeo Uthayan Yai
RELIGIOUS SITE | As you leave the park, stop at this wat to see a Si Satchanalai image of Lord Buddha, one of the few still remaining. ✉ *Si Satchanalai* *B150 (includes admission to entire Historical Park).*

Chapter 9

CAMBODIA

Updated by
Marco Ferrarese

Sights ★★★★★ | Restaurants ★★★★☆ | Hotels ★★★★☆ | Shopping ★★★☆☆ | Nightlife ★★☆☆☆

WELCOME TO CAMBODIA

TOP REASONS TO GO

★ **Angkor Temple Complex:** Hands-down Southeast Asia's most magnificent archaeological treasure, Angkor has hundreds of ruins, many still hidden deep in the jungle.

★ **Education and enlightenment:** You'll learn a heap about history, warfare and human tragedy, science, and archaeology.

★ **Off-the-beaten-path beaches:** Along the Gulf of Thailand lie a few of Southeast Asia's most unspoiled beaches and (generally) unpolluted waters. You'll eat some delicious seafood here.

★ **Philanthropy:** Work with street kids, give blood, buy a cookie to support the arts—if you're looking to do good while you travel, you'll find plenty of exciting and meaningful opportunities here—however, make sure that an organization is reputable, as scams abound.

★ **Southeast Asia's rising star:** Gradually earning worldwide attention, Siem Reap is developing into one of the hippest cities in Southeast Asia.

1 **Phnom Penh.** The lively capital city.

2 **Tonle Bati.** Small lake with a beach and temples.

3 **Phnom Chisor.** Stunning countryside views.

4 **Koh Dach.** Beach-day destination and home to Silk weavers.

5 **Udong.** Important pilgrimage destination for Cambodians.

6 **Kampong Cham.** Temple ruins and temple-topped hills.

7 **Kompong Thom Ruins.** Pre-Angkorian ruins.

8 **Kratie.** Freshwater Irrawaddy dolphins.

9 **Ratanakkiri Province.** A remote destination with a mystical lake.

10 **Battambang.** A city known for its temple ruins.

11 **Siem Reap.** The gateway to Angkor.

12 **Tonle Sap.** The biggest freshwater lake in Southeast Asia.

13 **Kulen Mountain.** A sacred place for modern Cambodians.

14 **Sihanoukville.** A base to explore islands.

15 **Kampot.** Lively riverside town.

16 **Kep.** Beautiful seaside getaway.

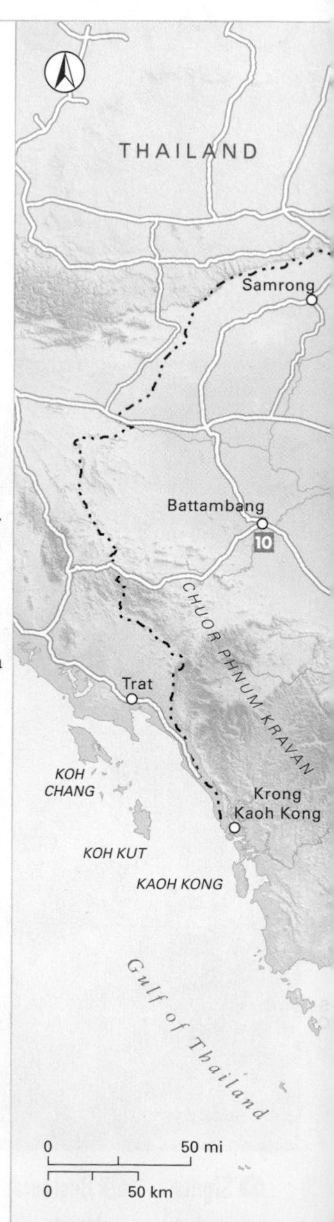

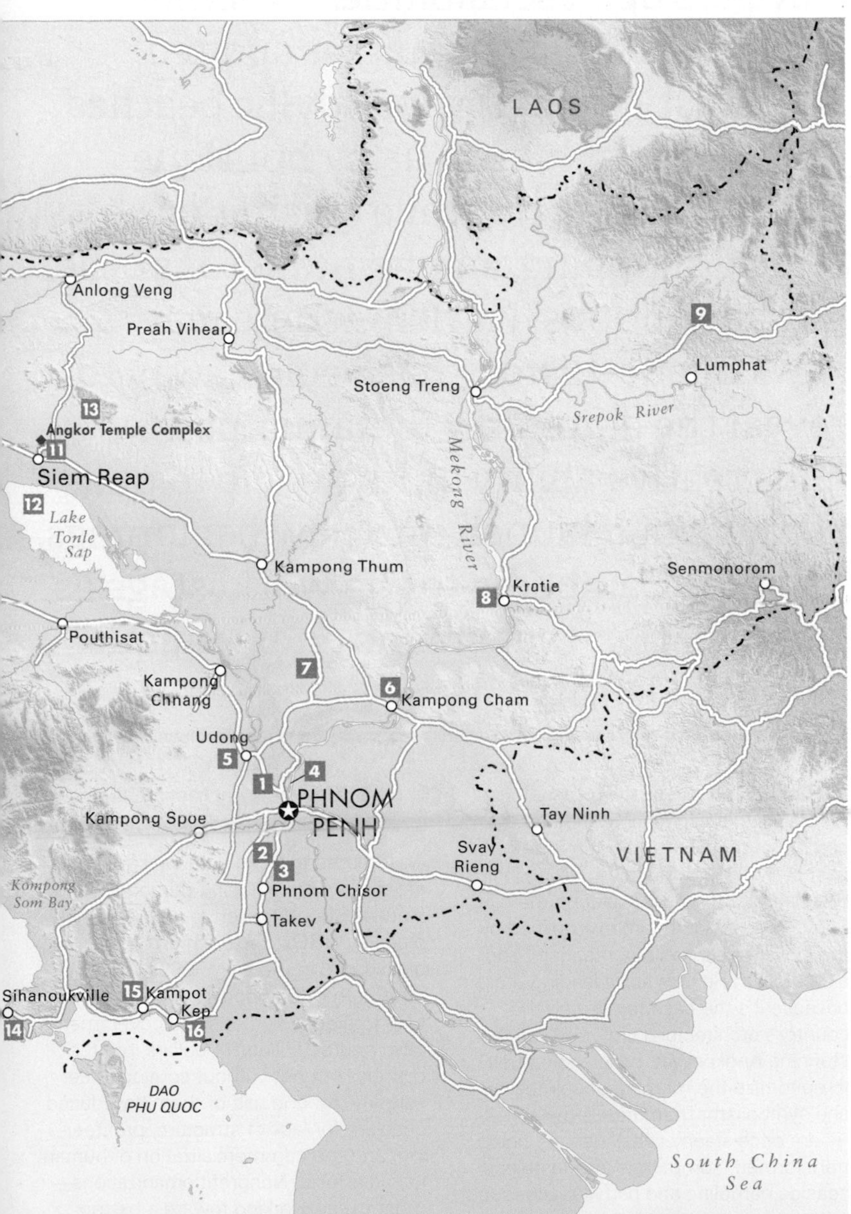
LAOS
Anlong Veng
Preah Vihear
Stoeng Treng
Lumphat
9
Srepok River
13
Angkor Temple Complex
11
Siem Reap
12
Lake Tonle Sap
Mekong River
Kampong Thum
Senmonorom
8
Kratie
Pouthisat
7
Kampong Chnang
6
Kampong Cham
Udong
5
1
4
PHNOM PENH
Kampong Spoe
Tay Ninh
2
Svay Rieng
VIETNAM
3
Kompong Som Bay
Phnom Chisor
Takev
Sihanoukville
15
Kampot
Kep
14
16
DAO PHU QUOC
South China Sea

It's not by chance that Cambodia has become highly popular among eclectic travelers of all sensibilities, whether they're seeking lush jungles spotted with dusty temple ruins, idyllic beaches with an air of luxury, artsy boutique hotels, exciting nouvelle cuisine, or ethical shopping, among numerous other vibrant options. Its rich—some may say loaded—history has peeled away to reveal the admirably dynamic, positive, and creative ability of its people to pull through and launch into new beginnings, bringing Cambodia to the world stage as a destination that stands on its unique cultural identity.

Phnom Penh is the bustling capital, where visitors can dip into the darkest corners of the country's traumatized past by walking through the Killing Fields one day, and the next exploring the hip, edgy, new design boom exemplified by the city's hotels, restaurants, bars, and shops. Siem Reap is still a leading draw because it's the base for visiting the country's architectural crown jewel, the stunning Angkor Wat, which continues to epitomize the merging of spirituality and symbolism. Then there's the south, where once-sleepy coastlines are being transformed, sometimes into tasteless seaside gambling and partying zones, but in other cases into enchanting havens of stylish beach chic.

An interesting trend with which tourists are met when exploring Cambodia is the staunch support given to local communities by NGOs, the creation of which blossomed in the early 1990s. In the aftermath of Cambodia's grueling civil war, foreign aid groups and governments have poured billions of dollars into the country, but not without coming under scrutiny. Around half of them have faced criticism for lack of structure, profiteering, and the commercialization of humanitarian efforts. Nonprofit organizations—in most cases working toward a better

Cambodia—address a wide range of humanitarian, cultural, and environmental issues. Today there are about 3,500 registered NGOs in Cambodia, which has the second-highest number of NGOs per capita in the world, after Rwanda. Many nonprofits now run accommodations, restaurants, and travel agencies that provide the visitor with more than they expect to receive on vacation—the chance to help and an education. But it's worth checking out the legitimacy of an organization before parting with your money.

MAJOR REGIONS

Phnom Penh and Nearby. In the capital, **Phnom Penh**, you'll find a great deal to see and do: a palace and war monuments, great food and fine wine, and ample opportunities for people-watching along the breezy riverfront. Roads heading out of the capital lead to day-trip destinations like the beaches of **Tonle Bati**, a small lake with a couple of temples nearby, the lovely temple at **Phnom Chisor** to the south, and the pagoda-topped hill of **Udong** and the Mekong island of **Koh Dach** in the north.

North of Phnom Penh. As you travel north, you'll see some of Asia's last remaining, but ever-decreasing jungles, where wildlife populations are actually increasing. For pre-Angkorian ruins, visit the ancient temple ruins at **Kampong Cham** and the **Kompong Thom ruins**, halfway between Phnom Penh and Siem Reap, which date to the 7th-century capital of Zhen La. Get a glimpse of the rare freshwater Irrawaddy dolphin at **Kratie**. There are still seven ethnic hill tribes, and some of the country's last remaining elephants, in the far north in **Ratanakkiri Province.** The city of **Battambang** (Cambodia's second largest) is a thriving center for the arts with exquisite colonial buildings, and is only three hours away from Siem Reap on a new road. Note that even if many of these destinations are quite removed from one another, it's now possible to visit most of them by simply hopping on and off buses between Phnom Penh, Siem Reap, and the Laos border.

Siem Reap and Angkor Temple Complex. Siem Reap, which means "Siam defeated," based on a 15th-century battle with Cambodia's neighbors to the west, has emerged as a modern, friendly, and elegantly low-key city with highly sophisticated shopping, dining, and nightlife options. It's a rapidly growing city, and the gateway to the **Angkor Temple Complex**, the largest religious structure ever built, and just one temple in a complex of hundreds. **Around Siem Reap**, **Tonle Sap** is the biggest freshwater lake in Southeast Asia while Kulen Mountain, considered a holy mountain during the Angkor Dynasty, has the ruins of ancient temples.

Southern Cambodia. The once-sleepy coast has perked up. Whether you stay at a high-end resort, in a hillside bungalow, or in an island hut, it remains a treat to enjoy the laid back-beach-ambience setting. **Sihanoukville** lies some 230 km (143 miles) southwest of Phnom Penh, a four-hour bus ride from the capital, and has suffered the dire consequences of Chinese-backed investments, becoming a grimy casino-strewn construction site, Don't linger: use it as a base to take boats to the offshore islands, which still remain relatively unexploited. **Kampot,** east of Sihanoukville, has now become the place to linger and with its caves, views, and pepper plantation, is worth a couple of days. **Kep** and the islands of the Koh Rong archipelago have reemerged as stylish getaways and you can find some of the world's best pepper plantations.

Planning

WHEN TO GO

Cambodia has two seasons, both affected by the monsoon winds. The northeastern monsoon blowing toward the coast ushers in the cool, dry season in November, which lasts through February, with temperatures between 65°F (18°C) and 80°F (27°C). December and January are the coolest months. It heats up to around 95°F (35°C) and higher in March and April, when the southwestern monsoon blows inland from the Gulf of Thailand, bringing downpours that last an hour or more most days. This rainy, humid season runs through October, with temperatures ranging from 80°F (27°C) to 95°F (35°C). The climate in Phnom Penh is always very humid. Thanks to climate change, Cambodia now experiences rainstorms in the dry season, cool temperatures in the hot season, and a lot of unpredictability. Bring your umbrella, although higher-end resorts usually offer one along with your bathrobe and slippers.

It's important to book in advance if you plan on visiting during mid-April's New Year celebrations, or for the Water Festival in Phnom Penh in November. Strangely, the New Year is one of the best times to see the capital—at least in terms of lower rates and crowds—because the majority of Phnom Penh residents come from somewhere else and they all go home for the holidays.

PLAN YOUR TIME

HASSLE FACTOR

High. There are no direct flights from the United States to Cambodia, but flights to nearby Asian hubs are frequent.

3 DAYS

Fly into Siem Reap. Explore the many temples of Angkor. By night visit Siem Reap's night markets and downtown.

1 WEEK

You have time to explore the temples of Angkor in more depth (there are some 300, but only the largest have been excavated). Then head to Phnom Penh and take a river cruise down the Mekong. If time permits, hit the beaches of Kep or spend a day in splendid Kampot.

2 WEEKS

Explore Angkor and Siem Reap in depth, followed by a trip to Battambang, Cambodia's second-largest city and a thriving hub of arts and culture. Then head to Phnom Penh, and a day trip up the Mekong to Koh Dach. Relax at the beaches of Koh Rong, and then check out Kep and Kampot.

GETTING HERE AND AROUND

AIR TRAVEL

After many years of "semi–aviation isolation" Phnom Penh is opening up to the rest of the world, with Qatar Airways being one of the first international carriers to fly here, although still not directly.

There are half a dozen flights from Vietnam's Ho Chi Minh City each day to Phnom Penh (prices start at $69 one way) and the travel time is about 45 minutes. Carriers who fly direct include Vietnam Airlines, Qatar Airways, and Cambodia Angkor Air. You can also fly to Siem Reap from Ho Chi Minh City with Cambodia Angkor Air. The flight takes about an hour 15 minutes and costs from $79 one way. There are about a dozen flights a day from Hanoi to Siem Reap; these take one hour 40 minutes, and fares start at $80 one way on VietJet Air.

Regular air service links Phnom Penh and Siem Reap to Bangkok and Vientiane. Domestic flights run between Phnom Penh and Siem Reap. Air Asia, Bangkok Airways, Lao Airlines, Royal Khmer Airlines, Siem Reap Airways, and Thai Airways have flights to Cambodia *(see Air Travel in Travel Smart Thailand)*.

CONTACTS Cambodia Angkor Air ✉ *17D Omkhun St., Siem Reap* ☎ *063/969–2681, 063/636–3666* 🌐 *www.cambodiaangkorair.com.* **Qatar Airways** ☎ *023/963800* 🌐 *www.qatarairways.com.* **Vietnam Airlines** ✉ *50 Samdech Pan Ave. (214), Phnom Penh* ☎ *023/990840, 023/215998 reservation and ticketing* 🌐 *www.vietnamairlines.com.*

BOAT TRAVEL

Boats do travel from Ho Chi Minh City to Phnom Penh, but they take three days and are a sightseeing option rather than quick A-to-B travel. From Phnom Penh, ferries called "bullet boats" travel along the Tonle Sap to reach Siem Reap and Angkor; they no longer ply waters between Sihanoukville and Koh Kong, however, so the only way to go is by road. You can buy tickets from a tour operator, your hotel's concierge, or at the port in Phnom Penh. **■TIP→ Bullet boats, though fast, can be dangerous.** Smaller (but noisy) ferries travel daily between Siem Reap's port and Battambang, on the Sangker River. Ask about water levels before booking a ticket; in dry season the water can get so low the boat may get stuck for hours at a time. For those who like to sit atop in the fresh air, take lots of suntan lotion.

BUS TRAVEL

Cambodia has a comprehensive bus network, and bus travel is cheap and generally of a good standard. It's also usually the safest cross-country transportation, aside from flying. Travel from neighboring countries is easy, reliable, and cheap. Buses from Thailand and Vietnam operate daily.

BUS CONTACTS Giant Ibis ✉ *7E0, Rd. 106, Sangkat Wat Phnom, Khan Doun Penh* ☎ *023/987808, 023/999333* 🌐 *www.giantibis.com.* **GST Express Bus** ✉ *13E0, St. 142, Phnom Penh* ☎ *010/677909.* **Mekong Express** ✉ *103 E0, Sisowath Quay, Phnom Penh* ☎ *012/787839 Head Office, 070/833399 Riverside branch* 🌐 *catmekongexpress.com.* **Virak Buntham** ✉ *St. Riverside, Khan Doun Penh* ✣ *North of night market* ☎ *016/786270* 🌐 *www.virakbuntham.com.*

CAR TRAVEL

If you want to get to a destination quickly, hiring a driver with a car is probably the most effective way, but it can be a hair-raising ride. A hired car with a driver costs about $50 a day, but agree on the price beforehand. **■TIP→ We strongly advise against driving yourself.** Foreign drivers licenses are not valid here, rules of the road aren't observed, most drivers drive dangerously, and most of the main roads are not in good condition.

MOTO AND TUK-TUK TRAVEL

Within cities and for shorter journeys, *motos* (motorcycle taxis) and *tuk-tuks* (three-wheeled cabs) are the best and cheapest ways of getting around. Tuk-tuk drivers will greet (or hassle) you at every street corner, providing you with the opportunity of learning to haggle. To get fixed and very affordable rates, download and use ride-sharing smartphone applications like Grab and PassApp Taxi, which work great in most Cambodian cities, and start at $0.10 per kilometer.

TRAIN TRAVEL

Cambodia revamped its train system in 2018. Trains run south between Phnom Penh, Takeo, Kampot, and Sihanoukville ($8) on Friday, Saturday, Sunday, Monday, and on public holidays. On alternate days, a second line runs west and south of the Tonle Sap to Poipet and the Thai border. The main stops are at Pursat and Battambang, and the complete journey takes about 10 hours through serene countryside. There is also one shuttle train service from Phnom Penh's railway station, in walking distance from the Central Market, to Phnom Penh International Airport. It runs almost every hour from 5:30 am to 2:15 am and costs $5. ☎ *078/888582* 🌐 *royal-railway.com/*

BORDER CROSSINGS

There are five main border crossings between Vietnam and Cambodia, the busiest and most popular being Moc Bai–Bavet, with a regular bus service between Ho Chi Minh City and Phnom Penh; this is the recommended way to go. When getting on the bus to return to Vietnam from Phnom Penh, the driver's assistant will ask you for your passport, which will be kept until you reach the

At A Glance

Capital: Phnom Penh

Population: 16,245,729

Currency: Riel

Money: ATMs in cities; U.S. dollars widely accepted (even preferred), credit cards only in tourist places.

Language: Khmer

Country Code: 855

Emergencies: Call local police.

Driving: On the right

Electricity: 230v/50 cycle; plugs are either U.S. standard two-prong, European standard with two round prongs, or U.K. standard three-prong. Power adapter needed.

Time: 11 hours ahead of New York during daylight savings; 12 hours otherwise

Documents: 30 days or more with valid passport; visa on arrival

Mobile Phones: GSM (900 and 1800 bands)

Major Mobile Companies: Metfone, Smart, Cellcard, QB

Websites

Ministry of Tourism:

🌐 *www.tourismcambodia.org*

Move to Cambodia:

🌐 *www.tourismcambodia.org*

Tourism Cambodia:

🌐 *www.tourismcambodia.com*

border. This may appear strange, but it's the standard procedure, so don't worry. Other crossings include Ving Xuong to Kaam Samnor, on the river from Chau Doc, if you're traveling by boat; Tinh Bien to Phnom Den, if you are traveling to or from Kep; and O Yadao to Le Thanh, if you want to cross into the north of the country. All border crossings have become more regulated over the past few years, but corruption and minor bribery remains. Travelers have reported the borders at Koh Kong, between Cambodia and Thailand, and Dom Kralor, between Cambodia and Laos, to be particularly stressful. Don't listen to any tout asking for money to "facilitate" your visa process, and don't be surprised if even the border officials will ask for a $2 "stamping fee" when entering or leaving the country, or as much as $5 extra for issuing a tourist visa on arrival. Don't lose your cool: smiling and insisting on the correct price may help, but don't expect it.

The following border points are open with Thailand (Thai border towns in parentheses): Koh Kong (Hat Lek), Pailin (Ban Pakard), Duan Lem (Ban Laem), Poipet (Aranyaprathet), O'Smach (Chong Jom), and Anlong Veng (Chong Sa Ngam). From Laos you can cross at Dom Kralor (Voeung Kam). Overland crossings through Poipet and Koh Kong are the most popular, but bear in mind that Cambodian roads remain arduous, particularly in the rainy season. Coming from Laos overland, the best way to continue into Cambodia is by catching one of the many bus services plying the route Pakse/Si Phan Don/Stung Treng. Asia Van Transfers connects the Laos/Cambodia border to Siem Reap daily for $20. Book your tickets online at least a day in advance. 🌐 *asiavantransfer.com*

PASSPORTS AND VISAS

One-month single-entry tourist visas, which cost $30, are available at all land border crossings and at the airports.

You may need a passport photo—if you don't have one with you, it's an added $2 to have it made there (no added wait; sometimes you might not even be asked for a photo). When crossing on the bus from Vietnam, bus operators will ask for a fee of $5 for helping "fix" your visa. This is not compulsory and you can arrange your own visa at the border, but it does make the crossing slightly less of a hassle. Don't forget that you must have your visa for Vietnam in advance, and the dates must be relevant to your entry. You can also get your visa in advance on the Kingdom of Cambodia's e-visa website. This service takes a maximum of three days, costs $30 plus $6 service charge, but it saves a passport page as no visa sticker is applied at the border, and can prevent overcharging at land borders. 🌐 *www.evisa.gov.kh.*

MONEY MATTERS

The Cambodian currency is the riel, but the U.S. dollar is accepted everywhere, with many high-end businesses actually requiring payment in dollars. Don't be surprised to get change in riel when you pay in dollars. *Most prices are given in dollars in this chapter.* Thai baht are usually accepted in bordering provinces.

The official exchange rate is approximately 4,000 riel to one U.S. dollar or 20,000 Vietnamese Dong. It's possible to change dollars to riel just about anywhere.

ATMs are available in all major cities and towns, mostly at ANZ and Canadia banks, although there are numerous other banks starting to install them. Using an ATM will cost you $5 per withdrawal. Credit cards are accepted at major hotels, restaurants, and at some boutiques. Cambodian banking hours are shorter than in many Western countries, generally from 8 am until 3 or 4 pm. ATMs are available 24 hours.

What It Costs in U.S. Dollars

	$	$$	$$$	$$$$
RESTAURANTS	under $8	$8–$12	$13–$16	over $16
HOTELS	under $50	$50–$100	$101–$150	over $150

HEALTH AND SAFETY

If a real health emergency arises, evacuation to Bangkok is the best option.

Cambodia is far safer than many people realize, but you still need to exercise common sense. Most violence occurs against Cambodians. A decade ago, tourists were often mugged and sometimes even killed in Phnom Penh and on the beaches of Sihanoukville. Keep most of your cash, valuables, and your passport in a hotel safe, and avoid walking on side streets after dark—and it's best to avoid abrupt or confrontational behavior overall. Siem Reap has less crime than the capital, but that's starting to change. **■ TIP→ Late at night use more secure ride-hail services like Grab and PassApp Taxi, whose vehicles and drivers are automatically tracked.**

Land mines laid during the civil war have been removed from most major tourist destinations. Unexploded ordnance is a concern, however, around off-the-beaten-track temples, where you should only travel with a knowledgeable guide. As a general rule, never walk in uncharted territory in Cambodia, unless you know it's safe.

Cambodia has one of Asia's most atrocious road records. Accidents are common in the chaotic traffic of Phnom Penh and on the highways, where people drive like maniacs and will not hesitate to make speedy U-turns on a busy two-way street. The better the road, the scarier the driving. Unfortunately, chauffeurs are some of the worst offenders. Wear a seat belt if they're available, and if you rent a moto, wear a helmet. If you are in a tuk-tuk, just hold on tight.

TOURS AND PACKAGES

5oceans Travel

GUIDED TOURS | This company, run by two dynamic women, has been at the forefront of tourism in Cambodia for more than a decade and is the official representative for most of the carriers flying to Cambodia. 5oceans arranges trips ranging from comprehensive daylong tours of Phnom Penh to bespoke one-month adventures around the country. ✉ *139 E0, St. 136 (Oknha In), Khan Daun Penh* ☎ *023/221537, 023/221869* 🌐 *www.5oceanscambodia.com* 🎫 *From $30.*

★ Beyond Unique Escapes

Expert and ethical, this tour operator for the Siem Reap area offers the usual Angkor Temple tours, but also some more unusual experiences like spotting sunrise or sunset at a remote ruin far from the crowds, or hiking to a waterfall in the jungle of Kulen National Park. Other highly rated options include trips to villages and volunteering at their own NGO project HUSK, a rural literacy and development program. ✉ *Shinta Mani St., Old Market* ✣ *Near ANZ Royal Bank* ☎ *077/562565, 063/969269* 🌐 *www.beyonduniqueescapes.com* 🎫 *From $20.*

Hanuman Travel

ADVENTURE TOURS | If it's adrenaline thrills you're after, a cultural experience, or an exploration filled with adventure, this tour operator will tailor your trip to suit your needs. They can also recommend and book your accommodations. ✉ *13E St. 830, Sangkat Tonle Bassac* ☎ *023/218396* 🌐 *www.hanumantravel.com* 🎫 *From $85.*

★ oSmoSe Conservation Ecotourism Education

An agent of positive change in the area, oSmoSe, a nonprofit organization, has been fighting to conserve the unique biosphere of Tonle Sap and Prek Toal by reeducating local villagers from poachers to protectors of the environment that sustains them. They also lobby against big commercial interests that have been involved in short-term exploitation of the ecosystem, and have successfully helped to reharmonize many aspects of human coexistence with nature. On their exceptional tours you get to visit a bird sanctuary with an expert guide and also experience floating villages in a fascinating and respectful way. ✉ *St. 27, Wat Bo* ☎ *012/832812, 063/765506* 🌐 *www.osmosetonlesap.net* 🎫 *From $105.*

VISITOR INFORMATION

Once you arrive, pick up a visitor's map (separate editions for Phnom Penh, Siem Reap, and Sihanoukville) by Angkor Path Publications (🌐 *www.angkorpath.com*), as well as any of the various pocket guides, the best of these being Cambodia Pocket Guide (🌐 *www.cambodiapocketguide.com*), widely available free at airports, hotels, and restaurants.

Canby Publications (🌐 *www.canbypublications.com*) is an excellent source of information, with city and nightlife guides, and up-to-date bus schedules to anywhere in the country. **Move to Cambodia** (🌐 *www.movetocambodia.com*), updated by long-term expats, offers a wealth of information on the best places to eat, drink, and party in all major Cambodian destinations.

The **Ministry of Tourism** (🌐 *www.tourism-cambodia.org*) has some information on its website. **Tourism Cambodia** (🌐 *www.tourismcambodia.com*) has more detailed descriptions of top attractions. You can also visit the Tourist Information Center in Phnom Penh at 262 Monivong Boulevard, Khan Daun Penh.

Phnom Penh

The capital of Cambodia, Phnom Penh is strategically positioned at the confluence of the Mekong, Tonle Sap, and Bassac rivers. The city dates back to 1372, when a wealthy woman named Penh, who lived at the eastern side of a small hill near the Tonle Sap, is said to have found four Buddha statues hidden in a large tree drifting down the river. With the help of her neighbors, she built a hill (a *phnom*) with a temple on top, and invited Buddhist monks to settle on its western slope. In 1434 King Ponhea Yat established his capital on the same spot and constructed a brick pagoda on top of the hill. The capital was later moved twice, first to Lovek and later to Udong. In 1866, during the reign of King Norodom, the capital was moved back to Phnom Penh.

It was approximately during this time that France colonized Cambodia, and the French influence in the city is palpable—the legacy of a 90-year period that saw the construction of many colonial buildings, including the grandiose post office and train station (both still standing, though the latter is threatened by potential development plans). Some of the era's art deco architecture remains, in varying degrees of disrepair. Much of Phnom Penh's era of modern development took place after independence in 1953, with the addition of tree-lined boulevards, large stretches of gardens, and the Independence Monument, built in 1958.

Today Phnom Penh has a population of about 2 million people. But during the Pol Pot regime's forced emigration of people from the cities, Phnom Penh had fewer than 1,000 residents. Buildings and roads deteriorated, and most side streets are still a mess. The main routes are now well paved, however, and the city's wats (temples) have fresh coats of paint, as do many homes. This is a city on the rebound, and its vibrancy is in part due to the abundance of young people, many of whom were born after the war years. Its wide streets are filled with motorcycles, which weave about in a complex ballet, making it a thrilling achievement merely to cross the street. You can try screwing up your courage and stepping straight into the flow, which should part for you as if by magic, but if you're not quite that brave—and people have been hit doing this—a good tip is to wait for locals to cross and tag along with them.

Beggars

Beggars will sometimes approach you in Cambodia. Many NGO workers who work with the homeless advise against giving handouts on the street. Instead, you should acknowledge the people who greet you, politely decline, and make a donation to an organization that operates larger-scale programs to aid beggars and street kids.

There are several wats and museums worth visiting, and the Old City has some attractive colonial buildings scattered about, though many disappear as time goes on. The wide park that lines the waterfront between the Royal Palace and Wat Phnom is a great place for a sunset stroll, particularly on weekend evenings when it fills with Khmer families, as do the other parks around town: Hun Sen Park, the Vietnamese monument area, and the promenade near the monstrous Naga Casino. On a breezy evening you'll find hundreds of Khmers out flying kites.

GETTING HERE AND AROUND

AIR TRAVEL

Vietnam Airlines flies direct to Phnom Penh from Ho Chi Minh City, four times a day. Flights take 45 minutes and prices start at $150. Qatar Air flies once every day and is slightly cheaper, with prices from $120.

Phnom Penh's modern Pochentong Airport is 10 km (6 miles) west of downtown. A taxi from the airport to downtown Phnom Penh costs beween $12 and $18 depending on your final destination, while motorcycles and tuk-tuks

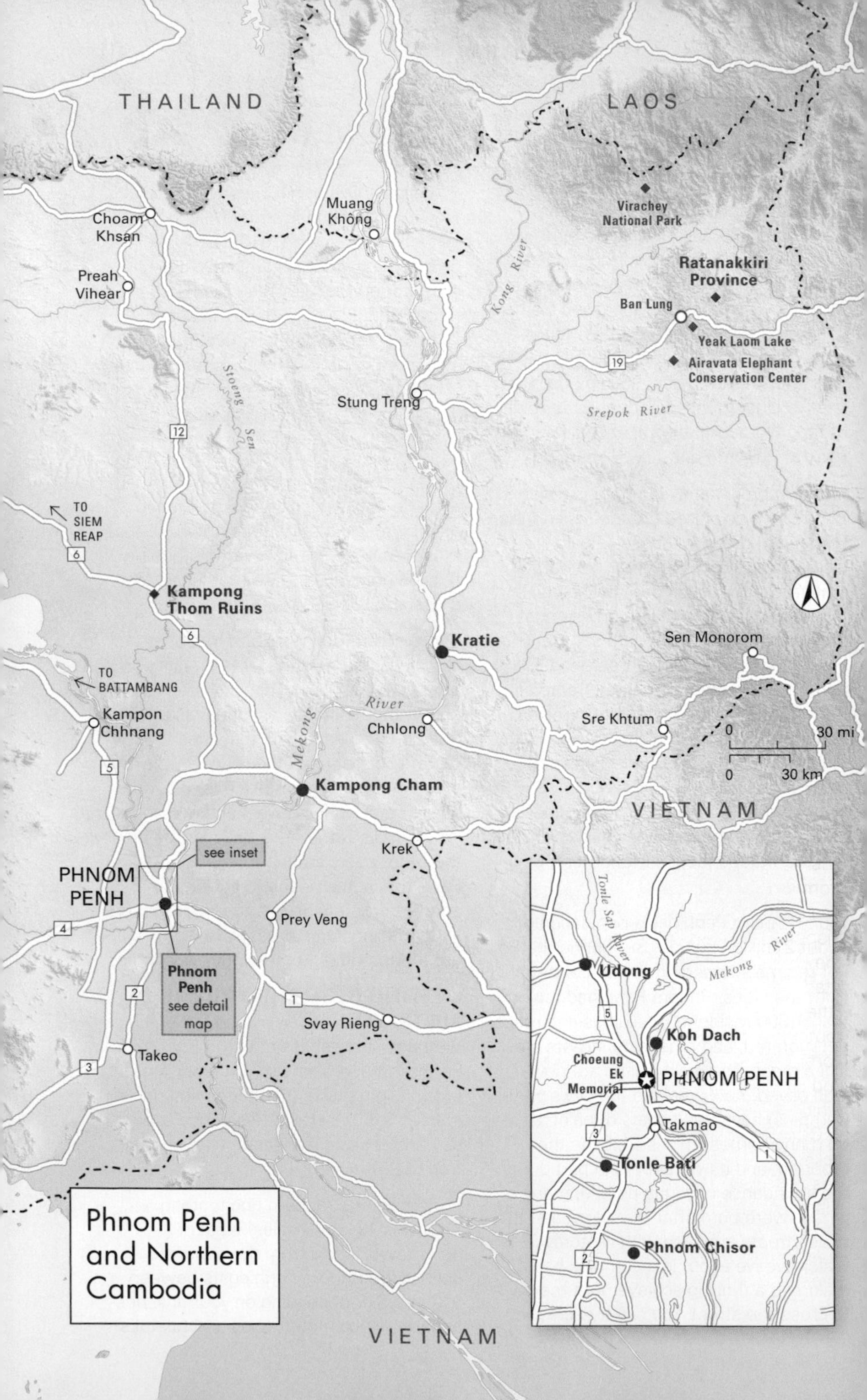

THAILAND
LAOS
Virachey National Park
Ratanakkiri Province
Ban Lung
Yeak Laom Lake
Airavata Elephant Conservation Center
Muang Không
Choam Khsan
Preah Vihear
Kong River
Stoeng Sen
Stung Treng
Srepok River
12
19
TO SIEM REAP
6
Kampong Thom Ruins
Kratie
Sen Monorom
TO BATTAMBANG
Kampon Chhnang
5
Mekong River
Chhlong
Sre Khtum
0
30 mi
0
30 km
Kampong Cham
VIETNAM
Krek
see inset
PHNOM PENH
4
Prey Veng
Phnom Penh see detail map
2
1
Svay Rieng
Takeo
3
Phnom Penh and Northern Cambodia
VIETNAM
Tonle Sap River
Mekong River
Udong
5
Koh Dach
Choeung Ek Memorial
PHNOM PENH
Takmao
3
1
Tonle Bati
Phnom Chisor
2

will set you back $3 and $7 respectively. There is also a train link to Phnom Penh Railway Station ($5) and the very convenient and air-conditioned Bus Line 3 (1,500 riel; prepare to have small change) that takes about 30 minutes to reach the Central Market. To find the bus stop to town, walk out of the airport's parking lot and turn left. ■ **TIP→ If using motorcycles and tuk-tuks, Grab and PassApp Taxi ride-hail apps get lower fares.**

AIRLINES Cambodia Angkor Air ✉ *House 206A, Preah Norodom Blvd.* ☎ *023/666–6786, 023/666–6788, 023/212564* 🌐 *www.cambodiaangkorair.com.* **Vietnam Airlines** ☎ *024/3832–0320* 🌐 *www.vietnamairlines.com.*

BUS TRAVEL

Phnom Penh has an efficient air-conditioned city bus system running from 5:30 am to 8:30 pm and costing only 1,500 riel per trip. The most useful line to tourist is number 3, which runs east to west from the night market, and stops at the Central Market and the Pochentong International Airport. ■ **TIP→ Download the Stops Near Me smartphone app to see all routes, bus stops, and real-time position of available buses, all in English.** There are also a half dozen or more private bus companies with regular service from all major Cambodian cities. Major bus stations include the Central Market, Sisowath Quay near the ferry port, and the Hua Lian Station near the Olympic Stadium. Mekong Express charges a little more than other bus companies, but routes are direct and buses are clean and comfortable, with onboard tour guides and a bathroom (bring your own paper, which is a golden rule anywhere public in Cambodia). Most long-distance bus tickets cost $6 to $25, depending on the destination and distance. Bus company Giant Ibis also provides free Wi-Fi. Tickets can be purchased at the bus companies' offices or through most hotels and guesthouses.

Even though there are regular buses from Ho Chi Minh City to Phnom Penh, and the reverse, it's advisable to book ahead. The trip takes six to seven hours and is pretty straightforward. There are a couple of stops en route as well as the lengthier layover at the border crossing; prices range from $10 to $20. Get a Vietnam visa before you set off.

TAXI, MOTO, AND CYCLO TRAVEL

The most common forms of transportation are the moto (motorcycle taxi) and tuk-tuk. They cruise the streets in abundance, and gather outside hotels and restaurants—wherever you walk, you'll attract them. The standard fare for a short trip on a moto is $1 to $2; tuk-tuks run a little higher, up to $4. Taxis don't cruise the streets, but there are usually a couple parked outside large hotels, and the receptionist can call one. Almost all drivers speak varying degrees of English, some fluently. Agree on an amount before you set off, or use ride-hail smartphone apps like Grab and PassApp Taxi for transparent, cheap, and no-hassle tuk-tuk and taxi booking.

VISITOR AND TOUR INFORMATION

Guides can also be hired right at the Royal Palace and National Museum.

Diethelm Travel

River cruises, bird-watching, biking adventures, and culinary experiences are some of the great packages on offer. ✉ *65 St. 240* ☎ *023/219151* 🌐 *www.diethelmtravel.com/cambodia* 🎫 *From $25.*

Exo Travel

Formerly know as Exotissimo, this company specializes in tours around Southeast Asia. Most of the tours are packages, but even so many shine a light on unique aspects local Khmer culture, past and present. Temple tours, cooking classes, and cycling trips are some of the experiences on offer. ✉ *SSN Center, 111 Norodom Blvd., 6th fl.* ☎ *023/218948* 🌐 *www.exotravel.com* 🎫 *From $160.*

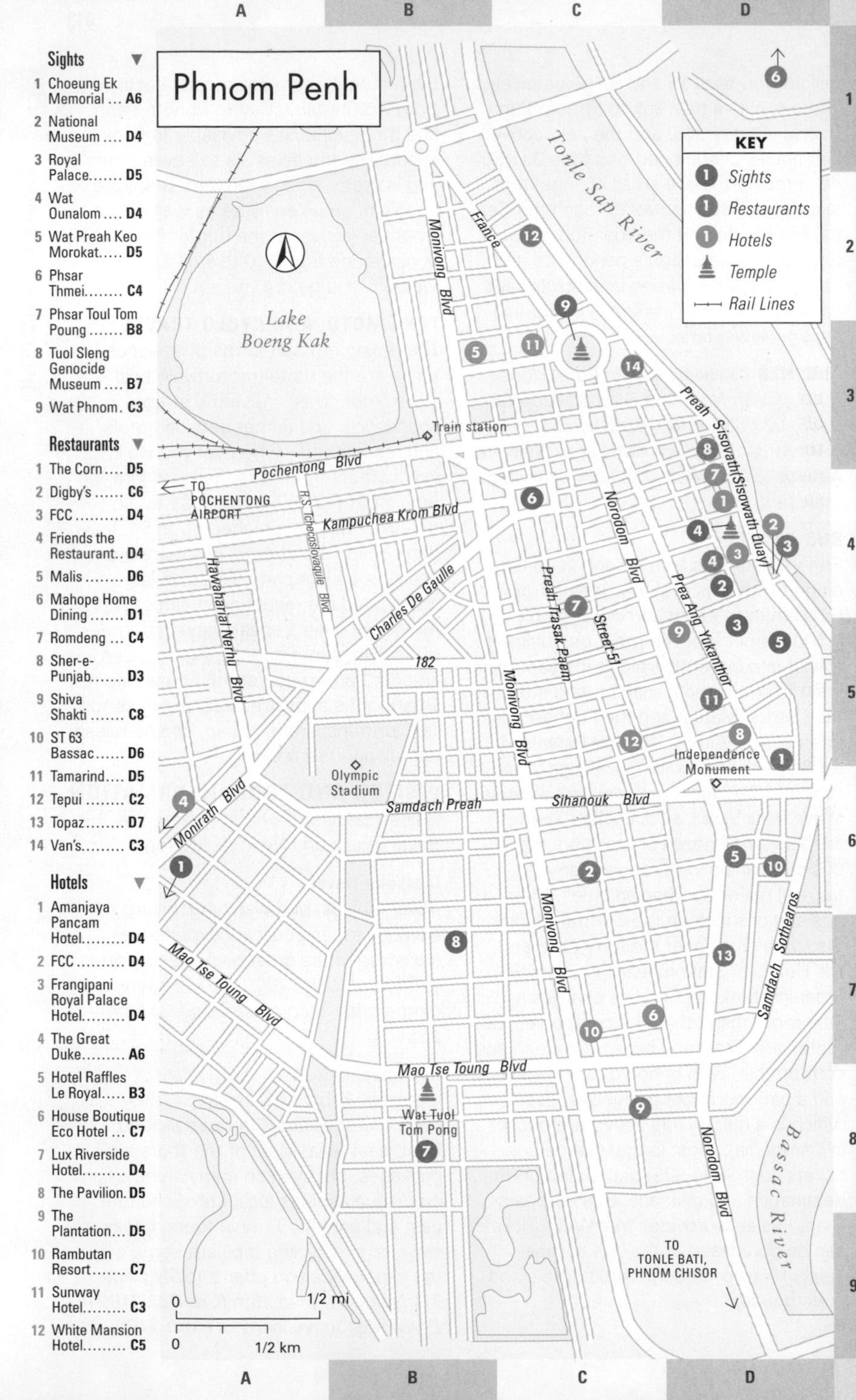

Phnom Penh
Sights
1 Choeung Ek Memorial ... A6
2 National Museum D4
3 Royal Palace....... D5
4 Wat Ounalom D4
5 Wat Preah Keo Morokat..... D5
6 Phsar Thmei........ C4
7 Phsar Toul Tom Poung B8
8 Tuol Sleng Genocide Museum B7
9 Wat Phnom. C3
Restaurants
1 The Corn D5
2 Digby's C6
3 FCC D4
4 Friends the Restaurant.. D4
5 Malis D6
6 Mahope Home Dining D1
7 Romdeng ... C4
8 Sher-e-Punjab....... D3
9 Shiva Shakti C8
10 ST 63 Bassac...... D6
11 Tamarind.... D5
12 Tepui C2
13 Topaz....... D7
14 Van's........ C3
Hotels
1 Amanjaya Pancam Hotel......... D4
2 FCC D4
3 Frangipani Royal Palace Hotel......... D4
4 The Great Duke....... A6
5 Hotel Raffles Le Royal..... B3
6 House Boutique Eco Hotel ... C7
7 Lux Riverside Hotel......... D4
8 The Pavilion. D5
9 The Plantation... D5
10 Rambutan Resort....... C7
11 Sunway Hotel......... C3
12 White Mansion Hotel......... C5
KEY
Sights
Restaurants
Hotels
Temple
Rail Lines
Tonle Sap River
Lake Boeng Kak
France
Monivong Blvd
Train station
Pochentong Blvd
TO POCHENTONG AIRPORT
R.S. Tchecoslovaquie Blvd
Kampuchea Krom Blvd
Norodom Blvd
Preah Sisovath/Sisowath Quay
Hawaharlal Nerhu Blvd
Charles De Gaulle
Preah Trasak Paem
Street 51
Prea Ang Yukanthor
182
Olympic Stadium
Independence Monument
Samdach Preah
Sihanouk Blvd
Monirath Blvd
Mao Tse Toung Blvd
Samdach Sothearos
Wat Tuol Tom Pong
Bassac River
TO TONLE BATI, PHNOM CHISOR
0
1/2 mi
1/2 km
A
B
C
D
1
2
3
4
5
6
7
8
9

Touring Phnom Penh

Start your tour early, just as the sun rises over the Tonle Sap. Take a tuk-tuk to **Wat Phnom**, then climb the staircase and head for the temple where King Ponhea Yat is venerated. After descending the hill, head east to the Tonle Sap and walk south along the riverfront promenade. Across the street you are greeted by a plethora of breakfast options; pick the restaurant of your choice. After eating, return to the riverfront, where you have a fine view of the Chroy Changvar Peninsula. The cobbled riverside path leads you to **Wat Ounalom**, one of Phnom Penh's largest and oldest pagodas.

After visiting the wat, continue south on Sisowath Quay, past a busy strip of bars and restaurants, and on to a huge lawn in front of the cheerful yellow **Royal Palace.** On the grounds of the palace is the must-see **Wat Preah Keo Morokat**, aka the Silver Pagoda. The palace closes for lunch from 11 am to 2 pm, so plan accordingly. On the northern side of the palace a side street leads to the traditional-style **National Museum**, which is a peaceful and quiet place to spend an hour or two.

By now you might be hungry again. As you exit the museum, head north on Street 13 to **Friends the Restaurant** for a light lunch and tasty drink. From there, if you think you can hack it, catch a tuk-tuk to the **Tuol Sleng Genocide Museum**, which will require an hour or more with a clear head. It's a somber, sobering experience, and most locals wouldn't dream of visiting. Afterward head to the trendy Street 240 for some good food and interesting shopping.

Tourist Information Center
✉ *373 Preah Sisowath Quay, Khan Daun Penh* ✣ *In front of Yisang Restaurant Riverside* ☎ *023/218585* 🌐 *www.tourism-cambodia.com.*

 Sights

Phnom Penh is an easy place to navigate and explore. There are markets, museums, and historical sites to visit. You will be able to explore the highlights of the city's tourist attractions in three to four days. All hotels will be able to arrange a range of transportation options for your tours around the city.

Choeung Ek Memorial (*Killing Fields*)
MEMORIAL | In the mid- to late 1970s thousands of Khmer Rouge prisoners who had been tortured at the infamous Tuol Sleng prison were taken to the Choeung Ek extermination camp for execution. Today the camp, 14 km (9 miles) southwest of downtown Phnom Penh, is a memorial, and the site consists of a monumental glass stupa built in 1989 and filled with 8,000 skulls, which were exhumed from mass graves nearby. It's an extremely disturbing sight: many of the skulls, which are grouped according to age and sex, bear the holes and slices from the blows that killed them. The site is at the end of a rough and dusty road, and can be reached in 30 minutes by motorbike, tuk-tuk ($12 is a reasonable price), or car. ■ **TIP→ The audio tour, available in English, is excellent and well worth the small additional fee.** ✉ *Sangkat Cheung Ek* 🌐 *www.phnompenh.gov.kh* 🎟 *$3, $6 with audio tour.*

National Museum
MUSEUM | This is one of Cambodia's two main museums and houses impressive relics that have survived war, genocide, and widespread plundering. More than 5,000 artifacts and works of art chronicle

the various stages of Khmer cultural development, from the pre-Angkor periods of Fu Nan and Zhen La (5th to 8th century) to the Indravarman period (9th century), the classical Angkor period (10th to 13th century), and post-Angkor period. A palm-shaded central courtyard with lotus ponds houses the museum's showpiece: a sandstone statue of the Hindu god Yama, the Leper King, housed in a pavilion. **Guides, who are usually waiting just inside the entrance, can add a lot to a visit here.** ✉ *Sts. 13 and 178* ☎ *023/217647 up to 48* 🌐 *cambodiamuseum.info* 🎫 *$10 adults.*

Phsar Thmei (*Central Market*)
MARKET | An inescapable sightseeing destination in Phnom Penh is the colonial-era Central Market, built in the late 1930s on land that was once a watery swamp. This wonderfully ornate building with a large dome retains some of the city's art-deco style. The market's Khmer name, Phsar Thmei, translates as "new" market to distinguish it from Phnom Penh's original market, Phsar Chas, near the Tonle Sap River; it's popularly known as Central Market, however. Entry into the market is through one of four grand doors that face the directions of the compass. The main entrance, facing east, is lined with souvenir and textile merchants hawking everything from cheap T-shirts and postcards to expensive silks, handicrafts, and silverware. Other stalls sell electronic goods, cell phones, watches, jewelry, household items, shoes, secondhand clothing, flowers, and just about anything else you can imagine. ✉ *Kampouchea Krom Blvd. and St. 130.*

Phsar Tuol Tom Ponug (*Russian Market*)
MARKET | This popular covered market earned its nickname in the 1980s, when the wives and daughters of Russian diplomats would often cruise the stalls on the lookout for curios and antiques. Today the market has a good selection of Cambodian handicrafts. Wood carvings and furniture abound, as do "spirit houses" used for offerings of food, flowers, and incense. Colorful straw mats and hats, as well as baskets, are in high demand. The market is the city's best source for art objects, including statues of the Buddha and Hindu gods; you can also buy valuable old Indochinese coins and paper money printed during different periods of Cambodia's turbulent modern history. A jumble of stalls concentrated at the market's south side sells CDs, videos, and electronics. It's also a great place to buy overstock clothes from Cambodia's numerous garment factories at a fraction of their official retail price. ✉ *Phnom Penh* ✥ *South of Mao Tse Tung Blvd., between Sts. 155 and 163.*

Royal Palace
BUILDING | A walled complex that covers several blocks near the river, the official residence of current King Preah Norodom Sihamoni and former residence of the late King Sihanouk and Queen Monineath Sihanouk, is a 1913 reconstruction of the timber palace built in 1866 by King Norodom. The residential areas of the palace are closed to the public, but within the pagoda-style compound are a number of structures worth visiting. These include Wat Preah Keo Morokat; the Throne Hall, with a tiered roof topped by a 200-foot-tall tower; and a pavilion donated by the Emperor Napoléon III and shipped here from France. Guides can be hired at the entrance for $10. ✉ *Sothearos* ✥ *Between Sts. 184 and 240* 🎫 *$6.50, plus $2 for a camera, $5 for a video camera.*

Tuol Sleng Genocide Museum
MUSEUM | This museum is a horrific reminder of the cruelty of which humans are capable. Once a neighborhood school, the building was seized by Pol Pot's Khmer Rouge and turned into a prison and interrogation center, the dreaded S-21. During the prison's four years of operation, some 14,000 Cambodians were tortured here; most were then taken to the infamous Killing Fields for execution. The four school buildings

The Royal Palace's Throne Hall is used today for ceremonies like coronations and royal weddings.

that made up S-21 have been left largely as they were when the Khmer Rouge left in January 1979. The prison kept extensive records and photos of the victims, and many of the documents are on display. Particularly chilling are the representations of torture scenes painted by S-21 survivor Vann Nath. Locals generally reveal they have never set foot here. ✉ *St. 113 (Boeng Keng Kang) and St. 350* 🎫 *$5.*

Wat Ounalom

RELIGIOUS SITE | On the riverfront, a little way north of the National Museum, the 15th-century Wat Ounalom is now the center of Cambodian Buddhism. Until 1999 it housed the Institute Buddhique, which originally contained a large religious library destroyed by the Khmer Rouge in the 1970s. Wat Ounalom's main *vihear* (temple hall), built in 1952 and still intact, has three floors; the top floor holds paintings illustrating the lives of the Buddha. The central feature of the complex is the large stupa, **Chetdai,** which dates to Angkorian times and is said to contain hair from one of the Buddha's eyebrows. Four niche rooms here hold priceless bronze sculptures of the Buddha. The sanctuary is dedicated to the Angkorian king Jayavarman VII (circa 1120–1215). In much more recent times the wat served as a temporary sanctuary for monks fleeing the police and soldiers in post-election political riots. ✉ *Sisowath Blvd.* ☎ *012/773361* 🎫 *Free.*

Wat Phnom

HISTORIC SITE | According to legend, a wealthy woman named Penh found four statues of the Buddha hidden in a tree floating down the river, and in 1372 she built this hill and commissioned this sanctuary to house them. It is this 90-foot knoll for which the city was named: Phnom Penh means "Hill of Penh." Sixty years later, King Ponhea Yat had a huge stupa built here to house his ashes after his death. You approach the temple by a flight of steps flanked by bronze friezes of chariots in battle and heavenly *apsara* (traditional Khmer dancing figures). Inside the temple hall, the vihear, are some fine wall paintings depicting scenes from the Buddha's lives, and on the north side is a charming Chinese shrine. The bottom of the hill swarms with vendors selling devotional candles and flowers, food stands (one with a monkey protecting a couple of dogs) with rather unappetizing food, and beggars. ✉ *Norodom Blvd. and St. 94* 🎫 *$1.*

★ **Wat Preah Keo Morokat** (*The Silver Pagoda*)
RELIGIOUS SITE | Within the Royal Palace grounds is Phnom Penh's greatest attraction: the Temple of the Emerald Buddha, built 1892 to 1902 and renovated in 1962. The temple is often referred to as the **Silver Pagoda** because of the 5,329 silver tiles—more than 5 tons of pure silver—that make up the floor in the main *vihear* (temple hall). At the back of the vihear is the venerated **Preah Keo Morokat** (Emerald Buddha)—some say it's carved from jade, whereas others maintain that it's Baccarat crystal. In front of the altar is a 200-pound solid-gold Buddha studded with 2,086 diamonds. Displayed in a glass case are the golden offerings donated by Queen Kossomak Nearyreath (King Norodom Sihamoni's grandmother) in 1969; gifts received by the royal family over the years are stored in other glass cases. The gallery walls surrounding the temple compound, which serves as the royal graveyard, are covered with murals depicting scenes from the Indian epic, the *Ramayana.* Pride of place is given to a bronze statue of King Norodom on horseback, completed in Paris in 1875 and brought here in 1892. There's a nearby shrine dedicated to the sacred bull Nandi. ✉ *Samdech Sothearos Blvd.* ✢ *Between Sts. 240 and 184* 🎫 *Included in admission to Royal Palace.*

Restaurants

Phnom Penh is quickly becoming one of the top culinary cities in Asia. With delectable Khmer food at all levels, from street stands to five-star establishments, plus an influx of international restaurants, you'll eat well in Phnom Penh. The country's colonial history means you'll find many French-inspired restaurants, too.

The Corn
$ | **CAMBODIAN** | The focus here is on delicately spiced Khmer-inspired vegan dishes. Try the rich, creamy sweet potato, pumpkin, and coconut curry, or a clean, crisp green mango, carrot, and herb salad with smoked tofu. **Known for:** gluten free; veggie amok; signature black rice. Ⓢ *Average main: $5* ✉ *26 Suramarit Blvd.* ☎ *017/773757* 🌐 *www.yourphnompenh.com/order/food/the-corn/* ▭ *No credit cards.*

Digby's
$$ | **AMERICAN** | A restaurant, coffee shop, butcher shop, and deli all rolled into one—if it's meat you're after, this is the place. Their locally sourced meat is all certified (a rarity in Cambodia) and all the gourmet sausages and cold cuts are prepared, cured, and smoked on the premises. **Known for:** popular happy hour; club sandwiches; hearty breakfasts. Ⓢ *Average main: $10* ✉ *No 34A, 306 St., Boeung Keng Kang 1* ☎ *023/226677* 🌐 *www.dnakcompany.com.*

FCC
$$ | **INTERNATIONAL** | You don't have to be a foreign correspondent to join the lively international crowd that gathers every day at this atmospheric French-colonial building. The beer is always cold, the cocktails icy, and you can grab a reliable burger or wood-fired pizza and enjoy the open river views if you're in need of a change from Khmer fare (having said that, the beef Lok Lak is one of the best in town). **Known for:** beer-battered fish-and-chips; lively meeting spot; occasional cultural events. Ⓢ *Average main: $8* ✉ *363 Sisowath Quay* ☎ *023/724014* 🌐 *www.fcccambodia.com.*

★ **Friends the Restaurant**
$ | **TAPAS** | Before Romdeng, there was Friends the Restaurant. This extremely

Cambodian Cuisine

Cambodian cuisine is distinct from that of neighbors Thailand, Laos, and Vietnam, although some dishes are common throughout the region. Fish and rice are the mainstays, and some of the world's tastiest fish dishes are to be had in Cambodia. The country has the benefit of a complex river system that feeds Southeast Asia's largest freshwater lake, plus a coastline famous for its shrimp and crab. Beyond all that, Cambodia's rice paddies grow some of the most succulent fish around. (Besides fish, Cambodians also eat a lot of pork, more so than beef, which tends to be tough.)

Be sure to try *prahok*, the Cambo dian lifeblood—a stinky-cheeselike fermented fish paste that nourishes the nation. *Amok*, too, is a sure delight. Done the old-fashioned way, it takes two days to make this fish-and-coconut concoction, which is steamed in a banana leaf.

Down south, Kampot Province grows world-renowned aromatic pepper. If you're coming from a northern climate, try a seafood dish with whole green peppercorns on the stalk. You won't find it (not fresh, anyway) in your home country.

Generally, the food in Cambodia is far tamer and less flavorsome that of Thailand or Laos, but seasoned heavily with fresh herbs. Curried dishes, known as *kari*, show the ties between Indian and Cambodian cuisine. As in Thailand, it is usual in Cambodian food to use fish sauce in soups, stir-fry, and as a dipping sauce. There are many variations of rice noodles, which give the cuisine a Chinese flavor. Beef noodle soup, known simply as *kuyteav*, is a popular dish brought to Cambodia by Chinese settlers. Also, *banh chiao*, a crepe-like pancake stuffed with pork, shrimp, and bean sprouts and then fried, is the Khmer version of the Vietnamese *bánh xèo*. Cambodian cuisine uses many vegetables. Mushrooms, cabbage, baby corn, bamboo shoots, fresh ginger, Chinese broccoli, snow peas, and bok choy are all found in Cambodian dishes from stir-fry to soup.

Usually, meals in Cambodia consist of three or four different dishes, reflecting the tastes of sweet, sour, salty, and bitter. The dishes are set out and you take from which dish you want and mix with your rice. Eating is usually a communal experience, and it is appropriate to share your food with others.

popular—best to book ahead—nonprofit eatery near the National Museum serves a huge range of small tapas, fruit juices, salads, and international dishes. **Known for:** falafel burger; attentive staff and service; international clientele and atmosphere. Ⓢ *Average main: $5* ✉ *215 St. 13* ☎ *012/802072* 🌐 *www.tree-alliance.org* ▭ *No credit cards.*

Mahope Home Dining

$$$$ | CAMBODIAN | This luxurious and intimate dining experience, curated by local Khmer chef Rotanak in her wooden stilt house, is scenically set 30 minutes north of the city center in a jungle garden along the Mekong. Both the setting and menu, which is prepared fresh every day with the produce that Chef Nak sources directly from her favorite markets, are perfectly choreographed to impress. **Known for:** exclusive location on a peaceful river bend; traditional music performances; ancient Khmer recipes. Ⓢ *Average main: $90* ✉ *2 Mekong River*

Rd., Prek Leap ⊕ Near Vearin Pagoda ☎ 012/906024 ⊕ www.rotanak.co/mahope-home-dining/.

Malis

$$$ | **CAMBODIAN** | The Phnom Penh elite frequent this upscale, traditional Khmer restaurant in a peaceful garden, as its chef Luu Meng is a Cambodian celebrity who has worked on TV with the likes of Gordon Ramsay. The long menu features a great variety of fresh fish and seafood, soups, complex curries, and grilled meats. **Known for:** rotating seasonal menu; fish prahok; creative curries. *$ Average main: $13 ✉ 136 St. 41 (Preah Norodom) ☎ 023/221022 ⊕ www.malis-restaurant.com/phnompenh/.*

Romdeng

$ | **CAMBODIAN** | Some of the country's tastiest provincial Khmer dishes are served at this gorgeously redesigned house in a residential area. Romdeng (which means "galangal" in Khmer) offers plenty of piquant soups, curries, salads, and meat dishes. **Known for:** Cambodia's signature fermented fish paste; pomelo salad; fried insects. *$ Average main: $7 ✉ 74 St. 174 ☎ 092/219565 ⊕ www.tree-alliance.org ▭ No credit cards.*

Sher-e-Punjab

$ | **INDIAN** | Follow the aroma of pungent spices into this restaurant and prepare for a hearty curry and all the essential sides at the capital's best Indian restaurant. The accommodating staff and exotically spiced fare more than compensate for the modest appearance of this much raved-about restaurant. **Known for:** tandoori chicken; wide selection of naan breads; perfectly cooked kebabs. *$ Average main: $6 ✉ 16 St. 130 ☎ 023/216360, 092/992901 ⊕ www.sherepunjabindianfood.com.*

Shiva Shakti

$$ | **INDIAN** | Succulent samosas, vegetable *pakoras* (fritters), spicy lamb masala, butter chicken, and prawn *biryani* (with rice and vegetables) are among the favorites served at this small Indian restaurant. In the pleasant dining room a statue of the elephant-headed Hindu god Ganesha stands by the door, and reproductions of Mogul art line the walls. *$ Average main: $9 ✉ 17 St. 63, Khan Chamkarmon ☎ 012/813817, 023/213062 ⊙ Closed Mon.*

★ ST 63 Bassac

$ | **CAMBODIAN** | ST 63 Bassac is run by a young Cambodian couple who aim to make international cuisine accessible and affordable for a local crowd, and at the same time showcase the best of Cambodian cuisine for foreign crowds. All the delicious dishes are well presented and amazingly well priced. **Known for:** Cha Kdao Sach Maon (spicy hot chicken with basil); refreshing cocktails; creamy smoothies. *$ Average main: $5 ✉ 2 St. 308, Boeung Keng Kang 1 (BKK1), Chamkamon District ☎ 015/647062.*

Tamarind

$ | **MOROCCAN** | The Mediterranean comes east at this popular three-story bar-restaurant in the heart of artsy Street 240. The menu extends from North African couscous and Spanish tapas, to Asian-fusion bites, served in a warm, jovial

Local Eats

For a local treat, try the afternoon **noodle shops** on Street 178 near the National Museum. These street-side eateries pack in the Khmer crowds, serving quick-fried noodles and rice-flour-and-onion cakes. They're popular among locals and cheap (less than a dollar per serving). You won't find the cleanest of restaurants here, but everything is well cooked, and you'll get a tasty snack with an eye for what it's like to eat Khmer-style. Don't get here before 4 pm.

atmosphere. $ *Average main: $6* ✉ *31 St. 240* ☎ *012/830139* 🌐 *bit.ly/2MYop6c.*

★ Tepui

$$$$ | SOUTH AMERICAN | Built in 1903, Chinese House (home to Tepui) is among the few colonial houses in Phnom Penh that remains in its original state. An impressive painting of a Chinese girl with ruby-red lips is the centerpiece in this sophisticated restaurant serving South American and Asian-fusion dishes, with specialties such as corn empanadas filled with beef picadillo and goat cheese cream, or red tuna tartare with wasabi emulsion. **Known for:** wine and cocktails; Pan-Asian cuisine; elegant outdoor terrace. $ *Average main: $17* ✉ *Chinese House, 45 Sisowath Quay, cross St. 84* ✥ *In front of Phnom Penh Port* ☎ *023/991514, 017/873101* 🌐 *www.chinesehouse.asia* ⊙ *Closed Sun. No lunch.*

Topaz

$$$$ | FRENCH | The first-class French specialties at this fine restaurant make it a longtime Phnom Penh favorite. Imported cuts of beef from Cape Grim in Tasmania and other highest quality ingredients cooked to perfection mean that Topaz remains one of the most feted places to dine in the city, even with its growing restaurant scene. **Known for:** extensive wine list; three-course set lunch menus; peaceful courtyard garden. $ *Average main: $25* ✉ *182 Norodom Blvd.* ☎ *089/211888, 023/221622* 🌐 *www.topaz-restaurant.com.*

Van's

$$$$ | FRENCH | In the elegant setting of the beautifully restored 1880's Indochina Bank Building, next to the post office, you can dine on exquisite French cuisine. Walk past the old vaults and up to the colonnaded dining area on the first floor. **Known for:** duck confit paupiette with duck liver; fillet of grouper with a matelote sauce; set lunch specials. $ *Average main: $25* ✉ *5 St. 102* ☎ *023/722067* 🌐 *vans-restaurant.com.*

Stocking the Fridge

Veggy's If your room or suite has a kitchenette or an ample mini-refrigerator, check out Veggy's, which features fine wines, cheeses, and meats from around the world. It also supplies imported dry goods and fresh veggies, as the name indicates. ✉ *23 St. 240* ☎ *023/211534.*

Hotels

These days the capital offers a plethora of accommodations for all budgets. Phnom Penh has several international-standard hotels, including the Cambodiana Hotel refurbishment of a 1960s building, a creation by the architect Lu Ban Hap, at the behest of the late King Sihanouk. Clean and comfortable boutique hotels and trendy guesthouses have sprung up across the city. Most charge less than $50 a night. If you haven't found what you're looking for, wander the riverfront and its side streets. You're bound to discover something to your liking among the dozens upon dozens of options.

■ **TIP→ When booking a hotel, check for special offers and promotions—many establishments offer deals.**

Amanjaya Pancam Hotel

$$$ | HOTEL | With chic rosewood furnishings and Khmer silk textiles in the rooms and soapstone-finished bathrooms, Amanjaya is the classiest hotel on the banks of the Tonle Sap River. **Pros:** glorious riverside location; great restaurant and bar; free smartphone for guest use in every room. **Cons:** faces one of Phnom Penh's busiest streets; no pool; small elevator. $ *Rooms from: $140* ✉ *1 St. 154, Sisowath Quay* ☎ *023/219579* 🌐 *www.amanjaya-suites-phnom-penh.com* *21 suites* *Free breakfast.*

FCC

$$ | **HOTEL** | Ideally located on the riverfront, cooled by the river breezes, and across from the National Museum, the Foreign Correspondents Club or FCC is well known as a hub for expats and visitors who hang out at its lively restaurant-bar on the second and third floors. **Pros:** charm of old-style correspondents' digs; lively restaurant-bar; excellent location. **Cons:** a little ragged around the edges; street noise; patchy hot water. *Rooms from: $50* *363 Sisowath Quay* *023/991641, 023/210142* *www.fcccambodia.com/fcc-hotel-phnom-penh/* *9 rooms* *Free breakfast.*

Frangipani Royal Palace Hotel

$$ | **HOTEL** | The fifth in a local chain, the Frangipani Palace Hotel is currently the only hotel in Phnom Penh with a rooftop pool, from where you can enjoy lovely panoramic views of the capital, especially at sunset. **Pros:** scenic rooftop pool and bar; good spa; high-end restaurant. **Cons:** not all rooms have a view; piped music throughout; only one elevator for eight floors. *Rooms from: $75* *27 St. 178, Sangkat Cheychumneas, Khan Daun Penh* *023/223320, 023/223340* *www.frangipanipalacehotel.com* *72 rooms* *Free breakfast.*

The Great Duke

$$$$ | **HOTEL** | One of Phnom Penh's finest hotels is on the far edge of town, where it's long been a favorite of business travelers and tycoons requiring VIP treatment. **Pros:** many amenities and services (including a concierge and executive floor); good selection of bars and restaurants; dramatic views. **Cons:** location in business district; far from city's main attractions; facilities a little outdated. *Rooms from: $250* *296 Blvd. Mao Tse Tung* *023/424888, 008/0031–221211 worldwide booking* *www.thegreatdukehotels.com.kh* *346 rooms* *Free breakfast.*

Hotel Raffles Le Royal

$$$$ | **HOTEL** | Phnom Penh's ritziest hotel, first opened in 1929, was practically destroyed during the Khmer Rouge years and was meticulously restored by the Raffles group in 1996. **Pros:** great location; old-world luxury; large swimming pool. **Cons:** style may not be to everyone's tastes; service has become quite lackadaisical; old premises start looking a bit worn out. *Rooms from: $200* *92 Rukhak Vithei Daun Penh* *023/981888, 800/768–9009 in U.S., 800/1–723–3537 international access* *www.raffles.com/phnom-penh/* *133 rooms* *Free breakfast.*

House Boutique Eco Hotel

$ | **HOTEL** | Excellent value for budget price, this quiet and airy hotel offers large, squeaky-clean, solar-powered rooms, some with balconies, fitted with upcycled wooden furniture. **Pros:** quiet environment; close to nightlife; good value. **Cons:** large plant at the center of the pool; breakfast not included; not all rooms have balconies. *Rooms from: $30* *76 St. 57, Boeung Keng Kang 1* *023/220884* *www.houseboutiquehotel.com* *32 rooms* *No meals.*

Lux Riverside Hotel

$$ | **HOTEL** | The rooms here are immaculate, spacious, and surprisingly pleasant for a budget property. **Pros:** river views; nice rooms; parking. **Cons:** noisy locale; no windows in back rooms; dodgy Wi-Fi reception in some rooms. *Rooms from: $50* *2 St. 136, Sangkat Phsar Kandal, Khan Daun Penh* *023/722828, 023/722318* *www.luxriversidehotels.com* *100 rooms, 2 apartments* *Free breakfast.*

★ The Pavilion

$$ | **HOTEL** | A discreet green oasis in the heart of bustling Phnom Penh, the Pavilion is in a lovingly restored building of the raging 1920s, with a swimming pool surrounded by palm, banana, and jackfruit trees. **Pros:** limo pickup service; good spa; great location. **Cons:** rooms and

bathrooms are a little small; no children under 16 allowed; fills quickly. *Rooms from: $65 ✉ 227 St. 19, Khan Daun Penh ☎ 023/222280 🌐 maads.asia/pavilion ⇄ 36 rooms 🍴 Free breakfast.*

★ The Plantation

$$ | HOTEL | This large boutique hotel is built around a grand 1930s villa in the heart of the city, with an open yard with a lotus filled pond in the middle. **Pros:** super restaurant; the larger of the two pools is only for guests; good location. **Cons:** only one shower at the main pool; slight overcharging for outsourced activities and transportation booked through reception; insects can be a nuisance in the garden. *Rooms from: $90 ✉ 28 St. 184 ☎ 023/215151 🌐 theplantation.asia ⇄ 70 rooms 🍴 Free breakfast.*

★ Rambutan Resort

$$ | HOTEL | This refurbished 1960's Khmer villa brings a touch of arty chic to Phnom Penh's central suburbs. **Pros:** excellent breakfast; great location; bathtub on the balcony. **Cons:** pool area can be busy; popular with the young flashpacker crowd; tucked in a side alley and not always easy to find tuk-tuks. *Rooms from: $50 ✉ 29 St. 71, Boeung Keng Kang 1 ☎ 023/993400 🌐 rambutanresort.com ⇄ 16 rooms 🍴 Free breakfast.*

Sunway Hotel

$$ | HOTEL | Near Wat Phnom and the U.S. embassy, this is a primary choice among business travelers. **Pros:** in the heart of the business district; excellent lounge bar; no smoking in all rooms. **Cons:** slightly dated architecture; only the suites have balconies; adjoining rooms can get noisy. *Rooms from: $60 ✉ 1 St. 92 ☎ 023/430333 🌐 phnompenh.sunwayhotels.com ⇄ 138 rooms 🍴 Free breakfast.*

White Mansion Hotel

$$ | HOTEL | FAMILY | This glossy boutique hotel on the hip, upscale Street 240 has suites on the top floors with balconies overlooking great vistas of the city, while rooms on the ground floor have terraces that lead directly to the pool. **Pros:** spacious rooms with espresso machines; child-friendly; nice monochrome design. **Cons:** open showers can be messy; elevator only goes up to third floor; set breakfast can be hit or miss. *Rooms from: $100 ✉ 26 St. 240 ☎ 023/555–0955 🌐 www.hotelphnompenh-whitemansion.com ⇄ 30 rooms 🍴 Free breakfast.*

Nightlife

What makes the nightlife here enjoyable is how easy it is to get from place to place in this compact city. Most of the dusk-to-dawn night spots are near the Tonle Sap riverside, along Streets 240 and 51. A useful website for upcoming events and venue information is 🌐 *www.lengpleng.com*, which is updated every Thursday or Friday. **■ TIP→ Keep your wits about you after dark in Phnom Penh—robberies are common, and although foreigners aren't specifically targeted, they are certainly not exempt from the rise in crime.**

BARS AND PUBS

Bassac Lane

BARS/PUBS | Once a sleepy residential lane, this road transformed into a highly celebrated expat drinking spot. As in a drinking catalogue of sorts, many tiny boutique bars sit wall to wall, each with its own peculiar style. From the biker Americana of **Hangar 44**, to the bibliophile heaven of **The Library,** or the black-and-white class of gin-and-wine bar **Cicada**, there's something to suit all tastes here. *✉ Bassac La., Boeung Keng Kang 1.*

Katy Peri Pizza

BARS/PUBS | Though not a bar, this food cart has to have a mention as a popular feature of Phnom Penh nightlife. It's a movable pizza oven attached to a moped, but mostly stations at popular nightlife hub Street 51, serving hot pizzas and Peri Peri chicken to all sorts of patrons. *✉ 172 St. 51, Boeung Keng Kang 1.*

Cambodia's Festivals

Like many Southeast Asian nations, Cambodia celebrates a lot of important festivals. Quite a few of them are closely tied to Buddhism, the country's predominant religion.

Meak Bochea: On the day of the full moon in February, this festival commemorates the Buddha's first sermon to 1,250 of his disciples. In the evening, Buddhists parade three times around their respective pagodas.

Khmer New Year: Celebrated at the same time as the Thai and Lao lunar new year (mid-April), it's a new-moon festival spread over the three days following the winter rice harvest. People celebrate by cleaning and decorating their houses, making offerings at their home altars, going to Buddhist temples, and splashing lots and lots of water on each other. Be forewarned: foreigners are fair game.

Visakha Bochea: This Buddhist festival on the day of the full moon in May celebrates the Buddha's birth, enlightenment, and death.

Chrat Preah Nongkol: The Royal Plowing Ceremony, a celebration of the start of the summer planting season, is held in front of the Royal Palace in Phnom Penh in May. The impressive ceremony includes soothsaying rites meant to predict the outcomes for the year's rice harvest.

Pchum Ben (All Souls' Day): In mid-October the spirits of deceased ancestors are honored according to Khmer tradition. People make special offerings at Buddhist temples to appease these spirits.

Bonn Om Touk: The Water Festival ushers in the fishing season, and marks the "miraculous" reversal of the Tonle Sap waters. It's celebrated in November throughout the country: longboat river races are held, and an illuminated flotilla of *naga*, or dragon boats, adds to the festive atmosphere. The biggest races are held in Phnom Penh in front of the Royal Palace, and the king traditionally presides.

Le Moon Rooftop Lounge
BARS/PUBS | This is an ideal spot to visit with a bunch of friends for a night of cocktails accompanied by sparkling views of the Tonle Sap and Mekong rivers, as well as Wat Ounalom. On the rooftop of the Amanjaya Pancam Hotel, the bar also serves finger food. ✉ *1 St. 154, Sisowath Quay* ☎ *023/214747* 🌐 *www.amanjaya-pancam-hotel.com.*

Score Sports Bar & Grill
BARS/PUBS | Open until 2 am every morning, this sports haunt is a favorite of expats, locals, and tourists who want to catch a game live on one of many LCD screens, while enjoying a tipple among a chatty, enthusiastic crowd. The food isn't the best in town, but most people don't come only to eat. ✉ *Wat Lanka, 5 St. 282* ✣ *Between Sts. 51 and 57* ☎ *023/221357.*

DANCE CLUBS

Blue Chilli
CABARET | Phnom Penh is a gay-friendly city, and Blue Chilli, behind the National Museum, is one of the most popular and oldest bars for locals, expats, and tourists. The lively, friendly bar hosts entertaining drag shows and other performances throughout the week, as well as DJ sets that will keep you dancing until the early hours. ✉ *36Eo St. 178* ☎ *012/566353* 🌐 *www.bluechillicambodia.com.*

Epic

DANCE CLUBS | As the name might suggest, this place, which opened in 2014, is for big nights out—a high-tech dance club, near the Russian embassy, that caters to the high fliers of the capital, including jet-setters, A-list celebrities, and serious ravers. The daily party goes on until 5 am. Check the website for details of upcoming events. ✉ *122B Sangkat Tonle Bassac, Chamkamon District* ☎ *023/210454, 010/600608* 🌐 *www.epic.com.kh.*

Pontoon Club and Lounge

DANCE CLUBS | The first club in the Cambodian capital that brings top DJs from around the world for happening live sets draws an accidental as well as a dedicated music-loving crowd. Thursdays are LGBT nights, with *Shameless*, Phnom Penh's most iconic drag cabaret show. ✉ *80 St. 172* ☎ *016/779966, 010/300400* 🌐 *www.pontoonclub.com.*

GATHERING PLACES

★ Samai

GATHERING PLACES | Difficult to find but well worth the effort, this microdistillery-bar, near the Aen Mall, is one of the trendiest joints in Phnom Phen's flourishing bar scene. Excellent Samai brand rum is distilled on-site in 200-year-old copper stills and makes a great base for the Moorish-Asian-inspired cocktails. The downside: it's only open on Thursday nights. ✉ *9b St. 830* ✣ *Off Sothearos Blvd.* ☎ *023/224143* 🌐 *www.samaidistillery.com.*

Show Box

BARS/PUBS | Very near Tuol Sleng, but quite a distance from the main "happening" spots in town, Show Box has a clever strategy to draw in customers—it gives out free beer every day from 6:30 to 7 pm. Once there, many end up staying all night for the laid-back vibe, live music, fun pub quiz Thursday nights, and the company of a youthful, artsy crowd. ✉ *11 St. 330, Chamkamon District* ☎ *017/275824.*

MUSIC CLUBS

Club Love

MUSIC CLUBS | Every night, the city's current dance club of choice packs guest DJs and a motley crew of expats, backpackers, and locals who strut their stuff and party till 4 am. ✉ *3 St. 278, Boeung Keng Kang 1* ✣ *Above Duplex* ☎ *070/856195.*

WINE BARS

Bouchon Wine Bar

WINE BARS—NIGHTLIFE | Bouchon serves a dapper selection of more than 40 French wines and accompanying light meals (well, light by French standards) or finger food, in a buzzily sophisticated, industrial, nouveau-pub atmosphere that attracts an eclectic international crowd. Wine labels are also stamped on the wooden tables, and you can sample different varieties by the bottle or by the glass. ✉ *3 St. 246* ☎ *077/881103.*

Crush Wine Bar

WINE BARS—NIGHTLIFE | Serious about its craft, Crush has temperature-controlled coolers and an air-conditioned storage room, offering at least 100 wines by the bottle and 20 by the glass. A trendy spot to enjoy a perfect drink. ✉ *12 St. 294, Sangkat Tonle Bassac.*

Performing Arts

Various Phnom Penh theaters and restaurants offer programs of traditional music and dancing, many organized by nonprofit groups that help Cambodian orphans, disadvantaged kids, and individuals with a disability. Siem Reap perhaps has more venues, but most there are run by for-profit companies in the tourism industry.

Chaktomuk Hall

CULTURAL FESTIVALS | This architectural landmark, built in 1960 by Vann Molyvann, hosts performances of traditional music and dance organized by the Ministry of Culture, and is also a venue for business events such as conferences.

Women parade near the Royal Palace in celebration of Bonn Om Touk, Cambodia's water festival.

Dates and times of the occasional shows are listed in the *Phnom Penh Post.* ✉ *Sisowath Quay* ✣ *North of St. 240* ☎ *023/725119.*

Meta House

ART GALLERIES—ARTS | The first floor of the German Cambodian Cultural Center is a trendy one-stop for culture in the capital. From free movie screenings to live music, DJ sets, and theater, Meta House boasts a consistent calendar of worthy events. Don't forget their bar, serving excellent cocktails and beers, and German food, including tasty Alsatian pizzas. ✉ *37 Sothearos Blvd., Sangkat Tonle Bassac* ☎ *023/218987* 🌐 *www.meta-house.com.*

Plae Pakaa

CONCERTS | **FAMILY** | Established to create work opportunities for talented local artists, Plae Pakaa puts on three shows, each performed twice a week at 7 pm (no show on Sunday). They are organized by the Marion Institute with Cambodian Living Arts and take place in the National Museum gardens. The beautifully staged performances showcase the rich diversity of Cambodian culture, from Apsara dances to traditional ceremonies, theater, music, and contemporary dance. If you're only in town for two or three days you can catch a different performance each night. ✉ *National Museum, St. 3* ✣ *Corner of St. 178* ☎ *017/998570* 🌐 *www.cambodianlivingarts.org* 🎫 *$15.*

Sovanna Phum Khmer Art Association

DANCE | The privately run association organizes educational workshops for young Cambodians in dance, music, and theater, and hosts performances featuring shadow puppets, folk dances, and traditional music every Friday and Saturday at its theater. ✉ *166 St. 99, Chamkamon District* ✣ *Corner of St. 484* ☎ *012/846020, 012/837056* 🌐 *sovannaphumtheatre.com.*

Shopping

The city has many shops and a few markets selling everything from fake antiques to fine jewelry, while several polished boutiques sell items made with local materials and offer sustenance to socially disadvantaged individuals. Prices are generally set at shops, so save your bargaining skills for the markets. The best shops are to be found on Streets 178 and 240.

ANTIQUES AND FINE ART

Couleurs d'Asie

ANTIQUES/COLLECTIBLES | As well as presenting regular exhibitions of contemporary and classic-style Khmer art, Couleurs d'Asie sells beautifully crafted accessories and home style items made by local artists in sumptuous silks and other locally sourced materials. The store closes at 3 pm on Sunday. ✉ *33 St. 240* ☎ *023/221075* 🌐 *www.couleursdasie.net.*

Le Lezard Bleu

ANTIQUES/COLLECTIBLES | Like its newer twin in Siem Reap, Le Lezard Bleu is a boutique-gallery-shop featuring housewares creations inspired by Cambodian culture and made by local artisans, as well as a collection of antique objets d'art. It mainly stocks posters, sculptures, prints, and silks. ✉ *61 St. 240* ☎ *023/986978.*

Waterlily

JEWELRY/ACCESSORIES | Enter a world of humorous fantasy, quirky chic, and illustrative color at the jewelry workshop-store of French designer Christine Gauthier. Buttons, beads, wires, and feathers shine in her eccentric designs, some of which are hidden like treasures in a chest with hundreds of little drawers for you to peek through. ✉ *37 St. 240* ☎ *012/812469.*

X-EM Design

ART GALLERIES | It's more of a showroom than a shop, where Em Riem showcases his own works as well as inviting other fresh Cambodian artists to exhibit here—a must for design and art lovers and collectors. ✉ *13 St. 178* ✣ *West of Norodom Blvd.* ☎ *023/722252.*

CLOTHING

Ambre

CLOTHING | After studying at Paris School of Fine Arts and the Esmod School of Fashion Design, Romyda Keth made her name for herself abroad. Since returning to her native Cambodia, she has opened her own fashion shop in an old colonial villa and showcases her creations there. Her designs are a big hit locally and internationally. ✉ *No. 37, 178 St.* ☎ *023/217935* 🌐 *www.romydaketh.net.*

CRAFTS

Daughters of Cambodia Boutique

CLOTHING | Within Phnom Penh's red-light district and offering employment opportunities to sex-trafficking victims, this boutique sells men's and women's clothing and accessories, children's toys, and home style items. There is also a lovely café and a spa on the premises. ✉ *321 Sisowath Quay* ☎ *089/910203* 🌐 *daughtersofcambodia.org.*

Friends 'n' Stuff

CRAFTS | Trendy, playful, and eco-friendly accessories can be found here, next to the ultrapopular Friends restaurant and just north of the National Museum. Check out the locally crafted laptop cases made from recycled bicycle tires, handbags made from food packets, glossy hardback books about Cambodia, and other fun stuff—and all for the worthy cause of helping street children achieve a quality of life. ✉ *215 St. 13, Khan Daun Penh* ☎ *023/220596* 🌐 *www.mithsamlanh.org.*

Rajana

BOOKS/STATIONERY | Interesting, locally handcrafted jewelry, silks, home style items, stationery, and clothing are sold at this shop next to the Russian Market, and the proceeds go toward the Rajana Association, which trains local artisans. **Check out the old war-scrap necklaces and recycled spark-plug figurines.** The association also has one shop in Street 240 and other locations in Sihanoukville and Siem Reap. ✉ *Psar Tuol Tom Poung (Russian*

Market), 61C St. 450 ☎ *023/993642* 🌐 *www.rajanacrafts.org.*

Watthan Artisans Cambodia
CLOTHING | This is an organization worth supporting, producing attractive women's accessories, decorative objects, and knickknacks in silk, cotton, wood, and clay—all made on-site by people with physical disabilities. Watthan Artisans products can also be found at the great Colours of Life store behind the FCC. ✉ *Wat Than Pagoda, 180 Norodom Blvd.* ☎ *023/216321* 🌐 *www.wac.khmerproducts.com.*

MARKETS

Psar Reatrey Night Market
OUTDOOR/FLEA/GREEN MARKETS | This lively riverfront market attracts locals and tourists alike for basic clothing, traditional handmade souvenirs, accessories, and gift shopping until midnight. Several stands sell freshly made local dishes as well as drinks like sugarcane and bean juices, and there is a large sitting area covered in rattan mats. ✉ *Sisowath Quay* ✣ *Between St. 106 and St. 108.*

Psar Thmei
CLOTHING | The largest market in Phnom Penh, popularly known as the Central Market, is an art deco-style structure in the center of the city that sells foodstuffs, household goods, fake antiques, and some silver and gold jewelry. You're expected to bargain—start off by offering half the named price and you'll probably end up paying about 70%. Take your time to find what you want, as the vendors can be pushy. It's busiest in the morning. ✉ *Blvd. 128 (Kampuchea Krom)* ✣ *At St. 76 and Neayok Souk St.*

Psar Tuol Tom Pong
OUTDOOR/FLEA/GREEN MARKETS | A popular location for discovering some of the best bargains in town, the Psar Tuol Tom Pong, or Russian Market, next to Wat Tuol Tom Pong, sells a great variety of Cambodian handicrafts, traditional krama scarves, Khmer wood carvings, baskets, knockoff electronics, and much more. ✉ *Sts. 155 and 440.*

SILK

Sayon Silkworks
HOUSEHOLD ITEMS/FURNITURE | Offering employment to impoverished women from remote regions, Sayon Silkworks has a fine collection of silk accessories, quilts, and other home elements, such as cushions and bolsters, in exquisite colors and patterns. ✉ *40 St. 178* ☎ *077/697280.*

Silk & Pepper
CLOTHING | Choose from made-to-order clothing, jewelry, gifts, and home accessories from this interesting fair-trade establishment in the heart of Phnom Penh. They are serious about their silks, and source only the best materials, crafted with the age-old ikat Cambodian weaving technique. ✉ *33 St. 178* ☎ *012/851234, 023/222692.*

Tonle Bati

33 km (20 miles) south of Phnom Penh.

On weekends Phnom Penh residents head for this small lake a half-hour drive south on Highway 2. It has a beach with refreshment stalls and souvenir stands. Note that you'll encounter many beggars and children clamoring for attention here. The nearby but more remote **Ta Phrom,** a 12th-century temple built around the time of Siem Reap's Angkor Thom and Bayon, is less chaotic. The five-chambered laterite temple has several well-preserved Hindu and Buddhist bas-reliefs. Nearby is an attractive, smaller temple, **Yeah Peau.** Admission to Ta Phrom and Tonle Bati is $3 and open to the public at all times. Phnom Tamao, Cambodia's leading zoo, is about 11 km (7 miles) farther south, but it's not worth a detour.

GETTING HERE AND AROUND

Hiring a car and driver in Phnom Penh is perhaps the easiest way to visit Tonle Bati (around $50 including waiting time), and if you do this, you can easily combine the trip with Phnom Chisor. The drive takes about 30 minutes.

Diethelm Travel *(see Phnom Penh Planner)* arranges tours to Tonle Bati.

Phnom Chisor

55 km (34 miles) south of Phnom Penh.

A trip to Phnom Chisor is worth the drive just for the view from the top of the hill of the same name. There's a road to the summit, but most visitors prefer the 20-minute walk to the top, where stunning vistas of the Cambodian countryside unfold. At the summit the 11th-century templeis a Khmer masterpiece of laterite, brick, and sandstone. Admission is $3.

GETTING HERE AND AROUND

Though the (decent) bus ride is cheap, you can combine Tonle Bati and Phnom Chisor in one trip if you hire a car and driver (about $50 per day), perhaps the easiest way to visit Phnom Chisor. The drive takes about 20 minutes from Tonle Bati or 40 minutes from Phnom Penh. Takeo-bound GST and Neak Krorhorm buses (departing from Phnom Penh every hour) stop at Prasat Neang Khmau; from there you can hire a moto to take you up the hill. The whole trip should take no more than an hour.

Diethelm Travel *(see Phnom Penh Planner)* and Hanuman Travel *(see Cambodia Planner)* arrange tours to Phnom Chisor.

Koh Dach

30 km (19 miles) north of Phnom Penh.

This Mekong River island's main attractions are its beach and its handicrafts community of silk weavers, wood carvers, potters, painters, and jewelry makers. The beach isn't spectacular by Southeast Asian standards, but it is convenient for Phnom Penh getaways. In all, the trip over to the island is quick; most people spend about half a day on this excursion, but you can dwell longer if you want a relaxing beach day.

GETTING HERE AND AROUND

Any tuk-tuk or moto driver can take you to Koh Dach from Phnom Penh. Alternatively, you can hire a car and driver for the day (about $50 per day). The trip takes approximately two hours each way, and involves a ferry trip to the island.

Diethelm Travel *(see Phnom Penh Planner)* and Hanuman Travel *(see Cambodia Planner)* arrange tours to Koh Dach.

Udong

45 km (28 miles) north of Phnom Penh.

This small town served as the Khmer capital from the early 1600s until 1866, when King Norodom moved the capital south to Phnom Penh. Today it's an important pilgrimage destination for Cambodians paying homage to their former kings. You can join them on the climb to the pagoda-studded hilltop, site of the revered Vihear Prah Ath Roes assembly hall, which still bears the scars of local conflicts from the Khmer Rouge era.

GETTING HERE AND AROUND

Udong is best reached by catching a Sorya bus to Kampong Chhnang from the Central Bus Station and getting off at the junction at the Km 37 mark. Motos and tuk-tuks will then take you to the temples. The bus costs around $2.

You can also take a boat from Phnom Penh; this can be arranged through your hotel or any travel agent.

Diethelm Travel, Exotissimo *(see Phnom Penh Planner)*, and Hanuman Travel *(see Cambodia Planner)* arrange tours to Udong.

Cambodia Then and Now

Internationally, Cambodia is best known for two contrasting chapters of its long history. The first is the Khmer Empire, which in its heyday covered most of modern-day Southeast Asia. Today the ruins of Angkor attest to the nation's immutable cultural heritage. The second chapter is the country's recent history and legacy of Khmer Rouge brutality, which left at least 1.7 million Cambodians dead. In 1993 the United Nations sponsored democratic elections that failed to honor the people's vote. Civil war continued until 1998, when another round of elections was held, and violent riots ensued in the aftermath. Cambodia's long-standing political turmoil—both on the battlefield and in much more subtle displays—continues to shape the nation's day-to-day workings. Through decades of war, a genocide, continued widespread government corruption, high rates of violence and mental illness, the provision of billions of dollars in international aid, and the disappearance of much of that money, Cambodia has suffered its demons. Yet Cambodians are a forward-thinking, sharp-minded, and friendly people, whose warm smiles are not yet jaded by tourism and do not belie the inordinate suffering their nation has so recently endured. Though practically destroyed by the regional conflict and homegrown repression of the 1970s, individual Cambodians have risen from those disasters, and a new, hard-working, and young middle class has blossomed.

Ecology

More than half of Cambodia was once blanketed in forests, but the landscape has changed in recent decades as a result of ruthless and mercenary deforestation. The country is blessed with powerful waters: the Mekong and Tonle Sap rivers, and Tonle Sap Lake, which feeds 70% of the nation. The surrounding mountain ranges, protecting Cambodia's long river valleys, are home to hill tribes and some of the region's rarest wildlife species.

The three ranges of low mountains—the northern Dangkrek, the exotically named Elephant Mountains in the south, and the country's highest range, the Cardamoms, in the southwest—formed natural barriers against invasion and were used as fortresses during the war years. Among these ranges is a depression in the northwest of Cambodia connecting the country with the lowlands in Thailand; by allowing communication between the two countries, this geographic feature played an important part in the history of the Khmer nation. In eastern Cambodia the land rises to a forested plateau that continues into the Annamite Cordillera, the backbone of neighboring Vietnam.

Colonization, War, and Invasion

As the seat of the Khmer Empire from the 9th to the 13th century, Cambodia developed a complex society based first on Hinduism and then on Buddhism. After the decline of the Khmers and the ascendancy of the Siamese, Cambodia was colonized by the French, who ruled from the mid-1860s until 1953.

Shortly after the end of World War II, during which the Japanese had occupied Cambodia, independence became the rallying cry for all of Indochina. Cambodia became a sovereign power with a monarchy ruled by King Norodom Sihanouk, who abdicated in favor of his father in 1955 and entered the public stage as a mercurial politician.

In the early 1970s the destabilizing consequences of the Vietnam War sparked a horrible chain of events. The U.S. government secretly bombed Cambodia, arranged a coup to oust the king, and invaded parts of the country in an attempt to rout the Vietcong. Civil war ensued, and in 1975 the Khmer Rouge, led by French-educated Pol Pot, emerged as the victors. A regime of terror followed. Under a program of Mao Tse-tung–inspired reeducation centered on forced agricultural collectives, the cities were emptied and hundreds of thousands of civilians were tortured and executed. Hundreds of thousands more succumbed to starvation and disease. During the four years of Khmer Rouge rule, somewhere between 1 and 2 million Cambodians—almost one-third of the population—were killed.

By 1979 the country lay in ruins. Vietnam, unified under the Hanoi government, invaded the country in response to a series of cross-border attacks and massacres in the Mekong Delta by the Khmer Rouge. The invasion forced the Khmer Rouge into the hills bordering Thailand, where they remained entrenched and fighting for years. United Nations–brokered peace accords were signed in 1991. International mediation allowed the return of Norodom Sihanouk as king and the formation of a coalition government that included Khmer Rouge elements after parliamentary elections in 1993. But civil war continued.

Reconciliation and Recovery?

In 1997 Second Prime Minister Hun Sen toppled First Prime Minister Norodom Ranariddh in a coup. During the following year's national elections, Hun Sen won a plurality and formed a new government, despite charges of election rigging. Pol Pot died in his mountain stronghold in April 1998, and the remaining Khmer Rouge elements lost any influence they still had.

It has taken years for the United Nations and the Cambodian government to establish a tribunal that will bring to justice the few surviving key leaders of the Khmer Rouge regime. Proceedings began in 2007, but only one former Khmer Rouge leader (Duch, the infamous head of Tuol Sleng) is in jail; Ta Mok, the so-called Butcher, was the only other Khmer Rouge leader to be imprisoned, but he died in 2006. The others remain free; many have blended with ease into current society, and some remain in the folds of the Cambodian government.

Foreign investment and the development of tourism have been very strong in recent years, but it remains to be seen whether domestic problems can truly be solved by Prime Minister Hun Sen (a former Khmer Rouge commander) and his hard-line rule.

Kampong Cham

125 km (78 miles) northeast of Phnom Penh.

Cambodia's third-largest city was also an ancient Khmer center of culture and power on the Mekong River, and it has a pre-Angkorian temple, **Wat Nokor.** (Sadly, the temple itself is in a state of disrepair and the $2 entry fee unmerited.) Just outside town are the twin temple-topped hills, Phnom Pros and Phnom Srei (included in the price). Ask a local guide to explain the interesting legend surrounding their creation. In the ecotourism village of Cheungkok, about 5 km (3 miles) south of town, you can see silk making, carving, and other traditional crafts in progress and also buy the wares directly from villagers. All profits are reinvested in the village.

Kampong Cham can be visited in a few hours, but with Cheungkok it is an all-day trip.

GETTING HERE AND AROUND

You can get to Kampong Cham from Phnom Penh by taxi or bus; the trip takes about three hours. Any guesthouse or hotel can arrange for a taxi. Expect to pay $6 for a single bus ticket and $50 for a taxi from Phnom Penh. The buses (Sorya, Giant Ibis, and Mekong Express) leave hourly from the bus station at the Central Market or their respective offices near the Night Market.

Restaurants

Kampong Cham has the usual local food stalls and shophouses, but few restaurants of note.

Smile

$ | **CAMBODIAN** | Buddhism for Social Development Action runs this experiential training restaurant. Even so, the dining experience (Khmer and Western, leaning heavily towards Italian, food served) on the whole is better than many professional setups. *Average main: $3* *6 Mort Tunle St. (aka Riverside St.)* *017/997709* *www.bsda-cambodia.org.*

Hotels

Monorom VIP Hotel

$ | **HOTEL** | The heavy, sculpted wooden furniture and ruffled curtains of the large rooms may be too much for some, but it's apparent that the owners of this hotel have made a real effort to create a pleasant and polished environment. **Pros:** central, riverside location; comfortable beds; nice views. **Cons:** bored, inattentive staff; no breakfast; not all rooms have views. *Rooms from: $20* *Mort Tunle St. (aka Riverside St.)* *097/733–2526, 092/777102* *www.monoromviphotel.com* *50 rooms, 1 suite* *Free breakfast.*

Rana

$ | **B&B/INN** | **FAMILY** | Rana offers a one-of-a-kind, well-organized experiential homestay for adults or families in the Cambodian countryside. **Pros:** unique window into local life; culturally educational; friendly owners. **Cons:** two-night minimum stay; a certain level of fitness is required for the activities; no electricity or running water. *Rooms from: $25* *Srey Siam* *012/686240* *rana-ruralhomestay-cambodia.webs.com* *No credit cards* *2 rooms* *Free breakfast.*

Kompong Thom Ruins

160 km (99 miles) north of Phnom Penh.

These ruins, exactly halfway between Phnom Penh and Siem Reap, are even older than those at Angkor. They are all that remain of the 7th-century Sambor Prei Kuk, the capital of Zhen La, a loose federation of city-states. The ruins, which are free and open to the public at all times, are near the Stung Sen River, 35 km (22 miles) northeast of the provincial town of Kampong.

GETTING HERE AND AROUND

The ruins are a day trip by taxi from Siem Reap (two hours; $50) or Phnom Penh (three hours; also $50, or $10 per person, shared). The journey can be dusty and hot in the dry season and muddy and wet in the rainy season. All buses between Phnom Penh and Siem Reap stop in Kompong Thom, but you will pay the full fare (about $10) regardless. Arrange local transportation via tuk-tuk or moto (about $25 for the full tour of the ruins).

Kratie

340 km (217 miles) northeast of Phnom Penh.

Kratie is famous for the colony of freshwater Irrawaddy dolphins that inhabits the Mekong River some 15 km (9 miles) north of town in the village of Kampi. ■ **TIP→ The dolphins are most active in the early morning and late afternoon.** Tuk-tuks and hired cars with driver from Kratie charge about $10 for the journey to the stretch of river where the dolphins can be observed. You will likely have to hire a local boatman to take you to where the dolphins are, as they move up and down the river. The trip costs $9 for two people, and $7 for three or more.

GETTING HERE AND AROUND

Several bus companies from Phnom Penh's Central Bus Station offer regular service to Kratie (six to seven hours; $10). Expect delays in the wet season. You can also get a shared taxi or hire your own driver, but as always buses are a far safer option.

Diethelm Travel *(see Phnom Penh Planner)* arranges tours to Kratie.

Restaurants

Kratie has an abundance of local food shops. Most guesthouses have simple menus, and there is a lively food-stall scene in town.

Tokae Restaurant

$ | **CAMBODIAN** | Next to Kratie's busy marketplace, this is one of the better places to eat in town. The kitchen provides decent and inexpensive traditional Khmer fare and Western-style comfort foods catering to a mostly tourist clientele. *Average main: $3 10 St.*

Hotels

★ Rajabori Villas Resort

$$ | **RESORT** | After the long bus or taxi trip to Kratie, it is another 20 minutes by boat and tuk-tuk to get to Rajabori Villas Resort, tucked on the northern end of the blissful island of Koh Trong. The traditional Khmer bungalows set in lush gardens have colonial-style wooden furniture and are decorated with Cambodian textiles and prints. **Pros:** free bikes for exploring the island; peaceful location (no cars); nature all around. **Cons:** food and drinks on the expensive side; getting to and from the resort can be challenging; nonguests pay $5 to use the pool. *Rooms from: $60 Koh Trong 012/770150, 012/959115 www.rajabori-kratie.com 15 bungalows Free breakfast*

Le Tonlé Guesthouse

$ | **B&B/INN** | Central guesthouse that provides hospitality vocational training to disadvantaged Cambodian youths. **Pros:** good service; quiet yet very central; homey atmosphere. **Cons:** few rooms means it's often full; some staff should improve English skills; not all rooms are en suite. *Rooms from: $20 724 St. 03 095/261448 www.letonle.org 4 rooms Free breakfast.*

Religion in Cambodia

As in neighboring Thailand, Laos, and Vietnam, Buddhism is the predominant religion in Cambodia. But animism and superstition continue to play strong roles in Khmer culture and society. Many people believe in powerful *neak ta*, or territorial guardian spirits. Spirit shrines are common in Khmer houses as well as on temple grounds and along roadsides. The Khmer Loeu hill tribes, who live in the remote mountain areas of Ratanakkiri and Mondulkiri provinces, and some tribes of the Cardamom Mountains are pure animists, believing in spirits living in trees, rocks, and water.

The main layer of Cambodian religion is a mix of Hinduism and Buddhism. These two religions reached the country from India about 2,000 years ago and played a pivotal role in the social and ideological life of the earliest kingdoms. Buddhism flourished in Cambodia in the 12th to 13th century, when King Jayavarman VII embraced Mahayana Buddhism. By the 15th century, influenced by Buddhist monks from Siam and Sri Lanka, most Cambodians practiced Theravada Buddhism.

Cambodian religious literature and royal classical dance draw on Hindu models, such as the *Reamker*, an ancient epic about an Indian prince searching for his abducted wife and fighting an evil king. Brahman priests still play an important role at court rituals.

Cambodia's Muslim Chams, who number a few hundred thousand, are the descendants of the Champa Kingdom that was based in what is today Vietnam. They have had a presence in this area since the 15th century, when they were forced from the original kingdom. The country's 60,000 Roman Catholics are mainly ethnic Vietnamese. A small Chinese minority follows Taoism.

Ratanakiri Province

Ban Lung is 635 km (395 miles) northeast of Phnom Penh.

Both Ratanakkiri and neighboring Mondulkiri provinces are mountainous and once covered with dense jungle, which is rapidly giving way to mainly rubber plantations, and together they are home to 12 different Khmer Loeu ethnic-minority groups. The government has developed four community-based projects in the region. The eventual aim is to reinvent large sections of the area as ecotourism destinations, making them self-sufficient and helping the communities reduce the impact on the natural resources.

GETTING HERE AND AROUND

From Phnom Penh there are several bus services to Ban Lung (10 hours; $8 to $14) on Virak Bunthambus lines. The journey is much improved from a few years ago with the opening of a paved road all the way to Banlung. There are no scheduled flights available, but charter companies do the trip regularly; visit any travel agent for details. Share-taxis are always an option.

Diethelm Travel *(see Phnom Penh Planner)* arranges tours to Ratanakiri.

In Ban Lung you can hire a jeep with a driver-guide or, if you're very adventurous, rent a motorcycle, to visit the fascinating destinations an hour or two away.

Sights

Ratanakkiri Province is remote, but it is slowly building a reputation as an ecotourism destination, and the government is trying hard to promote tourism to this part of Cambodia. Intrepid travelers will find natural and cultural attractions, including waterfalls, jungle treks, lakes, villages, and the Airavata Elephant Foundation.

Airavata Elephant Conservation Center

FARM/RANCH | FAMILY | Located a few kilometers south of Ratanakiri's capital Banlung, Airavata is a "new generation" elephant camp following responsible and ethical alternatives to mass tourism. In an effort to help save some of Cambodia's dwindling population of 300-odd elephants, they work under patronage of Cambodia's King Norodom Sihamoni. Travelers meet the animals in optimal natural conditions, guided by highly selected indigenous mahouts who treat elephants in the best possible way, as they enjoy their work. Guests can learn how to be a mahout for a day. ✉ *Banlung* ✣ *10 km south of Banlung, past Okatieng waterfall* ☎ *012/770650* 🌐 *www.airavata-cambodia.com.*

Ban Lung

TOWN | The provincial capital is a small, sleepy town that holds a certain romance as a far-flung capital, away from the influence of Phnom Penh, but otherwise offers little more than slow-paced local life and clouds of red dust in the dry season—or mud in the wet season. Arrive with everything you need, as Western goods are sometimes difficult to obtain. Most of the decent hotels are located around Kan Seng lake.

Bokeo

MINE | A visit to the gem mines of the Bokeo area, 30 km (20 miles) east of Ban Lung, can be arranged through your hotel, or any moto driver in Ban Lung can take you there. Some of the mines are increasingly deep, claustrophobic, man-sized potholes, and mining is for semiprecious stones such as zircon. As you drive through the villages in the area, the villagers line up to sell you their finds. *Bokeo* literally means "gem mine."

Virachey National Park

NATIONAL/STATE PARK | This lush and scenic jungle, 35 km (22 miles) northeast of Ban Lung, is home to the two-tiered Bu Sra Waterfall and lots of wildlife. Tuk-tuks and motos will take you here from Ban Lung ($15), but all treks and eco-activities should be prearranged in Ban Lung at the park's visitor information center. The best way to discover the area and possibly spot some of the ever dwindling rare species found here is through one of the local tour operators, like recommended DutchCo Trekking Cambodia (St. 78A 🌐 *www.trekkingcambodia.com),* who can arrange two- to seven-day trips. ✉ *Banlung* 🌐 *viracheyecotourism.blogspot.com* 🎫 *$5.*

★ Yeak Laom Lake

VOLCANO | FAMILY | Lodged in a volcanic crater 5 km (3 miles) east of Ban Lung, this mystical lake, bordered by jungle, is sacred to many of the Khmer Loeu hill tribes. It's a half mile in diameter and 154 feet deep, and there are three wooden jetties from which to launch yourself into the cool waters. Swing from a hammock in one of the wooden huts lining the shore—these cost $3 to rent for the day, but if you order food it's free. The local specialty is *prung,* bamboo stuffed with vegetables, meat, and local herbs and spices which are cooked over an open fire. Stalls at the entrance sell jungle honey, as well as the usual kramas and other craftwork cloths. Take a tuk-tuk ($3) or moto from Ban Lung. ✉ *Banlung* 🎫 *$1.50.*

Restaurants

Banlung Kitchen

$ | CAMBODIAN | This restaurant of the namesake bed-and-breakfast offers

Khmer and international dishes, creatively presented and highly praised by returning customers. Vegetables are sourced from the in-house garden, and the menu also caters to vegetarians and vegans. **Known for:** vegan burgers; friendly owners; eclectic menu. *Average main: $3* *148 St. 544, Banlung* *010/816529* *www.banlungkitchen.business.site* *No credit cards.*

Hotels

Terres Rouge Lodge and Restaurant
$$ | HOTEL | The former residence of the governor of Ratanakiri Province has been transformed into a scenic resort with a beautifully landscaped tropical garden. **Pros:** spacious rooms, some with lake views; beautiful colonial building; good restaurant and bar. **Cons:** sporadic service; some rooms are showing a little wear and tear; a little out of the town center. *Rooms from: $75* *Boeung Kan Siang Lake, Banlung* *012/770650* *www.ratanakiri-lodge.com* *22 rooms, 7 suites* *Free breakfast.*

Yaklom Hill Lodge
$ | B&B/INN | This popular lodge has an eco-friendly philosophy and offers clean, well-maintained wooden cottages and a traditional hill tribe house in a jungle setting at Yeak Laom Lake about 5 km (3 miles) outside the city. **Pros:** lush natural location; ecological (off the grid); some lodging options good for families or groups of up to eight people. **Cons:** no hot water most of the day; basic facilities only; definitely off the beaten track. *Rooms from: $15* *Rd. 78, Banlung* *011/790510* *yaklom.blogspot.com* *No credit cards* *15 cottages, 1 house* *Free breakfast.*

Battambang

290 km (180 miles) northwest of Phnom Penh.

Cambodia's second-largest city straddles the Sanker River in the center of the country's rice bowl. Dusty Battambang used to be bypassed by most visitors to Cambodia, but that's starting to change. The city not only has some fine old French colonial architecture, but also a charming old town filled with hip cafés, boutique hotels, and art galleries that deserve soaking up the atmosphere for a few days.

GETTING HERE AND AROUND

All the major bus companies depart daily from Phnom Penh's Central Market to Battambang (five hours; $9), and in some cases, on to Poipet. There is also a train service leaving Phnom Penh Railway Station at 6.30 am every other day, stopping at Pursat and Battambang (eight hours) en route to Poipet. Buses also leave from Siem Reap (three hours; 6$). For the more adventurous, lovely but lengthy boat trips are a good option. The ride to Siem Reap can take anywhere between 5 and 10 hours ($20). A hired car with a driver costs about $50 a day, but settle on the price before setting off.

TOURS

Capitol Tours
Covering most of Cambodia, this company offers interesting tour packages, including temple excursions, river rides, and bird-watching. *739 La Ae St.* *Near Boeung Chhouk Market* *053/953040, 092/277561* *www.capitoltourscambodia.com* *From $35.*

Sights

The few sights to see in and around town include some Angkor-era temple ruins and the Khmer Rouge "killing caves." The town is walkable and full of vibrant arts galleries and cafés, and strolling down to the river in the evening is a pleasant way to pass the time. Most of the out-of-town sights listed here can be visited in a day renting a tuk-tuk with driver for about $25.

Heritage Walk

BUILDING | The cluster of blocks between Street 1, parallel to the Sanker River, and Street 3, and all the way down to Street 127, house a great variety of historic architecture representing diverse phases of the city's legacy. Grab one of the annotated walking maps by Khmer Architecture Tours (🌐 *www/ka-tours.org) from Bric-à-*Brac hotel and explore on foot. **■ TIP→ Don't miss the very interesting and free museum at the Governor's Mansion, itself an exquisite piece of colonial architecture.** ✉ *Sangkat* 🌐 *www.ka-tours.org/.*

Phnom Banan

ARCHAEOLOGICAL SITE | In the countryside 25 km (15 miles) south from the city, this 11th-century hilltop temple has five impressive towers and is sometimes referred to as "the mini Angkor Wat." Reaching the temple involves a hike up 350 or so steps, so go after lunch when it's less hot. Tuk-tuks from Battambang charge $10–$15 for the round-trip. There is a mystical little cave round the side of the hill whose waters are supposed to induce visions. ✉ *Banan Hill* 🎫 *$2.*

Phnom Sampeou

CAVE | In addition to being the site of a temple, this hill, 10 km (7 miles) southwest of Battambang, was also used by the Khmer Rouge to execute prisoners in a group of killing caves. In one, which contains the skeletal remains of some of the victims, you can stand on the eerily dark floor and look up to a hole in the cave roof, with sunlight streaming through. The Khmer Rouge reportedly pushed their victims through that hole to their deaths on the rocks below. ✉ *Hwy. 57.*

Psar Nath Market

MARKET | Like most local markets, this is a great spot to buy fresh foods, and it's also known for gems and Battambang's famous fruit—lime-green oranges. Its vendors also sell everything from cheesy souvenirs to electronics imported from China. Some stalls have textiles, but most of these are imported. ✉ *On the Sangker River.*

Wat Ek Phnom

RELIGIOUS SITE | Long before the French arrived, Battambang was an important Khmer city, and among its many temples is this 11th-century Angkorian structure. Even though it was heavily looted, the temple still has a few fine stone carvings in excellent condition. In front of the ruins stands a newly built pagoda. It's 10 km (7 miles) north of the city and getting here via tuk-tuk or moto will cost around $10. **■ TIP→ Admission is free with a ticket to Wat Banan, but only on the same day.** ✉ *St. 1734* 🎫 *$3.*

Restaurants

There's a good selection of restaurants in town, including some Western cuisine. The places to eat here are all at the lower end of the price range. A Khmer food market down by the river is open in the late afternoon or early evening.

Jaan Bai

$ | **CAMBODIAN** | Meaning "rice bowl" in Khmer, this social enterprise restaurant curated by the Cambodian Children Trust dishes up tasty Khmer and Thai mains in a cozy and artsy atmosphere—rotating exhibits of local artworks hang from the wall, and it's often packed with young creatives in the evenings. Jaan Bai provides skills development and employment for disadvantaged Cambodians, and a share of the profits goes towards community development work. **Known for:** good set meals for sharing; locally brewed organic coffee; no MSG in the food. 💲 *Average main: $4* ✉ *St.*

2 ✣ Next to Psar Nat ☎ 078/263144 🌐 www.cambodianchildrenstrust.org/social-enterprises/.

Kinyei Cafe

$ | **BRASSERIE** | Hip and tiny coffee shop strewn with potted plants and managed by young, knowledgeable local baristas who serve a robust blend of beans from Thailand, Vietnam, and Cambodia. Their lunch options, such as the veggie rolls, are perfect for a quick bite. **Known for:** gluten-free choices; good breakfast sets; strong coffee. 💲 *Average main: $3* ✉ *229 St. 1.5* ☎ *010/644000* 🌐 *www.kinyei.org.*

Hotels

★ Battambang Resort

$$ | **RESORT** | A small paradise, this tranquil resort has a lush garden where you can relax in a hammock among exotic fruit trees and organically grown herbs, flowers, and vegetables, all used by its restaurant to create healthy Asian and European dishes. **Pros:** lovely pool; free use of bikes; free pickup and daily shuttle service to and from Battambang. **Cons:** a little out of the way; marriage venue nearby can be noisy; sandwiched between two high-rises that spoil part of the charm. 💲 *Rooms from: $70* ✉ *Wat Ko Village* ☎ *012/510100, 053/666–7001* 🌐 *www.battambangresort.com* *10 rooms* *Free breakfast.*

★ Bric-à-brac

$$ | **HOTEL** | Enter the special world of two expatriate Australian designers enamoured of Asia, who made Battambang their home, and leave as family, not a guest. **Pros:** customized service; breakfast can be served in bed; furnished with charming and rare Indochinese artifacts. **Cons:** very limited rooms, so it fills up fast; doesn't have a full restaurant menu; old staircase with no lift may put some guests off. 💲 *Rooms from: $100* ✉ *112 St. 2* ✣ *Corner of St. 119* ☎ *077/531562, 077 /531549* 🌐 *bric-a-brac.asia* *3 rooms* *Free breakfast.*

La Villa

$$ | **HOTEL** | This boutique hotel is in a beautifully restored 1930s colonial house, with well-maintained, spacious rooms that have an old-world charm and quaint art deco feel. **Pros:** beautiful architecture; lovely riverfront location; large, clean pool. **Cons:** not many facilities; service can lack attention to detail; starting to show some wear and tear. 💲 *Rooms from: $80* ✉ *185 Pom Romchek, 5 Kom, Rattanak Commune* ☎ *017/411880, 053/730151* 🌐 *www.lavilla-battambang.net* *3 rooms, 4 suites* *Free breakfast.*

Maisons Wat Kor Boutique

$$ | **RESORT** | Traditional Khmer villas set in lush garden surroundings about 3 km south of the Old Town.The pastel-hued rooms are all spacious, with their own verandas, and fitted with cooling wooden floors and furnishings. **Pros:** attentive service; beautiful natural setting; great value for the money. **Cons:** 10-minute drive from town; basic continental breakfast; not many activities in the area. 💲 *Rooms from: $70* ✉ *St. 800* ✣ *Wat Kor Village* ☎ *017/555377* 🌐 *www.maisonswatkor.com* *8 rooms.*

Nightlife

Miss Wong Battambang

WINE BARS—NIGHTLIFE | Siem Reap's popular drinking hole opened shop in Battambang. Indigo walls and decadent Chinese-themed decor lure patrons to a well-tested menu of Asian infusions, such as Kaffir lime, and established international mixology. Perfect place for a sophisticated, vintage night. ✉ *St. 2* ☎ *092/428332* 🌐 *bit.ly/2BfJ3h6.*

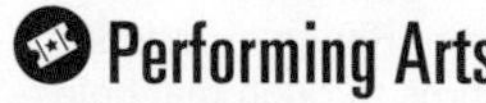

Performing Arts

Phare Battambang Circus

ARTS VENUE | **FAMILY** | The famous Cambodian Circus originated in Battambang: for more than 15 years, the Phare Ponleu Selpak center has offered quality arts training to locals. Their daily shows ($14) combine dance, theater, live music, and circus performances with Cambodian narratives. Shows start at 7 pm, and there are also guided visits of the campus ($5) from Monday to Friday until 3:30 pm. ✉ *Anh Chanh Village, Ochar Commune* ☎ *077/554413* 🌐 *www.phareps.org.*

Romcheik 5 Artspace

ART GALLERIES—ARTS | This hip art gallery hosts rotating exhibits of local artists on the ground floor. Upstairs a museum collects the best work from the four young co-founders, all graduates of the Phare Ponleu Selpak School, who were expelled from Thailand during childhood and shelterd by an NGO. Entry $2. ✉ *St. 201A* ☎ *089/373683, 086/677704* 🌐 *www.romcheik5.com.*

Sangker Gallery

ART GALLERIES—ARTS | A refurbished shophouse that functions as a social and artistic hub by collecting and showcasing paintings from up-and-coming Battambang artists. Rotating exhibits alternate monthly on the first floor. ✉ *194 St. 2* ☎ *06/962313* ☞ *Closed Mon.*

Tep Kao Sol Gallery & Boutique

ART GALLERIES—ARTS | A good place to buy watercolors, reproductions, and postcards by leading Cambodian artists. On the first floor, co-owner and artist Loeum Lorn exhibits his peculiar artworks created by printing photographs of ice on canvas. ✉ *129 St. 2* ☎ *017/982992.*

Siem Reap

315 km (195 miles) north of Phnom Penh.

Siem Reap, which means "Siam defeated," based on a 15th-century battle with Cambodia's neighbors to the west, has emerged as a modern, friendly, and elegantly low-key city with highly sophisticated shopping, dining, and nightlife options. After a long day at the Angkor Temple Complex, you'll be happy to spend your evening strolling along the Siem Reap River, and dining at an outdoor table on a back alley in the hip old French quarter or Alley West off the more boisterous Pub Street, which is closed to traffic in the evening.

The Old Market area is a big draw and the perfect place to shop for souvenirs; dig through the silk, wood, and silver ornaments and accessories and you may find your treasure. Many of the colonial buildings in the area were destroyed during the Khmer Rouge years, but many others have been restored and turned into world class resorts and restaurants.

You could spend an entire afternoon in the Old Market area, wandering from shop to shop, café to café, gallery to gallery. It changes every month, with ever more delights in store. Long gone are the days when high-end souvenirs (the legal kind) came from Thailand. Today numerous shops offer high-quality Cambodian silks, Kampot pepper and other Cambodian spices, and herbal soaps and toiletries made from natural Cambodian products.

GETTING HERE AND AROUND

AIR TRAVEL

Angkor Air has five daily flights from Phnom Penh to Siem Reap costing about $100 each way and taking 40 to 45 minutes. Vietnam Airlines have five direct flights daily to and from Hanoi's Noibai Airport ($160 each way) and six daily flights direct to and from Ho Chi Minh City ($145 each way). There are also daily charter flights, which may offer a cheaper alternative.

Bangkok Airways flies six times daily between Siem Reap and Bangkok (one hour; $300 round-trip). Lao Air flies three times a week to Siem Reap from both Pakse (50 minutes; $150 one-way) and Vientiane (80 minutes; also $150 one-way), in Laos.

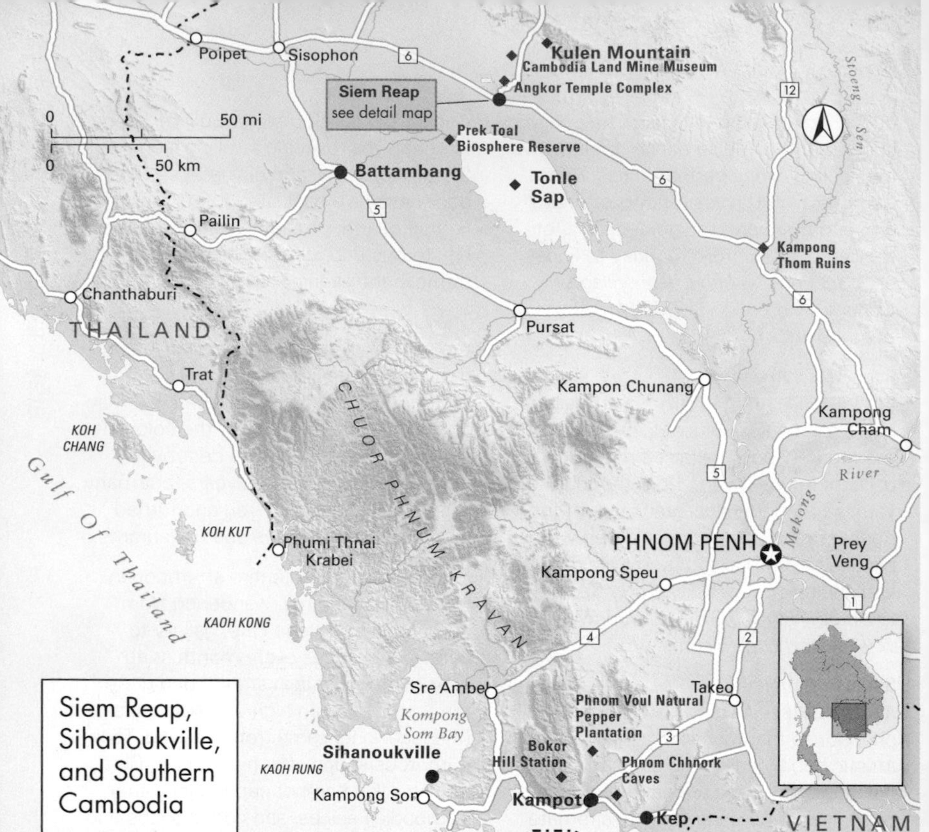

Royal Khmer Airlines and Angkor Air fly between Phnom Penh and Siem Reap (one hour; from $65 and up one-way). Siem Reap International Airport is 6 km (4 miles) northwest of town. The taxi fare to any hotel in Siem Reap is $5.

BOAT TRAVEL

The road to Phnom Penh was upgraded several years ago, but some tourists still prefer the six-hour boat trip on the Tonle Sap. High-speed ferries, or "bullet boats," depart from Phnom Penh for Siem Reap daily.

A daily boat travels from Battambang to Siem Reap (5 to 10 hours; $20) on the Tonle Sap. ■ **TIP→ In the dry season, the water level on the Tonle Sap is often low. Passengers may be required to switch boats, or boats might get stuck—a long ordeal.**

Boats arrive at the ferry port at Chong Khneas, 12 km (7½ miles) south of Siem Reap.

BUS TRAVEL

Siem Reap is accessible by direct bus from Phnom Penh (five to six hours; $5 to $13) on all major lines. Minvans also connect it to Kratie, Kampong Thom, and Battambang.

Travel agencies can help you arrange all bus trips.

CAR TRAVEL

The road to Siem Reap from Phnom Penh has greatly improved in recent years, and the trip by taxi takes four hours. Nevertheless, you'll be putting your life in the hands of daredevil drivers with little care for the rules of the road or the function of the brake pedal. Take the bus instead.

MOTO AND TUK-TUK TRAVEL

Tuk-tuk and moto drivers have kept apace with the growing number of tourists visiting Siem Reap: they'll find you—you won't need to find them. They charge about $2 to $4 for a trip within town, but be sure to settle on the fare before setting off, or use a ride-hail smartphone application like Grab and PassApp Taxi to secure a reasonable and fixed fare. There are no cruising taxis, but hotels can order one.

TOURS

Beyond Unique Escapes

BICYCLE TOURS | FAMILY | Temple tours, village trips, cooking classes, and a lot, lot more are offered by this tour operator, and it also runs the local NGO Husk, which has a real and positive impact on local communities. ✉ *717 St. 14* ☎ *077/562565, 063/969269* 🌐 *www.beyonduniqueescapes.co* 🎫 *From $25.*

Hanuman Travel

GUIDED TOURS | This is the Siem Reap branch of the tour operator based in Phnom Penh and offers the same services. A tried and tested operator, Hanuman, has good options for exploring this part of Cambodia on multiday tours with cultural, historical, and activity themes. ✉ *5 Krom 2, Phum Traeng* ☎ *023/218356, 012/807657* 🌐 *www.hanuman.travel.*

Indochine Exploration

ADVENTURE TOURS | Bespoke ecotourism options are offered throughout Cambodia by this company whose partners are conservationists and expert explorers. Many of the employees here previously worked for oSmoSe and other conservation groups, and this has become the preferred tour operator for all the established high-end hotels. A tour with Indochine Exploration will be a highlight of your trip to Siem Reap. ✉ *0108 Treang Village, Sloe Kran Commune* ☎ *092/650096* 🌐 *www.indochineex.com* 🎫 *From $65.*

★ oSmoSe Conservation Ecotourism Education

An agent of positive change in the area, oSmoSe, a nonprofit organization, has been fighting to conserve the unique biosphere of Tonle Sap and Prek Toal. On their exceptional tours you get to bird-watch at the bird sanctuary with an expert guide and also experience floating villages in a fascinating and respectful way. ✉ *Sala Kamroeuk* ✥ *Close to Wat Damnak* ☎ *012/832812, 063/765506* 🌐 *www.osmosetonlesap.net* 🎫 *From $105.*

Sights

Siem Reap is the base to use for exploring the temples at Angkor, but it has more to offer than that. It has its own great places to see, and there is something seductive about this city that makes visitors want to linger. You can wander around the contemporary Angkor National Museum, take a cooking class, visit a rural village, explore myriad art galleries, try a gourmet restaurant, or take a stroll down the central Pub Street. There's plenty to keep the temple-weary traveler occupied for two or three days, or even a week or more.

★ Angkor National Museum

MUSEUM | This modern, interactive museum, which opened in 2008, gracefully guides you through the rise and fall of the Angkorian Empires, covering the religions, kings, and geopolitics that drove the Khmer to create the monumental cities whose ruins are highly visible in modern-day Cambodia. With more than 1,300 artifacts on glossy display, complemented by multimedia installations, this museum experience helps demystify much of the material culture that visitors encounter at the archaeological parks and sites. The atmosphere is set in the impressive gallery of a thousand Buddhas, which plunges you into the serene spirituality that still dominates the region. Seven consequent galleries, set up chronologically, highlight the Funan and Chenia pre-Angkorian epochs, followed by the golden age of the Angkorian period led by the likes of King Soryavarman II, who built Angkor Wat. The final two galleries showcase stone inscriptions documenting some of the workings of the empires, and statues of Apsara, shedding light on the cult and fashions of these celestial dancers. The audio tour is excellent and well worth the extra $3. ✉ *968, Vithei Charles de Gaulle, Khrum 6, Phoum Salakanseng, Khom Svaydangum* ☎ *063/966601* 🌐 *www.angkornationalmuseum.com* 🎫 *$12.*

★ Angkor Temple Complex

ARCHAEOLOGICAL SITE | The temples of Angkor, hailed as "the eighth wonder of the world" by some, constitute one of the world's great ancient sites and Southeast Asia's most impressive archaeological treasure. The massive structures, surrounded by tropical forest, are comparable to Central America's Mayan ruins—and far exceed them in size. Angkor Wat is the world's largest religious structure—so large that it's hard to describe its breadth to someone who hasn't seen it. And that's just one temple in a complex of hundreds. In all, there are some 300 monuments reflecting Hindu and Buddhist influence scattered throughout the jungle, but only the largest have been excavated and only a few of those reconstructed. Most of these lie within a few miles of each other and can be seen in one day, though two or three days will allow you to better appreciate them. Most people visit the temples of Bayon and Baphuon, which face east, in the morning—the earlier you arrive, the better the light and the smaller the crowd—and west-facing Angkor Wat in the late afternoon, though this most famous of the temples can also be a stunning sight at sunrise. The woodland-surrounded Ta Prohm can be visited any time, though it is best photographed when cloudy, whereas the distant Banteay Srei is prettiest in the late-afternoon light. ✣ *5½ km (3½ miles) north of Siem Reap* 🌐 *www.autoriteapsara.org* 🎫 *$37 for 1 day, $62 for 3 days, $72 for 1 wk* ☞ *Skimpy clothing, such as short shorts and backless tops, violate the dress code of the complex. Shield yourself from the sun with light fabrics, and bring a wide-brimmed hat or an umbrella for shade.*

Cambodia Land Mine Museum

MUSEUM | Be sure to visit this museum, established by Aki Ra, a former child soldier who fought for the Khmer Rouge, the Vietnamese, and the Cambodian Army. Now he dedicates his life to removing the land mines he and thousands of others laid across Cambodia. His museum is a must-see, a sociopolitical eye-opener that portrays a different picture of Cambodia from the glorious temples and five-star hotels. Any tuk-tuk or taxi driver can find the museum. When in the Old Market area, visit the Akira Mine Action Gallery for more information on land mines and ways to help land-mine victims go to college. **■ TIP→ As it is a decent distance from Siem Reap, it's best to combine this with a visit to the Banteay Srey Temple complex.** ✣ *Off road to Angkor, 6 km (4 miles) south of Banteay Srey Temple, 25 km (15 miles) from Siem Reap* ☎ *015/674163* 🌐 *www.cambodialandminemuseum.org* 🎫 *$5.*

Restaurants

Abacus

$$$$ | **INTERNATIONAL** | Ideal for a romantic garden dinner or a fun, elegant night out with friends, Abacus offers an eclectic choice of French-international fusion cuisine. Through a weekly changing menu, chefs and co-owners Renaud and Pascal combine their creative talents and refined expertise to provide a high-quality, welcome change from traditional restaurants or bland hotel fare. **Known for:** foie gras; Abacus burger; impeccable service. [$] *Average main: $17* ✉ *Off Rd. 6* ✣ *Take Rd. 6 toward the airport, pass Angkor Hotel, and turn right at ACLEDA Bank.*

Continued on page 453

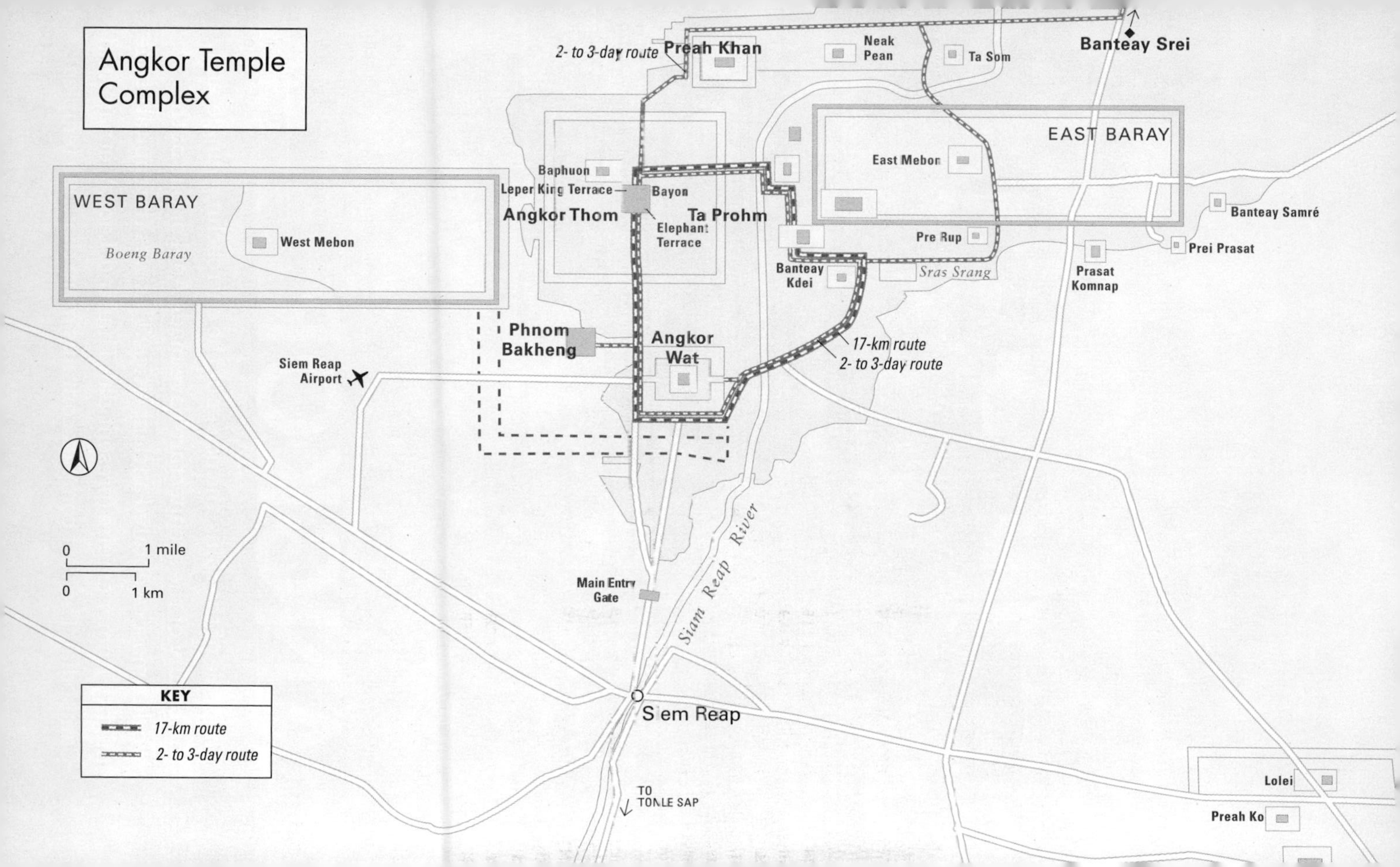
Angkor Temple Complex
2- to 3-day route
Preah Khan
Neak Pean
Ta Som
Banteay Srei
EAST BARAY
East Mebon
Baphuon
Leper King Terrace
Bayon
WEST BARAY
Angkor Thom
Ta Prohm
Elephant Terrace
Boeng Baray
West Mebon
Pre Rup
Banteay Samré
Prei Prasat
Banteay Kdei
Sras Srang
Prasat Komnap
Phnom Bakheng
Angkor Wat
17-km route
2- to 3-day route
Siem Reap Airport
0
1 mile
0
1 km
Main Entry Gate
Siam Reap River
KEY
17-km route
2- to 3-day route
Siem Reap
TO TONLE SAP
Lolei
Preah Ko

ANGKOR

by Christina Knight

The scale of the ruins, the power of the encroaching jungle, and the beauty of the architecture have made Angkor one of the world's most celebrated ancient cities. This was the capital of the mighty Khmer empire (present-day Thailand, Laos, Vietnam, and Cambodia). The vast complex contains more than 300 temples

and monuments that four centuries of kings built to honor the gods they believed they would become after they died. It's not just the size of the structures that takes your breath away; it's the otherworldly setting and a pervading sense of mystery.

THE CITY OF ANGKOR

Silk-cotton tree roots growing over the ruins at Ta Prohm.

CONSTRUCTION

Angkor, which simply means "city," was founded in 839 AD when King Jayavarman II completed the first temple, Phnom Bakheng, using sandstone from the Kulen mountains, northeast of Angkor. Jayavarman II had established the empire in 802, uniting various principalities, securing independence from Java (in present-day Indonesia), and declaring himself the world emperor as well as a "god who is king," or *devaraja*.

Over the next 400 years, each successive Khmer emperor added to Angkor, erecting a *wat*, or temple, to worship either Shiva or Vishnu. The Khmer empire was Hindu except during the rule of Jayavarman VII (1181–1220), who was a Mahayana Buddhist. Theravada Buddhism became the dominant religion in Cambodia after the decline of the Khmer empire, in the 15th century.

Kings situated buildings according to principles of cosmology and numerology, so the center of the city shifted over the centuries. Only the wats, built with reddish-brown laterite, ochre brick, or gray sandstone, have survived; wooden structures perished long ago.

Historians estimate that the royal city had a population of 100,000 in the late 13th century; at that time, London's population was roughly 80,000. The royal city was ringed by a larger medieval city about 3,000 square km (1,150 square mile)—the world's largest pre-industrial settlement and more than twice the size of present-day Los Angeles, with an estimated population of 1 million. At its height, the Khmer empire covered about 1 million square km (400,000 square mile), stretching east from the Burmese border to southern Vietnam and north from Malaysia to Laos.

Archaeologists have only excavated the largest of the hundreds of temples that once dotted the royal city, and even fewer have been restored. The most impressive and best preserved temple, Angkor Wat, is also the world's largest religious monument; it covers approximately 2 square km (¾ square mile), including its moat.

Angkor Wat.

Apsara bas-relief on a wall of Angkor Wat.

DECLINE AND RENEWAL

In 1431, Thailand's Ayutthaya kingdom invaded and sacked Angkor. The following year, the declining Khmer empire moved its kingdom to Phnom Penh, 315 km (195 mile) south. Though a handful of foreign adventurers visited Angkor in the following centuries, it wasn't until 1861, when Frenchman and naturalist Henri Mouhot published a book about the site, that Angkor became famous. By this time, looting foreigners and the insistent forces of time and nature had taken a toll on the complex. Restoration efforts began in the early 20th century but were interrupted by the Cambodian Civil War in the 1960s and '70s; in 1992, UNESCO declared Angkor a World Heritage Site. Since that time the number of visitors has risen an average of 2 million annually. You won't have the place to yourself, but it's unlikely to feel crowded in comparison to famous European sites.

ANGKOR WAT

A monk looking at Angkor Wat across the moat.

The best-preserved temple has become shorthand for the entire complex: Angkor Wat, built by King Suryavarman II in the early 12th century. The king dedicated Angkor Wat to Vishnu (the preserver and protector), breaking with tradition—Khmer kings usually built their temples to honor Shiva, the god of destruction and rebirth, whose powers the kings considered more cosmically essential than Vishnu's.

It helps to think of the ancient city as a series of concentric protective layers: a 190-m- (623-ft-) wide moat surrounds an outer wall that's 1,024 by 802 m (3,359 by 2,630 ft) long—walking around the outside of the wall is a more than 2-mi stroll. A royal city and palace once occupied the space inside the wall; you can still see traces of some streets, but the buildings did not survive. The temple itself sits on an elevated terrace that takes up about a tenth of the city.

APPROACHING THE TEMPLE

You'll reach the temple after crossing the moat, entering the western gateway (where you'll see a 10-foot, eight-armed Vishnu statue), and walking nearly a quarter of a mile along an unshaded causeway. Angkor Wat originally had nine towers (an auspicious number in Hindu mythology), though only five remain. These towers,

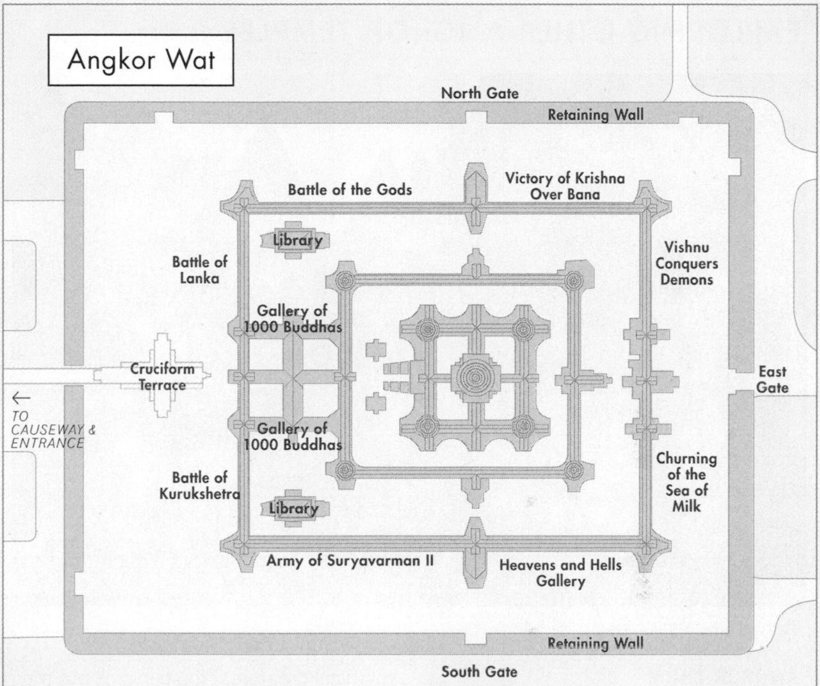

Angkor Wat

North Gate
Retaining Wall
Victory of Krishna Over Bana
Battle of the Gods
Library
Vishnu Conquers Demons
Battle of Lanka
Gallery of 1000 Buddhas
Cruciform Terrace
East Gate
← TO CAUSEWAY & ENTRANCE
Gallery of 1000 Buddhas
Churning of the Sea of Milk
Battle of Kurukshetra
Library
Army of Suryavarman II
Heavens and Hells Gallery
Retaining Wall
South Gate

which took 30 years to complete, are shaped like closed lotuses and form the center of the temple complex. Their ribbed appearance comes from rings of finials that also take the form of closed lotuses. These finials, along with statues of lions and multi-headed serpents called *nagas,* were believed to protect the temple from evil spirits.

Like the other major monuments at Angkor, the complex represents the Hindu universe. The central shrines symbolize Mt. Meru, mythical home of the Hindu gods, and the moats represent the seven oceans that surround Mt. Meru.

THE GALLERIES

Nearly 2,000 *Apsara*—celestial female dancers—are scattered in bas-relief on the outer entrances and columns of galleries. Inside the shaded galleries,

Bas-relief depicting a historical Khmer battle.

600 m (2,000 ft) of bas-reliefs tell epic tales from the *Ramayana,* the *Churning of the Sea of Milk* (gods and demons join forces to find the immortality elixir), the punishments of the 32 hells, and the less-imaginative rewards of the 37 heavens.

EXPLORING OTHER ANGKOR TEMPLES

Banteay Srei temple complex.

ANGKOR THOM

King Jayavarman VII built the massive city known as Angkor Thom in 1181 and changed the state religion to Buddhism (although subsequent kings reverted to Hinduism). At the center of the city stands the 12th-century **Bayon,** a large, ornate state temple that rises into many towers (37 remain today), most of which are topped with giant, serene, smiling boddhisattva faces on four sides. These faces, the most photogenic and beatific in all of Angkor, resemble both the king and the bodhisattva of compassion—a Buddhist twist on the king-as-a-god tradition.

On the walls of Bayon's central sanctuary are 1½ km (1 mile) of marvelous bas-relief murals depicting historic sea battles scenes from daily life, and Hindu gods and mythical creatures. You can pick out the Khmers in the reliefs because they are depicted with long earlobes; they frequently warred with the Cham, whose warriors wear headpieces that curl towards the jawline. Jayavarman VIII, a later king, added the Hindu iconography and destroyed some of his predecessor's Buddhist statuary.

King Jayavarman VII.

Just to the north of the Bayon is the slightly older **Baphuon,** which King Udayadityavarman II built in the mid-11th century as part of a small settlement that predated Angkor Thom. The king built the temple on a hill without proper supports, so it collapsed during a 16th-century earthquake. In that same century, a magnificent reclining Buddha was added to the three-tiered temple pyramid, which was originally a Shiva sanctuary. The temple is undergoing reconstruction and is not open to the public; however, the exterior gate and elevated walkway are open.

Once the foundation of the royal audience hall, the **Elephant Terrace** is adorned with carvings of *garudas* (bird-like creatures), lion-headed figures, and elephants tugging at strands of lotuses with their trunks.

Located at the north end of the Elephant Terrance, the **Terrace of the Leper King** area is named after a stone statue found here that now resides in the National Museum; a copy remains here. Precisely who the Leper King was and why he was so named remains uncertain, though several legends offer speculation. (One theory is that damage to the sculpture made the figure look leprous, leading people in later generations to believe the person depicted had been ill.) Today the terrace's two walls create a maze lined some seven layers high with gods, goddesses, and nagas.

TA PROHM

Jayavarman VII dedicated this large monastic complex to his mother. It once housed 2,700 monks and 615 royal dancers. Today the moss-covered ruins lie between tangles of silk-cotton and strangler fig trees whose gnarled offshoots drape window frames and grasp walls. This gorgeous, eerie spot gives you an idea of what the Angkor complex looked like when westerners first discovered it in the 19th century. Another famous mother—Angelina Jolie—shot scenes of *Lara Croft: Tomb Raider* here.

Sculptures of *devas* leading to Angkor Thom.

Two-storeyed pavilion at Preah Khan.

PHNOM BAKHENG

One of the oldest Angkor structures, dating from the 9th century, Bakheng temple was carved out of a rocky hilltop and occupied the center of the first royal city site. Phnom Bakheng is perhaps the most popular sunset destination, with views of the Tonle Sap Lake and the towers of Angkor Wat rising above the jungle. Climb a shaded trail or ride an elephant up the hill. You'll still have to climb steep stairs to reach the top of the temple.

PREAH KHAN

Dedicated to the Jayavarman VII's father, mossy Preah Khan was also a monastery. Its long, dim corridors are dramatically lit by openings where stones have fallen out. Preah Khan is the only Angkor site with an annex supported by rounded, not square, columns.

BANTEAY SREI

This restored 10th-century temple, whose name means "citadel of women," lies 38 km (24 mile) northeast of Siem Reap. Its scale is small (no stairs to climb), but its dark pink sandstone is celebrated for its intricate carvings of scenes from Hindu tales. The site is at least a 40-minute, somewhat-scenic drive from other Angkor sites; your driver will charge extra to take you here, but it's less crowded than other temples.

Did You Know?

Time has erased the red lacquer and gold leaf that originally accented Angkor's many bas-reliefs; oil from the hands of countless visitors has darkened the dancing *Asparas* and warring soldiers.

Planning Your Visit

Timing

You can see most of the significant temples and monuments in a one-day sprint, although a three-day visit is recommended. If you have just one day, stick to a 17-km (11-mile) route that takes in the south gate of Angkor Thom, Bayon, Baphuon, the Elephant Terrace and the Terrace of the Leper King, and Ta Prohm, ending with a visit to Angkor Wat. Leave the most time for the Bayon and Angkor Wat. If you have two or three days, cover ground at a more leisurely pace. You can also tack on additional sites such as Preah Khan, Neak Pean, Pre Rup, Phnom Bakheng, or Banteay Srei. Another option is East Mebon, a 10th-century ruin in the East Baray. Alternatively, visit the West Baray, once Angkor's largest reservoir it still fills with water during the rainy season. The best way to experience Angkor is with a guide, who can help you decode the bas-reliefs and architectural styles.

When to Go

Most people visit the east-facing temples of Bayon and Baphuon in the morning—the earlier you arrive, the better the light and the smaller the crowd. West-facing Angkor Wat gets the best light in the late afternoon, though these temples can also be stunning at sunrise. You can visit the woodland-surrounded Ta Prohm at any time, though photos will turn out best on cloudy days; the distant Banteay Srei is prettiest in late-afternoon light. If quiet is your priority, beat the crowds by visiting sunset spots in the morning and east-facing temples in the afternoon.

Getting Around

The entrance to the complex is 4 km (2½ miles) north of Siem Reap; you'll need to arrange transportation to get here and around. Most independent travelers hire a car and driver ($35 to $50 per day), moto (motorcycle) driver ($12 to $18), or tuk-tuk ($20 to $35, seats up to four). Renting bicycles ($3 to $5) or electric bikes ($5 to $8) is also an option if you're up for the exertion in the heat. Tourists may not drive motorized vehicles in the park. If you hire a driver, he'll stick with you for the whole day. Going with a guide is strongly recommended.

Admission

The Angkor complex is open from 5:30 am to 6 pm. Admission is $37 for one day, $62 for three consecutive days, and $72 for a week. You'll receive a ticket with your photo on it. Don't lose the ticket—you'll need it at each site and to access the restrooms. If you buy your ticket at 5 pm, you'll be admitted for the remaining open hour, in time to see the sunset from Phnom Bakeng to catch the last rays setting Angkor Wat aglow. Your ticket will also count for the following day.

What to Wear

Skimpy clothes, such as short shorts and backless tops, violate the park's dress code. Shield yourself from the sun with light fabrics, and bring a wide-brimmed hat or even a shade umbrella. Note, however, that those wearing Vietnamese-style conical hats will be turned away since they cause offense. Drivers remain with the vehicle, so you can leave items you don't want to carry.

Hiring an Angkor Guide

A guide can greatly enrich your appreciation of Angkor's temples, which are full of details you might miss on your own. English-speaking guides can be hired through the tourism office on Pokambor Avenue, across from the Raffles Grand Hotel d'Angkor. But the best way to find a guide is through your hotel or guesthouse. Ask around. Most guides who work for tour companies (and the tourism office) are freelancers, and often when you book through a tour company, you'll pay a higher price. Find a young staffer at your hotel or guesthouse and tell him or her what you want—the type of tour, what you hope to learn from your guide, your particular interests in the temples.

Prices usually run around $45 a day, not including transportation, for a well-informed, English-speaking guide. Your guide will meet you at your hotel, along with a tuk-tuk or car driver, whom you'll need to pay separately ($12 to $15 per day for a tuk-tuk; $25 for a car). Guides, who are almost always men, will typically cater to your interests and know how to avoid crowds. You aren't expected to join your guide for lunch. Usually your driver will drop you and your guide at a temple and pick you up at another entrance, meaning you won't have to double back on yourself.

Hanuman Travel. If you feel more comfortable booking through a travel company, Hanuman Travel is an excellent choice. The expert company, which works throughout Cambodia and surrounding countries, has established a foundation to help eradicate poverty in Cambodia's hinterlands. Your tourist dollars will go toward wells, water filters, mosquito nets, and other amenities that can greatly improve a rural family's life. ✉ *12 St. 310, Sangkat Tonle Bassac* ☎ *023/218396, 023/218398* 🌐 *www.hanuman.travel.*

After 100 meters turn left ☎ *063/763660, 012/644286* 🌐 *restaurantabacus.com* ⏲ *Closed June and 1 wk in mid-Apr.*

★ Cuisine Wat Damnak

$$$$ | ECLECTIC | Cuisine Wat Damnak offers a unique journey for the taste buds with its five- or six-course set menus (changing every fortnight). Beyond the sophisticated indoor sala and romantic garden, the concept here is Cambodian food remodeled into creative modern dishes by French chef Joannes Riviere, whose knowledge of the area allows him to source rare ingredients such as shellfish unique to the Mekong and Tonle Sap lake, fresh lotus seeds, wild lily stems, and edible flowers. **Known for:** good wine list; generous portions; Mekong langoustines with pineapple and herbs. 💲 *Average main: $26* ✉ *Chocolate Rd., Sala Kamreuk Commune* ✣ *Between Psa Dey Hoy market and Angkor High School* ☎ *077/347762* 🌐 *www.cuisinewatdamnak.com* ⏲ *Closed Sun., Mon., and Apr. No lunch.*

★ Devatas Restaurant

$ | CAMBODIAN | Delightful and authentic Khmer cuisine is served under thatched roofs in a tropical garden next to Bang Khnar, a pre-Angkorian lake strewn with lotus flowers. Hammocks and loungers encourage diners to linger longer for coffee, conversation, or a postmeal nap. **Known for:** fish amok; eggplant with minced meat; green papaya salad with shrimp and pork strips. 💲 *Average main: $5* ✉ *Banteay Srey* ✣ *500 meters (1/3 mile) from the Cambodian Landmine*

Museum ☎ 011/292142, 081/849632 🌐 www.devatas-restaurant.com.

Il Forno

$$ | **ITALIAN** | Rustic brick walls and aged-effect saffron walls give this "little corner of Italy" a homely feel. The Neapolitan wood-fire oven makes delicious pizza and calzone specialties, and there's an authentic variety of pasta dishes, platters for one or for sharing, and *primi piatti* on offer. **Known for:** good regional wines; dragon-fruit–and–passion-fruit panna cotta; four-cheese gnocchi. *Average main: $10 ✉ Pari's Alley, 16 The-Lane, Old Market ☎ 078/208174, 063/763380 🌐 ilforno.restaurant/siem-reap/.*

★ Mahob

$$ | **CAMBODIAN** | **FAMILY** | The name translates as "food," and if you're after a Cambodian menu that appeals to the Western palate but is not without an adventurous element, this is an excellent choice. Try deep-fried frogs' legs coated with crispy rice flakes, or wok-fried local beef with tree red ants served with rice. **Known for:** chef Sothea's attention to detail; curries; cooking classes. *Average main: $8 ✉ 137 Traing Village, Group 3 ✣ Off Charles de Gaulle Ave. ☎ 063/966986, 017/550206 🌐 www.mahobkhmer.com.*

★ Mie Cafe

$$ | **ASIAN** | This top-notch open-air garden restaurant, out-of-the-way from the noisier part of the city, reflects the forward-thinking new generation of postdisaster Cambodia, represented here by the visionary young owner, Siv Pola. Everything is prepared with sensitivity, creativity, and great skill: try the Tonle Sap Fish, a carpaccio of snakehead fish fillet, marinated in fresh picked herbs, with a tempura poached egg. **Known for:** spicy tuna tartare with mango; creamy chocolate cake; relaxing setting. *Average main: $9 ✉ 0085 Phum Treng, Khum Slorgram ☎ 012/791371, 069/999096 🌐 miecafe-siemreap.com ⏲ Closed Tues. and Oct.*

Moloppor

$ | **ASIAN** | This pleasant Japanese-style café by the river serves good snacks, small plates, desserts, and drinks. Try a cashew-nut shake—you'll probably want a second. *Average main: $4 ✉ E. River Rd. ☎ 063/504–6888 🌐 www.moloppor-cafe.com/restaurant/ ▭ No credit cards.*

★ The Sugar Palm

$$ | **CAMBODIAN** | Even superstar chef Gordon Ramsay swears by this Siem Reap institution, whose new location, set in a beautiful and breezy wooden sala, doesn't betray owner Khetana's colorful enthusiasm for the traditional Khmer cuisine she learned from her mother and grandmother. You can order à la carte or opt for one of the sampler platters ($15), which offer house signature specialties like crispy shrimp cakes with black-pepper sauce or pomelo salad with chicken. **Known for:** uniquely soufflélike fish amok made to order; prahok khtis; vegetarian options. *Average main: $8 ✉ St. 27 ✣ Opposite Pannasastra University ☎ 012/818143 🌐 www.thesugarpalm.com ⏲ Closed Sun.*

Tell Restaurant

$$ | **GERMAN** | German dishes, yummy cheese fondue, as well as Khmer and Asian specialties are served at this well-run restaurant. The portions of German pork knuckle and schnitzel are huge, and imported Bavarian wheat beer is an ideal accompaniment. *Average main: $8 ✉ 374 Sivatha Rd. ☎ 063/963289.*

The Village Cafe

$ | **FRENCH** | Possibly the most happening restaurant in Kandal Village, this French-owned and retro-themed bar and international bistro is the go-to place for French cuisine and Khmer staple dishes. Their good selection of wines and cocktails also attracts Siem Reap's drinking elite, especially on Funky Friday, their club night with live DJs. *Average main: $7 ✉ 586 Tep Vong St. ☎ 092/30540 ▭ No credit cards ⏲ No lunch.*

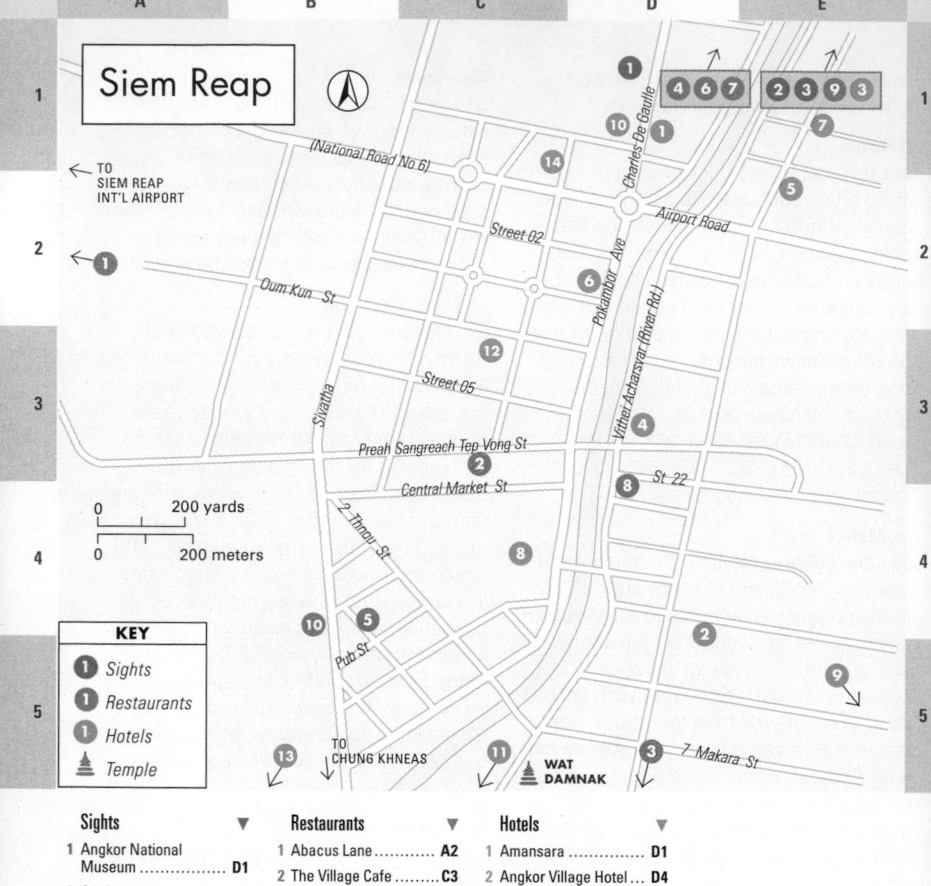

Sights

1 Angkor National Museum D1

2 Angkor Temple Complex E1

3 Cambodia Land Mine Museum E1

Restaurants

1 Abacus Lane A2

2 The Village Cafe C3

3 Cuisine Wat Damnak... D5

4 Devatas Restaurant.... D1

5 Il Forno.................. B4

6 Mahob D1

7 Mie Cafe................. D1

8 Moloppor D3

9 The Sugar Palm.......... E1

10 Tell Restaurant.......... B4

Hotels

1 Amansara D1

2 Angkor Village Hotel ... D4

3 Angkor Village Resort...................... E1

4 Belmond La Résidence d'Angkor D3

5 Borann, l'Auberge des Temples.............. E2

6 FCC Angkor.............. D2

7 Heritage Suites Hotel ... E1

8 Ivy Guesthouse & Bar... C4

9 Navutu Dreams E5

10 Raffles Grand Hôtel d'Angkor D1

11 Rambutan Resort........ C5

12 Shinta Mani Angkor..... C3

13 Sojourn Boutique Villas...................... B5

14 Victoria Angkor Resort & Spa C1

Hotels

★ Amansara

$$$$ | **RESORT** | The jewel in the crown of Siem Reap hotels, Amansara offers exceptional service, atmosphere, and accommodations in surroundings of understated luxury. **Pros:** some suites have private plunge pool; impressive attention to detail by friendly management and staff; 10 minutes from Angkor. **Cons:** pricey; no in-room TV; feels too proper. *Rooms from: $760 ✉ Road to Angkor ✥ Behind Tourism Dept. ☎ 063/760333 🌐 www.amanresorts.com 24 suites 🍽 No meals.*

Angkor Village Hotel

$$$ | **HOTEL** | This oasis of Khmer-style wooden buildings, lush gardens, and pools filled with lotus blossoms lies along a stone path a couple of blocks from the river in a green neighborhood. **Pros:** central location and easy access to tuk-tuks; spa with traditional therapies; the hotel organizes activities and trips. **Cons:** road can get congested during the rainy season; some rooms are looking a little worn; can get damp in rainy season. *Rooms from: $150 ✉ Wat Bo Rd. ☎ 063/963361 🌐 www.angkorvillagehotel.asia 38 rooms 🍽 Free breakfast.*

Angkor Village Resort

$$$ | **RESORT** | **FAMILY** | This resort, between Siem Reap and Angkor Wat, offers guests who value their time and privacy a real sense of retreat from the rest of the world after a busy day of sightseeing. **Pros:** unusual pool; spacious, comfortable rooms; good breakfast buffet. **Cons:** somewhat out of the way; noisy air-conditioning. *Rooms from: $130 ✉ Rd. 60, Phum Traeng ✥ Off Charles de Gaulle Ave. ☎ 063/963561 🌐 www.angkorvillage.com 80 cottages 🍽 Free breakfast.*

Belmond La Résidence d'Angkor

$$$$ | **RESORT** | **FAMILY** | Swathed in ancient Angkor style, this luxurious retreat, now part of the Belmond group, is within a walled compound with lovely gardens beside the river. **Pros:** attractive riverside location; family-friendly services; excellent restaurant. **Cons:** some rooms have less than spectacular views; River Road rooms can get traffic noise; steep room service cost. *Rooms from: $225 ✉ River Rd., Wat Bo ☎ 063/963390, 800/237–1236 reservations 🌐 www.residencedangkor.com 59 rooms 🍽 Free breakfast.*

Good Deeds

Angkor Hospital for Children. Not far from the Old Market on Achamen Street sits the Angkor Hospital for Children, founded in 1999 by Japanese photographer Kenro Izu. It provides pediatric care to more than 100,000 children each year. Give blood, save a life. *✉ Tep Vong (Achamean) Rd. and Oum Chhay St., Sangkat Svay Dangkum ☎ 063/963409 🌐 angkorhospital.org.*

Borann, l'Auberge des Temples

$$ | **HOTEL** | The accommodations are attractive and the rates reliable at this tranquil, small hotel, a couple of blocks east of the river behind La Noria. **Pros:** large rooms; traditional style; terrace for every room. **Cons:** small pool; patchy Wi-Fi. *Rooms from: $65 ✉ Wat Bo St., Wat Bo ✥ North of N6 ☎ 063/964242 🌐 www.borann.com 20 rooms 🍽 Free breakfast.*

FCC Angkor Hotel

$$$ | **HOTEL** | Next to the Royal Residence, the former French consulate has been turned into an inviting retreat along the river, removed from the noise of the city center. **Pros:** sleek contemporary design; riverside location; on-site spa. **Cons:** could do with a sprucing up; poor lighting in some rooms; expanding soon to another wing. *Rooms from: $125 ✉ Pokambor Ave. ☎ 063/760280, 023/992284 🌐 www.*

There are about 200 faces of Lokesvara, the bodhisattva of compassion, on Bayon's towers.

fcccambodia.com 🛏 *31 rooms* 🍽 *Free breakfast.*

★ Heritage Suites Hotel

$$$$ | **HOTEL** | In a quiet neighborhood, close to the town center and river, this iconic boutique hotel charms with its understated luxury and discrete attention to detail. **Pros:** warm, attentive staff; quiet, laid-back atmosphere; restaurant and bar are top drawer. **Cons:** hidden in Siem Reap's backstreets; daytime noise coming from nearby kindergarten; restaurant menu on the pricier side. 💲 *Rooms from: $210* ✉ *Wat Polanka Rd.* ☎ *063/969100* 🌐 *www.heritagesuiteshotel.com* 🛏 *26 rooms* 🍽 *Free breakfast.*

Ivy Guesthouse & Bar

$$ | **B&B/INN** | As one of the best backpacker's options, the Ivy offers cheap accommodations a short walking distance to most central spots. **Pros:** central location; low prices; near all local nightlife. **Cons:** rooms somewhat in need of an upgrade; breakfast not included; very basic. 💲 *Rooms from: $8* ✉ *Central Market St. and Shinta Mani St., Old Market* ☎ *012/800860 cell phone* 🌐 *ivy-guesthouse.com* 💳 *No credit cards* 🛏 *20 rooms* 🍽 *No meals.*

Navutu Dreams

$$ | **RESORT** | A slightly different Siem Reap experience is offered at this countryside bungalow resort, where the concept of well-being is promoted via resident yoga instructors, holistic practitioners, and healthy eating options. **Pros:** free yoga classes; free airport pickup; tuk-tuk shuttle package available. **Cons:** about 10 minutes out of town; limited breakfast options; some public spaces showing wear. 💲 *Rooms from: $100* ✉ *Navutu Rd.* ☎ *063/964864, 092/141694* 🌐 *navutudreams.com* 🕒 *Closed Sept.* 🛏 *26 rooms, 4 suites* 🍽 *Free breakfast.*

Raffles Grand Hotel d'Angkor

$$$$ | **HOTEL** | Built in 1932 and still featuring the cage elevator from that year in the lobby, this grande dame was restored and reopened after near destruction by occupying Khmer Rouge guerrillas. **Pros:** picturesque gardens; excellent restaurant; nicely designed and decorated.

Cons: somewhat dependant on their name and former glory; more impersonal than smaller hotels; outside the center of Siem Reap. $ *Rooms from: $190* ✉ *1 Vithei Charles de Gaulle, Khom Svaydangum* ☎ *063/963888* 🌐 *www.raffles.com/siem-reap* *99 rooms, 18 suites, 2 villas* 🍽 *Free breakfast.*

★ Rambutan Resort

$$ | **B&B/INN** | This gem of a getaway is one of the better boutique accommodations around, with highly curated rooms, most with balconies and outdoor bathtubs, grouped around a stone-and-palm-enclosed saltwater pool. **Pros:** good prices; friendly staff; tasty and curated breakfast. **Cons:** tricky access; small swimming pool; front door closes early. $ *Rooms from: $90* ✉ *Krom 10, Rambutan La., Wat Damnak* ☎ *012/654638* 🌐 *rambutansiemreap.com* *43 rooms* 🍽 *Free breakfast.*

★ Shinta Mani Angkor

$$$$ | **HOTEL** | Not only will you sleep and eat in luxurious style, your money will also help support projects bringing clean water, transportation, and jobs to underprivileged communities, via the Shinta Mani Foundation. **Pros:** Shinta Mani is a beacon in Siem Reap for the nonstop work it does to help and promote charitable causes; good location; great facilities. **Cons:** no elevator, which limits some accessibility; not very family-friendly; rooms' wardrobe space could be bigger. $ *Rooms from: $200* ✉ *Oun Khum and 14th Sts., Old French Quarter* ☎ *063/761998* 🌐 *www.shintamani.com* *62 rooms* 🍽 *Free breakfast.*

★ Sojourn Boutique Villas

$$$$ | **RESORT** | The layout of these villas, each with a pool or garden view, offers privacy and relaxation in lovingly maintained verdant grounds, and your stay will help the owners' ongoing support for underprivileged locals. **Pros:** poolside restaurant serves Khmer specialties; extremely knowledgeable management; quality spa. **Cons:** a 15-minute ride from town center; 1980s-style swim-up pool bar not for everyone; inconsistent Wi-Fi. $ *Rooms from: $180* ✉ *Treak Village Rd., Treak Village* ☎ *012/923437* 🌐 *www.sojournsiemreap.com* *11 rooms* 🍽 *Free breakfast.*

Night Flights

Around sunset, the sky fills with thousands of large bats, which make their homes in the trees behind the Preah Ang Chek Preah Ang Chorm Shrine, near the gardens in front of the Raffles hotel.

Victoria Angkor Resort & Spa

$$ | **RESORT** | Just west of the Royal Gardens stands this sophisticated resort modeled on a strong colonial aesthetic. **Pros:** attentive service; friendly staff; top-quality breakfast buffet. **Cons:** a bit of a commercial feel; spa leaves much to be desired; can get crowded with tour groups. $ *Rooms from: $100* ✉ *National Hwy. 6 and Sivatha Rd., Khom Svaydangum* ☎ *063/760428* 🌐 *www.victoriaangkorhotel.com/* *129 rooms* 🍽 *Free breakfast.*

Nightlife

Most of Siem Reap's nightlife is concentrated around the Old Market, particularly on vibrant Pub Street, and in Kandal Village, where some of the most popular spots are to be found. Just get a little lost, and you're sure to find a hangout that fits your style.

Asana Old Wooden House

BARS/PUBS | A grown-up playground strewn with hammocks, wooden bar stools, and tree-trunk tables, Asana is uniquely located in one of the few remaining old, traditional Khmer houses in Siem Reap. It attracts a fun, artsy crowd and hosts occasional performances. Among a list of regular snacks and drinks, try the signature cocktail—tamarind sauce, made with rum, tamarind juice, Kaffir leaf, and lemony rice-paddy herbs. You can sign up for a cocktail-making class, too. ✉ *St. 7 and The Lane, Old French Quarter* ☎ *092/987801* 🌐 *www.asana-cambodia.com.*

Balthazar Wine Bar

WINE BARS—NIGHTLIFE | This French-owned and brilliantly designed wine bar across the river has outdoor or indoor seating and a fantastic selection of international wines. Don't forget to try the "planches"—cold cuts and cheese platters—that make a night here all the more worthwhile. ✉ *Corner St. 24* ☎ *010/270645.*

Laundry Bar

BARS/PUBS | A favorite among visitors and expats yearning for a place to chill out, this bar is a little away from the madding crowds of Pub Street and features local and touring bands. When no live bands are playing, it's also popular for its creative cocktails and funky music playlists. ✉ *St. 9 and Psah Chas Alley 1, Old Market* ☎ *016/962026.*

Long's Bar

BARS/PUBS | A dimly lit, air-conditioned oasis of calm in the bustle of Siem Reap's tourist district. Owner Long, a skilled barista, is very passionate about his craft and always happy to entertain his patrons as he keeps ice-cold beers, good wines, and unique cocktails flowing. ✉ *Doung Hem St., Old Market* ✣ *Between St. 7 and The Lanes* ☎ *012/447363.*

★ Miss Wong

BARS/PUBS | A favorite haunt of creative types, eclectic expats, and guests from exclusive resorts, this bar stands out with its sexy 1920s Shanghai-kitsch aesthetic—red walls, gold lanterns, and low lighting. Immersed in an era of glamorous decadence, guests are easily seduced into tasting cocktails made using local herbs, such as the apricot liqueur and Kaffir lime–infused gin martini. Dim sum and Asian-fusion finger food are also on the menu. ✉ *The-Lane* ☎ *092/428332* 🌐 *www.misswong.net.*

Nest Angkor

BARS/PUBS | For a change of scene head to this restaurant-bar located in a landscaped garden, where guests are invited to sip their designer cocktails lying on canopied loungers. There are occasional DJ sets, too. ✉ *Sivatha Blvd.* ☎ *063/966381* 🌐 *nestangkor.com.*

Picasso Tapas Bar

BARS/PUBS | A real hub for foreign residents, the barrel-shaped Picasso is a fun option for those who crave a few tasty Spanish tapas dishes with their drinks to keep them going late into the night. ✉ *The Alley West, Old Market* 🌐 *www.picassostapas.com.*

★ The Yellow Sub

BARS/PUBS | This off-the-wall, four-story gastropub is the owners' gushing tribute to the Beatles, whose memorabilia—and even personal objects such as toys, paintings, and family photos—decks practically every surface. Wacky cocktails such as the bubblegum martini are complemented by snacks like crunchy popcorn-crusted prawns. It's a real hit with the expat crowd. ■ **TIP→ Take in the sunset over Siem Reap from the lovely fourth-floor terrace.** ✉ *9A The Lane, Old Market* ☎ *088/665–5335.*

Performing Arts

The 1961

ART GALLERIES—ARTS | Get inspired! A really interesting initiative, The 1961 is a gallery-art-events-cowork space. People gather for the quality exhibitions, to enjoy cool drinks in the outdoor pavilion, or just to find a quiet little spot to catch up on some work and have a coffee. The regular exhibitions feature local and international artists and aim to bring them closer to their audiences, showcasing classic to avant-garde, and visual to musical forms of art. ✉ *211 Osaphear St., Upper West River Side* ☎ *015/378088.*

★ Phare Cambodian Circus

CIRCUSES | FAMILY | Cambodia's answer to the Cirque du Soleil is a must-see show. Previously only a traveling show, it has now found a permanent home in Siem Reap, in a cool, pink, high-top tent behind Angkor National Museum, although one of its troupes continues to take the show on the road internationally. The high-energy performances combine Cambodian storytelling traditions with circus arts, dance, acrobatics, and acting to captivate audiences every night. The Phare School is a charitable organization that has a positive impact on poor communities. **■ TIP→ Most seating is first-come-first-served, so try to get there early.** ✉ *Comaille Rd.* ✣ *Off Charles de Gaulle Ave.* ☎ *015/499480, 092/225320* 🌐 *www.pharecambodiancircus.org* 🎟 *$35.*

Shopping

Angkor Night Market

MARKET | Here at this lively flea market, you can practice your bargaining skills and get lost in a maze that includes a food hall, massage stands, bars, and an enormous variety of clothes, accessories, souvenirs, food and cosmetic products, jewelry, and more. ✉ *Sivatha Blvd., Old Market* 🌐 *www.angkornightmarket.com.*

Artisans Angkor

CRAFTS | With 38 workshops in Siem Reap and more than 800 craftspeople employed around the country, Artisans Angkor offers a dazzling selection of Cambodian fine arts and crafts, accessories, and silverware from all over the country, and you can see skills such as woodworking, silk painting, and lacquering. It is refreshing that the movement toward the renewal and modernization of arts, crafts, and design is gathering momentum, with many of the high-grade products available in Siem Reap now manufactured locally. ✉ *Stung Thmey St.* ☎ *063/963330* 🌐 *www.artisansdangkor.com.*

The Best of the Best 

Reliable international chains have begun to open along the road to Angkor, and both the dusty airport road and the town's noisy thoroughfares are clogged with upper-end accommodations. Nevertheless, why settle for a lousy location? Siem Reap offers several superb options in the quaint and quiet river area. Booking a room in a high-price hotel in this quarter means that your view of the hotel pool won't include the neighbors' laundry line, and will delight you with natural splendor instead of traffic jams.

Eric Raisina Couture House

CLOTHING | Madagascar-born, French-raised fashion designer Eric Raisina has a couple of outlets in Siem Reap where he presents his impeccably stylish couture designs. The world-acclaimed designer uses stunning Khmer silks to create clothing and accessories that clearly stand a head above the rest. You'll find this outlet next to the Shinta Mani Hotel. **■ TIP→ You can also visit his atelier, at 75–81 Charles de Gaulle Avenue, by appointment only.** ✉ *Charles de Gaulle, Sangkat Svay Dangkum* ☎ *063/963207 atelier, for appointments, 063/963210 Cassia Gallery* 🌐 *www.ericraisina.com.*

★ Kandal Village

SHOPPING NEIGHBORHOODS | This exclusive area near the center of town is a great place to find a range of upscale shops and cafés offering tasty bites to maintain your energy levels. Get eccentric artworks from the cool Trunkh or elegant luxury gifts from talented designer

Louise Loubatieres. Clothing designer Sirivan Chak Dumas presents her collections at Sirivan, and you can pick up some exquisite handmade silks from the Takeo Province at Neary Khmer. If all this shopping makes you weary, treat yourself to a relaxing treatment at Frangipani Spa or check out some local art at For Art's Sake. ⊠ *Hap Guan St.*

Mekong Quilts
CRAFTS | Offering employment opportunities to disadvantaged women, Mekong Quilts sells beautiful handmade, durable quilts of all designs, colors, styles, and sizes. ⊠ *5 Sivatha Blvd., Old Market* ☎ *063/964498.*

Psar Chaa Old Market
OUTDOOR/FLEA/GREEN MARKETS | Perfect for last-minute shopping, you'll find just about everything here, from clothing to traditional woodcrafts, fabrics, and ceramic home-style items, kitschy souvenirs, attractive silverware, and all varieties of freshly cooked or packaged foods. ⊠ *Market St. and Pokombor Ave.*

Senteurs d'Angkor
FOOD/CANDY | This store transforms spices and herbs used traditionally in Cambodia into delightful cosmetic or deli food products. Here you can find Kampot pepper, Rattanakiri coffee, soaps made with lemongrass, turmeric, jasmine, or mango, and lots more. All the products make excellent gifts—especially for yourself. ⊠ *Alley West, Old Market* ☎ *012/954815, 063/964801* 🌐 *www.senteursdangkor.com.*

Theam's House
ART GALLERIES | This place specializes in unique lacquerware designs such as polychrome paintings and trademark colored elephants, as well as elegant traditional wood-carved Buddha statues and home style items. ⊠ *25 Phum Veal, Kokchak Commune* 🌐 *www.theamshouse.com.*

Tonle Sap

10 km (6 miles) south of Siem Reap.

Covering 2,600 square km (1,000 square miles) in the dry season, Cambodia's vast Tonle Sap is the biggest freshwater lake in Southeast Asia. Its unique annual cycle of flood expansion and retreat dictates Cambodia's rice production and supplies of fish. During the rainy season the Mekong River backs into the Tonle Sap River, pushing waters into the lake, which quadruples in size. In the dry season, as the Mekong lowers, the Tonle Sap River reverses its direction, draining the lake. Boats make the river journey to the lake from Phnom Penh and Battambang, tying up at Chong Khneas, 12 km (7½ miles) south of Siem Reap. Two-hour tours of the lake, costing $15 to $20, set out from Chong Khneas, and you can tour the floating villages, with prices starting at $20.

GETTING HERE AND AROUND

Boats make the river journey to the lake from Phnom Penh ($30) and Battambang ($20; usually during the wet season, May to October only), tying up at Chong Khneas, 12 km (7½ miles) south of Siem Reap.

Two-hour tours of the lake ($15) set out from Chong Khneas; arrange them at any travel agent in Siem Reap.

Transportation to and from the Tonle Sap can be arranged at any hotel or travel agent. Alternatively, ask any tuk-tuk or moto ($7 to $12).

Sights

★ Prek Toal Biosphere Reserve
NATURE PRESERVE | Between Chong Khneas and Battambang, this is mainland Southeast Asia's most important waterbird nesting site. It's a spectacular scene if you visit at the start of the dry season (November and December), when water remains high and thousands of rare

Did You Know?

The roots that creep over the ruins of Ta Prohm belong to either silk-cotton trees or thinner strangler fig trees. Strangler figs grow out of crevices in other trees, sometimes smothering their hosts over time.

Cambodia's Endangered Species

In an ironic contrast to the Khmer Rouge atrocities, at least some of Cambodia's wildlands and wildlife populations emerged from that period intact, and therefore the country has a far different scenario than that faced by its neighbors, where the rarest of species were expunged years ago.

The Prek Toal Biosphere Reserve is Southeast Asia's most important waterbird nesting site, home to several endangered species. Near Sre Ambel, in what was a Khmer Rouge hotbed, conservationists are working to save the Cambodian royal turtle, which was thought extinct until the early 2000s. In Kratie some of the world's last Irrawaddy dolphins swim the Mekong in another area long held by the Khmer Rouge; and in Mondulkiri, conservationists report an increase in wildlife species in recent years.

The more tourists who express interest in Cambodia's natural environment, the better the outlook for these species and others. The jungles remain threatened by illegal logging (just visit Stung Treng and Ratanakiri), and poaching is common. But if those in charge begin to see serious tourist dollars connected to conservation, there may be hope yet.

birds begin to nest. Visits can be booked through **oSmoSe Conservation Ecotourism Education**. Day tours and overnight stays at the Prek Toal Research Station can be arranged. Prices vary. ✉ *Siem Reap.*

Kulen Mountain

50 km (31 miles) north of Siem Reap.

King Jayavarman II established this mountain retreat 50 km (31 miles) northeast of Siem Reap in AD 802, the year regarded as the start of the Angkor dynasty. The area is strewn with the ruins of Khmer temples from that time, when the mountain was revered as holy, with a hallowed river and a waterfall. Admission to the area costs $20, and it is not included in the ticket price to the Angkor Temple Complex.

GETTING HERE AND AROUND

Tuk-tuks, motos, and local taxis can take you to Kulen Mountain; negotiate a price prior to departure, or ask your hotel to handle it (expect to pay around $20 for the trip). The journey should take no more than 50 minutes. Siem Reap tour companies also go here.

Sihanoukville

230 km (143 miles) southwest of Phnom Penh.

A half a century ago, Cambodia's main port city, Sihanoukville, was a sleepy backwater called Kampong Som. Then a series of world-shattering events overtook it and gave rise to the busy industrial center and coastal resort now prominent on every tourist map.

The French laid the foundations of Kampong Som back in the mid-1950s, before they lost control of the Mekong Delta and its ports following their retreat after the French-Indochina War. The town was renamed Sihanoukville in honor of the then king. A decade later, Sihanoukville received a further boost when it became an important transit post for weapons destined for American forces fighting in the Vietnam War. In the mid-1970s Sihanoukville itself came under American attack and suffered heavy casualties

Khmer: A Few Key Phrases

A knowledge of French may get you somewhere in francophone Cambodia, but these days it's far easier to find English speakers. The Cambodian language, Khmer, belongs to the Mon-Khmer family of languages, enriched by Indian Pali and Sanskrit vocabulary. It has many similarities to Thai and Lao, a reminder of their years as vassal lands in the Khmer Empire.

The following are some useful words and phrases:

Hello: joom reap soo-uh

Thank you: aw-koun

Yes: bah (male speaker), jah (female speaker)

No: aw-te

Excuse me: som-toh

Where?: ai nah?

How much?: t'lay pohn mahn?

Never mind: mun ay dtay

Zero: sohn

One: muay

Two: bpee

Three: bay

Four: buon

Five: bpram

Six: bpram muay

Seven: bpram pull

Eight: bpram bay

Nine: bpram buon

Ten: dop

Eleven: dop muay

Hundred: muay roi

Thousand: muay poan

Food: m'hohp

Water: dteuk

Expensive: t'lay nah

Morning: bprek

Night: youp

Today: tngay nee

Tomorrow: tngay sa-ik

Yesterday: mus'el mun

Bus: laan ch'nual

Ferry: salang

Village: pum

Island: koh

River: tonle

Doctor: bpet

Hospital: moonty bpet

Bank: tia-nia-kia

Post Office: praisinee

Toilet: baan tawp tdeuk

after Khmer Rouge forces captured the SS *Mayaguez,* a United States container ship.

Modern Sihanoukville has long been Cambodia's seaside playground. Its seven primary tourist beaches, all easily accessible from downtown by motorbike taxi or even a rented bicycle, attracted many backpackers and foreign investors throughout the area. But as of late, with the arrival of increasing numbers of Chinese investors, what was once a quiet and budget beach haven has transformed into an open-air construction site. Chinese developers have built 50 casinos, and there are 50 more in the pipeline.

Most beaches are dirty and backed by rows of cinder blocks, the roads unpaved and dusty. If that was not enough, prostitution and crime rates are rising, and so are the prices of accommodations and food. The city is fast losing most of its Cambodian character, and morphing into yet another Macau. All that said, there are some beautiful places to stay if you must base yourself here. ⚠ **We can no longer recommended a visit to Sihanoukville for more than what's necessary to catch an onward boat to the nearby islands.**

GETTING HERE AND AROUND

Sihanoukville airport has undergone modernization over the past few years and has five daily flights to different cities in China, one flight to Kuala Lumpur in Malaysia, and Cambodia Angkor Air flights to Siem Reap and Phnom Penh. Flights take one hour, with prices starting at $72.

Air-conditioned buses from Phnom Penh run several times daily ($8 to $10), departing from the Central Market or the Hua Lian Station near Olympic Stadium. Four hours later, they arrive a couple of kilometers outside of Sihanoukville, and getting off the bus you're enthusiastically greeted by the local tuk-tuk and moto drivers who jostle for your business. The farthest trip, to Otres, by tuk-tuk shouldn't cost more than $8, and going anywhere else shouldn't be more than $6 (there is a board with price suggestions at one end of the bus station). Prices for motos are half that of tuk-tuks, and taxis will cost double, but don't expect them to have a meter. Buses from Bangkok (10 hours; from $25) and other towns on Thailand's eastern seaboard connect to Sihanoukville via Koh Kong. At last, trains ($8) connect Phnom Penh to Sihanoukville, stopping at Takeo and Kampot, on Friday, Saturday, Sunday, Monday, and public holidays.

You can hire a private car and driver through your hotel or guesthouse for the trip to the coast from Phnom Penh (three to four hours; starting at $50 excluding gas). **■ TIP→ The highway to Sihanoukville is much improved and is now one of the better roads in Cambodia, but it is still hazardous to drive for anyone who is not familiar with roads in Cambodia.** Buses are almost as quick and often safer.

Taxis make the trip to and from Sihanoukville and Phnom Penh. The charge is $10 per person for five people, but if you want to be a little less cramped you can pay $13 to have only three seated in the back, or try and get the coveted front seat.

Sights

Sihanoukville is a beach town without a center. There is a market area with a surrounding business area that has all the banks and other basic facilities; however, the town's accommodations are spread out along the coast. There is a national park to visit that has mangroves and rivers, and is teeming with birdlife.

★ Koh Rong Samloem

ISLAND | The Sihanoukville coast is flanked by several islands, many of them untouristed and lightly populated by Khmer fishermen, and some are accessible by boat. **Koh Rong Samloem, Koh Tas, Koh Ta Kiev,** and **Koh Russei** are popular day-trip destinations for snorkeling and picnicking, but local guides can arrange overnight stays in rustic bungalows if you'd like to linger for a few days. Koh Rong Samloem is about 2½ hours by boat from the mainland (or 40 minutes in a speedboat), and there are some quiet and isolated beaches with a few basic bungalow options. The amenities vary depending where you go. **■ TIP→ The jungle interior of the island is home to some of the deadliest snakes in Cambodia. They are more afraid of you, of course, but be aware.** ✉ *Sihanoukville.*

Ream National Park

NATIONAL/STATE PARK | Encompassing 210 square km (81 square miles) of coastal land 16 km (10 miles) north of

The Road to the Coast

The four-hour bus journey from Phnom Penh to Sihanoukville along Highway 4 is an interesting one, winding through uplands, rice paddies, and orchards. Once you drive past Phnom Penh's Pochentong Airport and the prestigious Cambodia Golf & Country Club, and on through the area of Kompong Speu, the landscape turns rural, dotted with small villages where a major source of income seems to be the sale of firewood and charcoal. Somewhere around the entrance to Kirirom National Park all buses stop for refreshments at a roadside restaurant.

The halfway point of the journey lies at the top of the **Pich Nil mountain pass,** guarded by dozens of colorful spirit houses. These spirit houses were built for the legendary deity Yeah Mao, guardian of Sihanoukville and the coastal region. Legend has it that Yeah Mao was the wife of a village headman who worked in far-off Koh Kong, an island near today's border with Thailand. On a journey to visit him, Yeah Mao died when the boat transporting her sank in a storm—an all-too-believable story to anyone who has taken the boat from Sihanoukville to Koh Kong. Her spirit became the guardian of local villagers and fisherfolk.

At the small town of Chamcar Luang, a side road leads to the renowned smuggling port of Sre Ambel. The main highway threads along **Ream National Park,** with the Elephant Mountains as a backdrop. The national park is a highlight of Sihanoukville, with its mangroves, forests, waterfalls, and wildlife. The park is, unusually for Cambodia, well protected from the vagaries of modern development. The sprawling Angkor Beer brewery heralds the outskirts of Sihanoukville and the journey's end.

Getting Here and Around

You can hire a private car and driver through your hotel or guesthouse for the trip to the coast from Phnom Penh. The price varies, but starts at approximately $50, and can be split with other passengers if you prefer. The drive (four to five hours) is often an alarmingly fast and dangerous ride along the well-maintained highway. Nevertheless, it is common to see tourists who have rented motorcycles in Phnom Penh zipping past.

All major bus companies go to the coast, and Hunaman Travel and oSmoSe Conservation do tours.

Sihanoukville, this park includes mangrove forests, the Prek Tuk Sap estuary, two islands, isolated beaches, and offshore coral reefs. Macaques, pangolin (scaly anteaters), sun bears, and muntjac (barking deer) live in the forest. Tours can be booked from most hotels in town or directly with the park rangers who, however, receive mixed reviews in terms of their knowledge of local flora and fauna. ✉ *Airport Rd.* ☎ *012/875096, 016/767686* 🌐 *www.reamnationalpark.com* 🎫 *Walking tour $6 for 2 hrs, $10 for 5 hrs, boat tour $35 per 2 people.*

Restaurants

The most inexpensive guesthouses, restaurants, and other tourist services are on Victory (Weather Station) Hill, Serendipity Beach, and Ochheuteal Beach. Some of the lodgings in these areas are

Jayavarman VII built Preah Khan in 1191 to commemorate the Khmers' victory over Cham invaders.

quite attractive, although over the years these locations have become somewhat blighted by mass tourism.

Cafe Sushi

$ | **JAPANESE FUSION** | You can fish your own dinner right out of the Gulf of Siam on a trip arranged by this restaurant, then take a class to learn how to prepare it—or just choose whether to have it grilled or made into a tartare, sushi, nigiri, or tempura. By far the most authentic Japanese food in Sihanoukville, the menu is heavily reliant on the Japanese owner's whim and the fish caught that day. *Average main: $7 37 St. 705, Sangkat 3, Khan Mittapheap Inside Khmer Seafood Market 034/934800 www.cafesushizen.com No credit cards.*

Chhne Meas Restaurant

$ | **SEAFOOD** | Dine on the edge of Victory Beach, next to the crashing waves, at this lovely indoor-outdoor Cambodian restaurant. All manner of fresh fish and seafood, from stir-fries to clay pots to barbecues and curries, is available. **Known for:** sunset location; local crowd; stir-fried crab. *Average main: $6 Vithey Krong 012/340060 No credit cards.*

The Deck

$$ | **INTERNATIONAL** | In the Sokha Beach Resort, this outdoor beachfront restaurant is an idyllic dinner-and-drinks spot, from the dreamy sunset hour to late at night. The tapas menu is innovative and trendy, and Japanese dishes are authentic and refined. **Known for:** duck and vegetable spring rolls; happy hour; fresh seafood. *Average main: $12 Sokha Beach Resort, 2 Thnou St., Sokha Beach 034/935999 www.sokhahotels.com/sihanoukville/dining No lunch.*

Manoha

$ | **CAMBODIAN** | Simple, unpretentious, Manoha serves French-Khmer cuisine with a sophisticated air, prepared by a Cambodian chef who utilizes the best of fresh local ingredients and the catch of the day. You'll get excellent value here, with delicate dishes like fish carpaccio and tartare, or fruitier options like the Bai Cha Manoha (prawns in a spicy sauce, with rice served in a pineapple). **Known**

for: hearty breakfast; open 24 hours; big portions and extensive menu. *Average main: $5 Serendipity Beach Rd. 097/915–2814 No credit cards.*

★ Sandan

$ | **CAMBODIAN** | Operated by the Tree Alliance charity, this is a vocational training restaurant that consistently demonstrates just how good the training is—the service is attentive and the food exceptional. New and inventive Cambodian dishes are constantly being added, the specials change regularly, and the cocktails are pretty decent, too. **Known for:** grilled pork fillet stuffed with fresh-toasted coconut; Cambodian panfried noodles; fresh prawn ceviche. *Average main: $5 St. 10311, Krong Preah One block south of 7 Makara St. 034/452–4000 www.tree-alliance.org/our-restaurants/sandan.php.*

Starfish Bakery and Cafe

$ | **CAFÉ** | Here you can try a shake, house-made yogurt, or a brownie, indulge in a massage, and learn about volunteering opportunities in Sihanoukville. The café has Wi-Fi and a handicrafts shop upstairs. **Known for:** quiet garden setting; business with a cause; homemade pastries. *Average main: $4 Sihanoukville On unmarked road off 7 Makara St. 012/952011 www.starfishcambodia.org No credit cards.*

Hotels

Don Bosco Hotel School

$ | **HOTEL** | **FAMILY** | As the name suggests, this lodging doubles up as a school for trainees of the service industry, selected from a pool of local underprivileged young adults, but far from feeling like a guinea pig at a training facility, guests enjoy a high level of service and care. **Pros:** big swimming pool; shuttle services to town and beaches three times a day; excellent food. **Cons:** inconvenient location; part of a larger complex; somewhat impersonal. *Rooms from: $35 Group 13, Sangkat 4, Ou 5 034/933765, 016/919834 www.donboscohotel-school.com 31 rooms No meals.*

★ Lazy Beach, Koh Rong Samloem

$$ | **B&B/INN** | Jump on the hotel's boat from Ochheuteal Beach at midday and two hours later marvel at this beautiful tropical hideout, made up of wooden bungalows stretched out along the powdery beige sand. **Pros:** peaceful getaway; pretty, natural setting; friendly management and staff. **Cons:** a two-hour boat ride; no electricity; not much to do (except relax). *Rooms from: $60 Koh Rong Sanloem 016/214211, 017/456536 lazybeachcambodia.com No credit cards 10 rooms No meals.*

Sokha Beach Resort

$$$ | **RESORT** | **FAMILY** | This is the top address in Sihanoukville—a huge first-class resort hotel with all the facilities required for a fun-filled beach holiday. **Pros:** great for families; private beach; nice location. **Cons:** not geared to romantic getaways; a bit short on the luxury status it claims; close to a casino. *Rooms from: $120 2 Thnou St. 034/935999 www.sokhahotels.com 268 rooms, 20 suites, 79 villas Free breakfast.*

★ Song Saa Private Island

$$$$ | **RESORT** | Barefoot luxury are the buzzwords most used to describe this multiple-award-winning resort, set on two small islands (*Song Saa* is Khmer for "sweet hearts") a 40-minute speedboat trip from Sihanoukville. **Pros:** created with sustainability in mind; surrounding waters are part of a marine park; exceptional and discreet staff. **Cons:** limited accommodations so book early; stepping off the speedboat at Port 1, Gate 1 (Sihanoukville's harbor) at the end of your stay; surrounding waters have many sea urchins. *Rooms from: $1,400 Koh Ouen 0236/860360, 0239/890009 songsaa.com 27 villas All-inclusive.*

Most hotels and guesthouses arrange boat trips, which include packed lunches, to the many offshore islands. Several companies offer diving and snorkeling; two of the most popular dive centers are EcoSea Dive and Scuba Nation.

EcoSea Dive

DIVING/SNORKELING | Eco-friendly instruction comes at very competitive prices, and they even have a resort of their own on Koh Rong Samloem. Dives start from $30. ✉ *Between Serendipity Beach and Golden Lions traffic circle* ☎ *034/934631, 012/654104* 🌐 *www.ecoseadive.com.*

Scuba Nation

DIVING/SNORKELING | This was Cambodia's first certified PADI dive center and is still probably the best around, taking trips out to good underwater sites. They offer all the courses, up to advanced levels, and have some fun options for children. ✉ *Serendipity Beach Rd.* ✣ *Opposite Holiday Villa Nataya* ☎ *012/604680, 034/933700* 🌐 *www.divecambodia.com.*

Kampot

110 km (68 miles) east of Sihanoukville, 150 km (93 miles) south of Phnom Penh.

With the drastic changes happening in nearby Sihanoukville, this attractive riverside town at the foot of the Elephant Mountain range, not far from the sea, is attracting more and more tourists and expats, and is fast becoming the new "place to be" on the southern coast. Kampot is known for its French colonial architectural remnants—and for salt and pepper. In the dry season laborers can be seen along the highway to Kep, working long hours in the salt fields; pepper plantations are scattered around the province. Kampot is also the departure point for trips to the seaside resort of Kep and Bokor Hill Station. The coastal road from Sihanoukville to Kampot has been sealed and offers spectacular views. Several limestone caves speckle the landscape from Kampot to Kep to the Vietnam border. Plan at least a morning or afternoon excursion to see the cave and Hindu temple at Phnom Chhnork.

GETTING HERE AND AROUND

To get here, take a taxi or bus, or hire a car and driver through your hotel. The journey from Phnom Penh takes approximately four hours. A single bus ticket on Sorya Transport costs $7 from Phnom Penh's Central Market. Prices for a taxi or a car with driver start at $50. Hotels are the best source for tour information in and around Kampot.

Kampot has enough to keep the intrepid traveler busy for a couple of days. The town is artsy and relaxed, with a wide river marking the center of the town's dining and lodging area, whose epicenter is the cluster of streets around the Old Market. Kampot is the stepping-off point for nearby Kep, and it has rapids and a few caves to explore. Don't forget the world-renowned salt and pepper production. Bokor Hill Station remains the largest draw for visitors and is earmarked for a new spate of development.

Bokor Hill Station

MOUNTAIN—SIGHT | In the early 20th century, the French built this station as a retreat from the heat and humidity of the coast. It is now a collection of ruins, but it's worth visiting for the spectacular sea views from its 3,000-foot heights. It's 35 km (22 miles) west of Kampot, and travel here is extremely rough in the rainy season. Hiring a motorbike ($5) for the day is a fun way to experience the local scenery on the way up and down. Tour operators won't tell you that the charming old casino, believed to be haunted and the hill's main attraction, has been disappointingly transformed into a new hotel—and the new concrete shops and buildings are a bit of an eyesore. The waterfall and views, however, are still worth the excursion. ✉ *Kampot* 🌐 *phnombokor.com.*

Phnom Chhnork Caves

ARCHAEOLOGICAL SITE | The limestone caves shelter a pre-Angkorian ruin, over which the stalagmites and stalactites are gradually growing. The less appealing cave of Phnom Sia (flashlight required) is more for the fun of exploring in the depths of a cave. The white elephant cave, or Cave of Sasear, has a shrine where worshippers pray to an elephant-shaped limestone formation. Tuk-tuks from town cost $10 for the round-trip. Locals will ask $4 to guide you into the caves ✉ *On road from Kampot to Kep* 🎫 *$1.*

Phnom Voul Natural Pepper Plantation

FARM/RANCH | Kampot's world-renowned aromatic pepper is sold all around the town and surrounding areas, but there's nothing quite like visiting where it's grown, sampling it right off the plant, and paying its producers in person for a certified 100% organic product. This is one of the most respectable producers, where you can buy white, red, or black pepper in half- or one-kilogram bags. It's not cheap, but it is top quality. **■ TIP → As most pepper plantations are in the countryside along dusty, rocky roads, it's best to arrange a taxi ride—tuk-tuks across this kind of terrain can be exhausting.** ✉ *Chom Ka 3 Village, Pong Tek Commune, Dom nak Er district.*

Restaurants

Cafe Espresso Kampot

$ | CAFÉ | Caffeine lovers rejoice, for at Cafe Espresso you are guaranteed to find the perfect, most elegantly presented cup of coffee. Beans are locally grown, home roasted, and ground fresh for each order. **Known for:** Western comfort food; vegetarian options; family-friendly environment. $ *Average main: $5* ✉ *No. 17 down side street off Old Market St.* ✣ *Across from 333 bakery* ☎ *092/388736* 🌐 *kampotcoffee.wixsite.com/espresso* ⊗ *No dinner.*

★ Divino

$ | ITALIAN | Don't be misled by the simple appearance of this hole-in-the-wall Italian restaurant, as it truly dishes up the best pizzas and pastas in town. Michelin-starred Italian chef Marco brings northern Italian flavors to the table, mixing authentic family recipes with healthy doses of Kampot pepper and home-grown vegetables. **Known for:** crunchiest pizzas in town; good wine list; jovial atmosphere. $ *Average main: $5* ✉ *St. 724* ☎ *088/479–1027* 🌐 *divino-kampot.wixsite.com/divino-kampot.*

★ Epic Arts Cafe

$ | CAFÉ | FAMILY | Created as a positive, dynamic means of raising awareness and generating work opportunities for deaf or disabled people in the region, many of whom now work here, Epic Arts Cafe serves a good selection of tasty homemade breakfast dishes, including options like porridge, as well as lunch (try the BLT), dessert, and children's dishes, fresh-fruit smoothies, and iced coffees brewed from local beans. $ *Average main: $3* ✉ *1st May Rd., Kompong Kandal* ✣ *Across from new Kampot Market* ☎ *092/922069* 🌐 *www.epicarts.org.uk* ▬ *No credit cards* ⊗ *No dinner.*

The Fish Market

$$ | ASIAN FUSION | Completely renovated, Kampot's 1930 fish market upgraded to luxe riverfront bistro. It's a perfect spot for a stylish sundowner: the creative cocktails (from $17) blend local flavors into classic mixologies—think Kampot pepper Bloody Marys and lychee martinis. **Known for:** sunset views; creative cocktails; variety of seafood options. $ *Average main: $10* ✉ *Riverside Rd.* ✣ *Opposite the Old Market* ☎ *012/728884.*

Rikitikitavi

$ | **INTERNATIONAL** | This cheery second-floor terrace restaurant has a youthful vibe, and serves European and American favorites such as burgers, bruschetta, and salads, but the cuisine also has a strong Khmer undercurrent. Try the creamy Saraman beef curry with peanuts, local herbs, and spices. **Known for:** local ingredients; relaxing riverside location; extensive menu. *Average main: $7 ✉ Riverside Rd. ⇔ Next to post office ☎ 012/235102, 012/274820 ⊕ www.rikitikitavi-kampot.com.*

Hotels

Bokor Mountain Lodge

$ | **HOTEL** | Ideally set on the banks of Kampong Bay river in a restored colonial building, this centrally located boutique-style hotel offers a handful of clean, spacious, and affordable rooms. **Pros:** nice views; great restaurant; management knowledgeable about the area. **Cons:** light sleepers may be irked by the noisy next-door pub; a little rough around the edges. *Rooms from: $35 ✉ Riverfront Rd. ☎ 033/932314, 017/712062 ⊕ bit.ly/2Oh9c0v ⇨ 6 rooms ǀ◎ǀ Free breakfast.*

Ganesha Riverside Eco Resort

$ | **RESORT** | This little heaven for nature lovers offers a choice of budget, eco-friendly accommodations that are clean, spacious, and in a rustic local style. **Pros:** in the heart of nature; good service; yoga and meditation on offer. **Cons:** a little isolated ($4 tuk-tuk ride); not much to do here; prayer sound from nearby Buddhist temple and Muslim mosque. *Rooms from: $40 ✉ Kampong Kreang ☎ 092/724612 ⊕ www.ganesharesort.com ⇨ 8 rooms ǀ◎ǀ Free breakfast.*

Kampot View Boutique Hotel

$$ | **HOTEL** | This river-view boutique hotel right next to Kampot's new bridge has three floors of pristine rooms with minimalist-chic design and sliding glass doors, some with river and some with garden views. **Pros:** modern design; intimate swimming pool; convenient to center but still private. **Cons:** 1 km (half mile) from the Old Market; next to a trafficked road and can get noisy; ground-floor rooms next to the pool are less private. *Rooms from: $50 ✉ National Rd. 3, Thvi Village, Andong ⇔ Next to the new bridge, on the opposite side of the river from town ☎ 071/7181–11112 ⊕ kampotviewboutiquehotel.com ⇨ 22 rooms ǀ◎ǀ Free breakfast.*

Kep

25 km (16 miles) east of Kampot, 172 km (107 miles) south of Phnom Penh.

You'll never find another seaside getaway quite like Kep, with its narrow pebble-and-sand coastline bordered by the ghostly villa ruins of the Khmer Rouge era. What once was the coastal playground of Cambodia's elite and the international glitterati was destroyed in decades of war. Ever so slowly investors are refurbishing what's salvageable; most of the villas now being turned into resorts were bought for next to nothing in the early 1990s. When you arrive, tuk-tuk drivers and tour guides are sure to find you. Not much traffic comes through Kep, so the locals know the bus schedule. They're sure to offer you a tour of a nearby pepper plantation, which can be a rewarding experience but also a long, bumpy ride along dusty rural roads (a 4x4 or regular car is the best option). Kep grows some of the world's best pepper, which you can enjoy in its green, red, black, and white phases in a multitude of traditional dishes—the crab with Kampot pepper is especially good.

The beach in town is small and a popular picnic spot for locals who come to relax at the water's edge. Offshore, beautiful **Rabbit Island** has attracted a lot of tourists over the last few years, and the

Cambodia's Early History

The earliest prehistoric site excavated in Cambodia is the cave of Laang Spean in the northwest. Archaeologists estimate that hunters and gatherers lived in the cave 7,000 years ago. Some 4,000 years ago this prehistoric people began to settle in permanent villages. The Bronze Age settlement of Samrong Sen, near Kampong Chhnang, indicates that 3,000 years ago people knew how to cast bronze axes, drums, and gongs for use in religious ceremonies; at the same time, they domesticated cattle, pigs, and water buffaloes. Rice and fish were then, as now, the staple diet. By 500 BC ironworking had become widespread, rice production increased, and moats and embankments were being built to enclose their circular village settlements. It was at this stage that Indian traders and missionaries arrived—in a land then called Suvarnabhumi, or Golden Land.

Legend has it that in the 1st century AD the Indian Brahman Kaundinya arrived by ship in the Mekong Delta, where he met and married a local princess named Soma. The marriage led to the founding of the first kingdom on Cambodian soil. Archaeologists believe that the kingdom's capital was at Angkor Borei in Takeo Province.

In the 6th century the inland kingdom of Zhen La emerged. It comprised several small city-states in the Mekong River basin. A period of centralization followed, during which temples were built, cities enlarged, and land irrigated. Power later shifted to Siem Reap Province, where the history of the Khmer Empire started when a king of uncertain descent established the Devaraja line by becoming a "god-king." This royal line continues today.

unfortunate result is that it has become somewhat polluted. You can hire a boat to take you there for $7 to $10. If you are a true nature adventurer and choose to stay at one of the 30 or so bungalows here, be warned—there are snakes in the interior of the island and there is only sporadic electricity—and the nightly massing of bugs is not for the fainthearted; but, having said all this, the tropical paradise can inspire most to conquer their fears.

GETTING HERE AND AROUND

To get here, take a taxi or bus, or hire a car and driver through your hotel. The journey from Phnom Penh takes approximately 3½ hours. A single bus ticket is $7 from Phnom Penh's Central Market. Hiring a taxi or a car with driver will cost at least $50. Given the good condition of the coastal road and the distance of the sights, renting a scooter (around $6 per day) is the best way to move around town.

 Restaurants

A strip of simple eateries mainly run by local fishermen and their families can be found in the seafront Crab Market area. Here you can take your pick of these good-value local haunts, each serving tons of fresh seafood dishes—mainly finger lickin' crab—for around $6. Choices range from fresh salads and crunchy patties to succulent, spicy curries starring the famously flavorsome green, red, or black pepper from neighboring Kampot. Ideally, arrive around sunset to watch the fishermen returning with their catch, and to enjoy the mesmerizing colors play on the ocean before tucking into your dinner.

Don't expect anything fancy from these basic restaurants; overall, hygiene standards are adhered to, and service is polite.

Sailing Club

$$ | **INTERNATIONAL** | **FAMILY** | A great way to combine seaside eating and fun, especially for families, the Knai Bang Chatt hotel's Sailing Club is open throughout the day and welcomes all for seafood barbecues, a popular Sunday brunch, and light meals as well as beach volleyball, sailing, Hobie Cat rentals, and kayaking. Linger on until the evening to sip a cocktail and take in the stunning sunset views. **Known for:** sunset dinners; crab cakes; romantic location. *Average main: $10* *Phum Thmey, Sangkat Prey Thom* *036/210310* *www.knaibang-chatt.com* *Closed Mon.*

The Waterfront Beach Club & Lounge Bar

$$ | **SEAFOOD** | In tiny Kep, where you can quickly tire of the Crab Market options or your hotel restaurant, this beachfront spot is a refreshing alternative, serving local Samai-rum-based cocktails and wine in a romantic seaside setting. The artsy restaurant-lounge stands on a terrace in a pretty garden, where you can relax on loungers and enjoy the fresh sea breeze. *Average main: $8* *Rd. 33* *097/689–2738* *No credit cards.*

Hotels

★ Knai Bang Chatt

$$$$ | **RESORT** | In this scenic and luxurious resort you will experience the laissez-faire glamour of the Kep of the 1960s and 1970s, when it was a fashionable seaside escape for Cambodian royalty and the international elite. **Pros:** exclusive and luxurious; scenic beach location; old-fashioned elegance. **Cons:** a bit isolated; not the best beach in Cambodia; not all rooms have good natural light. *Rooms from: $200* *Phum Thmey, Sangkat Prey, Thom Khan, Kampot* *036/210310* *www.knaibangchatt.com* *18 rooms* *No meals.*

Le Bout du Monde

$$ | **RESORT** | Meaning "the end of the world" in French, Le Bout du Monde is perched on the top of a steep hill near the national park, with beautifully landscaped gardens, far-reaching views, and eco-friendly credentials. **Pros:** ecological and social ethics; wonderfully scenic; enjoyable hiking trails nearby. **Cons:** in-room humidity can be challenging in wet season; mattresses are a little hard; solar lights can be dim. *Rooms from: $55* *Preah Thom* *097/526–1846* *www.leboutdumondekep.com* *9 rooms* *Free breakfast.*

★ Samanea Beach Resort

$$$ | **RESORT** | **FAMILY** | Twelve Khmer-style villas, all with their own private verandas and charming open-roofed Balinese baths filled with plants and trees, fan around a large blue-tiled pool set amid peaceful gardens at this seafront resort. **Pros:** Olympic-size pool; first sushi restaurant in Kep; private beach and jetty. **Cons:** far from town; insects can easily enter the open-roofed bathrooms; limited dining options nearby. *Rooms from: $150* *33A Kep Rd.* *088/240–0600* *www.samanea-resort.com* *12 villas* *Free breakfast.*

Chapter 10

LAOS

Updated by
Marco Ferrarese

Sights	Restaurants	Hotels	Shopping	Nightlife
★★★★☆	★★★☆☆	★★★★☆	★★☆☆☆	★★☆☆☆

WELCOME TO LAOS

TOP REASONS TO GO

★ **Natural Beauty:** Laos is a beautiful country. Take a multiday trek or bike ride, or enjoy the fantastic mountain scenery from Luang Prabang to Vang Vieng. The far north from Luang Nam Tha to Phongsaly offers the best trekking and nature options.

★ **Archaeological Wonders:** The country's most unusual attraction is the Plain of Jars, which has 5-ton stone-and-clay jars of mysterious origin. Wat Phu, pre-Angkor Khmer ruins, is Laos's most recent UNESCO World Heritage site.

★ **Buddhist Customs:** Observing or participating in morning alms in Luang Prabang is a magical experience; so, too, is sitting in a temple to chat with a novice monk, surrounded by the sounds of chanting and chiming bells.

★ **The Mekong:** The Mekong River is the lifeline of Laos. You can travel down the mighty tributary on a slow cruise, or stop at one of 4,000 Islands for a chance to spot freshwater dolphins.

1 **Vientiane.**

2 **Nam Ngum Lake.**

3 **Phu Khao Khouay.**

4 **Plain of Jars.**

5 **Vang Veng.**

6 **Luang Prabang.**

7 **Tad Khuang Si Waterfall.**

8 **Tad Sae Waterfall.**

9 **Pak Ou Caves.**

10 **Bang Muang Ngoi.**

11 **Luang Nam Tha.**

12 **Muang Sing.**

13 **River Journey to Huay Xai.**

14 **Phongsaly.**

15 **Tha Khek.**

16 **Highway 13 South Along the Mekong.**

17 **Savannakhet.**

18 **Pakse.**

19 **Bolaven Plateau.**

20 **Tad Fane.**

21 **Champasak.**

22 **Si Phan Don and the 4,000 Islands.**

CHINA
0
100 mi
0
100 km
VIETNAM
Phongsaly
Muang Sing
Luang Nam Tha
Dien Bien Phu
HANOI
Haiphong
Meung
Oudomxay
Pak Mong
Xieng Khaw
Huay Xai
Pak Ou
Hua Muang
Pakbeng
Luang Prabang
Phonsavan
PLAIN OF JARS
Vang Vieng
Phu Bia 2820 m
Pakxan
Khamkeut
VIENTIANE
Mekong
Tha Kaek
VIETNAM
THAILAND
Savannakhet
Khon Kaen
River
BOLAVEN PLATEAU
Pakse
Attapeu
Nakhon Ratchasima
CAMBODIA

Despite a limited infrastructure, Laos is a wonderful country to visit. Laotians are some of the friendliest, gentlest people in Southeast Asia—devoutly Buddhist and traditional in many ways. Laos has a rich culture and history, and though it's been a battleground many times in the past, this is a peaceful, stable country today. Fewer than 7 million people live in this landlocked nation whose countryside is dominated by often impenetrable forested mountains. Not yet inured to countless visiting foreigners, locals volunteer assistance and offer a genuine welcome.

Luang Prabang and its historic sites are the country's primary claim to fame and the reason most tourists visit, but as a destination Laos also excels with its abundant nature and the chance the small towns and villages here provide to escape normally overcrowded Southeast Asia. In many ways a visit to Laos is a placid throwback to what travel in Thailand was like two decades or so ago. Many parts of the country—among them 4,000 Islands in the Mekong, or Phongsaly, Muang Ngoi, and Luang Nam Tha in the north—offer a fabulous opportunity to unwind, relax, and get away from the stresses of big cities and got-to-see-everything travel. Most visitors to Laos enter via Vientiane, but even here the rhythm of life is calmer than in its regional counterparts. As you venture forth from the capital city, as nearly all visitors do and should, the vibe becomes mellower still.

MAJOR REGIONS

Vientiane and Nearby. Vientiane is not only the capital of Laos but also the logical gateway to the country, as it's far more accessible to the outside world than Luang Prabang. Sitting along the Mekong River, the city is a curiosity—more like a small market town than a national capital—but it has some fine temples, many French colonial buildings, and a riverside boulevard unmatched elsewhere in Laos. North of Vientiane, you'll find beautiful daytrip destinations including **Nam Ngum**

Lake, the National Park **Phu Khao Khouay,** the archaeological wonder **Plain of Jars,** and **Vang Vieng** with its beautiful mountains, caves, waterfalls, and a laid-back, rural vibe.

Luang Prabang and Northern Laos. For all its popularity as a tourist destination, **Luang Prabang** remains one of the most isolated cities in Southeast Asia. Although a highway now runs north to the Chinese border, the hinterland of Luang Prabang is mostly off-the-beaten-track territory, a mountainous region of impenetrable forests and deep river valleys. Pleasant day trips from the city include to **Tad Khuang Si Waterfall, Tad Sae Waterfall,** and **Pak Ou Caves**. For trekking, ecotourism, gorgeous scenery, and hill tribe visits, the towns of **Ban Muang Ngoi**, northeast of Luang Prabang, and **Muang Sing** and **Luang Nam Tha,** north of Luang Prabang, are good bases. Despite Luang Prabang's air links to the rest of the country and the outside world, the Mekong River is still a preferred travel route, with various cruise and ferry boats departing Luang Prabang for the leisurely **River Journey to Huay Xai.** Farther north of Luang Prabang, **Phongsaly** offers even more adventure and trekking through forest-covered mountains.

Southern Laos. In some ways, Laos is really two countries: the south and north are as different as two sides of a coin. The mountainous north was for centuries virtually isolated from the more accessible south, where lowlands, the broad Mekong Valley, and high plateaus were easier to traverse and settle. The south does have its mountains, however: notably the Annamite range, called Phu Luang, home of the aboriginal Mon-Khmer ethnic groups who lived here long before Lao farmers and traders arrived from northern Laos and China. The Lao were followed by French colonists, who built the cities of **Thakhek, Savannakhet,** and **Pakse.** Although the French influence is still tangible, the southern Lao cling tenaciously to their old traditions, making the south a fascinating destination. The far southern region sees fewer tourists than other parts, but Pakseis an interesting town and a convenient base from which to explore the fabulous Wat Phu in **Champasak** and other ancient Khmer ruins, or explore the waterfalls and coffee plantations of the **Bolaven Plateau.** Fishing villages line the lower reaches of the Mekong River, a water wonderland with **Si Phan Don and the 4,000 Islands** and waterfalls at **Tad Fane.**

Planning

WHEN TO GO

Laos has a tropical climate with two distinct seasons: the dry season, from November through May, and the rainy season, from June through October. The cooler portion of the dry season, from November through February, is a comfortable time to tour Laos. By mid-March temperatures begin to soar. The country becomes baking hot, and because farmers burn their fields in spring, the air turns brown and hazy. In the rainy season, road and air travel can be slower and the days are often very hot and sticky; August and September see the most rain. On the upside, the country is greener and less crowded during the rains and prices are lower.

The yearly average temperature is about 82°F (28°C), rising to a maximum of 100°F (38°C) during April and May. In the mountainous areas around Luang Nam Tha, Phonsavan, and Phongsaly, however, temperatures can drop to 59°F (15°C) in winter and sometimes hit the freezing point at night.

Laos has a busy festival calendar and Vientiane and Luang Prabang, in particular, can get very crowded during the most important of these festivals, among them Lao New Year, in April, and Vientiane's That Luang Festival, in November. Book your hotel room well in advance during these periods.

PLAN YOUR TIME

HASSLE FACTOR

High. There are no direct flights from the United States to Laos but it is easily accessed by flight through other points in Southeast Asia.

3 DAYS

Experience the majesty of Luang Prabang, an entire city that has been declared a UNESCO World Heritage site. Take a day trip up the Mekong River to see villages and explore cliff-side caves.

1 WEEK

You have more time to spend in Luang Prabang and either take a Mekong River trip west to Huay Xai and do a three-day gibbon eco-adventure or go north to hit Laos's northernmost province, Luang Nam Tha, to join a trek to visit forest-dwelling ethnic minorities.

2 WEEKS

Spend a full week in northern Laos in Luang Prabang and Luang Nam Tha and go west to Huay Xai. While up north, try to head to Phonsavan to reach the Plain of Jars. Then head back to Luang Prabang and go south on serene Route 13 to Vang Vieng and then Vientiane.

PLANNING YOUR TIME

Given distances in Laos and its mountainous terrain, if you've only got a week to spend here, you'll have to choose between visiting the north or south. A popular strategy in the north would be to enter Laos in Huay Xai from Chiang Mai/Chiang Rai in Thailand, then take the two-day boat trip on the Mekong to Luang Prabang. If you are a mountain lover, you could skip the boat ride and take a minivan to Luang Nam Tha, and spend a couple of days here kayaking or trekking in the Nam Ha Reserve or visiting ethnic minority hill tribes. From here it takes a long day's journey to get to Luang Prabang, where you can relax in a colonial resort and enjoy the UNESCO World Heritage sites. Luang Prabang is more about the atmosphere than actual sights, so a few days can be enough for a quick visit. Afterward take a bus south to Vang Vieng, or else a van to the Plain of Jars, and spend a few days in either of these spots, with Vang Vieng the best option for nature and scenery lovers, and the Plain of Jars of interest for history and archaeology buffs. From Vang Vieng a few hours' drive by car will get you to Vientiane; from the Plain of Jars you can fly. Spend your last night in Vientiane, which has all services and connections out of the country. If you opt for seeing the 4,000 Islands and southern Laos, it's best to head here from Ubon Ratchathani in Thailand, crossing over to Pakse (or else flying from Vientiane if you have been up north). Pakse isn't worth more than a day, so head down to Champasak for a day exploring Wat Phu and staying in the quiet river town or else across on Don Daeng Island. Then head to Don Khong, Don Khon, or Don Det for a few days, where you can investigate the Irrawaddy dolphins in the Mekong, check out the spectacular waterfalls, and enjoy the sleepy island life. It's worth it from here to make a side trip up to the Tad Fane waterfall and the coffee-growing region on the Bolaven Plateau. With all these side trips, you'll need at least four days here.

GETTING HERE AND AROUND

AIR TRAVEL

Most of Laos's mountainous terrain is impenetrable jungle, and road travel here is very slow; the only practical way to tour the country in less than a week is by plane. Bangkok Air has daily flights from Bangkok to Luang Prabang; Thai Air flies to Vientiane; and Lao Airlines runs frequent, slightly more expensive flights from Bangkok to Luang Prabang and Vientiane, as well as provincial cities including Pakse and Savannakhet. (⇨ *See Air Travel in Travel Smart Thailand*).

■TIP→ An inexpensive and convenient option to is to fly Air Asia Thai Smile, or Nok Air from Bangkok to either Ubon Ratchathani or Udon Thani and then cross the border by land, putting you in Vientiane or Pakse in less than an hour.

BOAT TRAVEL

Running virtually the entire length of the country, the Mekong River is a natural highway. Because all main cities lie along the Mekong, boats are an exotic yet practical means of travel. Mekong Cruises operates two luxury cruise routes, the Luang Say (⇨ *River Journey to Huay Xai*) and the Vat Phou (⇨ *Pakse*). Shompoo Cruise (⇨ *River Journey to Huay Xai*) offers a mid-range alternative to the Luang Say cruise.

BUS TRAVEL

A network of bus services covers almost the entire country. Though cheap, bus travel is slow and not as comfortable as in Thailand. VIP buses, which connect Vientiane, Luang Prabang, and Pakse, are somewhat more comfortable—they have assigned seats and more legroom, and make fewer stops. Minivan service, common between cities, costs slightly more than the bus, but it's quicker and some companies pick up passengers at their hotels. **■TIP→ Sleeper buses travel between Vientiane and Pakse, but beds are less than 6 feet long, so tall folks may want to buy both spots in what is essentially one shared small bed.**

CAR TRAVEL

Although it's possible to enter Laos by car or motorbike and drive around on your own, this is not recommended, as driving conditions are difficult: nearly 90% of the country's 14,000 km (8,700 miles) of roads are unpaved; road signs are often indecipherable; and accidents will invariably be considered your fault. A better alternative is to hire a car and driver for about $50 per day.

SONGTHAEW AND TUK-TUK TRAVEL

Tuk-tuks and songthaews cruise the streets and are easy to flag down in most towns. Tuk-tuk drivers can be unscrupulous about fares, especially in Luang Prabang and Vientiane. **■TIP→ Do not believe the "official" prices placard displayed by drivers in Vientiane.** Don't get into a tuk-tuk before you've agreed on a fare and don't negotiate in dollars—get a quote in kip or baht. Expect to pay about 25% more than you would for a similar ride in Thailand.

BORDER CROSSINGS

In addition to the international airports in Vientiane, Luang Prabang, and Pakse, there are numerous land and river crossings into Laos. The busiest is the Friendship Bridge, between Laos and Thailand, which spans the Mekong River 29 km (12 miles) east of Vientiane. Other border crossings from Thailand to Laos are: Chiang Khong to Huay Xai (by bridge across the Mekong River); Nakhon Phanom to Tha Khek; Mukdahan to Savannakhet; and Chongmek to Vang Tao. There are also several new open crossings from the more remote Loei and Phrae provinces in northern Thailand. You can also enter Laos from Cambodia at Non Nok Khiene, and from Mohan, in China's Yunnan Province, at Boten. There are seven crossings between Laos and Vietnam, including Cau Treu to Nam Phao (from near Vinh, Vietnam, to Lak Xao in Laos); Nam Can to Nam Khan (Vinh to Phonsavan); and Lao Bao to Dansavan (on the Hue to Savannakhet route).

Border crossings are open daily from 8:30 to 5, except for the Friendship Bridge, which is open daily from 6 am to 10 pm.

MONEY MATTERS

The currency is the Lao kip (LAK), which comes in relatively small notes (the largest denomination equals about $12). Most prices in this chapter are listed in kip, sometimes with the U.S. dollar equivalent for reference. The Thai baht is accepted in Vientiane, Luang Prabang, and border towns. It's best to carry most of your cash in dollars or baht and exchange relatively small amounts of kip as you travel. At this writing, the official exchange rate is approximately 250 kip to the Thai baht and a little more than 8,400 kip to one U.S. dollar.

There are ATMs throughout the country so changing money is not a big issue.

Credit cards are accepted in most hotels and some restaurants but few shops. Banks in major tourist destinations will provide a cash advance on a MasterCard or Visa, typically for a 5% service charge. Western Union has branches in Vientiane and other major towns.

Exchange Rate

With an exchange rate of more than 8,100 Lao kip to the U.S. dollar, keeping track of what things cost can be difficult. Currency rates fluctuate daily, but below is a quick conversion chart, with kip figures rounded up or down as applicable.

8,400 kip = $1

42,500 kip = $5

85,000 kip = $10

168,000 kip = $20

424,000 kip = $50

848,000 kip = $100

1 million kip = $120

HEALTH AND SAFETY

■ TIP→ Laos's health care is nowhere near as good as Thailand's. If you will be traveling extensively, consider buying international health insurance that covers evacuation to Thailand.

Take the same health precautions in Laos that you would in Thailand *(see Health in Travel Smart Thailand)*. Pharmacies are stocked with Thai antibiotics and are often staffed with assistants who speak some English. Vientiane is malaria-free, but if you're visiting remote regions, consider taking prophylactics. HIV is widespread in border areas. Reliable Thai condoms are available in Laos.

Laos is fairly free of crime in tourist areas. Pickpocketing is rare, but you should still be careful in crowded areas. Never leave luggage unattended.

Penalties for drug possession are severe. Prostitution is illegal, and $500 fines can be levied against foreigners for having sexual relations with Lao citizens to whom they are not married (how this is enforced is unclear, but even public displays of affection may be interpreted as shady behavior).

■ TIP→ In the countryside, trekkers should watch out for unexploded ordnance left over from the Vietnam War, especially in Xieng Khuang (Plain of Jars) and Hua Phan provinces, and in southern Laos. Don't wander off well-traveled trails. Better yet, trek with a qualified guide. Do not photograph anything that may have military significance, such as airports or military installations.

PASSPORTS AND VISAS

You'll need a passport and a visa to enter Laos. Visas can be obtained on arrival at most entry points, but if you're taking the cross-border bus to Vientiane from Udon Thani or Nong Khai in Thailand, you'll need to get a visa in advance. You can do this at the Lao embassy in Bangkok or consulate in Khon Kaen in an hour or through an embassy or travel agency before you leave home. Tourist visas are good for 30 days, cost $35 for Americans ($42 for Canadians), and can be paid for in U.S. dollars (if you are buying a visa at the Lao border or in a Lao embassy or consulate in Thailand, you can pay in baht, but you will be charged B1,500, which is much more than $35). You'll need to have two passport-size photos

At A Glance

Capital: Vientiane

Population: 6,961,200

Currency: kip

Money: ATMs in cities; U.S. dollar and Thai bhat widely accepted; credit cards only in resort areas.

Language: Lao

Country Code: 856

Emergencies: Call local police

Driving: On the right

Electricity: 230v/50 cycle; plugs are either U.S. standard two- and three-prong or European standard with two round prongs. Power converter needed.

Time: 11 hours ahead of New York

Documents: Up to 30 days with valid passport; visa on arrival

Mobile Phones: GSM (900 and 1800 bands)

Major Mobile Companies: LaoTelecom, Unitel, Beeline, ETL Mobile

Websites

National Tourism Authority of the Lao People's Democratic Republic: 🌐 *www.tourismlaos.org*

Laos Hotel & Travel Guide: 🌐 *www.visit-mekong.com/laos*

Green Discovery Laos: 🌐 *www.greendiscoverylaos.com*

(one photo if buying at the border) with you. Bring photos from home, get them in Bangkok, or pay an extra 40 baht at the border for a photo. Occasionally immigration officials ask to see evidence of sufficient funds and a plane ticket out of the country. Showing them credit and ATM cards should be proof enough of funds. ■ **TIP→ Regulations change without warning, so check with the Lao embassy in your home country before setting out.**

EMBASSY Lao Embassy (Bangkok)
✉ *502/502/1–3 Soi Sahakarnpramoon, Pracha Uthit Rd., Wangthonglang, Bangkok* ☎ *02/539–6667.*

TOURS

Diethelm Travel

GUIDED TOURS | One of the oldest and most respected travel agencies offering package trips to Laos, Diethelm is a good source for travel information and tours in Laos. The agency's Taste of Laos tour focuses on the country's coffee industry. Multiday tours to Wat Phu take in other major attractions in southern Laos. ✉ *Ban Vat Nong, District 1, Luang Prabang* ☎ *020/9619–3264* 🌐 *www.diethelmtravel.com/laos* 🎫 *From 925,000 kip ($114) per person for 2 travelers (higher rate for 1 person, lower for more than 2).*

Green Discovery Laos

GUIDED TOURS | The top eco- and adventure-tour operator in Laos, Green Discovery offers a staggering array of adventure, eco, and cultural tours, from one day to one week, throughout the country. The company, which trains its guides well, is also the best source for local information. ✉ *54 Setthathirat Rd., Ban Xieng Ngeun, Nam Phou, Vientiane* ✣ *Next door to Kop Chai Deu* ☎ *021/223022* 🌐 *www.greendiscoverylaos.com* 🎫 *From 1,000,000 kip ($123) per person for 2 travelers.*

National Tourism Authority of the Lao People's Democratic Republic

The official government tourist agency has offices in Vientiane and all other provinces in Laos. The staff provides some printed materials and tries to be helpful, but you are probably better off going to private travel agencies for more detailed information. ✉ *Box 3556, Ave. Lane Xang, Vientiane* ✣ *East side of street near Dongpalane Rd.* ☎ *021/212248, 021/212251* 🌐 *www.tourismlaos.org.*

RESTAURANTS
Choices in Luang Prabang and Vientiane are endless, among them high-end French restaurants; Japanese, Thai, Indian, and pizza places; and fantastic bakeries and coffee shops. In smaller locales you might have to make do with sticky rice and grilled meats or fish, but most towns have at least one or two fancier places with decent menus. Lao food is similar to Thai but not quite as spicy or varied. Vietnamese pho noodles are widely available, as are baguette sandwiches.

HOTELS
Luang Prabang has some of the most elegant resorts in the world. Vientiane has a classic colonial luxury hotel, a few boutique options, and several international-caliber business-style hotels. Upscale options have opened around Champasak in the south. Otherwise, fancy resorts in Laos are few and far between, though there are perfectly adequate facilities in Pakse and the Plain of Jars. In Phongsaly, Muang Ngoi, 4,000 Islands, and other out-of-the-way places, amenities such as Wi-Fi connections and even basics like hot water may not be up to par.

What It Costs in Lao Kip

$	$$	$$$	$$$$
RESTAURANTS			
under 81,000 kip	81,000–122,000 kip	122,001–162,000 kip	over 162,000 kip
HOTELS			
under 410,000 kip	410,000–820,000 kip	820,001–1,230,000 kip	over 1,230,000 kip

Vientiane

Laos's capital is a low-key, pleasant city thanks to its small size, relative lack of traffic, and navigable layout. The pace here is as slow as the Mekong River, which flows along the edge of town. Aside from the magnificent lotus-shaped stupa Pha That Luang, there aren't too many must-sees, but the promenade along the Mekong and the many wats scattered about are great to explore by bicycle.

The abundance of ugly cement-block buildings and new Chinese-built high-rises gives Vientiane a superficially run-down appearance, but this only makes the remnants of elegant French colonial architecture stand out all the more. There are also dozens of temples—ornate, historic Buddhist structures that stand amid towering palms and flowering trees. First-time visitors often find Vientiane a drab, joyless city, but you only have to arrive during the weeklong That Luang Festival in November to be reminded that first impressions can be misleading.

GETTING HERE AND AROUND

AIR TRAVEL
Vientiane's Wattay International Airport is about 4 km (2½ miles) from the city center. You can take a metered taxi from the airport into the city for 80,000 kip; get a taxi voucher from the kiosk in the arrivals hall. The ride to the city center takes about 15 minutes. Alternatively, if you don't have much luggage, walk out the airport gate and take a tuk-tuk for 40,000 kip. The cheapest option is the air-conditioned Airport Shuttle bus to Talat Sao (Vientiane's morning market), which costs 15,000 kip.

BUS TRAVEL
Vientiane's city bus system was upgraded in 2018 and provides a few useful routes for the traveller. Note however that most services stop running between 5 and 6 pm. The city bus station is next

to Talat Sao (the morning market) and only handles city routes, the Airport Shuttle Bus, and through buses to Thailand. The Airport Shuttle Bus (#44) leaves roughly every 40 minutes from 8 am to 10:20 pm, and also stops in the city center next to several accommodation options. The Northern Bus Terminal for trips to and from northern Laos is 10 km (6.2 miles) northwest of the center, and is served from Talat Sao by Bus #8 (5,000 kip; every 30 minutes from 6 am to 5 pm). Buses bound for points in southern Laos leave from the Southern Bus Station, which is far out on the northern reaches of the city near to Highway 13, and is served by Bus #23 or #29 (4,000 kip; every 20 minutes from 6 am to 6 pm). Another useful route is Bus #20 (5,000 kip; every 30 minutes from 6:30 am to 5:20 pm) which stops at Wat That Luang. Check updated schedules at 🌐 *www.vientianebus.org.la*

The best way to get to Vientiane from Thailand via bus is to take one of the hourly buses from either Udon Thani (two hours; B80) or Nong Khai (one hour; B55). ■ **TIP→ These buses take you straight to Talat Sao, Vientiane's morning market, but you cannot board them unless you already have a Lao visa.**

If you don't have an advance visa, you can take a bus from Udon Thani to Nong Khai, then a tuk-tuk to the border (from B30 to B50), cross the Friendship Bridge on a B20 shuttle bus, and take a taxi (B350), tuk-tuk (B150), or public bus #14 (8,000 kip; every 15 minutes from 6 am to 6 pm) from the Lao side of the border into Vientiane's morning market. Bus #14 also stops at the interesting Buddha Park en route to the city.

TAXI AND TUK-TUK TRAVEL

You can cover Vientiane on foot, but tuk-tuks and jumbos, their larger brethren, are easy to flag down. Negotiate the price before setting off; you can expect to pay about 20,000 to 40,000 kip for a ride within the city if you are a firm negotiator. Taxis are available, but must be reserved, which you can do through your hotel or at the morning market. For day trips outside the city, ask your hotel or guesthouse to book a car with a driver.

SAFETY AND PRECAUTIONS

Vientiane is very safe, but beware of being fleeced by tuk-tuk drivers. Ask a local for correct fares.

TIMING

Most people stay in Vientiane a few days, time enough to tour That Luang and a few other monuments, soak up the sleepy ambience, and enjoy some creature comforts and a Beerlao on the Mekong before heading out into the wilds. If you throw in day trips to Nam Ngun or nearby national parks, you could make it a few more. Vientiane is also the place to take care of any business (onward visas, fax and computer connections, et cetera).

EMERGENCIES

The new Alliance International Medical Centre Clinic, affiliated with the Wattana Hospital in Thailand, is the best medical center in Laos. Most expats and embassy personnel head here to attend to their health needs. ■ **TIP→ For anything major, consider crossing the border to Thailand and going to Wattana Hospital in Nong Khai or Udon Thani.**

ESSENTIALS

AIR CONTACTS Lao Airlines ✉ *Wattay Airport, Hwy. 13* ☎ *021/510040 for ticketing and reservations, 021/513146 for international flights, 021/513032 for domestic flights* 🌐 *www.laoairlines.com.* **Thai Airways International** ✉ *M and N Building, ground fl., Souphanouvong Rd., Ban Kunta* ✣ *Just past Mercure Hotel on way to airport* ☎ *021/222527 up to 29 in Vientiane* 🌐 *www.thaiair.com.*

BANKS Bank of Lao PDR ✉ *Yonnet Rd.* ✣ *Just north of Nam Phu Sq.* ☎ *021/213300 up to 01* 🌐 *www.bol.gov.la.* **Banque Pour le Commerce Exterieur Lao (BCEL)** ✉ *1 Pangkham St., Ban*

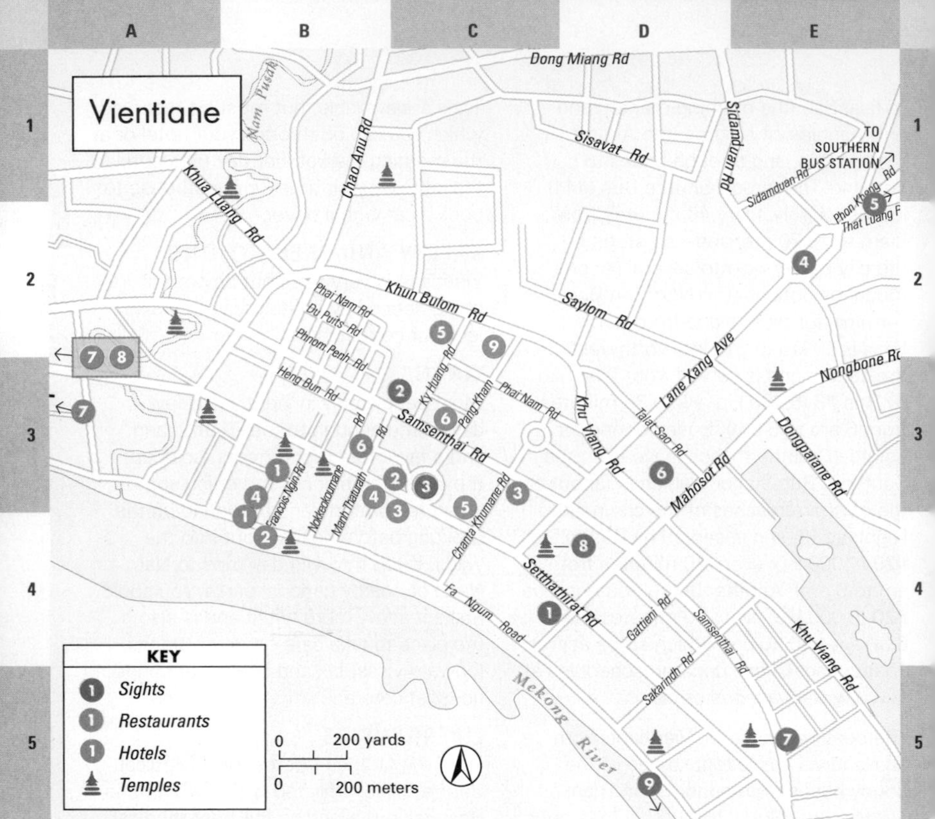

Sights	
1 Ho Phra Keo	C4
2 Lao National Museum	C3
3 Nam Phu Fountain	C3
4 Patuxay Monument	E2
5 Pha That Luang	E1
6 Talat Sao (Morning Market)	D3
7 Wat Si Muang	E5
8 Sisaket Temple	C4
9 Xieng Khuan Buddha Park	D5

Restaurants	
1 Acqua	B3
2 Khop Chai Deu	B3
3 Kualao	C3
4 La Signature	B3
5 Noy's Fruit Heaven	C2
6 Taj Mahal	B3
7 Villa Opera	A3

Hotels	
1 Ansara Hotel	B4
2 Best Western Vientiane	B4
3 Bloom Hotel & Cafe	C3
4 Dhavara Boutique Hotel	B3
5 Ibis Vientiane Nam Phu	C3
6 Lao Plaza Hotel	C3
7 Mercure Vientiane	A2
8 Salana Boutique Hotel	A2
9 Settha Palace	C2

Etiquette and Behavior

Laotians are generally gentle and polite, and visitors should take their lead from them—avoiding any public display of anger or impolite behavior. Even showing affection in public is frowned on.

Laotians traditionally greet others by pressing their palms together in a sort of prayer gesture known as a *nop*; it is also acceptable for men to shake hands. If you attempt a nop, remember that it's basically reserved for social greetings; don't greet a hotel or restaurant employee this way. The general greeting is *sabai di* ("good health"), invariably said with a smile.

Avoid touching or embracing a Laotian, and keep in mind that the head has spiritual significance; even patting a child affectionately on the head could be misinterpreted. Feet are considered "unclean," so when you sit, make sure your feet are not pointing directly at anyone, and never use your foot to point in any situation. Shoes must be removed before you enter a temple or private home, as well as some restaurants and offices.

Shorts and sleeveless tops should not be worn in temple compounds. When visiting a temple, be careful not to touch anything of spiritual significance, such as altars, Buddha images, or spirit houses. Ask permission from anyone before taking a photograph of him or her.

Xiengnheun ⊕ 1 block south of Nam Phu Sq. ☎ 021/213200 🌐 www.bcel.com.la.

CAR-RENTAL AGENCY Avis ✉ *Setthathirat and Hengbounnoy Rds. ☎ 021/223867 🌐 www.avrlaos.com.*

TRAVEL AGENCIES Green Discovery Laos ✉ *54 Setthathirat Rd., Ban Xieng Ngeun, Nam Phou ⊕ Next door to Kop Chai Deu ☎ 021/223022 🌐 www.greendiscovery-laos.com.*

Sights

Ho Phra Keo

RELIGIOUS SITE | There's a good reason why Ho Phra Keo, one of the city's oldest and most impressive temples, has a name so similar to the wat in Bangkok's Grand Palace. The original Ho Phra Keo here was built by King Setthathirat in 1565 to house the Emerald Buddha, which he had taken from Chiang Mai in Thailand. The king installed the sacred statue first in Luang Prabang and then in Vientiane at Ho Phra Keo, but the Siamese army recaptured the Buddha in 1778 and it was installed in Bangkok. The present temple, restored in 1936, is a national museum. On display are Buddha sculptures of different styles, some wonderful chiseled images of Khmer deities, and a fine collection of stone inscriptions. The masterpiece of the museum is a 16th-century lacquered door carved with Hindu images. ✉ *Setthathirat Rd. and Mahosot Rd. ☎ 021/212621 🎫 5,000 kip.*

Lao National Museum

MUSEUM | A two-story French colonial building houses this well-laid-out museum with interesting geological and historical displays. Exhibits touch on Laos's royal past, its colonial years, and its struggle for liberation. Other highlights include details about the country's 50 main ethnic groups, along with indigenous instruments that illustrate how they made music. ✉ *Samsenthai Rd., opposite Lao National Culture Hall ☎ 021/212460 🎫 10,000 kip.*

Nam Phu Square (*Fountain Square*)

PLAZA | The main square in Vientiane's tourist area, this used to reflect more emphatically the city's French influence, reinforced further by the cadre of very Gallic restaurants along the perimeter. Unfortunately, a recent renovation saw Nam Phu's namesake central fountain incorporated into a fancy new restaurant, visually disrupting the plazalike feel. The fountain is lit up multicolor at night, and bands perform for a crowd dominated on most days by tourists and Lao youth hanging out. The square and surrounding streets still contain many eateries. ✉ *Nam Phu Fountain, Rue Pangkham.*

★ **Pha That Luang**

MEMORIAL | The city's most sacred monument, this massive, 147-foot-high, gold-painted stupa is also the nation's most important cultural symbol, representing the unity of the Lao people. King Setthathirat had it built in 1566 to guard a relic of the Buddha's hair and to represent Mt. Meru, the holy mountain of Hindu mythology, the center and axis of the world. Surrounding the lotus-shape stupa are 30 pinnacles on the third level and a cloistered square on the ground with stone statues of the Buddha. Two brilliantly decorated temple halls, the survivors of four temples originally here, flank That Luang. On the avenue outside the west gate stands a bronze statue of King Setthathirat erected in the 1960s by a pious general. That Luang is the center of a major weeklong festival during November's full moon. The stupa is on the north end of town, a 10-minute songthaew ride from the city center. ✉ *That Luang Rd.* ✣ *End of That Luang Rd., northeast of Patuxay Monument* ☎ *20/9521–0600* 🎫 *5,000 kip.*

Patuxay Monument

MEMORIAL | An ersatz Arc de Triomphe, the monument is a prominent landmark, if minor attraction, between the city center and Pha That Luang. A disarmingly candid plaque describes Patuxay as a "monster of concrete." Harsh, if perhaps true, but if you have some time to kill during the day, you can scale its seven stories for a decent photo op and stroll the souvenir stalls on the second floor. ✉ *Ave. Lang Xang* ✣ *2½ km (1½ miles) southeast of Pha That Luang* 🎫 *3,000 kip.*

Talat Sao (*Morning Market*)

MARKET | To immerse yourself in Vientiane, visit this vast indoor bazaar that despite its name stays open all day. Shops within the bright and orderly space sell everything from handwoven fabrics and wooden Buddha figures to electric rice cookers and sneakers. Most vendors cater to locals, but there is plenty to interest travelers: fabric, handicrafts, intricate gold-and-silver work, jewelry, T-shirts, and bags and suitcases. Many products are imported from abroad. Fruits, confections, and noodle soups are sold at open-door stalls outside, where Vietnamese shoemakers also ply their trade. Near the main post office, the market is inside a large department store, Laos's first, and spills out into the surrounding area. ✉ *Ave. Lane Xang and Khu Vieng St.*

Wat Si Muang

PUBLIC ART | This wat that dates to 1563—its last major renovation was in 1956—guards the original city pillar, a revered foundation stone also from the 16th century. In a small park in front of the monastery stands a rare memorial to Laos's royal past: a large bronze statue of King Sisavang Vong. ✉ *Samsenthai Rd. at Setthathirat Rd.* ✣ *Near eastern end of Setthathirat Rd.* 🌐 *www.watsimuang.com* 🎫 *Free.*

Wat Sisaket Museum

RELIGIOUS SITE | A courtyard with 6,840 Buddha statues stops the show at this intriguing temple-monastery complex across from Ha Phra Keo. Built in 1818 by King Anu, the temple survived Vientiane's 1828 destruction by the Siamese army, and the monastery, still active, remains

Laos Festivals

Bun Bang Fai: The Rocket Festival is held in the middle of May. Rockets are fired and prayers are said in the paddy fields to bring rain in time for the planting of the rice seedlings.

Bun Khao Padab Din: This special rice ceremony takes place in August; the exact date depends on the harvest schedule. People make offerings at temples to keep alive the memory of spirits who have no relatives.

Bun Khao Salak: This rice ceremony whose date also depends on the harvest schedule happens in September. For this one, people visit temples to make offerings for their ancestors. Boat races are held on the Mekong, especially in Luang Prabang and Khammuan Province.

Bun Ok Pansa: The day of the full moon in October marks the end of Buddhist Lent, and is celebrated with donations to local temples. Candlelight processions are held, and colorful floats are set adrift on the Mekong River. The following day, boat races are held in Vientiane, Savannakhet, and Pakse.

Bun Pimai: Lao New Year takes place from April 13 to 15. At this water festival similar to Thailand's Songkran, all the important Buddha images are cleaned with scented water (and the public gets wet in the bargain). The festivities are particularly lively in Luang Prabang, where the holiday is celebrated for nearly a week.

Bun Visakhabucha (Buddha Day): On the day of the full moon in May, candlelight processions are held in temples to mark the birth, enlightenment, and death of the Buddha.

That Ing Hang Festival: This takes place in Savannakhet in December, and lasts several days on the grounds of the ancient Wat That Inhang, just outside the city. Events include sports contests, performances of traditional Lao music and dance, and a spectacular drumming competition.

That Luang Festival: This weeklong event in Vientiane in November ends with a grand fireworks display. Hundreds of monks gather to accept alms. The festival runs concurrently with an international trade fair showcasing the products of Laos and other countries of the Greater Mekong Subregion (GMS).

Wat Phu Festival: Also known as Makhabucha Day, this festival is held during the day of the first full moon in February at Wat Phu, near Champasak. Elephant races, buffalo fights, cockfights, and traditional Lao music-and-dance performances make for a very full schedule.

intact in its original form. The courtyard contains little niches and large platforms with Buddhas of all sizes. The impressive temple hall underwent some restoration in 1938, though it needs further repair. The intricately carved wooden ceiling and doors still impress, but time has taken its toll on the paintings that once covered the hall's walls. ✉ *Setthathirat Rd. at Ave. Lane Xang* ☎ *021/212622* 🎫 *10,000 kip.*

Xieng Khuan Buddha Park

RELIGIOUS SITE | The bizarre creation of an ecumenical monk, Luang Pa Bunleua Sulilat, who dreamed of a world religion embracing all faiths, this park is "peopled" by enormous Buddhist and Hindu

Thai invaders destroyed That Luang in 1828; it was restored in the 20th century.

sculptures spread across an attractive landscape of trees, shrubs, and flower gardens. Keep an eye out for the remarkable 165-foot-long sleeping Buddha. The park was laid out by the monk's followers in 1958 on a strip of land along the Mekong, opposite the Thai town of Nong Khai. Get there by taking public bus #14 from the Talat Sao bus station. ✉ *Thadeua Rd.* ✣ *Km 27–28, northeast of Thai-Lao Friendship Bridge* 🎫 *5,000 kip, 3,000 kip camera fee.*

Restaurants

★ Acqua

$$ | **ITALIAN** | With chic mosaics and a cool bar downstairs and private VIP dining areas upstairs, Acqua is visually stunning, and the food keeps pace with the decor. All the usual Italian stalwarts grace the menu, along with imported oysters and Wagyu beef. **Known for:** pizzas; lunch buffet; extensive wine list. [$] *Average main: 98,000 kip* ✉ *007/078 Rue Francois Ngin, Ban Mixay, Ban Mixay* ☎ *020/2811–7888* 💳 *No credit cards.*

Khop Chai Deu

$ | **ECLECTIC** | A popular downtown restaurant and bar inside a French colonial structure, this is an excellent stop for happy-hour cocktails or dinner. For a tasty introduction to traditional Lao cuisine, try the Lao Discovery, a set menu including *larb*, a semi-spicy salad; *tom yum*, a sour chili-and-lemongrass fish soup; *khao niaw*, Lao sticky rice; and a glass of *lao-lao* (rice whisky). **Known for:** happy-hour cocktails; Lao, Asian, and international dishes; live music. [$] *Average main: 60,000 kip* ✉ *54 Setthathirat Rd.* ✣ *Near Nam Phu Sq.* ☎ *021/263829.*

Kualao

$$ | **LAO** | The Lao cuisine at this restaurant inside a fading mansion is among Vientiane's best. Favorites include *mok pa fork* (steamed fish wrapped in banana leaves and cooked with eggs, onions, and coconut milk), and *gaeng panaeng,* a thick red curry with chicken, pork, or beef. **Known for:** classy ambience; Lao folk dancing evening performances; larb and black sticky rice. [$] *Average*

main: 85,000 kip ✉ 134 Samsenthai Rd. ✣ One block southeast of Nam Phu Sq. ☎ 021/214813 🌐 www.kualaorestaurant.com.

★ La Signature

$$$ | **FRENCH** | The charming restaurant of the boutique Ansara Hotel serves authentic French cuisine in a romantic garden setting. Appetizers on the varied menu might include anything from fish carpaccio or a warm goat-cheese salad to the over-the-top combo of fried duck and duck foie gras. **Known for:** superb wine selection; daily chef's plates; refined atmosphere. *$ Average main: 150,000 kip ✉ Ansara Hotel, Quai Fa Ngum, Ban Vat Cham Tha, Hom 5, Muang Chanthabury ✣ 100 meters up from river road on small side lane just past Wat Chan ☎ 021/213514 🌐 www.ansarahotel.com.*

★ Villa Opera

$$$ | **ITALIAN** | The new location of this longtime Italian restaurant, in a beautiful colonial villa with garden, sits a bit out of the main tourist center, but still reigns as a steady Vientiane's grande dame. Villa Opera serves authentic pastas, baked entrées, and fresh salads along with items like the Pizza de Laos, made with chilies and Lao sausage. **Known for:** homemade pasta; stylish renovation; homely but high-end. *$ Average main: 150,000 kip ✉ 42 Rue Panya Si, Si Thane Nuea ☎ 021/215099.*

Noy's Fruit Heaven

$ | **CAFÉ** | The family that runs this cute little café serves gourmet sandwiches, prepares various breakfasts, and can whip up just about any tropical fruit smoothie you can dream up. The sandwiches include imported feta, Camembert, or goat cheese melted onto fresh baguettes. *$ Average main: 30,000 kip ✉ 060 Hengbounnoy Rd. ☎ 020/5539–6898 ▭ No credit cards.*

Taj Mahal

$ | **INDIAN** | A nondescript eatery tucked behind the Lao National Culture Hall, Taj Mahal serves Indian food at ridiculously cheap prices. Excellent tandoori naan bread, a good selection of dal and meat and fish curries, and other northern Indian favorites are among the many menu choices. *$ Average main: 30,000 kip ✉ Setthathirat Rd. ✣ Off Nokkeokoumano Rd., behind Lao National Culture Hall ☎ 020/5561–1003 ▭ No credit cards.*

Beware: Happy Meals

When you see a sign for "Happy Pizza" or "Happy Shakes" in Vang Vieng, you might imagine there's a jolly local cook whipping up that pizza or shake. Well, the chef might indeed be jolly but you won't be if you are caught ingesting what is in actuality marijuana-laced pizza or shakes. Marijuana is illegal in Laos (but you'd never know the way restaurants openly advertise happy meals) so know that you can be fined and even jailed. Bummer.

★ Tamnak Lao

$ | **LAO** | A wonderful place to experience Lao cuisine and culture, the latter in the form of classical dances performed nightly, this restaurant provides a blissful retreat from the downtown tourist frenzy. You can dine either in the teakwood interior space or outside in the garden. **Known for:** local cuisine; French Colonial setting; fresh fish from the Mekong. *$ Average main: 60,000 kip ✉ 100 Phonxay, 23 Singha Rd., Saysettha ✣ Just northeast of Patuxay Monument ☎ 021/413562 🌐 / ⏲ Closed Sun.*

Hotels

★ Ansara Hotel

$$$ | **HOTEL** | A small boutique hotel on a quiet lane near the Mekong River, the Ansara is convenient to local attractions.

Lao Cuisine

It may not be as famous as Thai food, but Lao cuisine is similar and often just as good, though usually less spicy. Chilies are used as a condiment, but Lao cuisine also makes good use of ginger, lemongrass, coconut, tamarind, crushed peanuts, and fish paste. Because so much of the country is wilderness, there's usually game, such as venison or wild boar, on the menu. Fresh river prawns and fish—including the famous, massive Mekong catfish, the world's largest freshwater fish—are also standard fare, along with chicken, vegetables, and sticky rice.

As in Isan, *larb* (meat salad with shallots, lime juice, chilies, garlic, and other spices) is a staple, as are sticky rice and *tam mak hu*, the Lao version of green-papaya salad. Grilled chicken, pork, and duck stalls can be found in every bus station and market in the country. Northern Laos, especially Luang Prabang, is noted for its distinctive cuisine: specialties include grilled Mekong seaweed, sprinkled with sesame seeds and served with a spicy chili dip; and *orlam*, an eggplant-and-meat stew with bitter herbs. Sticky rice, served in bamboo baskets, is the bread and butter of Laos. Locals eat it with their hands, squeezing it into a solid ball or log and dipping it in other dishes.

Throughout the country you'll find *pho*, a Vietnamese–style noodle soup, served for breakfast. Fresh baguettes, a throwback to the French colonial days, are also available everywhere, often made into sandwiches with meat pâté, vegetables, and chili sauce. Laotians wash it all down with extra-strong Lao coffee sweetened with condensed milk, or the ubiquitous Beerlao, a slightly sweet lager.

Pros: extremely quiet; free laptops in rooms; free minibar replenished daily. **Cons:** expensive; a bit hard to find; lacks spa. *Rooms from: 1,100,000 kip* *Quai Fa Ngum, Ban Vat Cham Tha, Hom 5, Muang Chanthabury* *100 meters up from river road on small side lane just past Wat Chan* *021/213514* *www.ansarahotel.com* *28 rooms* *Free breakfast.*

Best Western Vientiane

$$ | **HOTEL** | With a convenient location in the heart of town near the Mekong River, and comfort at competitive rates, this hotel is popular with business travelers. **Pros:** fitness center and Jacuzzi; quiet pool area; great location near river and restaurants. **Cons:** small pool; no views; rooms feel slightly worn. *Rooms from: 690,000 kip* *2–12 Francois Ngin Rd., Ban Mixay* *021/216906 up to 09* *www.bestwesternvientiane.com* *44 rooms* *No meals.*

Bloom Hotel & Cafe

$$ | **HOTEL** | This small boutique hotel above the namesake Euro-inspired bistro offers a few good value, squeaky-clean rooms that range from basic-but-stylish doubles to larger mini–studio apartments. **Pros:** intimate; stretches the budget in style; central. **Cons:** no views; no swimming pool; dining options somewhat limited. *Rooms from: 443,406 kip* *Wat Xieng Ngeun Alley, Sethathirath Road* *021/21640* *https://bit.ly/2B0w-0ja* *16* *Free breakfast.*

Dhavara Boutique Hotel

$$$$ | **HOTEL** | This white-tinged hotel offers larger-than-life and spacious rooms in a very central yet quiet side street. **Pros:** no pool; central yet quiet location;

50% in low season. **Cons:** balconies only in deluxe rooms; views are not great; pricey. *$ Rooms from: 1,279,000 kip ✉ 25 Manthaturath Road, Xieng Ngeun Village ☎ 021/222238 🌐 www.dhavarahotel.com ⇌ 24 rooms 🍽 Free breakfast.*

Ibis Vientiane Nam Phu

$$ | HOTEL | This a good choice if you're after a trusted brand with clean and comfortable facilities, right next to the Nam Phu Fountain and the adjoining restaurant and bars. **Pros:** central Nam Phu Fountain location; blackout curtains on windows; trusted brand. **Cons:** no gym or pool; small rooms; breakfast not included. *$ Rooms from: 730,000 kip ✉ Box 2359, Nam Phu Sq. ☎ 021/262050 🌐 www.ibishotel.com ⇌ 64 rooms 🍽 No meals.*

Lao Plaza Hotel

$$$$ | HOTEL | Something of a local landmark, the Lao Plaza stands six stories tall in the center of town. **Pros:** large swimming pool and terrace; enormous beds; three restaurants. **Cons:** way overpriced for what you get; on very busy street; constant hassle from tuk-tuk drivers outside. *$ Rooms from: 1,700,000 kip ✉ 63 Samsenthai Rd. ☎ 021/218800, 021/218801 🌐 www.laoplazahotel.com ⇌ 142 rooms 🍽 Free breakfast.*

Mercure Vientiane

$$$ | HOTEL | A five-minute drive from the airport, this modern hotel with a sweeping art-nouveau facade has a pleasant location in front of Fa Ngum Park. **Pros:** tennis courts; full slate of amenities; good Internet discounts. **Cons:** out of town center; on very busy road; expensive. *$ Rooms from: 909,000 kip ✉ Unit 10, Samsenthai Rd., at Setthathirat Rd. ☎ 021/213570 🌐 www.accorhotels.com ⇌ 172 rooms 🍽 No meals.*

Salana Boutique Hotel

$$$ | HOTEL | Rooms with Lao textiles and decor, finely crafted wood floors, and modern amenities like flat-screen TVs and fast Wi-Fi make this boutique hotel on a quiet downtown street a splendid choice. **Pros:** in the heart of the city center; temple views from some rooms; chic, with fine wood floors and Lao decor. **Cons:** rooms are tiny; expensive for downtown; staff can be a bit arrogant. *$ Rooms from: 1,100,000 kip ✉ Chao Anou Rd., 112 Ban Wat Chan ☎ 021/254254 🌐 www.salanaboutique.com ⇌ 42 rooms 🍽 Free breakfast.*

★ Settha Palace

$$$$ | HOTEL | Rooms at this landmark property have high ceilings, hardwood floors, Oriental rugs, and period pieces that reflect its many histories—from its inception in the French colonial period to its life as a hotel in the 1930s and again in the 90s (with a period of expropriation by the Communist government in between). **Pros:** elegant and private; gorgeous furnishings; beautiful pool garden. **Cons:** often fully booked; no elevator; only four standard rooms. *$ Rooms from: 1,800,000 kip ✉ 6 Pang Kham Rd. ☎ 021/217581, 021/217582 🌐 www.setthapalace.com ⇌ 29 rooms 🍽 Free breakfast.*

Nightlife

The after-dark scene in Vientiane is very subdued, mostly confined to certain expensive hotels and a handful of bars and pubs along the Mekong River boulevard.

Bor Pen Yang

BARS/PUBS | Vientiane's most popular bar, also a restaurant serving international cuisine, occupies a prime spot on the Mekong, with great views from the rooftop setting. On most nights the place is packed with locals and travelers—plus an assortment of ladyboys and bar girls—but the views, music, and camaraderie are good enough to prevent it from becoming seedy. Bor Pen Yang is open from 10 am to midnight. *✉ Fah Ngum Quay, Ban Wat Chan ☎ 021/264544 office, 020/787–3965.*

Chokdee Café Belgian Beer Bar
BARS/PUBS | With an interesting Tintin-inspired decor and beers imported from Belgium (14 on tap and much more bottled), it's no wonder this casual bar is as popular as it is, albeit a little expensive for Vientiane. Dishes like the excellent mussels in garlic butter sauce greatly exceed pup-grub expectations. ✉ *Quai Fa Ngum* ✣ *On the riverside* ☎ *021/263847*.

Lao Bowling Center
GATHERING PLACES | The bowling alley around the corner from Settha Palace serves food and drink to a rowdy mix of locals and expats. ✉ *Khun Bulon Rd. and Rue Le Ky Huong* ☎ *021/218661, 021/223219*.

Traditional Lao Show
DANCE | The Lane Xang Hotel presents traditional Lao dancing and music nightly from 7 to 9 at its restaurant. The performances are free, though you'll likely want to have dinner or at least drinks. ✉ *Lane Xang Hotel, Rue Pangkham and Fa Ngum Rd.* ☎ *021/214100* *Free*.

Shopping

Carol Cassidy Lao Textiles
TEXTILES/SEWING | American-born textile expert Carol Cassidy runs this beautiful weaving studio inside a renovated French Colonial mansion. She and her team of local artisans, mostly women, create high-quality textiles and scarves, shawls, and wall hangings. ✉ *84–86 Nokkeokoumane Rd.* ☎ *021/212123* 🌐 *www.laotextiles.com* ⏲ *Closed Sun*.

Caruso Lao
CRAFTS | For exquisite handwoven Lao silk and fine wood carvings, head to this riverside craft shop, one of the best in Laos. ✉ *008 Fa Ngum Rd.* ✣ *A few blocks northwest of Don Chan Palace hotel* ☎ *021/223644* 🌐 *www.carusolao.com*.

Phaeng Mai Silk Gallery
TEXTILES/SEWING | This shop in Vientiane's old weaving district sells naturally dyed handwoven silk products. ✉ *110 Ban Nongbuathong Tai* ☎ *021/217341* ⏲ *Closed Sun*.

Saoban Crafts
CRAFTS | A fair-trade business that works with traditional artisans to preserve and promote Lao village crafts and empower local women, this shop sells silk and cotton textiles, recycled bomb products, bags, jewelry, and other items. ✉ *Chao Anou Rd., 97/1 Ban Watchan* ✣ *Near Wat Ong Teu* ☎ *020/5510–0034* 🌐 *www.saobancrafts.com*.

Talat Sao (*Morning Market*)
GIFTS/SOUVENIRS | With crafts, jewelry, T-shirts, and more, the morning market will satisfy most shoppers' needs. The adjacent indoor mall hosts many mobile phone sellers and electronics vendors. A visit to the morning market provides perspectives on modern Lao life and the lifestyles of young Laotians. ✉ *Lane Xang Ave. at Khao Vieng St*.

Nam Ngum Lake

90 km (56 miles) north of Vientiane.

GETTING HERE AND AROUND

You can take a bus from Talat Sao Bus Station to the Talat bus stop, where songthaews (15,000 kip) continue on to Nam Ngum. The trip takes three hours. To really experience the area, though, consider taking a full-day Green Discovery Laos (⇨ *Tours, in Planning, above*) adventure tour, which includes a boat ride on the lake. Hiring a car and driver for the day will run about 500,000 kip ($62). If you're driving, take Highway 10 north from Vientiane to the Lao Zoo; from there, follow the road for the Dansavanh Resort.

TIMING

This trip is best done as a day tour, but if you have extra time, spend the night in one of the area's many lodges.

Phu Khao Khouay

40 km (25 miles) northeast of Vientiane

GETTING HERE AND AROUND

This National Park is about three hours from Vientiane, via Highway 13 south to Tha Bok and then via a side road north from there. Green Discovery Laos (⇨ *Tours, in Planning, above*) runs reasonably priced one- to two-day treks and homestays; this is a good way to see the park, because hiring a car and driver is pricey. It's not recommended to go without a tour operator because the park itself no longer offers scheduled activities, and accommodations are run down and expensive. Should you decide to venture out on your own, buses run from Talat Sao to Tha Bok (25,000 kip); from there, songthaews go to Ban Hat Khai, where you can arrange treks.

TIMING

One day or an overnight trip is enough time to see the area.

Plain of Jars

390 km (242 miles) northeast of Vientiane, 270 km (162 miles) southeast of Luang Prabang.

How did they get here? is the question you will ask as you consider the hundreds of megalithic jars clustered together across the plains and throughout the province of Xieng Khuang. Interspersed between all those stone jars are trenches and bomb craters. From the early 19th century until 1975, the area was a recurring battle zone. Hundreds of unexploded ordinances have been cleared from the area but you won't want to wander beyond the markers... just in case.

GETTING HERE AND AROUND

A long day's drive along Highway 7 from either Vang Vieng or Luang Prabang (about seven or eight hours), the vast plain is difficult to reach but a wonder to behold. Travel agencies in Vientiane and Luang Prabang, among them Diethelm Travel *(see Laos Planner)*, offer tours. You'll fly into Xieng Khuang Airport in Phonsavan, which is 3 km (2 miles) outside town. Lao Airlines flies daily from Vientiane for about $100. There is also a paved road between Phonsavan and Pakxan, on the highway south of Vientiane. A trip on this road takes eight hours by bus. Most hotels and guesthouses in Phonsavan can arrange trips to the jar sites for 120,000 kip per person in a shared minivan; you can also take a taxi to the sites for about 250,000 kip.

The bus to Phonsavan from Luang Prabang costs 105,000 kip, and takes seven hours. From Vientiane the cost is 150,000 kip; the trip takes 10 hours or more.

SAFETY AND PRECAUTIONS

Stay on marked paths, and don't stray off into the countryside without a guide; the Plain of Jars area is still littered with unexploded ordnance.

TIMING

One day is enough to see the jar sites and visit some local villages. Nevertheless, Phonsavan is a friendly place that doesn't see many tourists other than visitors to the jars, and it may be worthwhile to spend an extra day exploring the pretty surrounding countryside, hot springs, and local villages.

TOURS

Sousath Travel

GUIDED TOURS | This is the best tour operator in town. Run by the Maly Hotel family, it conducts many different trips around the area, from basic Plain of Jars tours to Luang Prabang boat trips. The day trips to the jars and local villages and overnight treks to visit Hmong villages are an excellent way to experience rural Laos. ✉ *Xaysana Rd. (Hwy. 7), Phonsavan* ☎ *020/2296–7213* *From 120,000 kip.*

Restaurants

Bamboozle Restaurant and Bar

$ | **BURGER** | This cozy bamboo-walled restaurant dishes up some Western and Lao staples, in a central location close to the town's market. A bit expensive for Phonsavan's standards but a perfect spot for those longing for some comfort-foods. **Known for:** lemon honey margaritas; tasty hamburgers; pizzas. *Average main: 42,635 kip* ✉ *Number 73, Unit 5, Phonsavan* ☎ *020/7792–8959* *No credit cards.*

Nisha

$ | **INDIAN** | Here's a double surprise: some of the best food in Laos can be found in remote Phonsavan, and it's Indian to boot. Hole-in-the-wall Nisha, presided over by its amiable owners from Tamil Nadu, serves fantastic Indian cuisine. **Known for:** Chicken Lessani; full vegetarian menu; nan bread. *Average main: 40,000 kip* ✉ *7th Rd., Ban Thai, Phonsavan* ✥ *At eastern end of Phonsavan's main street (Hwy. 7)* ☎ *030/984–8435* *No credit cards.*

Hotels

Maly Hotel

$ | **HOTEL** | **FAMILY** | With nice enough rooms to let, a good restaurant, and a tour agency, the Maly Hotel is not as well looked after as it used to, but remains good value in Phonsavan. **Pros:** excellent in-house tour agency; good restaurant; discounts often available when hotel isn't

Who created the ancient jars on the Plain of Jars, and why, remains a mystery.

full. **Cons:** deluxe rooms overpriced; a bit of a hike to center of town; not the best value for Phonsavan. *Rooms from: 284,000 kip* ✉ *Muang Phouan Rd., Phonsavan* ✣ *East of Lao Mongol Hospital* ☎ *020/5550–6255* 🌐 *www.malyhotel.com* *26 rooms* *Free breakfast.*

Pukyo Guesthouse

$ | **B&B/INN** | This relaxing Lao-Belgian-run guesthouse set in a quiet neighborhood about 2 miles out of town offers five clean and large rooms, some with balconies, in an authentic Lao mansion. **Pros:** good breakfast included; authentic Lao house; free tea, coffee, and fruit all day. **Cons:** out of town; tiny en suite bathrooms; far from other dining options. *Rooms from: 341,082 kip* ✉ *56 Saylom Village, Phonsavan* ✣ *3 km from Phonsavan's center* ☎ *020/5955–6275* *5 rooms* *Free breakfast.*

Vang Vieng

160 km (99 miles) north of Vientiane.

Backpackers traveling between Vientiane and Luang Prabang on Highway 13 discovered the town of Vang Vieng in the mid-1990s. During the Vietnam War the United States maintained an airstrip in the town center; there are rumors that the abandoned tarmac will someday field direct flights from Luang Prabang or elsewhere. Vang Vieng became famous for its rope-swing party bars along the river, attracting a huge backpacker crowd. In 2012, due to a huge number of deaths caused by drinking, drugs, and drowning, the Lao government closed the bars along the river. Today Vang Vieng is starting to move slightly more upscale and trying to disassociate itself from the backpacker party scene, and it attracts a steady number of Korean and Chinese tour package groups. The town's cramped and overdeveloped main tourist strip is not that appealing anymore, but the natural scenery beyond the bridge is still worth visiting.

GETTING HERE AND AROUND

BUS TRAVEL

From Vientiane you can take a minibus (50,000 kip), which takes three to four hours to reach Vang Vieng.

VIP buses (105,000 kip) headed back to Vientiane from Luang Prabang stop here three times a day—the journey takes seven hours. Minivan rides to Vang Vieng can be arranged at travel agencies in both cities for about the same price as a VIP bus ticket.

A daily bus (110,000 kip) goes to Phonsavan (Plain of Jars), a six-hour ride.

SONGTHAEW TRAVEL

Songthaews run from the bus station, 2 km (1 mile) north of town, to all hotels for 20,000 kip per person. They can also be hired for excursions farther afield; prepare to bargain.

SAFETY AND PRECAUTIONS

Always double-check prices in Vang Vieng, as merchants are notorious for overcharging. Make sure to shop around and compare, as quotes for identical services may vary wildly.

The river can be fast flowing during rainy season. All but the strongest swimmers are advised to wear a life vest and take the necessary precautions when inner tubing or kayaking.

Do not under any circumstances accept offers for smoking marijuana or other drugs in Vang Vieng. Dealers are usually informants for the police, and visitors who are caught face paying a very large bribe or jail time.

TIMING

Vang Vieng itself is not all that pleasant, but the surrounding countryside merits investigation. One day to explore the caves and go farther afield, and one day to relax on the river should be plenty.

EMERGENCIES

HOSPITAL Provincial Hospital ✉ *Ban Vieng Keo, Vangviang* ✣ *Across from Ban Sabai Guesthouse, along river* ☎ *023/511604.*

TOURS

Green Discovery Laos

GUIDED TOURS | This established tour operator offers a variety of full and half-day tours exploring Vang Vieng's surroundings. Choose between kayak excursions on the Nam Song River, visits to the caves, experiences in local villages, or a combination of the three. ✉ *Kangmuong St., Vangviang* ☎ *023/511230* 🌐 *www.greendiscoverylaos.com* *Kayaking trip 592,000 kip ($73) per person for 2 people, less for larger groups.*

Sights

Vang Vieng

TOWN | Some of the most attractive scenery and countryside in Laos, including the Nam Song River and a dramatic range of jagged limestone mountains, surrounds this convenient stopover between Vientiane and Luang Prabang. These days the town center is jam-packed with bars and backpacker hangouts, but you can escape the noise and the crowds by making for the river, which is lined with guesthouses and restaurants catering to both backpackers and those on a more flexible budget. The river is clean and good for swimming and kayaking, and the mountains beyond are riddled with caves and small, pleasant swimming holes. River trips and caving expeditions are organized by every guesthouse and hotel. Treks to the caves can be fairly arduous, and some are only accessible by motorbike or bicycle, a popular alternative. Go via the toll bridge next to Riverside Boutique Hotel (4,000 kip on foot; 6,000 kip by bicycle; 10,000 kip by motorbike) and expect to pay between 10,000/20,000 kip to enter most caves. Less adventurous types can rent an inner tube for 55,000 kip and float down the

The pretty village of Vang Vieng is surrounded by spectacular limestone cliffs.

river for a few hours. ✉ *Along Hwy. 13, Vangviang.*

Restaurants

La Verandah Riverside

$ | **ECLECTIC** | This beautifully situated resort restaurant right on the river serves an impressive mix of Thai, Lao, French, and Western dishes. The penang curry is aromatic and full of flavor, as is the spaghetti *pad kee mao* (drunken noodles, with basil and chili sauce). **Known for:** good wine list; duck breast with honey and red wine sauce; affordable set menus. $ *Average main: 73,000 kip* ✉ *Villa Nam Song Resort, Unit 9, Ban Viengkeo, Vangviang* ☎ *023/511637* 🌐 *www.villanamsong.com.*

Restaurant du Crabe d'Or

$$ | **ECLECTIC** | Vang Vieng's haute cuisine restaurant offers an eclectic choice of Lao, traditional Asian, and French dishes—the Laotian sampling menu the top draw. The indoor and outdoor dining areas command majestic views of the river and towering limestone cliffs. **Known for:** salmon carpaccio and glazed duck breast; extensive list of French and Chilean wines; strong Lao coffee. $ *Average main: 95,000 kip* ✉ *Riverside Boutique Resort, Ban Viengkeo, Vangviang* ☎ *023/511726* 🌐 *www.riversidevangvieng.com/restaurant/.*

Hotels

Amari Vang Vieng

$$ | **RESORT** | Towering above the river in close proximity to Vang Vieng's tourist enclave, the Amari is popular with tour groups, but sleek rooms with wall windows and attractive river-view balconies offset that nuisance. **Pros:** trusted brand; large pool next to the river; spacious reception hall. **Cons:** breakfast is $15 extra; close to a noisy and ugly part of town; not all rooms have views. $ *Rooms from: 724,799 kip* ✉ *Song River Road, Sawang Village, Ban Savan* ☎ *023/511800 up to 09* 🌐 *www.amari.com/vang-vieng* 🛏 *160 rooms* 🍽 *No meals.*

Elephant Crossing Hotel

$$ | **RESORT** | Almost every room at this modern four-story hotel has a river view, a balcony, hardwood floors, and wooden trim constructed of recycled bits of old Lao houses. **Pros:** river views; free Wi-Fi; private balcony in each room. **Cons:** small rooms; fairly long walk to town center; often crowded with tour groups. *Rooms from: 410,000 kip ✉ Ban Viengkeo (Namsong Riverside), Vangviang ☎ 023/511232, 020/560–2830 🌐 www.theelephantcrossinghotel.com 35 rooms Free breakfast.*

Inthira Vang Vieng

$$$ | **HOTEL** | This central hotel's well-appointed rooms have wood floors, large and modern en suite bathrooms, and balconies offering stunning views of the Nam Song River and mountain backdrop. **Pros:** private river views; large pool; good restaurant. **Cons:** close to a busy part of town; lacks a spa; some bathrooms less modern. *Rooms from: 835,650 kip ✉ Ban Viengkeo, Vangviang ☎ 023/511088 🌐 www.inthirahotels.com/vangvieng 38 rooms Free breakfast.*

★ Riverside Boutique Resort

$$$ | **RESORT** | With the best riverside viewpoint in town, overlooking fabulous mountain scenery and an atmospheric wooden bridge, this upscale boutique hotel is blissfully, beautifully serene. **Pros:** best viewpoint in Vang Vieng; best swimming pool; quiet and away from the backpacking crowd. **Cons:** not all rooms have good river views; breakfast buffet a bit bland; expensive for the area. *Rooms from: 1,100,000 kip ✉ Ban Viengkeo, Vangviang ☎ 023/511726, 023/511727 🌐 www.riversidevangvieng.com 34 rooms Free breakfast.*

Luang Prabang

390 km (242 miles) north of Vientiane.

Luang Prabang is Laos's religious and artistic capital, and its combination of impressive natural surroundings, historic architecture, and friendly inhabitants make it one of the region's best stopovers. The abundance of ancient temples led UNESCO to declare Luang Prabang a World Heritage Site in 1995, and since then it's been bustling with construction and renovation activity.

But the charm of Luang Prabang is not exclusively architectural—just as appealing are the people, who seem to spend as much time on the streets as they do in their homes. Children play on the sidewalks while matrons gossip in the shade, young women in traditional dress zip past on motor scooters, and Buddhist monks in saffron robes stroll by with black umbrellas, which protect their shaven heads from the tropical sun. Some 36 temples are scattered around town, making Luang Prabang a fine place to explore on a rented bicycle or on foot. When you need a break from temple-hopping, there are plenty of appealing eateries and fashionable boutiques. Waking early one morning to watch the throngs of monks make their alms runs at dawn is highly recommended. Your hotel should be able to tell you what time to get up and suggest a good viewing spot.

■ TIP→ Locals may approach you to buy food from them to serve to the monks, but this is not wise. The locals often give packs of unsuitable rice or other junk to turn a profit. Speak to someone at your lodging or a reputable agency in town about how best to donate to the monks.

GETTING HERE AND AROUND

AIR TRAVEL

There are direct flights to Luang Prabang from Bangkok and Chiang Mai. Lao Airlines operates two flights daily from Bangkok and one from Chiang Mai, and Bangkok Airways flies twice daily from Bangkok. There is also service between Luang Prabang and Singapore, Hanoi, and, in Cambodia, Phnom Penh and Siem Reap. Lao Airlines also operates three flights a day between Vientiane and

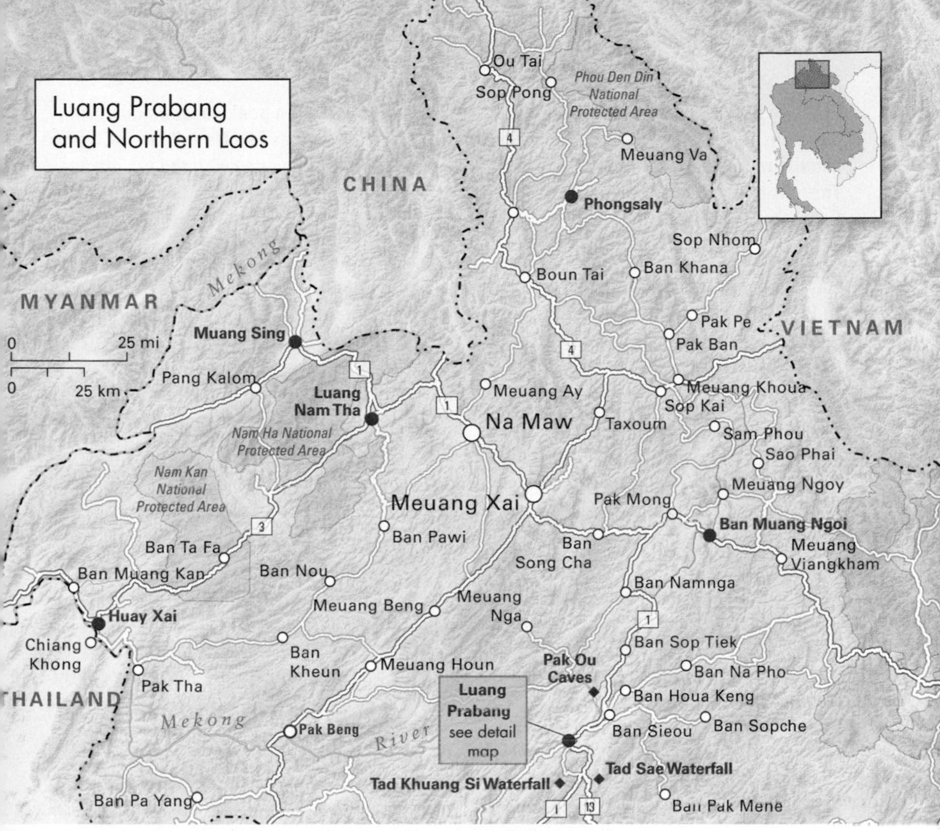

Luang Prabang, and one between Pakse and Luang Prabang.

Luang Prabang International Airport is 4 km (2½ miles) northeast of the city. The taxi ride to the city center costs 50,000 kip.

BIKE TRAVEL

Biking is one of the best ways to visit all the interesting sights within Luang Prabang, and many hotels provide bicycles for guests. If yours does not, you can rent one from shops in town for 20,000 to 30,000 kip per day.

BOAT AND FERRY TRAVEL

Boats for hire can be found just about anywhere along the entire length of the road bordering the Mekong River; the main jetty is on the river side of Wat Xieng Thong.

BUS AND MINIVAN TRAVEL

Buses from Vientiane arrive four or five times daily; the trip to Luang Prabang takes between 9 and 11 hours. You have your choice of VIP (usually with air-conditioning and toilets aboard), express, and regular buses; prices range from 130,000 to 150,000 kip. You'll pay more if you buy your ticket from an agency in town, though it is convenient. There are also buses to Phonsavan (eight hours; 100,000 kip), Vang Vieng (seven hours; 105,000 kip), Oudomxay (four hours; 60,000 kip), and Luang Nam Tha (nine hours; 100,000 kip), among other places. There are two bus terminals in Luang Prabang, the Northern Bus Terminal, out near the airport, and the Ban Naluang Southern Bus Terminal, in the south of town, with services to respective destinations. **■ TIP→ For about the same price as a bus, minivans make the trip to Luang**

Prabang and many other destinations far more comfortably and quickly, and service usually include pickup from your hotel. There is a minivan station opposite the Southern Bus Terminal.

CAR TRAVEL

Although you can drive from Vientiane to Luang Prabang, it takes from eight to nine hours to make the 365-km (240-mile) trip along the meandering, but paved, road up into the mountains.

TAXI, TUK-TUK, AND SONGTHAEW TRAVEL

Tuk-tuks and songthaews make up Luang Prabang's public transport system. They cruise all the streets and are easy to flag down, but the drivers are a pain to negotiate with and will attempt to charge extortionate prices. Plan on paying around 20,000 kip for a trip within the city. The few taxis in town must be booked through your hotel or guesthouse. ■**TIP→ There are now tramlike vehicles that cost only 5,000 kip. The locals use them and they are a great alternative to tuk-tuks, but they only run along fixed routes. If you'd like to use them, ask someone at your hotel for advice.**

SAFETY AND PRECAUTIONS

For medical and police emergencies, use the services of your hotel or guesthouse. The higher-end resorts have a doctor on call from Luang Prabang Provincial Hospital. For serious emergencies, one needs to fly to Bangkok or Vientiane.

Luang Prabang is safe, but beware of unscrupulous tuk-tuk drivers.

TIMING

Unless you are a temple addict, three or four days in Luang Prabang is more than enough, although with the waterfalls and cave side trips, it's easy to pass more time here. If you have the extra time, try to get farther north, where there are fewer tourists and fantastic nature.

■**TIP→ Despite scores of guesthouses, finding accommodations here can be a challenge in the peak season and during holidays such as Lao New Year or Chinese New Year. When you visit the top attractions, be prepared for crowds of tourists.**

TOURS

Tiger Trail

ECOTOURISM | Established in 2000, this tour operator focuses on sustainable tours, offering one-day to weeklong tailored itineraries through the country's most famous and remote reaches. ✉ *Sisavangvong Rd.* ✢ *Across the road from Luang Prabang Bakery* ☎ *030/ 996–6969* 🌐 *laos-adventures.com* 🎫 *From 400,000 kip (50$) per person.*

★ **White Elephant Adventures**

ADVENTURE TOURS | By far Luang Prabang's best tour operator, White Elephant conducts single and multiday hiking, biking, and kayaking adventures led by well-trained local guides. The company's foreign-born owners are as enthusiastic about sharing their adopted country as they are about making sure each visitor's touring experience is authentic and fulfilling. They also strive to ensure that the impact of their journeys on the local people and the environment is low. A great source of local information, the organization is involved with literacy projects for rural Lao girls and other self-help initiatives. ✉ *44/3 Sisavangvong Rd.* ✢ *Across street from Luang Prabang Bakery* 🌐 *www.white-elephant-adventures-laos.com* 🎫 *From 400,000 kip ($50) per person.*

Green Discovery Laos, Lao Youth Travel, and **Diethelm Travel** *(see Laos Planner)*have Luang Prabang branches.

Sights

★ **Laos Buffalo Dairy**

FARM/RANCH | **FAMILY** | Opened by a group of expatriates who complained that the cost of cheese in Luang Prabang was too high, this full-fledged water buffalo farm started as a social enterprise, and now welcomes tourists. Laos Buffalo Dairy

A Good Walk (or Ride)

Touring the city's major sights takes a full day—maybe longer if you climb Phu Si Hill, which has particularly lovely views at sunset. The evening bazaar on Sisavangvong Road starts around 6 pm. Though the distances between these attractions are walkable, you may not want to do this all on foot if it's really hot out. Rent a bike, or break this into a few shorter walks, and stay out of the sun during the heat of the day.

Start your tour of Luang Prabang at the **Tribal Market,** at the intersection of Sisavangvong Road and Setthathirat Road. From here head northeast along Sisavangvong, stopping on the left at one of the city's most beautiful temples, **Wat Mai.** Magnificent wood carvings and golden murals decorate the main pillars and portico entrance to the temple. Continue down Sisavangvong to the compound of the **Royal Palace,** with its large bronze statue of King Sisavangvong.

On leaving the palace grounds by the main entrance, climb the staircase to **Phu Si Hill.** The climb is steep and takes about 15 minutes, but you'll be rewarded with an unforgettable view of Luang Prabang and the surrounding countryside.

Back in front of the Royal Palace, follow Sisavangvong toward the confluence of the Mekong and Nam Khan rivers, where you can find another fascinating Luang Prabang temple, **Wat Xieng Thong.** Leaving the compound on the Mekong River side, walk back to the city center along the romantic waterside road, which is fronted by several French colonial houses and Lao traditional homes. Passing the port area behind the Royal Palace, continue on to the intersection with Wat Phu Xay; turn left here to return to the Tribal Market. Every evening there's a local night market, stretching from the Tribal Market to the Royal Palace.

helps local farmers by renting their pregnant buffaloes, taking care of them and returning them healthier to their owners, who are also welcome to join a series of practical workshops. Guests can try their hand at farming and milk-making activities while learning about the challenges that local farmers face every day. Don't forget to taste the delicious ricottas, feta cheeses, and cheesecakes on offer. Admission includes cake of the day and tea. ✉ *Ban Muang Khay* ✣ *After the turnoff to Kuang Si Waterfall* ☎ *030/969–0487* 🌐 *www.laosbuffalodairy.com* 🎫 *100,000 kip.*

★ Night Market

MARKET | The night market is a hub of activity, full of colorful local souvenirs and cheap, delicious food, and a meeting place for locals and tourists. Starting in the late afternoon, Sisavangvong Road is closed to vehicles from the tourist office down to the Royal Palace, and a tented area is set up, thronged with vendors selling lanterns, patterned cushion covers, Lao coffee and tea, hand-stitched bags, and many other local crafts. Small side streets are lined with food stalls selling everything from fried chicken to Mekong seaweed and other treats at a fraction of the price you'll pay in a restaurant. It's worth strolling the market just for the atmosphere. ✉ *Sisavangvong Rd., from Kitsarat Rd. to Royal Palace.*

Pha Tad Ke Botanical Garden

GARDEN | Set on 40 hectares of land on the opposite side of the Mekong, a 15-minute boat ride south of town, the

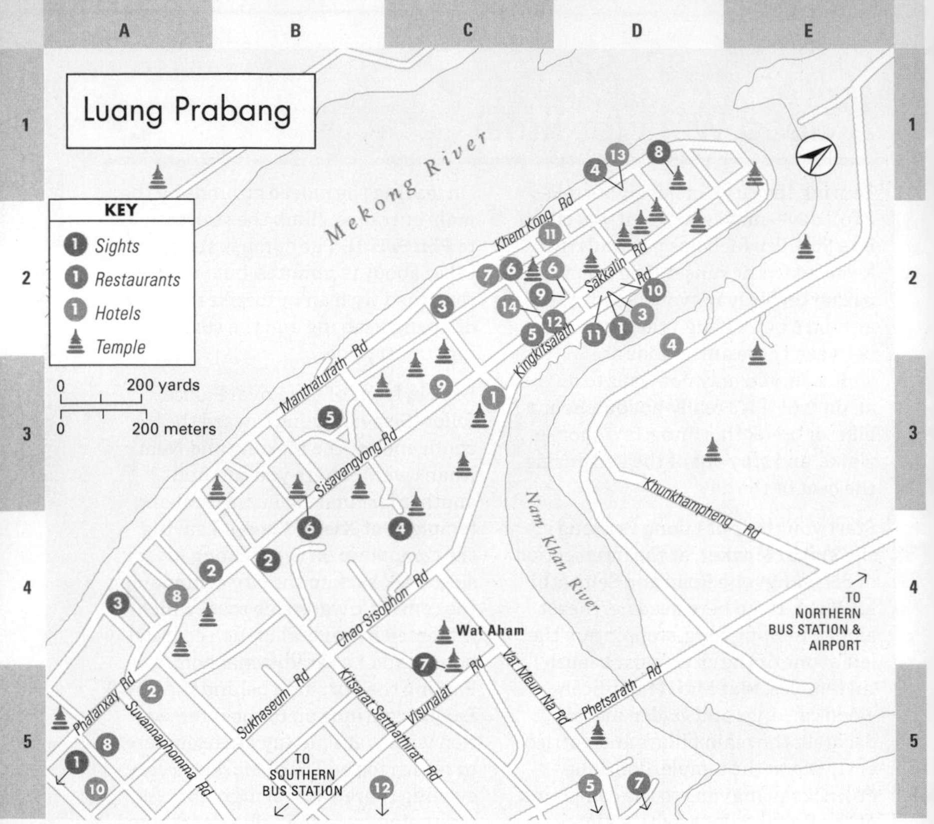

Sights

1 Laos Buffalo Dairy...... **A5**
2 Night Market............ **B4**
3 Pha Tad Ke Botanical Garden....... **A4**
4 Phu Si Hill................. **C4**
5 Royal Palace **B3**
6 Wat Mai.................. **B3**
7 Wat Visun................. **C4**
8 Wat Xieng Thong **D1**

Restaurants

1 Apsara Restaurant..... **D2**
2 Joma Bakery Café...... **B4**
3 Khaiphaen................ **C2**
4 Kitchen by the Mekong................. **D1**
5 Le Cafe et Restaurant Ban Vat Sene............ **C2**
6 L'Elephant Restaurant Français..... **C2**
7 Luang Prabang Bakery **D5**
8 Manda de Laos **A5**
9 Restaurant Les 3 Nagas **D2**
10 Rosella Fusion Restaurant.............. **D2**
11 Tamarind Restaurant and Cooking School.... **D2**
12 Tamnak Lao **C2**

Hotels

1 Amantaka................ **C3**
2 Angsana Maison Souvannaphoum......... **A5**
3 Apsara **D2**
4 Apsara Rive Droit........ **D2**
5 Belmond La Résidence Phou Vao Hotel........... **D5**
6 Hotel 3 Nagas............ **D2**
7 Le Calao Inn.............. **C2**
8 Rattana Guest House ... **A4**
9 Sackarinh Guest Room **C3**
10 Satri House.............. **A5**
11 Sayo River Guest House............. **C2**
12 Sofitel Hotel de la Paix **B5**
13 Victoria Xiengthong Palace.................. **D1**
14 Villa Sant................. **C2**

centerpiece of these botanical gardens is the ethno-botanic garden, where Laos's flora and its uses in daily life, rituals, and cuisine are richly explained. Gravel pathways bring visitors through an arboretum, a limestone habitat, and a ginger garden. This green oasis also boasts a café cum restaurant, a plant retail store, and a souvenir shop. A dedicated jetty near Wat That has hourly departures to and from the gardens until 4 pm. ✉ *Luang Prabang* ⊕ *Ticket office at Wat That* ☎ *071/261000* 🌐 *www.pha-tad-ke.com* 🎫 *210,000 kip* ⏲ *Closed Wed.*

Phu Si Hill

VIEWPOINT | Several shrines and temples and a golden stupa crown this forested hill, but the best reason to ascend its 328 steps is to enjoy the view from the summit: a panorama of Luang Prabang, the Nam Khan and Mekong rivers, and the surrounding mountains. It's a popular spot for watching the sunset (just be sure to bring insect repellent), but there are huge crowds, pickpockets, and the view from atop old Phu Si is probably better appreciated at sunrise, when you will have it all to yourself. If you're not game for the steep climb up the staircase, try the more enjoyable hike up the trail on the "back" side of the hill. ✉ *Luang Prabang* ⊕ *Between Sisavangvong and Phousi Rds.* ☎ 🎫 *20,000 kip.*

Royal Palace

CASTLE/PALACE | In a walled compound at the foot of Phu Si Hill stands this palace, the former home of the royal Savang family. Built at the beginning of the 20th century, the palace served as the royal residence until the Pathet Lao took over Laos in 1975 and exiled Crown Prince Savang Vatthana and his children to a remote region of the country (their fate has never been established). It still has the feel of a large family home—a maze of teak-floor rooms surprisingly modest in scale. The largest of them is the **Throne Room,** with its gilded furniture, colorful mosaic-covered walls, and display cases filled with rare Buddha images, royal regalia, and other priceless artifacts.

The walls of the **King's Reception Room** are decorated with scenes of traditional Lao life painted in 1930 by the French artist Alex de Fautereau. The **Queen's Reception Room** contains a collection of royal portraits by the Russian artist Ilya Glazunov. The room also has cabinets full of presents given to the royal couple by visiting heads of state; a model moon lander and a piece of moon rock from U.S. president Richard Nixon share shelf space with an exquisite Sèvres tea set presented by French president Charles de Gaulle and fine porcelain teacups from Chinese leader Mao Tse-tung. Other exhibits in this eclectic collection include friezes removed from local temples, Khmer drums, and elephant tusks with carved images of the Buddha.

The museum's most prized exhibit is the **Pha Bang,** a gold image of the Buddha slightly less than 3 feet tall and weighing more than 100 pounds. Its history goes back to the 1st century, when it was cast in Sri Lanka; it was brought to Luang Prabang from Cambodia in 1359 as a gift to King Fa Ngum. This event is celebrated as the introduction of Buddhism as an official religion to Laos, and Pha Bang is venerated as the protector of the faith. An ornate temple called Ho Pha Bang, near the entrance to the palace compound, is being restored to house the image.

Tucked away behind the palace is a crumbling wooden garage that houses the aging royal fleet of automobiles. You'll need about two hours to work through the Royal Palace's maze of rooms. ✉ *Sisavangvong Rd.* ⊕ *Across from Phu Si Hill* ☎ *071/212470* 🎫 *30,000 kip.*

Wat Mai

RELIGIOUS SITE | This small but lovely temple next to the Royal Palace compound dates from 1796. Its four-tier roof is characteristic of Luang Prabang's religious architecture, but more impressive are the magnificent wood carvings and gold-leaf murals on the main pillars and portico entrance to the temple. These intricate panels depict the last life of the Buddha, as well as various Asian animals. During the Bun Pimai festival (Lao New Year), the Prabang sacred Buddha image is carried from the Royal Palace compound to Wat Mai for ritual cleansing ceremonies. ✉ *Sisavangvong Rd.* ✣ *Near Royal Palace Museum* 🎫 *10,000 kip.*

Wat Visun

RELIGIOUS SITE | The 16th-century Wat Visun and neighboring **Wat Aham** play a central role in Lao New Year celebrations, when ancestral masks, called *phu gneu gna gneu,* are taken from Wat Aham and displayed in public. Wat Visun was built in 1503, during the reign of King Visunalat, who had the temple named after himself. Within the compound is a large and unusual watermelon-shaped stupa called **That Makmo** (literally Watermelon Stupa). The 100-foot-high mound is actually a royal tomb, where many small, precious Buddha statues were found when Chin Haw marauders destroyed the city in the late 19th century (these statues have since been moved to the Royal Palace). The temple hall was rebuilt in 1898 along the lines of the original wooden structure, and now houses an impressive collection of Buddha statues, stone inscriptions, and other Buddhist art. ✉ *Visunalat Rd.* ✣ *Near Vat Muen Na Rd.* 🎫 *10,000 kip.*

Wat Xieng Thong

RELIGIOUS SITE | Luang Prabang's most important and impressive temple complex is Wat Xieng Thong, a collection of ancient buildings near the tip of the peninsula where the Mekong and Nam Khan rivers meet. Erected in 1559 and 1560, the main temple is one of the few structures to have survived centuries of marauding Vietnamese, Chinese, and Siamese armies, and it's one of the region's best-preserved examples of Buddhist art and architecture. The intricate golden facades, colorful murals, sparkling glass mosaics, and low, sweeping roofs of the entire ensemble of buildings (which overlap to make complex patterns) all combine to create a feeling of harmony and peace.

The interior of the main temple has decorated wooden columns and a ceiling covered with wheels of dharma, representing the Lord Buddha's teaching. The exterior is just as impressive thanks to mosaics of colored glass that were added at the beginning of the 20th century. Several small **chapels** at the sides of the main hall are also covered with mosaics and contain various images of the Buddha. The bronze 16th-century reclining Buddha in one chapel was displayed in the 1931 Paris Exhibition. The mosaic on the back wall of that chapel commemorates the 2,500th anniversary of the Lord Buddha's birth with a depiction of Lao village life. The chapel near the compound's east gate, with a gilded facade, contains the royal family's funeral statuary and urns, including a 40-foot-long wooden boat that was used as a hearse. ✉ *Sisaleumsak Rd.* ✣ *Between Suvannakhamvong Rd. and Sakkarin Rd., where Mekong and Nam Khan rivers meet* ☎ *071/212470* 🎫 *20,000 kip.*

Restaurants

★ Apsara Restaurant

$$ | **INTERNATIONAL** | Occupying a lovely spot overlooking the Nam Khan River, Apsara serves delicious Lao cuisine, from baguette sandwiches for lunch to elegant set dinners starring dishes such as a whole Panin fish stuffed with lemongrass and served with tamarind dressing. It also hosts the first Lao branch of Paste, curated by award-winning Thai chef Bee Satongun. **Known for:** Lao set menus; slow-cooked buffalo cheeks with tamarind sauce and cabbage slaw; Penang pork neck curry. $ *Average main: 90,000 kip* ✉ *Ban Wat Sene, Kingkitsarath St., Ban Wat Sene* ☎ *071/254670* 🌐 *www.theapsara.com/the-apsara-restaurant.html.*

The Prabang Buddha

But for a few simple facts, the Pha Bang Buddha image, the namesake of Luang Prabang, is shrouded in mystery. This much *is* known: the Prabang image is approximately 33 inches tall and weighs 110 pounds. Both hands of the Buddha are raised in double *abhaya mudra* position (the meaning of which has predictably ambiguous symbolic interpretations, including dispelling fear, teaching reason, and offering protection, benevolence, and peace). Historically, the Prabang Buddha has been a symbol of religious and political authority, including the legitimate right to rule the kingdom of Laos.

It is believed that the image was cast in bronze in Ceylon (Sri Lanka) between the 1st and 9th century, although it has also been suggested that it is made primarily of gold, with silver and bronze alloys. Regardless of its composition, the double-raised palms indicate a later construction (14th century), and a possibly Khmer origin.

Nonetheless, in 1359 the Prabang was given to Fa Ngum, the son-in-law of the Khmer king at Angkor, and brought to Muang Swa, which was subsequently renamed Luang Prabang, the capital of the newly formed kingdom of Lang Xang. The Prabang Buddha became a symbol of the king's legitimacy and a means of promoting Theravada Buddhism throughout Laos.

In 1563 the Prabang image was relocated to the new capital city of Vientiane. In 1778 Siamese invaders ransacked Vientiane and made off with both the Prabang and Emerald Buddhas. The Prabang was returned to Laos in 1782 after political and social unrest in Siam was attributed to the image. Similar circumstances surrounded the subsequent capture and release of the Prabang by the Siamese in 1827 and 1867.

Following its return to Laos, the Prabang was housed in Wat Wisunalat, Luang Prabang's oldest temple, and then at Wat Mai. In 1963, during the reign of Sisavang Vatthana, Laos's final monarch, construction began on Haw Pha Bang, a temple to house the Prabang on the grounds of the palace.

But in 1975 the Communist Pathet Lao rose to power, dissolved the monarchy, and installed a Communist regime. The Communist government, having little respect for any symbol of royalty *or* Buddhism, may have handed over the Prabang to Moscow in exchange for assistance from the Soviet Union. Other accounts of the image have it spirited away to Vientiane for safekeeping in a vault, where it may still reside today.

Regardless, there is a 33-inch-tall Buddha statue, real or replica, housed behind bars in an unassuming room beside the entrance to the Royal Palace Museum (until Haw Pha Bang is completed). On the third day of every Lao New Year (April 13 to 15), the image is ferried via chariot to Wat Mai, where it is cleansed with water by reverent Laotians.

As for its authenticity, a respectable and reliable source told me simply this: "People believe that it is real because the Prabang Buddha belongs in Luang Prabang."

—Trevor Ranges

Joma Bakery Cafe

$ | **CAFÉ** | Canadians run this inexpensive self-service restaurant, where an in-house bakery turns out delicious pastries, bagels, pizzas, and French bread. The homemade soups are excellent, as are the breakfast burritos and wraps, and you can pick up standard coffee and espresso drinks. **Known for:** good coffee; Western comfort food; social atmosphere. *Average main: 30,000 kip* *Chao Fa Ngum Rd, Hua Xieng* *Near post office on Chao Fa Ngum* *071/252292* *www.joma.biz* *No credit cards.*

Khaiphaen

$ | **LAO** | One of the SE Asian Tree Alliance's training restaurants for marginalized youths, Khaiphaen's menu includes anything from a watermelon-and-goat-cheese salad to fusion Lao staples such as grilled buffalo steak with pickled daikon. **Known for:** humanitarian concept; mousse au chocolat; pork belly. *Average main: 45,000 kip* *100 Sisavong Vatana Rd., Ban Wat Nong* *030/515–5221* *www.khaiphaen-restaurant.org* *No credit cards.*

★ Kitchen by the Mekong

$ | **LAO** | The romantic restaurant of the boutique hotel that occupies the former royal residence serves exquisite cuisine in a serene, romantic setting. The Lao tasting menu, a good option, includes tamarind soup, orlam (spicy chicken stew), and *sai oua,* a homemade pork sausage, served with river weed and chili paste. **Known for:** creative French chef; affordable prices; scenic setting. *Average main: 80,000 kip* *Victoria Xiengthong Palace, Kounxoau Rd., Ban Phonehueng* *Near Wat Xiengthong* *071/213200* *www.victoriahotels.asia* *No credit cards.*

Le Café et Restaurant Ban Vat Sene

$ | **FRENCH** | Sidewalk seating and a retractable brown-striped awning contribute to the atmosphere of a traditional French café here. Freshly made quiche, baguettes, and *grandes tartines* (large slices of homemade bread with various toppings) are the menu highlights. **Known for:** organic garden; fully homemade menu; ice cream. *Average main: 50,000 kip* *Sakkarin Rd., Ban Wat Sene* *Across from Villa Santi Hotel* *071/252482* *www.elephant-restau.com/cafebanvatsene.*

★ L'Elephant Restaurant Français

$$$ | **FRENCH** | One of Luang Prabang's finest restaurants offers traditional French, with a dash of Lao influence, especially when it comes to the ingredients. Consider, for example, the *chevreuil au poivre vert* (local venison in a pepper sauce). **Known for:** tartare; coq au vin; buffalo steak. *Average main: 150,000 kip* *Ban Wat Nong, Kounxoua Rd.* *071/252482* *www.elephant-restau.com.*

Luang Prabang Bakery

$ | **CAFÉ** | With a central location and the most enticing atmosphere of several outdoor-seating restaurants in its part of town, the bakery is an ideal stop for people-watching and a cool drink or coffee and pastries. You can also sample some of the nearly two dozen Laotian dishes, such as *jo mart len pak lae kout noi* (steamed fresh vegetables with a spicy grilled-tomato sauce) served here, or satisfy a craving for Western food with a hamburger, a pizza, some pasta, or even a steak. **Known for:** cakes and pastries; coffee; sandwiches. *Average main: 50,000 kip* *Sisavangvong Rd., Ban Chomkong* *North of Royal Palace Museum on right* *71/252499, 71/254844* *luangprabang-bakery-guesthouse.com.*

★ Manda de Laos

$$ | **LAO** | With an unbeatable location over a UNESCO-classified lotus pond, this impressive wooden restaurant only serves traditional Lao food, all based on the owner's mother family recipes. The dishes, such as steamed fish Hor Mok–style or the delicious jungle honey-glazed spareribs, are presented in highly choreographic ways that help emphasize

the venue's authenticity. **Known for:** beautiful setting; authentic Lao cuisine; buffalo steak. *Average main: 90,000 kip* ✉ *10 Norrassan Rd, Ban That Luang* ✣ *Down the road from Satri House's back entrance* ☎ *020/5644–4847* 🌐 *www.mandadelaos.com.*

Restaurant les 3 Nagas

$ | **LAO** | River seaweed with spicy buffalo jam and steamed mushrooms in coconut mousse are just two of the local specialties served at this atmospheric restaurant. Set menus are available from 200,000 kip, and you can order à la carte. **Known for:** grilled buffalo with coffee sauce; mango sticky rice with pumpkin mousse; abundant sampler menus. *Average main: 80,000 kip* ✉ *Sakkarin Rd., Ban Wat Nong* ☎ *071/253888* 🌐 *www.3-nagas.com.*

Rosella Fusion

$ | **LAO** | This humble restaurant under a tent awning overlooking the Nam Khan River doesn't really churn out fusion, but superb Lao and Western dishes without overlapping influences. Chef Dit, who used to be the bartender at nearby Amantaka, also concocts frozen margaritas and mojitos that rival any in town. **Known for:** mok paa steamed fish; green curry; crunchy bruschettas. *Average main: 45,000 kip* ✉ *Kingkitsarat Rd., Ban Wat Sene* ✣ *100 ft after Apsara on river side* ☎ *020/7777–5753* *No credit cards.*

★ **Tamarind Restaurant and Cooking School**

$ | **LAO** | This riverside restaurant is *the* place to experience and understand Lao cuisine in Luang Prabang. The various tasting menus feature five traditional types of *jeaow*, or dips, to be eaten with vegetables or sticky rice; there's also a five-bites selection that includes dried buffalo, sai oua (flavored local sausage), and other delicacies. **Known for:** marinated buffalo; fresh-fruit smoothies; well-trained local staff. *Average main: 50,000 kip* ✉ *Kingkitsarath Rd., Ban Wat Sene* ✣ *Just before Apsara on Nam Khan River* ☎ *071/213128* 🌐 *www.tamarindlaos.com.*

Tamnak Lao

$ | **LAO** | The set menu is the way to sample a wide cross-selection of Lao dishes at this noted restaurant, cooking school, and (just for good measure) book exchange. Alternatively, you can order à la carte from a lengthy menu that includes *kaipan,* a crispy dried Mekong River plant covered with sesame seeds (it's the local equivalent of chips and salsa), and a local favorite, *orlam*, an eggplant "casserole" that can be compared to an exotic *gaeng kiew waan* (Thai green curry). **Known for:** bamboo shoots; cozy veranda; mango sticky rice. *Average main: 50,000 kip* ✉ *Sakkarin Rd., Ban Wat Sene* ✣ *Across from Villa Santi Hotel* ☎ *071/252525 restaurant, 071/212239 cooking school* 🌐 *www.tamnaklao.net.*

Hotels

New hotels are shooting up in Luang Prabang to accommodate the growing numbers of tourists. Many of the most attractive of them are in converted buildings dating from French colonial days, and several hotels are former royal properties.

Amantaka

$$$$ | **RESORT** | The queen of resorts in Luang Prabang, this gorgeous and tranquil oasis occupies an old French colonial building surrounded by leafy gardens and shaded verandas. **Pros:** spacious and private suites; excellent food served in the atmospheric restaurant; huge pool. **Cons:** extra 20% service charge; on the flight path into the LP airport, so jet noise when planes fly in; absurdly expensive. *Rooms from: 6,500,000 kip* ✉ *55/3 Kingkitsarath Rd., Ban Thongchaleun* ☎ *071/860333* 🌐 *www.amanresorts.com* *24 rooms* *Some meals.*

★ **Angsana Maison Souvannaphoum**

$$ | **B&B/INN** | The former residence of Prince Souvannaphoum, prime minister in the 1960s, has been transformed into one of Luang Prabang's top hotels. **Pros:**

Cooking Classes

Several Luang Prabang restaurants not only serve tasty Lao food, but also teach you how to cook it yourself. Classes cover Lao cuisine and its cultural influences, and the restaurants provide ingredients for recipes that students cook and then share as a meal. Daytime classes include a visit to a local food market to learn about the ingredients and how to select them; evening classes, which are shorter, lack this component. Class sizes are limited to a dozen or fewer students. The classes cost between 160,000 kip and 285,000 kip depending on the school and the length of the class. Tamarind Restaurant and Cooking School is by far—and deservedly—the most popular choice. Especially during high season, make reservations well ahead to ensure you get a space. Tamnak Lao, another good option, has been open since 1999. *See Restaurants for reviews of these restaurants and their contact information.*

spa; large claw-foot tubs in some rooms; exclusive, private feel. **Cons:** views not inspiring; on a fairly busy road; small bathrooms in some rooms. *Rooms from: 700,000 kip* *Chao Fa Ngum Rd.* *071/254609* *www.angsana.com/en/ap-laos-maison-souvannaphoum* *24 rooms* *Free breakfast.*

Apsara

$$ | **B&B/INN** | With its white facade and balustrades and riverside location, this French-style *maison* would be at home in southern France; instead, it's Luang Prabang's trendiest boutique hotel. **Pros:** quiet riverside location; beautifully furnished rooms; rain-style showerheads in some bathrooms. **Cons:** downstairs rooms have no views; standard rooms a bit dark; often fully booked. *Rooms from: 760,000 kip* *Kingkitsarat Rd., Ban Wat Sene* *Between Tamarind and Rosella restaurants* *071/254670* *www.theapsara.com* *13 rooms* *Free breakfast.*

Apsara Rive Droite

$$$$ | **B&B/INN** | For those looking for something even more glamorous and exclusive than the Apsara, this sister property across the Nam Khan River has a swimming pool, private verandas, and a free 24-hour shuttle-boat service to take guests across the river. **Pros:** luxurious isolation; quiet; nice swimming pool. **Cons:** across the river; little atmosphere in this neighborhood; only nine rooms, so often full. *Rooms from: 1,350,000 kip* *Ban Phanluang* *Across Nam Khan River from Apsara* *071/254670 reservations, 071/213053* *www.theapsara.com* *9 rooms* *Free breakfast.*

Belmond La Résidence Phou Vao Hotel

$$$$ | **RESORT** | Its prime position on Kite Hill gives this sumptuous hotel the best views in town. **Pros:** infinity pool; excellent restaurant; discounts for longer stays. **Cons:** garden rooms do not have great views; 20% service charge; not the best value. *Rooms from: 3,230,000 kip* *Phu Vao Hill 3* *071/212530 up to 33* *www.belmond.com/la-residence-phou-vao-luang-prabang* *34 rooms* *Free breakfast.*

★ Hotel 3 Nagas

$$ | **HOTEL** | This colonial mansion stands under official UNESCO World Heritage site protection, thanks in no small measure to the efforts of the former owner to retain its weathered but handsome look.

Pros: private patios; gorgeous garden; spacious bathrooms with claw-foot tubs. **Cons:** often fully booked; poor lighting in rooms; 20% service charge. *Rooms from: 780,000 kip ✉ Sakkarin Rd., Ban Wat Nong ☎ 071/253888 🌐 www.3-nagas.com 🛏 15 rooms 🍽 Free breakfast.*

Le Calao Inn

$$ | **B&B/INN** | Fronting the Mekong and just down the street from Wat Xieng Thong, this small hotel was resurrected from a ruined mansion built by a Portuguese merchant in 1904. **Pros:** quiet spot on the Mekong; upstairs rooms have private balconies with river views; atmospheric. **Cons:** almost always booked; interiors not as elegant as exterior; some rooms have unpleasant smell. *Rooms from: 650,000 kip ✉ Khem Kong Rd. ☎ 071/212100 🌐 le-calao-inn.hotelsinluangprabang.com/en/ 🛏 6 rooms 🍽 Free breakfast.*

Rattana Guest House

$ | **HOTEL** | Family-run guesthouses are common in Luang Prabang, but this one stands out for making patrons feel right at home. **Pros:** spotlessly clean; new building with teak floors; firm mattresses. **Cons:** bit of a walk to main dining and shopping area; smallish rooms in new wing; no views. *Rooms from: 125,000 kip ✉ Koksack St., 3/2 Ban What That ☎ 071/252255 No credit cards 🛏 14 rooms 🍽 No meals.*

Sackarinn Guest Room

$ | **HOTEL** | Spotless and super cheap, this place in the center of town is the ideal Luang Prabang guesthouse. **Pros:** ideal location; very clean; friendly staff. **Cons:** some rooms dark; low ceilings; often booked in high season. *Rooms from: 150,000 kip ✉ Sisavangvong Rd., Ban Xieng Mouane ✥ Near Luang Prabang Bakery ☎ 071/254512, 020/544–2001 No credit cards 🛏 15 rooms 🍽 No meals.*

★ Satri House

$$$$ | **HOTEL** | Formerly a prince's residence, this century-old property has been refurbished and expanded into a series of French colonial homes surrounded by pools and gardens and is one of Luang Prabang's best-kept secrets. **Pros:** beautiful colonial residence; quiet neighborhood but not far from night market; superior furnishings. **Cons:** not all rooms have terraces; a bit removed from the action; no TVs but available upon request. *Rooms from: 1,300,000 kip ✉ 057 Photisarath Rd., Ban Thatluang ✥ About 500 ft past Maison Souphannaboum on left ☎ 071/253491 🌐 www.satrihouse.com 🛏 31 rooms 🍽 Free breakfast.*

Sayo River Guest House

$$ | **B&B/INN** | A white colonial-style hotel with green shutters, the Sayo River Guest House is chic yet unpretentious. **Pros:** serene riverside location; spacious, well-furnished rooms; some rooms have balconies. **Cons:** some rooms lack big windows; often full in high season; a walk from central area. *Rooms from: 490,000 kip ✉ Khem Kong Rd., Ban Phone Meuang ☎ 071/212484 🌐 www.sayoguesthouse.com/sayo-river-eng 🛏 13 rooms 🍽 Free breakfast.*

Sofitel Hotel de la Paix

$$$$ | **HOTEL** | It doesn't get much more elegant than this in sleepy Laos. **Pros:** exquisite spa; exclusive retreat; spacious rooms all with plunge pools or hot tubs in their own private gardens. **Cons:** a trek to the town center; very expensive for Luang Prabang; not many shops or restaurants nearby. *Rooms from: 1,700,000 kip ✉ Ban Mano ✥ Off Manomai Rd. just past Lao Airlines office ☎ 071/260777 🌐 www.hoteldelapaixlp.com 🛏 23 rooms 🍽 Free breakfast.*

★ Victoria Xiengthong Palace

$$$ | **HOTEL** | The final residence of Laos's royal family has been renovated into one of the town's most luxurious hostelries. **Pros:** fantastic location; extremely quiet; elegant room furnishings. **Cons:** tight

spaces in some rooms; not all rooms have Mekong views or plunge pools; no swimming pool. *Rooms from: 850,000 kip ✉ Kounxoau Rd., Ban Phonehueng ✣ Where Mekong and Nam Khan rivers meet ☎ 071/213200 🌐 www.victoriahotels.asia 26 rooms Free breakfast.*

Villa Santi

$$$ | B&B/INN | A local princess's son-in-law converted this 19th-century royal residence in the heart of Luang Prabang into to a boutique hotel, and built a resort outside town. **Pros:** main property has central location; restaurant in pleasant garden; opulent Royal Suite rooms. **Cons:** tiny bathrooms; no balconies or views; overpriced. *Rooms from: 1,000,000 kip ✉ Sakkarin Rd., Ban Wat Sene ☎ 071/252157 🌐 www.villasantihotel.com 20 rooms Free breakfast.*

Nightlife

Luang Prabang's nightlife is limited—most places close by 11. On Souvannakhamphong Road, some bar-restaurants consisting of simple tables and chairs are located on the hill above the Mekong River. Over on Phu Si Hill are Lao Garden, a casual, open-air restaurant and bar, and the Hive Bar, where young backpackers congregate within a dimly lighted interior or around small outdoor "campfires" to mix, mingle, and share tales of the road. These two and L'etranger Books and Tea (⇨ *see below*) are near the corner of Phu Si and Phommathay streets.

Chez Matt

WINE BARS—NIGHTLIFE | At this cozy, sophisticated wine bar, you can sample good wines and Champagne and some mean martinis. The prices are decent, jazz plays in the background, and the place is close enough to Nam Khan River restaurants you can slip in for a drink before or after dinner or while waiting for your table. *✉ Sisavang Vatthana Rd., Ban Wat Sene ✣ Across street from Icon Klub just off Nam Khan River ☎ 020/7777–9497.*

Dao Fa

BARS/PUBS | Luang Prabang's young nouveau riche strut their stuff at Dao Fa. The action doesn't heat up until after 10, and the party's over at midnight due to curfew, but for those who like thumping beats, this is the only real nightclub in town. Because it's out by the southern bus station, you won't see many foreign faces here. *✉ Rd. 13 ✣ Across from National Stadium just near Southern Bus Terminal ☎ 071/260789.*

525 Cocktails and Tapas

TAPAS BARS | This is a perfect British-owned pub with a delightful outdoor patio and sleek minimal-chic interior design with excellent black-and-white photography from Southeast Asia on the walls. Cocktails are strong and well mixed, and their eclectic tapas range from Mexican empanadas to lemon meringue tartlets. The lively mixed crowd of locals and expats makes it all the more enjoyable for a night out. *✉ 100 Kingkitsarath Rd ☎ 071/212424 🌐 www.525cocktailsandtapas.com.*

Icon Klub

BARS/PUBS | An engaging Hungarian named Lisa runs this hole-in-the-wall bohemian-style hangout. It's the perfect place to grab a well-mixed whisky sour or mojito and find out about life in Luang Prabang. Most tourists don't discover her tiny, eclectically decorated white house, but many expats drink here, and everyone knows everyone. It's easy to strike up a conversation, and Lisa runs theme nights with swing music and holds book discussions to keep things stimulating. *✉ Sisavang Vatthana Rd., Ban Xiengmouane 51/4 ✣ Uphill from Saynamkhan Hotel between Nam Khan River and Sakkarin Rd., across from Chez Matt ☎ 071/254905, 020/9930–0788 🌐 www.iconklub.com.*

Did You Know?
Luang Prabang is designated a UNESCO World Heritage site for its fusion of traditional architecture and Lao urban structures with those built by the European colonial authorities in the 19th and 20th centuries.

L'etranger Books and Tea
RESTAURANT—SIGHT | From 7 am until 10 pm, patrons of this bookstore and hangout sip tea, coffee, and smoothies or nibble on snacks while reclining on comfortable and chic floor pillows. In the evening, the place fills up for DVD screenings. ✉ *Ban Aphay, next to Hive Bar* ☎ *071/260248* 🌐 *www.bookslaos.com.*

Performing Arts

Royal Ballet Theater Phralak-Phralam
DANCE | Three times a week this troupe performs at the Royal Palace museum. The program includes a *bai-si* welcoming ceremony, local folk songs, classical dances enacting episodes from the Indian *Ramayana* epic, and outdoor presentations of the music and dances of Lao minorities. ✉ *Royal Palace Museum, Sisavangvong Rd.* ✣ *Across from Phu Si Hill* ☎ *071/253705* 🌐 *phralakphralam.com/phralak_phralam_en/* 🎟 *100,000 kip–150,000 kip.*

Activities

Many of the tour operators in town offer interesting rafting and kayaking trips, plus cycling expeditions. Several shops rent bikes for about 20,000 kip a day.

Shopping

Luang Prabang has two principal markets where you can find handicrafts: the Dara Central Market, on Setthathirat Road, and the Tribal Market, on Sisavangvong Road. In the evening, most of Sisavangvong Road turns into an open bazaar, similar to Thailand's night markets. It's a pleasant place to stroll, bargain with hawkers, and stop for a simple meal and a beer at one of many roadside stalls.

Caruso Lao
CRAFTS | The well-regarded Vientiane boutique noted for its fine wood carvings and high-end Lao silks has opened a Luang Prabang branch. All the products are handwoven and carved by master artisans. ✉ *60 Sakkarin Rd., Ban Wat Sene* ✣ *Near Cafe Ban Vat Sene* ☎ *071/254574* 🌐 *www.carusolao.com.*

Ock Pop Tok Heritage Shop
TEXTILES/SEWING | This central boutique sells exquisite textiles produced with the help of more than 500 women in rural Laos. Browse among silk scarves, shirts, and even handmade dolls. Fifty percent of proceedings goes back to the weavers. ✉ *Sakkarin Rd., Ban Wat Sene* ☎ *071/254761* 🌐 *ockpoptok.com.*

Pathana Boupha Antique House
TEXTILES/SEWING | An antiques and textile shop and museum, Pathana Boupha claims to produce the costumes and ornaments for Luang Prabang's Miss New Year pageant in (an apparently prestigious endeavor). A dizzying array of goods is on display, many not for sale. Shoppers *can,* however, purchase textiles produced by various Laotian ethnic groups. It is worth coming here just to check out the beautiful old building and antiques collection. ✉ *26/2 Ban Visoun* ☎ *071/212262.*

Tribal Market
MARKET | Eclipsed by Luang Prabang's night market and these days less tribally oriented than its name might suggest, this covered market has piles of produce and household goods, including textiles and many Chinese-made items. ✉ *Sisavangvong Rd.* ✣ *At Setthathirat Rd.*

Tad Khuang Si Waterfall

29 km (18 miles) south of Luang Prabang.

This popular waterfall makes a pleasant half-day trip from Luang Prabang.

GETTING HERE AND AROUND

Tour operators in Luang Prabang offer day trips that combine Tad Khuang Si with a visit to a Khamu tribal village nearby for 55,000 kip. The drive, past rice farms and small Lao Lum tribal villages, is half the adventure. Taxi and tuk-tuk drivers in Luang Prabang all want to take you to the falls, quoting around 150,000 kip round-trip, but unless you have your own group, a tour is a better deal.

Sights

Tad Khuang Si Waterfall

BODY OF WATER | A series of cascades surrounded by lush foliage, this attraction is popular with Lao residents and foreigners. Many visitors merely view the falls from the lower pool, where picnic tables and food vendors invite lingering, but a steep path through the forest leads to pools above the falls that are perfect for a swim. Two nearby diversions most groups include on a waterfall outing are a **rescue center** that rehabilitates moon bears saved from poachers, and a recently opened **butterfly park** (closed on Tuesday). The best time to visit the area is between November and April, after the rainy season. Watch your footing around the falls. ✉ *Luang Prabang* 🎫 *30,000 kip.*

Restaurants

★ Carpe Diem

$$ | FRENCH FUSION | This excellent French and Lao restaurant has a serene garden and wooden decks overlooking the last stretch of the falls and a cocktail bar, La Terrasse, with an incredibly scenic setting for a quiet drink before or after a visit to Tad Khuang Si Waterfall park. After closing at 5 pm, this scenic venue can also be hired for private functions. **Known for:** natural setting with swimming hole; vegan options; good choice of fish and meats. $ *Average main: 100,000 kip* ✉ *Kuang Si Waterfalls, Luang Prabang* ✣ *Down a right-side lane before the park's main entrance* ☎ *020/9867–6741* 🌐 *www.carpediem.la.*

Tad Sae Waterfall

15 km (9 miles) east of Luang Prabang.

This dramatic cascade makes a worthy side trip from Luang Prabang, with opportunities for zip-lining, swimming, and more.

GETTING HERE AND AROUND

From Luang Prabang you can hire a tuk-tuk for about 150,000 kip for a return journey, but you are best to let a travel agency arrange a trip by boat. Adventure-tour agencies like White Elephant *(see Tour Information in Luang Prabang)* and Green Discovery *(see Laos Planner)* also organize kayaking day trips to the falls.

Sights

Tad Sae Waterfall

BODY OF WATER | Most scenically reached by boat, this waterfall is best visited during the rainy season, when the rivers are high and their combined waters form a thundering cascade. The waterfall has multilevel limestone formations divided into three steps with big pools beneath them—don't forget your bathing suit. Old waterwheels and new zip lines add an adventure component, and elephant riding also takes place. There is a small, simple resort nearby. You can get here by road, but it's delightful to arrive here by boat. Be careful on the slippery paths around the falls. ✉ *Luang Prabang* ✣ *Southeast of Luang Prabang, accessed by road from Ban Aen village* 🎫 *20,000 kip.*

Pak Ou Caves

25 km (16 miles) up the Mekong from Luang Prabang.

While the caves themselves leave some visitors underwhelmed, the scenery en route is pleasant and the area is worth spending a couple of hours exploring.

Laos: Then and Now

Early Settlers

Prehistoric remains show that the river valleys and lowland areas of Laos were settled as far back as 40,000 years ago, first by hunters and gatherers and later by more developed communities. The mysterious Plain of Jars—a stretch of land littered with ancient stone and clay jars at least 2,000 years old—indicates the early presence of a sophisticated society skilled in the manufacture of bronze and iron implements and ceramics. Starting in the 3rd century BC, cultural and trading links were forged with Chinese and Indian civilizations.

Between the 4th and 8th century, farming communities along the Mekong River began to organize themselves into communities called Muang—a term still used in both Laos and neighboring Thailand. This network of Muang gave rise in the mid-14th century to the first Lao monarchy, given the fanciful name of Lan Xang, or the Kingdom of a Million Elephants, for the large herds of the pachyderms that roamed the land.

Colonization and Independence

At the start of the 18th century, following fighting over the throne, the kingdom was partitioned into three realms: Luang Prabang, Vientiane, and Champasak. Throughout the latter part of the 18th century Laos was under the control of neighboring Siam. In the early 19th century Laos staged an uprising against the Siamese, but in 1828 an invading Siamese army under King Rama III sacked Vientiane and took firm control of most of Laos as a province of Siam. Siam maintained possession of Laos until the French established the Federation of French Indochina, which included Laos, Vietnam, and Cambodia, in 1893. In 1904 the Lao monarch Sisavang Vong set up court in Luang Prabang, but Laos remained part of French Indochina until 1949. For a brief period during World War II Laos was occupied by Japan, but reverted to French control at the end of the war. In 1953 the Lao PDR became an independent nation, which was confirmed by the passage of the Geneva Convention in 1954. The monarchy was finally dissolved in 1975, when the revolutionary group Pathet Lao, allied with North Vietnam's Communist movement during the Vietnam War, seized power after a long guerrilla war.

The Vietnam War and its Aftermath

During the Vietnam War the U.S. Air Force, in a vain attempt to disrupt the Ho Chi Minh Trail, dropped more tons of bombs on Laos than were dropped on Germany during World War II. Since the end of the Vietnam War the People's Democratic Party (formerly the Pathet Lao) has ruled the country, first on Marxist-Leninist lines and now on the basis of limited pro-market reforms. Overtures are being made to the outside, particularly to Thailand, Japan, and China, to assist in developing the country—not an easy task. The Friendship Bridge over the Mekong River connects Vientiane with Nong Khai in northeastern Thailand, making Laos more accessible to trade with neighboring countries. The Chinese have become a major player in Laos recently,

financing dam and road projects, along with starting a massive construction boom in Vientiane.

Gradual Growth

Decentralization of the state-controlled economy began in 1986, resulting in a steady annual growth rate of around 6%. The country has continued to grow steadily: Vientiane, Luang Prabang, and Pakse have new airports; visitors from most countries can now get a visa on arrival, and those from some ASEAN (Association of Southeast Asian Nations) countries need no visa at all. New hotels are constantly opening. Nonetheless, infrastructure in the country remains primitive in comparison to the rest of the world. Laos has no railways; communications technology and electricity are common only in more densely populated areas (cell phones outnumber landlines five to one), and many of the country's airports and airstrips are paved. The road from the current capital, Vientiane, to Laos's ancient capital, Luang Prabang, has been paved and upgraded—though it still takes eight hours to make the serpentine, 320-km (198-mile) journey north, and many of the nation's roads are in poor condition or unpaved. The upgraded road running south from Vientiane can now accommodate tour buses going all the way to the Cambodian border. Other border crossings have also opened up, especially along the Vietnamese border.

A low standard of living (the GDP per capita of $3,000 is one of the world's lowest, and 22% of the population lives below the poverty line) and a rugged landscape that hampers transportation and communication have long made the countryside of Laos a sleepy backwater. But Luang Prabang, boosted by its status as a World Heritage site, has become a busy and relatively prosperous tourist hub. Vientiane, despite its new hotels and restaurants, remains one of the world's sleepiest capital cities, but is getting set for some dramatic changes.

Despite their relative poverty, Lao people are frank, friendly, and outwardly cheerful people. Although Laos certainly has far to go economically, it is currently a member of the ASEAN trade group, has Normal Trade Relations status with the United States, and receives assistance from the European Union to help it acquire WTO membership. Growing investment in Laos and expanding numbers of tourists to both the main tourist centers and more remote areas should continue to benefit the people of Laos.

GETTING HERE AND AROUND

It takes 1½ hours to get to Pak Ou by boat from Luang Prabang. Many agencies in town organize tours for 90,000 kip per person, not including admission to the caves. Tours leave Luang Prabang around 8 am and include visits to waterside villages for a look at the rich variety of local handicrafts, a nip of lao-lao, and perhaps a bowl of noodles. You can also take a tuk-tuk to the village of Pak Ou, and then a quick boat ride across the Mekong, but few people use this option, as it is less scenic and pricier than taking a tour.

Sights

Pak Ou Caves

CAVE | In high limestone cliffs above the Mekong River, at the point where it meets the Nam Ou River from northern Laos, lie two sacred caves filled with thousands of Buddha statues dating from the 16th century. The lower cave, **Tham Thing,** is accessible from the river by a stairway and has enough daylight to allow you to find your way around. The stairway continues to the upper cave, **Tham Phum,** for which you need a flashlight. The admission charge of 30,000 kip includes a flashlight and a guide. Many visitors are not impressed by the caves or the tourist hordes but find that the scenery along the way makes the trip worth the effort. Ideally, it's best to visit the caves as part of a cruise tour to or from Huay Xai. Try to avoid visiting in the height of high tourist season, as it gets extremely crowded and unpleasant.

The town of Pak Ou, across the river from the caves and accessible by ferry, has several passable restaurants. It is possible to get to the cave by tuk-tuk from town, but then you'd miss the scenery, and you'll still have to catch a boat to reach the entrance.. ✉ *Luang Prabang* ⊹ *At confluence of Nam Ou and Mekong rivers* 🎫 *30,000 kip.*

Ban Muang Ngoi

150 km (93 miles) northeast of Luang Prabang.

This picturesque village sits on the eastern side of the Nam Ou River, which descends from Phongsaly Province in the north to meet the Mekong River opposite the famous Pak Ou Caves.

GETTING HERE AND AROUND

The journey here is an adventure in itself: a minivan takes you from Luang Prabang's Northern Bus Terminal to a pier at Nong Khiaw (four hours; 45,000 kip), where boats (25,000 kip) continue on a one-hour trip upstream to the village. Boats leave Nong Khiaw at 11 am and 2 pm, and return from Muang Ngoi at 9:30 am daily, which means that you need to charter your own boat or go on a tour if you don't want to spend the night. Also remember that scheduled afternoon boats may not run if there are not enough passengers. Just about any travel agent in Luang Prabang can arrange a guide or a tour. When the water is high enough, you can continue upriver from Muang Ngoi to Muang Khua, which has onward bus connections to Vietnam.

TIMING

Two or three days will give you a chance to go for some hikes or boat trips and just relax in one of Laos's more tranquil spots.

Sights

Ban Muang Ngoi

TOWN | The village, populated by Lao Lum and surrounded by unusual limestone peaks, has become a popular traveler hangout, with friendly locals, gorgeous scenery, and plenty of treks and river-touring options. All-day electricity has only recently arrived in Muang Ngoi, but Wi-Fi is now available and several fancy restaurants line its one street. With these upgrades the village looks poised to roll into the future, but accommodations remain pretty basic and may lack amenities travelers desire. **■ TIP→ There is no ATM here, so make sure to bring all the cash you need.** As of 2018, Lao Youth Travel is the only tour operator based in Muang Ngoi. They can organize hiking trips to nearby villages (210,000 kip per day/two persons) and kayaking expeditions (150,000 kip per person). Their office is near the boat landing 🌐 *youtheco@laotel.com.* ✉ *Ban Ngoy Nua.*

Ning Ning Guesthouse

$ | B&B/INN | Of Ban Muang Ngoi's many simple guesthouses, this is probably the best. **Pros:** good mosquito netting; riverside restaurant; quiet. **Cons:** bungalows lack river views; expensive for Muang Ngoi; crowded in high season. Ⓢ *Rooms from: 300,000 kip* ✉ *Ban Muang Ngoi, Ban Ngoy Nua* ✥ *Near boat landing* ☎ *020/2388–0122* ✉ *ningning_guesthouse@hotmail.com* ▬ *No credit cards* *10 bungalows* *Free breakfast.*

Luang Nam Tha

319 km (198 miles) north of Luang Prabang.

The capital of Laos's northernmost province is the headquarters of the groundbreaking Nam Ha Ecotourism. Nam Tha town itself isn't very exciting, but give yourself a couple of days to do an ecotour or trek, kayak, bicycle, or explore the sights along the Nam Tha River and the Nam Ha Protected Area.

GETTING HERE AND AROUND

Luang Nam Tha is tiny, and can be navigated on foot, although many places rent mountain bikes (from 10,000 kip to 25,000 kip per day) for exploring the surrounding countryside.

AIR TRAVEL

Lao Airlines flies from Vientiane to Luang Nam Tha on Monday, Wednesday, and Friday for $100. Tuk-tuks run from the airport and bus station into town for about 30,000 kip.

BOAT TRAVEL

Longtail boats can be arranged for the two-day trip on the Nam Tha River, running all the way down to Pak Tha, where the Nam Tha meets the Mekong, and on to Huay Xai. The same trip can also be done in reverse, although it makes more sense to go downriver. A boat costs about 1.8 million kip (about $220), and can take four to six passengers. Unless you speak Lao, it's best to make arrangements through the Boat Landing *(see Hotels, below)* or Forest Retreat *(see below)*. Note that the boats can only travel the Nam Tha during times of high water, basically from July to October.

BUS TRAVEL

The Luang Nam Tha bus station is 10 km (6 miles) out of town, past the airport. Buses go to Oudomxay three times a day (four hours; 40,000 kip); to Luang Prabang and Vientiane each morning (8 and 19 hours; 90,000 kip and 200,000 kip, respectively); and to Muang Sing every hour and a half (two hours; 25,000 kip).

SAFETY AND PRECAUTIONS

Be careful of snakes if trekking in the area, and know that leeches (harmless but very annoying) come out during the rainy season.

VISITOR AND TOUR INFORMATION

VISITOR AND TOUR INFORMATION

Forest Retreat Laos ✉ *Main St., Louang Namtha* ✥ *Next to Minority Restaurant* ☎ *020/5556–0007* 🌐 *www.forestretreatlaos.com.*

Nam Ha Ecotourism

TOWN | This ecotourism program, a model for Southeast Asia, actively encourages the involvement of local communities in the development and management of tourism policies. You can join a two- or three-day trek through the Nam Ha Protected Area, which provides some excellent opportunities for communing with nature, having outdoor adventures, and visiting ethnic minorities (Khamu, Akha, Lanten, and Yao tribes live in the dense forest). The Boat Landing Guesthouse, Forest Retreat Laos, Phou lu Travel and Green Discovery Laos (all in Luang Nam Tha) conduct or arrange tours. ✉ *Louang Namtha* ☎ *020/2239–0195* 🌐 *www.namha-npa.org.*

Restaurants

★ The Bamboo Lounge

$ | **INTERNATIONAL** | A husband-and-wife team from New Zealand opened this happening eatery that serves outstanding wood-fired pizzas, freshly baked bread, pastas, and other Western dishes you can enjoy with a real espresso or cappuccino. The restaurant, which opens at 7 am, is affiliated with Forest Retreat Laos, a trekking agency across the street that works with local people to create and promote sustainable tourism in the Nam Ha Protected Area. **Known for:** eclectic range of pizzas; tasty burritos; hummus. $ *Average main: 57,000 kip* ✉ *The Green Building, Main St., Louang Namtha* ☎ *020/5568–0031* 🌐 *bambooloungelaos.com* 💳 *No credit cards.*

Luang Nam Tha Night Market

$ | **LAO** | Local families mix with tourists under the night-market sky to sample grilled meats and fish served alongside papaya salad, noodle dishes, and other local specialties. For 30,000 kip you can score an entire chicken, dip it in hot sauce along with a finger full of sticky rice, and wash down the ensemble with a cold beer Lao. **Known for:** cheap eats; convivial atmosphere; local flavor. $ *Average main: 30,000 kip* ✉ *Nam Tha Rd., Louang Namtha* ✥ *Downtown next to Bank of Commerce, across street from Zuela Guesthouse* 💳 *No credit cards.*

Hotels

Boat Landing Guesthouse

$ | **B&B/INN** | The timber-and-bamboo bungalows at this eco-friendly place are comfortably furnished in rattan. **Pros:** open-air restaurant with traditional food; great source of local information; bicycles available. **Cons:** not convenient to town and restaurants; expensive for Luang Nam Tha; patchy Wi-Fi. $ *Rooms from: 382,000 kip* ✉ *Ban Kone, Louang Namtha* ✥ *Off Luang Rd.* ☎ *086/312398* 🌐 *www.theboatlanding.laopdr.com* *11 rooms* 🍽 *Free breakfast.*

Muang Sing

60 km (37 miles) north of Luang Nam Tha.

The appeal of Muang Sing lies in what is out of town. Unless you're coming here to trek and visit the hill tribes, the town isn't worth more than a day.

GETTING HERE AND AROUND

The only way in and out of Muang Sing is by bus from Luang Nam Tha. There are five to six departures each day; the two-hour journey costs 25,000 kip.

Sights

Muang Sing

TOWN | In the late 19th century this mountain-ringed town on the Sing Mountain River was the seat of a Tai Lue prince, Chao Fa Silino. Muang Sing lost its regional prominence, however, when French colonial forces occupied the town and established a garrison here. These days, it's known for its morning market, which draws throngs of traditional ethnic hill tribes. Shoppers from among the 20 different tribes living in the area, and even traders from China, visit the market to buy locally produced goods and handicrafts. The market is open daily throughout the day, but it is best to go from 6 to 8 before the minority groups return to their villages. ✉ *Muang Sing.*

Hotels

Adima Guesthouse

$ | **B&B/INN** | Adima's simple brick bungalows are set 6 miles out of town toward the Chinese border, where a cluster of nearby Yao, Haka and Thai Lue villages make for great walks. **Pros:** bucolic setting; hot-water bathrooms; breakfast included. **Cons:** kind of isolated; basic rooms; a bit run down. *Rooms from: 60,000 kip* ✉ *Muang Sing* *On the main road to China* *9 rooms* *No meals* *No credit cards.*

River Journey to Huay Xai

297 km (184 miles) up the Mekong from Luang Prabang

The 300-km (186-mile) trip along the Mekong River between Luang Prabang and Huay Xai is a leisurely journey on one of the world's most famous stretches of river. Your boat drifts along the meandering Mekong past a constantly changing primeval scene of towering cliffs, huge mud flats and sandbanks, rocky islands, and riverbanks smothered in thick jungle, the riverscape occasionally interrupted by swaths of cultivated land, mulberry trees, bananas, and tiny garlic fields. There are no roads, just forest paths linking dusty settlements where the boats tie up for refreshment stops.

There are several ways to make this journey: by regular "slow" boat, which holds about 50 passengers; by speedboat (not recommended), which seats about four; or on the midrange Shompoo Cruise boat or the luxury *Luang Say* boat of Mekong Cruises. All these trips can be arranged in Luang Prabang.

The only village of note is a halfway station, **Pakbeng,** which has many guesthouses and restaurants along its one main street and seems to exist solely to serve the boat passengers who arrive each night. Once you arrive in Huay Xai (which has little of interest in itself other than the Gibbon Experience), a good way to enter Thailand is to cross the river on the bridge to Chiang Khong and then take a bus to Chiang Rai, 60 km (37 miles) inland.

GETTING HERE AND AROUND

BOAT TRAVEL

You can journey from Luang Prabang to Huay Xai on regular "slow" boat, a speedboat, or a cruise liner.

The slow boat trip is a 12- to 14-hour journey over two days. Taking the slow boat allows you to soak in local color, but you will be sitting on uncomfortable wooden seats for the privilege. The night is spent in Pakbeng, in basic guesthouses whose owners come to greet the boats and corral guests. The fare is 220,000 kip per person; slow boats depart daily from a recently constructed pier 7 km (4½ miles) outside Luang Prabang.

Speedboats make the journey between Luang Prabang and Huay Xai in six hours. **■ TIP→ Speedboats may be fun for the first hour, but they are not safe, and become extremely uncomfortable after the novelty wears off.** The seats are hard, the engine noise is deafening (earplugs are advised), and the wind and spray can be chilling. If you're determined to take one, bring a warm, waterproof windbreaker, and make sure the boat driver provides you with a life jacket and crash helmet with a visor. Speedboats cost 340,000 kip per person, and leave daily from a pier on the outskirts of Huay Xai.

SAFETY AND PRECAUTIONS

Speedboats are uncomfortable and unsafe.

Sights

The Gibbon Experience

NATURE PRESERVE | Popular and unique, this experience combines a visit to the Bokeo Nature Reserve with jungle trekking, sleeping in canopy-level tree houses, traveling among the trees by zip lines, and watching gibbons and other wildlife. Profits benefit gibbon rehabilitation and sustainable conservation projects. Be prepared to rough it a bit. Groups are small, so book the experience well ahead. ✉ *Th. Saykhong, Ban Houayxay* ☎ *084/212021* 🌐 *gibbonexperience.org* 🎫 *2.5 million kip ($310) for 3-day all-inclusive package.*

Luang Say Lodge & Cruises

BOAT TOURS | The *Luang Say* luxury boat travels between Luang Prabang and Huay Xai along the Mekong River. Much more comfortable than the regular boats and speedboats that make this journey, the *Luang Say* is also far more expensive. English- and French-speaking guides accompany the voyages. Two-day, one-night up to four-day, three-night options are available, with meals and visits to a few sights included in the rates. Overnight stays are at the attractive Luang Say Lodge in Pakbeng. ✉ *50/4 Sakkarin Rd., Luang Prabang* ☎ *071/252553,* 🌐 *www.luangsay.com* 🎫 *5.3 million kip ($634) all-inclusive Oct.–Mar.; 3.7 million kip ($443) Apr.–Sept.* ☞ *Oct.–Apr. cruises 3 times a wk in each direction, May–Sept. twice; no cruises in June.*

Shompoo Cruise

BOAT TOURS | Providing a much-needed alternative to expensive cruises and the uncomfortable and crowded slow boats plying the Mekong River between Luang Prabang and Huay Xai, this new company operates affordable two-day journeys. Costs in high season range from $155, not including accommodations in Pakbeng, to $225 with higher-end lodgings. The boats travel with a maximum of 40 people, but will sail with as few as 10. Stops along the way include a local Khmu village and the Pak Ou Caves. ✉ *18/02 Ounkham Rd., Bat Wat Nong, Luang Prabang* ☎ *071/213189* 🌐 *www.shompoocruise.com* 🎫 *From $155 in high season.*

Restaurants

Daauw Home

$ | **LAO** | Inside a thatched hillside bungalow overlooking Huay Xai's main street, Daauw Home is run by a nongovernmental organization that helps local women and ethnic minorities empower themselves. Cooking over an open fire, the chefs prepare amazing dishes that diners enjoy with "mojitlao" cocktails. **Known for:** gai baan grilled chicken; pizzas; Hmong handicrafts for sale. [$] *Average main: 73,000 kip* ✉ *Wat Jom Kao Manilat, Ban Houayxay* ☎ *030/904–1296* 🌐 *daauwvillagelaos.com* 💳 *No credit cards.*

Terrasse Restaurant and Chill Place

$ | **LAO** | Next to the stairs of Wat Jom Khao Manilat, this no-frills bamboo-and-thatch restaurant is a good choice for French and Lao food that's cooked with market-fresh ingredients. The hammocks and beautiful views over the Mekong help stretch meals into lazy spells—a perfect past-time in this sleepy town. **Known for:** garlic chicken; selection of wines; big portions. [$] *Average main: 25,527 kip* ✉ *Ban Houayxay* 💳 *No credit cards.*

Hotels

Riverside Houayxay

$ | **HOTEL** | About a third of the wood-floor rooms in this midtown hotel have superb Mekong River views. **Pros:** centrally located; Mekong views from some rooms; good restaurant with memorable views. **Cons:** expensive for Huay Xai; river-facing rooms get very hot in the afternoon; often packed with noisy tour groups. [$] *Rooms from: 205,000 kip* ✉ *168 Centre Rd., Ban Houayxay* ☎ *084/211064*

Religion in Laos

The overwhelming majority of Laotians are Buddhists, yet as in neighboring Thailand, spirit worship is widespread, blending easily with temple traditions and rituals. A common belief holds that supernatural spirits called *phi* have power over individual and community life.

Laotians believe that each person has 32 *khwan*, or individual spirits, which must be appeased and kept "bound" to the body. If one of the khwan leaves the body, sickness can result, and then a ceremony must be performed to reattach the errant spirit. In this ritual, which is known as *bai-si*, white threads are tied to the wrist of the ailing person in order to fasten the spirits. Apart from the khwan, there are countless other spirits inhabiting the home, gardens, orchards, fields, forests, mountains, rivers, and even individual rocks and trees.

Luang Prabang has a team of ancestral guardian spirits, the Pu Nyeu Na Nyeu, who are lodged in a special temple, Wat Aham. In the south, the fierce guardian spirits of Wat Phu are appeased every year with the sacrifice of a buffalo to guarantee an abundance of rain during the rice-growing season.

Despite the common belief in a spirit world, more than 90% of Laotians are officially Theravada Buddhists, a conservative nontheistic form of Buddhism said to be derived directly from the words of the Lord Buddha. Buddhism arrived in Laos in the 3rd century BC by way of Ashoka, an Indian emperor who helped spread the religion. A later form of Buddhism, Mahayana, which arose in the 1st century AD, is also practiced in Laos, particularly in the cities. It differs from Theravada in that followers venerate the bodhisattvas. This northern school of Buddhism spread from India to Nepal, China, Korea, and Japan, and is practiced by Vietnamese and Chinese alike in all the bigger towns of Laos. The Chinese in Laos also follow Taoism and Confucianism.

Buddhism in Laos is so interlaced with daily life that you have a good chance of witnessing its practices and rituals firsthand—from the early-morning sight of women giving alms to monks on their rounds through the neighborhood to the evening routine of monks gathering for their temple recitations. If you visit temples on Buddhist holy days, which coincide with the new moon, you'll likely hear monks chanting texts of the Buddha's teachings.

Christianity is followed by a small minority of mostly French-educated, elite Laotians, although the faith also has adherents among hill tribe converts in areas that have been visited by foreign missionaries. Missionary activity has been curbed in recent years, however, as the Lao government forbids the dissemination of foreign religious materials.

Islam is practiced by a handful of Arab and Indian businesspeople in Vientiane. There are also some Muslims from Yunnan, China, called Chin Haw, in the northern part of Laos. More recently, a very small number of Cham refugees from Pol Pot's Cambodia (1975–79) took refuge in Vientiane, where they have established a mosque.

riverside_huayxai_laos_@hotmail.com *No credit cards* *38 rooms* *No meals.*

Phongsaly

425 km (264 miles) north of Luang Prabang.

If you're looking for off-the-beaten-track adventure, head for the provincial capital Phongsaly, in the far north of Laos. It's a hill station and market town nearly 5,000 feet above sea level in the country's most spectacular mountain range, Phu Fa. Trekking through this land of forest-covered mountains and rushing rivers may be as close as you'll ever get to the thrill of exploring virgin territory.

GETTING HERE AND AROUND

Buses from Oudomxay make the nine-hour run to Phongsaly (80,000 kip) daily at 8 am, with the journey taking slightly less time each year as the road receives upgrades. In town, tuk-tuks can take you wherever you need to go for 10,000 kip.

SAFETY AND PRECAUTIONS

Always trek with a local guide. The terrain is mountainous jungle, and it's easy to get lost. It is also close to the Chinese border, which is not always clearly marked. English is not widely spoken here.

TIMING

The only reason to come to Phongsaly is to go trekking, experience one of Laos's most untouched spots, and enjoy the cool weather and fabulous scenery. Plan on spending a minimum of three days to experience Phongsaly. If you're pressed for time, skip this area, as the journey is a difficult one.

TOURS

The Phongsaly Provincial Tourism office runs a good ecotourism program providing treks and homestays in hill tribe areas with English-speaking guides.

VISITOR AND TOUR INFORMATION

CONTACT Phongsaly Tourism Office *Downhill from the morning market* *020/5428–4600.*

 Sights

Tribal Museum

MUSEUM | For a break from trekking, drop by this museum whose exhibits provide a glimpse into the lives and culture of the area's 25 different ethnic groups. The tribal-costume display is delightfully kaleidoscopic. *Phôngsali* *Next to Agricultural Bank, near post office* *020/5657–6050* *5,000 kip.*

 Restaurants

★ Souphailin's Restaurant

$ | **LAO** | Despite its humble appearance, this small thatched-roof eatery serves the best food in Oudomxay, and is itself a reason to slip into this otherwise colorless town. The owner, Mrs. Souphailin, specializes in northern Lao cuisine. **Known for:** mok het khao (white mushrooms cooked in a banana leaf); kaeng naw som sai sin gai (bamboo soup with chicken); books filled with travelers' recommendations. *Average main: 40,000 kip* *Ban Vieng Hai, 13 Nua Rd., Muang Xay* *Across from Bank of Lao building, a few steps up side road* *081/211147, 020/5606–2474* *No credit cards.*

 Hotels

Litthavixay Guesthouse

$ | **HOTEL** | Rooms here are simple but clean, with comfortable beds, hot showers, TVs, air-conditioning, and fans—all luxuries in this neck of the woods. **Pros:** centrally located; best Wi-Fi in town; owners can speak English and assist tourists. **Cons:** noisy street outside; west-facing rooms get quite hot in the afternoon; rooms are starting to feel a bit worn out. *Rooms from: 73,000 kip* *Na Wan Noi, 13 Nua Rd., Muang Xay*

↔ 400 meters north of northern bus station on right ☎ 081/212175 ▭ No credit cards ⇆ 18 rooms ¶○| No meals.

Namkat Yorla Pa Resort

$$$ | **RESORT** | Opened in 2016, this eco-focused resort 10 miles out of Oudomxay's center tries hard to exploit the natural beauty of the Nam Kat waterfall and create some sort of novel "tourist attraction." The rooms and villas, some with private plunge pools, mix rattan, bamboo, and terra-cotta tiles, and for the moment are the most luxurious in the region. **Pros:** pretty forest surroundings; spa and gym; sauna. **Cons:** far from anything; nature activities are not included; re-created Khmu village is kitsch. $ *Rooms from: 851,521 kip ✉ Faen Village, Xay District, Muang Xay ☎ 020/5556–4359 🌐 www.namkatyorlapa.com ⇆ 60 ¶○| Free breakfast.*

Sengphachan Guesthouse

$ | **B&B/INN** | One of the newest offerings in Phongsaly, this guesthouse has large rooms with oversized beds equipped with cotton linens and an extra blanket for chilly nights. **Pros:** good Wi-Fi; good value; balcony overlooking the main road. **Cons:** some rooms are showing wear; owners live on the ground floor; poor English is spoken. $ *Rooms from: 120,000 kip ✉ Phôngsali ↔ On western side of the main road, west of the market and Amazing Lao Travel ☎ 020 /5519–4111 ⇆ 10 rooms ¶○| No meals ▭ No credit cards.*

Viphaphone Hotel

$ | **HOTEL** | Completely revamped in 2018, Viphaphone's exterior structure looks quite uninspiring, but its refurbished, spotless rooms have all the bells and whistles that travelers come to expect, even in such a remote part of Laos. **Pros:** spacious rooms; air-conditioner units with heater for the colder months; Western toilets. **Cons:** some staff speak little English; cheaper rooms are small; the odd hallway's structure sacrifces space in some rooms. $ *Rooms from: 100,000 kip ✉ Phôngsali ↔ On main road, east of market ☎ 020/9817–1031 ▭ No credit cards ⇆ 24 rooms ¶○| Free breakfast.*

Tha Khek

350 km (217 miles) south of Vientiane.

Tha Khek is a bustling Mekong River port in Khammuan Province with some of its ancient city wall still intact. Thailand's provincial capital of Nakhon Phanom sits across the Mekong River from Tha Khek: ferries and the third Thai-Lao Friendship Bridge over the Mekong connect the two cities. The main reason to linger here is the stunning countryside and karst (limestone caverns and sinkholes) surrounding the town, which can be visited as a popular counterclockwise motorbike loop that starts and ends in Tha Khek. The region contains dramatic limestone caves, most notably Tham Khong Lor, set about 180 km to the northeast. More than 6½ km (4 miles) long, this cave is so large that the Nam Hin Bun River runs through it. There is a 60,000-kip entry fee, which includes a sampan ride to the entrance of the cave, and an adventurous two-hour-long guided tour in a wooden longboat that fits a maximum of three people. The trip includes a stop on an exposed part of the cave so that visitors can walk among the impressive stalactites and stalagmites. When the boat reaches the other side of the cave, it turns and brings visitors back to the park's headquarters. It's recommended to use swimwear and rubber shoes or slippers as it's easy to get wet, especially in the rainy season, when water showers drip powerfully from holes in the cave's top.

GETTING HERE AND AROUND

To reach Tha Khek it is easier to fly to Nakhon Phanom in Thailand, which has a couple daily flights from Bangkok, rather than backtrack from Savannakhet or Pakse's airports.

Several buses leave Vientiane's Southern Bus Station to Tha Khek (about four

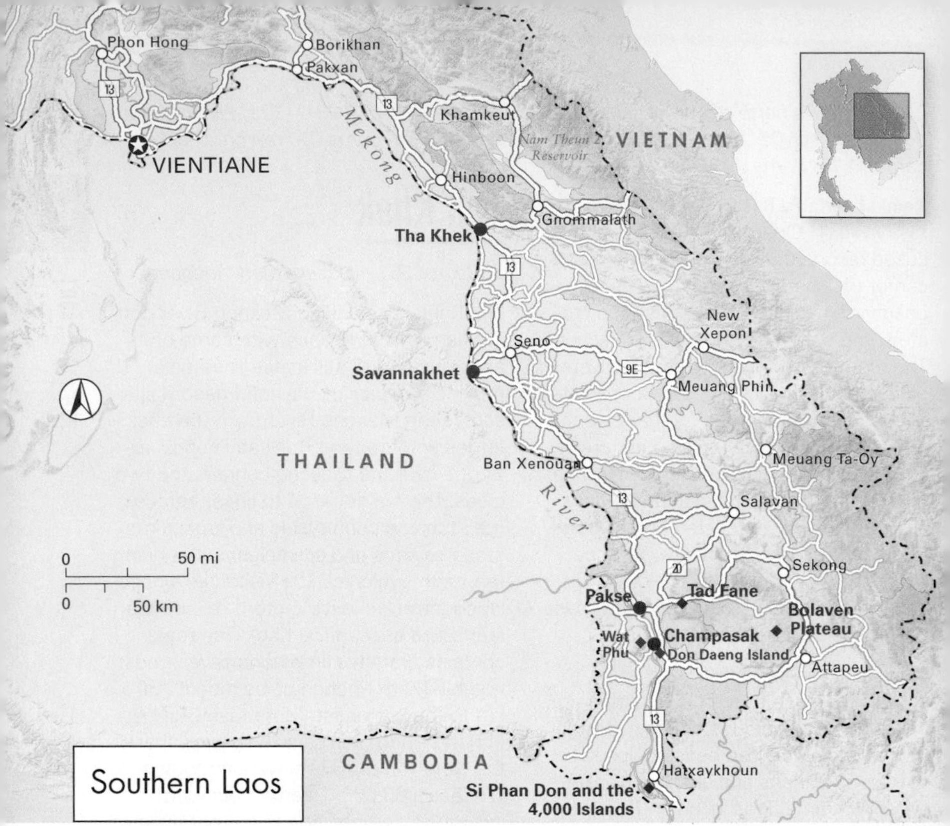

Southern Laos

hours; 40,000 kip), but if your final destination is Tham Khong Lor, it's easier to catch the direct bus (10 am, seven hours; 80,000 kip) to Ban Nahin, from where you'll have to change to a songtaew (25,000 kip) for the last 42 km to Khong Lor village.

The Khong Lor Loop is a popular 450-km motorbike circuit on completely sealed roads that starts and ends in Tha Khek. It's usually taken anti-clockwise, so that Tham Kong Lor remains one of the last highlights. Every hotel in town can rent motorbikes and hand out maps of the many caves and waterfalls to visit en route, but Wang Wang's, set in the town square by the river, and Mr Ku's, in-house at Thakek Travel Lodge, come recommended by travelers.

TIMING

The Khong Lor Loop can be done in three days, but a more leisurely four will help better enjoy the surroundings.

Hotels

Spring River Resort & Restaurant
$$ | **HOTEL** | Neatly arranged in a lush meadow that faces a blue lagoon sheltered by an impressive karst formation, this series of squeaky-clean bamboo bungalows is set 2 km from Khong Lor's entrance. **Pros:** picturesque location; excellent value; reliable Wi-Fi. **Cons:** a bit of a hike from Khong Lor; jungle setting means insects; breakfast is $5 extra.
$ Rooms from: 425,000 kip ✉ Near Konglor Cave, Ban Tiou Village ☎ 020/5963–6111 🌐 www.springriverresort.com 16 rooms 🍽 No meals.

Savannakhet

470 km (290 miles) south of Vientiane.

A former French colonial provincial center, the riverside town of Savannakhet is today the urban hub of a vast rice-growing plain. It's a good place to break the long journey between Vientiane and Pakse, distinguished by some fine examples of French colonial architecture around Talat Yen Plaza, home to a night market and the iconic Catholic church Eglise Sainte Therese (free admission). Nearby Wat Xayaphoum dates back to the 16th century and has an interesting Buddha statue workshop.

GETTING HERE AND AROUND

Lao Airlines flies from Vientiane to Savannakhet several times daily for 850,000 kip ($100). From Pakse buses depart hourly until midday for Savannakhet from the northern bus station (five hours; 45,000 kip). VIP buses (115,000 kip) from Vientiane's Southern Bus Terminal to Savannakhet depart daily at 8:30 pm and arrive about seven hours later. There are also several daily buses from Thakhek (30,000 kip), which stop at the bus station along Highway 13, a few miles out of town. Most bus tickets include a songthaew transfer into town, otherwise it will cost around 20,000 kip to most any point.

The Thai town of Mukdahan lies just across the Mekong River and is accessible by ferry or by crossing the third of four bridges connecting Thailand and Laos. The bridge, one of several established to create an East–West Economic Corridor connecting the Vietnamese port of Da Nang with Laos, Thailand, and Myanmar (Burma), also greatly facilitates tourist travel between Thailand and Laos. Eight to twelve buses shuttle passengers the 10 miles in either direction; buses depart daily from 7 am to 5:30 pm, stopping briefly at the border, where passengers must pay a fee of 10 Thai baht.

 Sights

Dinosaur Museum
MUSEUM | One of Savannakhet's curiosities is this dinosaur museum that displays fossils discovered in the area. ✉ *Kanthabuli Rd. and Chaimeuang Rd.* ☎ *041/212597* 🎫 *5,000 kip.*

Talat Yen Plaza
PLAZA | Savannakhet's center develops around this old square, at whose upper end stands the iconic Catholic church Eglise Sainte Therese. One of the few in Laos, it is surrounded by peaceful gardens, and can be visited throughout the day. All around Talat Yen Plaza, a grid of historical lanes boast several interesting yet crumbling art deco French buildings, perfect to explore on foot. From 5 pm Talat Yen Plaza fills up with a popular night market: you'll find souvenirs and stalls selling the usual Lao and Thai staples: stir-fried and noodle-based dishes. The series of little bars and cafés that dot the square's perimeter are among the best spots to have a coffee or a drink in town. ✉ *Savannakhet.*

 Restaurants

Lin's Cafe
$ | **INTERNATIONAL** | This bistro occupies a 1930s historical building in the corner of Talat Yen Square and offers a wide menu of Western-inspired comfort foods, from salads to pasta, rice dishes, and coffees. The good milk shakes, brews, and strong Wi-Fi make it popular with travelers. **Known for:** reasonable prices; exhibition of old Savannakhet on the first floor; icy drinks. $ *Average main: 30,000 kip* ✉ *Savannakhet* ✣ *Northeast corner of Talat Yen, in front of the Eglise Saint Therese* ☎ *030/533–2188.*

 Hotels

Aura Residence
$ | **HOTEL** | This modern and clean Thai-style flashpacker hotel within walking

distance of the bus station has large rooms, most with small balconies, sturdy beds and fresh linens, and decent size bathrooms—all great perks at this price range. **Pros:** very close to bus station and Thai consulate; good value; staff speak good English. **Cons:** a 25-minute walk to Talat Yen; karaoke nearby can be noisy; breakfast not included. *Rooms from: 200,000 kip ✉ Sisavangvong Rd. ✣ 250 meters south of bus station, beside Avalon Residence ☎ 041/252818 20 rooms 🍴 No meals No credit cards.*

Hostel Savan Cafe

$ | **B&B/INN** | Inspired and decorated in the old Chinese vintage style that hints more at Penang, Malaysia, than French-Indochina, this downtown option has a trendy ground-floor bistro, several good-value rooms, and a clean, functional dorm for those on a budget. **Pros:** scenic and homely; rooftop terrace with Mekong views; hallways have been turned into art galleries. **Cons:** few rooms so it can get booked solid; reception staff speaks little English; dorms with clean, yet shared, bathrooms. *Rooms from: 200,000 kip ✉ Savannakhet ✣ Old Town, on the same lane as the Tourism Information Centre ☎ 020/7656–0000 5 rooms 🍴 Free breakfast.*

Pakse

205 km (127 miles) south of Savannakhet, 675 km (420 miles) south of Vientiane.

Pakse is a former French colonial stronghold, linked now with neighboring Thailand by a bridge 40 km (25 miles) away. It plays a central role in an ambitious regional plan to create an "Emerald Triangle"—a trade and tourism community grouping Laos, Thailand, and Cambodia. The city has few attractions, most notably the riverside Wat Luang, Pakse's biggest temple. It's home to a Buddhist Monk School, and probably the best place in the country to see a monk almgiving ceremony—you'll be one of few visitors, compared to the throngs of tourists in Luang Prabang. Pakse is also the starting point for tours to the Khmer ruins at Wat Phu, the 4,000 Islands, and the Bolaven Plateau, which straddles the southern provinces of Saravan, Sekon, Attapeu, and Champasak.

GETTING HERE AND AROUND

AIR TRAVEL

Domestic: There are several Lao Airlines flights each day from Vientiane to Pakse, sometimes routed via Savannakhet, and a daily service to Luang Prabang; both flights take about an hour and costs about 800,000 kip ($100) one way. **International:** Lao Airlines also flies daily to Siem Reap, Cambodia; to Ho Chi Minh City in Vietnam on Tuesdays, Thursdays and Saturdays (from 1,500,000 kip/$180); and to Bangkok on Mondays, Wednesdays, Fridays, and weekends (from 1,700,000 kip/$200). A tuk-tuk from Pakse International Airport, which is 4 km (2 miles) northwest of the city center, costs from 30,000 kip to 40,000 kip.

BOAT TRAVEL

Vat Phou Cruises

BOAT TOURS | A luxurious double-decker houseboat, the *Vat Phou*, plies the southern length of the Mekong between Pakse and Si Phan Don. The all-inclusive cruises, which last three days and two nights, stop at Champasak, Vat Phou, Don Khong Island, a small village containing the temple of Oum Muong, and the waterfall at Phapheng, near Laos's border with Cambodia. The cruise guide speaks English, French, and Thai. *✉ Mekong Cruises (tour operator), 108 Th. 11, Ban Wat Luang ☎ 031/251446 🌐 www.vatphou.com From 6 million kip ($739) all-inclusive Oct.–Mar., 4.5 million kip ($518) Apr.–Sept. ☞ Oct.–Mar., Tues., Thurs., and Sat.; Apr.–Sept., Tues. and Sat.; no cruises in June.*

BUS TRAVEL

Pakse is the transportation hub for all destinations in the south. It has four bus stations: the Northern Bus Terminal, situated about 6 miles north of town, has hourly departures to Savannakhet (five hours; 40,000 kip) and other points north. The Southern Bus Terminal (aka KM8 Bus Terminal) is mostly used by locals to point south. The Kriang Kai Bus Terminal (aka Km2 Bus Terminal) has some night buses to Vientiane. At last, the most used bus station is the Chitpasong Bus Terminal next to the Sedone River in the center of town. From here, comfortable VIP bed buses make the overnight, 11-hour journey to and from Vientiane (200,000 kip from Vientiane, including transfer to bus station, 170,000 kip from Pakse to Vientiane). Buses leave Vientiane nightly at 8 or 8:30 pm and arrive in Pakse at 6:30 am; the times are the same from Pakse to Vientiane. If you're headed to Si Phan Don from Pakse, it's more convenient to take a minibus, which will pick you up at your hotel for 65,000 kip; all guesthouses sell tickets.

For international departures, you can get direct buses to Ubon in Thailand from Pakse as well as to Siem Reap and Phnom Penh in Cambodia.

CAR TRAVEL

Any travel agent in town can arrange car rental with a driver.

MOTORBIKE TRAVEL

Given the good quality of roads around Pakse, renting a scooter to visit the waterfalls, Champasak, or the Bolaven Plateau is a very popular option for the most adventurous.

TAXI, TUK-TUK, AND SONGTHAEW TRAVEL

Tuk-tuks around town cost 10,000 kip (although you will be hard-pressed to get this price as a tourist). Songthaews to Champasak (one hour; 30,000 kip) leave from the Dao Heuang market.

TIMING

Unless you are using Pakse as a base for visiting Champasak or elsewhere as a day tour, one night should be enough. Themain city sights can be covered in a day, but allow for two if you decide to explore the countryside by motorbike. Pakse is also a perfect place to book tickets, go to the bank, and deal with any kind of communications or business before moving on to Champasak, Tad Fane, or the 4,000 Islands. Allow for two to thee extra days if you decide to tackle the shorter or longer version of the Bolaven Plateau Loop.

TOURS

Miss Noy

ADVENTURE TOURS | Recommended Belgian-Lao run motorbike rental shop (from 30,000 kip per day) that also organizes tours and sells tickets for onward travel. ■ **TIP→ If you intend to explore the area independently, drop by Miss Noy at 6 pm for their daily brief on the best motorbike routes to Champasak and the Bolaven Plateau.** ✉ *13 National Hwy.* ✣ *Right opposite Jasmine restaurant* ☎ *020/2227–2278.*

Pakse Travel

This company arranges ecotours to Champasak, Si Phan Don, and farther afield, conducted by trained guides and with excellent transportation options. Day tours to the Bolaven Plateau, homestays on Don Daeng and in ethnic villages, tea-and coffee plantation tours are just some of the offerings. ✉ *108 Ban Thalung, Hwy. 13* ✣ *Next to Phi Dao Hotel downtown* ☎ *020/2227–7277, 020/7773–4567* 🌐 *www.paksetravel.com* ☞ *Prices vary depending on number of travelers.*

VISITOR AND TOUR INFORMATION

CONTACT Champasak Provincial Tourism ✉ *Th. 11, Ban Thasalakam* ✣ *Near BCEL bank* ☎ *031/212021.*

Lao: A Few Key Phrases

The official language is Lao, part of the extensive Thai family of languages of Southeast Asia spoken from Vietnam in the east to India in the west. Spoken Lao is very similar to the northern Thai language, as well as local dialects in the Shan states in Myanmar and Sipsongbanna in China. Lao is tonal, meaning a word can have several meanings according to the tone in which it's spoken.

Here are a few common and useful words:

Hello: sabai di (pronounced *sa-bye dee*)

Thank you: khop chai deu (pronounced *cop jai der*; use khop cheu neu in northern Laos)

Yes: heu (pronounced like deux) *or* thia

No: bor

Where?: iu sai (pronounced *you sai*)?

How much?: to dai (pronounced *tao dai*)?

Zero: sun (pronounced *soon*)

One: neung

Two: song

Three: sam

Four: si

Five: ha

Six: hok

Seven: tiet (pronounced *jee-yet*)

Eight: pet

Nine: kao

Ten: sip

Twenty: sao (rhymes with cow; different from Thai "yee sip")

Hundred: neung loi

Thousand: neung phan

To eat: kin khao (pronounced *kin cow*)

To drink: kin nam

Water: nam

Rice: khao

Expensive: peng

Bus: lot me (pronounced *lot may*)

House: ban

Road: thanon

Village: ban

Island: don

River: mae nam (pronounced *may nam*)

Doctor: maw

Hospital: hong mo (pronounced *hong maw*)

Post Office: paisani

Hotel: hong hem

Toilet: hong nam

Sights

Historical Heritage Museum

MUSEUM | Pakse's history museum displays stonework from the famous Wat Phu in Champasak, handicrafts from the Bolaven Plateau ethnic groups, and locally made musical instruments. ✉ *Hwy. 13* ✣ *1 km (½ mile) before Dao Heung Market turnoff* ☎ *020/5527–1733* 🎫 *10,000 kip.*

★ Wat Phou Salao

RELIGIOUS SITE | Built across the river on the way to Champasak in August 2011, this hilltop temple has an impressive

"Big Buddha" statue that dominates the peak. A long staircase flanked with nagas brings visitors to the top (allow 30 minutes for the climb) where there are great views of the river and the city, especially as they soak the crimson sunsets. There is also a newer, concrete road to the top. ✉ *Pakse* ✣ *Adjacent to the Japanese bridge.*

Restaurants

Jasmine

$ | **INDIAN** | A Pakse mainstay, this restaurant serves vegetarian and nonvegetarian Indian and Malay food, including excellent dosas and curries. Western-style breakfasts are prepared starting at 6:30 am—perfect for the early-morning minivan crowd heading to the 4,000 Islands. **Known for:** masala dosa; roti canai; rice and curries. $ *Average main: 40,000 kip* ✉ *385 Banthaluang, Rd. 13* ✣ *Across from Phi Dao Hotel* ☎ *031/251002* ▭ *No credit cards.*

Le Panorama

$ | **ASIAN FUSION** | The sixth-floor restaurant at the Pakse Hotel not only has the best view in town, but it also has the best food. Start with a sunset cocktail on the romantic rooftop terrace, and then move on to a romantic candlelight dinner under the stars. **Known for:** gai vat phou (chicken breast stuffed with crabmeat); international wines; excellent tam som (green papaya salad). $ *Average main: 50,000 kip* ✉ *Pakse Hotel, Th. 5, Ban Wat Luang* ☎ *031/212131, 031/252993* 🌐 *www.hotelpakse.com* ⊗ *No lunch.*

Hotels

Athena Hotel

$$ | **HOTEL** | The spacious and vintage-styled rooms all have wide windows that allow plenty of natural light to shine on the classy hardwood floors and furniture. **Pros:** large bathrooms; swimming pool; unlimited a la carte breakfast. **Cons:** rooms facing main road can get noisy; patchy Wi-Fi; central but not very close to the river. $ *Rooms from: 800,000 kip* ✉ *RN 13 South, Phabath Village* ☎ *031/214888* 🌐 *www.athenahotelpakse.com* ⇆ *25 rooms* 🍽 *Free breakfast.*

Pakse Hotel

$ | **HOTEL** | Pakse's oldest hotel was refurbished in 2018 and keeps offering well-maintained, centrally located rooms. **Pros:** great central location; comfortable rooms with plenty of light; attentive staff. **Cons:** small elevator; standard rooms don't have views; busy with tour groups. $ *Rooms from: 252,000 kip* ✉ *Th. 5, Ban Wat Luang* ☎ *031/212131, 031/252993* 🌐 *www.paksehotel.com* ⇆ *63 rooms* 🍽 *Free breakfast.*

★ Residence Sisouk

$$ | **HOTEL** | A premier boutique hotel refurbished from a historical corner building, Residence Sisouk is luxurious and charming with its original hardwood flooring, a mix of old and new furnishings, photography, and leafy plants. **Pros:** close to everything; colonial charm; good breakfast and café. **Cons:** not all rooms have river views; inconsistent service; old staircase. $ *Rooms from: 430,000 kip* ✉ *Bane Lakmuang* ✣ *Opposite Lao Air Lines office along the riverfront* ☎ *031/214716* 🌐 *www.residence-sisouk.com* ⇆ *25 rooms* 🍽 *Free breakfast.*

Bolaven Plateau

23km (14 miles) east of Pakse.

The volcanic soil of this plateau to the east of Pakse makes the vast region ideal for agriculture: it's the source of much of the country's prized coffee, tea, and spices. Despite its beauty and central role in the Lao economy, the plateau has minimal tourist infrastructure, and is pretty much off-the-beaten-track territory.

GETTING HERE AND AROUND

Most tour agents and hotels organize day trips to the Bolaven Plateau from Pakse. These usually take in Tad Fane waterfall and the countryside around Paksong, and are just a mere teaser of the beauty that awaits farther east. The best way to go is to hire a car and driver for a few days, or rent a motorbike and strike on the well-established Bolaven Plateau Loop, starting and ending in Pakse. Miss Noy is a reliable rental company ☎ *020/2227–2278.*

SAFETY AND PRECAUTIONS

The main roads are paved, but any side trip requires caution. Motorbike theft is a problem in some stops that your rental company should be able to indicate before you set off. Stick to normal precautions otherwise.

TIMING

Take a minimum of two days for the Small Loop and three for the Long Loop. Adding a few extra days makes the experience more enjoyable.

Sights

Bolaven Plateau Loop

BODY OF WATER | The waterfall is set on the border of the Dong Hua Sao National Park and up in the cool air of the Bolaven Plateau, Laos's premier coffee-growing region. There's good hiking here, and the cool temperatures are a relief from the heat and humidity down on the Mekong. The area is accessible as a day trip from Pakse, though there is a somewhat run-down and overpriced resort at the base of the falls should you care to stay. Aside from the easy stroll out to the viewing platform above the main falls, those who don't suffer vertigo can try the 400-meter-high zip line that soars over the falls, giving a bird's-eye view of the area ($40 per person). You can also take a guided walk down to the base of the falls, or venture onto one of the roundabout trails going up above the falls. These trails take in some minor falls and some fun swimming holes. Farther afield, the beautiful **Tat Yuang falls** can be reached in about an hour via a trail from Tad Fane, or from a turnout at Km 40 on the main road. Inquire at the resort about guides and trail information. ✉ *Pakse.*

Tad Fane

38 km (24 miles) east of Pakse.

Tad Fane is Laos's most impressive waterfall, pounding down through magnificent jungle foliage for almost 400 feet.

GETTING HERE AND AROUND

Buses and songthaews run from the Pakse bus station several times each morning. The trip up to Tad Fane and the Bolaven Plateau town of Paksong takes an hour and costs 40,000 kip.

SAFETY AND PRECAUTIONS

The trails around the falls are slippery and can be dangerous, especially during the rainy season (when the leeches come out). Proceed with caution and take a guide if you feel unsure about getting around on your own.

TIMING

Take one day for the falls and possibly another day to do some hiking in the park or explore the area around Paksong.

Sights

Tad Fane waterfall

BODY OF WATER | The waterfall is set on the border of the Dong Hua Sao National Park and up in the cool air of the Bolaven Plateau, Laos's premier coffee-growing region. There's good hiking here, and the cool temperatures are a relief from the heat and humidity down on the Mekong. The area is accessible as a day trip from Pakse, though there is a somewhat run-down and overpriced resort at the base of the falls should you care to stay. Aside from the easy stroll out to the viewing platform above the main falls, those who don't suffer vertigo can try the 400-meter-high zip line that soars over the falls, giving a bird's-eye view of the area ($40 per person). You can also take a guided walk down to the base of the falls, or venture onto one of the roundabout trails going up above the falls. These trails take in some minor falls and some fun swimming holes. Farther afield, the beautiful **Tat Yuang falls** can be reached in about an hour via a trail from Tad Fane or from a turnout at Km 40 on the main road. Inquire at the resort about guides and trail information. ✉ *Pakse.*

Champasak

40 km (25 miles) south of Pakse.

In the early 18th century the kingdom of Laos was partitioned into three realms: Luang Prabang, Vientiane, and Champasak. During the 18th and 19th centuries, this small village on the west bank of the Mekong River was the royal center of a wide area of what is today Thailand and Cambodia. The area's most unique lodging option, with a Robinson Crusoe feel, is La Folie on Don Daeng, an island near Champasak that remains largely untouched by tourism and is an excellent base for visiting Wat Phu and Champasak. The River Resort, just north of Champasak, is upscale and romantic.

GETTING HERE AND AROUND

Songthaews travel here from the Dao Heuang Market in Pakse three times each morning (one hour; 20,000 kip). Minibuses can be arranged through guesthouses and travel agencies in Pakse for 60,000 kip. While most tour agency minibuses take the road toward the 4,000 Islands and drop you off at the Ban Muang boat pier on the east bank of the Mekong—Don Daeng Island is accessed from here—a new road down the west side cuts out the need for a boat ride across if coming via local songthaew. A car with a driver can be hired from all tour agencies in Pakse for about 500,000 kip. Tuk-tuks run to Wat Phu from Champasak for 10,000 kip per person. You can also rent motorbikes (50/70,000 kip per day) as the road is perfectly sealed and sees sporadic traffic.

■ TIP→ These days the best way to get to Champasak from Pakse is by the new road; the ferry crossing gets far less use now, and you may find yourself stuck waiting for a boat.

If you do take a boat, the correct price for crossing is 10,000 kip, but the boatman will likely try to extract more unless you give the correct change.

TIMING

One day should be enough time to tour the ruins.

Sights

Don Daeng Island

ISLAND | In the middle of the Mekong opposite Wat Phu, this island is a fantastic escape. Nine km (5½ miles) long, Dong Daeng has gorgeous views of the river and the surrounding countryside. An ecotourism program and a long sandy beach have made it popular with visitors to Wat Phu as an alternative to staying in Pakse or Champasak. Bicycles can be rented on the island, and the Provincial Tourist Office in Pakse can arrange homestays. There's also a charming upscale hotel, La Folie Lodge. ✉ *Champasak.*

★ Wat Phu

RELIGIOUS SITE | This temple sits grandly on heights above the Mekong River, about 8 km (5 miles) south of Champasak, looking back on a centuries-old history that won it UNESCO recognition as a World Heritage site. Wat Phu predates Cambodia's Angkor Wat—Wat Phu's hilltop site was chosen by Khmer Hindus in the 6th century AD, probably because of a nearby spring of freshwater.

Construction of the wat continued into the 13th century, at which point it finally became a Buddhist temple. Much of the original Hindu sculpture remains unchanged, however, including representations on the temple's lintels of the Hindu gods Vishnu, Shiva, and Kala. The staircase is particularly beautiful, its protective *nagas* (mystical serpents) decorated with plumeria, the national flower of Laos. Many of the temple's treasures, including pre-Angkor–era inscriptions, are preserved in an archaeology museum that is part of the complex. An impressive festival takes place at the temple each January. ✉ *Rd. 14, 8 km (5 miles) south of town* ☎ *030/956–5325* 🌐 *www.vatphou-champassak.com/en* 🎫 *50,000 kip; 40,000 kip 6 am–8 am and 4:30–6, with no museum entry.*

Restaurants

★ The River Resort Restaurant

$ | **ECLECTIC** | The international team in the kitchen of the River Resort's elegant restaurant prepares fine Asian and Western dishes—the best food you will find in all southern Laos—with equal skill and panache. Highly recommended is the local Mekong fish, which can either be grilled and served with tamarind sauce and lime, or steamed in a banana leaf Lao-style. **Known for:** good wine list; grilled-asparagus starter; good prices for this range. $ *Average main: 80,000 kip* ✉ *Ban Phaphinnoy, Rd. 14A* ✥ *North of Champasak town, about 1 km (½ mile) north of boat-pier turnoff* ☎ *020/5685–0198* 🌐 *theriverresortlaos.com.*

Hotels

★ La Folie Lodge

$$$$ | **B&B/INN** | For a luxury Robinson Crusoe experience, nothing surpasses La Folie. **Pros:** stunning views; unique escapist experience; off-season discounts up to 40%. **Cons:** no other dining options nearby; very expensive; most staffers do not speak English. $ *Rooms from: 1,460,000 kip* ✉ *Don Daeng, Pathoumphone* ✥ *Opposite Champasak in middle of Mekong* ☎ *030/534–7603* 🌐 *www.lafolie-laos.com* 🛏 *24 rooms* 🍴 *Free breakfast.*

★ The River Resort

$$$ | **RESORT** | This gorgeous riverfront boutique resort with outdoor rain-style showers and truly cool air-conditioning is the perfect spot to start or end a southern Laos excursion. **Pros:** stunning Mekong River location and views; riverside swimming pool; free bicycles for guests. **Cons:** outside town; no facilities near resort; not convenient to Wat Phu. $ *Rooms from: 975,000 kip* ✉ *Ban Phaphinnoy, Rd. 14A* ✥ *North of Champasak town, about 1 km (½ mile) north of boat-pier turnoff* ☎ *020/5685–0198* 🌐 *theriverresortlaos.com* 🛏 *28 rooms* 🍴 *Free breakfast.*

Si Phan Don and the 4,000 Islands

80 km (50 miles) south of Champasak, 120 km (74 miles) south of Pakse.

If you've made it as far south as Champasak, then a visit to the Si Phan Don area—celebrated for its 4,000 Mekong River islands and freshwater dolphins—is a must. *Don* means "island," and two in this area are especially worth checking out: Don Khon (and its connected counterpart, Don Det) and the similarly named Don Khong. The Khone Phapheng Falls, on the mainland near Don Khon, are a highlight, and visiting them can be combined with seeing the freshwater Irrawaddy dolphins. You'll find many boat operators happy to escort you. Don Det, connected to Don Khon by a bridge, attracts the backpacker crowd. Don Khong has scenic rice fields and more upscale lodging choices and is far more peaceful than Don Khon, but is not as interesting or attractive. Most lodging options on Don Khon, Det, and Khong are fairly standard, but this is changing as progress comes to the islands.

GETTING HERE AND AROUND

Any travel agency in Pakse can help you make arrangements for getting to and from the islands. If going to Don Khong, consider taking a boat onward to Don Khon rather than taking the road. A boat usually makes the island-hop (40,000 kip) every morning at 8:30.

From Pakse you can take a minibus, arranged at any travel agency or guesthouse, to the boat crossing at either Hai Sai Khun (for Don Khong) or Nakasang (for Don Khon) with tickets for the small boat crossing to the islands included. The journey takes from two to three hours and costs between 60,000 and 70,000 kip depending which island you go to. A bridge connects Don Khong Island and Highway 13 on the Mekong's eastern bank, but the bridge is in the southern part of the island, so most minibuses still drop passengers at the boat pier farther north.

Boat crossings from the mainland to Don Khon (from Nakasang) cost 250,000 kip and take 15 minutes; to Don Khong (from Hat Sai Khun) it's a five-minute trip and costs 15,000 kip.

SAFETY AND PRECAUTIONS

Take care when kayaking on the Mekong. The water may appear still, but the currents are stronger than they seem, and eddies can suck you in. It's best to go with a guide. The name Liphi Falls means "spirit trap," and there's a lot of superstition surrounding them. It is considered offensive to swim here, so do refrain. Also, the rapids are strong, and there have been a number of tourist deaths in years past.

TIMING

The major sights can be seen in one day, but it would be a shame to not budget a few more days to relax and enjoy the local pace of life.

Sights

Don Khon Island

ISLAND | You can hike or bicycle to the beautiful Liphi waterfall on the island of Don Khon, though an even more stunning one, **Khone Phapheng,** is just east of Don Khon on the mainland. Day-trip tours that include visits to the Irrawaddy dolphins and the mainland's Phapheng fall set out from Don Khon. Also on Don Khon, and the connected Don Det, are the remains of a French-built railway. ✉ *Don Khon Island* 🎫 *Liphi waterfall 35,000 kip.*

Don Khong Island

ISLAND | The largest island in the area, Don Khong is inhabited by a community of fisherfolk living in small villages amid ancient Buddhist temples. The best way to explore is by bicycle—this a pretty big place. Far less visited than Don Det/ Don Khon, it's also a great spot to chill out along the river. A new bridge across the Mekong now connects Don Khong to the mainland, but minibuses still use the boat pier for travelers to cross. The bridge has yet to spoil the quiet pace of the island, which has beautiful rice fields in the middle. ✉ *Don Khong Island.*

Irrawaddy dolphins

NATURE PRESERVE | Downstream from Don Khon, at the border between Laos and Cambodia, freshwater Irrawaddy dolphins frolic in a protected area of the Mekong. Boat trips to view the dolphins set off from Tha Sanam Beach, south of Liphi Falls. Even better, head out to see the dolphins by kayak. All the guesthouses in town can arrange trips. ✢ *Boats depart from southern tip of Don Khon Island* 🎫 *70,000 kip per person, minimum of 3 people.*

The Irrawaddy Dolphin

The freshwater Irrawaddy dolphin, known as *pla ka* in Lao, is one of the world's most endangered species; according to a 2008 study, fewer than 50 now remain in the Mekong. The Irrawaddy has mythical origins. According to Lao and Khmer legend, a beautiful maiden, in despair over being forced to marry a snake, attempted suicide by jumping into the Mekong. But the gods intervened, saving her life by transforming her into a dolphin.

Lao people do not traditionally hunt the dolphins, but the Irrawaddy have been casualties of overfishing, getting tangled in nets. New dams in the Mekong have altered their ecosystem, further threatening their survival.

Catching a glimpse of these majestic animals—which look more like orcas than dolphins—can be a thrilling experience. The least obtrusive way to visit the Irrawaddy is in a kayak or other nonmotorized boat. If you go by motorboat and do spot dolphins, ask your driver to cut the engine when you're still 100 yards or so away. You can then paddle closer to the animals without disturbing them. Do not try to swim with the dolphins, and—of course—don't throw any trash into the water.

Restaurants

Seng Ahloune Restaurant
$ | **LAO** | This rickety restaurant on wooden planks just above the Mekong may not look like much, but its cooks consistently deliver tasty and authentic Lao food. The setting is intimate and romantic, though the place can get busy with tour groups staying at the family's decent guesthouse. **Known for:** river views; friendly staff; chicken biryani. *Average main: 50,000 kip* *Just west of bridge connecting Don Khon with Don Det* *031/260934* *No credit cards.*

Hotels

Pon Arena Hotel
$ | **HOTEL** | The enormous Mekong River–view rooms with terraces are the way to go at this inviting riverside property. **Pros:** large Mekong-view rooms with fabulous vistas; beautiful riverside pool; owner speaks fluent English. **Cons:** disappointing breakfast; standard and deluxe rooms lack views; Mekong-view rooms cost twice as much as standard ones. *Rooms from: 365,000 kip* *Ban Kang Khong, Don Khong Island* *To right of boat pier on Don Khong* *031/515018 reservations, 020/2227–0037 manager's cell* *www.ponarenahotel.com* *35 rooms* *Free breakfast.*

Sala Done Khone
$ | **B&B/INN** | The accommodations at this charming resort come in three flavors: French colonial–style rooms, adobe-style "green" rooms set in a garden, and atmospheric "raftels" floating on the Mekong. **Pros:** beautiful riverside location; most upmarket hotel on the island; some raftels have sunroofs. **Cons:** rooms book up quickly in high season; mosquitoes prevalent at sunset; rooms look a bit worn out. *Rooms from: 350,000 kip* *Just east of boat drop-off in Don Khon* *031/260940* *www.salalaoboutique.com/saladonekhone/* *30 rooms* *Free breakfast.*

Index

C

X

Y

Z

Photo Credits

Front Cover: Jill Krueger [Description: Wat Pho, Temple of the Reclining Buddha, Phra Nakhon District, Bangkok, Thailand.] Back cover, from left to right: Dudarev Mikhail/Shutterstock; Olives Jean-Michel/Shutterstock; Andy Lim/Shutterstock. Spine: Chaloemphan/Shutterstock. Interior, from left to right: 2005 Michael Yamashita/Aurora Photos (1). Eddy Galeotti / Shutterstock (2-3). Chapter 1: Experience Thailand: Ingolf Pompe 17 / Alamy (8-9). Luciano Mortula - LGM/Shutterstock (10-11). Yuttasak Chuntarothai/Shutterstock (11). Chirawan Thaiprasansap/Shutterstock (11). gagarych/Shutterstock (12). SantiPhotoSS/Shutterstock (12). Jill Krueger (13). Matyas Rehak/Shutterstock (14). Praphat Rattanayanon/Shutterstock (14). Shuttertong/Shutterstock (14). Tatiana Belova/Shutterstock (14). topten22photo/Shutterstock (15). OH studio image gallery/Shutterstock (15). korawat today/Shutterstock (15). The HippoZoom/Shutterstock (15). 9nong/Shutterstock (16). Ninara/Wikimedia Commons (16). hlphoto/Shutterstock (16). Nycscripts | Dreamstime.com (16). SantiPhotoSS/Shutterstock (17). Cocosbounty | Dreamstime.com (18). Watchrakorn Pakpan/Shutterstock (18). 501room/Shutterstock (18). vespaFoto/Shutterstock (18). HelloRF Zcool/ Shutterstock (19). pook_jun/Shutterstock (19). pratan/Shutterstock (22). Natsicha Wetchasart/Shutterstock (22). Virojt Changyencham/ Shutterstock (22). Africa Studio/Shutterstock (22). Nungning20/Shutterstock (23). Olga Kurguzova/Shutterstock (23). 9nong/Shutterstock (23). TONG4130/Shutterstock (23). saravutpics/Shutterstock (24). Panjaporn Nawathong/Shutterstock (24). Jes2u.photo/Shutterstock (24). Kamonkanok/Shutterstock (24). lidear21/Shutterstock (24). PtrT/Shutterstock (25). hlphoto/Shutterstock (25). Nor Gal/Shutterstock (25). v74/ Shutterstock (25). kungverylucky/Shutterstock (25). Nuwatphoto | Dreamstime.com (26). wk1003mike/Shutterstock (26). 501room/Shutterstock (26). Nuwatphoto | Dreamstime.com (27). cowardlion/Shutterstock (27). cowardlion/Shutterstock (28). Dmitry Chulov/Shutterstock (28). aroon phadee/Shutterstock (28). anek.soowannaphoom/Shutterstock (28). martinho Smart/Shutterstock (28). apiguide/Shutterstock (29). IVAN VIEITO GARCIA/Shutterstock (29). viewfinder/Shutterstock (29). jnara/Shutterstock (29). Inoprasom/Shutterstock (29). Master2 | Dreamstime.com (30). Jangnhut | Dreamstime.com (30). David Ionut/Shutterstock (30). Lakhesis | Dreamstime.com (31). Lakhesis | Dreamstime.com (31). NickPolanszky Photo/Shutterstock (32). think4photop/Shutterstock (32). Tiwakorn Dhupagupta/Shutterstock (32). Dudarev Mikhail/Shutterstock (33). Gubgib | Dreamstime.com (33). Aleksandar Todorovic/Shutterstock (34). JM Travel Photography/Shutterstock (34). julieleanne/Shutterstock (34). WeStudio/Shutterstock (35). Tooykrub/Shutterstock (35). North Wind Picture Archives/Alamy (43). Alvaro Leiva/age fotostock (44). Thomas Cockrem/Alamy (44), Genevieve Dietrich/Shutterstock (44). Juha Sompinmäki/Shutterstock (45). Thomas Cockrem/Alamy. (45). Bryan Busovicki/Shutterstock (45). Mary Evans Picture Library/Alamy (46)Content Mine International/Alamy (46). Public domain (46). Sam DCruz/Shutterstock (47). Newscom (47). Ivan Vdovin/age fotostock (47). Thor Jorgen Udvang/Shutterstock (48). AFP/Getty Images/Newscom(48). Chapter 3: Bangkok: Travel mania/Shutterstock (65). Chris L Jones/ Photolibrary.com (86-87). PCL / Alamy (88). John Hemmings/Shutterstock (88). Gina Smith/Shutterstock (88). Andy Lim/Shutterstock (90). Steve Vidler / eStock Photo (91). Heinrich Damm/ wikipedia.org (91). Plotnikoff/Shutterstock (91). do_ok/Shutterstock (91). Dave Stamboulis (92). P. Narayan / age fotostock (92). wayne planz/ Shutterstock (93). Travel Pix Collection (115). SuperStock (116). Juha Sompinmäki/Shutterstock (116). Mireille Vautier / Alamy (117). BlueMoon Stock / Alamy (117). john lander / Alamy (117). kd2/Shutterstock (117). David Kay/Shutterstock (118). Arco/I Schulz (118). jamalludin/ Shutterstock (118). Songchai W / Shutterstock (127). Luca Invernizzi Tettoni/Tips Italia/photolibrary.com (139). Chapter 4: Around Bangkok: Olympus/Shutterstock (141). Juriah Mosin/Shutterstock (151). Elena Elisseeva/Shutterstock (152). Andy Lim/Shutterstock (152). Robert Fried / Alamy (152). Ian Trower / Alamy (152). Juriah Mosin/Shutterstock (153). Jill Krueger (153). Ronald Sumners/Shutterstock (154). Asia / Alamy (154). dbimages / Alamy (155). Tourism Authority of Thailand (170). Chapter 5: The Gulf Coast Beaches: Jill Krueger (175). Jose Fuste Raga (190-191). Gonzalo Azumendi / age fotostock (193). Look Die Bildagentur der Fotografen GmbH / Alamy (193). Gavriel Jecan / age fotostock (195). Dave Stamboulis (195). Pla2na/Shutterstock (200). Guiziou Franck / age fotostock (214). Dmitry Zimin/Shutterstock (223). Makhh/Shutterstock (227). Chapter 6: Phuket and the Andaman Coast: Efired/Shutterstock (231). Torsak Thammachote/Shutterstock (234). William Berry/ Shutterstock (235). Dave Stamboulis (235). Dave Stamboulis (263). Pichugin Dmitry/Shutterstock (267). Andy Lim/Shutterstock (283). Chapter 7: Chiang Mai: NaughtyNut/Shutterstock (289). Valery Shanin/Shutterstock (300). Muellek/Shutterstock (303). Dave Stamboulis (308-309). Wikipedia.org (310). Wikipedia.org (310). mediacolor's / Alamy (310). Dave Stamboulis (310). Hemis / Alamy (310). Dave Stamboulis (311). Bryan Busovicki/Shutterstock (311). David Bleeker Photography.com / Alamy (311). Chapter 8: Northern Thailand: Paii VeGa/Shutterstock (333). Dave Stamboulis / Alamy (336). Andrea Skjold/Shutterstock (337). kentoh/Shutterstock (337). David South / Alamy (354). raffaele meucci (366). Stuart Pearce (367). SuperStock (368). SuperStock (368). KLJ Photographic Ltd/iStockphoto (369). Jon Arnold Images Ltd / Alamy (369). SuperStock (370). Anders Ryman / Alamy (370). Val Duncan/Kenebec Images / Alamy (371). Simon Podgorsek/iStockphoto (371). Robert Fried / Alamy (372). Luciano Mortula/Shutterstock (386). Juha Sompinmäki/Shutterstock (388-389). Chie Ushio (389). Khoo Si Lin/ Shutterstock (389). N. Frey Photography/Shutterstock (389). Idealink Photography / Alamy (390). Pipopthai | Dreamstime.com (391). SteveSPF/ Shutterstock (392). David Halbakken / Alamy (392). javarman/Shutterstock (393). Michele Falzone / Alamy (393). qingqing/Shutterstock (393). J Marshall - Tribaleye Images / Alamy (394). Juha Sompinmäki/Shutterstock (394). Julien Grondin/Shutterstock (394). Julien Grondin/ Shutterstock (395). hfng/Shutterstock (395). Jon Arnold Images Ltd / Alamy (395). Chapter 9: Cambodia: Efired/Shutterstock (401). Luciano Mortula/Shutterstock (417). Ryan Fox / age fotostock (426). Sakdawut Tangtongsap/Shutterstock (444-445). Raga Jose Fuste (446). Luciano Mortula/iStockphoto (447). Bruno Morandi / age fotostock (447). Jordi Camí / age fotostock (448). Colman Lerner Gerardo/Shutterstock (448). Brianna May/iStockphoto (449). Vladimir Renard/Wikimedia.org (450). R. Matina / age fotostock(450). Bernard O'Kane / Alamy (451). Paul Panayiotou / Alamy (451). Joris Van Ostaeyen/iStockphoto (452). Ben Heys/Shutterstock (458). Evan Wong/Shutterstock (463). Vladimir Korostyshevskiy/Shutterstock (468). Chapter 10: Laos: Guitar photographer/Shutterstock (475). Avigator Fortuner 887/Shutterstock (490). Mathes | Dreamstime.com (497). WitthayaP/Shutterstock (499). Phonepaseth Keosomsak/Shutterstock (513). About Our Writers: All photos are courtesy of the writers.

Notes

Notes

Notes

Notes

Notes

Notes

Notes

Notes

Notes

Notes

Notes

Notes

Fodor's ESSENTIAL THAILAND

Editorial: Douglas Stallings, *Editorial Director*; Margaret Kelly, Jacinta O'Halloran, *Senior Editors*; Kayla Becker, Alexis Kelly, Amanda Sadlowski, *Editors*; Teddy Minford, *Content Editor*; Rachael Roth, *Content Manager*

Design: Tina Malaney, *Design and Production Director*; Jessica Gonzalez, *Production Designer*

Photography: Jill Krueger, *Senior Photo Editor*

Maps: Rebecca Baer, *Senior Map Editor*; Henry Colomb and Mark Stroud (Moon Street Cartography), David Lindroth, *Cartographers*

Production: Jennifer DePrima, *Editorial Production Manager*; Carrie Parker, *Senior Production Editor*; Elyse Rozelle, *Production Editor*

Business & Operations: Chuck Hoover, *Chief Marketing Officer*; Robert Ames, *Vice President and General Manager*; Stephen Horowitz, *Director of Business Development and Revenue Operations*; Tara McCrillis, *Director of Publishing Operations*

Public Relations and Marketing: Joe Ewaskiw, *Manager*; Esther Su, *Marketing Manager*

Writers: Jacob Dean, Marco Ferrarese, Sophie Friedman, Simon Ostheimer, Andrew Parks, Barbara Woolsey

Editor: Jacinta O'Halloran

Production Editor: Elyse Rozelle

1st Edition

ISBN 978-1-64097-127-1

ISSN 2639-5967

Library of Congress Control Number 2018958615

SPECIAL SALES

This book is available at special discounts for bulk purchases for sales promotions or premiums. For more information, e-mail SpecialMarkets@fodors.com.

PRINTED IN THE UNITED STATES OF AMERICA

10 9 8 7 6 5 4 3 2 1

About Our Writers

From a home base in Penang, **Marco Ferrarese** covers Malaysia, India, and the larger Southeast Asian region for a number of international guidebooks and publications that include *Travel + Leisure Southeast Asia, the Guardian, BBC Travel,* and *Nikkei Asian Review*. His debut novel *Nazi Goreng* (2013) was a bestseller in Malaysia until it was banned by the Ministry of Home Affairs in 2015. Marco has also played guitar in Malaysian hardcore punk bands and written a book about it, *Banana Punk Rawk Trails* (2015), and earned a Ph.D in subcultural anthropology from Monash University Malaysia. He and his Malaysian photographer wife still call Penang home, even though they are on the road reporting from elsewhere most of the time. Know more about him and his books at 🌐 *www.marcoferrarese.com* and 🌐 *www.monkeyrockworld.com*.

Sophie Friedman bikes, drives, flies, walks, and rides trains around the globe. She has contributed to dozens of Fodor's Travel and Michelin Green Guide guidebooks. Her writing and photographs have appeared in print and online in AFAR, Bloomberg, Centurion, Conde Nast Traveler, Departures, Dubai Voyager, Forbes, Forbes Travel Guide, Jetsetter, JetStar Media, Jumeirah magazine, MSN, Oyster, and the *Wall Street Journal*. She always travels with sunscreen. She hopes that the ever-evolving, often amazing places listed in the Thailand guide will provide you with as many wonderful experiences and memories as they have her. Sophie updated the Experience and Chiang Mai chapters for this edition.

Simon N. Ostheimer resides in Phnom Penh, the latest stop in an Asian odyssey that has so far seen him live in Shanghai, Beijing, Hong Kong, Kuala Lumpur, Bangkok, and Phuket. He spent 5 years on the latter, and—having updated the Phuket and the Andaman Coast chapter for this guide—is now missing the many charms of his former island home. When not working for Fodor's, he also contributes to global inflight magazines, design tomes, and travel guides.

Andrew Parks spent three years traveling across the U.S., Asia and Australia—including a six-month stint in Bangkok—and fell in love with Minneapolis along the way. He's currently working on a new arts and culture site that celebrates the Twin Cities, along with freelance pieces for such publications as *Food & Wine, Travel + Leisure, Condé Nast Traveler, New York Magazine,* and *AFAR*. Andrew updated the Northern Thailand and Gulf Coast Beaches chapters for this edition.

Barbara Woolsey is a Canadian journalist who has criss-crossed Asia by plane, train and motorbike. She has lived in Bangkok for several periods since 2010, including stints reporting for the Bangkok Post, hosting and producing for *TrueVisions* TV, and writing a nightlife column. She currently spends most of her time in Berlin, producing for Reuters TV and contributing to publications such as *The Guardian, The Telegraph,* and Thrillist. Barbara updated the Bangkok, Around Bangkok, and Travel Smart chapters for this edition.